~ BLOOMS ~
OF BRESSINGHAM
GARDEN
PLANTS

~BLOOMS~
OF BRESSINGHAM
GARDEN
PLANTS

ALAN & ADRIAN BLOOM

CHOOSING THE BEST HARDY
PLANTS FOR YOUR GARDEN

HarperCollins*Publishers*

Acknowledgements

We would like to thank the following people who have given assistance with this book:
John Elsley, our transatlantic friend presently living in South Carolina,
for his time and knowledge in assessing the USA hardiness zones for all chapters,
and for some very pertinent advice on plant behaviour in North America;
Bob Pearson, for his valuable assistance with all sections of the book,
but in particular alpines and the roses within the shrubs chapter;
Michael Warren and family, of Photos Horticultural, for providing so many excellent
photographs, most of which were taken at Bressingham;
Richard Bonson, from nearby Diss, who provided such attractive original
colour illustrations to add an extra dimension to the book;
Allen J. Coombes, for his assistance with nomenclature;
Susan Conder, for the difficult task of editing the text;
Caroline Churton and Caroline Hill, of HarperCollins, for their skills in editing
and design, and not least for their fortitude during the long final haul.
Alan and Adrian Bloom

In addition, I would also like to thank the following:
John Bond, MVO, VMH, friend and Keeper of the Gardens at Savill Gardens,
Windsor Great Park, for his knowledgeable advice and guidance on the shrubs chapter;
and lastly, but hardly least, my wife Rosemary, who not only unscrambled my writing to
type it, but who also, despite our nearly five years of involvement in the book,
remained patient and supportive throughout.
Adrian Bloom

First published in 1992 by HarperCollins Publishers, London

© Alan and Adrian Bloom, 1992

A CIP catalogue record for this book is available from the British Library
ISBN 0 00 412329 8

Project Editor:	Caroline Churton
Editor:	Susan Conder
Additional editorial assistance from:	Mary Davies, Barbara Dixon, Joan Field,
	Caroline Holden, Susanna Longley, Robert Pearson
Art Editor:	Caroline Hill
Assistant Designer:	Paul Griffin
Picture Researcher:	Jane Lewis
Colour illustrations:	Richard Bonson
Planting plans:	Adrian Bloom
Line illustrations:	Tig Sutton
Photographs:	Adrian Bloom, Photos Horticultural, Harry Smith,
	Ed Barber, Eric Crichton, A-Z Botanical Collection

FRONTISPIECE: Alan and Adrian Bloom in the Dell garden at Bressingham

Set in Caslon 540 & 3, by Brown Packaging Limited, 257 Liverpool Road, London N1
Colour origination in Hong Kong
Printed and bound in Great Britain by HarperCollins Manufacturing, Glasgow

CONTENTS

FOREWORD

We do not always realize how fortunate we are to live in Great Britain, because our temperate climate enables us to grow in our gardens an enormously wide range of plants. At a time when gardening has never enjoyed a greater following, the main difficulty for gardeners has become one of choice, as the selection of plants from which to choose is now so extensive. Garden centres have proliferated, gardening programmes on television draw vast audiences, gardens open to the public and flower shows attract millions of visitors. The national thirst for soundly based horticultural knowledge seems to have no bounds and generates a continuing need for professional guidance for the amateur gardener.

This is where the contribution of the internationally renowned Alan and Adrian Bloom can offer authoritative advice. The skills of this exceptional father and son team complement each other admirably, as is clearly evident in the unique gardens they have created at Bressingham. Now they have brought together in one volume all the knowledge needed to establish, develop and improve a garden. Their plant introductions are legion and many of the best are attractively illustrated in this book. Because of the authors' proven skills in selection, plant lovers will find it an invaluable aid to their gardening. Those who have admired the outstanding exhibits staged from Bressingham at RHS Shows both at Chelsea and Vincent Square and who aspire to creating similar effects in their own gardens can now, with the help of this book, fulfil their dreams.

I am confident that this is a book to which gardeners will return again and again, and that for many it will become a really well-thumbed friend.

Robin Herbert, VMH
President of the Royal Horticultural Society

PREFACE

B *looms of Bressingham Garden Plants* is a guide for all gardeners who want to make the most of the garden space they have, by using hardy perennials, grasses and ferns, alpines, conifers, heaths and heathers, and shrubs to best advantage.

What we, as gardeners, have learned from practical experience is set out concisely in the sections that follow. This includes observations on the suitability of each plant described for soil, climate and aspect, to ensure its success and the satisfaction of the gardener. However restricted or enormous the space and whatever the prevailing conditions, there are plants that can be grown, bringing beauty and joy. We hope our advice regarding these will be helpful.

Tastes, as well as the basic approach to gardening, vary with the individual. Gardening is a tiresome chore for some and an abiding passion for others, but between these extremes is a latent longing in many people's minds to achieve greater rewards for their gardening efforts. Some people grow plants as a form of relaxation from the pressures of modern life, while others use gardening to express individual creativity; but whatever the initial motivation, the crux is that both ongoing mental and physical exertion are also needed.

The effort we have put into this book reflects the effort which has gone into each of our own, large, comprehensive gardens. Any sense of achievement falls very short of pride, because we are still learning and will never know all the answers, nor will we cease finding still more plants worth growing, for love and beauty's sake. Some will find a place in our nursery catalogue or Plant Centre, along with thousands of others, to be offered to the gardening public.

This is, we believe, a gardening book with a difference, the advice given being based on our practical experience as gardeners and nurserymen and on observations made in different situations all over the world.

Alan Bloom   *Adrian Bloom*

ALAN BLOOM'S INTRODUCTION

There was scarcely any garden at Bressingham when I bought the 220-acre Hall Farm in 1946; but the house stood well back from the road, screened by a shelter belt, and mature trees studded its park-like meadow. Here was the ideal setting for a garden, but moving my Hardy Plant Nursery from near Cambridge was hampered by the grim winter of 1946-7. By 1948 I admitted defeat and moved to Canada – a disastrous move, but my return in 1950 was the start of a more realistic phase.

By 1953 the nursery had nearly 40 acres of perennials and alpines, grown for the trade. With the new emphasis on low-maintenance forms of gardening, in 1955 I created five island beds in the big lawn in front of the house, leaving wide, grassy paths between. In these beds plants were grouped, with more space around each group than between the individual plants comprising it. Plants were graded down in height, from tall ones placed in the centre of each bed to perimeter subjects only 15-30cm/6-12in high. Growth was sturdier and weeding easier than in the old-fashioned, one-sided borders, and the plants could be viewed all round.

This success sparked off an urge to collect a greater variety, beyond the 2000 or so I already grew. Extensions and improvements followed, including the creation of the Dell garden, until, by 1962, there were forty-seven island beds and about 5000 species and varieties, covering 5 acres. Since then, perennials have returned to popularity, and island beds are widely accepted as an excellent way to grow them.

The popular conception of a rock garden is even more labour-intensive. A miniature mountain seemed out of place in rockless, flat East Anglia, so in 1952 I made raised beds, using few rocks and thus providing more space for plants and minimizing stooping. Adrian also made a conifer and heather garden for me, and my whole garden is now open to the public on a regular basis.

I still collect and introduce new plants; though I know that perfection is unobtainable, the urge to pursue it remains a challenge.

Alan Bloom in his garden at Bressingham Hall

PERENNIALS

The recent upsurge of interest in perennials is due partly to the realization that they offer immense variety in form, colour and continuity, and partly to the more rational approach in growing them. The old, traditional 'herbaceous border' was fine when labour-saving was not an issue; then, the one-sided border crammed with flowers was the popular ideal. Staking was often needed, because growth was lanky due to lack of light and air. With the need to reduce labour-intensive gardening, shrubs and ground covers replaced many herbaceous borders, which were indeed troublesome.

The new approach avoids cramming and uses more compact, shorter subjects and well-spaced groups of each kind to encourage sturdy growth. This can be achieved in one-sided borders, but island beds are more reliable and effective, with very little staking needed, since they seem to be less vulnerable to wind and rain. Access for maintenance is much easier and such beds allow all-round viewing.

CHOOSING PERENNIALS

The range is so wide that almost any sized bed can hold a choice of subjects which will give pleasure for most of the year. The important factor is to choose kinds adaptable to a given site, soil and situation.

Decide at the outset whether variety or impact counts most. Whereas a wide variety, perhaps only one of each plant in a small garden, may be more botanically interesting, where space allows, grouping several plants of each type has more visual impact, especially in terms of colour, and is more practical.

As well as matching plants to soil and site, satisfying personal preferences for colour, flowering period, or type of growth is equally valid. A garden, after all, is for most people the place where their individuality and creativity can be given free expression, as well as a place for relaxation. The specialist approach of collecting and

Alan Bloom's Dell garden at Bressingham in June. The bold blue leaves of *Hosta sieboldiana* 'Elegans' make the main impact in the shade and moisture bed in the foreground, whilst *Mimulus*, *Aruncus*, *Primula* and *Dactylorhiza* provide a palette of colour and form around it

Lupinus 'Noble Maiden' (Russell Hybrids) and *Anchusa azurea* 'Loddon Royalist' create a dramatic contrast in midsummer

growing a wide variety of a favourite genus can also be of absorbing interest. Some British gardeners are designated as holding a haven for plants under the National Council for the Conservation of Plants and Gardens, the National Collections fostering body. Dozens of genera have by this means found a permanent home and, largely by swapping, each collection becomes richer and closer to completion.

A sense of 'rightness' within the garden setting may not come readily to those who have not had enough time or experience to study plant harmony. It can be cultivated by observing the relationship between various plants in a bed and, in the larger sense, the bed's relationship to the immediate environment. The formal, straight boundaries that most gardens have make rectangular or gently curving informal beds more pleasing aesthetically than intricately complex ones. The degree of privacy available, the choice of front or rear garden, and the presence of mature trees also affect the siting of beds. An established tree may provide welcome shade, but its far-ranging roots can inhibit plant growth, from lack of sun, nutrients or moisture.

Within a bed, initial harmony is less vital; if mistakes are made, such as a subject growing taller than expected and obscuring a shorter one behind, they can easily be remedied by repositioning after the first season. Placing spiky flowers between clumps of rounded or flattish flowers usually works. Subjects having abundant, shapely foliage, such as *Hemerocallis, Kniphofia, Heuchera* and *Hosta*, should be placed next to those which are rather bare-stemmed, such as *Helenium, Aconitum* and the taller anemones. Early-flowering subjects which become unattractive later through lack of foliage are best kept away from frontal positions, which are ideal for evergreen plants or ones which retain foliage until the end of the season.

For an effective display, intersperse spiky perennials with those of a flattish or rounded appearance

Place the tallest plants at the back of one-sided borders and in the centres of island beds. Graduate heights down to the perimeter; along the front, use dwarfer-growing subjects less than 60cm/2ft high. Occasionally, a few taller subjects can be used towards the front to provide variety, but only those with good base foliage and erect stems, such as *Kniphofia, Crinum, Crocosmia* or *Hemerocallis*. Avoid tall subjects for narrow beds or borders because they will overhang dwarfer plants, or need supports, and in general will look ungainly. A guide would be to restrict the choice of taller subjects to those which, when in flower, will be about half the width of the border in height, and even then, choose only a few and ones of shapely appearance. Spacing between plants, whether singly or in groups, should vary with expected height and spread from 15cm/6in to 60cm/2ft or more. The space between groups of one type should be 20 to 25 per cent more than between individual plants comprising the group, to allow for access and to encourage sturdy growth.

Spacing of individual plants in relation to groups of perennials

In the end, however, harmony submits to no hard and fast rules and the final decisions rest with individual appreciation. In the process of trying to achieve harmony as one sees it, lie the joy and satisfaction which come from knowing and loving perennials.

SOME CULTURAL ADVICE

Many different types of soil exist, as do variations in climate, which also affect growing conditions. Perfection in both is rarely found, if ever, but you can make the best of your soil even if the climate is beyond your control. Good drainage is a basic essential, but shallow, sandy, chalky or stony soils are apt to dry out quickly. These need extra humus added. Well-rotted compost or manure contains more nutrient than peat, and if the latter or substitutes such as leaf mould or bark are used, organic fertilizer should be added.

Heavy soil, whether alkaline or acid, is less likely to dry out, but is liable to be obdurate, wet and sticky in winter or rainy summers and lacking friability when dry. Humus alone will not improve its structure. I firmly believe that the answer is digging in sharp or gritty sand (soft 'builder's' sand is unsuitable): the soil becomes less sticky, more friable, and plant growth is much improved. The sand can be applied on bare ground or dug in between established plants, but the deeper it is, the better the results. If need be, fertility can then be improved by adding humus.

Irrigation

Excessive irrigation, whether from rain or manually applied, has a detrimental effect. Overhead watering is best in the form of dense mist, not large drops; nor should more be given than will moisten the soil down to where moisture already exists. This can be discovered by checking and feeling by hand, or by using a rod to test for soil dampness. Knowing how much to apply in a dry period comes from making a studied estimate beforehand on how much water is needed; this will vary according to soil type and discretion must be used. Often it is simply a question of trial and error. Too little water is of course harmful, but so is too much.

Irrigation is also important when planting, whether container-grown or bare-rooted plants. Water if the soil surface is dry and the soil trickles back into the planting hole. 'Puddling' is the best method. Insert the plant at the correct depth and pull the dry soil round it to three quarters of the depth of the hole. Then fill up the hole with water. Once this soaks in, draw the rest of the soil around to restore the level, and gently firm. This ensures survival far better than an overall, overhead splash, prevents the surface becoming crusty as it dries, and, lastly, encourages vital capillary action.

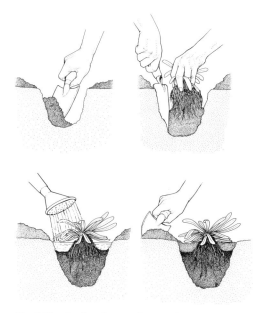

'Puddling': planting and watering to retain moisture

Dealing with weeds

Annual weeds are easy to control and inevitably need hoeing after a bed is planted, but perennial weeds, such as couch grass, mare's tail, ground elder and bindweed, must be meticulously forked out or sprayed well before planting. The most pernicious weeds can only be eliminated with a potent systemic weedkiller, used with the utmost care on weeds in full leaf. Repeated applications for certain weeds are sometimes necessary. What kills one may not affect another, and in this case expert advice should be taken. Couch grass is better forked

A bright association of some popular perennials. The large-flowered blue *Delphinium* makes a good background to the yellow *Hemerocallis* 'Lark Song' and *Helenium* 'Morheim Beauty'

out, but bindweed is more effectively killed by chemicals applied to the leaves. Failure to do this will be bitterly regretted in the years to come.

Weedkillers are, however, no alternative to hoeing among perennials. It is highly risky to spray weeds between plants because a contact weedkiller does not discriminate and always affects a wider area than that actually treated. Contact sprays for annual weeds, even where used well away from plants, soon leave a greenish film on the soil surface, inhibiting soil aeration and creating a seed bed for weeds, until it is stirred with a hoe.

I find that hoeing is, in most cases, far more efficacious than spraying, just as hand digging is much superior to any mechanical cultivator. Both tasks provide, in addition, healthy exercise.

General maintenance

Staking should be reduced to the minimum. The need to support plants – among the most tedious tasks – is greatly reduced if a bed or border is not crammed and compact plants are chosen.

Supports for less than tidy plants, such as potentillas and geraniums, are a matter of personal preference. I let anything under about 60cm/2ft loll somewhat, if this is its nature. What I omit sometimes to do in time is to reduce the height of tall, late-summer subjects, such as heleniums, by taking off the tip shoots when they are about half the height they would be in flower. Do this about six or seven weeks before flowering time and it often eliminates the need for staking. This applies, however, only to plants liable to reach

Removing the tip of tall, late-summer flowering perennials when half their ultimate height

1.5-1.8m/5-6ft and almost entirely to members of the daisy, or *Compositae*, family, never to spike-forming subjects.

Dead-heading is a matter of personal preference rather than obligatory. Some plants do not look at all unsightly after flowering, and their seed heads can be a positive attraction. It is true that others flower for longer if dead-headed, especially achilleas, salvias, scabiosa, delphiniums and lupins, and some gardeners consider it worth the trouble. They would also find it worthwhile to cut hard back after flowering those plants which flower between mid-spring and midsummer, to encourage a second crop or fresh green foliage.

Another optional task for those aiming for perfection is to thin out clumps of stems that become congested in full growth. Snip off the weakest or thinnest stems close to the base to encourage larger, fuller flowers. Again, this applies only to *Compositae* plants, phlox and a few other subjects.

Seasonal work

Staking and supporting are successful only if done while growth is still erect. Mid- to late spring is the time to stake in most localities. Spring is also the time to curb excessive surface growth. Subjects such as some achilleas and monardas make vigorous, mat-like growth which, within a year or two, may encroach on weaker neighbours. It does no harm to chop back any excessive growth with a spade.

There is no set time for clearing up when the season ends. If you prefer a tidy appearance, then late autumn is best. I often leave mine until late winter or early spring, to cut back and fork between plants in one operation. This has the advantage of treading only once on winter wet soil. With heavy soil, however, this task is best done before winter, so that frost breaks down lumps.

Late autumn is the time to give less than hardy subjects winter protection. Where annual snow cover is assured, many tender plants can survive without extra covering; some plants come through severe frosts in Moscow or Montreal better than in milder, damper, temperate climates, such as in Britain. I use mounded oak or beech leaves, weighted down with twigs to prevent them blowing away, to protect plants. Straw and hedge clippings can also be used in low mounds or around plants such as *Kniphofia* and *Penstemon* from late autumn until spring growth begins, but avoid material liable to turn mushy and wet, since frost penetrates wetness much more quickly.

Probably 90 per cent of the perennials and alpines I have listed are fully hardy in the United Kingdom, and scarcely any of the tender types I grow are lifted in autumn and kept frost-free during winter. Over the years, hard winters have caused losses for me from the combined effect of frost and poor drainage.

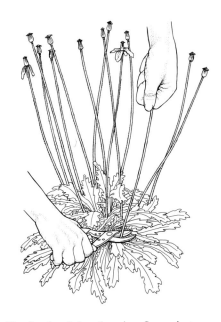

Cutting back hard spring-flowering plants to encourage a second crop of flowers or fresh green foliage

Thinning large, congested clumps close to the base of the plant

Protecting vulnerable species in winter by covering them with mounded oak leaves

These exotic shade-loving perennials are headed by the beautiful but rare, double white *Trillium grandiflorum* 'Flore Pleno', backed by the yellow, hanging flowers of *Disporum flavens*. In the foreground the curling leaves of *Hosta undulata* 'Medio Variegata' provide foliage contrast with *Primula sieboldii* 'Snowflake' and 'Mikado'

Planting

Except in the case of container-grown plants, planting, too, is best done according to season. My very general rule is to plant, or divide and replant, in spring those plants which flower after midsummer, such as *Aster amellus* and its forms. Spring or early-summer flowering subjects I plant in autumn, but in damp weather many are quite safe to plant in late summer. However, there are exceptions to the rule. Pyrethrums and scabiosa, unless pot-grown, are unlikely to over-winter if planted later than late summer.

As with container-grown stock, plants whose roots carry a good ball of soil can be safely moved more or less any time. Discretion is of course needed where soil is intractable due to frost or waterlogging. Always, however, ensure adequate watering-in if the soil is dry, and loosen the surface after planting if the soil is wet and sticky.

PLANT NAMES

I feel strongly that those who grow plants for their beauty find a deeper satisfaction if they know the plants' proper names. To avoid botanical names on the grounds that they are difficult to master or memorize is not valid. Nor is it valid to protest that common or folk names are preferable, since they are variable and impracticable, especially with single-genus collections, and in books, catalogues and, above all, garden centres.

A note for the newcomer on nomenclature is appropriate. The first name of any plant is its genus, such as *Geranium*; it is often abbreviated to its first letter after the genus has been fully mentioned once in texts or catalogues. Secondly comes its species, or specific, name, such as *G. endressii* or *G. sanguineum*. Sometimes botanical varieties or sub-species provide a third name, such as *G. sanguineum lancastriense*, as a natural variation on the typical form. Then there are selected garden forms, or cultivars, which may be hybrids, such as *G.* 'Johnson's Blue', or forms of a species, such as *G. cinereum* 'Ballerina'. Today, cultivars are given names in ordinary language, but older cultivars often have Latin names, such as *G. pratense* 'Album'. Whoever introduces or originates a new cultivar is entitled to name it, but botanical names come under the international rules of nomenclature.

Unfortunately, nomenclature authorities, or taxonomists, are apt to change names from time to time, on the basis of correcting historical mistakes or of newly discovered botanical similarities or differences. Such changes gradually filter through to the more practical users and can cause confusion and annoyance. For example, some species of the *Orchis* genus were found to have a slightly different root from others and were given the unlovely generic name of *Dactylorhiza*.

Labelling plants *in situ* in the garden is an excellent way of remembering names. Several types of label exist, some less obtrusive than others, and indelible ink is available.

QUALITY CONTROL

My own definition of quality, as applied to perennials or alpines for sale, is that they should be large enough to flower in the first year. With few exceptions due to the nature of certain plants, reputable, reliable producers or retailers sell plants which have been grown for at least one season. They will have seen it flowering in the nursery and will vouch for it being true to name; they will also replace it if for some reason it fails to survive in the customer's garden.

Many garden centres are merely retailers and buy in stock, mostly container-grown, from wholesale producers. Quality then depends on whether the retailer sets the standard, but there are some whose standards are governed by price and profits rather than by quality and reliable service.

Since the resurgence of demand for hardy plants, there has been a marked increase in the number of small producers setting up in business. Often the emphasis is on unusual plants and several erstwhile amateurs with sizeable gardens now issue lists or catalogues of what they have to offer. In general, compared with most well-established producers their prices tend to be considerably lower, but in my experience the quality may also be low: small plants, scarcely better than rooted cuttings or seedlings, or divisions of older plants.

Generally, good-quality plants are better value than immature stock, in the long run. Luckily, newcomers to the business of growing hardy plants for sale who stay the course can learn how to achieve the right standards of price versus quality.

Lastly, beware of advertisements in the weekend national or gardening press for plant 'bargains': they are often misleading.

This striking association of shrubs and perennials in July includes (from left to right) *Buddleia davidii* 'Pink Delight', *Coreopsis verticillata* 'Golden Gain', the deep blue *Delphinium* × *belladonna* 'Peace' and *Chrysanthemum maximum* 'Summer Snowball', fronted by the silver-grey foliage of *Artemisia canescens*

PERENNIALS DIRECTORY

Acanthus spinosus

This obviously cannot be complete, but it is based on garden-worthiness and availability, and on nearly seventy years' intimate experience. The directory includes a few alpines, since they are technically perennials. Some make first-class, front-of-the-border subjects, while others are excellent dwarf ground cover.

Key

H: Approximate height
W: Approximate width
F: Months in flower
Z: Relevant hardiness zone(s)

ACANTHUS Bear's breeches

Most of these stately plants have handsome, elegant, divided leaves, much featured in Corinthian architecture, and imposing flower spikes of overlapping bracts, good for drying. They are best in large clumps, sited where the whole plant can be seen, in sun and well-drained soil.

Achillea 'Anthea'

Achillea Galaxy Hybrids

Protect young plants with a mulch where winters are cold. The deep, fleshy roots are difficult to eradicate, once established.
A. balcanicus (syn. *A. longifolius*). This has spikes of mauve flowers above dark green, deeply lobed leaves, often over 60cm/2ft long. It needs space, and spikes may need support. H1-1.2m/39-48in, W60cm/2ft. F7-9. Z6-10.
A. longifolius. See *A. balcanicus*.
A. mollis and *mollis latifolius*. Both have large, rounded but deeply indented, almost pinnately lobed leaves and pink flowers, less free than *A. spinosus*, but of good overall appearance. The form *latifolius* is more robust, with glossy, arching leaves, and though less free-flowering, is most often grown. H1.2-1.35m/48-53in, W60cm/2ft. F7-9. Z6-10.
A. perringii. A dwarf species with narrow, saw-edged leaves and spikes of pinkish flowers. Grows compactly but is deep-rooting. H30cm/1ft, W30cm/1ft. F6-8. Z7-9.
A. spinosus. This most spectacular and reliable species has deeply cut, dark green, lanceolate leaves and spikes of purplish, foxglove-like flowers, protected by sharp spines. H1.2m/4ft, W60cm/2ft. F7-9. Z7-10. The form *spinosissimus* is a rarely seen plant with stiff, dense, prickly and somewhat silvery, finely cut leaves and occasional spikes of pinkish mauve flowers. H60cm/2ft, W60cm/2ft. F7-9. Z7-10.

ACHILLEA Yarrow, milfoil

This useful genus contains a wide range of species, 10-150cm/4-60in high, most with delicate, ferny leaves and tight heads or loose clusters of tiny flowers. Some listed under Alpines are equally at home as frontal groups of perennials, but all much prefer sun and well-drained soil. Most taller kinds are good for cutting and the flat-headed yellow kinds will dry for winter decoration. They flower for a longer period if cut back when faded.
A. 'Anthea'. This outstanding hybrid is more erect than *A.* 'Moonshine' and the foliage, soft and silvery, even more attractive. The flower heads, 8-10cm/3-4in across, are primrose-yellow and fade to creamy yellow, making for perfect harmony in flower and foliage. Cut out faded stems to prolong the flowering season. H60cm/2ft, W30cm/1ft. F6-8. Z4-8.
A. clypeolata. The true species, seldom offered, carries deep yellow, flat flower

heads above narrow, serrated, strikingly silver-grey, hairy foliage. Dislikes winter wet, and needs regular lifting, dividing and replanting. H50cm/20in, W40cm/16in. F6-9. Z4-8.
A. 'Coronation Gold'. This bushy variety, more compact than its parent, *A. filipendulina*, has small, flat heads of deep yellow flowers above greyish foliage. H90cm/3ft, W60cm/2ft. F7-9. Z4-8.
A. decolorans **'W. B. Child'**. This has clumps of green foliage and white, green-eyed, daisy-like florets forming heads 8-10cm/3-4in across. Good for cutting. H60cm/2ft, W60cm/2ft. F6-9. Z4-8.
A. filipendulina. Only cultivars are now available, the most popular being **'Gold Plate'**, with wide heads of bright yellow flowers on leafy stems, and fingered, aromatic foliage. H1.2-1.5m/4-5ft, W45cm/18in. F6-9. Z4-8.
A. 'Flowers of Sulphur' (syn. 'Schwefelblüte'). This slow-spreading hybrid is like a compact *A. millefolium* in habit, with small heads of sulphur-yellow flowers. H60cm/2ft, W30cm/1ft. F6-9. Z5-8.
A. millefolium. The common yarrow is invasive and free-seeding, and most selections need curbing annually to prevent excessive spread. **'Cerise Queen'** is probably the best older variety, with cherry-red flowers. H60cm/2ft, W38cm/15in. F6-9. Z3-8. Until recently, pink and cherry-red were the only improvements on the wild type, but thanks to breeding work undertaken in Germany, there now exist several attractive selections arising from *A. millefolium* and *A. taygetea*. The following, known as Galaxy Hybrids, grow robustly with deep green, filigree foliage. **'Apple Blossom'** (syn. 'Apfelblüte'), light lilac-pink. H40cm/16in, W60cm/2ft. F6-9. Z4-8. **'Great Expectations'** (syn. 'Hoffnung'), buff-primrose flowers. H60cm/2ft, W38cm/15in. F6-9. Z4-8. **'Lilac Beauty'**, wide heads of distinctive lilac shade, erect-growing. H60cm/2ft, W38cm/15in. F6-9. Z3-8. **'Salmon Beauty'** (syn. 'Lachsschönheit'), light salmon-pink. H60cm/2ft, W38cm/15in. F6-9. Z4-8. **'The Beacon'** (syn. 'Fanal'), very bright red, almost scarlet flowers, with yellow centres. H60cm/2ft, W38cm/15in. F6-9. Z4-8.

Achillea 'Moonshine'

A. 'Moonbeam'. This hybrid has clear, light yellow heads for many weeks and is especially good for cutting and drying. Vigorous but not invasive. H90cm/3ft, W38cm/15in. F6-9. Z4-8.

A. 'Moonshine'. This variation, which I selected, is very popular for its showy, flat heads of lemon-yellow above silvery filigree foliage. I rank it as one of the best plants ever raised and named. H60cm/2ft, W45cm/18in. F6-9. Z4-8.

A. *ptarmica*. Those forms of sneezewort in cultivation, variously named **'Boule de Neige'**, **'Perry's Variety'** and **'The Pearl'**, all have branching heads of pure white, double, button flowers. Although good for cutting, the roots are apt to be very invasive, like couch grass roots, and need annual curbing. H75cm/30in, W75cm/30in. F6-7. Z4-9.

A. 'Schwellenburg', from Germany, is free-flowering, with profuse flat heads of deep mustard-yellow on 50cm/20in stems. It has abundant silvery foliage and a clumpy habit. H38cm/15in, W30cm/1ft. F6-8. Z4-8.

A. *taygetea*. This forms neat silver-grey clumps and light yellow, flat heads, fading to primrose with age, on stiff stems. Good for cutting. H45cm/18in, W45cm/18in. F6-8. Z5-8.

ACONITUM Aconite, monkshood

Almost all have distinctive, hooded flowers, hence the common name. They are under-rated as garden plants, though less trouble than their delphinium cousins, and many flower in late summer and autumn, when few perennials are in bloom. Aconitums appreciate good soil and respond to spring mulching. All are fully hardy, but tend to become congested after two to three years and so suffer from starvation. When replanting, use only the largest pieces and enrich the soil with compost; bury surplus roots 23-25cm/9-10in deep, to destroy them. Aconites are adaptable to semi-shade and heavy soil; tall types may need staking. The roots are poisonous, in the unlikely event of being eaten.

A. 'Blue Sceptre'. A striking cultivar with stiffly erect, well-foliaged spikes of violet-

Aconitum henryi 'Sparks Variety'

blue and white flowers. H75cm/30in, W45cm/18in. F7-9. Z4-8.

A. 'Bressingham Spire'. This forms a strong-stemmed, perfect, narrow pyramid, well-clothed with handsome, deeply cut leaves. As each terminal spike of deep violet-blue opens, supporting side spikes come into flower. H90-100cm/36-39in, W45cm/18in. F7-9. Z4-8.

A. *carmichaelii* 'Arendsii'. A fine German selection with deeply-divided leaves and erect stems topped in autumn with short spikes of deep amethyst-blue flowers. Moist soil preferred. H1.8m/6ft, W30cm/1ft. F9-10. Z3-8.

A. *henryi* 'Sparks Variety'. Widely branching stems carry profuse deep violet, hooded flowers. It may need staking on exposed sites. H1-1.2m/39-48in, W45cm/18in. F6-8. Z4-8.

A. 'Ivorine'. A distinctive cultivar having a more bushy habit with ample foliage. The flowers are ivory-white on branching spikes. H up to 90cm/3ft, W75cm/30in. F6-8. Z5-8.

A. *japonicum*. This flowers early, with clusters of amethyst flowers on leafy stems. The leaves are larger and lighter green than most, and rapid root growth makes for congestion after two to three years. H1m/39in, W45cm/18in. F6-8. Z5-8.

A. *lycoctonum* (syn. *A. vulparia*). This has a

Aconitum 'Ivorine'

bushy, leafy habit with branching spikes of small, creamy yellow flowers on wiry stems. It has a long flowering season, but is prone to flopping. H1.1m/43in, W45cm/18in. F6-8. Z4-8.

A. *napellus* 'Album'. The typical flowers are white and held on fairly erect stems. H1-1.2m/39-48in, W30cm/1ft. F6-8. Z5-8. **'Bicolor'** is distinctive for its blue and white flowers on branching stems. A first-rate plant. H1.1m/43in, W45cm/18in. F6-8. Z4-8. The form *carneum* is the nearest to pink, but is a very pale shade. H1.2m/4ft, W38cm/15in. F6-8. Z5-8.

A. *vilmorinianum*. Rarely offered, but has slender, wiry stems and short terminal

Adonis amurensis

Agapanthus 'Bressingham Blue'

spikes of deep blue. H1.5m/5ft, W30cm/1ft. F6-8. Z4-8.

A. vulparia. See *A. lycoctonum*.

ACTAEA Baneberry

A. alba. The white baneberry has clumps of astilbe-like leaves, fluffy white flowers and bright red stalks, contrasting effectively with the white berries in autumn. The berries of all species are poisonous. Cool, fertile, moist soils are most suitable. H90cm/3ft, W45cm/18in. F7-8. Z3-8.

A. rubra. Similar to the above, but with ferny leaves and glistening red berries, carried well above the foliage. H45cm/18in, W30cm/1ft. F7-8. Z3-8.

A. spicata. This unspectacular, shade-loving species, sometimes known as herb Christopher, is interesting for its short spikes of small white flowers, outstanding foliage and, above all, shiny, currant-like black berries in autumn. Cultivate as above. H45cm/18in, W45cm/18in. F7-8. Z3-8.

ADENOPHORA

A. tashiroi. Closely related to campanulas, this fleshy-rooted plant has clear blue bells dangling from arching, branching stems. It makes a little basal expansion, but is not difficult in good, well-drained soil and sun. Leaves are small and greyish, and it flowers

for a long time. H40-60cm/16-24in, W25cm/10in. F6-9. Z4-8.

ADONIS

These are appealing, slow-growing harbingers of spring, with bowl-shaped yellow flowers on leafy stems. The first two below are adaptable as alpines or for the front of the border. All prefer light but not poor or dry soil, shelter and sun, and are long-lived with fibrous roots. They are best lifted and divided for replanting when dormant, from midsummer to late autumn. Because of their long dormancy period, the spot should be marked to avoid damage when hoeing, and adjacent plants chosen to provide cover during this period.

A. amurensis. Its glistening green-tinged yellow flowers appear as early as winter aconites, but are four times the size. H15cm/6in, W25cm/10in. F1-3. Z4-7. In 'Plena' the large, double yellow, green-centred flowers open on short stems and are followed by a mound of lacy greenery until midsummer, when they become dormant. H15cm/6in, W25cm/10in. F3-5. Z4-7.

A. vernalis. This choice species makes erect little bushes of delicate greenery set with bright yellow, single, buttercup-like flowers. Remains green until late summer. H30cm/1ft, W30cm/1ft. F4-5. Z4-7.

A. volgensis. Probably a geographical form of *A. vernalis*, this flowers a little earlier. H25-30cm/10-12in, W30cm/1ft. F4-5. Z4-7.

AGAPANTHUS African lily

Terminal clusters of blue or white, lily-like flowers on smooth, leafless stems make a splendid display. The strap-like leaves form dense clumps, growing from thick, long-lived roots. In general, the broader the leaf, the less hardy the plant. The newer, hardy kinds are deservedly popular. Beyond a preference for sun and good, well-drained, deep soil, they are trouble-free and can remain in one place for years, although are best covered with litter over winter in the coldest districts. Old clumps, if flowering declines, may be divided on site with a spade thrust vertically into the rootball, but ample feeding and watering usually keep them flowering well. They are best moved in spring, when new growth is about to begin. All below, Z8-10.

A. 'Blue Giant'. The tallest listed here, it has wide, rich blue trumpets. H1.1m/43in, W45cm/18in. F7-9.

A. 'Bressingham Blue'. Acknowledged as the deepest amethyst-blue in cultivation, this is profuse and first-class. H80-90cm/32-36in, W45cm/18in. F7-9.

A. 'Bressingham Bounty'. This recent selection has extra-large, bright blue heads. H80cm/32in, W38cm/15in. F7-9.

A. 'Bressingham White'. Outstandingly free-flowering, with pure white blooms. H90cm/3ft, W45cm/18in. F7-9.

A. 'Headbourne Hybrids'. This strain varies from light to deep blue and is acclaimed for hardiness, though no more so than the named varieties listed. H70-90cm/28-36in, W38-90cm/15-36in. F7-9.

A. 'Isis' (formerly *A. weillighii*). An older, but reliable cultivar with blue flowers. H80cm/32in, W45cm/18in. F7-9.

A. 'Lilliput'. This is almost a miniature,

Agapanthus 'Bressingham White'

with relatively small, rich blue flowers on slender stems. H15cm/6in, W10cm/4in. F7-8.

A. 'Loch Hope'. This is taller and later than most others. Dark blue flowers. H90-120cm/3-4ft, W45cm/18in. F8-9.

A. patens. Clear, light blue and a little later, this fills a need with large heads lasting well into early autumn. H90cm/3ft, W45cm/18in. F8-9.

A. 'Profusion'. This lives up to its name. The flowers are a mid-blue and, like all the others, it eventually forms a large clump.

Agapanthus 'Lilliput'

Alchemilla mollis

H90cm/3ft, W45cm/18in. F6-8.
A. weillighii. See *A*. 'Isis'.

ALCHEMILLA Lady's mantle

These adaptable, clump-forming plants with clouds of tiny, acid-green flowers are useful for ground cover in sun or shade, damp or dry soil. *A. mollis* is the most popular; it grows almost anywhere, except in waterlogged soil.

A. alpina. This silvery ground cover has small but close-set foliage and short sprays of buff flowers. H15cm/6in, W15cm/6in. F6-8. Z3-7.

A. erythropoda. Steady spread of grey foliage and heads of greenish yellow flowers. H15cm/6in, W15cm/6in. F6-8. Z3-7.

A. hookeri. Good ground cover of silvery grey, low mounds with greenish buff flowers. H20cm/8in, W15cm/6in. F6-8. Z3-7.

A. mollis. An excellent subject as a foil, but with a beauty of its own. The grey-green leaves are rounded, slightly hairy, and hold raindrops. The loose sprays of tiny, yellow-green flowers are attractive for many weeks and useful in cut-flower displays. Self-seeds freely. H45cm/18in, W60cm/2ft. F6-8. Z4-8.

ALLIUM Ornamental onion

This vast genus includes edible onions and contains good garden plants as well as weedy ones. Never introduce alliums into the garden without knowing their habit of growth, since some can be invasive, either by self-seeding or from bulbils. The list below contains those which do not have rapid spread or which quickly die back after flowering, and some are nearly evergreen.

A. bulgaricum, **A. giganteum**, and several others which die back to just a bulb after flowering may still appeal to a few, but I cannot recommend them as worthy perennials. Almost any soil suits them but they prefer sun. A few are quite tiny and are described in the Alpines chapter. H1m/39in, W25cm/10in. F6-7. Z4-8.

A. cernuum. Long succession of terminal heads of dangling, violet-mauve tubular flowers, followed by pretty seed heads; the leaves, unusually attractive for alliums, are narrow. Plants form a neat clump. H45cm/18in, W15cm/6in. F6-8. Z3-8.

A. nuttallii. Erect, smooth stems carry round heads of soft lavender flowers, from a sturdy, trouble-free clump. H60cm/2ft, W15cm/6in. F6-9. Z4-8.

A. pulchellum. Narrow, greyish foliage and heads of lilac-mauve. Self-seeds freely. H25cm/10in, W15cm/6in. F6-9. Z6-9.

A. pyrenaicum. Deep green, almost evergreen, strap-like leaves and graceful, long-lasting heads of lavender flowers. H50cm/20in, W15cm/6in. F7-9. Z4-8.

A. schoenoprasum. This is the culinary chive, but **'Forescate'** has bright purple-crimson blooms, worthy of a place in a

Allium pyrenaicum

Allium schoenoprasum 'Forescate'

border. H30cm/1ft, W23cm/9in. F6-8. Z3-9. The giant form **'Majus'** has pretty heads of rosy lavender flowers. H35cm/14in, W23cm/9in. F6-8. Z3-9.

A. senescens. This gives a bright, late-flowering display of flesh-pink from neat-growing, almost evergreen clumps.

A. flavum and **A. glaucum** are similar, retaining much of their foliage permanently, and their yellow flower clusters, 20-30cm/8-12in high, make a good show for frontal positions. H25cm/10in, W15cm/6in. F7-9. Z4-8.

A. stellatum. This has glaucous foliage and pale pink flowers. H35cm/14in, W15cm/6in. F6-8. Z4-8.

ALSTROEMERIA Peruvian lily

Beautiful, lily-like flower clusters on tall, leafy stems make these very tempting and much loved by flower arrangers, but such deep-rooting types as *A. aurantiaca* and the Ligtu Hybrids are best grown in isolation, as they can be invasive. *A. pulchella*, however, has tubers nearer the surface and is easier to control. A sunny position, shelter and well-drained, deep, light soil are best.

A. Ligtu Hybrids. These are many shades of colour from pink to salmon, yellow and orange. They need to be planted 15cm/6in deep, from young seed-raised stock, in

Amsonia tabernaemontana

Anchusa azurea 'Loddon Royalist'

Anemone × hybrida 'Hadspen Abundance'

Anemone × hybrida 'Lady Gilmour'

ANAPHALIS Pearl everlasting

These easy-to-grow, grey- or silver-leaved plants have loose heads of small, fluffy white flowers. The taller species are useful for cutting and can be dried for winter decoration. Although not deep-rooting, they spread fairly rapidly in good soil, but they also tolerate quite poor or dry conditions and do not deteriorate if left for several years. Unlike most other silver-leaved subjects, some tolerate light shade.

A. margaritacea. This has silvery foliage, robust, branching growth and heads of profuse, crispy white flowers. It tolerates some shade. H30-45cm/12-18in, W30-45cm/12-18in. F7-9. Z3-8.

A. nubigena. More compact, otherwise of similar growth to the above, with woolly leaves. H20cm/8in, W23cm/9in. F7-9. Z4-8.

A. triplinervis. Good ground cover, this is also similar to *A. margaritacea*, with tidy growth and silvery, woolly leaves. **'Summer Snow'** flowers more freely and is closer to pure white. H25cm/10in, W60cm/2ft. F7-9. Z4-9.

A. yedoensis. This has relatively tall stems and fairly tight heads of ivory-white flowers. It is excellent for cutting, and the whole plant makes a leafy, silvery bush. Its vigorous roots spread steadily. H75cm/30in, W30cm/1ft. F8-10. Z4-8.

ANCHUSA

These are not without faults but are valued for their bright display of blue in early summer. From black fleshy roots come rather rough leaves and branching stems carrying scores of clear blue, bell-shaped flowers. They much prefer sun and well-drained soil, and often die out in winter in badly drained soil. Their main fault lies in leaving a bare gap for some weeks when flowering is over by midsummer because the basal leaves also fade away. This can sometimes be avoided, however, if the plant is cut hard back when flowering ends. Larger forms may need staking. The following, all Z4-8.

A. azurea (syn. *A. italica*). There are many named forms. **'Little John'**, a valuable dwarf, leafy and long-flowering. H35cm/14in, W30cm/1ft. F5-8. **'Loddon Royalist'**, gentian-blue flowers. H1.5m/5ft, W60cm/2ft. F5-7. **'Opal'**, light blue. H1.1m/43in, W60cm/2ft. F5-7. **'Royal Blue'**, dark blue. H1.1m/43in, W60cm/2ft. F5-7. These have now superseded the old **'Dropmore'**.

A. italica. See *A. azurea*.

ANEMONE

Only true herbaceous perennials are included here, those growing from corms being classed as bulbs. The pasque flower, formerly *A. pulsatilla*, now has its own, separate genus, *Pulsatilla vulgaris*. By far

light soil and sun. Old plants resent being moved or disturbed. H80cm/32in, W30cm/1ft. F6-8. Z6-11.

A. pulchella. Although the parrot lily needs protecting by litter in cold districts, it is remarkably hardy in well-drained soil and sun. Its leafy stems terminate in a cluster of rich reddish brown, green-tipped tubular flowers. H60cm/2ft, W30cm/1ft. F8-9. Z8-10.

AMSONIA

A. tabernaemontana (syn. *A. salicifolia*). This appears to be the primary species in cultivation. It makes a stout, long-lived clump with narrow leaves on arching, willowy stems tipped with small, blue, periwinkle-like flowers for many weeks. Charmingly graceful and adaptable to almost any soil, in sun or a little shade. H75cm/30in, W45cm/18in. F6-9. Z4-9.

the most valuable anemones are the Japanese types (*A.* × *hybrida*), which make a fine display in later summer and autumn, but others mentioned below are also garden-worthy. Almost all are long-lived, given well-drained soil and sun, though the Japanese kinds are apt to spread freely. The yellow stamens add to the beauty of the cup-, saucer- or bowl-shaped flowers.

A. × *hybrida*. This and the hybrids are too interbred to separate. All are easy in well-drained soil and sun, but do not transplant well except as pot-grown plants raised from root cuttings. None needs staking, and they revel in limy soil. **'Bressingham Glow'**, the best rich deep pink, semi-double flowers. H60cm/2ft, W45cm/18in. F8-10. Z5-8. **'Hadspen Abundance'**, deep rose-pink, almost semi-double flowers, prominent golden-yellow stamens, very free-flowering. H60cm/2ft, W30cm/1ft. F8-10. Z5-9.

'Lady Gilmour', large, ivy-type basal leaves, large, semi-double, clear pink flowers. H60cm/2ft, W45cm/18in. F7-10. Z5-8. **'Lorelei'**, erect, wiry stems carrying soft deep pink flowers, fairly rapid spread. H70cm/28in, W45cm/18in. F7-10. Z5-8. **'Louise Uhink'**, pure white, finer than the old **'Honorine Jobert'** or **'Whirlwind'**. H90cm/3ft, W30cm/1ft. F8-10. Z5-8; **'September Charm'**, dainty, profuse, single, soft pink flowers. H40cm/16in, W30cm/1ft. F7-10. Z5-9. **'White Giant'**, the tallest, with the largest flowers of all. H90cm/3ft, W45cm/18in. F7-10. Z5-8.

A. × *lesseri*. A hybrid ideal for good, deep soil that does not dry out and light shade. It has deeply divided leaves and erect stems bearing small but profuse, glowing, rosy red flowers in early summer, and often again in early autumn. It has fibrous, non-invasive roots and is slow-growing. H45cm/18in, W30cm/1ft. F5-6. Z5-8.

A. magellanica. There are two forms, the larger being better. Finely cut leaves and erect stems carry cream, cup-shaped flowers for several weeks. H35cm/14in, W25cm/10in. F5-7 . Z2-9.

A. rivularis. Worthy of greater use, its slow-spreading roots send up deep green, divided leaves and stiff, branching stems carrying white flowers, sometimes bluish on the reverse. Humus-rich soil is preferred. H60cm/2ft, W30cm/1ft. F6-8. Z6-8.

A. sylvestris. The snowdrop anemone, happy in sun or semi-shade and heavy or light soil, has pure white cups above soft green mounds of foliage. The fluffy seed heads are also attractive. H35cm/14in, W30cm/1ft. F6-8. Z4-9.

A. tomentosa and *A. vitifolia*. Both are similar to the Japanese anemones (*A.* × *hybrida*), but are less colourful and can be invasive. Both H90cm/3ft, W38cm/15in. F8-10. Z4-8.

Anthemis cupaniana

ANTHEMIS

A genus of marguerite-type flowers and finely divided foliage from a compact rootstock. Some are short-lived if allowed to overflower. Easy-to-grow sun lovers for open positions and well-drained soil.

A. cupaniana. This makes rapid surface growth in summer of greyish, aromatic leaves, forming a low blanket below a long succession of white, yellow-centred daisies. Needs fairly frequent lifting, dividing and replanting in spring. H25cm/10in, W75cm/30in. F5-8. Z5-8.

A. rudolphiana (syn. *A. biebersteinana*). See under Alpines.

A. sancti-johannis. It is doubtful whether the true plant is now available, but under this name in the trade is a well-foliaged twiggy plant of deep green, topped with short-stemmed, rich orange-yellow daisies. H60cm/2ft, W60cm/2ft. F6-8. Z4-9.

A. tinctoria. Only hybrid forms of the golden marguerite are seen now. Its floppy stems are somewhat woody, with tiny leaves; plants can be untidy and short-lived. All flower profusely and if not cut back to near ground level after fading are apt to die for lack of new basal growth. **'Grallach Gold'** is deep yellow, but seldom long-lived. **'Mrs Buxton'** ('E.C. Buxton') and **'Wargrave'** are both primrose-yellow. All H90cm/3ft, W90cm/3ft. F6-8. Z4-8.

ANTHERICUM

These clump-forming plants are easy to grow in any good, light soil and make a pleasing display in early summer. They have glossy leaves and smooth, erect stems topped with a sheaf of small, white, trumpet-type flowers. Some confusion has resulted in separating St Bernard's lily, *A. liliago*, from what was St Bruno's lily, *A. liliastrum*, now classified as *Paradisea liliastrum*. Only slight differences exist.

A. algeriense. This is similar to *A. liliago*, but less robust and it rarely sets seed. H75cm/30in, W25cm/10in. F5-7. Z6-9.

A. liliago. This has narrow basal leaves, smooth stems and pure white flowers in early summer, followed by attractive seed heads. It self-seeds if happy. H60cm/2ft, W30cm/1ft. F5-7. Z5-9.

Anthericum liliago

ANTHOLYZA See under CROCOSMIA.

AQUILEGIA Columbine

These are old favourites but few are long-lived; flowering can be brief on dry soils and some self-seed too much. Not many can be relied upon to come true from seed, but this is virtually the only means of increase. All prefer a mainly sunny position.

A. canadensis. Wiry stems end in bright yellow and red flowers. H60cm/2ft, W30cm/1ft. F5-7. Z4-9.

A. flabellata. Less graceful but stockier and longer-lived than most, with chubby, lilac-tinged white flowers. Best in the rich blue dwarf form, *nana*, and the white **'Nana**

Aquilegia vulgaris 'Nora Barlow'

Alba'. All will come reasonably true from seed. H30cm/1ft, W30cm/1ft. F5-7. Z4-9.

A. longissima. This has extra-long, bright yellow spurs to its pale yellow flowers. Short-lived. H60cm/2ft, W45cm/18in. F5-7. Z4-9.

A. vulgaris. Commonly known as Granny's bonnet, this is mostly seen in various colours. The clustered flowers come in profusion in white, pink, indigo, violet and crimson. H60cm/2ft, W45cm/18in. F5-7. Z5-9. **'Granny's Gold'** is distinctive for its golden foliage, which contrasts well with the purplish flowers. H60cm/2ft, W30cm/1ft. F6-7. Z5-9. **'Nora Barlow'** is an intriguing variation which comes 90 per cent true

Armeria plantaginea 'Bees Ruby'

Artemisia canescens

Aruncus dioicus 'Plumosus'

from seed and is quite long-lived. The tightly bunched pink, red and green flowers are double, almost quilled. Other doubles are appearing in various colours from dark purple to light blue and white. H70cm/28in, W45cm/18in. F5-7. Z5-9. **'White Bonnet'** grows strongly and has double white quilled flowers. H75cm/30in, W30cm/1ft. F6-7. Z5-9.

Hybrids. **'Biedermeier'**, colourful dwarf mixture, with bunched heads of erect flowers. H40cm/16in, W30cm/1ft. F5-7. Z3-9. **'Crimson Star'**, good-sized crimson and white bicolour flowers on slender stems. H50cm/20in, W30cm/1ft. F5-7. Z3-9. **'McKana Hybrids'**, mixed colours with extra-long spurs, superseding the old 'Scott Elliot' strain. H75cm/30in, W30cm/1ft. F5-7. Z3-9.

ARISAEMA
These arum-like plants have divided foliage, tuberous roots and spathes. They are hardy in all but very cold areas, and prefer humus-rich soil in sun or light shade. They are fussy about planting depth, and need to be set 13cm/5in or so deep, when dormant.
A. candidissimum. A lovely species for cool shade, with pure white, hooded spathes, followed by lobed leaves and orange berries, if several types are planted close together. H30cm/1ft, W45cm/18in. F6-8. Z7-9.
A. consanguineum. This has slender, erect stems and umbrella-like leaves, with large, brown-striped, greenish spathes. H60cm/2ft, W30cm/1ft. F6-7. Z8-9.

ARMERIA Thrift, sea pink
These are all more or less evergreen, forming grassy tufts or mats topped by tight, rounded flower heads on wiry stems. All need sun and well-drained soil.
A. **'Formosa Hybrids'**. This mixed strain includes white, pink and salmon, deep carmine and unusual terracotta shades. H30cm/1ft, W30cm/1ft. F6-8. Z6-7.
A. leucocephala **'Corsica'**. This has rosy salmon flower heads. H25cm/10in, W30cm/1ft. F6-8. Z4-9.
A. maritima. Although often classed as alpines, some named cultivars are perfect as frontal subjects to perennials or as edging. **'Alba'** is white, **'Dusseldorf Pride'** is nearest to red, and **'Vindictive'** is deep pink. The rosy red hybrids **'Bloodstone'** and **'Ruby Glow'** are a little taller and later. All H13-15cm/5-6in, W30cm/1ft. F5-7. Z3-7.
A. plantaginea. This is one of the taller species, with stout stalked flowers varying from carmine to white. It is usually represented in cultivation by **'Bees Ruby'**, with splendid, deep 'shocking' pink flower heads up to 4cm/1¹/2in across. H40cm/16in, W30cm/1ft. F6-8. Z4-9.

ARNEBIA The prophet flower
A. echioides. Still a rarity though easy to please in deep, light soil and sun. It has basal leaves and sprays of pure yellow flowers. On opening, each petal has a maroon spot, said to be the imprint of Mohammed's fingers. An intriguing plant and not only for its rarity. H20cm/8in, W20cm/8in. F5-6. Z4-7.

ARTEMISIA
With one exception these are best regarded as foliage plants, with flowers of little significance. All are greyish or silvery, with toothed or finely cut leaves, and have varying degrees of spread, acting as ground cover or as foils to more colourful subjects. They are best in sun, but are not fussy as to soil if it is well drained. They need pruning in spring if becoming unshapely.
A. canescens. This has the most delicate, silvery, almost hoary or filigree leaves. It is compact and somewhat shrubby, making excellent ground cover. H30cm/1ft, W30cm/1ft. Z5-9.
A. lactiflora. This is the exception, with green, deeply cut leaves and stiff stems carrying creamy white plumes in late summer. A very effective plant, but not happy in dry, poor soil. H1.5m/5ft, W60cm/2ft. F8-10. Z4-9.
A. ludoviciana **'Silver Queen'**. Rapid-spreading, with willow-like, silvery leaves and leafy stems, this is more compact and slightly floppier than the species. H80cm/32in, W60cm/2ft. Z4-9.
A. nutans. This neat-growing, shrubby but non-invasive species has very pretty, delicate laced foliage. H50cm/20in, W30cm/1ft. Z8-9.
A. pontica. Roman wormwood has silver-grey, finely cut foliage, making a good carpet. H25cm/10in, W50cm/20in. Z5-8.
A. stelleriana. Felted silver leaves, deeply cut and larger than most, are carried on ground-hugging stems. It makes good, evergreen ground cover, neatest in **'Boughton Silver'**. H30cm/1ft, W60cm/2ft. Z4-8.
A. villarsii. This has graceful sprays of delicate silver-grey from a compact-growing rootstock. H40cm/16in, W45cm/18in. Z5-9.

ARUNCUS Goat's beard
These showy plants, closely related to *Spiraea*, are fairly adaptable, but prefer moist soil and some shade. Established clumps can be left alone for many years. They are especially suited to waterside planting.
A. aethusifolius. A miniature species with creamy white spikes on crispy, dissected foliage. H20cm/8in, W25cm/10in. F6-7. Z4-8.
A. dioicus (syn. *A. sylvester*). Imposing, creamy white plumes are carried above a mass of fern-like foliage. H1.5-2.1m/5-7ft, W1.2m/4ft. F6-7. Z3-8. The choice **'Kneiffii'** is dwarfer, with dark green, deeply cut leaves, wiry stems and flower plumes. H90cm/3ft, W45cm/18in. F6-7. Z3-8. **'Plumosus'** and the **'Glasnevin'** form have shapely, creamy white plumes on erect stems. H1.2m/4ft, W45cm/18in. F6-7. Z3-8.
A. sylvester. See *A. dioicus*.

Asarum europaeum

ASARUM Wild ginger

All these evergreen ground-covering plants for shade make mounds of rounded leaves and insignificant flowers.

A. caudatum. This vigorous, mat-forming species has quite large, heart-shaped, fairly glossy leaves and small, brownish red, bell-shaped flowers. H25cm/10in, W45cm/18in. F6-7. Z5-8.

A. europaeum. A neat, clump-forming, evergreen ground cover, with highly glossy, kidney-shaped leaves and brownish flowers. H20cm/8in, W30cm/1ft. F5-6. Z4-7.

ASCLEPIAS Butterfly weed, milkweed

Few species are in cultivation. They have fleshy roots, small, waxy, upward-facing flowers, and silky seed heads. All are sun lovers for deep soil. A. hallii and A. syriaca should be avoided as invasive.

A. incarnata. A reliable clump-forming plant, its strong stems carry heads of glistening deep lilac-pink. Best in moist soil. H1.2m/4ft, W40cm/16in. F7-9. Z4-9.

A. tuberosa. The best known but not the easiest to grow, this seems to prefer an acid sandy or peaty soil to produce its wide heads of burnished deep orange. I have never managed to keep this alive for more than two or three years. H45cm/18in, W30cm/1ft. F7-9. Z4-9.

ASPERULA

A. odorata. The native British woodruff is useful beneath shrubs, but its tiny white

Asphodeline lutea 'Gelbkerze'

flowers have no impact. H15cm/6in, W30cm/1ft. F6-7. Z4-8.

A. tinctoria. A pleasing, but unspectacular, species with profuse, small white flowers giving an airy appearance. H30cm/1ft, W30cm/1ft. F5-7. Z4-8.

ASPHODELINE

A. liburnica. This has narrow, glaucous leaves and pale yellow flowers on slender spikes. H1m/39in, W30cm/1ft. F6-8. Z6-8.

A. lutea. King's spear, or asphodel, is more evergreen than A. liburnica, with clumps of narrow, glaucous leaves and strong spikes of bright yellow starry flowers, followed by attractive seed heads. The German cultivar 'Gelbkerze' has larger, slightly brighter flowers. Both H1m/39in, W30cm/1ft. F6-8. Z6-8.

ASPHODELUS

Full sun and well-drained soil suit these members of the lily family.

A. cerasiferus. A central fleshy root produces long, pointed, grey-green leaves and quite large, branching spikes of white flowers, suffused with reddish brown and with orange anthers. After flowering, it loses its foliage as it enters dormancy, which detracts from its merit. H1.5m/5ft, W60cm/2ft. F5-6. Z5-9.

Aster amellus 'Vanity'

ASTER

This vast and varied genus is not confined to Michaelmas daisies but has many other species of garden value, varying in height from 10cm/4in to 2.1m/7ft, and flowering from mid-spring to late autumn. Very few are difficult to grow, but most prefer sun and well-drained soil. Many are valuable for cutting; some can be invasive.

A. acris. See A. sedifolius.

A. amellus. This covers a range of first-rate, trouble-free varieties, all single rayed, yellow-centred flowers seldom needing support and having no faults or diseases. All are long-lived, slow-growing, non-invasive and long-flowering. For autumn planting, pot-grown plants are best. All F8-10, Z5-8.

'Bessie Chapman', deep blue, dark foliage. H75cm/30in, W45cm/18in. 'King George', an old, violet-blue favourite. H60cm/2ft, W45cm/18in. 'Lady Hindlip', deep pink. H75cm/30in, W45cm/18in. 'Nocturne', rich lilac-lavender. H75cm/30in, W45cm/18in. 'Pink Zenith', the most prolific pink variety. H75cm/30in, W45cm/18in. 'Sonia', clear mid-pink. H75cm/30in, W45cm/18in. 'Vanity', prolific, large-flowered, mid-blue. H70cm/28in, W45cm/18in. 'Violet Queen', masses of deep violet-blue flowers. H60cm/2ft, W45cm/18in.

Aster novae-angliae 'Harrington's Pink'

Aster novi-belgii 'Jenny'

Aster thomsonii 'Nanus'

A. cordifolius. This has heart-shaped leaves, wiry stems and graceful sprays of silvery blue flowers. **'Photograph'**, H1.3m/51in, W45cm/18in, and **'Silver Spray'**, H1.6m/63in, W45cm/18in, are both good. F9-10. Z3-8.

A. dumosus. See *A. novi-belgii* dwarf hybrids.

A. ericoides. This type makes stiff but shapely bushes, with tiny leaves and profuse, tiny flowers covering the plant. Undeservedly neglected, they are trouble-free, largely self-supporting and can remain for several years without being divided. White, pale blue and pale yellowish flower varieties exist. H70-90cm/28-36in, W30cm/1ft. F7-9. Z3-8.

A. farreri. See *A. tongolensis*.

A. 'Flora's Delight'. This and *A. × frikartii* are the results of crossing *A. amellus* and *A. thomsonii*. The former is a long-flowering, neat-growing plant with lilac-pink rayed flowers. It needs very well-drained soil. H50cm/20in, W40cm/16in. F7-9. Z4-9.

A. × frikartii 'Wunder von Stäfa' (syn. 'Wonder of Stäfa'). Taller, more branching and leafier than the type, it has clear lavender-blue flowers for many weeks. H1m/39in, W40cm/16in. F7-9. Z5-8. The very long-flowering **'Mönch'** is similar but less branching in habit.

A. laevis. Not often seen but an attractive, easy plant with strong stems carrying rounded sheaves of 2.5cm/1in wide, lavender-blue flowers. H80cm/32in, W38cm/15in. F8-10. Z4-8.

A. lateriflorus 'Horizontalis'. This has slender, twiggy, upright stems and horizontal sprays of small white or bluish flowers with pink stamens. Its diminutive leaves turn an attractive purple-bronze in early autumn. H1.5m/5ft, W38cm/15in. F9-11. Z4-8.

A. linosyris. So-called 'goldilocks' is willowy-stemmed and leaved, topped with rounded heads of small, button-like, fluffy yellow flowers. The form **'Gold Dust'** is best, with larger, deep yellow plumes. Both H90cm/3ft, W30cm/1ft. F7-9. Z3-8.

A. 'Little Carlow'. An unusual hybrid. Its small, bright blue flowers are carried on robust, branching stems. H1.1m/43in, W30cm/1ft. F9-11. Z3-8.

A. novae-angliae. New England asters make stout clumps from fibrous roots. They are reliable in any but waterlogged soil and the brownish stems carry single, yellow-centred, rayed petalled flowers in loose heads. Support may be needed in rich or moist soil or when overcrowded. All F9-10, Z4-8. **'Alma Pötschke'**, striking, warm salmon-rose. H1.5m/5ft, W60cm/2ft. **'Autumn Snow'** (syn. 'Herbstschnee'),

large white flowers in bushy heads. H1.5m/5ft, W50cm/20in. **'Harrington's Pink'**, clear pink. H1.5m/5ft, W60cm/2ft. **'Lye End Beauty'**, rosy lavender. H1.8m/6ft, W60cm/2ft.

A. novi-belgii. The true Michaelmas daisies have fallen out of favour, due to over-breeding and over-propagation, and vulnerability to wilt and mildew. Many varieties have stood the test of time and are well worth including for their autumn colour. Avoid tall kinds, which are liable to be top-heavy and need support, and lift and divide in spring every two to three years to prevent clumps degenerating. All Z4-8.

'Ada Ballard', large mauve-blue flowers. H90cm/3ft, W45cm/18in. F8-10. **'Bonanza'**, vivid red. H90cm/3ft, W45cm/18in. F9-10. **'Carnival'**, intense, semi-double cherry-red, erect-growing. H60cm/2ft, W45cm/18in. F9-10. **'Coombe Rosemary'**, fully double violet-purple flowers 3-5cm/1^1/4-2in across. H90cm/3ft, W45cm/18in. F9-10. **'Fellowship'**, very fine pink flowers. H90cm/3ft, W45cm/18in. F9-10. **'Marie Ballard'**, fine double light blue. H90cm/3ft. W45cm/18in. F9-10. **'Royal Ruby'**, semi-double rich, deep red. H50cm/20in, W45cm/18in. F9-10. **'White Ladies'**, strong-growing, white flowers, dark foliage. H1.2m/4ft, W45cm/18in. F9-10.

Dwarf hybrids, sometimes listed under *A. dumosus*, are less prone to diseases, grow vigorously and do not need support. Colours range from white to shades of pink, crimson, blue and lilac. **'Audrey'**, mauve-blue single, one of the best. H30cm/1ft, W45cm/18in. F9-10. **'Jenny'**, double red. H30cm/1ft, W45cm/18in. F9-10. **'Lady in Blue'**, compact, with masses of semi-double blue flowers. H25cm/10in, W45cm/18in. F8-10. **'Little Pink Beauty'**, the best semi-double pink. H40cm/16in, W45cm/18in. F9-10. **'Professor A. Kippenburg'**, an old favourite, the best clear blue. H30cm/1ft, W45cm/18in. F9-10. **'Snow Cushion'**, low-growing, compact, with white flowers. H30cm/1ft, W45cm/18in. F9-10.

A. pringlei 'Monte Cassino'. Very late-flowering cut-flower variety, a mass of white in late autumn. H1.2m/4ft, W60cm/2ft. F9-11. Z4-8.

A. purdomi. See *A. tongolensis*.

A. sedifolius (syn. *A. acris*). This has two forms, the dwarfer **'Nanus'** being preferable to the taller types, which have widely branched stems carrying myriad small blue flowers, making them top-heavy and floppy. Leaves are narrow and plants are clump-forming. 'Nanus': H40-50cm/16-20in, W38cm/15in; others: H80cm/32in, W38cm/15in. F7-9. Z4-7.

A. spectabilis. I rate this uncommon, late-flowering dwarf highly. It is mat-forming, with dark, leathery foliage, wiry stems and

Astilbe chinensis 'Pumila'

Astilbe simplicifolia 'Sprite'

Astilbe simplicifolia 'Bronze Elegance'

sprays of blue, yellow-centred flowers for several weeks. Disease-resistant. H30cm/1ft, W25cm/10in. F8-10. Z4-9.

A. subcaeruleus. See *A. tongolensis*.

A. **'Summer Greeting'**. A pretty hybrid of neat habit and long flowering, with light lavender rayed petals and a yellow centre. H30cm/1ft, W30cm/1ft. F6-8. Z4-8.

A. thomsonii **'Nanus'**. This very good plant has a shapely, bushy habit, set with greyish foliage and rayed, light blue, starry flowers for weeks on end. Best left undisturbed. H40cm/16in, W25cm/10in. F7-10. Z4-9.

A. tongolensis (syn. *A. yunnanensis*). Several allied species, including *A. farreri*, *A. purdomi* and *A. subcaeruleus*, are placed together because they are best represented by the named cultivars. All flower in early summer from mat-like growth and have single-stemmed flowers with bright orange centres. Useful cut flowers. Divide every two or three years after flowering. All F5-7, Z5-8. **'Berggarten'**, 5cm/2in wide, clear lavender-blue flowers. H40cm/16in, W30cm/1ft. **'Napsbury'**, deeper blue, finely rayed flowers. H35cm/14in, W30cm/1ft.

A. tradescantii. This may vary a little in height, but not in its form. Slender, erect stems carry longish, toothed leaves and heads of whitish, yellow-centred daisies. An easy, trouble-free species, valuable for late flowering and good for cutting. H1.2m/4ft, W45cm/18in. F9-10. Z4-8.

A. vimineus **'Ptarmicoides'**. This forms neat tufts, bearing slender, rigid stems with branches of small, whitish rayed flowers. H35cm/14in, W30cm/1ft. F7-9. Z5-8.

A. yunnanensis. See *A. tongolensis*.

ASTILBE

In common with several other genera, the species have been so interbred that classification under separate species is difficult, and pointless for those whose main interest is garden value. The entries below are adjusted accordingly. Without exception, astilbes do best in rich soil which does not dry out. They tolerate some dryness and flower longer if not in full sun, and thrive in a sunny place if continually moist, but only a few put up with wet, boggy conditions. These are generally the taller kinds; the very dwarf ones are the shade lovers. A spring mulch of enriched peat or leaf mould is beneficial for all, and the rewards for caring are high. All are hardy, self-supporting and long-lived.

A. × *arendsii.* See Hybrids below.

A. chinensis. The form *davidii* has imposing, magenta-pink spikes. H1.8m/6ft, W50cm/20in. F7-8. Z4-8. **'Pumila'** has a vigorous spread of deeply cut, ground-hugging foliage and stubby, lilac-pink flower spikes. Longer-flowering and more adaptable than most; excellent ground cover. H30cm/1ft, W25cm/10in. F7-9. Z4-8.

A. × *crispa* **'Liliput'**. This true dwarf has short, deep pink spikes above deep green, crispy leaves. **'Perkeo'** is similar, but lighter pink. Both H15cm/6in, W15cm/6in. F7-8. Z4-8.

A. grandis. This is white-plumed, with strong stems and downy leaves. H1.5m/5ft, W90cm/3ft. F6-8. Z4-8.

A. japonica. See Hybrids below.

A. rivularis. The tallest species, this has a vigorous spread, attractive, deeply divided, lobed leaves and strong stems carrying arching white plumes. It needs damp conditions. H2.1m/7ft, W1.2m/4ft. F7-8. Z4-8.

A. simplicifolia. This is the pink parent of several good dwarf hybrids. H30cm/1ft, W20cm/8in. F6-8. All Z4-8. **'Atrorosea'**, very full, intense pink, long-lasting spikes. H40cm/16in, W30cm/1ft. F6-8. **'Bronze Elegance'**, pink flowers, pretty bronze-tinged leaves, very compact habit. H20cm/8in, W20cm/8in. F6-8. **'Dunkellachs'**, narrow, graceful spikes of light salmon-pink flowers, needs humus-rich soil. H50cm/20in, W30cm/1ft. F6-8. **'Nana'**, miniature, with dainty, clear pink spikes. H15cm/6in, W15cm/6in. F6-8. **'Praecox Alba'**, bushy, pure white spikes. H35cm/14in, W30cm/1ft. F6-8. **'Sprite'**, abundant, wide-branching sprays of white, pink-tinged flowers above delicate dark greenery. It is rather gratifying to have raised this, since it has become so widely popular. H25-30cm/10-12in, W30cm/1ft. F7-9.

Astilbe 'Elizabeth Bloom'

Hybrids. The following are sometimes classified as *A. × arendsii* or *A. japonica*, but are best now listed alphabetically regardless. All Z4-8. **'Amethyst'**, full, lilac-rose spikes. H90cm/3ft, W60cm/2ft. F6-7. **'Bressingham Beauty'**, fine pink spikes on strong stems above attractive foliage. H1m/39in, W60cm/2ft. F6-8. **'Cologne'**, intense pink, quite dwarf, early. H50cm/20in, W45cm/18in. F6-7. **'Deutschland'**, compact, dazzling white. H50cm/20in, W45cm/18in. F6-7. **'Dusseldorf'**, bright cerise-pink. H50cm/20in, W45cm/18in. F6-7. **'Elizabeth Bloom'**, very free-flowering, rich pink, abundant greenery. H60cm/2ft, W60cm/2ft. F6-8. **'Fanal'**, dwarf, long-flowering red, short, dense spikes. H50cm/20in, W45cm/18in. F6-8. **'Federsee'**, sturdy, full, rosy red plumes. H60cm/2ft, W60cm/2ft. F6-8. **'Fire'**, intense cherry-red, feathery. H80cm/32in, W60cm/2ft. F6-8.

 'Glow', deep red, feathery, very dark foliage. H80cm/32in, W60cm/2ft. F6-8. **'Irrlicht'**, dark foliage, white flowers. H50cm/20in, W45cm/18in. F6-8. **'Jo Ophurst'**, stiff, tapering, ruby-red spikes. H60cm/2ft, W60cm/2ft. F6-8. **'Mainz'**, one of the earliest, deep pink. H45cm/18in, W45cm/18in. F6-7. **'Montgomery'**, almost flame-red. H60cm/2ft, W60cm/2ft. F6-8. **'Ostrich Plume'**, distinctive, arching, salmon-pink plumes. H80cm/32in, W60cm/2ft. F7-8.

 'Red Sentinel', almost brick-red, loose spikes, dark foliage. H75cm/30in, W60cm/2ft. F6-8. **'Rheinland'**, an old favourite, compact, upright, rich pink spikes. H50cm/20in, W45cm/18in. F6-7. **'Salland'**, tall, imposing, carmine-pink. H1.8m/6ft, W60cm/2ft. F7-8. **'Serenade'**, rosy red, quite dwarf. H40cm/16in, W45cm/18in. F6-8. **'Sheila Haxton'**, outstanding compact pink with a hint of lilac. H40cm/16in, W30cm/1ft. F6-8. **'Snowdrift'**, bright green mounds of cut foliage, clear white plumes, perfect contrast to 'Fanal' and deeper colours. H60cm/2ft, W45cm/18in. F6-8. **'Venus'**, tall, leafy, light pink. H1.2m/4ft, W60cm/2ft. F6-8.

ASTILBOIDES
A. tabularis. See *Rodgersia tabularis*.

ASTRANTIA Masterwort
Despite their lack of bright colour, these have become popular, especially for their value in flower arrangements. Most have a hint of green in their curiously shaped flowers, each with a dome of tiny florets backed by a collar-like bract. All are clump-forming, making useful ground cover, and are easy to grow in any soil which does not become baked in summer. All Z4-8.
A. carniolica rubra. Its deep crimson-green flowers are carried above mounds of finely divided foliage. Best in moist, rich soil. H45cm/18in, W30cm/1ft. F6-8.
A. helleborifolia. See *A. maxima*.
A. major. The most common species, this has much divided, lobed leaves and flowers on the greenish side of white, with a light green collar. H75cm/30in, W45cm/18in. F6-8. The form *involucrata* and **'Margery Fish'** (syn. 'Shaggy') are much alike, having extra-large bracts. H75cm/30in, W45cm/18in. F6-9. **'Rosea'** may cover more than one seedling selection but at its best has a neat habit and deep rose-red flowers. H75cm/30in, W45cm/18in. F6-8. **'Ruby Lustre'** has handsome deep pink blooms on erect stems above mounded foliage. H75cm/30in, W45cm/18in. F6-8. **'Sunningdale Variegated'** has very attractive foliage in spring and early summer, the leaves streaked white then cream, but this effect fades when greenish white flowers appear. A striking but not difficult plant. H80cm/32in, W45cm/18in. F6-8.
A. maxima (syn. *A. helleborifolia*). This is distinct for its pink flowers above a greenish pink collar on slender stems. Three-lobed leaves are not unlike those of ground elder and plants have quite a rapid spread in good soil. H75cm/30in, W45cm/18in. F6-9.

Astrantia major involucrata

Astrantia maxima

Begonia evansiana

ASYNEUMA See under PHYTEUMA.

BAPTISIA
B. australis. This long-lived, bushy plant has abundant blue-green foliage topped by short spikes of indigo-blue, lupin-like flowers, followed by attractive seed pods. A good, non-invasive plant for any reasonable soil. Often listed as *B. a. exaltata*. H90cm/3ft, W60cm/2ft. F6-8. Z3-9.

BEGONIA
B. evansiana (syn. *B. grandis*). This is hardy in most districts. Its semi-fibrous roots produce shiny, puckered, heart-shaped leaves with red undersides and arching sprays of small pink flowers, red in bud. There is also the white-flowered form **'Alba'**. Best in light soil and full sun. They increase by making small bulbils. Both H30cm/1ft, W45cm/18in. F7-9. Z6-9.

BERGENIA
Popular for weed-smothering ground cover, these make a good show except if spoiled by late frost. The mainly evergreen, shiny leaves vary in size up to 25cm/10in across. They are adaptable for sun or shade and are surface-expanding from shallow-rooting rhizomes. The hybrids are listed separately.
B. ciliata. Handsome, large hairy leaves and heads of blush-pink flowers make this outstanding; but it is rare and, although the roots are hardy, top growth is rather susceptible to spring frosts. H30cm/1ft, W45cm/18in. F3-5. Z5-8.
B. cordifolia. A reliable species, with

crinkly edged, rounded leaves, almost evergreen, and short spikes of lilac-pink flowers. H35cm/14in, W60cm/2ft. F3-5. Z3-8. **'Purpurea'** is outstanding for its purplish leaves in winter, followed by red-stemmed spikes of magenta-pink flowers. H50cm/20in, W60cm/2ft. F3-5. Z3-8.
B. crassifolia. Large, shiny, recurved, spoon-shaped leaves, tinted mahogany in winter, are combined with graceful sprays of light mauve-pink spikes. H35cm/14in, W45cm/18in. F3-5. Z3-8.
B. purpurascens. The narrow leaves turn almost beetroot-red in winter, brownish red underneath, and make especially good ground cover among shrubs. Deep pink flowers. H30cm/1ft, W30cm/1ft. F3-5. Z3-8.
B. × schmidtii. This early-flowering hybrid has dense, shiny leaves and pink flowers. H30cm/1ft, W30cm/1ft. F3-5. Z4-8.
B. stracheyi. This makes neat, compact, slow-spreading rosettes. It is early-flowering, with pale pink flowers. The white-flowered **'Alba'** is equally early. Both H20cm/8in, W30cm/1ft. F3-5. Z4-8.

Hybrids. Bred from all the above species, these include **'Abendglut'** (syn. 'Evening

Bergenia 'Bressingham Ruby'

Bergenia 'Baby Doll'

Glow'), slow-spreading, almost prostrate purplish leaves, purple-red stumpy spikes. H25cm/10in, W30cm/1ft. F3-5. Z3-8. **'Baby Doll'**, close-set spikes of sugar-pink flowers. H20cm/8in, W30cm/1ft. F3-5. Z4-8. **'Ballawley'** (formerly 'Delbees'), very large shiny leaves, handsome bright rose-pink spikes. H40cm/16in, W30cm/1ft. F3-5. Z4-8. **'Bressingham Bountiful'**, raised by the late Mr Pugsley, a fine light pink. H30cm/1ft, W30cm/1ft. F3-5. Z4-8. **'Bressingham Ruby'**, new, intense, deep red flowers and almost beetroot-red leaves in winter. H35cm/14in, W30cm/1ft. F3-5. Z3-8. **'Bressingham Salmon'**, a new, distinct, salmon shade. H30cm/1ft, W30cm/1ft. F3-5. Z4-8. **'Bressingham White'**, white flowers, handsome rounded leaves. H30cm/1ft, W30cm/1ft. F3-5, Z4-8.

'Glockenturm', purplish leaves, deep pink flowers. H25cm/10in, W30cm/1ft. F3-5. Z4-8. **'Morgenröte'**, dwarf, bright pink flowers, often flowering a second time. H30cm/1ft, W30cm/1ft. F3-5. Z3-8. **'Silberlicht'** (syn. 'Silver Light'), not quite white, not as neat as most, but free-flowering. H30cm/1ft, W30cm/1ft. F3-5. Z3-8. **'Sunningdale'**, good shiny leaves and pink flowers. H30cm/1ft, W30cm/1ft. F3-5. Z3-8.

BERKHEYA
B. macrocephala. This somewhat thistly species has long, divided, deep green leaves and strong, leafy, branching spikes of bright yellow daisy flowers, with spiny bracts. Full sun and fertile, well-drained soil are best. H1.2m/4ft, W90cm/3ft. F6-8. Z9-10.

BETONICA See under STACHYS.

BIDENS
B. atrosanguinea. See *Cosmos atrosanguineus.*

BOLTONIA
B. latisquana **'Snowbank'.** Very tall and branching, but makes a fine late display of small, white, Michaelmas daisy-type flowers. Sun or shade in any fertile soil; support is usually needed. Lift, divide and replant every two or three years. H2.1m/7ft, W60cm/2ft. F10-11. Z4-9.

BOYKINIA
B. aconitifolia. This demure but graceful little plant forms tufty, cut-leaved mounds, above which come dainty sprays of starry, white, yellow-centred flowers. Prefers cool shade and lime-free soil. H25cm/10in, W30cm/1ft. F5-7. Z5-9.
B. tellimoides (syn. *Peltiphyllum tellimoides*). Rounded, hand-sized, jagged leaves and open heads of small white flowers. Sun or shade where not too dry; lime-free soil. H30cm/1ft, W30cm/1ft. F5-6. Z5-9.

Brunnera macrophylla 'Variegata'

Calamintha nepetoides 'White Cloud'

BRUNNERA
B. macrophylla. This robust, adaptable plant has large, heart-shaped, light green leaves, following the intense blue forget-me-not flowers in spring. Good ground cover for all but hot, dry positions. H40cm/16in, W60cm/2ft. F4-6. All Z4-8. **'Hadspen Cream'** has wide, creamy buff-edged leaves. H35cm/14in, W60cm/2ft. F5-6. The similar **'Langtrees'** has small white blotches on the leaves. H40cm/16in, W60cm/2ft. F4-6. **'Variegata'** has bright leaf variegation, but needs shelter from sun. H40cm/16in, W60cm/2ft. F4-6.

BUPHTHALMUM See under INULA.

CALAMINTHA
These relatives of mint are non-invasive and flower for a long time in well-drained soil and sun or partial shade.
C. grandiflora. This makes mounds of light green, aromatic foliage set with short sprays of deep pink, sage-like flowers. H45cm/18in, W45cm/18in. F6-8. Z5-9.
C. nepetoides. One of my autumn favourites. Tiny, mauve, thyme-like flowers in profusion are borne on branching stems. H50cm/20in, W45cm/18in. F8-10. Z5-9. More compact is **'White Cloud'**. H30cm/1ft, W30cm/1ft. F8-10. Z5-9.

CALTHA Kingcup, marsh marigold
These early-flowering plants make a fine show, with shiny yellow, orange or occasionally white, buttercup-like flowers. Though moisture loving, they grow in any

Caltha palustris 'Plena'

Camassia leichtlinii 'Plena'

soil which does not dry out in summer. They prefer full sun, but on drier soil summer shade can be beneficial.

C. leptosepala. This choice, demure North American species has erect stems above a neat mound of foliage, carrying white, yellow-centred flowers. H15-20cm/6-8in, W30cm/1ft. F4-6. Z5-9.

C. palustris. The well-loved marsh marigold is best as a waterside subject, with impressive round leaves and rich yellow flowers. H30cm/1ft, W45cm/18in. The white form *alba* is very early and more compact at 15cm/6in. Both F3-5, Z4-9. 'Monstrosa Plena', has ranunculus-like double flowers, 4cm/1½ in across, on almost prostrate branching stems. H15cm/6in, W20cm/8in. F4-6. Z4-9. 'Plena' makes a splendid show with its glistening, perfect double flowers spraying out from neat, glossy foliage. This is so bright and cheerful that it pays to water copiously in summer. H15cm/6in, W20cm/8in. F3-5. Z4-9. 'Tyermanii' is similar, with single flowers, as if varnished, of bright yellow. H20cm/8in, W30cm/1ft. F4-5. Z4-9.

C. polypetala. The tallest and most luxuriant, with large leaves and glossy yellow flowers, this is a lush waterside plant. It spreads rapidly by its rooting stems and will even colonize the surface of the water. H60cm/2ft, W90cm/3ft. F4-6. Z4-9.

CAMASSIA

Bulbous, trouble-free plants for a sunny place with one fault of early dormancy, beginning in late summer and continuing until the following mid-spring. With their strap-shaped leaves and starry white to blue-violet flowers, they are good for naturalizing in rough grass or a wild garden, as well as in borders. Plant the bulbs 10cm/4in deep.

C. leichtlinii. As a type, this has whitish or bluish flowers on slender spikes above narrow leaves. H90-100cm/36-39in, W25cm/10in. F5-7. Z4-10. 'Plena' has more fulsome, creamy yellow flower spikes topping the smooth erect stems. H80cm/32in, W23cm/9in. F6-7. Z4-10.

CAMPANULA

This vast and varied genus gives us some first-rate subjects, including many alpines (q.v.). In general, they are easy to grow in any well-drained, fertile soil and sun, but a few prefer a little shade. There exists such a wealth of alpine and perennial species as to tempt one's collecting urges, as it has mine.

C. alaskana. Large, clustered heads of light blue make a massed display. H90cm/3ft, W40cm/16in. F6-8. Z3-7.

C. alliariifolia. The spurred bellflower is very adaptable and long-flowering. A clump-forming plant with heart-shaped leaves, its arching sprays of ivory-white bells continue for weeks. Drought-resistant. The form 'Ivory Bells' is best. H50cm/20in, W45cm/18in. F6-8. Z4-8.

C. 'Burghaltii'. Distinctive for its large, elongated bells of smoky lavender-blue hanging from short, leafy stems. H60cm/2ft, W30cm/1ft. F6-8. Z4-8.

C. carpatica. A borderline species, adaptable and effective as frontal groups with perennials, but listed under Alpines.

C. glomerata. The clustered bellflower is a variable species, with violet-blue flowers in tight, round heads or clasping the stems. Some forms spread quickly, and can be invasive. H30-90cm/1-3ft, W60cm/2ft. F6-8. All Z3-8. The form *acaulis* is almost stemless and very seldom seen. H15cm/6in, W45cm/18in. F6-8. Var. *dahurica* is a geographical form with purple flowers in wide clusters; quite vigorous spread. H50cm/20in, W60cm/2ft. F6-8. 'Joan Elliott' is early, with quite large violet-purple flowers. H30cm/1ft, W30cm/1ft. F5-8. 'Nana Alba' has sturdy spikes of white, outward-facing bells. H30cm/1ft, W30cm/1ft. F6-8. 'Purple Pixie', late, with dark foliage, has deep blue flowers on stiff spikes. H35cm/14in, W30cm/1ft. F7-9. 'Superba', largest of the vigorous, clustered-flower types, with large, rich purple-violet flowers, can be invasive. H80cm/32in, W60cm/2ft. F6-8.

C. grandis. See *C. latiloba*.

C. lactiflora. Variable in height and colour, most milky bellflowers have lavender-blue bells on branching stems. They are adaptable to sun or light shade; tall forms

Campanula alaskana

Campanula 'Burghaltii'

Campanula lactiflora 'Prichard's Variety'

may need support. All Z4-8. 'Alba' is tall with milky white flowers. H1.8m/6ft, W60cm/2ft. F6-8. 'Loddon Anna' is very tall, with unusual, flesh-pink flowers. H1.8m/6ft, W60cm/2ft. F6-8. 'Pouffe', a perfect miniature, forms dense mounds of light green foliage, with light lavender-blue flowers. This occurred as a pretty, self-sown seedling in my garden. H25cm/10in, W25cm/10in. F6-9. 'Prichard's Variety' is sturdy, with a splendid show of lavender-blue flowers. H1m/39in, W60cm/2ft. F6-8. **'White Pouffe'** is similar to 'Pouffe'; both flower best in sun. H25cm/10in, W25cm/10in. F6-9.

C. latifolia. The giant bellflower has strong, leafy stems growing from dense clumps of basal leaves and carrying large, drooping, violet-blue bells near and on top. Not averse to some shade, but dislikes very dry conditions. Self-seeds freely. H1.1m/43in, W60cm/2ft. F6-8. Z4-8. **'Gloaming'** is an appealing smoky blue with a hint of lavender. **'White Ladies'** has large, white blooms. H1.2m/4ft, W60cm/2ft. F6-8. Z4-8.

C. latiloba (formerly *C. grandis*). This forms light green rosettes from spreading roots, and slender stems clasped by stalkless, saucer-shaped flowers. Good ground cover. The white form **'Alba'** is now rare. The best form is **'Percy Piper'**, rich violet-blue though not very different from the old **'Highcliffe Variety'**. All H80cm/32in, W45cm/18in. F6-8. All Z4-8.

C. persicifolia. The peach-leaved bellflower is widely grown. Evergreen rosettes of pointed, dark green leaves produce slender stems studded with nodding, cup-shaped flowers varying from white to pale and deep blue. Good for cutting. H70-80cm/28-32in, W30cm/1ft. F6-8. All Z4-8. Several single-flowered selections have been named, but very few are cultivated; self-sown seedlings may be nondescript, so named varieties need to be increased by division. **'Fleur de Neige'** is a double white. H60cm/2ft, W30cm/1ft. F6-8. **'Hampstead White'** has a unique 'cup and saucer' formation of extra, ruff-like petals behind the flower. H70cm/28in, W30cm/1ft. F6-8. **'Pride of Exmouth'** is a double light blue. H60cm/2ft, W30cm/1ft. F6-8. **'Telham Beauty'**, a large-flowered rich blue, was the best-known, but the true original stock is rarely offered nowadays.

C. rapunculoides. This has insidious roots, which are liable to infest other plants and are very difficult to eradicate. It has nettle-like leaves and quite pretty lavender-blue, starry flowers, but should be strictly confined to a wild garden. H60-90cm/2-3ft, W60cm/2ft. F5-6. Z3-8.

C. sarmatica. See under Alpines.

C. takesimana. A Korean species of spreading habit, with flushed lilac bells, maroon inside, clinging to arching spikes. H60cm/2ft, W30cm/1ft. F6-8. Z4-8.

C. trachelium (syn. *C. urticifolia*). The nettle-leaf bellflower, or Coventry bells, is a seldom offered species, forming compact, tufty plants with bells carried all the way up the stems. There are single and double forms, in white and blue. All Z4-8. **'Bernice'**, the best and most reliable, forms a neat, clumpy plant, with fully double, china-blue flowers on erect stems.

Cardamine pratensis 'Flore Pleno'

H50cm/20in, W30cm/1ft. F6-8.

C. urticifolia. See *C. trachelium*.

*C. **'Van Houttei'**. This is a hybrid akin to *C.* 'Burghaltii' in habit, but the long, bell-shaped, dangling flowers are purple-blue. H30cm/1ft, W30cm/1ft. F6-9.

CARDAMINE

C. latifolia. This makes a fine spring show, with its large, lilac, thistle flowers borne on branching heads above a vigorous, almost evergreen, matted base. H30cm/1ft, W30cm/1ft. F3-5. Z3-9.

C. pratensis. Cuckoo flower, or lady's smock, has garden merit, with its mats of pinnate leaves and typical *Cruciferae* flowers, but is seldom cultivated. **'Flore Pleno'** has shorter, erect sprays, with double lilac or mauve flowers. Grow in fairly moist soil; lift and divide frequently. H25cm/10in, W25cm/10in. F4-5. Z3-8.

C. trifolia. An easy-going species, this has rounded heads of white flowers in early spring. H20cm/8in, W20cm/8in. F3-5. Z5-7.

CARDIOCRINUM

C. giganteum (formerly *Lilium giganteum*). This striking bulbous subject is worth the extra effort required to grow it. Provide deep, humus-rich soil, moist but well-drained, and light shade. Although virtually monocarpic, dying after flowering, it takes five years or so to reach flowering size if care is taken with bulbils or seedlings. Stiff, erect stems above large, deep green, heart-shaped leaves carry pure white, maroon-throated trumpets, clustered and outfacing at the top. Clumps of various-aged plants

Cardiocrinum giganteum

Cautleya robusta

will provide a yearly show. H2.4-3m/8-10ft, W90cm/3ft. F6-8. Z7-9.

CAUTLEYA

C. lutea. This small, slim species is sometimes seen. Its glossy leaves are purplish beneath, and its flowers yellow. H45cm/18in, W23cm/9in. F7-9. Z7-9.

C. robusta. Another subject for rich, damp soil and some shade. The shallow-rooting tubers are fleshy, radiating from a central crown. Lance-shaped foliage sheaths the erect, reddish stems carrying spikes of yellow-tipped, canna-like flowers, and makes an attractive mass of greenery. H90cm/3ft, W30cm/1ft. F7-9. Z7-9.

Centaurea macrocephala

Centaurea hypoleuca 'John Coutts'

CENTAUREA Knapweed

Also called perennial cornflowers, these include some very garden-worthy species, usually with purple, thistle-like flowers. All are easy to grow in open, sunny positions.
C. **'Bella'**. This pretty little grey-leaved, mat-forming species has lilac-pink flowers. H20cm/8in, W20cm/8in. F5-7. Z5-8.
C. cynaroides. See *C. rhaponticum*.
C. dealbata. The perennial cornflower is a vigorous, deep-rooting species with long, jagged leaves, silver beneath, and reddish purple thistles. May need staking. Dead-head to prolong flowering; may flower again in autumn. H60cm/2ft, W60cm/2ft. F5-7. Z4-8. **'Steenbergii'** is similar except for larger, rich rosy red flowers above abundant, longer, grey leaves. Can be invasive. H60cm/2ft, W60cm/2ft. F5-7. Z4-8.
C. glastifolia. This rare species has light green foliage and branches carrying yellow thistles with silvery calyces. H1.2m/4ft, W60cm/2ft. F6-8. Z3-8.
C. hypoleuca. This mounded ground cover has deeply lobed grey leaves and slender stems of clear pink flowers over a long period, often with a second flush in autumn. A charming, deserving plant. H40cm/16in,

Centranthus ruber 'Albus'

W40cm/16in. F5-7. Z4-8. **'John Coutts'** has 6cm/2¹⁄₂in wide, glistening pink flowers above ample grey foliage. It quickly forms large clumps and is long-lived, with attractive, daisy-like seed heads. H70cm/28in, W45cm/18in. F5-7. Z4-8.
C. macrocephala. The globe centaurea grows massively, with large, lance-shaped, mid-green leaves and stout stems topped by large yellow thistles, good for drying. H1.8m/6ft, W60cm/2ft. F6-8. Z3-8.
C. montana. The mountain bluet, or mountain knapweed, is an early-flowering species which tends to spread just below the surface, but not invasively. The leaves are lance-shaped, grey and slightly hairy; and flowers on single stalks have one row of toothed or lacy petals around a central cone. Colours vary from white to pink, light blue, lilac and violet-blue. Only a few cultivars are offered, such as the light lavender **'Parham'** and the deep blue **'Violetta'**; others carry the descriptive Latin epithets of *alba*, *caerulea rosea*, or *rubra*. Excellent on chalk and poor soil. All H30cm/1ft, W30cm/1ft. F5-6. Z3-8.
C. pulchra **'Major'**. Very stately with handsome, deeply cut, arching grey leaves and ramrod stems topped by large, deep pink thistles. It took me over ten years to restore stocks from the one plant remaining in 1946 when I moved to Bressingham. H90cm/3ft, W30cm/1ft. F6-8. Z7-8.
C. rhaponticum. Both this and *C. cynaroides* make handsome clumps of large, deeply cut leaves, from deep-rooting plants. The tufty, deep pink thistle flowers are also large, but sparse in relation to the foliage. H90cm/3ft, W45cm/18in. F6-8. Z4-8.
C. ruthenica. This trouble-free, drought-resistant plant has canary-yellow flowers on slender, branching stems. The ferny leaves are deep green. H1.2m/4ft, W40cm/16in. F6-8. Z5-8.
C. salonitana. This rare but valuable

species also has light yellow flowers on branching stems, but with deeply cut greyish foliage. Can be invasive. H1.2m/4ft, W60cm/2ft. F6-8. Z6-8.
C. simplicicaulis. A useful, grey-leaved ground-cover or foreground plant, with prettily indented leaves below slender stalks carrying clear pink flowers. H23cm/9in, W23cm/9in. F6-7. Z3-8.

CENTRANTHUS Red Valerian

C. ruber. This old favourite will colonize almost anywhere from self-sown seed, given sun and good drainage, even in the poorest soil, on walls and rocky banks, especially on limestone. **'Albus'** is a good white form, but colours are mostly pink to brick-red. All have fleshy leaves. H80cm/32in, W45cm/18in. F6-9. Z5-8.

CEPHALARIA Great scabious

C. gigantea. Sometimes listed as *C. tatarica*, this makes a massive plant, with dense clumps of divided leaves and a long succession of pale yellow, pincushion flowers on short, ribbed, branching stems. It is a good background subject for any soil and sun. H1.8-2.1m/6-7ft, W1.2m/4ft. F6-9. Z3-8.

CERATOSTIGMA Hardy plumbago

In cool temperate climates these shrubs usually behave like perennials, dying back to ground level in winter. They are valuable for their blue periwinkle flowers, late in the season, given a sunny place and well-drained, fertile soil, ideally against a wall in cold areas.
C. plumbaginoides. This dwarf, spreading plant has neat, leathery leaves, reddish in autumn, following the sparse display of blue flowers. It can be invasive. H15-20cm/6-8in, W30cm/1ft. F7-9. Z5-8.
C. willmottianum. See under Shrubs.

CHELONE Turtle head

These are close relatives of penstemon, but the flowers are more like those of the snapdragon, hence the folk name. Full sun and well-drained, acid soil are ideal.
C. barbata. Sometimes listed as *Penstemon barbatus*, its slender stems hold the tubular flowers, which have an open end and a hairy lip, obliquely. Colours vary from pink to salmon and red. They are not all long-lived. H60-80cm/24-32in, W45cm/18in. F6-8. Z4-8.
C. glabra. This forms a rosette of shiny green leaves and has pink flowers on unbranched spikes. H25cm/10in, W30cm/1ft. F6-8. Z3-8.
C. lyonii. Unlike the two above, the light green leaves of this neat little plant die down over winter to a small rootstock. It

Chelone obliqua

carries stumpy spikes of quite large, lilac-pink, snapdragon flowers, each with a yellow 'beard'. A white form exists. H60cm/2ft, W30cm/1ft. F6-8. Z3-8.
C. obliqua. From a slow but steady creeping stock come erect, leafy stems tipped with a good display of ruby-pink flowers. A reliable, weather-resistant plant which should be more widely grown. The white form **'Alba'** is also worth growing. Both H80cm/32in, W45cm/18in. F7-9. Z4-9.

CHRYSANTHEMUM

With so many named varieties of what most people regard as florists' flowers, one is apt to overlook several true species of garden value which are hardy and reliable perennials. Though now usually split into several genera, they are kept together here for convenience. Garden hybrids are available in great variety, but only those which make new basal growth in autumn will survive the winter.
C. arcticum. See *C. yezoense*.
C. coccineum (syn. *Pyrethrum roseum*; correctly, *Tanacetum coccineum*). These showy, early summer, pink, red and white daisies, some double, have become quite scarce, whereas fifty years ago over fifty varieties were in cultivation, especially for cutting. All are sun lovers for well-drained, ideally limy, soil, with finely cut, more or less evergreen foliage, fibrous roots and a clumpy habit. Plant pot-grown plants in autumn. All flower from late spring to midsummer, and often again later if cut back promptly. Double-flowered forms are less tall and may need support. All F5-7, Z5-9.

'Avalanche', robust, single white. H80cm/32in, W45cm/18in. **'Brenda'**, strong-growing deep pink, single. H80cm/32in, W45cm/18in. **'Bressingham Red'**, blood-red, single rayed flowers. H70cm/28in, W45cm/18in. **'Eileen May**

Robinson', still supreme as a single clear pink. H70cm/28in, W45cm/18in.
'Evenglow', single, deep salmon flowers. H60cm/2ft, W45cm/18in. **'J. N. Twerdy'**, very fine, double crimson-red. H70cm/28in, W45cm/18in. **'Philippa'**, double, glowing deep carmine. H70cm/28in, W45cm/18in. **'Princess Mary'**, light rose-pink, double. H70cm/28in, W45cm/18in. **'Vanessa'**, suffused deep pink, double. H70cm/28in, W45cm/18in.

The following dwarf cultivars are all vigorous: **'Laurin'**, single pink. H38cm/15in, W30cm/1ft. **'Peter Pan'**, almost double carmine-red. H30cm/1ft, W20cm/8in. **'Pink Petite'**, the same clear pink as **'E. M. Robinson'**. H38cm/15in, W25cm/10in. **'Red Dwarf'** (syn. 'Rote Zwerg'), as compact a variety as I have come across, with yellow centres and bright crimson petals. H30cm/ 1ft, W20cm/8in.
C. corymbosum (also sold as *Pyrethrum corymbosum*; correctly, *Tanacetum corymbosum*). This clump-forming plant with deeply cut foliage and tall white daisies makes a fine display in early summer. Worth wider use. H1.2m/4ft, W30cm/1ft. F5-7. Z6-9.
C. leucanthemum (correctly, *Leucanthemum vulgare*). The early-flowering marguerite, or ox-eye daisy, has slender stems carrying rayed white daisies, good for cutting. H50-70cm/20-28in, W30cm/1ft. F5-7. Z4-9.
C. maximum (correctly, *Leucanthemum maximum*). The shasta daisy includes single and double flowers, such as the well-known double **'Esther Read'** and **'Wirral Supreme'**. H50-75cm/20-30in, W30cm/1ft. Forms with lacy-edged petals include **'Aglaia'** and **'Thomas Killin'**. H75cm/30in, W30cm/1ft. The dwarf single **'Snowcap'** has intensely white flowers massed on stems only 35cm/14in tall. W30cm/1ft. **'Summer Snowball'** is an outstanding pure white, fully double. H75cm/30in, W30cm/1ft. Support may be needed. All F6-8, Z4-8.
C. nipponicum (correctly, *Nipponanthemum nipponicum*). Very dwarf, very vigorous and very late to flower, this semi-shrubby species carries wide rayed daisies above dark greenery. Well-drained soil and a sheltered, warm spot give best results. H15cm/6in, W38cm/15in. F9-11. Z5-9.
C. parthenium (syn. *Pyrethrum parthenium*; correctly, *Tanacetum parthenium*). **'White Bonnet'**, a double-flowered feverfew, is more reliably perennial than others and makes a dazzling display of pure white 'button' flowers above deeply divided pungent foliage. H75cm/30in, W38cm/15in. F6-8. Z4-8.
C. rubellum (correctly, *Dendranthema rubella*). Probably a hybrid which has produced a few good varieties, most fully hardy, with a fairly vigorous, bushy spread. All are single ray petalled, with yellow eyes.

Chrysanthemum coccineum 'Red Dwarf'

Replant every year or two to avoid overcongestion. **'Clara Curtis'** is the original clear pink and is still in demand. **'Duchess of Edinburgh'** is a bright bronzy crimson and **'Mary Stoker'** is yellow. All H60-90cm/2-3ft, W60cm/2ft. F8-9. Z5-9.
C. uliginosum (correctly, *Leucanthemella serotina*). Very tall, but valuable for late flowering, its stems are topped by white daisies in autumn. In rich, moist soil, excessive height can be controlled by cutting back a few centimetres/inches in early summer. H2.1m/7ft, W60cm/2ft. F9-11. Z4-9.
C. yezoense (syn. *C. arcticum*; correctly, *Dendranthema yezoense*). This forms spreading, clumpy growth of close indented leaves and gives a good display of branching sprays of white flowers, tinged pink. Full sun, well-drained soil. H20cm/8in, W45cm/18in. F9-10. Z5-9.

Hybrids. Not many so-called 'Koreans' have stood the test of time, but some of the old, button-flowered kinds have, and live on

Chrysanthemum maximum 'Snowcap'

Cimicifuga ramosa (background)

Clematis heracleifolia 'Crepuscule'

from year to year, making clumpy plants and tight, bushy growth, up to 80cm/32in tall and flowering well into autumn. The old, 80cm/32in high, purplish carmine **'Anastasia'** is still to be seen flowering in mid- to late autumn. W45cm/18in. Z7-9.

Dwarf, earlier varieties include the deep rose **'Mei-kyo'**, the browny orange **'Peterkin'** and the yellow **'Sunbeam'**, all vigorous, with quilled, button flowers, 2.5-5cm/1-2in across. H50-60cm/20-24in, W30-38cm/12-15in. F8-11. Z7-9. Of the wide range of early chrysanthemums which I've tried, both sprays and doubles, I still value the late summer-, early autumn-flowering double pink **'Madeleine'**, the double orange **'Mandarin'** and the single pink **'Peter Sare'**. H50-75cm/20-30in, W30-38cm/12-15in. F7-11. Z7-9. For those who care to take the trouble, many other late summer varieties are available, but most are best raised from spring-rooted cuttings every year, rather than by leaving them in the ground over winter.

CICHORIUM Chicory
C. intybus. The species is pretty, with its clear blue daisies up the stems, but few people would consider it garden-worthy. There is, however, a most attractive pink form, **'Roseum'**. The fluffy, open flowers closely attached to the branching stems are long-lasting. Full sun and well-drained soil. H1m/39in, W60cm/2ft. F6-9. Z4-8.

CIMICIFUGA Bugbane
These rank highly as beautiful, trouble-free plants for sun or partial shade, in good deep soil, not too dry or limy. They have

Cimicifuga ramosa 'Brunette'

slender but strong stems and are graceful with outspreading, deeply divided foliage, oddly scented in some species, and bottlebrush spikes of small white or cream flowers in late summer or autumn. The clumps become large in time with a mass of fibrous roots; the leaves often turn yellow in autumn. Support not necessary.
C. acerina. The smallest species, with wiry spikes and good leafage. **'Silverax'** has slightly fuller spikes. H1m/39in, W60cm/2ft. F8-9. Z4-8.
C. cordifolia. This has deep green, broad foliage and tapering spikes of white on wiry, purplish stems. H90-120cm/3-4ft, W60cm/2ft. F8-9. Z4-8.
C. dahurica. Taller and earlier to flower, this has graceful, branching spikes of small, fluffy, creamy white flowers. H2.1m/7ft, W60cm/2ft. F7-8. Z4-8.
C. racemosa. Clumps of bright green, divided leaves and spikes of ivory-white, often with later flushes. H1.8m/6ft, W60cm/2ft. F7-8. Z3-8.

C. ramosa. Large, divided leaves and lofty, tapering, branching spikes, creamy white, late in the season. H2.1m/7ft, W60cm/2ft. F8-9. Z4-8. **'Atropurpurea'** is outstanding for its purplish leaves and stems, contrasting effectively with the white flowers. H2.1m/7ft, W60cm/2ft. F8-9. Z4-8. **'Brunette'** has even more striking black-purple foliage. H1.8m/6ft, W60cm/2ft. F8-10. Z4-8.
C. simplex **'White Pearl'**. The latest to flower, with full, arching spikes of pure white to brighten the autumn scene. Deservedly popular. **'Elstead'** is similar, but with purplish buds. H1.2m/4ft, W60cm/2ft. F9-10. Z4-8.

CLEMATIS
It is not generally known that there are non-climbing species of real garden value. They are reliably hardy and long-lived, needing minimal attention in any reasonable soil.
C. davidiana. See *C. heracleifolia*.
C. × eriostemon **'Hendersonii'**. Nodding flowers with deep blue, reflexed petals appear from late spring to midsummer, followed by pretty seed heads. Though lax in habit, staking is not necessary. H60-70cm/24-28in if supported, otherwise 40cm/16in, W60cm/2ft. F5-7. Z4-9.
C. heracleifolia (sometimes listed as *C. davidiana*). **'Crepuscule'** makes a woody-based, leafy bush with hyacinth-like clusters of light blue, scented flowers for many weeks, followed by attractive seed heads. Though dying down over winter, its lush summer growth needs ample space. H90cm/3ft, W60cm/2ft. F6-9. Z4-9. **'Wyevale'** is of similar growth, but the flowers are a slightly deeper blue.
C. recta **'Macrantha'**. This needs support for its slender, leafy stems and heads of small, creamy white, scented flowers, followed by silvery, fluffy seed heads. **'Purpurea'** has purple-tinged foliage. H75cm/30in, W40cm/16in. F6-8. Z3-9.

COREOPSIS Tickseed
These yellow daisies, with yellow or orange central discs, are for full sun and any reasonable soil.

Coreopsis verticillata 'Moonbeam'

C. grandiflora. The best-known is not the most reliable, and the types easily raised from seed are not long-lived. These include **'Badengold'**, which is very shy to flower though fully perennial, the old **'Mayfield Giant'** and the newer, double **'Sunray'**. Cut hard back as flowering ends. All H75cm/30in, W38cm/15in. F6-8. Z4-9.
C. lanceolata. Reliably perennial. H60cm/2ft, W45cm/18in. F6-9. Z4-9.
'Goldfink' has neat tufts and very short stems of large yellow flowers. H25cm/10in, W25cm/10in. F6-9. Z4-9.
C. rosea. Unique for its small, pale pink flowers on narrow-leaved stems. Spreads below ground. H30cm/1ft, W30cm/1ft. F8-9. Z3-9.
C. tripteris. Not exciting but strong stems carry branched heads of yellow flowers. H1.8m/6ft, W45cm/18in. F7-9. Z4-9.
C. verticillata. This makes shapely bushes of finely divided leaves. Studded with small, bright yellow flowers for many weeks. H40cm/16in, W45cm/18in. F7-9. Z4-9. **'Golden Gain'** has larger flowers and an even more robust habit. H60cm/2ft, W38cm/15in. F7-9. Z4-9. **'Grandiflora'** has larger, deeper yellow flowers. H50cm/20in, W45cm/18in. F7-9. Z4-9. **'Moonbeam'** provides welcome variety with light lemon-yellow flowers, scented foliage and a relaxed, multi-branched growth. H40cm/16in, W30cm/1ft. F7-9, Z3-9. **'Zagreb'** has clear yellow flowers, dwarf bushy growth. H35cm/14in, W30cm/1ft. F7-9. Z3-9.

CORONILLA
C. montana. This has a low, twiggy, bushy habit and gives a good show of yellow pea-type flowers. Needs sun and good drainage. H30cm/1ft, W30cm/1ft. F6-8. Z3-7.

COSMOS
C. atrosanguineus (syn. *Bidens atrosanguinea*). This tender species is not fully appreciated for its long succession of rich deep crimson, single, dahlia-like flowers. These are chocolate-scented and come on slender stalks above bushy, dark green, divided foliage from a tuberous root. It needs a warm, sunny spot and survives outdoors only if covered to prevent frost

Crinum × powellii 'Album'

penetration. Roots may, however, be lifted and stored as for dahlias. H80cm/32in, W38cm/15in. F7-10. Z8-9.

CRAMBE Seakale
The ornamental species of seakale make an exciting display but leave a gap, with only a few basal leaves, when they return to dormancy. They have deep, fleshy roots and need well-drained soil and sun.
C. cordifolia. The best-known, this has widely branching stems carrying myriads of white, gypsophila-like flowers, 1.5cm/$\frac{1}{2}$in across, above mounds of large, rounded, deeply lobed leaves. H1.8m/6ft, W1.8m/6ft. F6-7. Z6-9.
C. maritima. Seakale is pretty enough to use as a decorative subject. Leaves are wide, glaucous and lobed, above which come broad heads of white flowers. H60cm/2ft, W60cm/2ft. F6-7. Z6-9.

CRINUM
These large, South African bulbs are hardy in most places, especially given the protection of a sunny wall, the reflected heat of which encourages flowering. Left alone, they produce glossy leaves and smooth stems carrying terminal clusters of outward-facing, trumpet-like, scented flowers. Plant with the tapering neck of the bulb just above ground level.
C. bulbispermum (syn. *C. capense*). This has white flowers, flushed pink outside, above light green leaves. H60cm/2ft, W60cm/2ft. F7-9. Z9-10.
C. capense. See *C. bulbispermum*.
C. × powellii. Huge bulbs produce large pink flowers, making a fine show. **'Album'**

is uncommonly beautiful, but scarce. H90cm/3ft, W90cm/3ft. F7-9. Z7-10.

CROCOSMIA
So much confusion exists over the generic names of this and allied cormous plants that grouping them under one heading is justified, regardless. Crocosmia is the 'correct' name for the cheerful, orange-flowered herbaceous perennial still popularly known as montbretia, and valuable for its late summer and early autumn flowers. The others include *Curtonus paniculatus*, formerly known as *Antholyza paniculata*, by cottage gardeners as Aunt Eliza and now, more correctly, *Crocosmia paniculata*; and *Tritonia*. The list below indicates *Monbretia* types with (M). These are less hardy and of more slender growth than those having *Crocosmia masonorum* and *C. paniculata* parentage. With the exception of *C. × crocosmiiflora* and *C. pottsii*, all grow best in sun and well-drained soil. Plant 8-10cm/3-4in deep and 15-20cm/6-8in apart, to form an outward-spreading clump. Crocosmias spread rapidly and if overcrowded stop flowering; if this happens, simply lift and divide the plants in early spring, adding a bit of fertilizer to the soil before replanting. The Bressingham cultivars originated from crossing *C. masonorum* with both *C. paniculata* and montbretia cultivars (*C. × crocosmiiflora*).
C. 'Bressingham Blaze'. The open-throated flowers are intense flame-orange. H75cm/30in, W15cm/6in. F7-8. Z5-9.
C. 'Citronella' (M). This old but pretty montbretia has soft yellow flowers and

Crocosmia 'Spitfire'

Crocosmia 'Lucifer'

Crocosmia 'Jenny Bloom'

spreads quite quickly. H60cm/2ft, W15cm/6in. F7-8. Z6-9.

C. × *crocosmiiflora* and *C. pottsii*. These two, and some others, are sometimes listed under *Montbretia*. Though colourful, with bright flame-orange flowers, they are rather invasive. In mild, damp regions they are sometimes regarded as weeds.

C. '**Bressingham Beacon**' is a strong-growing, flame-orange cultivar. H60cm/2ft, W15cm/6in. F7-8. Z5-9.

C. '**Emberglow**'. A glowing, burnt-orange shade with abundant, rush-like foliage. H60cm/2ft, W15cm/6in. F7-9. Z5-9.

C. '**Emily MacKenzie**' (M). A large-flowered late variety with deep orange petals and a mahogany-crimson throat. H50cm/20in, W15cm/6in. F8-9. Z6-9.

C. '**Jackanapes**' (M). A charming, vigorous bicolour, with yellow and deep orange-red flowers. H60cm/2ft, W15cm/6in. F7-9. Z6-9.

C. '**Jenny Bloom**'. This has soft butter-yellow flowers, and is strong-growing and prolific. H80cm/32in, W15cm/6in. F7-9. Z5-9.

C. '**Lucifer**'. A vast improvement on one of its parents, *Antholyza* (syn. *C. paniculata*), but it lacks nothing of the latter's hardiness and vigour. The flowers on wiry, upstanding spikes are deep flame-red, and a mature

group is a picture of outstanding brilliance above the attractive, sword-like foliage. It is also the earliest to flower and the tallest. A faultless plant. H1.1m/43in, W15cm/6in. F6-8. Z5-9.

C. masonorum. The parent of some of the Bressingham hybrids, selected for its hardiness and arching stems, which reveal wide-petalled, upward-facing, vermilion-orange flowers. The foliage is broad and handsome. H80cm/32in, W15cm/6in. F7-9. Z7-9. '**Firebird**' was originally selected as a single corm among many seedlings of *C. masonorum*, and stock was slowly built up from this. Quite the best form ever seen, with its large, flame-orange flowers on arching stems. H80cm/32in, W15cm/6in. F7-9. Z6-9.

C. '**Rowallane Yellow**'. Pure yellow with large flower heads. Certain to prove popular. H90cm/3ft, W15cm/6in. F6-9. Z7-9.

C. '**Solfatare**' (M). An old and somewhat tender variety, still in demand for its warm orange flowers above bronzy foliage. H60cm/2ft, W15cm/6in. F7-8. Z7-9.

C. '**Spitfire**'. This is another hybrid of real brilliance and attraction, with fiery orange flowers on strong stems. H75cm/30in, W15cm/6in. F7-9. Z5-9.

C. rosea (M). This has the distinction of pink flowers which, though not large, are attractive, and narrow, rushy foliage. H60cm/2ft, W15cm/6in. F6-8. Z6-9.

C. '**Vulcan**'. Deep flame-orange. Compact habit. H60cm/2ft, W15cm/6in. F7-9. Z5-9.

CRUCIANELLA
C. stylosa. See *Phuopsis stylosa*.

CYNARA Globe artichoke
C. scolymus. This can be eaten as a delicacy, but is a very ornamental species for the decorative garden. Strong stems rise to carry terminal thistle flowers with scaly-bracts enclosing a large purple-mauve tuft. The basal foliage is alone a feature, with very silvery, deeply jagged leaves up to 60cm/2ft long, and handsome all summer. Best in deep, light soil and full sun. H1.8-2.1m/6-7ft, W60cm/2ft. F7-8. Z7-9.

CYNOGLOSSUM Hound's tongue
These are seldom seen in gardens, but two species are worthwhile for their intensely blue, bell-shaped flowers that top leafy stems and clumps of narrow, basal leaves. Both flower early and for several weeks. Roots are somewhat fleshy. Grow in sun and any ordinary soil; very rich soil tends to result in floppy stems.

C. grande. Though somewhat lax, staking is not essential to give a good display in early summer of blue, white-centred flowers. H60cm/2ft, W30cm/1ft. F6-7. Z4-8.

C. nervosum. Much dwarfer than the above, with slightly grey, tongue-shaped leaves and

arching sprays of deep blue flowers.
H45cm/18in, W30cm/1ft. F6-8. Z5-8.

DACTYLORHIZA See under ORCHIS.

DEINANTHE
D. bifida. A rarity for cool shade and
shelter, this has handsome, upstanding
foliage, each leaf with a deep notch, and
clusters of small, nodding, blue-tinged,
waxy white flowers. H70cm/28in,
W45cm/18in. F6-7. Z5-9.
D. caerulea. Little clusters of waxy blue
flowers, with blue stamens, nestle above
handsome clumps of puckered hairy leaves.
For shade and sandy peaty soil.
H45cm/18in, W45cm/18in. F6-8. Z5-9.

DELPHINIUM
Large-flowered varieties are still offered by
specialists, but not many gardeners are
inclined to take the trouble to grow them to
their majestic perfection, since this involves
well-prepared and fed soil and staking
every spike, some of which grow 2.1-
2.4m/7-8ft high.

Seed-raised strains are more popular and
less expensive, but the Pacific Hybrids are
relatively short-lived. Breeders have
introduced compact spikes with large
flowers, such as *D.* **'Blue Heaven'**,
although there is much to be said for the
Belladonna Hybrids for display and
reliability. Hybridizers are still trying to
widen the colour range of the large-
flowered delphiniums to incorporate strong
perennial growth.

Of all border perennials delphiniums are
in greatest need of supporting before the
spikes become tall. Grow in deep, rich,
moist but well-drained soil and sun, but not
extreme heat.
D. × *belladonna*. This type is single-
flowered, producing an abundance of
graceful, loose racemes of flowers and
deeply cut leaves. If cut back after
flowering, most flower again. All Z3-8.
'Blue Bees', a favourite with sky-blue
flowers. H1m/39in, W60cm/2ft. F6-7.
'Lamartine', shapely, Oxford-blue spikes.
H1.2m/4ft, W60cm/2ft. F6-7. **'Peace'**, the
finest, brightest mid-blue. H1.2m/4ft,
W60cm/2ft. F6-7. **'Wendy'**, deep blue, with
dark foliage. H1.2m/4ft, W60cm/2ft. F6-7.
D. chinense, *D. grandiflorum* and
D. tatsienense are all short-lived, dwarf
species. *D. c.* **'Blue Butterfly'** is especially
popular for its brilliance. All make
outstanding frontal groups. All H25-
30cm/10-12in, W25cm/10in. F6-8. Z4-9.
D. grandiflorum. See under *D. chinense*.
D. **'Pink Sensation'** is a unique hybrid. It
has soft rose-pink branching spikes, but
needs very well-drained soil to avoid winter
rot. H1m/39in, W60cm/2ft. F6-8.

Cynara scolymus

Delphinium × *belladonna* 'Blue Bees'

Delphinium × *belladonna* 'Peace'

D. tatsienense. See *D. chinense*.
D. zalil. This distinct species has slender
spikes of light yellow flowers and dark
green foliage. Decidedly interesting and
reasonably long-lived; needs excellent
drainage and a warm, sunny site.
H80cm/32in, W30cm/1ft. F6-8. Z8-9.

DENDRANTHEMA See under CHRYSANTHEMUM.

DENTARIA Toothwort
Sometimes placed under *Cardamine*, these
all have similar broad flower heads making
a bright but brief display in early spring.
The white, tuberous roots which give the
plant its common name are clumpy but not
deep. If they have a long dormant period
they are quite adaptable to grow between
shrubs or beneath late-flowering plants.
Cool shade is ideal.
D. digitata. See *D. pentaphyllos*.

Dentaria pinnata

D. pentaphyllos (syn. *D. digitata*). This has
light green, fingery leaves with racemes of
pale purple flowers above. H30cm/1ft,
W15cm/6in. F3-5. Z6-8.
D. pinnata. Deeply divided leaves form
dense clumps, topped by heads of white
flowers, especially welcome in spring.
H30cm/1ft, W30cm/1ft. F3-5. Z5-9.

Dianthus barbatus 'Casser's Pink'

Diascia rigescens

Dicentra 'Snowflakes'

Dicentra spectabilis

DIANTHUS

Most belong in the Alpines chapter but the range of garden pinks and a few species must be included here. No garden is complete without pinks, for both perfume and colour. To meet a renewed demand in garden pinks, specialists are offering a wide range of varieties, especially old favourites. Some of these were popular up to 200 years ago, and it is pleasing to welcome them back from obscurity. Sun, shelter and light, well-drained, sandy or gritty soil are best.

D. barbatus. The species which produced sweet William also parented other, longer-lived hybrids and are still occasionally offered. **'Casser's Pink'** has typical deep green leaves forming a low mound, topped by a head of deep pink double flowers for many weeks. H30cm/1ft, W20cm/8in. F6-9. Z3-8. Probably synonymous with **'Prince Bismarck'**.

D. knappii. Grown for its yellow flowers on wiry stems, this makes little basal growth and needs sharp drainage. Short-lived. H30cm/1ft, W30cm/1ft. F6-8. Z3-8.

D. plumarius. The parent of most garden pinks, including the Allwoodii range. Altogether there are over 100 varieties in cultivation, both single- and double-flowered, in colours ranging from white through to pink and deep red. The following are a small selection. **'Brympton Red'**, large, single red. **'Constance Finnis'**, single pink, speckled red. **'Dad's Favourite'**, pale pink, blotched red. **'Doris'**, soft pink, fully double. **'Emperor'**, double red. **'Haytor'**, fully double, pure white. **'Mrs Sinkins'**, double white, very scented. **'Rose du Mai'**, pale pink, red-centred. All H25-40cm/10-16in, W30-38cm/12-15in. F6-8. Z4-8.

DIASCIA

These South African plants are noteworthy for long flowering, producing spurred, shell-like blooms. Though not fully hardy they are easy in light soil and sun. It is good practice to take cuttings in late summer, to ensure continuity in the event of cold winters.

D. cordata. This mat-forming species is for a frontal position. It has small, rounded, deep green leaves and short stems carrying a succession of pink flowers, deeper in the vigorous **'Ruby Field'**. H20cm/8in, W30cm/1ft. F6-9. Z7-9.

D. rigescens. Although showy and long-flowering, with dusky pink sprays, this is not hardy except in the mildest areas. H40cm/16in, W40cm/16in. F6-9. Z7-9.

D. vigilis (syn. *D. elegans*). This is one of the hardier species, recently introduced from South Africa. It makes deep green, slow-spreading mats and sprays of small pink flowers for many weeks. H25cm/10in, W30cm/1ft. F6-9. Z8-9.

DICENTRA Bleeding heart

A deservedly popular genus. *D. formosa* and *D. eximia* make pretty mounds of glaucous, ferny foliage and arching racemes of little, locket-like, dangling flowers. These are less fleshy-rooted and less fragile than the true bleeding heart, *D. spectabilis*, but all grow happily in good, light soil and a cool spot.

D. eximia and **D. formosa**. The species are much alike, the deep pink flowers having a long season; admirable for frontal positions. **D. e. 'Alba'** has pure white flowers and lush, deeply divided greenery, but is not reliable everywhere. H60cm/2ft, W60cm/2ft. F5-7. Z4-8.

Hybrids include the following. All Z4-8. **'Adrian Bloom'**, profuse crimson-rose flowers. H25cm/10in, W20cm/8in. F5-8. **'Bacchanal'**, small, deep crimson flowers. H20cm/8in, W20cm/8in. F5-7. **'Bountiful'**, slightly lighter crimson. H25cm/10in, W20cm/8in. F5-8. **'Luxuriant'**, very similar to 'Adrian Bloom'. H25cm/10in, W20cm/8in. F5-8. **'Pearl Drops'**, best white, flowers on arching tips above a mass of bluish green foliage. H30cm/1ft, W45cm/18in. F5-8. **'Snowflakes'**, long succession of pure white flowers from early spring. H25cm/10in, W25cm/10in. F4-9. **'Spring Morning'**, pink-tinged, ivory-white flowers. H20cm/8in, W20cm/8in. F5-8.

D. spectabilis. The true bleeding heart, with its fascinating, deep pink and white lockets dangling above light green, paeony-like foliage. Its enemies are cutting winds, spring frosts and winter wet. The ivory-white **'Alba'** is also charming, with lighter green foliage. Both H60cm/2ft, W45cm/18in. F5-7. Z3-8.

DICTAMNUS Burning bush

On hot days when the seed pods are ripening, the plant gives off a volatile gas which ignites if lit with a match, hence its common name. Never attempt to divide these plants, because they resent any disturbance. They can only be raised from seed and must be planted young.

D. albus (syn. *D. fraxinella albus*). Also called dittany or fraxinella, this has strongly aromatic, pinnate, light green leaves and stiff spikes of white flowers with prominent stamens. The form *purpureus* has soft lilac flowers. Well-drained, fertile, light soil and sun. H80cm/32in, W60cm/2ft. F6-8. Z3-8.

DIERAMA

The so-called fairy's wand, wand flower or angel's fishing rod are charming plants, good in light, moist soil but not reliably hardy in the coldest districts. The narrow, rush-like leaves are semi-evergreen and for a short period send up arching, wiry stems which branch at the top and carry dangling, light pink, trumpet-shaped flowers. The corms multiply to form a congested clump and

Digitalis × mertonensis

Diplarrhena moraea

where suited can stay undisturbed for several years; they also self-seed.

D. pulcherrimum. The wand-like stems with their pink flowers, opening from the tip downwards and encased in silver calyces, wave in a breeze above the rushy foliage. H1.5m/5ft, W30cm/1ft. F7-8. Z7-9.

D. pumilum (syn. *D. dracomontanum*). Also known as 'Hermia'. Compact-growing, with satiny pink flowers on wiry stems. H75cm/30in, W38cm/15in. F7-8. Z8-9.

DIGITALIS Foxglove

These must be included in spite of many having a short life. Some, such as the Excelsior Hybrids, which are biennial and seed around, are excellent for naturalizing and will colonize shady places, but only those suitable among other perennials are included below. Almost any soil, in sun or partial shade, is suitable.

D. ambigua. See *D. grandiflora*.

D. ferruginea. Tall spikes from evergreen rosettes carry small, rust-red flowers. H90cm/3ft, W30cm/1ft. F6-8. Z4-8.

D. grandiflora (syn. *D. ambigua*). Most live for three or four years, with spikes of

Dictamnus albus purpureus

primrose-yellow flowers on compact plants. H60cm/2ft, W30cm/1ft. F6-8. Z4-8.

D. lanata and **D. lutea**. Both have small, creamy yellow flowers on slender stems. Reliably perennial. H60cm/2ft, W30cm/1ft. F6-8. *D. lanata*: Z5-9; *D. lutea*: Z4-8.

D. × mertonensis. This has large flowers of an appealing, crushed-strawberry colour. Lift and divide regularly, after flowering; it also breeds true from seed. H60cm/2ft, W30cm/1ft. F6-8. Z5-9.

DIMORPHOTHECA See under OSTEOSPERMUM.

DIPHYLLEIA Umbrella leaf

D. cymosa. An unusual plant for a cool, shady place; woodland conditions are ideal. Large, lobed leaves, up to 30cm/1ft across; inconspicuous flowers followed by bright indigo-blue berries on red stalks. H70cm/28in, W30cm/1ft. F7-8. Z7-9.

DIPLARRHENA

D. moraea. This is borderline hardy, but worth protecting from frost in cold areas. The dark green, grassy foliage is evergreen and clump-forming; slender, wiry stems carry flat-petalled, iris-like white flowers, with tiny yellow and purple inner petals. A treasure for those with a warm, sunny spot and light, well-drained soil. H60cm/2ft, W25cm/10in. F5-7. Z9-10.

DISPORUM Fairy bells
These dwarf woodland plants, related to and resembling Solomon's seal, are fairly adaptable, making attractive mounds of greenery. They are rhizomatous and long-lived, preferring light, humus-rich soil and some shade. All Z4-9.

D. oreganum. This has low clumps of stalkless, heart-shaped leaves, in which nestle hanging white bells, followed by orange-yellow berries. *D. smithii* is not markedly different in general appearance. H25cm/10in, W25cm/10in. F6-7.

D. pullum. This has purplish flowers, tinged green, above pointed green leaves and dark stems. H90cm/3ft, W30cm/1ft. F5-6.

D. sessile 'Variegatum'. This spreads just below the soil surface, producing pretty, creamy white-striped foliage. Greenish flowers. H30cm/1ft, W30cm/1ft. F5-6.

DODECATHEON Shooting star
Star-like, reflexed petals and prominent orange stamens give this fibrous-rooted, primula-like plant its common name. It is not averse to shade and likes humus-rich soil, but dies down after flowering. A long dormant period follows. Variations among the following are not great.

D. clevelandii, *D. jeffreyi* and *D. meadia* all have arching stems topped by rosy red to magenta flowers with a central yellow ring, and narrow, greeny brown leaves. All H20-30cm/8-12in, W20cm/8in. F5-6. Z5-7.

D. pulchellum 'Red Wings'. This is outstanding for its bright crimson flowers. H30cm/1ft, W15cm/6in. F5-6. Z5-7.

DORONICUM Leopard's bane
These yellow daisies are easy to grow and are invaluable early spring flowers. Their toothed, heart-shaped leaves usually die down in hot summers. Adaptable in reasonably moist soil and sun or part shade, most form clumps and need replanting every three years to renew vigour. Good for cutting.

D. austriacum and *D. caucasicum*. These are much alike, with bright yellow daisies 8cm/3in across. H45cm/18in, W30cm/1ft. F4-5. Z5-8. *D. c.* 'Goldzwerg' is the best dwarf form. H25cm/10in, W30cm/1ft. F4-6. Z4-8.

D. cordatum. This species, with its leafy clumps and fine yellow daisies, is best in dampish soil. H45cm/18in, W30cm/1ft. F4-6. Z4-8.

D. 'Harpur Crewe' (syn. *D. plantagineum* 'Excelsum'). This old favourite, being the tallest, is well loved for cutting. H90cm/3ft, W60cm/2ft. F5-6. Z4-8.

D. 'Miss Mason', a hybrid, makes a fine show for several weeks, with persistent, clump-forming leaves. H50cm/20in, W60cm/2ft. F4-6. Z4-8.

D. 'Spring Beauty' has fully double flowers. H30cm/1ft, W30cm/1ft. F4-6. Z4-8.

D. plantagineum 'Excelsum'. See *D.* 'Harpur Crewe'.

DRACOCEPHALUM Dragon's head
The shape of the hooded, labiate flowers gives this plant its common name. The few species cultivated are akin to *Salvia* and *Nepeta* and are easy to grow in well-drained soil and sun.

D. ruyschianum. This makes neat, narrow-leaved bushy growth with short spikes of deep violet-blue. H40cm/16in, W30cm/1ft. F6-8. Z4-8.

D. sibiricum. Now classed as *Nepeta sibirica*, but this has upright, leafy stems and clear blue flowers. H90cm/3ft, W30cm/1ft. F6-8. Z4-8.

ECHINACEA Purple coneflower
These reliable, daisy-like perennials always attract attention, with their prominent dark centres and radiating, crimson-magenta petals, often with lighter tips. Good, light soil and sun are appreciated.

E. purpurea. The original type is virtually non-existent in gardens, having been replaced by hybrids. All Z4-9.

'Abendsonne', an old German variety, is not very robust but has rosy pink flowers. H90cm/3ft, W45cm/18in. F7-9.

'Bressingham Hybrids' are similar to 'Robert Bloom'. H1m/39in, W45cm/18in. F7-9. 'Magnus' is an outstanding newcomer on account of the size of its ray petalled flowers. These are almost 10cm/4in across, a warm purplish rose, and borne on sturdy stems for a long period. H90cm/3ft, W38cm/15in. F7-10. 'Robert Bloom', an improvement on 'Abendsonne', has an even richer glow. The stems are sturdy and, unlike the former, the petals do not droop. H90cm/3ft, W38cm/15in. F7-9.

'The King' has overlong stems, and although the flowers are large the petals droop, as do the branching stems. H1.2m/4ft, W45cm/18in. F7-9. **'White**

Disporum sessile 'Variegatum'

Doronicum 'Miss Mason'

Lustre' has yellow-centred, ivory-white flowers. H90cm/3ft, W45cm/18in. F7-9.

ECHINOPS Globe thistle

These distinctive perennials have deeply jagged, mostly greyish, prickly foliage and spherical, metallic blue flower heads on branching stems. Some taller species are space-demanding and may need staking, apart from the nuisance of self-seeding. All are butterfly plants. They require full sun and ordinary or even poor, chalky or sandy soil. Drought-resistant.

E. bannaticus. This massive but handsome background plant is best for the wild garden. H2.1m/7ft, W60cm/2ft. F7-8. Z3-8.

E. humilis. This deep-rooting species is also tall and usually offered as **'Taplow Blue'.** The flowers are light blue and the leaves cobwebbed on the upper surfaces. H2.2m/88in, W60cm/2ft. F7-8. Z3-9.

E. **'Nivalis'** has very grey foliage and nearly white flowers, good for contrast. H1.8m/6ft, W60cm/2ft. F7-8. Z3-8.

E. ritro. More compact, with abundant, mid-blue flowers above greyish, thistly foliage. A first-class plant. **'Veitch's Blue'** is a good selection with smaller, lighter blue heads. Both H1.2m/4ft, W60cm/2ft. F7-8. Z3-9.

ELSHOLTZIA

E. stauntonii. This mint-like, clump-forming sub-shrub is interesting, and useful for late flowering. Erect stems have narrow, aromatic leaves and thin spikes of tiny purplish flowers. Grow in sun and well-drained soil; cut back to ground level in late winter. H1m/39in, W60cm/2ft. F10-11. Z5-7.

EOMECON

E. chionantha. A useful spring subject, with rounded, glaucous foliage and white, nodding, cup-shaped flowers on short stems. It is adaptable for shade or some sun, but needs moist, cool soil; it spreads quickly in light soil. Roots are fleshy, shallow and brittle; the sap is orange-red. H20cm/8in, W20cm/8in. F4-6. Z7-9.

EPILOBIUM

These include the pretty weed rose-bay willow-herb (*E. angustifolium*), but also other species quite safe to grow and providing a long season of subtle colour, followed by fluffy seed heads. Needs well-drained soil and sun.

E. dodonaei (syn. *E. rosmarinifolium*). This distinct, first-class species has long-lasting sprays of small pink flowers on erect, grey-leaved spikes. It seldom needs curbing or other attention. H1m/39in, W30cm/1ft. F6-9. Z3-7.

E. fleischeri. A clump former with narrow, greyish foliage, slim spikes of small pinkish

Echinacea purpurea 'Magnus'

Echinops ritro

Epimedium × rubrum

flowers and rather lax growth. H60cm/2ft, W30cm/1ft. F6-8. Z4-7.

E. rosmarinifolium. See *E. dodonaei.*

EPIMEDIUM Barrenwort

These are of real value for spring flowering and ground cover in sun or shade, as long as the soil is not bone-dry. The twiggy roots spread slowly and some forms are virtually evergreen, with pretty, fresh green leaves on wiry stems. The small flowers are spidery or starry and appear in spring before the new leaves.

E. alpinum. The young foliage is flecked with bronzy red and the yellow and reddish, short-spurred flowers are carried in sprays. There is a rare white form. H25cm/10in, W25cm/10in. F3-5. Z4-9.

E. × cantabrigiense. A hybrid of vigorous growth and orange-brown flowers. H25cm/10in, W25cm/10in. F3-5. Z5-9.

E. diphyllum. This good ground cover has paired leaves and pinkish flowers. H25cm/10in, W25cm/10in. F3-5. Z5-8.

E. grandiflorum (syn. *E. macranthum*). The

typical form is dwarf, with pale pink, starry flowers; **'Rose Queen'** has larger, deeper pink flowers with white-tipped spurs. Slow-growing and worthy of a fertile spot. Both H20cm/8in, W20cm/8in. F3-5. Z5-8.

E. macranthum. See *E. grandiflorum.*

E. × perralchicum. This evergreen hybrid has quite large, yellow flowers. H30cm/1ft, W30cm/1ft. F3-5. Z5-9. **'Fröhnleiten'**, a neater form, has yellow flowers and marbled foliage. Evergreen. H25cm/10in, W25cm/10in. F4-5. Z5-9.

E. perralderianum. This strong-growing species has evergreen, glossy leaves, bright green and bronzy red when young, copper-bronze in winter, and yellow flowers. H35cm/14in, W35cm/14in. F3-5. Z5-9.

E. pinnatum colchicum. Its semi-evergreen foliage is brightly coloured in autumn and winter. Profuse, large yellow flowers. H25cm/10in, W25cm/10in. F3-5. Z5-9.

E. × rubrum. Compact clumps of rounded foliage, attractively coloured when young, and deep pink, white-spurred, starry flowers. H20cm/8in, W20cm/8in. F3-5. Z4-9.

Epimedium × youngianum

Eremurus robustus

Erigeron 'Prosperity'

E. sagittatum. As its specific name suggests, this has arrow-shaped leaves and pink flowers. H20cm/8in, W20cm/8in. F3-5. Z5-9.

E. × versicolor. This has prettily tinted leaves in spring and again in autumn. There are several named forms, with pink or yellow flowers. **'Cupreum'** is copper-yellow. **'Sulphureum'** has pale yellow flowers with red spurs. **'Versicolor'** has pink sepals. All H30cm/1ft, W30cm/1ft. F3-5. Z5-9.

E. × warleyense. A splendid hybrid with abundant, light green leafage and a good show of deep orange flowers. H30cm/1ft, W30cm/1ft. F3-5. Z5-9.

E. × youngianum. This forms shapely little mounds of foliage and pink flowers. H20cm/8in, W20cm/8in. F3-5. Z5-8. The compact form **'Niveum'** has white flowers and attractive foliage. H20cm/8in, W20cm/8in. F3-5. Z5-8.

EREMURUS Foxtail lily

These stately and spectacular plants form clumps of strap-shaped leaves which die down in summer at flowering time, smooth leafless stalks and terminal spikes of small, starry, lily-like flowers with prominent stamens. They need sun and well-drained soil. Their fleshy roots radiate from a central crown like the spokes of a wheel and are sensitive to planting depth, so plant the crowns just below the surface, on a bed of sand, and mulch after flowering.

E. × bungei. The popular name for what is now *E. stenophyllus*, this has rich yellow flowers, fading to orange-brown. H1.5m/5ft, W60cm/2ft. F6-7. Z6-9.

E. himalaicus. These are mostly white, occasionally pink, and early-flowering. H90cm/3ft, W30cm/1ft. F6-7. Z5-8. **'Ruiter Hybrids'** are mainly yellow shades. H1.2m/4ft, W30cm/1ft. F6-7. Z6-9.

E. robustus. A giant species, this needs space for its wide-spreading roots. Its clear pink flowers, with green and brown markings, last for several weeks. H2.4m/8ft, W90cm/3ft. F6-7. Z5-8.

E. stenophyllus. See *E. × bungei*.

ERIGERON Fleabane

An indispensable genus with daisy-like flowers and lance-shaped leaves. Almost all plants now in cultivation are hybrids, the most recent of which often have bright colours and semi-double flowers. They are easy to grow in sun and well-drained soil, and are tolerant of maritime conditions, but they dislike being divided in autumn. Some may benefit from twiggy branch supports; almost all are good for cutting. Those with names ending in 'ity' were selected from a cross we made in 1951 as distinctive hybrids.

E. aurantiacus. A variable species with velvety leaves and flowers ranging from light to deep orange-yellow, but short-lived and seedlings are usually offered. H25-30cm/10-12in, W25cm/10in. F6-8. Z4-8.

E. caucasicus. This mat-forming evergreen has single, lavender-blue flowers. H25cm/10in, W25cm/10in. F6-8. Z5-8.

E. philadelphicus. Light pink flowers are carried above soft green leaves. Short-lived and apt to self-seed, becoming a nuisance. H60cm/2ft, W30cm/1ft. F6-7. Z4-8.

E. salsuginosus. A compact species with white, pink-tinged flowers over a long period. H20cm/8in, W20cm/8in. F5-7. Z5-8.

E. simplex. Leafy tufts give a charming display of white daisies in late spring. H25cm/10in, W25cm/10in. F5-7. Z5-8.

Hybrids. **'Adria'**, the best tall variety, has multiple rows of lavender-blue petals around a central yellow disc. H75cm/30in, W45cm/18in. F6-8. Z4-8. It supersedes **'Merstham Glory'**, **'Strahlenmeer'** and **'Wuppertal'**. Others worth growing include the following: **'Amity'**, single, lilac-pink flowers. H70cm/28in, W45cm/18in. F6-8. Z5-8. **'Charity'**, single, clear light pink. H60cm/2ft, W45cm/18in. F6-8. Z5-8. **'Dignity'**, long-

flowering, deep violet-blue single.
H45cm/18in, W45cm/18in. F6-8. Z5-8.
'Dimity', tufty light green leaves,
obliquely held sprays of large pink flowers.
H25cm/10in, W25cm/10in. F6-8. Z4-8.
'Foerster's Liebling', still popular for its
deep pink, semi-double flowers.
H40cm/16in, W45cm/18in. F6-8. Z5-8.
'Prosperity', dwarf and prolific, near
double, light blue flowers. II35cm/14in,
W45cm/18in. F6-8. Z5-8. **'Quakeress'**, old
but still worthy single, delicate lilac-pink.
H60cm/2ft, W45cm/18in. F6-8. Z5-8.
'Rose Triumph', semi-double pink.
H50cm/20in, W45cm/18in. F6-8. Z5-8.
'Rotes Meer', near red, finely rayed
petals. H60cm/2ft, W45cm/18in. F6-8.
Z5-8. **'Schwarzes Meer'**, deep violet,
with prominent yellow disc, superseding
the older **'Darkest of All'** and **'Violetta'**.
H60cm/2ft, W45cm/18in. F6-8. Z5-8.

ERYNGIUM Sea holly
These distinctive sun lovers have very
attractive foliage as well as long-lasting,
rounded, teazle-like flowers, or bracts,
excellent for drying. The only British
native, *E. maritimum*, is sometimes seen in
gardens, but the range is quite diverse and
none is fussy about soil, if well-drained; a
sunny, open site is best. A new range has
recently been introduced, but many are still
on trial. A few are quite promising,
including some with variegated basal
leaves. Others, however, can be faulted for
refusing to grow erectly without support.
E. agavifolium. Serrated, sword-like
evergreen leaves form a loose basal rosette,
and stiff stems carry stumpy green flower
heads. H1.5m/5ft, W60cm/2ft. F7-9. Z9-10.
E. alpinum. This has rounded, green, basal
leaves and smooth, branching, blue stems
with large, steely blue bracts, each with a
decorative calyx 'ruff'. **'Donard'** is an
improvement. H90cm/3ft, W45cm/18in.
F6-8. Z5-8.
E. amethystinum. The name denotes the
colour of the flowers; the jagged leaves are
green. The true plant is rare, but **'Jewel'**
and **'Violetta'** are sometimes offered.
All H60cm/2ft, W60cm/2ft. F6-8. Z3-8.
E. bourgatii. Striking silver, jagged basal
leaves are attractively veined white; wiry,
much branched stems carry blue teazles,
with the upper stems also blue. H60cm/2ft,
W30cm/1ft. F6-9. Z5-9.
E. bromeliifolium. Evergreen foliage and
small, whitish green flowers are graceful,
without the need for showy colour.
H1.2m/4ft, W60cm/2ft. F7-8. Z9-10.
E. leavenworthii. Seldom seen but
worthy, this has deeply set leaves and
branching stems of steely blue bracts.
H70cm/28in, W38cm/15in. F6-8. Z9-10.
E. × *oliverianum*. This fleshy-rooted
hybrid has fresh green, jagged foliage,

Eryngium × oliverianum

steely blue stems and large, steely blue
bracts. H90cm/3ft, W45cm/18in. F6-8. Z5-8.
E. planum. With rounded, deep green
leaves and branching heads of small blue
flowers and greeny blue, spiky bracts, , this
is useful for cutting, but **'Blue Dwarf'** is
the best garden form. H60-70cm/24-28in,
W45cm/18in. F6-8. Z5-9.
E. proteiflorum. Long, narrow, prickly,
evergreen leaves, each with a white midrib,
are partnered with imposing, bluish white
flower heads, enclosed in similarly coloured
leafy bracts. H90cm/3ft, W60cm/2ft. F6-8.
Z9-10.
E. serra. Another South American with
evergreen foliage, this time doubly serrate,
and erect stems of small greenish bracts.
H1.3m/51in, W45cm/18in. F6-8. Z9-10.
E. tripartitum. This has much branched,
wiry stems carrying small blue flower heads,
each with a deep blue, spiky bract, above
lush green basal rosettes. H90cm/3ft,
W60cm/2ft. F6-8. Z5-8.
E. variifolium. The rounded, evergreen
leaves are prickly, but with attractive white
veining. The flowers, borne stiffly on
branching stems, are bluish, with prominent
spiny bracts. H50cm/20in, W25cm/10in.
F7-9. Z5-9.

Eryngium bourgatii

E. zabelii. This seldom seen species is
erect-growing, with branching stems and
steely blue flowers. H70cm/28in,
W45cm/18in. F7-9. Z5-8.

EUPATORIUM
Easy to grow, these have small, fuzzy flower
heads. They are long-lived but best in good
soil that does not dry out.
E. ageratoides. See *E. fraseri*.
E. cannabinum. Hemp agrimony is a
British native. The double form, **'Flore
Pleno'**, is sometimes used, but the loose
purple-mauve heads are rather dull.
H1.2m/4ft, W60cm/2ft. F7-8. Z3-9.

Eupatorium purpureum 'Atropurpureum'

Euphorbia griffithii 'Fireglow'

Euphorbia palustris

Euphorbia amygdaloides 'Rubra'

Euphorbia myrsinites

E. fraseri (syn. *E. ageratoides*). This forms dense, bushy clumps of light green leaves and effective heads of puffy white flowers. H1.2m/4ft, W60cm/2ft. F8-9. Z4-9.

E. maculatum. A dwarf species, this makes leafy stems with lavender-purple heads. H70cm/28in, W35cm/14in. F7-9. Z2-9.

E. purpureum. The American Joe Pye weed is a stately, late-flowering background plant, its stiff stems, with whorls of pointed leaves, carrying wide, flat, rosy purple flower heads. An improved form with purply stems and leaves is 'Atropurpureum'; the white 'Album' is also attractive. H1.8-2.1m/6-7ft, W90cm/3ft. F8-10. Z3-9.

EUPHORBIA Spurge

Almost all those in cultivation have sulphur-yellow flowers, more accurately bracts, but this lack of colour variation is no deterrent to their popularity. Sulphur-yellow goes well with other colours and, in addition, so many varieties possess attractive form and green or glaucous foliage.

They are generally sun lovers and prefer poor, dryish soil to a rich, moist one. The evergreen, bush-forming types resent wet conditions and some, such as *E. wulfenii*, are liable to be cut back in severe winters. This type usually deteriorates after a couple of years' display, but self-sown seedlings are often to be found nearby. Those which die back each year to a strong clump are fully hardy, and the renewed spring growth of some makes them colourful long before the flowers appear.

Many which tolerate shade and dry soil are likely to luxuriate in sunny conditions.

Only these and the truly herbaceous types are amenable to division. Others are increased by seed and cuttings. Gloves should be worn when taking cuttings, as their white sap can irritate skin.

E. amygdaloides. Wood spurge has fast-spreading roots, deep green leaves and sprays of greenish yellow flowers. It is best in the wild garden and more attractive in **'Rubra'**, the purple-leaved form. H30cm/1ft, W30cm/1ft. F4-5. Z7-9.

E. characias. This is still confused with *E. wulfenii*. The former has brown centres to the greenish yellow flowers; the latter has yellow-centred flowers, carried in broader spikes. Both have evergreen, glaucous foliage and bushy growth habits; stems die back to the base after flowering. H1.2m/4ft, W90cm/3ft. F3-5. Z7-10.

E. corallioides. A useful, compact species, this has green leaves and sulphury heads for several weeks. H50cm/20in, W25cm/10in. F5-7. Z4-9.

E. cyparissias. The cypress spurge creeps far and wide, producing dainty, glaucous, cypress-like foliage and sprays of yellowish flowers. H15cm/6in, W30cm/1ft. F5-7. Z4-9.

E. epithymoides. See *E. polychroma*.

E. griffithii **'Fireglow'**. This striking, slow-spreading plant emerges in spring with purplish shoots that develop into a bushy mass of greenery, carrying fiery orange flowers. The foliage of the variety **'Dixter'** has a slightly darker hue. All are best in sun and poorish soil. H1m/39in, W60cm/2ft. F4-6. Z4-9.

E. longifolia. Long-lived, long-flowering and very handsome, with erect stems, good foliage, and wide heads of greenish yellow. H1.2m/4ft, W60cm/2ft. F6-8. Z6-9.

E. × martinii. Shapely, evergreen, bushy growth and flower heads of the usual colour. It does not appear to set seed, but the old flower heads are attractive, left on until autumn. H60cm/2ft, W50cm/20in. F6-7. Z7-9.

E. myrsinites. This has attractive, blue-grey, fleshy leaves closely set along the trailing stems which carry heads of sulphur-yellow flowers. H15cm/6in, W30cm/1ft. F5-7. Z5-8.

E. nicaeensis. This may be a form of *E. seguieriana*, with congested basal stems, small, narrow leaves and wide, sulphury yellow flower heads lasting for many weeks. Unfortunately, not long-lived. H30-50cm/12-20in, W40cm/16in. F5-7. Z5-8.

E. palustris. A lusty, clump-forming and deep-rooted species, its huge, greeny yellow flower heads make a spectacular late spring display, and the foliage turns orange and yellow in autumn. It is worthy of the space it needs. H1m/39in, W1m/39in. F5-6. Z5-8.

E. polychroma (syn. *E. epithymoides*). Compact and clump-forming, its outstanding yellowish flowers appear before the foliage. As the flowers fade to green, the whole plant becomes a neat leafy bush. **'Purpurea'** has purple-tinged foliage. Both H50cm/20in, W50cm/20in. F4-5. Z4-9.

E. robbiae. This good, evergreen ground cover for sun or shade has deep green, rounded leaves forming attractive basal rosettes, and flattish heads of almost green flowers. Roots spread quite rapidly but are easily curbed. H50cm/20in, W50cm/20in. F3-5. Z8-9.

E. schillingii. Another bushy, evergreen species, like a shorter *E. longifolia* with broader leaves. H50cm/20in, W50cm/20in. F6-7. Z7-9.

E. sikkimensis. Distinctive for its gracefully erect, willow-leaved stems, terminating in a broad head of greenish yellow flowers. The new spring shoots are attractive reddish shades, later turning soft green. Wide-spreading roots, especially in damp soil. H1.5m/5ft, W45cm/18in. F6-7. Z6-9.

E. wulfenii. Though correctly a form of *E. characias*, this is usually listed separately. Its flowers are clear yellow-green with no brown centres, and are carried in broader spikes, but both have the same sturdy habit, with glaucous leaves. An especially good form is **'Lambrook Gold'**. H1.2m/4ft, W90cm/3ft. F3-5. Z7-10.

FERULA Giant fennel

F. tingitana. Mounds of lacy, finely dissected leaves, 60cm/2ft high, eventually produce towering stems of huge, yellow, umbellifer flowers. It does best in full sun and well-drained soil; its long taproot resents disturbance, so young, seed-raised plants are safest. H2.1m/7ft, W90cm/3ft. F6-8. Z7-9.

FILIPENDULA

Formerly listed under *Spiraea* and naming is still somewhat confused, but these now represent a genus which includes the native meadow sweet. All have fingered or palmate leaves and feathery, flattened flower heads comprised of tiny flowers; none has a long flowering season but they make up for this with intense colourings. All but one prefer moist soil.

F. camtschatica (syn. *F. gigantea*). This is sometimes listed under *F. palmata*. A very imposing plant in the right place, it has strong, leafy stems and pink flower heads up to 30cm/1ft across. H2.4m/8ft, W60cm/2ft. F6-7. Z3-9.

F. digitata. See *F. palmata.*

F. gigantea. See *F. camtschatica.*

F. hexapetala (syn. *F. vulgaris*). Dropwort forms mats of ferny foliage and branching stems carrying typical plumes of white flowers. It does not need moist soil. All are deep-rooting. H60cm/2ft, W45cm/18in. F6-7. Z4-9. **'Flore Pleno'** is fully double and

Filipendula purpurea

intensely white above pretty, deep green filigree foliage. H40cm/16in, W30cm/1ft. F6-7. Z4-9. **'Grandiflora'** has rather lax stems of faintly scented, larger flowers on broadly branching heads. H60cm/2ft, W45cm/18in. F5-7. Z4-9.

F. palmata (syn. *F. digitata*). An old and perhaps invalid name, but it describes plants with hand-like leaves. There are several forms, with varying heights. Both **'Elegans'** and **'Elegantissima'** have indented foliage, wiry stems and heads of clear pink. H75-100cm/30-39in, W60cm/2ft. F6-7. Z3-9. **'Nana'** has heads of bright pink well displayed, but height varies with soil and moisture. H20-35cm/8-14in, W30cm/1ft. F6-8. Z3-9.

F. purpurea (formerly *F. palmata* 'Rubra'). This is the brightest of all, with dense, flattish heads of glistening, deep rose flowers. Does best in light shade and rich, moist, deep soil. **'Alba'** is a less striking white-flowered form. Both H90cm/3ft, W60cm/2ft. F6-7. Z4-9.

F. rubra (formerly *F. venusta magnifica*). Called queen of the prairies in the USA, this grows lustily in moist soil with an outspreading root system, and soon demands space. The strong leafy stems carry wide heads of clear pink flowers. H2.1m/7ft, W1.2m/4ft. F6-8. Z3-9.

F. ulmaria **'Aurea'**. Meadowsweet is a desirable foliage plant with divided, golden-green leaves, brighter if the nondescript flowers are cut back. This also prevents green-leaved seedlings. Best in cool, moist shade. H60cm/2ft, W45cm/18in. F7-8. Z3-9.

F. vulgaris. See *F. hexapetala.*

Filipendula hexapetala 'Flore Pleno'

Filipendula ulmaria 'Aurea'

Fritillaria imperialis

Galtonia candicans

Gaillardia grandiflora 'Mandarin'

FRANCOA

These are akin to heucheras and in mild districts retain their hairy, soft green foliage over winter. Elsewhere, they are not reliably hardy, but are easy to protect. The graceful flower spikes carry wand-like clusters of small, mainly pale pink flowers. They can be trained to form an arch or circle, hence the folk name, bridal wreath. Grow in light shade.
F. appendiculata, *F. ramosa* and *F. sonchifolia* are all much alike. H60-90cm/2-3ft, W38cm/15in. F6-8. Z7-9.

FRITILLARIA

Early-flowering bulbs often leave a bare patch after flowering, and these are no exception. Their nodding, bell- or lily-like flowers are so attractive, however, that they are worth the space, which can then be filled with annuals or other short-term

plants. Rich, moisture-retentive but well-drained soil is best.
F. imperialis. The crown imperial is available in orange-red and yellow forms, each with large clustered bells from a terminal spike, topped by a tuft of fresh green leaves. It flowers best in sun. The bulbs, which emit a strong smell when touched, may be left undisturbed for a few years. Plant new bulbs and lift, divide and replant old, congested clumps as soon as they die down in summer. H90cm/3ft, W45cm/18in. F4-5. Z5-9.
F. verticillata. This has small, greenish, bell-shaped flowers, slightly chequered on the inside, on stems carrying gracefully curling, greyish leaves. Best in cool shade. H60cm/2ft, W30cm/1ft. F5-6. Z6-8.

GAILLARDIA Blanket flower

G. grandiflora. Only hybrids of this species are grown as garden perennials. The flowers are gaily coloured in yellow, flame and mahogany-red shades, often parti-coloured, all with rayed petals and a rich brown centre. They flower for a long time, but need support. Good drainage is important, as is cutting hard back when flowering is finished. Excellent for cutting. Full sun and gritty, well-drained soil are best. All F6-8, Z3-8. **'Croftway Yellow'**, free-flowering monochrome. H60cm/2ft, W45cm/18in. **'Goblin'**, dwarf red and yellow. H30cm/1ft, W30cm/1ft. **'Ipswich Beauty'**, reddish centres, deep yellow petals. H60cm/2ft, W45cm/18in. **'Mandarin'**, deep flame-orange monochrome. H60cm/2ft, W45cm/18in. **'Wirral Flame'**, brownish red, scarcely tipped yellow. H60cm/2ft, W45cm/18in.

GALAX

G. aphylla. A choice and rarely seen plant for cool shade and acid soil. Its evergreen, rounded, leathery leaves give fine autumn and winter colour and slender sprays of tiny white flowers are carried in midsummer. Valuable foliage for flower arranging. H45cm/18in, W30cm/1ft. F8-9. Z5-8.

GALEGA Goat's rue

These excellent space fillers make robust leafy plants in any soil in sun. They have pinnate leaves and their short spikes of pea-shaped flowers are carried for several weeks. Support may be necessary.
G. officinalis. Available only in named forms, these include the white **'Alba'**, light pink **'Carnea'**, rosy mauve **'Her Majesty'** and purplish **'Lady Wilson'**. All H1.5m/5ft, W90cm/3ft. F6-8. Z4-8.
G. orientalis. This is less robust, with deep green leaves and royal blue flowers on short, erect spikes. Its roots are invasive. H80cm/32in, W60cm/2ft. F6-8. Z5-8.

GALTONIA Summer hyacinth

The connection is obvious, but the common name applies only to *G. candicans*. All are fully hardy bulbs, adaptable except for deep shade, and make a good summer display. Plant 8-10cm/3-4in deep.
G. candicans. The tallest and best-known species, this has smooth stems carrying drooping, white, slightly fragrant trumpets, followed by attractive seed pods. The long leaves are lax at the base. Quite effective for planting among smallish shrubs, or to follow early-flowering subjects, such as yellow alyssum or geum. H1.2m/4ft, W30cm/1ft. F7-8. Z7-10.

G. princeps. This has smaller flowers tinged green at the tip. Good for flower arranging. Bulbs increase naturally. H90cm/3ft, W30cm/1ft. F7-9. Z7-10.

GAURA
G. lindheimeri. An easy but untidy plant, useful where choicer plants cannot be grown. The willowy, branching stems carry a long succession of small, pinkish white flowers. A short-lived plant for full sun and well-drained soil, but self-seeds easily. H1.2m/4ft, W90cm/3ft. F7-9. Z6-9.

GENTIANA Gentian
Though perhaps better known as alpine plants, a few are valuable perennials and some are adaptable for frontal positions and rock gardens. Most summer-flowering kinds (unlike the autumn-flowering ones) tolerate lime, but they do like good, deep, humus-rich soil.
G. asclepiadea. The willow gentian is not for dry, open positions but will naturalize in cool, moist shade. Its wiry stems have willow-like leaves, terminating in many pairs of deep blue trumpets. Colour varies a little; the form **'Alba'** is white. These are lovely plants for late summer, given the right conditions. H60-70cm/24-28in, W60cm/2ft. F8-10. Z6-9.
G. lutea. Although not easy to establish, this is an imposing plant in every way. Stout, central crowns send up aspidistra-like leaves and stiff, unbranched spikes carrying clusters of yellow trumpets, each cluster surrounded by a green bract, and followed by attractive seed pods. Grow in deep, rich soil and sun. H90-120cm/3-4ft, W60cm/2ft. F6-8. Z7-8.

Gentiana lutea

Geranium clarkei 'Kashmir White'

G. makinoi. A rarity to delight those who can grow it. Sun and good drainage are essential, but rearing and establishment are difficult. Where happy, rich blue, upward-facing trumpets cluster on erect stems. H40cm/16in, W25cm/10in. F7-9. Z6-8.
G. septemfida. This and others akin to it, including *G.* × *doeringiana* and *G.* × *hascombensis*, are excellent for frontal positions or as alpines. Their lax, leafy stems carry clusters of typical gentian trumpets for several weeks. H15-20cm/6-8in, W30cm/1ft. F6-9. Z4-8.

GERANIUM Crane's bill
The garden value of hardy geraniums has at last been recognized. The range now available is steadily increasing and at Bressingham there are over 100 species and cultivars being evaluated in our trials, though it would be quite uneconomic to make them all available for sale. If several hardy geraniums are dwarf enough to be classed as alpines, some of these are quite suitable for positions in front of taller perennials. Very few are fussy about soil and only a few require full sun, while some will grow in quite dry shade and make good ground cover. See also under Alpines.
G. 'Ann Folkard'. Wide-spreading, with magenta-purple, saucer-shaped flowers. H30cm/1ft, W30cm/1ft. F6-9. Z5-8.
G. armenum (syn. *G. psilostemon*). A splendid subject if placed where its fierce magenta does not clash with other colours. Its habit is bushy and somewhat lax; the saucer-shaped, black-eyed flowers almost smother the deeply cut leaves, which colour well in autumn. **'Bressingham Flair'** is similar but the magenta is toned

Geranium × *cantabrigiense* 'Cambridge'

down with a hint of carmine. Sun preferred. Both H90cm/3ft, W90cm/3ft. F6-8. Z4-8.
G. atlanticum. See *G. malviflorum*.
G. × *cantabrigiense* **'Biokovo'**. This is a low-growing discovery from Yugoslavia, and has delicate pink flowers with deeper pink centres. Distinct. H20cm/8in, W30cm/1ft. F5-8. Z4-8. **'Cambridge'** is a hybrid between *G. dalmaticum* and *G. macrorrhizum* and was found in Cambridge Botanic Gardens, England. It has glossy green leaves and rose-pink flowers. H25cm/10in, W30cm/1ft. F5-8. Z4-8.
G. **'Claridge Druce'**. A most adaptable hybrid and excellent, clump-forming ground cover, with near evergreen, greyish, divided leaves and a vigorous surface spread, in sun or even quite dry shade. The flowers are magenta-pink but not glaringly so, and continue for several weeks just above the foliage. H60cm/2ft, W90cm/3ft. F6-9. Z4-8.
G. clarkei. **'Kashmir Purple'** and **'Kashmir White'**, formerly listed under *G. rectum*, have low, leafy growth and drooping

Geranium pratense 'Plenum Caeruleum'

Geranium macrorrhizum 'Bevan's Variety'

purple and white flowers, respectively. Both H30cm/1ft, W45cm/18in. F6-8. Z4-8.

G. delavayi. A demure species with deep green, upstanding, finely cut foliage and lilac-pink flowers. H30cm/1ft, W30cm/1ft. F6-7. Z5-8.

G. endressii. This forms hefty clumps of light green, evergreen leaves and carries outspreading sprays of clear pink flowers. The varieties **'A. T. Johnson'**, with silvery pink flowers, and the clear salmon-pink **'Wargrave Pink'** are offered as improvements, but the difference between them is insignificant. All H40cm/16in, W60cm/2ft. F6-8. Z4-8.

G. grandiflorum. See *G. himalayense*.

G. grevilleanum. This makes a wide-spreading, leafy ground cover when in growth, but dies back to a relatively compact plant in autumn. It has a long succession of nodding, lilac-pink flowers with reflexed petals. H35cm/14in, W30cm/1ft. F6-9. Z4-8.

G. himalayense (syn. *G. grandiflorum*). This rapidly expands into large clumps of low, deeply divided leaves, which colour

beautifully in autumn, and blue, bowl-shaped flowers, attractively veined red. H30cm/1ft, W60cm/2ft. F6-7. Z4-8. The vigorous **'Plenum'**, or **'Birch Double'**, has smaller but fully double blue flowers. H30cm/1ft, W60cm/2ft. F6-7. Z4-8.

G. ibericum. See *G. × magnificum*.

G. incisum. Pretty but not spectacular, this has finely cut, silky leaves on fairly erect stems and clusters of purplish, darker-veined flowers. H30cm/1ft, W30cm/1ft. F6-8. Z5-8.

G. 'Johnson's Blue', an outstanding hybrid, is neat, adaptable and makes a fine show of clear blue, darker-veined flowers above a dense cover of handsome, deeply divided leaves. H30cm/1ft, W30cm/1ft. F6-8. Z4-8.

G. libani. This makes an early display of light blue flowers, but by midsummer dies back to its brittle, fleshy roots until fresh leaves appear in autumn. H50cm/20in, W38cm/15in. F5-6. Z5-8.

G. macrorrhizum. This has semi-evergreen sweet briar-scented leaves, colouring well in autumn, somewhat woody stems and short sprays of magenta flowers, 4cm/1$\frac{1}{2}$in

across. The form ***album*** is white, **'Ingwersen's Variety'** is soft pink, and **'Variegatum'** has variegated leaves. **'Bevan's Variety'** and **'Depre'** are similar, as improvements on the type, with deep pink flowers. Good, quick-spreading, weed-proof ground cover for sun or shade. All H25cm/10in, W60cm/2ft. F6-7. Z4-8.

G. maculatum. This desirable plant is early-flowering, with a stout, clump-forming habit, fresh green fingered leaves and lots of lilac-pink flowers. H60cm/2ft, W45cm/18in. F5-7. Z4-8.

G. × magnificum (syn. *G. ibericum*). This makes a very bright show in early summer with masses of rich blue, dark-veined flowers over deeply cut, rounded leaves, but it tends to flop. Good autumn foliage colour. H60cm/2ft, W60cm/2ft. F6-7. Z4-8.

G. malviflorum (syn. *G. atlanticum*). This makes a leafy carpet of foliage from spreading tuberous roots from winter to spring. Saucer-shaped, light blue flowers are attractive, but dormancy follows. H23cm/9in, W23cm/9in. F4-6. Z4-8.

G. nodosum. This has slender stems, small, glossy leaves and small, purple-red flowers. It is rarely offered, but valuable for its tolerance of deep shade. Self-seeds freely. H40cm/16in, W40cm/16in. F6-8. Z5-8.

G. phaeum. The mourning widow is named for its small, nodding, purple-black flowers, clustered above slender, leafy stems. A very tolerant species, even in dry shade. H60cm/2ft, W60cm/2ft. F5-7. Z4-8.

'Album' has a profusion of flowers in early summer. H60cm/2ft, W60cm/2ft. F5-7. Z4-8. The form *lividum* is similar, but with greyish mauve flowers. H60cm/2ft, W60cm/2ft. F5-7. Z4-8.

G. pratense. The meadow cranesbill is a British native with deeply cut, rounded leaves colouring well in autumn, and sprays of saucer-shaped flowers. Singles can self-seed a little too freely and include the blue **'Mrs Kendall Clarke'**, and the rare white **'Album'** and pale pink **'Roseum'**. All have quite deep roots and need good drainage. The doubles are less vigorous and the flowers are smaller; **'Plenum Album'** is white, **'Plenum Caeruleum'** light blue, tinged lavender, and **'Plenum Violaceum'** deep blue. All H60cm/2ft, W60cm/2ft. F6-7. Z5-8.

G. procurrens. This wide-spreading species with self-rooting runners forms rapid ground cover of light green leaves and pale magenta flowers. H15cm/6in, W60cm/2ft. F6-9. Z5-8.

G. psilostemon. See *G. armenum*.

G. reflexum. Its purplish red, cyclamen-like flowers have reflexed petals and are carried above deeply cut leaves. Best in light shade. H60cm/2ft, W60cm/2ft. F5-7. Z5-8.

G. renardii. Its attractive, large, rounded, grey-green, puckered leaves make a shapely

Geranium pratense 'Mrs Kendall Clarke'

dome 25cm/10in high, above which is a brief show of pale lilac, purple-veined flowers. Good in poorish soil. H35cm/14in, W30cm/1ft. F5-6. Z6-8.

G. 'Russell Prichard'. A long-flowering hybrid, its vivid magenta-rose flowers are carried on outspread sprays. Greyish foliage adds to its value and in frontal or sloping positions with full sun, its sprawling habit is a bonus. H15cm/6in, W45cm/18in. F6-9. Z6-8.

G. sanguineum. The bloody cranesbill also has many variants, the type making tightly mounded clumps of vigorous growth in almost any soil, with deeply divided leaves and 2.5cm/1in wide, magenta-red flowers on short stems. H25cm/10in, W45cm/18in. F6-8. Z4-8. **'Album'** has lighter greenery and white flowers. H25cm/10in, W45cm/18in. F6-8. Z4-8. **'Holden's Variety'** is more mounded, with larger, bright pink flowers. H25cm/10in, W45cm/18in. F6-9. Z4-8. The form *lancastriense* **'Splendens'** is more prostrate, with sprays of clear pink, crimson-veined flowers for many weeks. H15cm/6in, W30cm/1ft. F6-8. Z4-8. **'Plenum'**, though not fully double, is a softer shade. H25cm/10in, W45cm/18in. F6-8. Z4-8.

G. sylvaticum. Another clump-forming species with variations. All are sturdy, early-flowering and best cut back after flowering to induce fresh growth. **'Album'** has ample, light green foliage and pleasing white flowers, 4cm/1½in across, on branching stems. **'Mayflower'** is a fine blue form. All H60cm/2ft, W60cm/2ft. F5-7. Z4-8. The form *wanneri* has flowers of an almost shell-pink tint, with deeper suffusions. H50cm/20in, W30cm/1ft. F5-7. Z4-8.

G. tuberosum. Fleshy roots send up ample light green leaves and small, pinkish flowers over a long period. H40cm/16in, W30cm/1ft. F6-9. Z5-8.

G. wallichianum. Though often used as an alpine, this is wonderful for a frontal position. Given a sunny slope in good, well-drained soil, it produces dense, deep green summer growth studded for weeks with lavender-blue, saucer-shaped flowers, white at the centre. **'Buxton's Variety'** is invariably the form listed. H30cm/1ft, W90cm/3ft. F6-10. Z4-8.

G. wlassovianum. Another species with spreading, mounded summer growth and a good show of lavender-blue, darker-veined flowers above dark, velvety leaves. H30cm/1ft, W30cm/1ft. F6-8. Z5-8.

GEUM Avens

This genus remains steadily popular, not only for rich flower colour, but for general reliability. All are easy-going sun lovers, though some flower less freely if allowed to become old clumps, and regular lifting, dividing and replanting is sensible. A few

Geranium × magnificum

Geranium renardii

hybrids which years ago were popular and in plentiful supply appear to have lost vigour for some reason; my few remaining plants of **'Dolly North'**, **'Fire Opal'**, **'Princess Juliana'** and **'Rubin'** are only just alive and flower sparsely, though as far as I can tell they are not diseased, and I have not seen them offered elsewhere for many years.

The following hybrids, however, are all good. **'Borisii'**, an old hybrid, and one of the earliest to flower, forms low, light green,

Geranium sylvaticum 'Album'

Geranium sanguineum lancastriense 'Splendens'

evergreen mounds and has orange-scarlet flowers, 1.5cm/½in across, on 15cm/6in sprays in late spring and sometimes later. H15-30cm/6-12in, W30cm/1ft. F5-7. Z5-8. **'Coppertone'**, a new variety, has semi-drooping sprays of coppery orange, cup-shaped flowers. H15-30cm/6-12in, W30cm/1ft. F5-7. Z5-8. **'Georgenberg'** has early, cup-shaped, light orange flowers. H30cm/1ft, W30cm/1ft. F5-7. Z5-8. **'Lady Stratheden'** and **'Mrs Bradshaw'** are relatively short-lived but free-flowering,

Geranium 'Russell Prichard'

the former double yellow and the latter double red, 2.5-4cm/1-1½in across. Both H60cm/2ft, W30cm/1ft. F6-8. Z5-9.
'Lionel Cox' has slightly arching sprays of light yellow flowers. H30cm/1ft, W30cm/1ft. F6-8. Z3-8. **'Nordek'**, recently introduced, is vigorous, with fiery orange flowers in late spring and again sporadically through mild winters. H40cm/16in, W30cm/1ft. Z5-8.
G. pyrenaicum. A parent of most mound-forming kinds, it has semi-drooping sprays of pale yellow, cup-shaped flowers. H25cm/10in, W30cm/1ft. F5-7. Z5-7.
G. × rhaeticum. Mat-forming, this has yellow flowers, followed by fluffy seed heads. H15cm/6in, W30cm/1ft. F5-6. Z5-8.
G. rivale. Vigorous leafy clumps of hairy, dark green, rounded leaves and slender, branching sprays of pink, bell-shaped flowers, best in the strawberry-pink **'Leonard's Variety'**. Both thrive in wet soil. H40cm/16in, W30cm/1ft. F6-7. Z3-8.
G. rossii. This has distinctive, carrot-like foliage and sprays of bright yellow flowers. H20cm/8in, W25cm/10in. F5-7. Z5-8.

GILLENIA
G. trifoliata. This long-lived, tough-rooted plant has erect, reddish, willowy stems and narrow leaves ending in terminal sprays of small white flowers with long-lasting red calyces. An unusual plant of much charm for sun or partial shade where not dry. H80-90cm/32-36in, W60cm/2ft. F6-8. Z4-8.

GUNNERA
G. manicata. This spectacular waterside subject has huge, jagged, deeply lobed leaves 1.2m/4ft high and across. The brownish green flowers appear on short, stiff, congested spikes. Best given ample space and a waterside position. Needs winter protection in all but the mildest climates; bending the old leaves over the furry crowns to protect them is traditional. H1.8m/6ft, W1.2m/4ft. F6-7. Z7-10.

Geum rivale 'Leonard's Variety'

Gillenia trifoliata

Gunnera manicata

GYPSOPHILA Baby's breath
All are sun-loving, drought-resistant, deciduous plants with vigorous, wide-spreading, bushy annual growth and delicate flowers valuable for filling space left by early-flowering plants, and for use in cut-flower displays. Some prostrate kinds are listed under Alpines. Well-drained, limy soil is preferable; they resent disturbance once established.
G. paniculata. The single-flowered perennial baby's breath has deep, fleshy roots, much branched, airy stems, small, greyish leaves and masses of tiny white flowers. H90cm/3ft, W90cm/3ft. F6-8. All Z4-9. The double white **'Bristol Fairy'** is a little less robust but the flowers are larger. H90cm/3ft, W90cm/3ft. F6-8. **'Compacta Plena'** is a very reliable double white. H50cm/20in, W45cm/18in. F6-9. **'Flamingo'**, a light pink double and glaucous-leaved, is shorter-lived and good drainage is essential. H90cm/3ft, W90cm/3ft. F6-8. **'Pink Star'** makes ample, low growth set with pale pink, semi-double flowers. H30cm/1ft, W45cm/18in. F6-9. **'Rosy Veil'** is almost prostrate, with bluish green narrow leaves and light pink flowers. H30cm/1ft, W45cm/18in. F6-9.

HACQUETIA
H. epipactis. This uncommon spring-flowering plant has tight umbels of tiny, sulphur-yellow flowers set in leafy bracts, followed by a mound of tufted, deeply lobed, dark green leaves. A cool, moist,

shady spot is best. A form with variegated leaves is an attractive rarity. H15cm/6in, W23cm/9in. F3-5. Z5-7.

HELENIUM Sneezeweed
Most of these well-loved plants bloom in late summer, producing daisy flowers in bright shades of yellow, orange and browny crimson with a central conical disc. All are easy to grow in sun, but the stem leaves of neglected, old or starved plants may wither prematurely, and tall types may need staking where damp or windy. Lift, divide and replant regularly. The following hybrids are derived largely from *H. autumnale.* All Z4-8.
'Bressingham Gold', deep yellow, crimson-streaked flowers, long, spear-shaped stem leaves. H1.1m/43in, W45cm/18in. F7-8. **'Bruno'**, late-flowering crimson-mahogany. H1.2m/4ft, W45cm/18in. F8-9. **'Butterpat'**, pure yellow, late-flowering. H1.1m/43in, W45cm/18in. F8-9. **'Coppelia'**, warm coppery orange, sturdy growth. H1m/39in, W45cm/18in. F8-9. All four above were raised at Bressingham.
'Copper Spray' (syn. 'Kupfersprudel'), coppery orange. H1.1m/43in, W45cm/18in. F8-9. **'Crimson Beauty'**, more brown than crimson, early and very dwarf. H60cm/2ft, W45cm/18in. F6-8. **'Gold Fox'**, fine tawny orange flowers. H1m/39in, W40cm/16in. F7-8. **'Golden Youth'**, the best early-flowering yellow. H90cm/3ft, W45cm/18in. F6-8. **'Mahogany'**, deep yellow and browny red. H90cm/3ft, W45cm/18in. F7-8. **'Mme Canivet'**, bright yellow, upright growth. H90cm/3ft, W45cm/18in. F7-8. **'Morheim Beauty'**, bronze-red flowers and a sturdy habit. H1.1m/43in, W45cm/18in. F7-8.
'Waldtraud', extra-large flowers, orange-brown, tall but strong. H1.2m/4ft, W45cm/18in. F8-9. **'Wyndley'**, compact, leafy, orange-brown flecked flowers for a long period. H70cm/28in, W45cm/18in. F6-8.

Gypsophila paniculata 'Rosy Veil'

Helenium 'Coppelia'

H. hoopesii. This is quite distinct. It has rosettes of large, leathery, greyish leaves and yellow flowers. H60cm/2ft, W45cm/18in. F6-8. Z3-7.

H. pumilum 'Magnificum'. Deep yellow flowers, floppy habit. H70cm/28in, W45cm/18in. F6-7. Z4-8.

HELIANTHUS Perennial sunflower

Those below make compact clumps and strong stems topped by single, double, or semi-double flowers in late summer, needing only sun and reasonable soil to give a good, trouble-free display. Others exist which are very invasive and are best avoided: *H. atrorubens*, *H. rigidus* and *H. spaicefolius*, and old hybrids such as *H.* 'Miss Melish' and *H.* 'Rev. Wolley-Dodd'.

H. decapetalus (syn. *H. multiflorus*) **'Loddon Gold'.** This has fully double flowers, 5cm/2in across, above leafy stems which need no supporting. Other hybrids and cultivars are **'Morning Sun'**, also sturdy, with anemone-centred, semi-double yellow flowers, and **'Capenoch Star'** and **'Capenoch Supreme'**, which are both similar. All H1.5m/5ft, W60cm/2ft. F7-9. Z5-8.

H. multiflorus. See *H. decapetalus*.
H. orygalis. See *H. salicifolius*.
H. salicifolius (syn. *H. orygalis*). Distinctive for its long, willow-like stem, foliage and

Helianthus decapetalus 'Loddon Gold'

Heliopsis scabra 'Golden Plume'

sprays of yellow flowers. Tall but attractive. H2.1m/7ft, W60cm/2ft. F9-10. Z6-9.

HELICHRYSUM

These sun-loving, drought-resistant plants need only good drainage. They vary in height and habit, some being suitable only as rock garden or alpine-house plants. Others are semi-shrubby and should be sited where they are not overshadowed by taller perennials. Very few are suitable for wet, cold districts. See also under Alpines.

H. alveolatum. See *H. splendidum*.
H. angustifolium. Its twiggy, grey-leaved stems have an aroma of curry powder and its button flowers are rusty orange. H30cm/1ft, W45cm/18in. F6-8. Z8-10.

H. orientale. This forms silvery, woolly carpets and straw-yellow flower heads, but is very vulnerable to winter wet. H30cm/1ft, W30cm/1ft. F6-8. Z8-9.

H. splendidum (syn. *H. alveolatum*). This makes an evergreen bush of silvery stems and foliage with orange-yellow button flowers in summer. Cut hard back in spring to keep it compact. H60cm/2ft, W75cm/30in. F7-9. Z8-10.

H. 'Sulphur Light'. Grey silvery stems and leaves topped by branching orange-yellow flower heads. It dies back in winter. H25cm/10in, W30cm/1ft. F6-9. Z5-9.

HELIOPSIS

H. scabra. All the following cultivars are good, reliable perennials which thrive in any reasonable soil and seldom need

staking. The single, semi-double or double yellow flowers, on branching, leafy stems, are 5-8cm/2-3in across. All F6-9, Z4-9.
'Ballerina', very free-flowering, single yellow. H1m/39in, W60cm/2ft. **'Desert King'**, large, rich yellow flowers. H1.1m/43in, W60cm/2ft. **'Gigantea'**, the tallest, single deep yellow. H1.2m/4ft, W60cm/2ft. **'Gold Green Heart'**, semi-double, lemon-yellow. H1.1m/43in, W60cm/2ft. **'Golden Plume'**, almost double, bushy habit. H1.1m/43in, W60cm/2ft. **'Incomparabilis'**, an old orange-yellow variety, still popular, semi-double. H1.1m/43in, W60cm/2ft.

HELLEBORUS Christmas rose, Lenten rose

The cup- or bowl-shaped flowers, which appear in winter or spring, have prominent stamens and thick petals. They come in a subtle range of colours and colour combinations, and can be startlingly beautiful, examined up close. All prefer some shade, ideally a north-facing position, but not excessive competition from tree roots. They are not fussy about soil, but enjoy a light mulch of humus to retain soil moisture. Some make good ground cover, with leathery, evergreen leaves.

Success is more likely with young plants as hellebores resent disturbance; most flourish for years if left alone. Divided plants of *H. niger* are apt to sulk, producing only occasional flowers and little foliage thereafter, but it seldom varies from seed.

While several other hellebores are not as resentful of being divided, this usually spoils the first season's flower display after planting. Sow seed as soon as ripe and divide in early autumn. *H. orientalis*-type seedlings seldom breed true and take about three years to reach flowering size from germination, which itself may take up to a year.

Foliage is vital for food manufacture and free flowering; a healthy plant remains evergreen at least until early winter. Most *orientalis* types make new sets of leaves after flowering, providing a shady canopy for the seeds to ripen slowly, and shield the soil beneath from the sun. Even though they appear to be drought-resistant, lack of summer foliage inhibits full development. Inter-breeding has made some original species obscure.

H. argutifolius (formerly *H. corsicus*). Evergreen, but rather lax in habit, producing grey-green, attractively veined, divided leaves and large clusters of pale apple-green flowers. H60cm/2ft, W90cm/3ft. F3-5. Z7-9.

H. atrorubens. As grown in gardens this is almost identical with *H. abschasicus*. Both

Helleborus foetidus 'Westerflisk'

Helleborus niger

flower in midwinter, with golden-stamened, deep maroon, cup-shaped flowers rising from a clumpy plant; but the latter does not set seed and foliage is withered by early winter, while the former may retain a few deep green leaves at flowering time. Both H30cm/1ft, W45cm/18in. F1-3. Z5-9.

H. colchicus. Close to *H. orientalis*, but it is well foliaged and has purplish flowers in early spring and sometimes again in autumn. H35cm/14in, W60cm/2ft. F2-4. Z4-9.

H. corsicus. See *H. argutifolius*.

H. cyclophyllus. Another *H. orientalis* type with pinkish flowers above the large, rounded and fingered leaves. H40cm/16in, W60cm/2ft. F2-4. Z6-9.

H. foetidus. This has deep green, upright growth, with fingered, dark evergreen leaves and greenish flowers with maroon-edged petals in spring. It is not long-lived but naturalizes by self-seeding. 'Westerflisk', with purplish leaves, is more attractive. H60cm/2ft, W60cm/2ft. F2-4. Z6-9.

H. guttatus. This dies back in autumn and has white or greeny pink flowers, often spotted with maroon inside. H30cm/1ft, W45cm/18in. F2-4. Z4-9.

H. lividus. This may suffer in cold winters but has handsome, tripartite evergreen foliage, which is attractively patterned with grey, and greenish purple, slightly scented flowers. H45cm/18in, W30cm/1ft. F3-5. Z8-9.

H. niger. The Christmas rose, with its nodding white flowers, often tinged greeny pink, and dark green, leathery leaves, usually flowers after Christmas and carries on until early spring. It resents being moved or divided and young seedling plants do best. Named clones, with larger, pure white flowers, include **'Potter's Wheel'** and **'White Magic'**; **'Altifolius'** is also good. All H25-30cm/10-12in, W45cm/18in. F1-3. Z4-8.

H. × nigercors. This is a cross between

H. argutifolius and *H. niger*. It has handsome, dark leaves and rather loose stems carrying sprays of open, creamy flowers. H30cm/1ft, W45cm/18in. F2-4. Z6-9.

H. orientalis. The Lenten rose is scarcely obtainable now in the true species, but hybrid strains are excellent, including white, greenish yellow, pink and maroon shades. Named varieties true to colour are **'Albion Otto'**, white; **'Heartsease'**, maroon; and **'Winter Cheer'**, flushed pink. Some splendid selections from Mrs Helen Ballard and others have widened the colour range to include sulphur- and primrose-yellow. All are virtually evergreen, with new leaves following the flowers, and they make good ground cover. All H30-60cm/1-2ft, W30-60cm/1-2ft. F2-4. Z4-9.

H. viridis. This has near evergreen, deeply cut foliage and abundant clear green flowers on upright stems. The sub-species *occidentalis* has smaller flowers. Both hold their colour for several weeks. Both H40cm/16in, W45cm/18in. F3-5. Z6-8.

HEMEROCALLIS Day lily

These first-class plants with fresh green, arching leaves and lily-like, often fragrant, flowers are immensely popular, with hybridists, especially in the USA, raising and naming vast numbers. (This makes trials for even the best a difficult task, though exciting developments are continually happening which more than compensate for the confusion.) All are reliable, adaptable for sun or partial shade and, though preferring good soil, not fussy. The earliest begin flowering in late spring, but the peak period is midsummer. Only a few species are now offered and these, from which hybrids have been bred, are mentioned below.

H. citrina. Its lemon-yellow, fragrant flowers open in the evening, from typical rushy growth. H70cm/28in, W60cm/2ft. F6-7. Z3-9.

H. dumortieri. This has early, deep yellow, fragrant flowers, dark brown in bud. H70cm/28in, W45cm/18in. F5-7. Z3-9.

H. flava (syn. *H. lilio-asphodelus*). This tall, yellow species is rare but nonetheless worthy, with its heavily fragrant flowers and wide-spreading habit. H75cm/30in, W45cm/18in. F6-8. Z3-9.

H. fulva. Another wide-spreading species, this has brownish orange flowers on erect stems. **'Kwanso Flore Pleno'** is double and has rather untidy growth. The variegated-leaved form is apt to revert to green. H80cm/32in, W60cm/2ft. F6-8. Z3-9.

H. lilio-asphodelus. See *H. flava*.

H. middendorffii. This is early-flowering and fully garden-worthy, though the fragrant, orange flowers are relatively small. H70cm/28in, W45cm/18in. F6-7. Z3-9.

H. minor. This has yellow flowers and is

Helleborus orientalis

Hemerocallis 'Stella D'Oro'

used as a parent for breeding some of the dwarfer cultivars. H45cm/18in, W45cm/18in. F5-6. Z4-9.

Hybrids. There are innumerable hybrids in cultivation so only a limited range can be described here. All Z4-9. **'Anzac'** is as near to true red as you are likely to find. H75cm/30in, W45cm/18in. F6-8. **'Black Magic'**. An old variety, deepest maroon. H70cm/28in, W45cm/18in. F6-8. **'Bonanza'** has a brownish centre to the light orange petals. H75cm/30in, W45cm/18in. F7-9. **'Burning Daylight'**. Deep glowing orange. H90cm/3ft, W60cm/2ft. F7-9. **'Buzz Bomb'**. Very close to 'Anzac', but dwarfer. H60cm/2ft, W45cm/18in. F6-8. **'Canary Glow'**. Large-flowered, warm yellow. H80cm/32in, W60cm/2ft. F6-8. **'Catherine Woodbury'**. Deep pink, pale pink and greenish white flowers. H90cm/3ft, W60cm/2ft. F6-8. **'Cherry Cheeks'** has extra-large, cherry-pink flowers. H80cm/32in, W60cm/2ft. F6-8. **'Chicago Royal Robe'**. Outstanding deep purple. H80cm/32in, W60cm/2ft. F6-8. **'Franz Hals'**. Bright orange, red-striped petals. H90cm/3ft, W60cm/2ft. F6-8. **'Golden Chimes'**. Fairly dwarf and very free to flower. H70cm/28in, W45cm/18in. F6-8. **'Hyperion'** has long been a favourite, with scented, pure yellow flowers. H90cm/3ft, W45cm/18in. F6-8. **'Lark Song'**. Light canary-yellow. H90cm/3ft, W45cm/18in. F6-8. **'Luxury Lace'**. Light satiny pink, with ruffled edges to the petals. H80cm/32in, W60cm/2ft. F6-8. **'Neyron Rose'**. Rosy red with an orange throat. H1m/39in, W90cm/3ft. F7-8. **'Pink Damask'**. Still a favourite pink. H80cm/32in, W60cm/2ft. F6-8. **'Stafford'**. Rich red with a deep yellow throat. H90cm/3ft, W90cm/3ft. F7-9. **'Stella D'Oro'**. Distinctive for its dwarf, dense clumps of leaves and long season of pale gold flowers. H50cm/20in, W45cm/18in. F6-10. **'Varsity'**. Large, peach flowers, maroon in the centre. H75cm/30in, W45cm/18in. F6-8.

Hemerocallis 'Stafford'

Hemerocallis 'Catherine Woodbury'

Hepatica nobilis

HEPATICA

These are well loved for their anemone-like, early spring flowers, but they can be difficult. If the single-flowered forms of *H. nobilis* resent division and are not always easy to please, the doubles are even more capricious. My original group of ten plants is now reduced to two, neither of which is likely to survive much longer; but there are the fortunate few gardeners who can grow them. Where happy, the slow-growing plants with ivy-like leaves may be left alone for years. They need an open, moist and not too acid soil, and are ideal in woodland gardens.

H. nobilis (syn. *H. triloba*). This has three-lobed leaves, and carried just above, in earliest spring, are little cup-shaped flowers. Blue shades predominate but white, light and deep pink forms exist. The doubles – blue, white and deep pink – are much in demand, though seldom offered. H15cm/6in, W20cm/8in. F3-4. Z4-8.

H. transsilvanica. This and its variants and hybrids are a little larger and later to flower. Light blues prevail, good in 'Loddon Blue' and the larger-flowered but rare 'Ballardii'. 'Nivea' is white. All H10cm/4in, W23cm/9in. F3-4. Z5-8.

H. triloba. See *H. nobilis*.

HESPERIS Sweet rocket, dame's violet

H. matronalis. Though not fully perennial, it makes a good display of small, scented, lilac-blue flowers on stout, branching stems, and seeds freely. H1m/39in, W30cm/1ft. F6-

Heuchera 'Red Spangles'

Heuchera micrantha 'Bressingham Bronze'

7. Z4-9. **'Lilacina Flore Pleno'** is a rare and charming plant, with an abundance of pale lilac flowers, very fragrant, especially in the evenings. Best on well-drained neutral or limy soil. H1.2m/4ft, W30cm/1ft. F6-8. Z4-9. The white double, **'Plena'**, is perennial but rare because it is so difficult to propagate. H60cm/2ft, W30cm/1ft. F6-7. Z4-9.

HEUCHERA

These distinctive plants have the three virtues of neat, evergreen, basal growth, a long flowering season, and very bright colours, as well as being good for cutting. They often begin in late spring with slender stems carrying many small, bell-shaped flowers, attractive to bees, and continue well into midsummer. The light green or marbled leaves are somewhat ivy-shaped, and the rather woody crowns do not suffer from dry conditions. Good drainage is essential, and though responsive to mulching, any good garden soil in sun or partial shade suits them. When replanting, discard the old woody sections; the fibrous roots encourage free flowering.

Most of those below were raised by us, having been a Bloom speciality since 1920.

Heuchera villosa

At that time my father was growing *H. brizoides* 'Gracillima' for cutting. He also invested in some of the larger-flowered *sanguinea* varieties. In due course these were crossed and produced a more colourful form of *brizoides*; and 'Bloom's Variety' gained an Award of Merit from the Royal Horticultural Society in 1928. I carried on hybridizing, and introduced some more varieties from 1931 on. In the 1950s, in the *Heuchera* trials at Wisley, Surrey, England, all but one of the awards went to Bressingham varieties.

H. bakeri. This may be a hybrid, with upright sprays of soft pink flowers. H40cm/16in, W30cm/1ft. F6-8. Z4-8.
H. × brizoides. This is best in the form **'Gracillima'**, with light pink flowers, though **'Pink Spray'** may be even better. **'Coral Cloud'** has larger, richer-coloured bells; **'Pearl Drops'** is white. All H60-70cm/24-28in, W30cm/1ft. F6-8. Z3-8.
H. cyclindrica. A vigorous species with close-set, greenish white bells and dense clumps of heart-shaped, deep green leaves. **'Green Ivory'** and **'Greenfinch'** are both sturdy, taller improvements, much loved by flower arrangers. All H60-70cm/24-28in, W30cm/1ft. F6-8. Z4-8.
H. micrantha. This variable species has sprays of small, greenish brown flowers, but the leaves of some are tinged purple. The first cultivar selected, **'Palace Purple'**, is an excellent garden-worthy form whose leaves are large, glossy and richly coloured, almost beetroot-red. It is variable from seed and **'Bressingham Bronze'** is a reliable selection. The tiny flowers have a hint of white. H70cm/28in, W30cm/1ft. F6-8. Z4-8.
H. pubescens. This has one or two cultivars with close-set flowers on erect stalks. **'Edge Hall'** is an old one of a soft pink shade; the newer **'Jubilee'** has larger flowers and is more reliable. All H50cm/20in, W30cm/1ft. F5-7. Z4-8.
H. sanguinea. The larger-flowered, brightly coloured hybrids (see below) come under this species, itself bright red but eclipsed by them. H30cm/1ft, W30cm/1ft. F5-8. Z3-8.
H. villosa. This has light green leaves and airy sprays of tiny white flowers, tinged green. In demand by flower arrangers. H50cm/20in, W30cm/1ft. F7-9. Z6-9.

Hybrids. As a mixed strain 'Bressingham hybrids' have an international reputation. Those below are named cultivars of proven worth. All W30cm/1ft, F5-7 or F5-8 where suited in fertile soil. **'Bressingham Blaze'**.

Bright coral-red bells. H50cm/20in. Z3-8.
'**Charles Bloom**'. Large, pure pink flowers.
H50cm/20in. Z4-8. '**Firebird**'. Intensely
red, upright sprays. H50cm/20in. Z4-8.
'**Freedom**'. Lives up to its name with
freely borne, soft pink flowers. H40cm/16in.
Z4-8. '**Gloriana**'. Rosy crimson, erect
sprays. H50cm/20in. Z4-8. '**Hyperion**'.
Deep pink bells on strong, clustered spikes.
H80cm/32in. Z4-8. '**Oakington Jewel**'.
Handsome marbled foliage, coral-red
flowers. H60cm/2ft. Z3-8. '**Pretty Polly**'.
Compact, but with large, pure pink flowers.
H35cm/14in. Z4-8. '**Red Spangles**'.
Intensely blood-red flowers. H50cm/20in.
Z3-8. '**Scintillation**'. Red-tipped, deep
pink flowers. H50cm/20in. Z3-8. '**Shere
Variety**'. Fairly dwarf with intense red
flowers. H40cm/16in. Z3-8. '**Snowstorm**'.
Notable for its white and green leaves,
which contrast with the bright cerise
flowers. H40cm/16in. Z4-8. '**Sunset**'. Warm
crimson-red flowers, later than most.
H50cm/20in. Z4-8.

× HEUCHERELLA

These are crosses between *Heuchera* and
Tiarella and as such are non-seeding
'mules'.

× *H*. '**Bridget Bloom**'. Named after my
eldest daughter, this makes compact little
mounds of pretty evergreen foliage and
starry pink flowers. Where suited in sandy,
humus-rich soil and part shade it often
flowers a second time in late summer.
H35cm/14in, W30cm/1ft. F5-7. Z4-8.
× *H*. *tiarelloides* makes a soft, golden-green
carpet and though not as free to produce its
sprays of pink flowers as the above, it is
easier to grow in any soil. Excellent ground
cover. H25cm/10in, W30cm/1ft. F5-6. Z4-8.

HIERACEUM Hawkweed

Only a few are garden-worthy, but they are
easy to grow in sun and any soil, especially
poor, dry ones. The following form basal
rosettes and dandelion-like flowers on
stiff stems.
H. × *rubrum*. This carries orange-red
flowers above tufts of green leaves; it can
be a little invasive. H30cm/1ft, W30cm/1ft.
F6-7. Z4-8.
H. *villosum*. Shaggy hawkweed makes
compact tufts of silvery, woolly leaves and
4cm/1^1/2in wide dandelion flowers. A good
little plant for a sunny place and light soil.
H15-20cm/6-8in, W23cm/9in. F6-8. Z4-8.
H. *waldsteinii*. This has prettily marked,
green and blue-grey foliage. H60cm/2ft,
W30cm/1ft. F6-7. Z3-8.

HOSTA Plantain lily

These clump-forming foliage plants vary in
height from 15cm/6in to 1.5m/5ft. Leaf
sizes are equally variable, from not much
more than finger size to the size of a dining

chair seat. Though easy to grow in any
reasonable soil, take care when siting, not
only because they vary so much in size, but
because some, especially variegated forms,
are best in light shade. All are shade-
tolerant, but they flourish better where not
too dry, so avoid siting where they are in
competition with tree roots. Their value,
especially as foliage plants, accounts for the
vast range of hybrids, of which only a few
can be mentioned. Their lily-like, white or
mauve flowers are attractive. All Z3-9.
H. '**August Moon**'. This has golden-green
leaves, in sun or shade. Pale mauve flowers.
H60cm/2ft, W45cm/18in. F8-9.
H. '**Big Daddy**'. Large, puckered leaves,
decidedly bluish, make a fine specimen
plant in semi- or full shade. H90cm/3ft,
W60cm/2ft. F8-9.
H. '**Blue Moon**'. This has round, blue,
ribbed leaves and profuse light mauve
flowers. H30cm/1ft, W30cm/1ft. F7-8.

Hosta 'Blue Moon'

H. *clausa*. The true form is green-leaved
but remarkable for its long display of
lavender-blue flowers and ample spread.
H35cm/14in, W45cm/18in. F6-9.
H. *fortunei*. This is green-leaved and early-
flowering. H90cm/3ft, W60cm/2ft. F6-7.
'**Albo-marginata**' is much more striking,
with leaves margined creamy white.
H80cm/32in, W60cm/2ft. F6-8. '**Aureo-
marginata**' is similar, but with a yellow leaf
margin. The vigorous '**Francee**' has wide,
oval, white-edged leaves making a splendid
clump. H60cm/2ft, W50cm/20in. F8-9.
'**Picta**' is more white variegated than green
in spring, but leaves turn green after
flowering. H80cm/32in, W60cm/2ft. F6-7.
H. '**Frances Williams**' is outstanding and
deservedly popular with its huge glaucous
leaves and buff variegations. H1m/39in,
W60cm/2ft. F6-8.
H. '**Ginko Craig**'. A dwarf with a rapid,
mound-forming spread, it has lance-shaped,

Hosta fortunei 'Francee'

Hosta 'Frances Williams'

Hosta 'Thomas Hogg'

Hosta 'Halcyon'

Hosta sieboldiana 'Elegans'

Hosta undulata 'Medio Variegata'

white-edged leaves and mauve flowers. H20cm/8in, W45cm/18in. F6-8.

H. 'Gold Edger'. Showy, green-gold, overlapping leaves and mauve flowers make this ideal for edging in sun or shade. H25cm/10in, W38cm/15in. F6-7.

H. 'Gold Standard'. This strong-growing, free-flowering form has leaves with green outer edges and colourful golden centres. H60cm/2ft, W50cm/20in. F7-8.

H. 'Ground Master'. This makes a dense spread of green and white variegated foliage for sun or shade and gives a good display of purple flowers. H30cm/1ft, W45cm/18in. F6-7.

H. 'Hadspen Blue'. Its leaves are decidedly blue and the flowers are mauve. H40cm/16in, W45cm/18in. F6-8.

H. 'Halcyon'. Very glaucous blue foliage and a good show of mauve flowers make this English variety, just one of many hybrids sometimes listed under *H.* × *tardiana*, especially garden-worthy. H45cm/18in, W45cm/18in. F7-8.

H. 'Krossa Regal'. This is strong-growing and glaucous-leaved, with purple flowers. H80cm/32in, W60cm/2ft. F6-8.

H. lancifolia. This species is attractive for its deep green, shiny, overlapping leaves and its late- and free-flowering habit. H35cm/14in, W30cm/1ft. F7-9.

H. minor. Late-flowering and green-leaved, it has deep mauve flowers, or white in 'Alba'. H20cm/8in, W30cm/1ft. F8-9.

H. plantaginea grandiflora. Also late, its white flowers are faintly scented and carried above light green leaves. Excellent for container growing. H90cm/3ft, W60cm/2ft. F8-9.

H. rectifolia 'Tallboy'. This is remarkable for its profuse, stately spikes of lavender-blue flowers on erect stems above strong-growing clumps of green leaves. H90cm/3ft, W60cm/2ft. F7-9.

H. 'Royal Standard'. A robust, green-leaved favourite, this has white, slightly scented flowers. H90cm/3ft, W60cm/2ft. F8-9.

H. 'Shade Fanfare'. This has green leaves in shade, yellowish in sun, with plenty of mauve flowers and a rapid spread. H40cm/16in, W45cm/18in. F7-8.

H. sieboldiana. This is glaucous-leaved with mauve flowers 80cm/32in high; 'Elegans' is much larger, with leaves up to 50cm/20in across and 1m/39in high spikes. 'Bressingham Blue' is equally robust but the leaves have a distinctive bluish tinge. All H90cm/3ft, W60cm/2ft. F7-8.

H. tardiflora. Low-growing and late-flowering; narrow, shiny, deep green leaves and relatively large, light purple flowers. H25cm/10in, W25cm/10in. F8-9.

H. 'Thomas Hogg'. Probably over a century old, this has wide, glaucous leaves with a buff edge, and light mauve, early flowers. One of the best pale-edged forms. H80cm/32in, W60cm/2ft. F6-8.

H. undulata. A species with variations, but basically undulate or twisted leaves with a white centre and dark green edges. The flowers are lilac-purple. 'Medio Variegata' has a yellow central blotch. H50cm/20in, W45cm/18in. F6-7.

H. ventricosa. Available in green-leaved or variegated forms, all are very upstanding, reliable and free-flowering, with lavender flowers. 'Variegata' is spectacular, with flowers similar to the green type. I introduced this to the USA in the 1960s, where it gained the premier award in 1987 given by the US Hosta Society. Though I had nothing to do with its submission for the award, I could never dispute the plant's worthiness, and was glad to accept the handsome, engraved commemorative plaque. H90cm/3ft, W60cm/2ft. F7-8.

HOUTTUYNIA

H. cordata. This spreads quickly in moist soil, with short, branching red stems of heart-shaped, bronzy leaves and faintly scented white flowers with central green cones and white bracts. **'Chameleon'.** Some forms are more variegated than others, but this is the brightest now in circulation. The name is not very apt, for although reversion is liable to take place to less colourful leaves, its notable feature is the range of colours on each leaf. It is less invasive than 'Plena', the foliage is rather later to appear, and the flowers are less significant. H20cm/8in, W30cm/1ft. F6-8. Z5-9. The double-flowered **'Plena'** is most often offered. Best as a waterside plant. H15cm/6in, W30cm/1ft. F6-8. Z5-9.

HYLOMECON

H. japonicum (syn. *H. vernalis*). A charming little subject, this has 5cm/2in, poppy-like, yellow flowers above fresh spring greenery. Plant in cool, not too dry soil and light shade. H30cm/1ft, W23cm/9in. F4-5. Z5-8.

Inula ensifolia 'Compacta'

Incarvillea mairei

HYSSOPUS

H. aristatus. This semi-shrubby plant, much loved by bees, has tiny but intensely deep blue flowers for several weeks. Best in well-drained, ideally chalky, soil and sun. H30cm/1ft, W30cm/1ft. F6-8. Z6-9.

H. officinalis. Another bee plant, this has bushy growth with lance-shaped leaves and deep blue flowers on short spikes. Prefers well-drained, ideally chalky, soil and sun. A pink form, **'Roseus'**, exists. H50cm/20in, W30cm/1ft. F6-8. Z6-9.

Inula royleana

INCARVILLEA

These taprooted plants need good, well-drained soil and sun. They do not appear above ground till mid-spring and then, two to three weeks later, show their quite large, trumpet-shaped flowers, followed by deeply cut leaves.

I. arguta. This forms a lax bush of small, indented leaves set with lilac-pink flowers, but is doubtfully hardy and rarely offered. H60cm/2ft, W30cm/1ft. F6-8. Z8-9.

I. delavayi. A very good garden plant. It has open-mouthed, mimula-like, rosy red flowers borne on spikes which expand from a few centimetres (inches) to nearly 60cm/2ft by the time flowering ends. The leaves are dark green and jagged, and attractive seed pods follow the flowers. H60cm/2ft, W30cm/1ft. F5-7. Z6-8. **'Bees' Pink'** is less reliable, but the colour, almost salmon-pink, is distinct. H40cm/16in, W30cm/1ft. F5-7. Z6-8.

I. mairei (formerly *I. grandiflora*). Its large, deep pink flowers appear before the pinnate leaves. H30cm/1ft, W30cm/1ft. F5-7. Z7-8.

INULA

A genus of yellow, narrow-petalled, daisy-like flowers, easy to grow in any well-drained soil and sun, and varying in height from 15cm/6in to 1.8m/6ft.

I. barbata. This forms matted clumps of soft greyish green foliage topped by 5-6cm/2-2¹/₂in flowers. H45cm/18in, W45cm/18in. F6-8. Z4-9.

I. ensifolia **'Compacta'**. A long season of 4cm/1¹/₂in flowers, carried on slender stalks, and dense, compact plants make this very pretty and an ideal frontal subject. H30cm/1ft, W30cm/1ft. F6-9. Z4-9.

I. 'Golden Beauty'. This is long-flowering, with the flowers carried on individual stems. H60cm/2ft, W60cm/2ft. F6-9. Z4-9. It is very similar to what is sometimes listed as *Buphthalmum salicifolium*, of which **'Dora'** is an improvement, with larger flowers and a more compact habit. H50cm/20in, W30cm/1ft. F6-9. Z4-9.

I. hookeri. Much like *I. barbata*, but taller and with green-tinged flowers. Best in damp soil; can be invasive. H75cm/30in, W60cm/2ft. F6-8. Z4-8.

I. magnifica. Given space, this is a most imposing subject, with strong stems, large leaves and rayed flowers 10cm/4in or more across from deep-rooting, long-lived clumps. H1.8-2.1m/6-7ft, W60cm/2ft. F6-8. Z4-8.

I. orientalis. This has rayed flowers and, though early, a rather short season. H60cm/2ft, W60cm/2ft. F6-7. Z4-8.

I. royleana. Finely rayed, bright yellow flowers at least 10cm/4in across are carried singly above quite large, tongue-shaped leaves. Best in light soil and a sunny spot. H50cm/20in, W45cm/18in. F6-8. Z4-8.

IRIS

Iris are, as a group, near ideal garden perennials. Most are easy to grow, long-lived, handsome in flower and foliage, and self-supporting. This large and much loved genus is so varied that, for ease of use, it is divided into sections below. Species can be had in flower every month, but most flower in spring and early summer. Few dwarf iris are alpines, in the technical sense, since they prefer shelter to the traditionally open, exposed position of an alpine bed, but they can usually be accommodated.

I. barbata (syn. *I. pumila*). These are often listed as 'Dwarf Bearded'. They flower early, producing blooms smaller than but similar to *I. germanica*, and have the same tuberous rhizomes, which grow on the soil surface. **'Blue Denim'** is mid-blue. H25cm/10in, W25cm/10in. **'Bright Eyes'** is lemon-yellow, flushed blue. **'Cherry Gardens'** is maroon and purple-pink. **'Lemon Flare'** is self-descriptive. **'Red Heart'** is rich violet and maroon. Cultivation is the same as for *I. germanica*: grow in sun and well-drained soil, and lift and replant after flowering. All H30cm/1ft, W20cm/8in. F4-5. Z4-9.

I. chrysographes. A narrow-leaved species best in the free-flowering cultivar **'Black Knight'**, with branching stems of flowers just a shade on the purple side of black, and delicately marked with gold, set among rush-like leaves. It prefers moist conditions. H70cm/28in, W30cm/1ft. F6-7. Z4-9.

I. clarkei. This beardless Siberian iris makes clumpy little plants with branching stems of violet-blue flowers. H20cm/8in, W30cm/1ft. F6-7. Z4-9. **'Blue Jimmy'**, maybe a hybrid, grows reliably and has violet-blue flowers. Moist soil is best. H30cm/1ft, W23cm/9in. F6-7. Z4-9.

I. douglasiana. This has deep green, wide-spreading, evergreen leaves and branching stems of blue, orchid-like flowers flecked with white and with attractively veined lower petals, or falls. Moist soil is best. H50cm/20in, W45cm/18in. F6-7. Z7-9.

I. ensata (syn. *I. kaempferi*). Large-flowered, in a fair range of self colours, the Japanese iris dislikes lime, heavy clay and excessive winter wet, but does best where not dry in summer. It is deciduous, and its single or double flowers, up to 20cm/8in across, have been the subject of hybridizers' interest since the seventeenth century; a huge variety of shapes, colours and sizes is now available, in seed mixtures and named varieties. **'Higo Strain'** has very large flowers in blue, mauve and white. H70-80cm/28-32in, W45cm/18in. F6-8. Z5-9. **'Snowdrift'** is a reliable pure white. H80cm/32in, W45cm/18in. F6-7. Z5-9. **'Variegata'** has violet-blue flowers, but leaf variegation fades with flowering. H60-80cm/24-32in, W45cm/18in. F6-7. Z5-9.

I. **'Florentina'**. The fleur-de-lys grows like *I. germanica*, but with large, fragrant, light blue-grey flowers. It is of interest also for its historical associations, and as the source of orris root, used in pot-pourri and perfumery. H60cm/2ft, W30cm/1ft. F6-7. Z4-9.

I. foetidissima. The gladwyn iris, or gladdon, will grow almost anywhere, including dry shade under trees. Its buff-yellow flowers are insignificant but they are followed in the autumn by decorative scarlet or orange seed pods, valued in dried-flower arranging. H60-70cm/24-28in, W45cm/18in. Z5-9. The evergreen, creamy white variegated form, **'Variegata'**, shows up brightly in winter, though it seldom flowers. H50cm/20in, W45cm/18in. Z5-9.

I. germanica. Flag, bearded or June-flowering iris are the popular, large-flowered perennials of which many hundreds of varieties have been introduced. Their rhizomes should not be fully covered when planted, with only the thin, lower roots well down. They are not fussy about soil, but need good drainage and like lime. Late summer or autumn planting is best, in mainly sunny places. The following are good colour representatives, but, ideally, select from where a large number can be seen in flower. **'Berkeley Gold'**, deep

Iris germanica 'Frost and Flame'

Iris germanica 'Black Swan'

Iris germanica 'Berkeley Gold'

Iris germanica 'Kent Pride'

yellow. **'Black Swan'**, nearly black. **'Braithwaite'**, lavender and purple. **'Edward Windsor'**, pastel pink. **'Frost and Flame'**, snow-white, with tangerine beard. **'Jane Phillips'**, light blue. **'Kent Pride'**, chestnut-brown, with yellow and white markings. **'Party Dress'**, peach-pink and tangerine-yellow. **'Rajah'**, orange and crimson. **'St Crispin'**, clear lemon-yellow. **'Tall Chief'**, purple and maroon. **'Wabash'**, white and violet. All H60-90cm/2-3ft, W30cm/1ft. F6. Z4-9.

I. graminea. Scented purplish flowers, with the falls veined blue on white, nestle singly in the dense, grassy leaves. Best in sun. H20cm/8in, W25cm/10in. F5-6. Z5-9.

I. innominata. This is usually available as a mixed strain in a range of colours, including white, yellow, orange, rose-pink, lilac, purple and magenta. The delicately veined flowers appear above narrow, deep green leaves. Where happy, in sun and moist soil, it makes a good show, but it dislikes lime. H25cm/10in, W30cm/1ft. F6-7. Z4-9.

I. japonica. This has bright green leaves and occasional, orchid-like, light blue, yellow-crested flowers, marked with yellow and dark lilac, and carried on branched stems. Both this and its creamy white variegated form, **'Variegata'**, are rather tender and need a warm, sunny spot and very well-drained soil. Both H30cm/1ft, W30cm/1ft. F6-7. Z8-9.

I. kaempferi. See *I. ensata*.

I. laevigata. Moisture-loving, this will grow in shallow water. Its flowers are quite large, upfacing, light blue and self-coloured, carried above wide, light green leaves. Lime-tolerant. H70cm/28in, W30cm/1ft. F6-7. All Z5-9. **'Monstrosa'**, short stems, large, light blue flowers. H50cm/20in, W30cm/1ft. F6-7. **'Rose Queen'**, soft pink, long-flowering. H70cm/28in, W30cm/1ft. F6-7. **'Variegata'**, light blue flowers, creamy white striped leaves. H70cm/28in, W30cm/1ft. F6-7.

I. mandschurica. Like a giant flag iris, this has bright yellow flowers on robust growth. H1.5m/5ft, W50cm/20in. F6-7. Z4-9.

I. milesii. This pretty dwarf species has light green leaves and light mauve-blue flowers with yellow-crested, crinkled petals. It needs a hot, sunny spot to thrive. H30cm/1ft, W30cm/1ft. F6-7. Z8-9.

I. missouriensis. With its branching stems of profuse, light blue, open flowers, this species deserves to be better known. H50cm/20in, W30cm/1ft. F6-7. Z5-9.

I. ochroleuca. Quite stately, the butterfly iris has clumps of 90cm/3ft high, greyish leaves, erect stems and creamy white, yellow-blotched flowers. H1.2m/4ft, W90cm/3ft. F6-7. Z4-9.

I. pallida. The most commonly grown form, *dalmatica*, has sword-like, grey-green leaves and fragrant pale blue flowers. More popular is **'Argentea'** (formerly *I. p.* 'Variegata'), with white and grey striped leaves, and **'Variegata'** (formerly *I. p.* 'Aurea Variegata'), with golden-yellow stripes. Both have clear blue flowers. All easy in sun or light shade. All H60-75cm/24-30in, W30cm/1ft. F6-7. Z4-8.

I. pseudacorus. The waterside flag iris will grow in any fairly moist soil. H1-1.2m/39-48in, W30cm/1ft. F6-7. Z5-9. **'Variegata'** has very bright, yellow-striped foliage except at flowering time. H1m/39in, W30cm/1ft. F6-7. Z5-9.

I. pumila. See *I. barbata*.

I. setosa. A dwarf, free-flowering species which has branching stems of light blue flowers with broad falls, and dense, light green, clump-forming, deciduous leaves. H30cm/1ft, W30cm/1ft. F6-7. Z4-9. **'Alaska Variety'** is much more robust and free. H60cm/2ft, W45cm/18in. F6-7. Z4-9.

I. sibirica. These are easy to grow in sun and moist soil, especially as waterside subjects. They are fibrous-rooted and form vigorous clumps of upright, bushy foliage. Erect stems carry graceful, beardless flowers. Some thirty named varieties exist, but the following are a good colour representation. All F6-7, Z3-9. **'Ego'**, bright blue, deepening towards the centre.

Iris missouriensis

Iris pallida 'Argentea'

Iris sibirica 'Persimmon'

Kniphofia caulescens

Kirengeshoma palmata

Kniphofia rooperi

H80cm/32in, W25cm/10in. **'Papillon'**, soft, light blue. H90cm/3ft, W25cm/10in. **'Persimmon'**, mid-blue. H90cm/3ft, W25cm/10in. **'Reheboth Gem'**, rich violet-blue. H90cm/3ft, W25cm/10in. **'Tycoon'**, deep violet. H90cm/3ft, W25cm/10in. **'White Swirl'**, pure white, H90cm/3ft, W25cm/10in.
I. stylosa (syn. *I. unguicularis*). This mainly winter-flowering iris is always worth a place in a sunny, sheltered spot, such as against a wall or fence, and will stay put for years, often sending up the occasional flower from early autumn through to mid-spring. The light blue flowers, deeper in **'Mary Barnard'**, are fulsome. Hot sun and poor, dry soil give the best results. H30cm/1ft, W30cm/1ft. F1-3. Z8-9.
I. unguicularis. See *I. stylosa*.

KIRENGESHOMA

These are very distinctive, with lobed leaves and sprays of waxy yellow flowers. They grow vigorously planted in cool, moist shade and rich, lime-free soil, and flower for several weeks.
K. koreana. This has erect stems with dull green, whorled leaves and erect, soft

yellow flowers, 5cm/2in across. H1m/39in, W60cm/2ft. F7-8. Z5-8.
K. palmata. This is bushier than the above, with an abundance of fresh green leaves and gracefully dangling, light yellow flowers. H90cm/3ft, W60cm/2ft. F7-9. Z5-8.

KNAUTIA
K. macedonica. See *Scabiosa rumelica*.

KNIPHOFIA Red hot poker
These are indispensable for their architectural value, but need plenty of space. They vary from 35cm/14in to 1.8m/6ft in height, flower from May to October according to type, and are not fussy about soil, although good drainage and sun are essential. Recently, some named varieties were decimated by virus, but this is now largely overcome. Seed-raised plants are immune, but vary in colour.
K. **'Ada'** has upstanding spikes of bright orange-yellow. H1.2m/4ft, W60cm/2ft. F7-8. Z5-9.
K. **'Atlanta'** (syn. *K. tuckii*) is early-flowering, with heavy spikes of yellow and red above broad glaucous foliage. H90cm/3ft, W60cm/2ft. F5-7. Z6-9.

K. **'Bressingham Comet'** has bright orange, red-tipped spikes and grassy leaves. H60cm/2ft, W45cm/18in. F8-10. Z6-9.
K. **'Candlelight'** is a grassy, shapely plant with a fine show of pure yellow spikes. H60cm/2ft, W45cm/18in. F6-8. Z6-9.
K. caulescens. Its large glaucous-leaved rosettes are more like a yucca; its stumpy flower spikes are yellow-tipped red. H70cm/28in, W60cm/2ft. F9-10. Z6-9.
K. **'C.M. Prichard'**. See *K. rooperi*.
K. **'Fiery Fred'** and *K.* **'Firefly'** are similar, with orange-red flowers and green leaves. H90cm/3ft, W60cm/2ft. F6-8. Z6-9.
K. **'Gold Else'** is an old, early-flowering yellow. H80cm/32in, W45cm/18in. F6-7. Z6-9.
K. **'Green Ice'** has large, ivory-buff, green-tinged spikes. H1.1m/43in, W60cm/2ft. F7-9. Z6-9.
K. **'Little Maid'** is a charmer with narrow leaves and profuse, ivory-white spikes. H60cm/2ft, W45cm/18in. F7-9. Z5-9.
K. **'Percy's Pride'** is robust, with sulphur-yellow flowers. H1.1m/43in, W60cm/2ft. F8-10. Z6-9.
K. praecox. See *K. primulina*.
K. primulina (syn. *K. praecox*). Early-

Kniphofia 'Percy's Pride'

Kniphofia 'Shining Sceptre'

flowering, with red and yellow spikes.
H70cm/28in, W60cm/2ft. F5-7. Z6-9.
K. 'Prince Igor' is one of the tallest
hybrids, at over 2.1m/7ft, and makes a
spectacular show of fiery red. W60cm/2ft.
F7-9. Z6-9.
K. rooperi (syn. *K.* 'C.M. Prichard'). One of
the latest to flower, its deep orange spikes
rise from broad foliage. H12m/4ft,
W60cm/2ft. F9-10. Z6-9.
K. 'Shining Sceptre'. Glowing, orange-gold
spikes. H90cm/3ft, W60cm/2ft. F7-9. Z6-9.
K. triangularis. This desirable species has
erect, narrow foliage and blazing, orange-
scarlet pokers. H80cm/32in, W50cm/20in.
F6-8. Z6-9.
K. tuckii. See *K.* 'Atlanta'.

LAMIUM Deadnettle
This genus includes useful ground-cover
plants and a few of greater garden value.
They thrive in shade, including under trees,
but some merit a good, deep soil.
L. galeobdolon 'Florentinum' (syn.
'Variegatum').This surface-rooting, rapid
spreader belongs in a wild garden. Its
silvery green leaves are carried on straggly
stems, and in spring it gives a brief, patchy

show of yellow flowers. H25-30cm/10-12in,
W30cm/1ft. F5-6. Z4-8. 'Herman's Pride'
is compact, with free-flowering yellow
blooms. 'Silver Carpet', also with yellow
flowers, is slower and less vigorous.
H15cm/6in, W20cm/8in. F4-7. Z4-8.
L. garganicum. This spreads modestly,
forming light green, almost evergreen, leafy
clumps with clear pink flowers in early
summer. Useful between shrubs in other
than dry soil. 'Golden Carpet' has gold-
tinted leaves. H15-20cm/6-8in, W60cm/2ft.
F5-6. Z6-8.
L. maculatum. This popular ground cover
has silver-pink speckled leaves and
purplish pink flowers. 'Aureum' is a less
vigorous form with bright golden-yellow
leaves and pink flowers. 'Beacon Silver' is
one of the best for leaf colour, with leaves
completely silvered, and has 15cm/6in high
pink flowers in early summer. 'White
Nancy' has similar foliage and pure white
flowers. 'Beedham's White' flowers
freely, from golden carpets, and 'Chequers'
has small leaves. 'Roseum' has pale pink
flowers. All are shallow-rooting and easy to
curb, if necessary. All are adaptable except
'Aureum' and 'Beedham's White', which
need a cool or moist, shady place. H to
30cm/1ft, W60cm/2ft. F4-7. Z4-8.
L. orvala. This has distinctive, erect
growth, coming from a deep-rooting, non-
spreading rootstock. It has shapely, deep
green foliage, and the stems carry plum-red
hooded flowers in late spring. The white
form 'Alba' is less attractive. Both
H50cm/20in, W38cm/15in. F5-6. Z4-8.

Lamium maculatum 'Beacon Silver'

Lathyrus vernus 'Spring Melody'

LATHYRUS Perennial sweet pea
L. latifolius. The white-flowered perennial
sweet pea makes climbing annual growth
from a taproot. H1.2m/4ft, W45cm/18in.
F6-8. Z5-9.
L. luteus 'Aureus' (sometimes listed as
Orobus aurantiacus). Small orange flowers
above low, bushy, yellow-green growth.
H40cm/16in, W60cm/2ft. F5-6. Z5-10.
L. vernus. Its purplish colour varies but its
habit is constant, making a mound of deep
green, forked leaves. Fine for any but wet
soil. 'Spring Delight' has violet-blue

Liatris spicata 'Kobold'

flowers. 'Spring Melody' is two shades of
pink, the paler merging with the deeper. All
H40cm/16in, W45cm/18in. F4-5. Z5-9.

LAVANDULA See under Shrubs.

LEUCANTHEMELLA See under CHRYSANTHEMUM.

LEUCANTHEMUM See under CHRYSANTHEMUM.

LIATRIS Gayfeather, blazing star
These spike-forming plants are unusual in
opening from the tip down, and make a
bright display with narrow leaves and
mostly light purple, fluffy pokers. The
plants are fleshy but not deep-rooted and
any reasonable soil in sun suits them.
L. callilepis. See *L. spicata.*
L. spicata (syn. *L. callilepis*). This has stiff
spikes of bright lilac-purple flowers.
H60cm/2ft, W25cm/10in. F6-8. Z4-9.
'Floristan White' is an attractive variation.
H60cm/2ft, W25cm/10in. F6-8. Z4-9.
'Kobold' (syn. 'Gnome') is mauve-pink,
with shorter, sturdy spikes. H40cm/16in,
W23cm/9in. F6-8. Z4-9.

Libertia formosa

LIBERTIA

These evergreen, sword-leaved clumpy plants need a warm, well-drained spot. They carry branching sprays of small, white, saucer-shaped flowers with yellow stamens in early summer, followed by attractive orange seed pods.

L. formosa. This is the hardiest and best known. *L. grandiflora* is virtually identical. H70cm/28in, W60cm/2ft. F5-6. Z9-10.

L. ixioides. Golden-tinged, narrow leaves and sprays of white flowers 1cm/^{1}/3in across. H45cm/18in, W60cm/2ft. F6-7. Z9-10.

LIGULARIA

The species were once part of the large *Senecio* genus and confusion over nomenclature still exists. All below are partial to moisture but most thrive in any good soil and sun. The leaves often droop in strong sunlight, but become turgid again by nightfall unless the soil is very dry. Almost all have yellow, daisy-type flowers; some make massive plants with large, handsome leaves. Heights vary somewhat according to soil moisture or richness.

L. clivorum. See *L. dentata*.

L. dentata (syn. *L. clivorum*) **'Desdemona'**. This massive plant has very large, leathery, heart-shaped, brownish green leaves, purplish beneath, and branching stems of orange flowers. H1.2m/4ft, W60cm/2ft. F7-8. Z4-8.

L. 'Gregynog Gold'. A hybrid with conical spikes of vivid orange flowers. H1.2m/4ft, W75cm/30in. F7-8. Z4-8.

Ligularia przewalskii 'The Rocket'

Limonium latifolium

L. × hessei. Grows stoutly with large, light green leaves and imposing spikes of deep yellow. H1.2m/4ft, W75cm/30in. F7-8. Z4-8.

L. hodgsonii. Rich orange-yellow flowers, 5cm/2in across, are carried above toothed leaves 15-20cm/6-8in across. Ideal for small gardens. H75cm/30in, W60cm/2ft. F6-7. Z4-8.

L. japonica. This has rounded, jagged edged leaves and branching spikes of yellow. H1.2m/4ft, W90cm/3ft. F6-8. Z4-8.

L. macrophylla. This distinctive species has stout stems, dock-like, grey-green leaves and terminal branching heads of yellow flowers. H1.8m/6ft, W60cm/2ft. F6-8. Z4-8.

L. przewalskii. Outstanding for its deeply cut, elegant foliage; black slender stems and yellow spidery flowers. H1.8m/6ft, W45cm/18in. F7-8. Z4-8. **'The Rocket'** is a striking variation, showier, and with leaves more rounded and toothed. H2.1m/7ft, W60cm/2ft. F7-8. Z4-8.

L. 'Sungold'. This is probably a natural hybrid and a first-class plant, adaptable, bushy and with a fine display of deep golden-orange flowers on branching stems. H1.5m/5ft, W60cm/2ft. F7-8. Z4-8.

L. veitchiana. Seldom offered, this has large rounded leaves and stiff spikes of yellow flowers. H1.5m/5ft, W60cm/2ft. F7-8. Z4-8.

LIMONIUM Statice, sea lavender

Wild sea lavenders are not good garden plants, but those listed below are, needing sun and well-drained soil. All have leathery basal leaves and everlasting flowers, ideal for winter displays.

L. incanum. This makes wide heads of small pink flowers above a rosette of leaves. The form *dumosum* is usually offered and is widely grown as a cut flower for drying. H35cm/14in, W45cm/18in. F7-9. Z5-9.

L. latifolium. This needs a warm, dry place to produce its wide heads of twiggy sprays of tiny blue flowers in late summer. These are a deeper shade in the variety **'Violetta'**. H80cm/32in, W60cm/2ft. F7-9. Z4-9.

'Robert Butler' is more compact, with erect, open heads of small, deep blue flowers. H30cm/1ft, W60cm/2ft. F7-9. Z4-9.

LINARIA Toadflax

Those below are free-flowering, spike-forming plants for sun and light – even poor – soil, but are rather short-lived. Both species come readily from seed; self-sown seedlings often appear as replenishments.

L. dalmatica. This pretty but rather short-lived plant has small glaucous foliage and tapering, branching spikes of light yellow, snapdragon-like flowers for many weeks. H75cm/30in, W60cm/2ft. F6-8. Z5-8.

Linum narbonense

Liriope muscari

L. purpurea. Erect, close-set spikes of many tiny purple flowers, each with an orange spot on the lower lip, are produced all summer long; the leaves are glaucous, small and narrow. **'Canon J. Went'** is a light pink variation. Both H90cm/3ft, W45cm/18in. F6-8. Z5-8.

LINUM Flax
Flaxes are sun lovers and need well-drained soil to reach their usual three- to five-year life span. Their flowers are upfacing little saucers and are produced over a long period. See also under Alpines.
L. austriacum and *L. perenne* are much alike, forming wiry-stemmed, somewhat bushy growth, with narrow leaves and terminal clear blue flowers. Both are short-lived. H45cm/18in, W30cm/1ft. F6-8. Z4-9.
L. flavum. The golden flax is yellow-flowered, with slightly shrubby growth, broader leaves and profuse flowers, up to 2.5cm/1in across. H30-60cm/1-2ft, W30cm/1ft. F6-8. Z5-8.
L. narbonense. This is more reliable than *L. perenne*, with bright blue, silky, funnel-shaped flowers 1cm/^{1}/$_3$in across for many weeks on erect, narrow-leaved wiry stems. It is evergreen in mild areas. The white-flowered **'Saphyr'** is distinct. All H45-60cm/18-24in, W30cm/1ft. F6-9. Z5-8.

LIRIOPE
These evergreen perennials have broadly grassy, mostly deep green, leaves, and erect spikes of bead-like lilac flowers from midsummer to mid-autumn. Some make good ground cover even in shade, but

flower more freely in the open. They are drought-resistant and slow-spreading, and thrive in any well-drained soil. There are a vast number of selections, including some with variegated leaves, in cultivation in the USA, but in northern Europe, *Liriope muscari* is the most successful and freest to flower. The brightly variegated forms perform best only where hot summers prevail. See also the closely related **Ophiopogon**.
L. hyacinthiflora. See *Reineckia carnea*.
L. **'Majestic'** is a hybrid with very full spikes, but is shy to flower. H30cm/1ft, W30cm/1ft. F8-10. Z6-10.
L. macrophylla. See *L. muscari*.
L. muscari (syn. *L. macrophylla*). This is an outstanding plant, too long neglected. It forms tussocks of deep green, blade-like leaves, evergreen except for a little winter fading. From late summer to late autumn it makes a bright display of short spikes set with grape hyacinth-like flowers of lilac-purple. Long-living and drought-resistant, it only needs good drainage. H30cm/1ft, W30cm/1ft. F8-10. Z6-10.
L. spicata. This spreads fairly quickly by means of rhizomes, again with deep green blades and thin spikes of small purplish flowers. H20cm/8in, W45cm/18in. F7-8. Z4-9. **'Alba'** is similar, except for colour.

LOBELIA
Some taller perennial kinds are still used for formal bedding and are well worth growing as border plants. The old practice of overwintering in a cold frame is unnecessary if the plants are grown in rich, moist soil and are lifted and divided in spring regularly. Cultivars are best covered by litter over winter if left *in situ*.
L. cardinalis. The true plant has a basal rosette of green leaves and enormous spikes of scarlet, lipped flowers. Though a hardy wild flower in the central USA, the cardinal flower does not overwinter well in Britain and tends to be short-lived. H75cm/30in, W30cm/1ft. F7-9. Z3-9.
L. fulgens. The main parent of many hybrids, this has downy purple stems, purple leaves and bright red flowers. H75cm/30in, W30cm/1ft. F8-10. Z8-9. The following are some of the hybrids. **'Bees' Flame'** has large, very bright scarlet flowers and beetroot-red foliage. H80cm/32in, W30cm/1ft. F7-10. Z4-8. **'Dark Crusader'** has similar leaves and deep crimson-purple flowers. H80cm/32in, W30cm/1ft. F7-10. Z4-8. **'Queen Victoria'**, an old favourite, has purple foliage and bright red flowers. H80cm/32in, W30cm/1ft. F7-10. Z4-8. **'Will Scarlet'** is green-leaved, with red flowers. H80cm/32in, W30cm/1ft. F7-10. Z4-8.

Lobelia 'Will Scarlet'

Lunaria rediviva

Lychnis flos-jovis 'Hort's Variety'

L. siphilitica. This has green basal rosettes and erect spikes of small, bright blue flowers over a period of many weeks. Short-lived but self-seeding, needing a warm spot and deep soil. H60cm/2ft, W30cm/1ft. F7-9. Z5-9.
L. × vedrariensis. This thereabouts hardy hybrid carries starry, rich purple flowers on lofty spikes and breeds reasonably true from seed. H1.2m/4ft, W30cm/1ft. F7-10. Z5-8.

LUNARIA Honesty
L. rediviva. The perennial honesty has fleshy roots and is long-lived. One of the earliest perennials to flower in spring, its stout leafy stems carry sprays of four-petalled, pale mauve flowers above basal rosettes, followed by the well-known white, papery seed pods, valuable for winter decoration indoors. Apt to seed itself freely. H1.2m/4ft, W30cm/1ft. F5-6. Z3-6.

LUPINUS Lupin
Although these are indispensable, they are not long-lived, reliable perennials. Over-propagation allowed disease virtually to wipe out the named **Russell Lupins** to colour. Nowadays, one has to settle for the mixed, seed-raised **Russell Hybrids**; although some can now come true from seed, they are still relatively short-lived. They come in self- and multi-colours, in white and all shades of pink, yellow, red, blue, purple and orange. All prefer neutral to acid soil. Dead-head to prevent unwanted seedlings and to encourage long flowering. H60-120cm/2-4ft, W60cm/2ft. F6. Z3-6.

LYCHNIS
This genus includes flowers of brilliant red and magenta. All are easy to grow in any reasonable, well-drained soil and sun, and are good for cutting.
L. × arkwrightii. This hybrid has intense vermilion-scarlet open flowers, 2.5cm/1in or more across, above purple-flushed foliage, but is rather short-lived. H30cm/1ft, W25cm/10in. F6-8. Z6-8.
L. chalcedonica. The Maltese cross, or Jerusalem cross, has leafy stems crowned by cross-shaped, scarlet-vermilion flowers, 1.5cm/^{1}/2in across, in heads up to 13cm/5in wide. It prefers reasonably moist soil. H1.1m/43in, W30cm/1ft. F6-8. Z4-8. 'Plena' is a rare double red form. H90cm/3ft, W30cm/1ft. F6-8. Z4-8. 'Rosea' has pale rose-pink single flowers. H90cm/3ft, W30cm/1ft. F6-8. Z4-8.
L. coronaria. The rose campion or mullein pink has rosettes of hairy, silver leaves, and branching stems carrying many open-petalled, magenta flowers for several weeks. Poor, dry soil is ideal. 'Abbotswood Rose' is intensely bright carmine; 'Alba' is white; 'Atrosanguinea' is purple-red; 'Oculata' has red-eyed, white flowers. All H60-80cm/24-32in, W45cm/18in. F6-8. Z4-8.
L. dioica. See *Silene dioica*.
L. flos-jovis. The flower of Jove has felty grey foliage, a dense, tufty habit, and sprays of purple-red flowers for several weeks. 'Hort's Variety' has clear bright pink flowers. Both H45cm/18in, W30cm/1ft. F6-8. Z5-9.
L. viscaria. The German catchfly makes deep green tufts and wiry stems topped by cerise-pink flowers. 'Alba' is white, with

Lychnis viscaria 'Splendens Plena'

light green leaves. 'Splendens Plena' has dark leaves and much fuller flowers than the species. All H25cm/10in, W30cm/1ft. F6-7. Z3-8.

LYSICHITON Skunk cabbage
Both species are bog plants with a deep-rooting, long-lived rootstock, huge leaves and bold arum flowers, made of flower-like spathes surrounding a fleshy spike, or spadix, which actually carries the tiny true flowers. They take several years to flower from seed, and old plants are difficult to divide and transplant. Young, pot-grown plants establish more effectively.
L. americanus. A spectacular waterside or bog plant when its huge, unpleasantly scented yellow spathes appear in early

Lysichiton americanus

Lythrum salicaria 'Firecandle'

spring. Large, paddle-shaped leaves follow as the spathes fade to green. H1.2m/4ft, W60cm/2ft. F3-5. Z7-9.
L. camtschatensis. The Asiatic skunk cabbage has smaller, sweetly scented white spathes and smaller leaves than *L. americanus.* H90cm/3ft, W60cm/2ft. F3-5. Z7-9.

LYSIMACHIA
This genus includes such diverse species as yellow loosestrife and creeping Jenny. All revel in rich, moist soil and will take some shade; some are inclined to become invasive.
L. ciliata. Though pretty, it needs annual curbing to keep within bounds. Basal rosettes carry upright stems, set with small, clear yellow, nodding flowers in the leaf axils. H90cm/3ft, W60cm/2ft. F6-8. Z3-9.
L. clethroides. This, too, may need curbing, having roots which creep and shoot afresh. The leafy stems carry short, terminal white-spikes, held obliquely like a small buddleia — very effective in late summer. The lance-

shaped leaves are often red in autumn. H1.2m/4ft, W60cm/2ft. F8-10. Z4-9.
L. ephemerum. This makes a leafy, glaucous, non-invasive clump. The spikes are upstanding and gracefully tapered, set with myriads of small white flowers. H1.2m/4ft, W30cm/1ft. F6-9. Z7-9.
L. punctata. The vigorous yellow loosestrife is not to be despised. It makes a splendid display of yellow flowers on leafy stems, but needs curbing in the moist soil it prefers. It grows in sun or part shade. H90cm/3ft, W60cm/2ft. F6-8. Z4-8.

LYTHRUM Purple loosestrife
These are among the most adaptable and long-lived perennials. They grow in sun or shade, and though happiest in moist soil, tolerating even boggy conditions, they still flower where quite dry. They make stout, woody roots and twiggy branching stems. Their flowers are especially welcome in late summer and their foliage often has brilliant autumn colour. Dead-head to prevent self-seeding. Hybrids of both species below are the only ones in circulation, with richer colours than the species.
L. salicaria 'Firecandle' has graceful, tapering spikes of small but intense rosy red flowers. H1.2m/4ft, W45cm/18in. F7-9. Z4-9. 'Robert' has a bushier, leafier habit and clear pink flowers. H80cm/32in, W45cm/18in. F7-9. Z4-9. 'The Beacon' is also bushy, with strong stems and full spikes of rosy red. H1.2m/4ft, W45cm/18in. F7-9. Z4-9.
L. virgatum 'Rose Queen' has twiggy spikes of clear rose-pink flowers. H80cm/32in, W45cm/18in. F7-9. Z4-9.

Macleaya cordata 'Flamingo'

'The Rocket' has erect, slender spikes, close to red. H90cm/3ft, W45cm/18in. F7-9. Z4-9.

MACLEAYA Plume poppy
Both species make good background plants with their lofty spikes set with terminal sprays of flowers. Their deeply lobed purplish leaves are handsome enough not to need concealing by foreground plants, and they also make excellent specimen clumps. Roots are inclined to wander but not to be a serious nuisance. Despite their height, these plants rarely need staking.
M. cordata. Tiny, ivory-white tubular flowers come on leafy spikes in late summer, in sun or partial shade. 'Flamingo' has pink-tinged flowers. Both H1.8m/6ft, W60cm/2ft. F8-9. Z4-9.
M. microcarpa 'Coral Plume' has terminal sprays of purplish flowers, glaucous stems and bluish purple leaves, grey-white beneath. H2.1m/7ft, W90cm/3ft. F7-9. Z4-9.

Lysimachia clethroides

Meconopsis regia

Meconopsis × sheldonii

MALVA Mallow

Few are garden-worthy and these are rather short-lived. The common musk mallow (*M. moschata*), with pink and white flowers, self-seeds too freely.

M. alcea. This lives for about three years and makes a good long display of clear pink, saucer-shaped flowers on branching stems. The form most often offered is *fastigiata*, with an erect, bushy habit. H1.2m/4ft, W60cm/2ft. F6-9. Z4-8.

MARRUBIUM

M. cylleneum. This has mounds of soft silvery foliage all year round. The yellowish flower heads are not showy. H30cm/1ft, W30cm/1ft. F7-9. Z3-8.

M. incanum is larger, with whitish flowers. H60cm/2ft, W60cm/2ft. F7-9. Z3-9.

MECONOPSIS

These poppy-like flowers, valued largely for their clear blue colour, prefer light shade, moist but not wet, humus-rich, lime-free soil and a cool atmosphere. Provide shelter from drying winds. Some species are monocarpic, dying after flowering, and most have to be reared from seed.

M. baileyi. See *M. betonicifolia*.

M. betonicifolia (syn. *M. baileyi*). The Himalayan blue poppy is widely popular. Buy young, pot-grown plants and prevent them flowering the first year to encourage perennial growth. The large sky-blue flowers with golden centres always appeal. H up to 1.2m/4ft, W45cm/18in. F5-7. Z7-8.

M. cambrica. The Welsh poppy, in shades of orange and yellow, is pretty, but self-sown seedlings can be a nuisance. Doubles

Meconopsis chelidoniifolia

exist but are rarely offered as they seldom seed and do not readily divide. H45cm/18in, W30cm/1ft. F5-8. Z6-8.

M. chelidoniifolia. This has wiry, leafy, erect, branching stems, green, lobed leaves and soft yellow, bell-shaped flowers, 5-8cm/2-3in across. H75cm/30in, W38cm/15in. F6-8. Z6-8.

M. grandis. Reliably perennial, this forms a clump of narrow, hairy leaves. The strong stems carry clusters of large, blue, saucer-shaped flowers. Clones vary a little. H90-150cm/3-5ft, W60cm/2ft. F6-7. Z7-8.

M. quintuplinervia. The harebell poppy is fully perennial with nodding, light lavender-blue, cup-shaped flowers. H30cm/1ft, W30cm/1ft. F5-7. Z7-8.

M. regia. It may take three years for this monocarpic species to flower, but it is very striking, with its huge rosettes of greyish, deeply cut foliage. Primrose flowers are carried on heavy spikes. H1.2m/4ft, W60cm/2ft. F6-7. Z7-8.

M. × sheldonii. A beautiful hybrid, seldom

offered. Its slender stems produce large nodding flowers of the purest blue. Best in humus-rich moist soil. H1m/39in, W40cm/16in. F6-7. Z7-8. **'Slieve Donard'** also has pure blue flowers, of satiny texture. H90cm/3ft, W38cm/15in. F6-7. Z7-8. **'Branklyn'** has light violet-blue flowers. H90cm/3ft, W38cm/15in. F6-7. Z7-8.

M. villosa. Also perennial, this has hairy rosettes of indented, rounded leaves and wide, nodding, clear yellow flowers. H60cm/2ft, W30cm/1ft. F6-7. Z7-8.

MELANDRIUM See *Silene dioica*.

MELISSA Balm

M. officinalis 'All Gold'. The leaves are not as strongly scented as the green form, but this is garden-worthy purely for its bright golden early foliage. Flowers are insignificant. Cut back to 15cm/6in above ground as soon as it reaches flowering height, to promote colourful foliage. H70cm/28in, W45cm/18in. F6-8. Z4-9.

Melissa officinalis 'All Gold'

Melittis melissophyllum

Mimulus 'Puck'

Mertensia virginica

MELITTIS Bastard balm
M. melissophyllum. A choice plant for partial shade, especially among trees and shrubs, with a clump-forming habit, nettle-like leaves and erect spikes of lipped, tubular flowers, cream and pink. H50cm/20in, W50cm/20in. F5-7. Z6-9.

MENTHA Mint
M. rotundifolia '**Variegata**'. Most mints are invasive and not to be grown with slower-growing plants. One or two variegated forms may be listed; 'Variegata' is the most attractive. Its round, creamy white and green variegated leaves are quite bright, but its short spikes of small, bluish flowers are very modest. Grow in light shade and moist soil. H45cm/18in, W45cm/18in. F6-7. Z5-9.

MERTENSIA
These are valued for their clear blue flowers in spring and early summer. All prefer some shade and well-drained, fertile soil.
M. asiatica. This is half-way between an alpine and a border plant, with striking, bluish silver foliage on lax stems set with small, sky-blue flowers. Plant in light, humus-rich soil in sun or light shade. H15cm/6in, W30cm/1ft. F6-9. Z4-9.
M. ciliata. Fleshy roots produce glaucous foliage and loose sprays of small, dangling, blue, bell-shaped flowers, pink in bud. H60cm/2ft, W30cm/1ft. F5-7. Z4-8.
M. coventryana. See under Alpines.
M. echioides. See under Alpines.
M. paniculata. This is like a taller *M. ciliata*. H60cm/2ft, W60cm/2ft. F6-8. Z4-8.
M. virginica. A real gem for cool woodland

conditions but becoming rare. Its black fleshy roots produce purplish blue shoots in spring, unfurling to fragile branching stems from which dangle sky-blue, bell-shaped flowers. With a long dormant period, markers are advisable. H60cm/2ft, W30cm/1ft. F4-5. Z4-9.

MEUM
M. anthamanticum. This has very attractive, aromatic, rich green filigree-like foliage, and wide, cow parsley-like heads of tiny white flowers. Plants are deep-rooting, dense and long-lived. H60cm/2ft, W60cm/2ft. F6-7. Z5-8.

MIMULUS Monkey flower
These are snapdragon-like, lipped flowers, often blotched or spotted with contrasting colours. Most like sun and moisture, otherwise they are not fussy, though mat-forming kinds either need replanting every year or two, or a light mulch every autumn.
M. bartonianus (syn. *M. lewisii*). Pink, lipped flowers on fairly upright branching stems with greyish leaves. Grow in good soil and divide and replant every spring. H70cm/28in, W45cm/18in. F6-9. Z6-9.
M. × burnetii. See under Alpines.
M. cardinalis. The scarlet monkey flower has greener stems and leaves, and orange-scarlet to cerise flowers. H70cm/28in, W45cm/18in. F6-9. Z7-10.
M. guttatus and *M. luteus* have produced several sturdy hybrids and cultivars, listed below, with fascinating bright colours. All F6-8, Z8-10. '**A. T. Johnson**' has large yellow flowers with brown blotches. H30cm/1ft, W30cm/1ft. '**Firedragon**' has

flame-orange, dark-spotted flowers. H25cm/10in, W30cm/1ft. '**Harlequin**' is primrose-yellow and brown. H25cm/10in, W30cm/1ft. '**Ochrid**' is multi-coloured yellow and mahogany. H25cm/10in, W30cm/1ft. '**Puck**' is a vigorous, mound-forming hybrid, covered in butter-yellow flowers, tinged orange. H15cm/6in, W25cm/10in. '**Shep**' has orange and red-brown flowers. H25cm/10in, W30cm/1ft.
M. lewisii. See *M. bartonianus*.
M. ringens. A good waterside plant, this has erect spikes with deep green leaves and small, tubular flowers of a pleasing light mauve-blue. H60cm/2ft, W30cm/1ft. F7-9. Z4-9.

MONARDA Sweet bergamot
These showy plants have leafy, square stems topped by heads of sage-like, hooded flowers emerging from prominent calyces. Heights vary with soils, and although they flower best in rich conditions they are then taller and less upright. Plants are surface-rooting and quickly form mats of aromatic leaves. They need to be kept young by regular division.
M. didyma. Bee balm, or Oswego tea, is the

Monarda didyma 'Prairie Night'

Monarda didyma 'Melissa'

main species, but crosses with **M. fistulosa** have produced hybrids, and only these are in circulation. **'Adam'** is bright red. **'Blue Stocking'** is lavender-blue. **'Cambridge Scarlet'** is an old red favourite. **'Croftway Pink'** is the best rosy pink. **'Melissa'** is a large-flowered pink. **'Prairie Glow'** is salmon-red. **'Prairie Night'** is violet-purple. **'Snow Maiden'** is white, but less vigorous. All H75-90cm/30-36in, W45cm/18in. F6-8. Z4-9.

MONTBRETIA See under CROCOSMIA.

MORAEA Butterfly iris
M. spathacea. This has strap-like leaves and wiry, leafy stems of yellow, iris-like flowers. Plant in full sun and well-drained soil. H60cm/2ft, W30cm/1ft. F5-7. Z9-10.

MORINA
M. longifolia. A distinctive, deep-rooted plant making thistle-like rosettes of long, pointed, serrated, shiny leaves. Erect spikes of pink, lipped flowers come for many weeks, though only a few at a time. Easy in any well-drained soil. There is also a white form. H70cm/28in, W30cm/1ft. F6-9. Z5-8.

MYOSOTIS Forget-me-not
M. palustris. See *M. scorpioides*.
M. scorpioides (syn. *M. palustris*).
'Mermaid' makes green mats of foliage and sprays of sky-blue flowers. This is a fully perennial and hardy forget-me-not. H15cm/6in, W30cm/1ft. F6-8. Z4-10.

NEPETA Catmint
These include good garden plants, easy to grow in a well-drained, mainly sunny, spot. Most have a long season of small flowered spikes and aromatic leaves.
N. 'Blue Beauty'. See *N.* 'Souvenir d'André Chaudron'.
N. × faassenii. See *N. mussinii*.
N. govaniana. This makes leafy, bushy, pale green growth and spikes of unusual, light yellow flowers for many weeks. Cool, moist conditions are best. H90cm/3ft, W60cm/2ft. F6-9. Z5-9.
N. mussinii. A name preferred to *N. × faassenii*, now said to be correct. This is the favourite catmint for bedding and edging, but is apt to suffer from winter wet. H30cm/1ft, W30cm/1ft. F6-9. Z3-8. **'Six Hills'** is similar, but twice as tall and grey-leaved. H60cm/2ft, W60cm/2ft. F6-9. Z4-8.
N. nervosa. A neat-growing, showy species, with a long display of short, violet-blue spikes. Quite distinct and worthwhile.

H25cm/10in, W30cm/1ft. F6-8. Z5-8.
N. 'Souvenir d'André Chaudron' (syn. *N.* 'Blue Beauty'). A rapidly spreading, potentially invasive hybrid, with lavender-blue flowers. Best with annual dividing and replanting. H45cm/18in, W45cm/18in. F6-8. Z5-9.

NERINE
These are easy and reasonably hardy bulbs, except in cold regions, with strap-like leaves for most of the year. They are valuable for their terminal flower clusters carried on leafless stems in autumn. Plant shallowly, against a wall or as edging, in light, well-drained soil and in full sun or part shade.
N. bowdenii. Its late-autumn display of clear pink, lily-like trumpets always appeals. H35cm/14in, W23cm/9in. F9-11. Z8-10. **'Fenwick's Variety'** is a little taller and larger-flowered. H40cm/16in, W23cm/9in. F9-11. Z8-10.
N. flexuosa 'Alba'. This is rare but very beautiful, with white flowers and deep

Nerine bowdenii

green leaves. Tender. H30cm/1ft, W15cm/6in. F9-11. Z9-10.
N. 'Pink Triumph'. A vigorous hybrid, but its silvery pink flowers are less freely borne. H30cm/1ft, W23cm/9in. F9-11. Z8-10.

NIPPONANTHEMUM See under CHRYSANTHEMUM.

OENOTHERA Evening primrose
The true evening primrose, *O. biennis*, the flowers of which open in the evening, is biennial, but many perennial kinds are garden-worthy, often with large, saucer-shaped flowers for a long period. Almost any well-drained soil in sun suits them. Some confusion over names still exists.
O. cinaeus. Similar to *O.* 'Fireworks', but its spring leaves are more brightly coloured. H30cm/1ft, W30cm/1ft. F6-8. Z5-8.

Oenothera 'Fireworks'

Orchis elata

O. **'Fireworks'** (syn. 'Fyrverkeri'). This rosette-forming, shallow-rooting hybrid often has multi-coloured leaves in spring, followed by sprays of sizeable yellow flowers. H35cm/14in, W30cm/1ft. F6-8. Z5-9.

O. fruticosa (syn. *O. tetragona*). Variable, but usually with lax, soft, bushy growth and light yellow flowers, 2.5cm/1in wide, open in the daytime. H25cm/10in, W30cm/1ft. F6-9. Z5-9.

O. glaber. A most attractive species with erect stems, slightly purplish leaves and open, pure yellow flowers, 5cm/2in across. H40cm/16in, W30cm/1ft. F6-8. Z5-9.

O. **'Highlight'** (syn. 'Hoheslicht'). Robust and showy, with bright yellow flowers, but stems become lax in rich soil. H60cm/2ft, W38cm/15in. F6-8. Z5-9.

O. linearis. Arching, wiry stems carry narrow leaves and masses of small yellow flowers. H35cm/14in, W25cm/10in. F6-9. Z5-8.

O. missouriensis. Its light yellow flowers, 8-10cm/3-4in across, last for weeks on end, followed by huge seed pods, useful in dried flower displays. Its sprawling habit lends itself to sloping ground, but as a deep-rooting hardy plant it is invaluable. H23cm/9in, W60cm/2ft. F6-9. Z5-8.

O. **'Sonnenwende'** is less tall, but neat and free-flowering, with maroon young leaves and flower buds. H50cm/20in, W30cm/1ft. F6-8. Z5-9.

O. tetragona. See *O. fruticosa.*

ORCHIS (including Dactylorhiza) Orchid

Though there is disagreement over the specific names of those most garden-worthy, no-one would question their beauty when well grown. A peaty or humus-rich, well-drained soil in light shade is best. As each flowering stem dies, together with its little tuberous root, it is replaced by, usually, two new ones. They are best left alone for at least two seasons, though my own enthusiasm for building up stocks has, until recently, precluded this. Lift and replant in autumn; a beneficial fungus is said to give them extra vigour so, theoretically, the soil in which plants have flourished should be added to any new planting site, together with extra humus. The most suitable species for gardens have been given the unlovely name *Dactylorhiza* and make a clear case for keeping to the old name!

O. elata. Spikes of close-set, speckled flowers of bright lilac-purple make a superb display. The leaves are broadly strap-shaped. Grow in well-drained but not dry, humus-rich soil, in light shade. H75cm/30in, W30cm/1ft. F6-7. Z6-8.

O. foliosa (syn. *O. maderensis*). This has folded, shiny green leaves and purple-lilac spikes, though colours do vary somewhat. H50-60cm/20-24in, W20cm/8in. F6-7. Z7-8.

O. fuchsii. The spotted orchid, a native of Britain, has brown-speckled, deep green leaves. The species is variable in height and colour. **'Bressingham Bonus'** was selected from a colony at Bressingham as being finer than any, with spikes of bright lilac-purple. It is very similar to *O. majalis*. H50-60cm/20-24in, W15cm/6in. F6-7. Z5-8.

O. latifolia. See *O. majalis.*

O. maderensis. See *O. foliosa.*

O. majalis (syn. *O. latifolia*). The marsh orchid varies in colour from pinkish lilac to purple, with narrow leaves, and grows

Origanum 'Herrenhausen'

best in rich, moist soil. H50cm/20in, W30cm/1ft. F6-7. Z5-8.

ORIGANUM Marjoram

Several are worth growing, each very different in appearance and doing best in full sun.

O. **'Herrenhausen'.** This hybrid is mauve-pink and has a similar habit to *O.* 'Nymphenburg'. H60cm/2ft, W30cm/1ft. F7-10. Z5-8.

O. laevigatum. This sends up dense, twiggy sprays of tiny, deep purple-violet flowers in late summer, with small, rounded, glaucous leaves. **'Hopleys'** has

Paeonia lactiflora 'Bowl of Beauty'

brighter, deep blue flowers. H40cm/16in, W30cm/1ft. F8-10. Z5-9.
O. **'Nymphenburg'** has pinkish flowers and a rather lax habit. H50cm/20in, W30cm/1ft. F7-9. Z5-9.
O. vulgare. The culinary marjoram has a more or less evergreen, golden-leaved form, **'Aureum'.** The flowers are insignificant but plants make good ground cover.

Paeonia mlokosewitschii

Paeonia tenuifolia

H15cm/6in, W30cm/1ft. Z4-8. Other variants exist of the green type with small lilac or pinkish flowers.

OSTEOSPERMUM
(syn. DIMORPHOTHECA)
These low-growing, leafy perennials are not reliably hardy but have a long season. Daisy-like flowers, up to 8cm/3in across, are light purple in *O. jucundum* and *O. barberiae*, but other shades exist. Grow in full sun and well-drained, light soil. Dead-head to prolong flowering.
O. barberiae. The only species with any pretension to hardiness; forms are worth protecting in winter because they flower on and on. H45cm/18in, W30cm/1ft. F6-10. Z10. **'Compacta'** is the hardiest, but flowers less freely, with single, pale magenta daisies from a sparsely leaved base. H15cm/6in, W40cm/16in. F6-10. Z9-10. **'Langtrees'** is much showier, the pink-tinged flowers 5cm/2in across. H25cm/10in, W30cm/1ft. F6-10. Z9-11.

OURISIA
O. macrophylla. This forms mats of deep green, round leaves and, where happy, gives a fine show of white, mimulus-like, lipped flowers, carried in whorls up the stems. Sadly, it is not quite hardy and needs winter cover. A rich, moist, peaty soil suits it best. H30cm/1ft, W30cm/1ft. F5-7. Z7-8. **'Loch Ewe'** is similar, with pinkish flowers.

PAEONIA Peony
As long-lived perennials, these are of unfailing appeal, both for their fine, large,

richly coloured flowers and their foliage. Many emerge in spring with red or purplish leaves, and some are attractive for autumn tints. Flowering, according to species, begins in mid-spring, but large-flowered types are at their best in early summer. Plant in autumn in well-prepared, enriched, deep soil, with the nubs or buds about 2.5cm/1in below the surface; deeper planting inhibits flowering. Because they grow into large clumps after a few years, ample spacing is advised. Paeonies are sometimes attacked by botrytis, which makes stems turn black and soft. Cut off infected stems at the base and dust with fungicide, which can also be used as a preventative in autumn or early spring. Tree paeonies (*P. suffruticosa*) are covered in the Shrubs chapter.
P. × *anemonaeflora* (syn. *P. officinalis* 'Anemoniflora') is semi-double, rosy red. H50cm/20in, W60cm/2ft. F5-6. Z5-8.
P. anemoniflora. See *P. officinalis.*
P. anomala × *smouthii.* This has single, crimson, loose, nodding flowers. H60cm/2ft, W60cm/2ft. F5-6. Z2-8.
P. arietina. This has slightly glaucous foliage from a strong-growing rootstock. **'Northern Glory'** is most likely to be available, with bowl-shaped, single, silky flowers in deep carmine, with pale yellow stamens. H75cm/30in, W60cm/2ft. F5-7. Z5-8.
P. lactiflora. This covers the majority of the early-summer flowering varieties. Some of those listed below have been in cultivation for well over a century, but a wider range of cultivars will be available from specialists. All H75-100cm/30-39in, W60cm/2ft. F6. Z3-9. **'Bowl of Beauty'**, very large flowers, more single than double, of glowing deep pink and fairly tall at 1m/39in. **'Claire Dubois'**, double satiny pink. **'Couronne d'Or'**, creamy white double, yellowing at the centre. **'Duchesse de Nemours'**, a favourite double white. **'Edulis Superba'**, fully double, soft pink and scented. **'Felix Crousse'**, free-flowering, carmine-red double.

'Festiva Maxima', large double white, flecked crimson. **'G. F. Hemerick'**, deep pink semi-double. **'Gayborder June'**, semi-double pink. **'Karl Rosenfield'**, tall double wine-red. **'Le Cygne'**, purest white double, large-flowered. **'Martin Cahuzac'**, carmine-red, fully double. **'Président Poincaré'**, very deep pink double. **'Sarah Bernhardt'**, still the most popular double soft pink. **'Shirley Temple'**, large, deep rose double. **'Solange'**, pale salmon double with a hint of orange.
P. **'Le Printemps'.** A vigorous hybrid, but the creamy pink flowers are rather small. H50cm/20in, W60cm/2ft. F5-6. Z5-8.
P. lobata. See *P. peregrina.*
P. mlokosewitschii. This teasing name

Papaver orientale 'Black and White'

belongs to the early-flowering, soft grey-foliaged, single yellow which always appeals and is commonly known as Molly the Witch. H70cm/28in, W60cm/2ft. F4-5. Z5-8.

P. obovata alba is a single white of great charm. '**Grandiflora**' has larger, creamy white flowers with orange-tinged centres. Both are early, so provide shelter from cold spring winds. H90cm/3ft, W60cm/2ft. F5-6. Z5-8.

P. officinalis (syn. *P. anemoniflora*). The old-fashioned paeony rose flowers a little earlier than *P. lactiflora* varieties. All are strong-growing, usually H80-90cm/32-36in, W60cm/2ft. F5-6. Z3-9. '**Alba Plena**', a large double white. '**Lize van Veen**', a double blush-pink. '**Rosea Superba**', a bright pink, large double, and '**Rubra Plena**', deep crimson-red double.

P. peregrina (syn. *P. lobata*). '**Sunshine**' is a good example of the type, which is fairly short and slow-spreading. The single flowers are intense salmon-flame. H60cm/2ft, W60cm/2ft. F5-6. Z5-8.

P. tenuifolia. This lacy-leaved species, especially the double-flowered form, '**Plena**', is rare. Both the species and the double are warm deep red. H45cm/18in, W45cm/18in. F5-6. Z4-8. A salmon-pink single exists but is seldom available.

PAPAVER Poppy

These showy, sun-loving plants prefer ordinary or poor, deep soil, dryish rather than moist.

P. 'Fireball'. This resembles a miniature *P. orientale*, except for its spreading habit and shallower roots. The flowers, 5cm/2in or so across, are early and fully double orange-scarlet. H30cm/1ft, W30cm/1ft. F5-7. Z4-9.

P. lateritium. Not often seen but pretty, with glaucous hairy leaves and a wealth of deep orange flowers, 8cm/3in across. H45cm/18in, W45cm/18in. F5-7. Z4-9.

P. orientale. Although oriental poppies are quite outstanding for size and brilliance,

Papaver orientale 'Turkish Delight'

they have some faults: the gap they leave after flowering, unless new foliage is induced by cutting back; some flowers so huge that they are top-heavy and difficult to support; and in other than well-drained soil fleshy roots which are apt to rot in winter. That said, most gardeners would not be without some of the best. All F5-7. Z4-9.

'**Beauty of Livermere**' (syn. 'Goliath'), one of the most reliable, a fine upstanding blood-red single. H1.1m/43in, W60cm/2ft. '**Black and White**', striking with its white petals and black centre. H75cm/30in, W60cm/2ft. '**Blue Moon**', huge, mauve-pink flowers with maroon specks. H1m/39in, W60cm/2ft. '**Glowing Embers**', fairly erect with glowing orange-red ruffled petals. H1m/39in, W60cm/2ft. '**Harvest Moon**', deep orange, semi-double flowers, effective until they begin to fade. H1m/39in, W60cm/2ft. '**Helen Elizabeth**', warm pink flowers and a neat, erect habit. H70cm/28in, W60cm/2ft.

'**Ladybird**', large, vermilion-red flowers. H60cm/2ft, W60cm/2ft. '**Marcus Perry**' has stood the test of time as a good, upstanding orange-scarlet. H80cm/32in, W60cm/2ft. '**Perry's White**', an old

Papaver orientale 'Picotée'

favourite. H90cm/3ft, W60cm/2ft. '**Picotée**', frilly white petals suffused scarlet. H70cm/28in, W60cm/2ft. '**Turkish Delight**', glowing flesh-pink. H75cm/30in, W60cm/2ft.

P. rupifragum. The Spanish poppy forms sizeable clumps of deeply cut leaves and orange flowers, but is shorter-lived than the similar, deep-rooting **P. heldreichii**, with glabrous leaves and orange flowers. Both H60cm/2ft, W60cm/2ft. F5-7. Z4-9.

PARADISIA

This and *Anthericum* are much alike, one being St Bernard's and this the St Bruno's lily.

P. liliastrum. This makes clumps of greyish foliage and a sheaf of small, white trumpet flowers on smooth, erect stems. Long-lived and quite easy to grow in sun and any well-drained soil. Its broadly grassy foliage tends to fade after flowering. H60-70cm/24-28in, W30cm/1ft. F6-7. Z5-9.

PARAHEBE

P. perfoliata (syn. *Veronica perfoliata*). Distinctive for its stem-clasping, glaucous leaves and twigginess, with small, light blue dangling flowers. Needs a warm spot. H60cm/2ft, W30cm/1ft. F7-9. Z8-11.

PELTIPHYLLUM

P. peltatum. From thick, lateral surface roots, the umbrella plant sends up round heads of leafless, starry, pink flowers in spring, followed by rhubarb-like leaves that provide complete cover over a wide area. A useful subject for any damp or even boggy soil. H up to 1m/39in, W60cm/2ft. F4-5. Z5-9. The half-sized form **'Nanum'** is valuable in a restricted space.

P. tellimoides. See *Boykinia tellimoides*.

PENSTEMON

This is a much larger and more diverse genus than is realized. It includes some species with vivid colours, and low-growing, semi-shrubby alpines. Some of the showiest and most suitable for beds and borders are not fully hardy, but several are well worth considering. Most garden cultivars come under *P. hartwegii* and need winter protection in cold regions. It is good

Peltiphyllum peltatum

practice to take cuttings in early autumn and overwinter them under glass, to replace any losses. Most prefer full sun and fertile, moist, but well-drained soil.

P. barbatus. See *Chelone barbata*.

P. campanulatus. Unusual for its pinkish flowers. H30cm/1ft, W30cm/1ft. F6-8. Z8-9. The best-known form is **'Evelyn'**, with tubular pink flowers on slender, narrow-leaved stems. It is bushy, with a small rootstock, like bedding penstemons, but not reliably hardy. H60cm/2ft, W60cm/2ft. F7-10. Z6-8.

Penstemon gloxinioides 'Pink Endurance'

Penstemon gloxinioides 'Sour Grapes'

Penstemon gloxinioides 'Garnet'

P. **'Catherine de la Mare'**. A hybrid making leafy, low bushes with a long display of deep lilac-blue spikes. H25cm/10in, W30cm/1ft. F6-9. Z6-8.

P. **'Dainty'**. This is distinctly dwarf, round and twiggy at the base. The flowers are large and colours range from pale blue to lilac-purple. It is fully hardy and flowers for a very long time. H30cm/1ft, W30cm/1ft. F6-10. Z6-8.

P. deustus. This has low-growing green mats, and short sprays of deep blue flowers. H20cm/8in, W30cm/1ft. F6-8. Z8-9.

P. digitalis. This resembles a foxglove and is fairly reliable, with plenty of basal foliage. The lilac flowers are carried on erect spikes. The form *purpurea*, or *venusta*, has purplish foliage. H60cm/2ft, W38cm/15in. F6-8. Z3-9.

P. fruticosus. See under Alpines.

P. glaber. Pink flowers are carried on stubby spikes. H25cm/10in, W30cm/1ft. F6-8. Z6-8.

P. gloxinioides. This species has to cover the 'bedding' varieties and hybrids, some of which are allied to *P. hartwegii* as a parental species. All are showy and large-flowered for mainly sunny positions and most soils, but hardy only in mild winters or districts. A mulch of leaves, bracken or peat around plants usually protects them enough to ensure new basal spring growth. All F6-10, unless otherwise noted. All Z9-10.

Hybrids include the following. **'Firebird'**, bright red. H40cm/16in, W45cm/18in. **'Garnet'**, wine-red. H50cm/20in, W45cm/18in. **'King George'**, salmon-red with a white throat. H60cm/2ft, W45cm/18in. **'Pink Endurance'**, clear pink, smaller-flowered but fairly reliable. H60cm/2ft, W45cm/18in. **'Rubicunda'**, large, warm red. H60cm/2ft, W45cm/18in. **'Ruby'**, blood-red, free-flowering. H50cm/20in, W45cm/18in. **'Sour Grapes'**, large, pale purple flowers, strong-growing. H70cm/28in, W45cm/18in. F6-9. **'Snowstorm'**, distinctive white flowers. H70cm/28in, W45cm/18in. F6-9.

P. heterophyllus. Though apt to be short-lived, the hybrid **'Blue Springs'** is worth growing for its intensely blue flowers. H35cm/14in, W45cm/18in. F6-8. Z7-8.

PHLOMIS See also under Shrubs.

P. russeliana (syn. *P. samia*). A sturdy plant with large, basal, evergreen leaves and whorls of hooded yellow flowers on strong stems. The clumpy, trouble-free rootstock grows freely in any soil, but is best in a fairly sunny place. H90cm/3ft, W60cm/2ft. F6-8. Z4-9.

P. samia. See *P. russeliana*.

P. tuberosa **'Amazone'**. An imposing recent introduction with deep green foliage and spikes with rose-pink hooded flowers. H1.5m/5ft, W45cm/18in. F6-8. Z6-8.

Phlomis russeliana

PHLOX

Although these are amongst the indispensables, phlox can be difficult. They are best in light soil and least happy in alkaline clays, which, nevertheless, can be improved by the addition of sharp sand. Eelworm and mildew are sometimes problems; generally, the brightest reds are most susceptible. Symptoms of eelworm infestation include distorted and withered stems. Although chemicals can be applied to treat early stages, they are potentially dangerous to use. If doing away with badly infected plants, choose a fresh site for replacements.

Over the years hundreds of named varieties have been raised and introduced; while many have not stood the test of time, a few of those listed below are still good after fifty to sixty years. In that period I have grown over 250 varieties. They are now considered to belong to *P. paniculata*, but this species is much taller than the cultivars and it could be that the old specific name of *P. decussata* is valid. At any rate, all have the panicle-type of flower head or truss.

P. × *arendsii*. These hybrids are showy and dwarf but not very robust. **'Anja'** is a reddish purple, **'Hilda'** a pink-eyed lavender, and **'Suzanne'** a red-eyed white. All flower fairly early. H35cm/14in, W30cm/1ft. F6-8. Z4-8.

P. divaricata. This has small but attractive heads of blue flowers from somewhat creeping basal growth. Cool shade and humus-rich soil are preferred. The form *laphamii* is mostly listed, but **'Fuller's White'** is worth looking for. H25cm/10in, W25cm/10in. F5-7. Z3-9.

P. maculata. This grows from a congested mat of fibrous roots and sends up narrow-leaved, slender stems crowned with charming, cylindrical flower trusses. Where suited in light soil they make a fine show and, like most larger hybrids, are pleasantly fragrant. **'Alpha'** is pink and **'Omega'** is white with a red eye. All H90cm/3ft, W30cm/1ft. F7-9. Z4-8.

P. paniculata. The following cultivars all F7-9, Z4-8. **'Bill Green'**, large heads of clear pink with a red eye. H80cm/32in, W30cm/1ft. **'Blue Ice'**, intense white with a slight bluish tinge. H90cm/3ft, W30cm/1ft. **'Border Gem'**, violet-purple, still good after sixty years. H80cm/32in, W30cm/1ft. **'Branklyn'**, short, stocky habit and a long season of deep lilac flowers. H60cm/2ft, W30cm/1ft. **'Caroline van den Berg'**, as near a blue as can be, though fifty years old. H80cm/32in, W30cm/1ft. **'Eva Cullum'**, strong and leafy, warm pink, red eye. H80cm/32in, W30cm/1ft. **'Franz Schubert'**, lilac, long-flowering and reliable. H90cm/3ft, W30cm/1ft.

'Fujiyama', vigorous white, not at all fussy, and having a distinct kinship with *P. paniculata*. H1m/39in, W30cm/1ft. **'Marlborough'**, violet-purple with dark foliage. H90cm/3ft, W30cm/1ft. **'Mary Fox'**, warm salmon, red eye, large heads and long-flowering. H80cm/32in, W30cm/1ft. **'Prince of Orange'**, outstanding salmon-orange. H90cm/3ft, W30cm/1ft. **'Prospero'**, strong-growing, light lilac. H1m/39in, W30cm/1ft. **'Red Indian'**, deep crimson-red. H90cm/3ft, W30cm/1ft. **'Rijnstroom'**, still the best pure pink after sixty years. H90cm/3ft,

W30cm/1ft. **'San Antonio'**, well-tried, deep magenta-purple. H90cm/3ft, W30cm/1ft. **'Sandringham'**, cyclamen-pink, with a darker centre. An old but still worthwhile cultivar. H75cm/30in, W75cm/30in. **'Skylight'**, lavender-blue, with dark foliage. H1m/39in, W30cm/1ft. **'Starfire'**, unsurpassed bright deep red. H90cm/3ft, W30cm/1ft. **'Vintage Wine'**, large heads of wine-red. H80cm/32in, W30cm/1ft. **'White Admiral'**, the best large-flowered white. H75cm/30in, W30cm/1ft. **'Windsor'**, deep carmine with a magenta eye. H80cm/32in, W30cm/1ft.

Forms with variegated foliage lack the vigour of others and need light, rich soil. **'Harlequin'** has buff-yellow streaked leaves and a good show of violet-purple flowers. H80cm/32in, W30cm/1ft. **'Norah Leigh'** is more brightly variegated, but the pale lilac-purple flowers are less attractive. H80cm/32in, W30cm/1ft.

P. pilosa. An early-flowering species of some merit. It makes a mound of light green foliage and has panicles of bright pinkish flowers. Vigorous habit. H50cm/20in, W38cm/15in. F5-6. Z4-9.

Phlox paniculata 'White Admiral'

Phlox paniculata 'Franz Schubert'

Phlox paniculata 'Eva Cullum'

Phlox paniculata 'Branklyn'

Phuopsis stylosa 'Purpurea'

Phygelius aequalis 'African Queen'

Physostegia virginiana 'Vivid'

Platycodon grandiflorus 'Apoyama'

PHUOPSIS

P. stylosa (syn. *Crucianella stylosa*). This rather rampant, low-growing perennial has tiny leaves and heads of bright pink flowers. It is quite showy and long-flowering but should not be placed close to choicer subjects, and it has a smell rather than a fragrance! Plant in any fertile soil and full sun. There is an improved form of some merit with deeper rose-pink flowers named **'Purpurea'**. Both H25cm/10in, W60cm/2ft. F6-8. Z5-8.

PHYGELIUS

Like *Perovskia*, these are technically shrubs, but best treated as perennials, cut back in late winter or early spring. All need all the sun they can get and are drought-resistant.
P. aequalis. An unusual, slow-spreading plant for a warm spot, against a sunny wall in cool climates, and well-drained soil, this has reddish buff tubular flowers dangling from pyramidal spikes. The leaves are deep green, spear-shaped. H60cm/2ft, W45cm/18in. F7-10. Z7-9. Having tried other varieties, I rate **'African Queen'**, with large, profuse, distinctly orange flowers and upright, bushy growth, as by far the best. **'Yellow Trumpet'** is inclined to make more growth and spread, at the expense of flowering. Both H90cm/3ft, W45cm/18in. F7-10. Z7-9.
P. capensis. The Cape figwort is best against a sunny wall, though fairly hardy. In an open border it flowers none too freely with spikes of orange-scarlet, tubular flowers. H1.2m/4ft, W60cm/2ft. F7-10. Z8-9.

PHYSALIS Cape gooseberry, Chinese lantern

P. franchetii. The best-known of this genus, all of which are rapid, invasive spreaders and incompatible with most border plants. Its insignificant white flowers are followed by a bright orange inverted cone, or 'lantern', in autumn, within which is a gooseberry-sized orange berry. Its floppy stems add little to the garden scene, but the 'lanterns' are excellent for drying. Any soil, sun or shade. H60-80cm/24-32in, W90cm/3ft. F8-10. Z5-8.

PHYSOSTEGIA Obedient plant

If pushed to one side, the individual tubular flowers, each on a hinged stalk, stay put for a time, hence the common name. The roots are spreading but easy to curb. Any reasonably moist soil and sun are fine; frequent lifting, dividing and replanting is advisable.
P. speciosa. See *P. virginiana*.
P. virginiana (syn. *P. speciosa*). This produces an abundance of erect spikes of mauve-pink, snapdragon-like flowers. H1.1m/43in, W60cm/2ft. F7-9. All Z4-8. Cultivars include the following. **'Rose Bouquet'**, rosy lilac. H80cm/32in, W60cm/2ft. F7-9. **'Summer Snow'**, white. H70cm/28in, W60cm/2ft. F7-9. **'Summer Spire'**, rosy pink on slender spikes. H80cm/32in, W60cm/2ft. F7-9. **'Variegata'**, quite tall, with lilac-pink spikes and variegated leaves. H50cm/20in, W45cm/18in. F8-10. **'Vivid'**, much dwarfer and later, deep pink. H50cm/20in, W45cm/18in. F8-10.

PHYTEUMA

P. campanuloides (syn. *Asyneuma campanuloides*). A very different member of the *Campanula* family, with narrow-leaved, compact growth and spikes of little, starry, violet-blue flowers on erect stems. Sun or light shade in any well-drained soil. H60cm/2ft, W30cm/1ft. F6-8. Z5-8.

PIMPINELLA

P. major **'Rosea'**. This would be more valuable if it were compact, since it tends to wander and needs annual attention. It has dissected, ferny leaves and flattish, cow parsley-like heads of light pink flowers. H60cm/2ft, W30cm/1ft. F6-8. Z5-9.

PLATYCODON Balloon flower

These close relatives of campanulas have buds that swell into little spheres before they fully open into saucer-shaped flowers, hence the common name. They are easily grown, long-lived, dwarfish plants, dying back to fleshy roots over winter. Sun and moist, fertile soil are ideal, but they are adaptable to partial shade.
P. grandiflorus. The parent species of several forms, including the white **'Album'**, the dwarf, deep blue **'Apoyama'**, **'Mariesii'**, in shades of light blue, and the pale pink **'Mother of Pearl'**. Semi-doubles are sometimes offered. All H40-50cm/16-20in, W45cm/18in, except for 'Apoyama' H20cm/8in, W30cm/1ft. F6-8. Z4-9.

PODOPHYLLUM

Unusual plants for humus-rich, moist soil and some shade, with attractive leaves, flowers and seed capsules.

P. emodi (syn. *P. hexandrum*). Pairs of deeply lobed leaves unfurl to resemble small umbrellas. The cup-shaped, nodding, pale pink flowers are rather sparse in late spring but are followed by large, red, plum-shaped pods. The form **'Majus'** is preferable. H35cm/14in, W30cm/1ft. F4-5. Z5-8.

P. hexandrum. See *P. emodi*.

P. peltatum. The may apple is quite handsome, with each plant producing a single, large leaf, and each creamy white flower followed by pinkish fruit. This also has a steady root spread in a damp spot. H70cm/28in, W45cm/18in. F4-5. Z4-9.

P. foliosissimum. The best tall species, with ample foliage and lavender-blue flowers with yellow stamens in a tight bunch. H80cm/32in, W60cm/2ft. F5-8. Z4-8.

P. 'Lambrook Mauve'. Compact and free-flowering, with sprays of mauve flowers over a long period. Non-seeding. H45cm/18in, W35cm/14in. F5-7. Z4-8.

P. pulcherrimum. This has abundant, light green leaves and sky-blue, yellow-centred flowers on shapely spikes for a long time. H40cm/16in, W35cm/14in. F5-7. Z3-8.

P. reptans. Creeping Jacob's ladder is quite dwarf, with lolling sprays, best in the early-flowering **'Blue Pearl'**. H20cm/8in, W30cm/1ft. F5-6. Z2-8.

P. × richardsonii is a hybrid with light blue flowers on erect stems. The similar **'Newark Park'** is also blue. H70cm/28in,

dense, leafy, arching stems and tiny, dangling, white flowers. **'Variegatum'** has white-edged leaves. H60cm/2ft, W30cm/1ft. F5-6. Z4-9.

P. giganteum (syn. *P. biflorum*). The best name for the tallest, strong-growing species, the giant Solomon's seal. A superb plant in every way. H1m/39in or more in good soil, W60cm/2ft. F5-7. Z4-9.

P. × hybridum. See *P. multiflorum*.

P. japonicum. See *P. falcatum*.

P. multiflorum (syn. *P. × hybridum*). A somewhat variable species. This also has a striking variegated form **'Variegatum'**. H50-60cm/20-24in, W30cm/1ft. F5-7. Z3-9.

P. odoratum. Faintly scented, this is a little taller than *P. multiflorum*. H70cm/28in, W30cm/1ft. F5-7. Z4-9.

P. verticillatum. This has tall, erect, slender stems carrying minute purplish flowers. Not very striking, though **'Purpureum'**, with purplish stems and leaves, is more attractive. H1.2m/4ft, W45cm/18in. F5-6. Z4-9.

Polemonium caeruleum 'Dawn Flight'

Podophyllum emodi

POLEMONIUM Jacob's ladder

The ladder-like leaf arrangement suggested the folk name. Most have blue or white flowers with rich yellow stamens and basal clumps of ferny foliage. They are easy to grow, preferring a mainly sunny position. Regular lifting, dividing and replanting is advisable.

P. caeruleum. The best-known but not the most reliable, and apt to seed itself. It has heads of lavender-blue, saucer-shaped flowers. H60cm/2ft, W60cm/2ft. F5-7. Z4-8.

'Dawn Flight' is reliably perennial with light green, ferny foliage and a fine display of white flowers. H70cm/28in, W60cm/2ft. F5-7. Z4-8.

P. carneum is not really pink, but lilac. The silky flowers dangle above low, clumpy growth. H25cm/10in, W30cm/1ft. F6-7. Z4-9.

W38cm/15in. F5-7. Z4-8.

P. 'Sapphire' is a clumpy, compact grower, with sheaves of light blue flowers on erect stems. H30cm/1ft, W30cm/1ft. F5-6. Z4-8.

POLYGONATUM Solomon's seal

There are many more kinds of Solomon's seal than is generally known. All are shade lovers with spreading, fleshy roots, but in good soil most grow quite well in sun. All give of their best if left alone and take a year or two to become established. The little, white, bell-shaped flowers dangle from strong, leafy stems, arching in the taller species. Variegated forms are very attractive. All flower in late spring to early summer. Nomenclature is fairly confused.

P. biflorum. See *P. giganteum*.

P. falcatum (syn. *P. japonicum*). The name generally applies to a dwarf species with

Polemonium foliosissimum

Polygonatum giganteum

Polygonum amplexicaule 'Inverleith'

POLYGONUM Knotweed

This large genus includes some first-rate, long-flowering species, valuable for their bright pink and red flowers, as well as some which are a menace. They vary in height from 10cm/4in to 2.1m/7ft and though some garden-worthy kinds prefer moisture, most are not fussy about soil and tolerate some shade. Almost all are fully hardy. Avoid *P. cuspidatum*, its form **'Compactum Roseum'** (syn. 'Reynoutria') and *P. sachaliense* unless for the wildest places; they are invasive and defy eradication except by poison.

P. affine. A surface spreader with shallow roots, giving good ground cover except for a tendency to die back patchily. Leaves are narrow and leathery and flowers are poker-like. H15-23cm/6-9in, W38cm/15in. F6-7. Z3-9. **'Darjeeling Red'** has spikes of deep pink. H20cm/8in, W45-60cm/18-24in. F6-8. Z3-9. **'Dimity'** has fuller, long-lasting pink spikes and is more reliable, with good autumn colour. H15cm/6in, W45cm/18in. F6-7. Z3-9. **'Donald Lowndes'** has fulsome pink pokers, but is prone to die back patchily. H20cm/8in, W60cm/2ft. F6-7. Z3-9.

P. amplexicaule. This makes abundant, bushy growth with a long succession of thin terminal spikes before dying back to a sturdy but not invasive root. H1.2m/4ft, W75cm/30in. F6-9. Z5-9. **'Arun Gem'** (syn. 'Pendula') has distinct bright pink tassels dangling above a leafy, compact base. H30cm/1ft, W75cm/30in. F6-9. Z5-9. **'Atrosanguineum'** is a deep crimson. H1m/39in, W60cm/2ft. F6-9. Z5-9. **'Firetail'** is an outstanding bright red. H1.2m/4ft, W1.2m/4ft. F6-10. Z5-9. **'Inverleith'**, dwarf but wide-spreading, is crimson. H35cm/14in, W60cm/2ft. F6-9. Z5-9. A self-sown seedling, which I have named **'Taurus'**, is much the same intense colour as 'Firetail', but only half the height and with a wider summer spread. H60cm/2ft, W1.2m/4ft. F6-10. Z5-9.

P. bistorta **'Superbum'**. From vigorous basal growth come handsome, finger-sized, light pink pokers on erect stems. Best in a damp spot. H80cm/32in, W60cm/2ft. F5-7, but may repeat. Z4-8.

P. campanulatum. This is a fine subject for a dampish place. From shallow, spreading roots comes dense, leafy growth with light pink flower heads for weeks on end until the frost. H90cm/3ft, W90cm/3ft. F7-11. Z5-9.

P. carneum. Like a more compact *P. bistorta*, these clumpy plants throw up profuse, deep pink pokers. H50cm/20in, W30cm/1ft. F6-7. Z4-8.

P. macrophyllum. Large, deep green, wavy-edged leaves and distinct, finger-sized, clear light pink flower spikes on erect stems. A choice and beautiful plant. H45cm/18in, W45cm/18in. F7-9. Z4-9.

P. milletii. Choice for good, moist, deep soil in sun or partial shade, this has clumps of narrow leaves and intensely crimson-red pokers on and off all summer. H30cm/1ft, W30cm/1ft. Mainly F6-8. Z5-9.

P. regelianum. This makes hefty clumps of ample, dock-like foliage from a somewhat fleshy but non-invasive rootstock and has a long display of erect spikes of light pink pokers. H90cm/3ft, W90cm/3ft. F6-9. Z4-9.

P. sphaerostachyum. This disputably named species is one of the longest-flowering perennials. In reasonably good, moist soil its compact roots throw up a continuous array of branching stems tipped with short, deep pink pokers from late spring onwards. A trim in midsummer helps continuity. H60cm/2ft, W30cm/1ft. F5-9. Z4-9.

P. weyrichii. This with *P. molle* and *P. paniculatum* comprise a group of lusty-growing species with clusters of white or cream pokers topping tall, leafy stems. All are spreaders, but roots can be curbed. They are good background subjects, but take over from less robust perennials if allowed to do so. All H1.5-2.1m/5-7ft, W90cm/3ft. F8-10. Z5-9.

POTENTILLA Cinquefoil

A wide range of non-shrubby kinds exists, of real garden value. Most are sun lovers for ordinary, well-drained soil and have strawberry-like leaves and brightly coloured, saucer-shaped flowers, especially the hybrids, some of which have been grown for over a century. When I was a schoolboy, these appealed to me so much that I bought myself twelve different hybrids, one of each for ten shillings. Some I still have in my garden.

P. alba. This makes good basal, mat-forming greenery and has short sprays of white, golden-eyed flowers. H20cm/8in, W30cm/1ft. F5-7. Z4-7.

P. argyrophylla. Clumps of silvery leaves and branching sprays of yellow flowers. H40cm/16in, W60cm/2ft. F5-7. Z6-9.

P. atrosanguinea. Similar to the above, but with red flowers; these two are probably the parents of several of the hybrids which follow. All Z5-8. **'Blazeaway'**, suffused orange-red, with greyish leaves. H30cm/1ft, W45cm/18in. F6-8. **'Flamenco'**, robust, early, blood-red. H50cm/20in, W60cm/2ft. F5-7. **'Gibson's Scarlet'**, popular, glowing red, long season. H60cm/2ft, W60cm/2ft. F6-9. **'Glory of Nancy'** and the very similar **'Monsieur Rouillard'**, both large, almost double, mahogany-red and orange. H35cm/14in, W45cm/18in. F6-8. **'William Rollison'**, intensely bright flame-orange, semi-double. H40cm/16in, W45cm/18in. F6-8. **'Yellow Queen'**, silvery leaves, shining yellow flowers. H25cm/10in, W45cm/18in. F5-7.

Polygonum affine 'Dimity'

Polygonum bistorta 'Superbum'

Potentilla atrosanguinea 'Blazeaway'

P. fragiformis. This has bright yellow flowers and silvery felted leaves. H20cm/8in, W25cm/10in. F5-7. Z5-7.
P. nepalensis 'Firedance'. This has brilliant orange flowers, but is apt to revert to yellow. H40cm/16in, W40cm/16in. F6-8. Z5-8. 'Helen Jane', with bright pink flowers on branching stems, has now eclipsed 'Miss Willmott', a favourite pink form. H45cm/18in, W40cm/16in. F6-9. Z5-8. 'Roxana' is suffused rosy orange. H40cm/16in, W40cm/16in. F6-8. Z5-8.
P. recta 'Warrenii'. Erect-growing, with branching heads of smallish yellow flowers above dissected greenery. A showy, easy plant, of which a paler yellow form exists. H70cm/28in, W30cm/1ft. F6-8. Z4-8.
P. rupestris 'Gold Kugel'. A useful front-of-the-border subject, with a modest spread of greenery and a bright show of yellow flowers. H20cm/8in, W30cm/1ft. F5-7. Z5-8.
P. thurberi. Unusual for its glowing, deep crimson flowers on short sprays above pretty foliage. H30cm/1ft, W25cm/10in. F6-9. Z5-8.

POTERIUM See under SANGUISORBA.

PRIMULA
Only the taller kinds are included here, most of which need rich, moist soil for success. A few are by nature short-lived, and if some prefer cool shade, others are happy in sun if well fed and watered. Although often referred to as bog primulas, very few prefer really boggy conditions to a more open, rich soil. Bogginess inhibits deep root penetration. Those selected as

suitable hardy perennials are listed in sections according to habit and adaptability.

Auricula primulas
These have round, somewhat leathery and sometimes powdery, or farinose, leaves from slow-spreading rhizomes. Flowers are carried in open clusters on 13-18cm/5-7in stems in spring and early summer. Most are easy to grow in sun or partial shade and do not object to heavy soil. The basic type is yellow, but many other shades exist from white to mauve and bluish ones, while some have two colours, ringed. There are innumerable cultivars. Sometimes classed with alpines.

Candelabra primulas
These include most tall kinds and moisture lovers for sun or part shade. Flowers are

Potentilla nepalensis 'Miss Willmott'

carried in whorls up tall stems. Heights vary according to soil fertility and moisture content.
P. anisodora is aromatic, with green-centred, purple flowers. H50cm/20in, W30cm/1ft. F5-7. Z6-8.
P. aurantiaca. Orange-yellow flowers are carried on brownish red stems. H40cm/16in, W20cm/8in. F5-6. Z6-8.
P. beesiana. This has rosy carmine flowers with yellow centres and light green, slightly farinose leaves. H60-70cm/24-28in, W45cm/18in. F5-7. Z5-8.
P. × bulleesiana is a strain of mixed colours, in shades of cream, yellow, apricot, pink, orange, red and purple, resulting from the species above and below being crossed. It is also known as 'Asthore Hybrids'. H50-60cm/20-24in, W30cm/1ft. F5-7. Z5-8.
P. bulleyana. A popular plant, with dark green leaves and warm deep orange flowers. H60-80cm/24-32in, W45cm/18in. F5-7. Z6-8.
P. burmanica has purple-red, yellow-eyed flowers and long, whitish, dusty leaves. H60-70cm/24-28in, W45cm/18in. F5-7. Z5-8.
P. chungensis. This has tufts of shallowly lobed leaves and red-centred, bright orange flowers. H50-60cm/20-24in, W45cm/18in. F5-7. Z6-8.
P. × chunglenta. A brilliant flame-orange hybrid. H50-60cm/20-24in, W45cm/18in. F5-7. Z6-8.
P. cockburniana. Like a more refined *P. chungensis*, less tall and apt to be short-lived. H30-40cm/12-16in, W30cm/1ft. F5-7. Z6-8.
P. helodoxa gives a fine display of pure yellow flowers and glossy, semi-evergreen leaves. H60-80cm/24-32in, W45cm/18in. F5-7. Z6-8.
P. 'Inverewe' is a non-seeding variety, with warm salmon-orange flowers. H50-60cm/20-24in, W45cm/18in. F5-7. Z6-8.
P. japonica. The Japanese primrose has leafy growth resembling young cabbages, and pink flowers, near red with a black eye

Primula × bulleesiana

Primula denticulata 'Alba'

in **'Miller's Crimson'**, and white with a yellow eye in **'Postford White'**. All H60-80cm/24-32in, W45cm/18in. F5-7. Z6-8.

P. nepalensis. This long-lived species has whorls of deep yellow flowers. H30cm/1ft, W30cm/1ft. F5-7. Z6-8.

P. pulverulenta. Brilliant rosy red flowers are carried above crinkled leaves, so profusely that this plant tends to flower itself to death. H40-50cm/16-20in, W45cm/18in. F5-6. Z6-8.

P. **'Rowallane'** is a strong-growing, sterile, bright orange-rose hybrid. H60-70cm/24-28in, W45cm/18in. F5-7. Z6-8.

There are also several mixed, mostly longer-lived candelabra strains, such as **'Bressingham Strain'** and **'Inshriach Hybrids'**.

Cortusoides primulas. Including *P. sieboldii*. See under Alpines.

Denticulata primulas

The drumstick primulas have dense, round heads of flowers on single stalks in spring. They are easy to grow where not too dry, in sun or part shade. Colours range from white to mauve, lilac, lavender-blues and deep pink. They are deep-rooting and long-lived. Many selections have been named and must be propagated by root cuttings. **'Alba'** may cover many white forms. **'Rubin'** perhaps many with red drumstick flowers, whilst **'Bressingham Beauty'** is a free-flowering powder-blue. One bluish selection, **'Karyann'**, has variegated leaves all summer. H30-45cm/12-18in, W25cm/10in. F4-5. Z6-8.

P. rosea. A decided moisture lover, this sends up short sprays of bright pink flowers in early spring. As these lengthen the leaves open. **'Delight'** is the best cultivar. H25cm/10in, W25cm/10in. F3-5. Z6-8.

P. vialii. This very distinct species has red hot poker-type, lavender-blue flower spikes on smooth stalks above a small and rather

Primula florindae

Prunella grandiflora 'Pink Loveliness'

sparsely leaved rootstock. It is quite spectacular in some shade in well-drained but moist humus-rich soil, flowering later than most primulas. It is, sadly, not long-lived, despite being ranked as a perennial. H30-50cm/12-20in, W23cm/9in. F6-8. Z6-8.

Sikkimensis primulas

These prefer some light shade and good, moist soil, but are otherwise quite reliable. They have drooping, somewhat tubular flowers clustered on top of a smooth stalk.

P. alpicola. The moonlight primula is variable in colour, the white being very beautiful. Other shades seldom offered are violet (*violacea*), pale purple and light yellow. Best for a moist, shaded position. H30-40cm/12-16in, W30cm/1ft. F5-7. Z6-8.

P. florindae. This grows exuberantly with ample foliage and tall heads of soft yellow flowers on quite large clusters. Orange-shaded forms also exist. These are good waterside subjects in sun or partial shade, long-lived and faintly scented. H60-80cm/24-32in, W60cm/2ft. F6-8. Z6-8.

Vernalis primulas

These include the cowslips, oxlips and primroses as well as the polyanthus. Although most are adaptable as front-of-the-border plants to be used with taller perennials, all are low-growing and are described under Alpines.

PRUNELLA Self-heal

These easily grown, mat-forming plants, closely related to *Stachys*, are useful for front-of-the-border groups.

P. grandiflora. This has dense spikes of tubular, purple-violet flowers. It is best in the three **'Loveliness'** varieties – **'Blue Loveliness'**, **'Pink Loveliness'** and **'White Loveliness'**. All H20cm/8in, W45cm/18in. F6-8. Z5-8. **'Little Red Riding Hood'** makes a fine show of rosy red. H15cm/6in, W25cm/10in. F6-8. Z5-8.

P. × *webbiana.* Hybrid with deep pink flowers and fingery leaves. H15cm/6in, W40cm/16in. F6-8. Z5-8.

Pulmonaria angustifolia azurea

Pulmonaria rubra 'Redstart'

PULMONARIA Lungwort

These are at last being appreciated for their early spring display and for the attractive, weed-smothering, ground-covering foliage which many possess, and which lasts until the first hard frost. They are not fussy about soil, are adaptable to sun or shade, and make good infill between deciduous shrubs. Though tolerant, they still respond to good treatment.

P. angustifolia. Makes up for deciduous foliage by being the first to flower in early spring. The narrow, unspotted leaves follow the flowers. The form *azurea* is the earliest and is intensely blue. H15cm/6in, W30cm/1ft. F3-4. Z3-8. **'Munstead Blue'** is a shade deeper and slightly later. H15cm/6in, W30cm/1ft. F3-4. Z3-8.

P. longifolia. This has conspicuously spotted leaves 15cm/6in long with blue flowers on terminal sprays; white in the form *alba*. Two excellent selections of note are **'Bertram Anderson'**, with deep violet-blue flowers, and **'Roy Davidson'**, with lighter blue flowers. All H25cm/10in, W45cm/18in. F4-5. Z5-8.

P. mollis. This is large and leafy, with velvety leaves and deep blue flowers, fading to purple-red. H40cm/16in, W60cm/2ft. F4-5. Z4-8.

P. officinalis. The Jerusalem cowslip, or spotted dog, varies considerably, some forms having spotted leaves. Flowers are usually pink, fading to pale blue. H25cm/10in, W45cm/18in. F4-5. Z4-8.

P. rubra. This is early-flowering, with coral-red blooms, and its evergreen leaves are softer than most. **'Bowles' Red'** is usually listed, but **'Redstart'** is superior. H30cm/1ft, W60cm/2ft. F3-4. Z5-8.

P. saccharata. The Bethlehem sage gives the widest range of choice, with evergreen leaves overlapping in a most pleasing way. Almost all have pink flowers which fade to blue on short sprays. All Z4-8. **'Argentea'**, leaves almost entirely silvered. H25cm/10in,

Pulmonaria saccharata 'Highdown'

Pulmonaria saccharata 'Sissinghurst White'

W60cm/2ft. F3-5. **'Highdown'**, less silvery than 'Argentea', a good blue. H30cm/1ft, W60cm/2ft. F3-5. **'Pink Dawn'**, spotted silver all summer. H25cm/10in, W45cm/18in. F3-5. **'Sissinghurst White'**, white sprays above green leaves. H25cm/10in, W60cm/2ft. F3-5.

PULSATILLA Pasque flower

Closely related to the anemone, these have deep, cup-shaped, hoary flowers with yellow stamens in spring, above greyish, ferny foliage. They like well-drained, gritty and limy soil. Once established, they resent disturbance and dividing old clumps is seldom successful. Seeds should be sown as soon as ripe, but *P. caucasica* has baffled me for years and I am still trying to work up a

good stock. Attractive seed heads.
P. caucasica. With lovely soft yellow above ferny foliage, this is less vigorous but worth trying. H30cm/1ft, W20cm/8in. F4-5. Z5-7.
P. vulgaris. This varies in height and colour, mauve and purple shades most often seen, but pink, red and white are also available. H25-30cm/10-12in, W30cm/1ft. F4-5. Z5-7.

PYRETHRUM See under CHRYSANTHEMUM.

RANUNCULUS Buttercup

Though generally moisture-loving, good, well-drained soil and a mainly sunny spot suit those below. None is evergreen, but all are fully hardy and most have jagged leaves.
R. aconitifolius. This robust species is best in the form *platanifolius*, which makes bushy, leafy growth with branching stems of profuse, smallish, single white flowers. H1m/39in, W90cm/3ft. F5-6. Z5-9.
'Flore Pleno' is a choice and lovely form with dazzling, fully double white flowers. Also known as 'The Fair Maids of France', or 'The Fair Maids of Kent', this is worth fussing over and providing the humus-rich soil on which height and vigour depend. H40-70cm/16-28in, W60cm/2ft. F5-6. Z5-9.
R. acris **'Flore Pleno'**. This is also fully double, with bright yellow, buttercup-like flowers and a wide-spreading habit. H60cm/2ft, W45cm/18in. F5-7. Z4-8.
R. amplexicaulis. This demure species has 2.5cm/1in white flowers, larger in **'Grandiflorus'**, above smooth glaucous, narrow leaves. H30cm/1ft, W20cm/8in. F6-7. Z4-8.
R. cortusifolius. Glistening yellow buttercups of good size on branching stems, given a warm, sunny spot and very well-drained soil. H60cm/2ft, W30cm/1ft. F5-7. Z8-9.
R. gouanii. A neat-growing clumpy buttercup yellow. H20cm/8in, W23cm/9in. F5-7. Z4-8.

Ranunculus acris 'Flore Pleno'

R. gramineus. The grassy leaves are glaucous and the bright yellow flower sprays are abundant. The habit is neatly clumpy. H30cm/1ft, W25cm/10in. F5-7. Z6-8.

R. 'Speciosus Plenus'. This may be a form of *R. bulbosus*, although the roots do not suggest it. Leafy clumps provide a fine display of quite large, fully double flowers. H25cm/10in, W25cm/10in. F5-7. Z4-8.

REINECKIA

R. carnea (syn. *Liriope hyacinthiflora*). This makes a carpet of tufty evergreen foliage with lily of the valley-like leaves, in which nestle short spikes of tiny pale pink flowers. An unusual ground cover for humus-rich soil in light shade. H15cm/6in, W15cm/6in. F6-7. Z4-8.

RHAZYA

R. orientalis. Closely related to *Amsonia*, this has willowy leaves and sprays of small, slate-blue, starry flowers on wiry stems. Best in well-drained soil and sun. H40cm/16in, W30cm/1ft. F6-8. Z5-8.

RHEUM Ornamental rhubarb

These vary in height from a few centimetres/inches to 2.1m/7ft or more. The taller ones are quite spectacular in spring, but take up much space which becomes more or less bare after early summer. Rich, moist soil and full sun.

R. 'Ace of Spades' has dark green, pointed leaves and white flowers. H1.2m/4ft, W1.2m/4ft. F5-6. Z5-9.

R. alexandrae. This has shiny, deep green

quite vigorous habit. Little plumes of pale pink are carried above round leaves. H30cm/1ft, W30cm/1ft. F5-7. Z5-9.

R. palmatum has glossy leaves, purplish red when young and even larger than those of rhubarb, from an equally hefty root. **'Atrosanguineum'** has bright reddish leaves in spring and tall spikes of creamy white. H2.1m/7ft, W2.1m/7ft. F5-6. Z5-9. **'Rubrum'** also has colourful leaves in spring, but the spikes are deep pink, almost red. H2.1m/7ft, W2.1m/7ft. F5-6. Z5-9.

RHODIOLA

R. rosea. See *Sedum rosea*.

RODGERSIA

These are among the elite of hardy perennials. All have handsome leaves, at least 60cm/2ft across, held well above ground level on sturdy stalks, and imposing flower spikes in summer. Most species have creamy white plumes, not unlike some astilbes. Roots are thick, shallow and spread slowly outwards in the good moist soil they prefer. Though adaptable for sun or shade, or as marginal plants, they are not for places where it is both dry and sunny. Some species are much alike, with only minor variations in the shape of leaves.

R. aesculifolia. The specific name means chestnut-leaved, describing the crinkled, bronzy foliage, with conical creamy white flower spikes. **'Irish Bronze'** has purple-tinted leaves and stems, and white flowers. Both H1.2m/4ft, W60cm/2ft. F6-8. Z5-8.

R. pinnata. This has paired, fingery, deeply divided leaves and white flowers. The form **'Elegans'** is freer to flower with imposing creamy spikes. H1.2m/4ft, W60cm/2ft. F6-8. Z5-8. **'Superba'** lives up to its name; not only is the foliage tinted purple, but the flowers are a glistening rose-pink. H1.2m/4ft, W50cm/20in. F6-7. Z5-8.

Rheum palmatum 'Atrosanguineum'

Rheum alexandrae

Rodgersia aesculifolia 'Irish Bronze'

Rodgersia pinnata 'Superba'

leaves of no great size, and sends up spikes carrying flowers partly hidden by large, creamy yellow bracts which redden with age. Its one fault, shyness in flowering, is a matter of chance and/or good drainage. H1m/39in, W60cm/2ft. F5-7. Z6-8.

R. kialense. This is a midget, but with a

R. sambucifolia. Rather similar to *R. pinnata* with more delicate white flowers and elder-like leaves. H1m/39in, W60cm/2ft. F6-8. Z5-8.

R. tabularis (syn. *Astilboides tabularis*). The large, round, light green leaves are only slightly lobed. They are carried umbrella fashion, and well above the creamy white flowers. H1m/39in, W45cm/18in. F6-8. Z5-8.

ROMNEYA California tree poppy
These are not good mixers, since their deep roots, when well established, shoot up well away from the original plant. They need a sunny spot in very well-drained or stony soil. Glaucous-leaved and semi-shrubby, they have white, scented, poppy-like flowers carried over a long period. They are difficult to divide, so pot-grown plants are best.

R. coulteri. This has large, yellow-centred white flowers and is the species most likely to be available. In any case, the only other species, **R. trichocalyx**, is fairly similar,

Roscoea cautleoides

Roscoea humeana

Romneya coulteri

although it branches lower down. Both H2.1m/7ft, W90cm/3ft. F7-10. Z8-10.

ROSCOEA
These fleshy-rooted perennials have hitherto been undeservedly neglected. All are very beautiful, quite distinctive and easy to grow in sun or part shade. The fleshy, thong-like roots are not large, nor annoyingly deep. When dormant the tips show little signs of buds, but when they break the surface in spring they soon produce light green, sheath-like leaves and spikes of orchid-like flowers on erect stems. In two to three years a single root will make a clump of up to a dozen in good, well-drained soil. All flower before their foliage is fully developed, and this is to their credit, as the bladed greenery becomes lush until autumn.

R. auriculata. This grows with vigour and ample leafage, with lavender-blue flowers paling towards the centre. H35cm/14in, W15cm/6in. F6-8. Z7-9.

R. beesiana. Its stiff, closely bunched stems carry buff and lilac lipped flowers. H30cm/1ft, W15cm/6in. F6-8. Z7-9.

R. cautleoides. Early and of a more open, slender habit than the above two species, the flowers are soft primrose-yellow. H40cm/16in, W20cm/8in. F5-7. Z7-9.

R. humeana. Its broad leaves sheath the flower stems and splay out at the tips. The flowers are quite large, mostly rich purple,

Rudbeckia 'Goldsturm'

but lilac, yellow and white forms exist. In cultivation two purple forms exist, one H30cm/1ft, W15cm/6in and the other H50cm/20in, W30cm/1ft. Both F6-8. Z7-9.

R. 'Kew Beauty'. This is like a glorified *R. cautleoides*, though later to flower. Its leafy stalks sheathe large, primrose-yellow flowers. H35cm/14in, W15cm/6in. F6-8. Z7-9.

R. procera. The finest blue-flowered species, this has large, deep violet-blue flowers above abundant greenery. H35cm/14in, W15cm/6in. F6-8. Z6-9.

R. purpurea. Also violet-blue, this has smaller flowers and leaves. H35cm/14in, W15cm/6in. F6-8. Z6-9.

RUDBECKIA Cone flower, black-eyed Susan
All these North American, daisy-like flowers possess a central cone and rayed petals. They are easy to grow in any reasonable soil and prefer sun. Some are over-tall for small gardens, but others provide first-rate displays of yellow, mainly in late summer and autumn.

R. deamii. This makes wide clumps of grey leaves and masses of yellow flowers. H80cm/32in, W38cm/15in. F7-9. Z4-9.

R. 'Goldsturm', one of the finest plants ever raised, has deep yellow rayed, black-centred flowers that continue for weeks, given good, moist soil. Dark green leaves on slow-spreading plants. H70cm/28in, W30cm/1ft. F6-10. Z4-9.

R. laciniata and **R. nitida** are much alike, with shiny, deep green basal foliage and green-coned, yellow flowers. Both are tall and usually need staking. They are seldom offered as species, but the large-flowered **R. n. 'Autumn Sun'** (syn. 'Herbstsonne') is garden-worthy. H2.1m/7ft, W60cm/2ft.

Rudbeckia laciniata 'Goldquelle'

F7-9. Z5-9. **R. l. 'Goldquelle'** is dwarfer and very beautiful, with leafy, deep green bushy growth covered in fully double, chrome-yellow flowers, 8cm/3in across. H1m/39in, W60cm/2ft. F7-9. Z3-9.

R. maxima. Seldom seen, but has good, broad glaucous foliage and large, drooping, golden rayed petals with a huge black cone. H1.2m/4ft, W60cm/2ft. F7-9. Z6-9.

R. mollis. This is vigorous, with hairy leaves and erect stems carrying yellow flowers with a browny green cone. It dislikes winter wet. H1m/39in, W38cm/15in. F7-9. Z6-9.

R. newmanii. See *R. speciosa*.

R. speciosa (syn. *R. newmanii*). Probably the original black-eyed Susan, this is inferior to *R.* 'Goldsturm'. H70cm/28in, W60cm/2ft. F7-9. Z4-9.

R. subtomentosa. This has greyish hairy foliage and stout stems carrying typical rayed flowers for several weeks. H1.1m/43in, W60cm/2ft. F7-9. Z4-9.

SALVIA

This vast genus includes some good garden plants but, sadly, some of the brightest colours are not hardy. All need sun and well-drained soil. Many are aromatic and most have hairy leaves; colourful bracts are also common. Some tender salvias are worth the extra care required to keep them over winter: the dwarf red *S. blepharophylla*, the silver-leaved, blue-flowered *S. farinacea*, the carmine-red *S. involucrata* **'Bethellii'** and the taller red *S. neurepia* give a bright display in a congenial location. Most are best lifted, divided and replanted every three or four years.

S. ambigens. This makes shapely bushes of small, deep green leaves and short spikes of royal blue flowers. Protect by covering with leaf mould, bark or litter in cold districts. H1.1m/43in, W45cm/18in. F7-10. Z5-8.

Salvia 'May Night'

Salvia 'Blauhügel'

S. argentea. Though hardy, it is rather short-lived. The large basal leaves are silvery and felted. Sprays of white hooded flowers and grey calyces on oblique branching stems are a prelude to a lingering demise. H80cm/32in, W35cm/14in. F6-7. Z5-8.

S. 'Blauhügel' (syn. 'Bluehills'). A reliable, long-lived plant with blue spikes. Could become a classic. H60cm/2ft, W30cm/1ft. F7-8. Z5-9.

S. blepharophylla. Low-growing, mounded and sub-shrubby, this has bright red flowers in maroon calyces, but is hardy only in the warmest areas. Where happy, it can be invasive. H25cm/10in, W25cm/10in. F7-9. Z9-10.

S. bulleyana. Rosette-like, crinkled, light green leaves are topped by close-set spikes of yellow, maroon-lipped flowers. A neat-growing, interesting species. H30cm/1ft, W30cm/1ft. F6-8. Z9-10.

S. 'East Friesland'. Violet-purple and similar to *S.* 'Superba', but not as high. H45cm/18in, W30cm/1ft. F6-8. Z5-9.

S. glutinosa. Quite reliable but not choice, this produces hefty clumps of coarse foliage and pale yellow flowers. H1.2m/4ft, W90cm/3ft. F6-8. Z5-8.

S. haematodes. Though not long-lived, it may seed itself. The dark green basal rosette produces much-branched stems of profuse, pale-throated, lavender-blue flowers. H1m/39in, W45cm/18in. F6-8. Z6-9. The hybrid **'Indigo'** is more reliable. H1m/39in, W45cm/18in. F6-8. Z6-9.

S. involucrata 'Bethellii'. Not very hardy, but showy enough to warrant the extra effort of covering well over winter. It has sturdy, shrubby growth and short spikes of large, bright rosy red flowers with pink bracts. H1.2m/4ft, W90cm/3ft. F8-10. Z7-9.

Saponaria × lempergii 'Max Frei'

Saxifraga fortunei 'Rubrifolia'

Saxifraga × urbium

Satureia montana

S. **'Lubeca'.** Violet-purple and again of similar habit to *S.* 'Superba', this is intermediate at H75cm/30in, W30cm/1ft. F6-8. Z5-9.
S. **'May Night'.** Its indigo-blue flowers appear earlier than those of *S.* 'Superba' and it flowers again if trimmed. H45cm/18in, W30cm/1ft. F5-8. Z5-9.
S. przewalskii. A rare but attractive species, this has bold branching spikes of small, purplish flowers above clumps of large, heart-shaped leaves. H80cm/32in, W38cm/15in. F6-8. Z5-9.
S. **'Rose Queen'.** This has rather small, pink flowers on thin spikes. H80cm/32in, W30cm/1ft. F6-8. Z5-9.
S. **'Superba'.** This much-loved hybrid has fine violet-blue upstanding spikes, with crimson-purple bracts, a splendid contrast with yellow, daisy-type subjects. H1.2m/4ft, W60cm/2ft. F6-8. Z5-9.
S. uliginosa. A tall, distinctive, late species, with delicate sprays of long-lasting, sky-blue flowers above deep green leafage. It prefers moist soil and a warm, sheltered spot, and needs supporting. H1.5m/5ft, W45cm/18in. F9-11. Z8-9.

SANGUINARIA Bloodroot
S. canadensis. This choice subject for well-drained, peaty soil and cool shade has large,

white, cup-shaped flowers with golden stamens and deeply lobed glaucous foliage that dies down in late summer. Its slow-spreading fleshy root has orange-red sap, hence its common name. The double form **'Plena'** is most attractive but the flowering period is all too fleeting. H25cm/10in, W30cm/1ft. F4. Z3-9.

SANGUISORBA Burnet
These strong-growing perennials have elegant, pinnate foliage and bottlebrush flowers, especially welcome in late summer. Full sun is ideal. Most need supporting. The first three below are tough-rooted plants, hardy and long-lived.
S. canadense has tall, narrowly branching spikes and fingered leaves topped by white pokers. H1.5m/5ft, W60cm/2ft. F8-10. Z3-8.
S. **'Magnificum Album'.** A dubious name for a robust plant with obliquely held, white pokers above abundant foliage. H80cm/32in, W60cm/2ft. F6-8. Z3-8.
S. obtusum. The Japanese bottlebrush, or Japanese burnet, has pink flower spikes carried above greyish leaves. A white variant, **'Album'**, exists. H70cm/28in, W60cm/2ft. F6-8. Z4-8.
S. sitchensis (syn. *S. stipulata*). A stout, upstanding plant with short, rosy red pokers on branching stems. H1.5m/5ft, W45cm/18in. F7-9. Z4-9.
S. stipluta. See *S. sitchensis.*
S. tenuifolia. A graceful species with finely cut leaves and small, drooping pink flowers held above the foliage. **'Alba'**, with white flowers, is particularly effective. H1.2m/4ft, W60cm/2ft. F6-8. Z4-8.

SAPONARIA Soapwort
These are untidy, invasive plants with campion-like flowers and spreading roots, perhaps best in a wild garden. The lather made from its leaves is used to clean delicate fabrics, hence its common name. Any well-drained soil, full sun; provide twiggy support.
S. × lempergii **'Max Frei'.** Fairly compact habit with single, bright pink flowers. H25cm/10in, W30cm/1ft. F7-9. Z4-8.

S. officinalis. Only the double forms are worth growing: **'Albo Plena'** in white; **'Roseo Plena'** in light pink; and the deep pink **'Rubra Plena'**. All H70cm/28in, W90cm/3ft. F6-8. Z4-8.

SATUREIA Winter savory
S. montana. Tiny blue flowers on low, twiggy, almost evergreen sub-shrubs make this a very good late subject for the front of a sunny, well-drained border. Shear in spring to keep compact. The slightly bitter leaves are used to flavour savoury dishes. H25cm/10in, W25cm/10in. F8-10. Z6-10.

SAXIFRAGA
Only two sections of this large genus can be included here as most plants are more at home in rock gardens.
S. fortunei and its variants are best in shade with light, humus-rich soil. They are shallow-rooting plants, producing in spring attractive rosettes of round, glistening leaves, red beneath, and, in mid-autumn, a sudden show of airy sprays of starry white flowers. They appreciate shelter, a light spring mulch and, in cold areas, some winter cover. H30-45cm/12-18in, W30cm/1ft. F10-11. Z4-7. **'Rubrifolia'** has reddish foliage. H25cm/10in, W20cm/8in. F10-11. Z6-7. **'Wada's Variety'** has leaves close to beetroot-red. H25cm/10in, W20cm/8in. F10-11. Z6-7.
S. umbrosa. See *S. × urbium.*
S. × urbium (syn. *S. umbrosa*). Commonly called London pride, this is closely related to *S. × geum.* Both make good, evergreen, shallow-rooting ground cover in shady or more open places. Both have leathery leaves and sprays of dainty white or pink flowers. Occasional replanting keeps them tidy. H20-25cm/8-10in, W35cm/14in. F5-6. Z6-7.

SCABIOSA Scabious, pincushion flower
Dense basal clumps of narrow, glaucous leaves and round, flat flowers over a long season make these firm favourites.

Scabiosa caucasica 'Miss Willmott'

Schizostylis coccinea 'Major'

S. 'Butterfly Blue'. This produces blue flowers all summer. H20cm/8in, W25cm/10in. F5-9. Z5-8.

S. caucasica. Ever popular and much valued for cutting, there are fewer named varieties now than fifty years ago. They prefer sun and well-drained soil, ideally with lime. Flowering is prolonged by cutting the flowers for decoration or by dead-heading. All H60-80cm/24-32in, W45-60cm/18-24in. F6-9. Z4-9. **'Blue Mountain'** is a strong-growing, deep blue. **'Bressingham White'** and **'Miss Willmott'** are both good whites, the latter more ivory. **'Clive Greaves'**, a prolific mid-blue, has stood the test of time. **'Moonlight'** is a fairly tall light blue.

S. columbaria. This makes a loose mound, carrying a long succession of pincushion lilac-blue flowers with deep purple centres. H75cm/30in, W75cm/30in. F6-9. Z5-8.

S. graminifolia. One of the finest plants for frontal groups, it makes dense mats of narrow, silver-grey leaves and a long show of light blue flowers. H30cm/1ft, W30cm/1ft. F6-9. Z7-9. **'Pink Cushion'**, from Bressingham, is light pink and less robust. Sun and light soil suit both. H25cm/10in, W25cm/10in. F6-9. Z7-9.

S. lucida. Deep green leafy clumps produce rosy lilac flowers. H35cm/14in, W30cm/1ft. F6-9. Z5-8.

S. minoana. Grey-leaved, low and bushy, its single stalks carry lilac-pink flowers. Evergreen. H50cm/20in, W45cm/18in. F6-8. Z6-8.

S. ochroleuca. Much like *S. columbaria* in habit, this has unusual, pale yellow flowers

on wiry stems, carried over a long period. Self-seeds freely. H75cm/30in, W75cm/30in. F6-9. Z4-7.

S. rumelica (syn. *Knautia macedonica*). This makes lax, bushy growth and a long succession of pure crimson, double flowers, 5cm/2in across, carried on branching stems. H75cm/30in, W75cm/30in. F6-9. Z5-9.

SCHIZOSTYLIS Kaffir lily

Valuable for late flowering but needing some fussing over, these spread rapidly by means of shallow, mat-forming roots in the moist, rich soil they prefer. Cover with leaves or bark in cold districts, to protect in winter. Adaptable for sun or shade, ideally in a slightly humid atmosphere.

S. coccinea. This is the only species now represented by named varieties, all like daintier versions of gladioli. All F9-11. Z6-9. **'Major'**, fine crimson-red. H60cm/2ft, W23cm/9in. **'Mrs Hegarty'**, older, pale pink variety. H50cm/20in, W23cm/9in. **'November Cheer'**, a Bressingham sport from 'Major', clear pink. H50cm/20in, W23cm/9in. **'Snow Maiden'**, a newly discovered white. H50cm/20in, W23cm/9in. **'Sunrise'**, almost salmon. H60cm/2ft, W23cm/9in. **'Viscountess Byng'**, another old pink. H50cm/20in, W23cm/9in.

SCILLA Squill

S. peruviana. Though technically a bulb, it is included here because it has a very short dormant season, retains its broad green, floppy leaves after flowering and has little spread. Short, thick spikes carry dense umbels of mostly violet-blue, starry flowers. A white form also exists. Best in a hot, sunny spot. H40cm/16in, W25cm/10in. F5-6. Z7-10.

SCOPOLIA

S. carniolica hladnikiana. An interesting plant for shade and rich, dryish soil. It has yellow flowers in early spring, followed by the leaves, which grow increasingly large and coarse as the season progresses. H60cm/2ft, W60cm/2ft. F3-4. Z5-8.

SCROPHULARIA Water figwort

S. aquatica 'Variegata'. This is the only form worth growing, and then mainly for its clumps of evergreen, cream-striped and -splashed foliage, which improves when the thin spikes of brownish flowers are cut back. Best in fairly moist soil and semi-shade. H1.2m/4ft, W30cm/1ft. F6-8. Z5-9.

Scilla peruviana

Sedum spectabile 'Brilliant'

SCUTELLARIA

This pretty but rare perennial has mostly fibrous roots and bushy, leafy growth. It is easily grown in sun and ordinary soil.

S. baicalensis. This has a deep, fleshy root and very little spread. Rich blue flowers are carried on narrow-leaved, twiggy bushes. H40cm/16in, W45cm/18in. F7-9. Z6-8.
S. canadensis. Somewhat similar to the following species, but with green leaves. H80cm/32in, W60cm/2ft. F7-9. Z4-9.
S. canescens. See *S. incana.*
S. incana (syn. *S. canescens*). This is my favourite tall species, with ash-grey leaves, bushy growth and sky-blue, lipped flowers. H90cm/3ft, W60cm/2ft. F7-9. Z4-9.

SEDUM Stonecrop

Several are of great value, flowering from spring to autumn. All are easy to grow in any well-drained soil, rich or poor, and in mainly sunny spots. Their flat or domed heads of starry flowers also attract butterflies.

S. aizoon. This is an early-flowering species, with fleshy green foliage and heads of yellow flowers. H35cm/14in, W35cm/14in. F6-8. Z4-9. **'Aurantiacum'** is preferable because of its bronzy stems and leaves and its deeper yellow, almost orange, flowers. H30cm/1ft, W30cm/1ft. F6-8. Z4-9.
S. alboroseum **'Mediovariegatum'** (syn. *S. spectabile* 'Variegatum'). Pale pink heads above pretty, creamy yellow variegated foliage. Watch out for reversion and pull off any all-green shoots as soon as seen. H40cm/16in, W40cm/16in. F8-10. Z4-9.
S. **'Autumn Joy'** (syn. 'Herbstfreude').

One of the best plants ever raised, this German hybrid has spring growth of glaucous, fleshy stems and leaves that remain attractive all summer. The flower heads widen as the season progresses into glistening pink plates up to 25cm/10in across, turning a deep bronze, then coppery red. Divide and replant regularly. H50cm/20in, W50cm/20in. F8-10. Z3-10.
S. ellacombeanum. This makes low green clumps with a profusion of yellow flowers. H20cm/8in, W25cm/10in. F6-8. Z3-8.
S. ewersii. This varies but all are pink-flowered above small glaucous leaves. H20cm/8in, W25cm/10in. F6-8. Z5-9.

S. floriferum **'Weihenstephaner Gold'**. A splendid frontal subject, this makes spreading, dark green mats and a long succession of orange-gold heads. H15-18cm/6-7in, W45cm/18in. F6-9. Z4-8.
S. heterodontum. Small round heads of orange-yellow flowers grow from a fleshy root in spring. H20cm/8in, W30cm/1ft. F4-5. Z4-8.
S. kirilowii. A rarity with green, needle-like foliage and yellow flowers. A variation with deep orange flowers, **'Rubrum'**, is even rarer. Both H20cm/8in, W30cm/1ft. F4-6. Z5-8.
S. maximum **'Atropurpureum'**. A striking plant, this has fleshy, plum-purple stems and leaves, and heads of reddish pink flowers. H60cm/2ft, W60cm/2ft. F7-9. Z4-9.
S. rhodiola. See *S. rosea.*
S. rosea (syn. *S. rhodiola*). The spring-flowering rose root is now given generic status, as *Rhodiola rosea*, but remains under *Sedum* for practical purposes. Its fleshy roots produce crowded stems of grey, toothed leaves, topped by fluffy yellow flower heads, coppery in bud. H25cm/10in, W25cm/10in. F4-5. Z2-8.
S. **'Ruby Glow'**. Another German hybrid with bluish foliage and a good display of ruby-red flowers, 10cm/4in across. H20cm/8in, W20cm/8in. F7-9. Z4-8.
S. spectabile. Sometimes called ice plants, their fleshy glaucous foliage is effective infill all summer before their wide heads of chalky pink flowers appear. Not much variation in the varieties offered. **'Brilliant'**, **'Indian Chief'**, **'Meteor'** and **'September Glow'** all have more vivid flowers. H30-40cm/12-16in, W30-40cm/12-16in. F8-10. Z4-9. **'Variegatum'**. See *S. alboroseum* 'Mediovariegatum'.
S. telephium. As a plain species this is not garden-worthy. The form *maximum*

Sedum 'Autumn Joy'

Sedum maximum 'Atropurpureum'

Selinum tenuifolium

'**Atropurpureum**' has handsome purple-red leaves and heads of glistening rosy red. H50cm/20in, W30cm/1ft. F7-8. Z5-9. '**Variegata**' has pretty foliage but very pale sulphur-yellow flowers. H50cm/20in, W30cm/1ft. F7-8. Z5-9. *S.* '**Vera Jameson**'. This has bluish purple leaves and loose heads of warm pink flowers. '**Sunset Cloud**', with wine-purple flowers, is somewhat similar. H25cm/10in, W25cm/10in. F7-9. Z4-9.

SELINUM
S. tenuifolium. Though it received a Royal Horticultural Society Award of Merit in 1881, it is now comparatively rare in gardens, perhaps because of its large size. It is like a much glorified cow parsley or Queen Anne's lace, with finely cut, outspreading foliage and imposing, flat heads of tiny white flowers with black anthers. In good, light soil it is a superb plant for mainly sun. H1.2-1.5m/4-5ft, W60cm/2ft. F7-9. Z6-9.

SENECIO
Many species formerly in this genus are now classified as *Ligularia*. Some below are moisture- and sun-loving.
S. cineraria. The name usually given to

the bright silver dusty miller, a sub-shrub often used for summer bedding. Its long, fingery leaves are very effective but flowering is insignificant. Hardy only in mildest districts. '**Colchester White**' is especially silvery. H60cm/2ft, W60cm/2ft. Z8-9.
S. doronicum. This gives a good display of yellow, ray-petalled daisy flowers, up to 5cm/2in across, from a compact, leafy rootstock. '**Sunburst**' is orange-gold and is not for dry soil. H40cm/16in, W40cm/16in. F5-6. Z5-9.
S. pulcher. This needs rich, light soil and a warm spot to produce its brilliant, magenta-pink, yellow-centred daisies in autumn, carried above dark green, leathery leaves. H30cm/1ft, W30cm/1ft. F8-10. Z8-10.
S. tanguticus. If allowed, its spreading underground shoots will romp in any moist or good soil. The leaves are jagged; the goldenrod-like, conical flower heads are bright yellow and carried on erect stems. Fluffy, long-lasting seed heads follow. H1.5m/5ft, W60cm/2ft. F8-10. Z6-9.

SERRATULA
These are of the knapweed tribe, with fluffy flowers on stiff, branching stems, and deeply divided deep green leaves, for a

good late summer display. Easy in any fertile soil and sun. Some taller species are now listed under *Jurinea*; *J.* 'Glycantha', for example, is similar to those listed below, except for its height and early flowering.
S. macrocephala. Makes shapely, bushy growth with profuse, small violet flowers. H30cm/1ft, W25cm/10in. F7-9. Z5-8.
S. seoanei (syn. *S. shawii*). Similar to above but shorter, with more delicate leaves. H25cm/10in, W25cm/10in. F8-10. Z5-8.
S. shawii. See *S. seoanei*.

SIDALCEA
These are valuable for providing flower spikes in contrast to flatter or rounder blooms. All are easy to grow and have silky, hollyhock-like flowers, graceful divided foliage and a clumpy, ground-covering base.
S. candida and *S. malviflora*. Only hybrids of these species are listed. Some taller ones may need support. All F6-8, Z5-8.
'**Croftway Red**', deep rose. H1m/39in, W45cm/18in. '**Elsie Heugh**', upstanding clear pink, fringed petals. H1.2m/4ft, W45cm/18in. '**Loveliness**', warm pink, compact. H80cm/32in, W45cm/18in. '**Mary Martin**', graceful slender stems, clear pink flowers. H1-1.2m/39-48in, W45cm/18in. '**Mrs Anderson**', deep pink, heavy foliage. H1.2m/4ft, W45cm/18in. '**Oberon**', shell-pink, erect, self-supporting. H80cm/32in, W45cm/18in. '**Puck**', similar to 'Oberon' but deeper pink. '**Rose Queen**', mid-pink, leafy stems. H1m/39in, W45cm/18in. '**William Smith**', salmon-pink. H1.2m/4ft, W45cm/18in.

SILENE Sea campion
S. dioica (syn. *Lychnis dioica* and *Melandrium rubrum*). These form hummocks of soft green leaves. The plant sometimes offered as '**Emneth Variety**' is very similar to '**Rosea Plena**', both with double, dianthus-like flowers in early summer. '**Plena**' is double. '**Rubra**' produces sprays of rosy red flowers. All H30cm/1ft, W30cm/1ft. F5-7. Z4-7.
S. maritima. See under Alpines.
S. schafta. See under Alpines.

Sidalcea 'William Smith'

Sisyrinchium striatum

SISYRINCHIUM

These have iris-like leaves and fibrous roots. Most are rock-garden plants but the following are tall enough to include here and are easy in any soil and sun.

S. idahoense. This has narrow, erect leaves and short sprays of violet-blue, yellow-centred flowers. H35cm/14in, W15cm/6in. F6-8. Z7-8.

S. striatum. This has broader, light green evergreen leaves and light yellow flowers. Tolerates light shade. Not long-lived but self-seeding. The creamy yellow variegated form **'Aunt May'** has some attraction. H60cm/2ft, W23cm/9in. F6-8. Z7-8.

SMILACENA False spikenard

S. racemosa. Has little, fluffy, scented flower plumes at the top of leafy stems, occasionally followed by red berries. Not for limy soil or a sunny, dry spot. H75cm/30in, W45cm/18in. F5-6. Z4-9.

Solidago 'Crown of Rays'

Solidago 'Golden Thumb'

Stachys macrantha 'Robusta'

SOLIDAGO Goldenrod

These range in height from a few centimetres/inches to 2.1m/7ft. Some are rather weedy; all are easy to grow in sun or light shade and any reasonable, even poor, soil. Their main fault is flowering too briefly before fading; and some can be invasive or self-seed too freely. Hybrids come in considerable variety, but the best are in the 50-90cm/20-36in height range. Taller ones, with the occasional exception, should be avoided, because they need supporting and/or become weedy. All Z4-9. **'Cloth of Gold'**, dwarf, abundant foliage, wide heads. H40cm/16in, W30cm/1ft. F6-8. **'Crown of Rays'**, similar, but a little taller. H45cm/18in, W30cm/1ft. F7-8. **'Golden Shower'**, attractive splayed plumes. H70cm/28in, W45cm/18in. F7-8. **'Golden Thumb'** (syn. 'Queenie'), neat, small, light-leaved bush, short yellow spikes. H25cm/10in, W25cm/10in. F8-9. **'Goldenmosa'**, light golden-green foliage, rich yellow plumes, neat-growing. H70cm/28in, W45cm/18in. F7-8. **'Goldstrahl'**, tall, with fine golden plumes. H90cm/3ft, W60cm/2ft. F7-8. **'Lemore'**, soft primrose-yellow. H70cm/28in, W45cm/18in. F7-8. **'Mimosa'**, the best tall form, golden yellow. H1.2m/4ft, W60cm/2ft. F8-9. **'Praecox'**, early-flowering and reliable. H90cm/3ft, W60cm/2ft. F6-7.

SPEIRANTHA

S. gardenii. An accommodating little evergreen plant for shade and any good, humus-rich soil, not too dry. It is related to lily of the valley but is not invasive. Its sprays of starry white flowers are scented. H15cm/6in, W15cm/6in. F4-6. Z6-8.

STACHYS

This genus now includes plants formerly listed under *Betonica*. All are easy to grow in mainly sun and any well-drained soil.

S. byzantina (syn. *S. lanata* and *S. olympica*). Lamb's tongue, or lamb's ear, is vigorous but shallow-rooting, with lilac labiate flowers above mats of downy leaves. H45cm/18in, W30cm/1ft. F5-6. Z4-9. Now available in several forms, all good silvery ground cover. Sprays of small pink flowers are secondary, some showier than others. **'Cotton Boll'** (syn. 'Sheila McQueen'), seed heads last over winter. H60cm/2ft, W30cm/1ft. F6-8. Z4-9. **'Primrose Heron'**, new felted leaves which emerge golden in spring and last for many weeks. H45cm/18in, W30cm/1ft. F5-6. Z4-9. **'Silver Carpet'** is a non-flowering, excellent carpeter. H20cm/8in, W30cm/1ft. Z4-9.

S. lanata. See *S. byzantina*.

S. macrantha. A very showy plant with dark green, downy foliage and spikes of deep lilac. H45cm/18in, W23cm/9in. F6-8. Z4-8. **'Robusta'**, stiff growth, crinkly, bright green leaves, deep pink spikes. H40cm/16in, W23cm/9in. F6-8. Z4-8. The form *rosea* is a more decided pink than the species. H45cm/18in, W23cm/9in. F6-8. Z4-8. **'Spicata Rosea'**, brighter than 'Robusta'. H30cm/1ft, W30cm/1ft. F6-8. Z4-8. **'Stricta Alba'**, erect little spikes of pure white above a deep green compact base. H20cm/8in, W20cm/8in. F6-8. Z4-8.

S. olympica. See *S. byzantina*.

STOKESIA Stoke's aster, cornflower aster

S. laevis. Formerly *S. cyanea*, this has leathery, broad, strap-like basal leaves of rich green, and large, solitary, cornflower-like flowers on short stems for many weeks. They are wide-petalled, in shades of blue and, less commonly, white, with fluffy centres. They are ideal for the front of a sunny border with well-drained soil. **'Blue Star'** and the taller **'White Star'** are good. The deepest blue is **'Wyoming'**. All H25-30cm/10-12in, W30cm/1ft. F6-9. Z5-8.

STROBILANTHES

S. atropurpureus. This useful but little-known perennial makes a stout, salvia-like bush with greyish leaves and a long succession of violet-blue hooded flowers. In any good soil and sun it makes a hefty, long-lived, unusual plant. H1.2m/4ft, W60cm/2ft. F7-10. Z7-9.

STYLOPHORUM Celandine poppy, wood poppy

S. diphyllum. This has clusters of rich yellow, poppy-like flowers, followed by silvery seed pods, above very handsome, glaucous foliage, deeply lobed and downy. Roots somewhat fleshy. Light soil and cool conditions. H30cm/1ft, W30cm/1ft. F4-6. Z5-8.

SYMPHYTUM Comfrey

Most comfreys have coarse, hairy leaves and drooping, tubular flowers. They make rapid growth from fleshy, deeply penetrating roots, even small pieces of which will sprout again if left in the ground. Adaptable in sun or shade and not fussy about soil, though cool, moist soil is ideal.
S. caucasicum. This has clustered sprays of sky-blue, bell-shaped flowers, but is best in a wild garden. H60cm/2ft, W60cm/2ft. F5-7. Z4-9.
S. grandiflorum. A lush carpeter, potentially invasive, with white flowers in **'Album'**, lilac-blue in **'Hidcote Blue'**, and rose-pink in **'Hidcote Pink'**. There is also a pretty gold and green variegated form, **'Variegata'** (syn. 'Goldsmith'). All H20cm/8in, W60cm/2ft. F4-6. Z5-9.
S. orientale. This grows almost anywhere except in wet soil, with a show of creamy white flowers. If not long-lived, it self-seeds freely. H40cm/16in, W45cm/18in. F5-7. Z4-9.
S. rubrum. This distinct and probably hybrid plant is slow-growing and needs fertile, moist soil to give of its best. The tubular, dangling, crimson-red flowers last for several weeks. H40cm/16in, W45cm/18in. F5-7. Z4-9.
S. × uplandicum. Also a hybrid, Russian comfrey has large hairy leaves and arching clusters of blue flowers, pink in bud, on

Strobilanthes atropurpureus

winged stems. H1.2m/4ft, W1.2m/4ft. F5-7. Z4-9. **'Variegatum'** has grey-green, white-edged leaves so bright that the flowers are best cut early, for a foliage display lasting many months. Sun or shade where not very dry. H1m/39in, W60cm/2ft. F5-7. Z4-9.

TANACETUM See also under CHRYSANTHEMUM

T. herderi. This makes evergreen bushes of filigree silver-grey leaves with a few yellow button flowers. Any soil and full sun. H20cm/8in, W30cm/1ft. F6-8. Z8-9.

TELLIMA Fringecup

T. grandiflora. This relative of *Heuchera* has the same mounded, evergreen leafage, but the flowers on hairy-stemmed sprays are creamy green. The purplish-leaved **'Rubra'** (syn. 'Purpurea') is more effective. Both flourish in sun or quite dry shade, even in poor soil. They can fill an awkward spot and are good in town gardens. Both H50cm/20in, W50cm/20in. F5-7. Z4-9.

TEUCRIUM Germander

T. chamaedrys. Wall germander makes low, evergreen bushes with shiny, crinkled leaves and short sprays of deep pink flowers. It makes quite a good frontal

Stylophorum diphyllum

Symphytum grandiflorum 'Variegata'

Thalictrum dipterocarpum

subject or edging, easy in sun and well-drained soil. It may be trimmed. H30cm/1ft, W30cm/1ft. F6-7. Z4-9.

T. scordium 'Crispum'. This has crimpled evergreen foliage, a compact habit and greenish cream flowers. H30cm/1ft, W30cm/1ft. F6-8. Z4-9.

THALICTRUM Meadow rue

These wide-ranging plants have a distinctive charm. Some grow robustly up to 2.1m/7ft, while others, 5cm/2in high, are decidedly choice and even difficult. All like deep, fertile soil, with humus for the less robust. Their foliage fully complements the flowers, but none is evergreen.

T. adiantifolium. See *T. minus* 'Adiantifolium'.

T. angustifolium. This has bright green, narrow foliage on tall, erect stems topped by heads of sulphury yellow flowers. H1.8m/6ft, W45cm/18in. F6-8. Z5-9.

T. aquilegiifolium. This clump-forming species makes an early display of columbine-like leaves and fluffy flowers in rounded terminal clusters. The flowers are small, rounded and purplish except in **'Album'**, where they are white. H1m/39in, W30cm/1ft. F5-7. Z5-9. **'Purpureum'** is purple-lilac, but shades and heights vary

considerably. H80-120cm/32-48in, W30cm/1ft. F5-7. Z5-9.

T. delavayi. See *T. dipterocarpum*.

T. diffusiflorum. This charmer refuses to flourish in hot, dry soils and atmospheres. The dainty little bushes with divided foliage and relatively large, pendant lilac-mauve flowers come from a very small rootstock and need much fussing over. H60cm/2ft, W30cm/1ft. F7-9. Z5-9.

T. dipterocarpum (syn. *T. delavayi*). Small mauve-blue flowers with yellow centres appear in great profusion on widely branching stems, apt to tangle. For rich soil. H1.2m/4ft, W45cm/18in. F7-9. Z5-9. The white **album** is not often seen but is very attractive, with lighter green foliage. It comes true from seed. H1m/39in, W45cm/18in. F7-9. Z5-9. **'Hewitt's Double'** prefers shade and needs rich, well-drained soil, but is a choice and beautiful plant. H90cm/3ft, W30cm/1ft. F7-9. Z5-9.

T. flavum. Yellow meadow rue is green-leaved, with yellow flowers in terminal clusters on strong stems. H1.5m/5ft, W45cm/18in. F6-8. Z6-9.

T. glaucum. This is similar to the above, but with bluish foliage. H1.5m/5ft, W45cm/18in. F6-8. Z6-9.

T. minus 'Adiantifolium' (syn. *T. adiantifolium*) produces myriads of small, grey-green maidenhair-type leaves on branching stems, but the flowers lack petals, having only the yellowish stamens. Plants form vigorous clumps. H60-90cm/2-3ft, W30cm/1ft. F6-7. Z3-7.

T. rochenbrunianum. An imposing plant for deep, fertile soil, in sun or part shade. Strong, erect stems carry sprays of glaucous leaves, candelabra fashion, and loose panicles of yellow-centred mauve flowers. H1.8m/6ft, W60cm/2ft. F7-9. Z5-9.

THERMOPSIS False lupin

These are lupin-like in appearance, with palmate leaves and racemes of yellow flowers. Though fairly long-lived plants, the only one I know which can safely be divided is the rather rampant *T. montana*. With the others, seed-raised plants give much the best results. Those with deep roots resent being moved once established. All are sun lovers and easy, given deep, well-drained soil.

T. angustifolia, **T. caroliniana** and **T. mollis** are clump-forming, sun-loving plants with no faults, giving a good display from leafy bushes. All are yellow and are seldom offered. All H80-100cm/32-39in, W60cm/2ft. F5-7. Z3-9.

T. montana. The species usually listed, but it is somewhat invasive, with bright yellow, pea-like flower spikes on smooth stems. H75cm/30in, W60cm/2ft. F6-7. Z3-8.

Thalictrum aquilegiifolium

Thermopsis montana

TIARELLA Foam flower
Dwarf, shade-loving plants allied to *Heuchera*, these are shallow-rooting and like sandy, humus-rich, cool and well-drained soil.

T. collina. A dainty subject for some shade, this mounded leafy plant produces sprays of pink-tinged creamy white flowers. H25cm/10in, W25cm/10in. F5-7. Z3-8.

T. cordifolia. This carpets shady places with pretty evergreen leaves, bronzy in winter, and gives a charming display of small white flowers. Spreads by runners. H15cm/6in, W45cm/18in. F5-6. Z3-8.

T. polyphylla. This forms low green hummocks of lobed, toothed leaves and tiny, pearl-like, white or pink-tinged flowers. H20cm/8in, W30cm/1ft. F5-7. Z5-8.

T. 'Rosalie'. This is a charming hybrid, having abundant greenery with each leaf centrally blotched a bronzy hue. Sprays carry pink flowers over a long period. H23cm/9in, W25cm/10in. F5-7. Z4-8.

T. trifoliata. This makes leafy clumps and produces a long succession of tiny, pearl-white flowers on short, branching stems. It prefers part shade. H20cm/8in, W30cm/1ft. F5-8. Z6-8.

T. wherryi. Well-foliaged, with creamy or pinkish white flowers. Tufty growth. H25cm/10in, W30cm/1ft. F5-7. Z3-8.

TOLMIEA Piggyback plant
T. menziesii. The piggyback plant, so named because baby plants form at the base of its ivy-shaped leaves, is good ground cover for cool shade, though the flowers are small and whitish. Less vigorous but attractive is **'Taff's Gold'**, with golden-green leaves. Both H20cm/8in, W40cm/16in. F5-6. Z6-9.

TOVARA
T. virginiana. This is a clump-forming relation of *Polygonum*, with thin, dun-coloured pokery spikes above a leafy bush. The form well worth growing for its multi-coloured brown, pink and green foliage alone is **'Painter's Palette'**, colourful for months. Likes any fertile soil, not too dry,

Tovara virginiana 'Painter's Palette'

Tradescantia virginiana 'Osprey'

Tricyrtis hirta

and shelter. Both H80cm/32in, W60cm/2ft. F6-10. Z3-9.

TRACHYSTEMON
T. orientalis. This grows vigorously, even invasively, almost anywhere. Short sprays of starry, purplish blue flowers come before the large, coarse, hairy, heart-shaped leaves in spring. Ideal under trees and shrubs. H40cm/16in, W60cm/2ft. F4-5. Z5-9.

TRADESCANTIA
T. virginiana. All those in circulation are cultivars, usually listed under this species. Easy to grow and long-flowering, preferring sun. Bright, three-petalled flowers are carried amid copious narrow foliage. Apt to become untidy with lolling stalks, but still worth growing. A dozen or so named varieties exist to cover the full colour range from white to light and mid-blue, purple and magenta. **'Caerulea Plena'**, double light blue flowers. **'Carmine Glow'**, crimson flowers, neat

habit. **'Iris Prichard'**, white flowers stained azure-blue. **'Isis'**, warm Oxford blue. **'Osprey'**, white, lilac-centred flowers. **'Pauline'**, light lilac-pink flowers. **'Purple Dome'**, rich velvety purple flowers. All approx. H50cm/20in, W50cm/20in. F6-9. Z5-9.

TRICYRTIS Toad lily
A wider range now exists of these charming and distinctive plants. Most have spotted, bell-shaped flowers and grow reliably in good, deep soil, in sun or part shade. As well as those listed, there are several other more recently introduced species.

T. formosana. This makes a clumpy plant, best in sun, with erect leafy stems carrying open heads of mauve, yellow-throated flowers with a hint of brown. H75cm/30in, W45cm/18in. F8-10. Z5-9.

T. hirta. The flowers along the stems are near white, heavily spotted lilac; the leaves are hairy. H90cm/3ft, W60cm/2ft. F8-10. Z4-9.

T. latifolia. This is yellow-flowered, spotted purple. H80cm/32in, W60cm/2ft. F8-10. Z6-9.

T. macropoda. The greenish yellow flowers are purple-spotted and the leaves are broad. H1m/39in, W60cm/2ft. F9-10. Z5-9.

T. stolonifera. A little paler than *T. formosana*, this has quite a vigorous spread. H90cm/3ft, W60cm/2ft. F8-10. Z5-9.

TRILLIUM Wood lily, wake robin
These have great appeal to keen gardeners for the charming display they give in spring. The flowers have three petals and three calyces; three leaves form a ruff-like whorl beneath each flower. All are in nature woodland subjects and respond to good treatment, humus-rich, moist but well-drained soil and light shade. They are generally slow-growing, from fibrous-rooted crowns, and once they settle satisfactorily they can be left alone for years, expanding into clumps having more and more flowers. It takes up to five or six years to produce a good flowering-sized crown from seed, which can take up to a year to germinate, or by division of double forms which do not set seed, so flowering-sized trilliums are quite expensive to buy. However, they are treasures to possess and care for. At Bressingham, for example, I began with nine plants of *T. grandiflorum* 'Flore Pleno' and held back from parting with any for fourteen years. I was then able to let only fifty go, while still slowly increasing reserve stocks.

T. cernuum. The nodding trillium has rather small flowers which nestle amongst the deep green leaves. White petals are recurving, showing a maroon centre. H35cm/14in, W30cm/1ft. F4-5. Z4-9.

T. chloropetalum. This name is sometimes applied to *T. sessile*, but is used here for the form having pale buff-yellow flowers with upstanding petals and grey-marbled leaves. H40cm/16in, W30cm/1ft. F4-6. Z6-9.

T. erectum. This has maroon nodding flowers with recurving petals, but there is also the white **'Album'**. Unpleasant scent. Both H30cm/1ft, W30cm/1ft. F4-6. Z4-9.

T. grandiflorum. The much-loved wake robin has large, pure white flowers, but most prized of all is the sumptuous double white **'Flore Pleno'**, which remains lovely for a long time. So does the rare, single, clear pink **'Roseum'**. All H30cm/1ft, W30cm/1ft. F4-6. Z4-9.

T. ovatum. This, too, has large white flowers a little earlier than *T. grandiflorum*, but the petals are slightly narrower and they fade to a pink shade. H30cm/1ft, W30cm/1ft. F3-5. Z5-9.

T. sessile. The maroon flowers have narrow, slightly twisted petals and stand erectly above the beautifully marbled, grey and dark green leaves. H45cm/18in, W30cm/1ft. F4-6. Z5-9.

TRITONIA See under CROCOSMIA.

TROLLIUS Globe flower
These make a fine display in early summer of mainly globe- or bowl-shaped, buttercup-like flowers. They have dense, hairy roots and thrive in deep, fertile soil which does not dry out, and they prefer sun. Flowers vary from pale primrose to yellow and orange, and are carried above deeply divided leaves. They often flower a second time where suited.

T. chinensis (syn. *T. ledebourii*). **'Golden Queen'** and **'Imperial Orange'** are distinctive in having open, deep yellow flowers with a central tuft of fiery orange, petal-like stamens. Later than most to flower. H90cm/3ft, W45cm/18in. F6-7. Z4-8.

T. × cultorum. These are hybrids between *T. chinensis*, *T. europaeus* and *T. asiaticus*. The following provide a good colour range. All F5-7, Z4-8. **'Alabaster'**, pale primrose, less robust than most. H50cm/20in, W45cm/18in. **'Bressingham Sunshine'**, pure, glistening yellow, vigorous. H75cm/30in, W45cm/18in. **'Canary Bird'**, self-descriptive. H75cm/30in, W45cm/18in. **'Commander in Chief'**, extra-large flowers, warm orange-gold. H70cm/28in, W45cm/18in. **'Earliest of All'**, flowers pure yellow, early and prolific. H70cm/28in, W45cm/18in. **'Fireglobe'**, upstanding, deep orange. H75cm/30in, W45cm/18in. **'Goldquelle'**, large-flowered, mid-yellow. H75cm/30in, W45cm/18in. **'May Gold'**, early-flowering, golden-yellow. H70cm/28in, W45cm/18in. **'Orange Princess'**, deep yellow. H75cm/30in, W45cm/18in.

T. ledebourii. See *T. chinensis*.

T. pumilus. Also dwarf, with bright yellow, open flowers. Suitable for rock gardens. H30cm/1ft, W30cm/1ft. F5-7. Z4-7.

T. stenopetalus. Somewhat similar to the species below, but taller, with stately stems carrying light yellow flowers above attractively divided foliage. H65cm/26in, W45cm/18in. F6-7. Z5-8.

T. yunnanensis. This makes a leafy base of lobed, light green leaves and has large, glistening, yellow flowers, sometimes green-tipped, on wiry, branching stems. H40cm/16in, W23cm/9in. F5-7. Z5-8.

Trillium grandiflorum 'Flore Pleno'

Trillium sessile

Trillium grandiflorum

Trollius × cultorum 'Goldquelle'

Tropaeolum tuberosum

Uvularia grandiflora

TROPAEOLUM

Only one of the three perennial species, all related to the annual nasturtium, is included here because *T. polyphyllum* and *T. speciosum* are climbers.
T. tuberosum. This has roots like small potatoes and growth is much more controllable than the others, but it does, however, need pea sticks or a fence on which to climb. It has dense, palmate, glaucous leaves and orange, scarlet-tipped, spurred flowers. Protect in winter with ample leaf mould as the tubers are not frost-proof. H1.5m/5ft, W90cm/3ft. F8-10. Z8-10.

UROSPERMUM

U. dalechampii. A charming plant for a sunny place and fertile soil, with a long display of light canary-yellow, dandelion-like flowers. The leaves are greyish with toothed edges. Good for a frontal position or rock garden. H40cm/16in, W60cm/2ft. F6-9. Z6-9.

UVULARIA Merrybells

U. grandiflora. This relative of Solomon's seal has arching, leafy stems carrying dangling, butter-yellow, lily-like flowers. One of the spring beauties for humus-rich soil and some shade. *U. perfoliata* is almost identical. H60cm/2ft, W23cm/9in. F4-6. Z5-9.

VALERIANA Valerian

The few species extant are rather coarse-growing and short-lived.
V. phu 'Aurea'. This has golden young foliage in spring only, followed by insignificant small white flowers. The young foliage is valuable in flower arranging. Full sun is needed for the best colour. H90cm/3ft, W45cm/18in. F5-6. Z5-8.

VANCOUVERIA

V. hexandra. A close relative of *Epimedium*, this is the only species available. It has attractive leaves, divided into rounded leaflets, and makes good ground cover in some shade and not-too-dry soil, though it can be slow to start. The flowers, carried in sprays, are starry and white. It keeps closer to the ground than *Epimedium*. H15cm/6in, W23cm/9in. F4-5. Z5-8.

VERATRUM

Given rich, fairly moist soil and some shade, these can remain undisturbed for years to provide lush, deep green foliage and imposing flower spikes. The flowers themselves are small and in subdued shades, but still very distinctive. Veratrums resent disturbance and it is best to begin with young, pot-grown plants.
V. album. The white or false helleborine falls short of white by having a tinge of green to its tiny, bowl-shaped flowers, clustered in dense, spiky heads on sturdy stems. H2.1m/7ft, W60cm/2ft. F7-9. Z4-7.
V. caudatum. This has large, ribbed leaves and brownish flowers. H1.8m/6ft, W60cm/2ft. F7-9. Z4-7.
V. nigrum. A firm favourite with its spectacular pleated leaves and branching spikes of densely packed, maroon-black flowers, followed by attractive seed heads. H2.1m/7ft, W60cm/2ft. F7-9. Z4-8.
V. viride. Freshly green overall, including

Veratrum nigrum

Verbena bonariensis

Verbascum 'Gainsborough'

Veronica gentianoides

the little bell-shaped flowers on dense spikes. H1.5m/5ft, W60cm/2ft. F7-9. Z3-7.

VERBASCUM Mullein
These are all spike-forming and stand out well against more rounded subjects. Perennial types have fleshy roots, need very well-drained soil and sun, and will thrive in quite poor soil. Some of the more colourful hybrids come from the short-lived species *V. phoeniceum*. All Z5-9.

V. chaixii. This has imposing, very erect spikes of yellow, rather small flowers with mauve eyes rising from a leafy base. H1.1m/43in, W45cm/18in. F6-8. **'Album'** has mauve-centred white flowers; both forms are inclined to self-seed in my garden. H1.1m/43in, W45cm/18in. F6-8.

V. densiflorum (syn. *V. thapsiforme*). From a large-leaved base come statuesque spikes of bright yellow. Good ground cover. H1.2m/4ft, W60cm/2ft. F6-8. Z5-9.

V. thapsiforme. See *V. densiflorum*.

Hybrids. There are three very similar **'Cotswold'**s – **'Beauty'**, **'Gem'** and **'Queen'** – all with branching stems and flowers of varying buff-yellow shades, with purple or mauve centres. All H1m/39in, W45cm/18in. F6-8. **'Gainsborough'**, woolly grey foliage, light yellow spikes. H1.1m/43in, W45cm/18in. F6-8. **'Golden Bush'**, distinctive, masses of tiny, clear yellow flowers on compact, twiggy growth, long flowering period. H50cm/20in, W30cm/1ft. F6-9. **'Hartleyi'**, robust, buff-yellow flowers with purple centres. H1.2m/4ft, W45cm/18in. F6-8. **'Mont Blanc'**, the finest white, felty grey leaves, short-lived. H1.1m/43in, W45cm/18in. F6-8. **'Pink Domino'**, deep green leaves, full, deep rosy pink flowers. H1m/39in, W45cm/18in. F6-8.

VERBENA
This genus includes several non-hardy species, but those below are hardy in most districts. All are best in sun and well-drained soil.

V. bonariensis. This has little heads of lavender-blue, fragrant flowers above slender, sparsely leaved, branching stems. Pretty as a group and long-flowering. Not very long-lived, but self-seeds freely.

H1.5m/5ft, W60cm/2ft. F6-9. Z7-10.

V. hastata. Stiffly erect with pointed leaves and a long succession of tiny, violet-purple flowers with purple bracts carried on branching stems. H1.1m/43in, W60cm/2ft. F6-9. Z4-8.

VERNONIA
V. crinita. The best-known of this autumn-flowering genus, it forms large clumps and tall stems carrying terminal clusters of small, purple-crimson, daisy flowers. By no means choice, its chief value is its lateness. Any soil; full sun. H2.1m/7ft, W60cm/2ft. F9-11. Z5-9.

VERONICA Speedwell
This widely varying genus provides some good, reliable perennials as well as alpines. The spike-forming kinds are especially useful and almost all are hardy and easy to grow in mainly sunny positions.

V. austriaca teucrium. See *V. teucrium*.

V. exaltata. Has leafy, fairly erect spikes of clear light blue flowers. Does not need staking. H1.2m/4ft, W30cm/1ft. F7-9. Z4-8.

V. gentianoides. This forms basal, light green, rosette-type foliage with ample spread and pleasing early spikes of light blue. **'Nana'** is half the height of the type and **'Variegata'** has creamy variegated leaves. All H35cm/14in, W35cm/14in. F5-6. Z5-8.

V. longifolia. The true species is not exciting, but good forms exist, with short, full spikes of rich deep blue and even white

Veronica pinnata 'Blue Eyes'

flowers. Rich soil and sun preferred for
'Blue Peter', **'Blue Spire'**, **'Foerster's
Blue'** and the compact, royal blue
subsessilis. Support may be necessary for
taller types. All H50-90cm/20-36in,
W38cm/15in. F7-9. Z4-8.
V. perfoliata. See *Parahebe perfoliata*.
V. pinnata **'Blue Eyes'**. This easy-going
perennial has compact, bushy growth and
bright blue flower spikes. H20cm/8in,
W25cm/10in. F5-7. Z3-8.
V. spicata. This is represented almost
entirely by tussock- or mat-forming,
deciduous cultivars and hybrids, many with
greyish foliage. All Z4-8. **'Barcarolle'**,
deep rosy pink spikes, green foliage.
H30cm/1ft, W45cm/18in. F7-9. **'Blue
Fox'**, lavender-blue spikes, green-leaved.
H30cm/1ft, W45cm/18in. F7-9.
'Heidekind', short, rosy red, not vigorous.
H20cm/8in, W30cm/1ft. F7-9. The form
incana, beautiful spreading mat of silvery,
evergreen leaves, violet-blue spikes,
sometimes sparsely produced. H30cm/1ft,
W30cm/1ft. F6-7. Z3-7. **'Lavender
Charm'**, long, pointed, lavender spikes.
H90cm/3ft, W45cm/18in. F7-9. **'Minuet'**,
soft grey foliage, clear pink flowers.
H30cm/1ft, W30cm/1ft. F7-9. **'Romiley
Purple'**, large, purple flower spikes.
H90cm/3ft, W45cm/18in. F7-9.
'Saraband', violet-blue, free-flowering,
grey foliage. H40cm/16in, W30cm/1ft. F7-9.
'Wendy', freer to flower but its foliage is
less grey. H40cm/16in, W30cm/1ft. F6-7.
V. teucrium (syn. *V. austriaca teucrium*).
Reliable, clump-forming plants with fresh
green, deciduous foliage and profuse
spikes of tiny flowers. All have bright mid-
to deep blue flowers, but vary in height. All
Z5-8. **'Blue Fountain'**, rich blue.
H50cm/20in, W30cm/1ft. F6-8. **'Crater
Lake Blue'**, dark blue. H30cm/1ft,
W30cm/1ft. F6-8. **'Kapitan'**, bright blue.
H25cm/10in, W30cm/1ft. F5-7. **'Shirley
Blue'**, brilliant blue. H20cm/8in,
W30cm/1ft. F6-8.

Veronica teucrium 'Blue Fountain'

Veronica virginica 'Alba'

V. virginica (syn. *Veronicastrum virginicum*).
An erect-growing, long-lived species, with
tapering, thin flower spikes above whorls of
dark green, horizontal leaves. The pale
blue and pale pink are much inferior to the
white and are seldom offered. **'Alba'** is
splendid for sun or part shade, given
reasonably good soil. The spikes stand
boldly above serrated foliage and remain
attractive for several weeks. H1.5m/5ft,
W45cm/18in. F7-9. Z4-8.

VERONICASTRUM
V. virginicum. See *Veronica virginica*.

VINCA Periwinkle
These can be awkward or invasive grown
with border perennials and are too large and
spreading to be classed as alpines. They are
best grown as self-rooting ground cover
between shrubs, and thrive in sun or semi-
shade and any soil.
V. major. The greater periwinkle has
much larger, rounded leaves and is taller
than the lesser periwinkle, *V. minor*. In the
type the blue flowers are sparse, but the
bright foliage makes up for this in the
cream variegated **'Variegata'** (syn.

'Elegantissima'). Both H30cm/1ft, W90cm/3ft. F4-5. Z7-9.

V. minor. The lesser periwinkle, or trailing myrtle in the USA, has many colour variations and flowers more freely than *V. major.* Its leaves are narrow and dark green, except in the single white, **'Alba'.** There are pale and deep blue singles as well as some double-flowered forms. The best light blue is **'Bowles' Variety'**, which makes a bright spring display and is not too rampant. All H15cm/6in, W90cm/3ft. F5-7. Z4-9.

VIOLA

Many are too low-growing for perennial beds and borders, but others can play an important role in frontal groups, or for underplanting trees and shrubs. Grow in fertile soil, in sun or part shade.

V. cornuta and its variants and hybrids certainly qualify. The type has masses of small, violet-purple flowers for many weeks, and clumps of rich green leaves making effective ground cover. H15-25cm/6-10in, W30cm/1ft. F5-7. Z5-8. **'Alba'** has white flowers. H15cm/6in, W30cm/1ft. F4-7. Z5-8.

V. cucullata. The marsh violet has white flowers on erect stems and tolerates damp soil. H8-15cm/3-6in, W15cm/6in. F4-5. Z4-9. **'Freckles'.** This hybrid has palest blue flowers with purple spots. H15cm/6in, W15cm/6in. F4-5. Z4-9.

V. labradorica **'Purpurea'.** See under Alpines.

V. septentrionalis. Similar to *V. cucullata.* Mat-forming and long-lived; white flowers. H20cm/8in, W15cm/6in. F4-5. Z4-8.

Hybrids. The following hybrids, all Z5-7, are garden-worthy. **'Ardross Gem'**, light blue flowers, flushed with gold. H13cm/5in, W30cm/1ft. F4-7. **'Boughton Blue'**, charming ethereal blue. H15cm/6in, W30cm/1ft. F4-7. **'Bullion'**, the most reliable pure yellow. H15cm/6in, W30cm/1ft. F5-8. **'Clementina'**, large violet flowers, vigorous. H15cm/6in, W30cm/1ft. F4-9. **'Irish Molly'**, softly suffused colours. H15cm/6in, W30cm/1ft. F5-8. **'Jackanapes'**, yellow and maroon. H15cm/6in, W30cm/1ft. F5-8. **'Maggie Mott'**, light blue and scented. H13cm/5in, W30cm/1ft. F5-8. **'Norah Leigh'**, mid-blue. H13cm/5in, W30cm/1ft. F4-7.

WALDSTEINIA

W. ternata. Good ground cover in sun or shade, this has strawberry-like, lobed evergreen leaves and a brief splash of bright yellow flowers. H10cm/4in, W30cm/1ft. F4-5. Z4-8.

YUCCA

These evergreen plants are best as isolated specimens to display their sword-like foliage to advantage. They are generally hardy and long-lived, though some flower irregularly. Spectacular ivory-white or pink-tinged, lily-like flowers on stiff spikes. Full sun and well-drained soil are essential.

Y. filamentosa. The most reliable species, Adam's needle is almost stemless and has greyish foliage with hair-like fibres along the edges. There are a few variations, all with basically ivory-white, bell-shaped flowers most years. H1.5m/5ft, W1.5m/5ft. F7-8. Z5-10. **'Bright Edge'** and **'Variegata'** have brightly variegated leaves and are worth a little cosseting in cold districts, but are less spectacular in flower. Both H90cm/3ft, W60cm/2ft. F7-8. Z5-9.

Y. flaccida. Notable for flowering most seasons, it is similar to the above, but with narrower, less rigid leaves. H1.5m/5ft, W1.5m/5ft. F7-8. Z5-10.

Y. gloriosa. The Spanish dagger grows massively and lacks nothing in spectacle – when it flowers. This is spasmodic in my garden but it flowers more frequently than the reputed seven-year intervals. It grows quite large, and it is necessary to avoid contact with its dagger-tipped leaves. Definitely a plant best grown in isolation! H2.1-3m/7-10ft, W1.5m/5ft. F8-9. Z7-10.

Y. recurvifolia. Also shy to flower, but a clump of its arching, narrow leaves inevitably becomes a focal point. H2.1-2.4m/7-8ft, W1.5m/5ft. F8-9. Z5-10.

ZANTEDESCHIA Arum lily, calla lily

Z. aethiopica. This is hardy given ample covering from mid-autumn to mid-spring in cold districts. **'Crowborough'** is now widely accepted as the most reliable, with handsome white spathes above large, shiny green leaves. Although moisture-loving and able to grow in mud in 15-30cm/6-12in deep water, it is surprisingly adaptable to any fertile soil. One or two other forms exist, including **'Green Goddess'**, with greenish flower spathes scarcely different in colour from the lush foliage, and **'Little Gem'**, only half the height. H1.2m/4ft, W60cm/2ft. F7-9. Z8-10.

ZAUSCHNERIA

A warm spot and light soil are essential for these plants, which make a bright late display.

Z. californica **'Glasnevin'.** This has green leaves and intensely red flowers. H35cm/14in, W35cm/14in. F8-10. Z8-10.

Z. canescens. This has twiggy summer growth, small grey leaves and brilliant, trumpet-shaped, orange-scarlet flowers. H35cm/14in, W35cm/14in. F8-10. Z8-10.

ZIGADENUS

The species listed are demurely charming and prefer light soil in a fairly sunny place.

Z. elegans. This has grassy leaves and short sheaves of greenish white, starry flowers. H50cm/20in, W20cm/8in. F7-9. Z5-9.

Z. muscitoxicus. This newcomer is quite promising, with profuse greenish white flowers on branching stems. H50cm/20in, W20cm/8in. F7-9. Z5-9.

Z. nutallii. Somewhat similar to *Z. elegans* but with broader leaves. H50cm/20in, W20cm/8in. F7-9. Z5-9.

Yucca gloriosa

Zigadenus elegans

Colourful Island Bed of Sun-loving Perennials

The prime colour period for this bed of first-rate perennials is late midsummer, but both foliage and flowers will also provide interest earlier and later than this. The *Dicentra*, for instance, can be expected to flower in April or early May, and the *Iris* and *Miscanthus* will be attractive from spring until autumn. Balance of colour is important, too, with the foliage of individual groups contrasting with the brightness of the flowers: the soft, green background provided by the *Miscanthus* sets off the stronger colours of the other plants, particularly the brilliant scarlet *Crocosmia*. The true island bed would have dwarf plants around the outside, short ones in the front and taller plants towards the middle. As shown here, this border could also be planted against a hedge or a wall. The peak season of interest is mid- to late summer.

1 *Dicentra* 'Luxuriant' (× 5)
2 *Iris pallida* 'Argentea' (× 5)
3 *Phlox paniculata* 'Sandringham' (× 5)
4 *Hemerocallis* 'Hyperion' (× 5)
5 *Miscanthus sinensis* 'Gracillimus' (× 3)
6 *Crocosmia* 'Lucifer' (× 5)
7 *Scabiosa caucasica* 'Clive Greaves' (× 5)
8 *Artemisia canescens* (× 5)

Area required:
approx. 7 sq. m/7 sq. yd

PERENNIALS FOR A SHADED CORNER

These flowering and foliage perennials are ideal for light shade where not too dry. This could be under trees, or against a hedge or wall, perhaps where the sun reaches it for only part of the day. All prefer some shade and reasonable moisture during the growing season, and will reward the gardener with an early display of colour, mainly in late spring, although many of the plants will continue to provide foliage interest all summer. The *Rodgersia* has both attractive foliage early in the season and heads of pink flowers in mid- to late summer, and may perhaps be joined by the reblooming × *Heucherella*, as long as conditions are suitable. Foliage interest is continued by the *Hosta* and *Pulmonaria*. The peak period of interest is mid-spring to midsummer.

1 × *Heucherella* 'Bridget Bloom' (× 5)
2 *Brunnera macrophylla* 'Hadspen Cream' (× 3)
3 *Dicentra spectabilis* 'Alba' (× 3)
4 *Rodgersia pinnata* 'Superba' (× 3)
5 *Euphorbia polychroma* (× 5)
6 *Pulmonaria saccharata* 'Highdown' (× 3)
7 *Hosta* 'Blue Moon' (× 5)

Area required:
approx. 5 sq. m/5 sq. yd

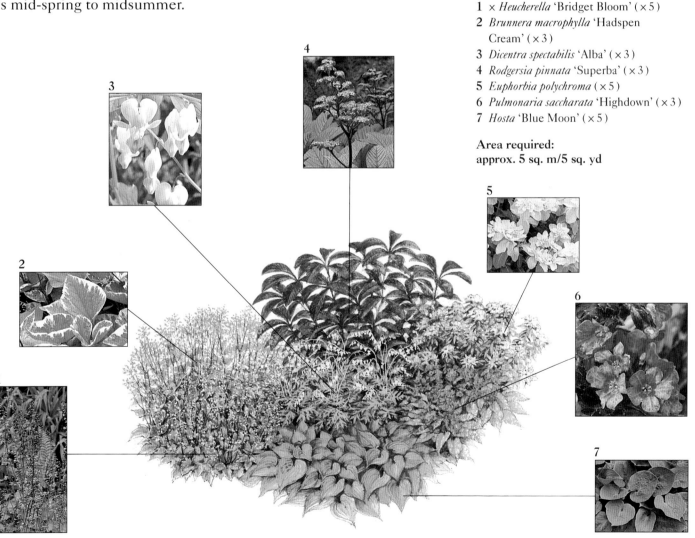

DWARF PERENNIALS FOR A LONG SEASON OF INTEREST

Here is a selection of excellent perennials which can be relied upon to give a long period of flower and attractive foliage. The grouping could be used as an island bed or a frontal border, the plants succeeding best in a sunny position in any reasonable soil that is not too dry. The tallest plant is an ornamental grass, *Deschampsia*, the heads of which turn from green to golden-brown as the brighter colours of the surrounding plants become more prominent in summer. A striking colour combination can be achieved with the purple leaves of the *Heuchera* and the icy blue *Festuca*, set against the summer-long magenta flowers of the *Geranium*. The latter will still be in flower when the *Liriope* is at its best in mid-autumn. The peak interest period is midsummer to mid-autumn.

1 *Geranium* 'Russell Prichard' (× 5)
2 *Festuca glauca* (× 5)
3 *Heuchera micrantha* 'Palace Purple' (× 7)
4 *Hemerocallis* 'Stella D'Oro' (× 7)
5 *Deschampsia caespitosa* 'Golden Dew' (× 5)
6 *Aster thomsonii* 'Nanus' (× 7)
7 *Polygonum affine* 'Dimity' (× 5)
8 *Liriope muscari* (× 7)

**Area required:
approx. 9 sq. m/9 sq. yd**

PERENNIALS FOR A MOISTURE BED

The rich mixture of flower colour and form with foliage colour, form and texture makes this grouping particularly attractive. Ideally, for all plants to do their best, a fertile soil in which moisture can be retained throughout the summer is needed. Although not a bog garden, this bed could be planted alongside a lake or pond, either in full sun or part shade. With perennials it is important to achieve a balance of height and a variety of foliage and flower types. Here spikes of *Ligularia*, *Hosta* and *Astilbe* contrast with the broader and flatter heads of the other flowers. The *Miscanthus* separates and therefore emphasizes the brighter colours of the flowers surrounding it, where a little 'seasonal licence' has been taken with regard to their flowering periods. The peak season of interest is mid- to late summer.

1 *Hosta ventricosa* 'Variegata' (× 5)
2 *Rudbeckia* 'Goldsturm' (× 5)
3 *Filipendula purpurea* (× 7)
4 *Miscanthus sinensis* 'Variegatus' (× 1)
5 *Iris sibirica* 'White Swirl' (× 5)
6 *Ligularia przewalskii* 'The Rocket' (× 5)
7 *Astilbe* 'Bressingham Beauty' (× 7)
8 *Tradescantia virginiana* 'Isis' (× 7)

Area required:
approx. 8 sq. m/8 sq. yd

GRASSES & HARDY FERNS

Grasses do not have colourful flowers, but many possess beautiful foliage which enlivens and contrasts with other perennials. Grasses can be brightly variegated, substantial enough to act as specimen plants, tall enough to act as a screen, or perfect for dwarf edging, and a thoughtful selection enhances the general decorative effect of perennials and shrubs.

In general, grasses are easy to grow and are adaptable to a wide variety of soils. The vast majority of grasses prefer an open position, well-drained soil and sun. Most kinds respond to division and the safest time for this is in spring as new growth begins.

Scarcely a garden exists in which some ferns would be out of place. The belief that they all need shade and moisture is widely held, but inaccurate. The majority do best in some shade, but as with many other perennials, the shade/moisture factor is variable. Some with a shade preference grow quite well in more open situations if moisture is present, and some moisture lovers do better in shade if not in competition with established tree or shrub roots.

For the more discerning gardener, ferns, with their cool, elegant beauty, have a unique value as decorative plants. Some prefer an open situation and tolerate quite dry soil once established. Some are herbaceous, dying down in winter; others are evergreen. Many small species with fronds only a few centimetres/inches long have a mat-forming or creeping habit, while others form, in time, large clumps with fronds up to 1.2m/4ft high. The latter need careful siting, for they are the most difficult to move or divide. With virtually all ferns, moving or dividing is best done after new spring growth has begun.

Most ferns prefer a good, open soil and dislike heavy clay. A mixture of peat, or finely composted bark, and coarse sand is the best soil conditioner, and peat or leaf mould where soil is thin, gravelly or chalky. It is important to give ferns a good start because, once established, most can remain undisturbed for years, building up fertility from decayed fronds.

A mixed bed of ornamental grasses and colourful, summer-flowering perennials, mostly of South African origin, including *Crocosmia*, *Agapanthus* and *Kniphofia*. The grasses vary from low-growing types, such as *Hakonechloa*, at the front to taller *Miscanthus* varieties at the back

GRASSES DIRECTORY

The value of grasses is slowly becoming recognized and a few specialists are currently introducing new species and cultivars. The grasses listed here are all reliable garden-worthy plants. Some sedges are also included.

Key

H: Approximate height
W: Approximate width
F: Months in flower
Z: Relevant hardiness zone(s)

ACORUS

A. gramineus. This looks like a grass but belongs to the *Araceae* family. Its fan-like evergreen blades appear on slow-spreading rhizomes. The golden-leaved 'Ogon', a recent arrival from Japan and possibly a different species, has 1.5cm/¹/2in wide blades, 15cm/6in long, of a bright gold, barely tinted green. It retains its colour all year round. Not to be compared with this, but more interesting than the plain-leaved species, is the variegated form 'Variegatus'. All prefer damp soil. All H20cm/8in, W15cm/6in. Z4-10.

AGROPYRON

A. pubiflorum (syn. *A. magellanicum*). Silvery blue, needle-like blades make this clump-forming species outstanding. It prefers sun and good drainage. H60cm/2ft, W60cm/2ft. Z5-8.

ANDROPOGON

A. scoparius. This is upright, shapely and evergreen, with narrow blades of a bluish coppery hue. Slow-growing, it prefers ligh soil and full sun. H60cm/2ft, W60cm/2ft. Z5-8.

ARUNDO Giant reed

A. donax. This is a giant among grasses, having strong stems with floppy, wide, somewhat sheathed glaucous leaves. It does not flower in cool temperate climates but is still worthwhile where space allows, in any reasonable or moist soil and sun. The creamy white striped variegated form 'Versicolor' (syn. 'Variegata') is less vigorous and decidedly tender. Both up to H3m/10ft, W1.2m/4ft. Z7-10.

AVENA Blue oat grass

A. candida. A much nicer name than *Helictotrichon sempervirens*, now said to be correct. This is a clumpy evergreen grass with bluish, narrow blades and arching, straw-coloured plumes. H80cm/32in, W60cm/2ft. F5-7. Z4-9.

BOUTELOUA Mosquito grass

B. gracilis (syn. *B. oligostachya*). This has short sprays of curious, brownish flower

Agropyron pubiflorum

spikes, at right angles to the stems, above a tufty, semi-evergreen, deep green base. H25cm/10in, W20cm/8in. F6-8. Z5-9.

BRIZA Common quaking grass

B. media. The common name comes from the way the tiny, greenish purple, locket-like flowers nod in a breeze, but the tuft-forming evergreen foliage is dull. The flowers are popular for drying. H90cm/3ft, W30cm/1ft. F6-8. Z5-9.

CALAMAGROSTIS

C. × acutiflora. 'Karl Foerster'. This is an attractive hybrid with an erect habit, its foliage a rich green followed by plum-brown spikes which remain until spring growth is renewed. H1.3m/51in, W60cm/2ft. F7-8. Z5-9.

CAREX Sedge

Though members of the *Cyperaceae* family, these are grass-like in appearance and are identifiable by their stems, which are triangular in section.
C. atrata. Evergreen and tolerant of dry conditions in sun or shade, this has erect, deep green blades and dangling brownish tassles. H70cm/28in, W60cm/2ft. F7-8. Z6-9.
C. buchananii. The leatherleaf sedge is evergreen, with erect tufts of unusual, coppery brown, thin, needly blades, reddish towards the base. H60cm/2ft, W20cm/8in. Z6-9.
C. comans. This has a more mounded, clumpy habit. The thin, dense growth has a decidedly brownish hue, held all year

Acorus gramineus 'Ogon'

round. Flowers are not conspicuous. H50cm/20in, W50cm/20in. F6-8. Z6-9.

C. elata (syn. *C. stricta*). **'Aurea'**, sometimes listed as Bowles' golden sedge, has bright leaves for most of the year, turning greenish in late summer, but is not fully reliable. Best in fairly moist soil and sun. H50cm/20in, W45cm/18in. F6-8. Z5-9.

C. morrowii (syn. *C. oshimensis*). The Japanese sedge has dark evergreen foliage in long-lived clumps, but rarely flowers. **'Evergold'** is one of the brightest year-round plants, forming large clumps in which flowers would be superfluous. Both H25cm/10in, W25cm/10in. Z7-9.

C. oshimensis. See *C. morrowii*.

C. pilulifera **'Tinney's Gold'** has low tussocks of year-round variegation, gold and green. H15cm/6in, W10cm/4in. Z7-9.

C. stricta. See *C. elata*.

CORTADERIA Pampas grass

This popular ornamental grass is almost perfect as a specimen and should never be in a mixed bed or border. Evergreen in mild climates, but dies back to ground level in cold ones; the plumes are excellent for drying.

C. selloana. There are several variations, from 1.2m/4ft to 3m/10ft high, making large clumps and silvery white plumes in autumn. **'Gold Band'** has narrow, golden-green striped leaves and silvery plumes. H1.5m/5ft, W90cm/3ft. F9-10. Z8-10. **'Pumila'** is compact and free-flowering. H1.2m/4ft, W90cm/3ft. F9-11. Z7-10. **'Silver Comet'** has leaves margined white and a good display of flowers, but needs a warm, sheltered spot. H1.2m/4ft, W90cm/3ft. F9-10. Z8-10. The finely plumed, free-flowering **'Sunningdale Silver'** is strong-stemmed. H1.8-2.1m/6-7ft, W1.8m/6ft. F9-11. Z7-10.

DESCHAMPSIA Tufted hair grass

D. caespitosa. This forms large tufts of narrow, deep green leaves and sheaves of very graceful spikes, valuable for cutting. A British grass of real garden merit for a sunny spot and any but dry soils. Self-seeds freely. **'Bronze Veil'** (syn. 'Bronzeschleier') is

Cortaderia selloana 'Gold Band'

Cortaderia selloana 'Pumila'

Deschampsia caespitosa 'Golden Dew'

Carex morrowii 'Evergold'

Deschampsia caespitosa 'Bronze Veil'

even more effective. Two recently introduced German variations include **'Gold Veil'** (syn. 'Goldschleier') and **'Golden Dew'** (syn. 'Goldtau'), which both make strong, clumpy, evergreen growth. 'Gold Veil' has plumes of green stems and flowers which turn a warm golden-yellow. H90cm/3ft, W90cm/3ft. F6-8. Z4-9. 'Golden Dew' has fountains of green stems and flowers which mature to a rich golden-brown. Good, compact form. H70cm/28in, W50cm/20in. F6-9. Z4-9.

D. flexuosa. Somewhat similar to the above species, but less tall. Tolerates light shade. H70cm/28in, W70cm/28in. F6-8. Z4-9.

FESTUCA Fescue

F. glauca. Blue fescue makes neat, bluish evergreen tufts, useful as edging, ground cover or frontal groups. Easy to grow in any sunny position. There are several selections available, but none is strikingly different. Flowers are insignificant. H25cm/10in, W25cm/10in. F6-7. Z4-8.

F. scoparia. This has small grey-buff flowers and makes very green cushions. H20cm/8in, W20cm/8in. F6-7. Z4-8.

GLYCERIA Manna grass

G. aquatica (syn. *G. maxima*). This has bright, seasonal, bladed leaves but is invasive in moist or good soil. **'Variegata'**, with green, white and yellow variegated leaves, flushed pink in spring, is the showiest form. Both H60cm/2ft, W45cm/18in. F6-7. Z5-9.

Festuca glauca

Hakonechloa macra 'Alboaurea'

HAKONECHLOA

H. macra 'Alboaurea'. A long name for one of the best of all dwarf grasses. Although not evergreen, spring brings a lovely show of green- and yellow-striped leaves, gradually ageing to ruddy brown and effective until late autumn. Plants spread slowly, appreciating good soil and a sunny place. H25cm/10in, W38cm/15in. Z7-9.

HELICTOTRICHON

H. sempervirens. See *Avena candida*.

HOLCUS Creeping soft grass

H. mollis 'Variegatus'. This has soft, deciduous foliage with pale buff variegations. Mat-forming, it is good for ground cover or edging. H30cm/1ft, W30cm/1ft. Z5-9.

KOELERIA

K. glauca. This compact species has slightly purplish, evergreen leaves, thin stems and greeny buff pokers. H30cm/1ft, W50cm/20in. F6-8. Z5-9.

LUZULA Woodrush

L. nivea. Snowy woodrush is a shade-loving, broad-leaved, evergreen grass with showy, dense heads of near white flowers.

H45cm/18in, W45cm/18in. F5-6. Z4-9.
L. sylvatica. Greater woodrush has bright green leaves, a slow-spreading, tufted habit, and open heads of greenish flowers. Good ground cover for dry shade. 'Marginata' (syn. 'Aureomarginata') has white leaf margins. Both H30cm/1ft, W30cm/1ft. F5-6. Z5-9.

MILIUM

M. effusum 'Aureum'. The so-called Bowles' golden grass is a short-lived, arching, golden-leaved perennial. It seeds itself freely and breeds true. Flowers are of no value. Best in light shade and rich, moist soil. H45cm/18in, W30cm/1ft. Z5-8.

MISCANTHUS Silver grass

This genus includes some very good grasses, all fairly tall and clump-forming, with an annual crop of strong stems with bladed leaves. They are good as windbreaks and for specimen planting. Though none is evergreen, the foliage remains attractive over winter, and is then cut down in spring. They flower best in hot summers. Some good selections have been introduced, mainly raised by Ernst Pagels in northern Germany, which flower regularly in cooler, northerly climates. A number are quite dwarf and so are excellent for the smaller garden.

M. sacchariflorus. Much like a bamboo in appearance with a wealth of long blades, Amur silver grass makes an effective screen from early summer until the following early spring. Does not flower in Britain. 'Variegatus' has white-striped leaves. Both H3m/10ft, W90cm/3ft. F9-10. Z5-10.
M. sinensis. Formerly called *Eulalia*, this has ample foliage, and green tassled flower sprays. H1.8m/6ft, W90cm/3ft. F7-9. Z5-10. It has many variations, reliable for erect growth and non-invasive habits. All Z5-10. 'Gracillimus' has elegant, narrow leaves and a shapely habit. H1.5m/5ft, W45cm/18in. F7-9. 'Purpureus' is more effective, with purplish leaves and profuse flowers. H1.5m/5ft, W90cm/3ft. F8-9. 'Silver Feather' is outstanding for the splendid show of pinkish white arching sprays of flowers which remain effective into winter. The leaves are long and the whole plant majestic. H2.1m/7ft, W90cm/3ft. F7-9. 'Strictus' has a stiff, columnar habit and green leaves. H90cm/3ft, W50-60cm/20-24in. 'Variegatus' is stately and brightly variegated with vertical white stripes. H1.5m/5ft, W90cm/3ft. 'Zebrinus', or zebra grass, is distinctive for having lateral bands of gold across green leaves. H1.5m/5ft, W90cm/3ft. 'Zebrinus Strictus' is similar, but of more rigid growth. H1.5m/5ft, W90cm/3ft. The last four seldom flower in northern temperate regions.

Miscanthus sinensis 'Variegatus'

Miscanthus sinensis 'Zebrinus'

MOLINIA Moor grass

M. altissima. Strong-growing and free-flowering, this has good autumn colour as stems fade. The terminal flower sprays are green, turning brown in autumn. H1.5m/5ft, W60cm/2ft. F8-10. Z5-9.

M. caerulea. Purple moor grass, a native of Britain, is for damp, acid soils. **'Moorhexe'** is a good green-leaved selection. H40cm/16in, W40cm/16in. F8-9. Z5-9. For garden use, however, **'Variegata'** is best. It makes stout clumps of soft, deciduous, creamy yellow-green leaves and long-lasting, charming, small, purplish buff flowers. Prefers a light, deep soil, and sun. H60cm/2ft, W60cm/2ft. F7-10. Z5-9.

PANICUM Switch grass

P. virgatum **'Strictum'**. This vigorous cultivar has erect, narrow, brown-tinted foliage, yellow in autumn, and profuse, feathery flowers. H1.5m/5ft, W90cm/3ft. F8-9. Z5-9.

PENNISETUM

These form large, deciduous tussocks, reliably long-lived, but not all produce their airy, feathery flowers freely. The grey-green leaves are long, arching and narrow. Good specimen plants; full sun required.

P. alopecuroides (syn. *P. compressum*). Chinese pennisetum, or rose fountain grass, is shy to flower but **'Hameln'**, a German variety, and **'Woodside'** are much freer, and their flowers are attractive well into winter. **'Viridescens'** has brighter green foliage. All H90cm/3ft, W60cm/2ft. F8-10. Z5-10.

P. compressum. See *P. alopecuroides*.

P. orientale. This has hairy blades on modest tufty growth. Its bottlebrush, silvery pink flowers are long-lasting and reliable. H45cm/18in, W30cm/1ft. F7-9. Z6-9.

P. villosum. Feathertop would be first-class if it were hardier, but it will not survive hard frosts. Tuft-forming, it produces panicles of near white bottlebrushes, with long, bearded bristles. It can also be grown as a half-hardy annual. H60cm/2ft, W45cm/18in. F8-10. Z8-10.

PHALARIS Gardener's garters

P. arundinacea **'Picta'**. This variegated-leaved grass, its creamy green and white stripes brightest in spring, should be planted only where its invasive habit can do no harm. H90cm/3ft, W60cm/2ft. Z4-9.

PHLEUM

P. phleoides. This has greenish brown pokers above semi-evergreen, tufty growth. H60cm/2ft, W30cm/1ft. F7-8. Z7-10.

SCIRPUS

S. lacustris. A round-stemmed rush which is aquatic in nature, thriving in up to 15cm/6in of water, but the sub-species

Molinia caerulea 'Variegata'

Pennisetum orientale

Stipa gigantea

tabernaemontani **'Zebrinus'**, with its lateral gold stripes, also grows in damp soil. It seldom flowers and spreads where suited. Both H90cm/3ft, W50cm/20in. Z4-9.

SPARTINA

S. pectinata. Cord grass has long, deciduous, ribbon-like, arching blades and greeny purple flowers. The variegated **'Aureo Marginata'** (syn. 'Aureo Variegata') has marginal yellow stripes. Vigorous, but controllable. Good by water. Both H1.8m/6ft, W90cm/3ft. F8-10. Z5-9.

STIPA Feather grass, needle grass

The following are attractive, with feathery flowers and narrow foliage, but are unreliable as perennials.

S. barbata. This is compact, with arching, fine stems ending in long, pale beige plumes. H60cm/2ft, W45cm/18in. F7-8. Z7-9.

S. calamagrostis. A vigorously clump-forming species which flowers freely with dense buff-white plumes 10-15cm/4-6in long. These tend to arch over and, being heavy, need supporting for best effect. H1.2m/4ft, W60cm/2ft. F7-9. Z5-10.

S. gigantea. This makes imposing specimen clumps, with somewhat silvery, thin blades up to about 60cm/2ft long. The tall stems remain erect, carrying oat-like flowers for many weeks. H1.8-2.1m/6-7ft, W60-75cm/24-30in. F6-8. Z5-10.

S. pennata. Common feather grass has silvery, long-awled flowers, ideal for drying. H90cm/3ft, W45cm/18in. F7-8. Z7-9.

S. tenuifolia. A beautiful ornamental grass forming a dense clump topped in midsummer by fluffy plumes which turn from beige to white, arching and flowing with every breeze. H60cm/2ft, W45cm/18in. F6-9. Z7-10.

Stipa calamagrostis

HARDY FERNS DIRECTORY

This lists examples of the main species of hardy ferns. Would-be collectors, however, will find that most have cultivars with subtle variations, detectable perhaps only on a second glance and obtainable solely from specialist sources.

Key
H: Approximate height
W: Approximate width
Z: Relevant hardiness zone(s)

ADIANTUM Maidenhair fern
These are native to various parts of the world. The following are deciduous, spreading below ground with new growth appearing in spring and lasting until winter. Humus-rich soil and some shade preferred.
A. pedatum. The American or northern maidenhair has branching fronds made up of many toothed lobes on slender black stems. H45cm/18in, W30cm/1ft. Z3-8. The form *aleuticum* (more correctly, *A. p. subpumilum*) is more compact, the fronds shorter and closer together, with glaucous green foliage often retained until midwinter. H15cm/6in, W30cm/1ft. Z3-8.

Adiantum pedatum

Adiantum venustum

'Minus' is one of the best dwarf forms, with overlapping, finely dissected fronds. H15cm/6in, W30cm/1ft. Z3-8.
A. venustum. This makes a carpet of delicate greenery from shallow roots which spread quickly in light, humus-rich soil and shade. The little leaves turn brown as winter comes, and remain until spring. Avoid deep planting. H15-20cm/6-8in, W15-23cm/6-9in. Z4-8.

ASPLENIUM
This genus of evergreen lime lovers now includes what were formerly *Phyllitis* and *Scolopendrium*.
A. scolopendrium. The hart's tongue, a British native, is well known for its long, leathery leaves. Given shade it is easy to grow, even in crevices or on walls. H up to 35cm/14in, W40cm/16in. Z4-8. 'Cristatum' has curiously dissected crests on the light green fronds. H35cm/14in, W40cm/16in. Z4-8. 'Kaye's Variety' has broad, almost oval fronds, toothed and ending in intricate crests. H30cm/1ft, W30cm/1ft. Z4-8. 'Undulatum' has narrow fronds with attractive wavy edges. H30-40cm/12-16in, W30-45cm/12-18in. Z4-8.

Asplenium scolopendrium 'Undulatum'

A. trichomanes. The maidenhair spleenwort varies, but usually has dark green, semi-evergreen, deeply cut fronds, and makes a good rock plant, ideally in cool crevices. H15cm/6in, W15cm/6in. Z3-8.
A. viride. This is another excellent rock plant, vivid green all year round. H8-13cm/3-5in, W25cm/10in. Z3-8.

ATHYRIUM
A. filix-femina. The lady fern has lacy, light green, deciduous fronds. Damp shade is best. H60-100cm/24-39in, W60cm/2ft. Z4-9. There are many variations. 'Minutum' (syn. 'Minimum', 'Minutissimum') is smaller but still makes large clumps, and can grow taller in shade and rich soil. Average H20cm/8in, W20cm/8in. Z4-9. 'Plumosum' has elegant, leathery, golden-green fronds. H90cm/3ft, W60cm/2ft. Z4-9. 'Regale' has crested tips. H90cm/3ft, W60cm/2ft. Z4-9. 'Vernoniae' has distinctive, crispy, triangular fronds and strong growth. H up to 1m/39in, W60cm/2ft. Z4-9. 'Victoriae' is a noble, strong-growing, crested form with narrow, lanceolate fronds having a criss-crossed, lattice-like pattern. It makes a splendid specimen plant. H up to 90cm/3ft, W60cm/2ft. Z4-9.
A. nipponicum 'Pictum' (syn. 'Metallicum'). Formerly named after the infamous Goering, the Japanese fern is low-spreading, with dark red, arching stems and silvery fronds. It needs shelter. The all-green type is also worthy. H30-60cm/1-2ft, W45cm/18in. Z3-8.

BLECHNUM Hard fern
Most have a moderately spreading habit and deep green, fairly narrow, leathery, evergreen fronds. They dislike lime, but tolerate a dry atmosphere.
B. penna-marina. This forms a dense, low carpet of fronds with deeply serrated edges. H15cm/6in, W30cm/1ft. Z3-8. The dwarf form 'Cristatum', 5cm/2in high, is ideal with alpines.
B. spicant. The common hard fern, or deer fern, produces two types of pinnate frond: arching, spreading, sterile ones and erect, spore-bearing, deciduous ones. A clump-forming species for humus-rich soil. H30-60cm/1-2ft, W45cm/18in. Z4-8.
B. tabulare. This shade lover is reliably hardy only in mild districts. Where suited, it forms a spreading mass of leathery fronds, each plant composed of outer, sterile, lance-shaped fronds and inner, brownish, fringed, fertile fronds. H up to 90cm/3ft, W30-60cm/1-2ft. Z7-9.

CYSTOPTERIS Bladder fern
C. bulbifera. The berry, or bulbil, bladder fern forms hummocks of feathery, densely packed, fresh green, deciduous fronds,

bearing bulbils along the edges. Ideal for limy soil and damp rockeries. H15-30cm/6-12in, W20-40cm/8-16in. Z3-7.

DRYOPTERIS Buckler fern
This genus is widely variable but most species are long-lived, vigorous, hardy and deciduous, and form stout clumps which rise above soil level.

D. borreri (syn. *D. affinis* and *D. pseudomas*). **'Crispa'** is a select form with arching, deep green, crisped fronds. The form *cristata* **'The King'**, a selection of the golden-scaled male fern, has evenly crested, arching fronds from a symmetrical central crown. Tolerates dry soil. Both H80-90cm/32-36in, W80-90cm/32-36in. Z4-8.

D. erythrosora. The Japanese shield fern has unusual pink- or bronze-tinged young fronds that mature to light green. Deciduous, but the leaves remain until midwinter. Provide shade and humus-rich soil. H60cm/2ft, W30cm/1ft. Z5-9.

D. filix-mas. The male fern is common, and adaptable to almost any but parched places. H90cm/ 3ft, W90cm/3ft. Z4-8. There are many varieties. **'Crispa Cristata'** has arching, crisp, bright green, crested fronds. H30cm/1ft, W30cm/1ft. Z4-8. **'Linearis'** has tall, finely divided fronds, with a pleasing airiness. H75cm/30in, W38cm/15in. Z4-8. **'Uniformis'** makes dense, bright greenery and good ground cover. H30cm/1ft, W30cm/1ft. Z4-8.

HYPOLEPIS
H. millefolia. The thousand-leaved fern creeps inoffensively, creating masses of evergreen, lacy, bracken-like greenery. It will tolerate sun. H25cm/10in, W60cm/2ft. Z7-9.

MATTEUCCIA Ostrich fern, shuttlecock fern
M. struthiopteris. This is quite spectacular, with large, shapely fronds forming shuttlecock-like rosettes from stout stocks and spreading runners which are likely to colonize in rich, moist soil. Shade not vital. H1m/39in, W60-90cm/2-3ft. Z2-8.

ONOCLEA Sensitive fern
O. sensibilis. This woodland fern has a spreading habit but somewhat sparse fronds: light green, triangular, sterile ones, turning brown in autumn, and narrow, persistent, fertile ones, with bead-like frondlets. A pretty, wild-garden subject for moist soil. H60cm/2ft, W90cm/3ft. Z4-8.

OSMUNDA Royal fern
O. regalis. This is a majestic specimen for damp, humus-rich, lime-free soil, sun or shade. It forms a massive crown above ground from which sprout deciduous fronds, coppery when young, then fresh

Dryopteris erythrosora

Dryopteris borreri 'Crispa'

green and, finally, yellow-brown in autumn. The tufts of fertile fronds look like dried flowers when mature. Moisture-loving. H up to 1.8m/6ft, W1.8m/6ft. Z3-9.

PHYLLITIS See under ASPLENIUM.

POLYPODIUM Common polypody
P. cambricum. With a mass of evergreen fronds in mounded clumps, this is adaptable to fairly dry soil. H25cm/10in, W45-60cm/18-24in. Z5-8.

P. vulgare **'Pulcherrimum'**. This is good as ground cover and for rock gardens or wall crevices, and occasionally grows as an epiphyte. The evergreen fronds are fresh green, tinted in autumn. Tolerant of dry soil but less vigorous in alkaline soil. H25cm/10in, W40cm/16in. Z5-8.

POLYSTICHUM Shield fern, holly fern
These evergreen ferns have large, broad fronds, with many variations in their intricate form. Most are fully hardy and adaptable even where soil is poor, dry or limy, if they are given a good start. Shade is best.

Matteuccia struthiopteris

Polystichum aculeatum

P. aculeatum. The hard shield fern has bold, deep, lacy, feathery fronds. Good drainage preferred. H60-75cm/24-30in, W60cm/2ft. Z4-8.

P. polyblepharum. This gives year-round elegant greenery with broad, shining fronds from hairy central crowns. Hardy and reliable. H50cm/20in, W30cm/1ft. Z5-8.

P. setiferum. The soft shield fern produces bulbils, or potential babies, along its midrib, adding to its charm. The several forms differ in the pattern of the broad, deeply cleft fronds, arching from a stout central crown. H up to 90cm/3ft, W90-120cm/3-4ft. Z5-8. **'Divisilobum'** has finely divided fronds and tolerates fairly dry conditions. H50cm/20in, W50cm/20in. Z5-8. **'Plumosum'** has soft, semi-prostrate, densely clothed, evergreen fronds. H30cm/1ft, W50cm/20in. Z5-8.

SCOLOPENDRIUM See under ASPLENIUM.

WOODSIA
W. polystichoides. This neat little tufted fern is of value amongst alpines, in sun or shade. H10cm/4in, W15cm/6in. Z4-8.

MIXED BED OF GRASSES AND PERENNIALS

Few gardeners realize what a wide range of ornamental grasses and sedges is available for use in the garden – or how these might best be used. Ornamental grasses planted on their own can create an attractive feature, with even their dead foliage in autumn and winter looking effective. However, the addition of other perennials can result in a very striking association throughout the summer, with their brighter colours standing out vividly against the usually more subtle colours and forms of the grasses. Some plants of South African origin, such as *Kniphofia*, *Agapanthus* and *Crocosmia*, seem to work admirably, but many other perennials are equally good. All the plants featured are happy in reasonably well-drained soil and sun where not too dry. The peak period of interest is midsummer to mid-autumn.

1 *Carex comans* (× 5)
2 *Kniphofia* 'Bressingham Comet' (× 7)
3 *Miscanthus sinensis* 'Zebrinus' (× 5)
4 *Stipa gigantea* (× 1)
5 *Agapanthus* 'Bressingham Blue' (× 7)
6 *Crocosmia* 'Emberglow' (× 9)
7 *Agropyron pubiflorum* (× 7)
8 *Pennisetum orientale* (× 5)

Area required:
approx. 9 sq. m/9 sq. yd

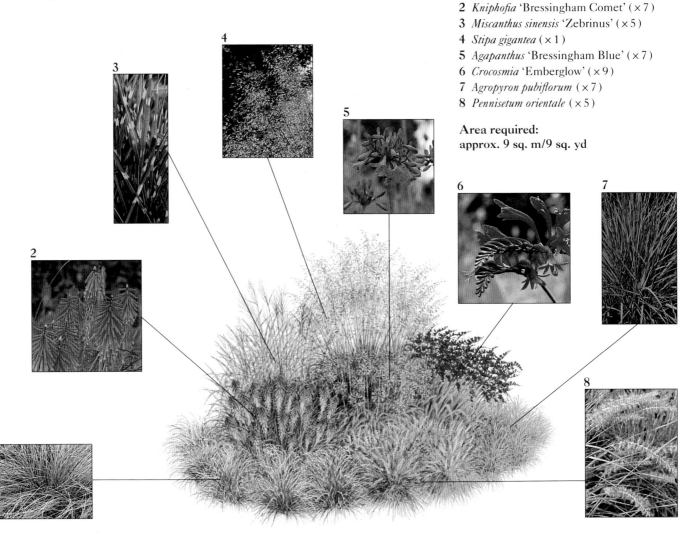

HARDY FERNS COMBINED WITH PERENNIALS

However small the garden there are usually a few shady spots in it which are ideal for planting hardy ferns. By and large, most ferns prefer soil that is not too dry, though once established they will often tolerate such conditions. This bed could be planted on the shady side of a house or wall, or under trees and shrubs, given reasonable light and some moisture. A mulch of leaf mould or other weed-free material would help to retain moisture in summer. The texture, form and generally subtle colours of ferns should be balanced with splashes of colour from other plants: here the foliage of the *Hosta* and *Saxifraga* is as important as the flower. Early spring colour could be provided by bulbs. The peak season of interest is early to late summer, although the foliage will provide year-round appeal.

1 *Gentiana septemfida* (×7)
2 *Dicentra* 'Snowflakes' (×5)
3 *Adiantum pedatum* (×5)
4 *Hosta fortunei* 'Francee' (×3)
5 *Dryopteris erythrosora* (×3)
6 *Polygonatum multiflorum* (×5)
7 *Athyrium nipponicum* 'Pictum' (×5)
8 *Saxifraga fortunei* 'Rubrifolia' (×5)

**Area required:
approx. 7 sq. m/7 sq. yd**

ALPINES

The popularity of the traditional rockery or rock garden has waned during recent years, but interest in alpine plants has grown. This is no paradox, but rather a natural consequence as other, more rational ways of growing alpines become widespread. A rockery or rock garden is, after all, aesthetically out of place in the vast majority of gardens, where rocks are not indigenous and where boundaries are usually straight. Nor do alpine plants necessarily grow better among rocks, which not only take up space, but also create problems of maintenance and weed control.

Alpines are best regarded as long-term investments. The better one comes to know them, the more joy and satisfaction they give, and their infinite variety can provide a fascinating study. A familiarity with their names is recommended, and the case for unobtrusive labelling is very strong as a collection increases.

WHERE TO GROW ALPINES

The best way to grow alpines is in a raised bed. This can be made from low retaining walls of rock forming a terrace or series of terraces on a slope, or from free-standing walls of stone, brick or even wood on a level site; whichever construction is chosen, the bed should be filled with the free-draining soil mix which almost all alpines prefer. Peat blocks can also be used as walls, especially for the range of plants which prefer a lime-free, peaty bed. The latter are best in a north-facing position, since many calcifuges also like some shade.

Raised beds are obviously convenient to maintain and offer dwarf plants more prominence, but, provided a site is well drained, an alpine bed can also be effective at ground level. Segregation between slow and rapid growers, which makes for simpler maintenance, is easier to attain this way than in a raised bed or rock garden, and construction costs are minimal. Apart from the disadvantages of

A mixed planting of alpines, shrubs, conifers, perennials and grasses – an effective combination of foliage and flower. The yellow *Genista sagittalis* in the foreground is complemented by the pendulous flowers of *Chiastophyllum oppositifolium*, behind which the multi-coloured leaves of *Ajuga reptans* 'Burgundy Glow' make a bright contrast

Two sharply contrasting alpine campanulas growing in unison, the blue, spreading *Campanula poscharskyana* 'Stella' intertwined with *Campanula carpatica* 'Bressingham White'

having to stoop, access can be a problem, too, in large, 'walk-about' beds, but paving-slab paths are an attractive solution. Slight undulations are quite in order where no natural slope prevails, but avoid steep slopes, since soil erosion from heavy rain or watering harms plants and quickly spoils one's efforts. Slopes of no more than 1 in 12 are best, though some vigorous, mat-forming plants prevent erosion once established. A few dwarf shrubs and conifers can help to relieve flatness, but, except in large beds, avoid spreaders such as prostrate junipers and cotoneasters.

Another alternative to a raised bed, if space is limited, is a stone sink or trough. Even in a restricted area such as this, many alpines will thrive happily as long as the drainage is good.

MAKING A SELECTION

The traditional term 'alpine', now more favoured than 'rock plant', is quite inadequate to describe the vast range of dwarf plants now available, from tiny hummocks, through mat-forming and semi-shrubby types to tuberous or mossy subjects. All are hardy perennials, but by no means all come from mountainous regions. As with the taller border perennials, most prefer an open situation and all have limits of adaptability, so it is up to the gardener to provide conditions in which they can flourish. Many alpines can be used at the front of a border, but there are some, especially those from high, dry altitudes, that need an alpine house because they cannot tolerate winter dampness with variable temperatures. Winter wet is much more harmful to alpines than frost alone. Some choice kinds, however, will tolerate winter dampness if extra grit or crushed stone is added to the soil mix for sharp drainage.

The great majority of alpines flower in spring and early summer. For continuity of display, some that flower in late summer and autumn should be chosen: the directory includes sufficient subjects to provide late-season interest. Almost all alpines are pot-grown commercially and can be planted at virtually any time.

There are, of course, prima donnas that need cossetting, but at the other extreme are alpines that romp away in quite ordinary soil, or even in wall crevices. Rapid growth may appeal to some, but avoid invasive plants such as snow-in-summer (*Cerastium tomentosum*) if you plan to grow less rampant kinds as well. Knowing a plant's likely spread and speed of growth is important if you are to segregate lusty growers from those they might otherwise smother within a year or two. The creeping kinds, whether spreading just below the surface or rooting as they grow, cause most problems, but with those that spread from a compact rootstock, such as *Aubrieta* and *Helianthemum*, shearing back excessive growth makes for easy control.

SOME CULTURAL ADVICE

Good drainage is so vital for most alpines that it should never be neglected, especially when establishing a new bed. The soil mix should also relate to the type of plants grown. If segregation is practised, quick-growing kinds need only ordinary, free-draining, weed-free soil; add sharp sand to heavy soil to improve texture and drainage. Choice subjects are more demanding, sun lovers often requiring ample grit and shade lovers extra humus to encourage growth. In general, sun lovers are less in need of humus-rich soil than those alpines preferring cool shade. Lime haters need their own area with more peat, and with sharp sand in a more acid loam. My own mix for acid-loving plants is made up of 40 per cent lime-free soil mixed with 25 per cent peat, 25 per cent fine-grade bark, and 10 per cent lime-free sharp sand.

A layer of small shingle or stone chippings among alpines is not a necessity, even amongst choice, slow-growing types, but it prevents

Covering the ground with shingle or stone chippings to reduce weeding, prevent splash, and assist surface drainage

The curious stems and flower heads of one of the houseleeks, *Sempervivum* 'Engle's Rubrum', make an arresting display in July

the surface drying out, helps to keep weeds down, and reduces the need for irrigation in dry periods.

Planting

Bearing in mind the soil considerations mentioned above, planting alpines is reasonably straightforward, most being planted from small pots. Space according to expected growth rates and try to please cultural preferences as indicated in the directory.

You should observe plants carefully during the first couple of seasons. If it is necessary to make some adjustments to keep the spreaders and slow growers apart, choose a propitious time, usually spring or early autumn, when plants do not suffer from being removed or replanted. Having decided on a more suitable position, prepare the hole, making it large enough to take the soil around the plant's roots, too. Then carefully carry out the transfer, watering the plant well beforehand if the soil is at all dry and continuing to water regularly until the plant is seen to be in growth.

Dealing with weeds

Alpine plants are usually more difficult to keep weed-free than taller, upright perennials. Hand weeding is necessary, since the creeping habit or low, mounded growth of so many rules out the use of a hoe, and bare places are best scratched over with a hand fork. A sterilized soil mix should be used initially, if possible, but annual weed seeds will inevitably drift in and germinate.

Those such as groundsel and shepherd's purse are easily pulled out, but annual grass is not, and this, in my experience, is the worst offender. It quickly reproduces and should be dealt with before it reseeds itself; seedlings too small to be pulled out should be scooped with a hand fork or trowel and turned over to rot away.

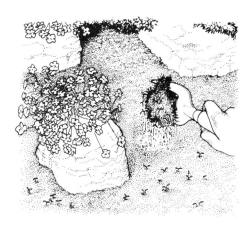

Scooping up and turning over small weeds, which will then rot away

ALPINES DIRECTORY

The selection which follows is by no means comprehensive, but it covers the most desirable subjects loosely termed alpines or rock plants, which will flourish without problems of cultivation for the average keen gardener.

Key
H: Approximate height after 2 years
W: Approximate width after 2 years
F: Months in flower
Z: Relevant hardiness zone(s)

ACAENA New Zealand burr
These fast-growing, mat-forming, mainly evergreen plants root as they spread, and can be invasive. Most are better as ground cover, especially overplanting dwarf bulbs or between paving, than in rockeries. Insignificant flowers in summer are followed by burr-like seed heads. Full sun and any, even poor, soil.
A. adscendens. This has reddish burrs and grey-green serrated foliage. H15cm/6in, W60cm/2ft. F7-8. Z6-8.
A. 'Blue Haze'. Has bluish grey leaves and brown burrs. H10cm/4in, W60cm/2ft. F7-8. Z6-8.
A. buchananii. Forms apple-green mats and greenish burrs. H5cm/2in, W60cm/2ft. F6-8. Z6-9.
A. inermis 'Copper Carpet'. This has distinctive, bronzed foliage and reddish flowers. H5cm/2in, W60cm/2ft. F6-8. Z6-9.
A. microphylla. The neatest, most commonly grown species makes ground-hugging, bronzy mats with bright red burrs. H2.5cm/1in, W60cm/2ft. F7-9. Z5-8.
'Pulchella' forms coppery, evergreen mats, with red burrs. H8cm/3in, W60cm/2ft. F7-8. Z5-8.

ACANTHOLIMON Prickly heath, prickly thrift
This sun lover needs light, gritty soil, and dislikes root disturbance.
A. glumaceum. This makes an evergreen cushion of hard, spiny foliage and stumpy spikes of starry, clear pink flowers. It prefers full sun and well-drained, light soil. Dislikes damp winters. H10cm/4in, W20cm/8in. F5-6. Z7-9.

ACHILLEA
The alpine dwarf yarrows make modestly spreading mats of soft filigree or divided foliage. All have white or yellow flowers and are easy to grow in sun and well-drained, poor soil. For foliage schemes, remove the flowers while still in bud.
A. argentea. This, more correctly *Tanacetum argenteum*, is one of several somewhat similar, silvery leaved, white-flowered species, the others being *A. ageratifolia* and *A. umbellata.* All are mat-forming, usually evergreen perennials. H13-15cm/5-6in, W13-15cm/5-6in. F5-6. Z5-7.
A. aurea. See *A. chrysocoma.*
A. chrysocoma (syn. *A. aurea*). This makes close furry mats of soft, silvery green foliage and mustard-yellow flowers. H15cm/6in, W25cm/10in. F5-6. Z4-8.
A. × lewisii 'King Edward'. This has primrose-yellow flowers and is less vigorous, needing frequent replanting. H10cm/4in, W20cm/8in. F5-8. Z4-8.
A. tomentosa. Woolly yarrow, the most popular species, has grey-green, filigree mats and dense, golden-yellow heads. H15cm/6in, W30cm/1ft. F5-7. Z3-7.

ACINOS
A. corsicus. See *Micromeria corsica.*

ACTINELLA
A. scaposa. A distinctive plant with numerous, bright yellow daisies above leathery, strap-like, green leaves. It is easy to grow in any well-drained soil in a sunny position. H20cm/8in, W23cm/9in. F5-6. Z5-8.

AETHIONEMA Stone cress
These plants have semi-shrubby growth with tiny leaves and rounded flower heads which are showy for several weeks. All need sun and free-draining, gritty soil. Short-lived but worth growing. All Z5-8.
A. grandiflorum (syn. *A. pulchellum*). Persian stone cress is charming, with delicate pink flowers on bluish green bushlets. H25cm/10in, W30-45cm/12-18in. F5-7.
A. iberideum. This iberis-like species forms grey-green, silvery mats bearing small, white flowers. H10cm/4in, W30cm/1ft. F5-7.
A. pulchellum. See *A. grandiflorum.*
A. 'Warley Rose'. This compact hybrid, one of the most popular alpines, makes a

Acaena microphylla

Achillea × lewisii 'King Edward'

Acaena 'Blue Haze'

Aethionema 'Warley Rose'

Ajuga reptans 'Burgundy Glow'

Allium beesianum

neat, bluish bush, well covered with rich, rose-pink flowers. Suffers from occasional dieback. H13cm/5in, W30cm/1ft. F5-7.

AJUGA Bugle

All but one species spread rapidly from runners, but make useful ground cover, especially under trees and shrubs, with their colourful leaves and short spikes of mainly blue flowers. They grow best in some shade and moist soil, and are unsuitable for hot, dry positions. All benefit from fairly frequent replanting. All Z3-9.

A. pyramidalis. This is the exception to the rule, being non-rampant. In cool, fairly moist shade it makes leafy clumps, and a good show of rich blue flowers. H25cm/10in, W15cm/6in. F4-6. The form 'Metallica Crispa' has close mats of deep purple-bronze, crisped foliage. H15cm/6in, W30-45cm/12-18in. F5-6.

A. reptans. Carpet, or common, bugle is mat-forming. Its many colourful varieties do best in some sun. 'Braunherz' has shiny purple-bronze leaves and blue flowers. H15cm/6in, W30-45cm/12-18in. F5-6. 'Burgundy Glow' has light blue flowers and wine-red, bronze and cream leaves. H15cm/6in, W30-45cm/12-18in. F5-6. 'Jungle Beauty' has large leaves, suffused purple in spring. H20cm/8in, W45cm/18in. F5-6. 'Rainbow' (syn. 'Multicolor') is an apt name for this colourful cultivar, which has bronze, pink and yellow leaves. H15cm/6in, W30-45cm/12-18in. F5-6. 'Variegata' has grey-green and cream leaves. H10cm/4in, W30-45cm/12-18in. F5-6.

Alyssum saxatile 'Flore Pleno'

ALCHEMILLA See under Perennials.

ALLIUM Ornamental onion

A few of the smallest of this extensive genus are worth growing as alpines, especially those which retain their grassy foliage all summer. All like well-drained, light soil in sun or light shade.

A. beesianum. Dainty, blue flower clusters above deep green, grassy leaves. H30cm/1ft, W15cm/6in. F6-8. Z5-10.

A. glaucum. This species has pink flowers and glaucous foliage. H15cm/6in, W8cm/3in. F6-8. Z5-9.

A. oreophilum (syn. *A. ostrowskianum*). Makes deep pink, starry flowers. The leaves are narrow and grass-like. H10cm/4in, W10cm/4in. F6-8. Z3-9.

A. ostrowskianum. See *A. oreophilum*.

A. splendens. This has clumpy, glaucous leaves and starry, yellow clusters. H20cm/8in, W25cm/10in. F6-8. Z4-9.

A. tibeticum. An attractive, free-flowering species with grassy green foliage and pendulous lilac-purple flower heads. H15-25cm/6-10in, W15-25cm/6-10in. F6-8. Z5-10.

ALYSSUM

A. saxatile (correctly, *Aurinia saxitalis*). Popularly known as gold dust, this species, with *Aubrieta*, is the highlight of the alpine

garden in spring, but the discerning gardener is not content with seed-raised types, or the lemon-yellow 'Citrinum', which become untidy. 'Dudley Neville' is a compact cultivar with silvery leaves and deep primrose-yellow flowers. 'Dudley Neville Variegated' has variegated leaves. Both make leafy mounds. Both H25cm/10in, W45cm/18in. F4-6. Z3-7. 'Flore Pleno' (syn. 'Plenum') is even more compact, with double, deep yellow flowers. H20cm/8in, W45cm/18in. F4-6. Z3-7.

ANACYCLUS Atlas Mountain daisy

A. depressus. This needs a sunny spot and well-drained soil, and will not tolerate winter wet. It has large, white, daisy flowers, red on the reverse of the petals, and rosettes of greyish, filigree foliage. H8-10cm/3-4in, W30cm/1ft. F5-7. Z6-8.

ANCHUSA Tufted alkanet

A. caespitosa. This choice but demanding plant needs gritty soil. Its short, bright blue sprays are carried above tufts of narrow, dark green leaves. H8cm/3in, W20cm/8in. F5-8. Z5-7.

ANDROSACE Rock jasmine

A truly alpine genus which includes some choice cushion-forming high alpines that hate winter wet and are best grown in an alpine house. Those below are reliable in an open, very well-drained position. All are rosette-forming, either in close hummocks or with a modest spread; most have soft, greyish leaves.

A. carnea. This species has several minor variations, all with dark green, narrow leaves and small heads of pink (rarely white) flowers. The form *laggeri* is the best, with larger, yellow-eyed, pink flowers. H8cm/3in, W20cm/8in. F5-6. Z4-7.

A. ciliata. Makes neat hummocks set with rose-pink, yellow-centred flowers.

Anacyclus depressus

Androsace sarmentosa 'Chumbyi'

Anthemis nobilis 'Flore Pleno'

Anthyllis montana 'Rubra'

H5cm/2in, W20cm/8in. F5-6. Z4-7.
A. lanuginosa. Forms silvery, trailing mats, with pink, dark-eyed flowers. H5cm/2in, W30-45cm/12-18in. F6-8. Z4-5.
A. microphylla. Its prostrate rosettes feature white, sweetly scented flowers. H5cm/2in, W20cm/8in. F5-6. Z4-7.
A. primuloides. See *A. sarmentosa*.
A. sarmentosa (syn. *A. primuloides*). This species has soft, silvery rosettes and little heads of clear pink flowers. 'Chumbyi', 'Salmon's Variety' and *watkinsii* are similar, all with pink flowers and all needing full sun and good drainage. All H30cm/1ft, W60cm/2ft. F5-6. Z4-7.
A. villosa. The small, hairy, silvery rosettes spread by stolons and bear little heads of white, pink-eyed flowers. H5cm/2in, W25cm/10in. F5-6. Z4-7.

ANDRYALA
A. agardhii. This charming bushlet needs a well-drained, sunny position. It has shiny, silvery, spatula-shaped leaves and yellow daisies for many weeks. H20cm/8in, W23cm/9in. F5-8. Z5-7.

ANTENNARIA
A genus of plants which form modestly spreading, grey-green or silvery carpets, ideal between paving slabs or as ground cover for bulbs. All are quite easy to grow, except in damp soil, and have button-like flowers on erect stems.
A. aprica. This species spreads fairly rapidly with silvery leaves and clusters of white flowers. H15cm/6in, W30-45cm/12-18in. F5-7. Z3-7.

A. dioica. A more compact plant, with white flowers, but the pink varieties 'Nyewoods', 'Rosea' and 'Rubra' are showier. All H10cm/4in, W30-45cm/12-18in. F5-7. Z3-8. 'Minima' is a small form with light pink flower heads. H8cm/3in, W30cm/1ft. F5-7. Z3-8.

ANTHEMIS
Most alpine forms of these sun-loving, daisy-like plants are more reliable than the taller forms, but very few are in circulation. All are easily grown in well-drained soil and a sunny position. None is long-lived, but they are easily propagated by division or seed.
A. biebersteiniana. See *A. rudolphiana*.

Antennaria dioica 'Rubra'

A. nobilis (syn. *Chamaemelum nobile*). Chamomile is not recommended as an alpine, except perhaps as a space filler. It has deep green, spreading, aromatic mats of filigree foliage and white flowers, the double form, 'Flore Pleno', being preferable. H20cm/8in, W40cm/16in. F6-8. Z6-9. For non-flowering, fragrant lawns or paths, evergreen 'Treneague' is best.
A. rudolphiana (syn. *A. biebersteiniana*). A charming little plant forming neat clumps of silvery, filigree leaves and golden-yellow daisies. H15cm/6in, W20cm/8in. F5-7. Z4-7.

ANTHYLLIS
These sun-loving, drought-resistant, shrubby plants have pea-shaped flowers and finely divided leaves. Well-drained soil is essential. All Z6-8.
A. hermanniae. This species has a rather lanky and tangled habit, but 'Minor' is neater, with a succession of yellow flowers above grey-green foliage. Both H15cm/6in, W60cm/2ft. F5-7.
A. montana. This deep-rooting, slow-spreading subject becomes woody with age. It is fully reliable and makes a fine show of trailing, downy grey foliage and pink flower clusters, deep pink in 'Rubra'. Both H15cm/6in, W30cm/1ft. F5-7.
A. vulneraria. Lady's fingers is more or less prostrate from a central root. The outspreading stems carry clustered flower heads, varying from pink to purplish and red. 'Rubra' is an intense orange-red. Neither is long-lived but self-sown seedlings usually appear in or near old plants. Both H10cm/4in, W30cm/1ft. F5-7.

Aquilegia glandulosa

Arenaria montana

Arabis caucasica 'Corfe Castle'

Armeria caespitosa

AQUILEGIA Columbine

Few of this well-loved genus, including the alpine species, are long-lived, and they can be propagated only from seed. Those who invest in them would do well to save some seed for continuity, for only a few specialists offer them. Some species are best grown in an alpine house. Good, not too dry, soil is best, and sun or light shade.
A. bertolonii. This species carries one large, rich blue flower, with a curved spur, on each stem. H15cm/6in, W15cm/6in. Z3-9.
A. discolor. This forms a cushion of finely cut leaves and light blue and cream bicoloured flowers. H10cm/4in, W15cm/6in. F5-6. Z3-8.
A. einseleana. Its violet-blue flowers are borne on slender stems. H25cm/10in, W15cm/6in. F5-6. Z3-8.
A. flabellata. See under Perennials.
A. glandulosa. This beautiful plant is quite rare and seedlings offered are seldom the true species. The blue and white flowers with hooked spurs are fulsome, and are carried in clusters. H30cm/1ft, W20cm/8in. F5-6. Z3-8.

ARABIS Rock cress

This genus flowers for several weeks in spring. Some spread rapidly, whereas others grow more compactly, flowering from small rosettes. They all prefer sun and light soil.
A. caucasica (formerly *A. albida*). The single-flowered, common white arabis is less attractive than the double white **'Plena'**

but both make a rapid surface spread, excellent on walls and dry banks but too invasive in small rock gardens. Flower sprays are 20cm/8in high, above more or less evergreen foliage. **'Corfe Castle'** has short sprays of deep pink flowers above neat mounds of foliage, almost as bright as the short-lived *A. blepharophylla*, which is too unreliable to recommend. **'Variegata'** has single, white flowers and creamy white and gold leaves. All H20cm/8in, W45cm/18in. F3-5. Z4-7.
A. ferdinandi-coburgii. The green-leaved species has dainty sprays of small, white flowers on deep green, spreading, matted rosettes. More exciting are the self-descriptive **'All Gold'**, which shows up boldly on its evergreen mat, and the slightly less variegated, green and cream evergreen **'Variegata'**, again with white flowers. All H10cm/4in, W20cm/8in. F4-6. Z5-7.
A. × sturii. This forms neat, low, green hummocks set with short spikes of sizeable, white flowers. H8-10cm/3-4in, W20cm/8in. F4-5. Z4-7.

ARENARIA Sandwort

Taxonomists have placed some species under *Minuartia*, *Alsine* or *Sagina*. Most are easy to grow, of mat or tufty form, for sun and any reasonable soil.
A. balearica. This species forms an evergreen film over the surface or in crevices of damp rock, but is less than hardy in cold regions. It prefers light shade. The tiny, white flowers are borne on wiry stems.

H5cm/2in, W30-45cm/12-18in. F5-6. Z4-7.
A. graminifolia. A plant which could be mistaken for tufty grass until its white flowers appear. H20cm/8in, W25cm/10in. F5-7. Z3-5.
A. laricifolia. See *Minuartia laricifolia*.
A. montana. Produces a cascade of white, saucer-shaped flowers over low, spreading, mounded mats. H15cm/6in, W30-45cm/12-18in. F5-7. Z3-5.
A. pinifolia. Forms a wide, tight, evergreen mat and sprays of tiny, white flowers. H10cm/4in, W45cm/18in. F5-7. Z3-5.
A. purpurascens. Scarcely purple, but pink sandwort's flowers still depart from the usual white, and are carried above neat, light green mats. H5cm/2in, W30-45cm/12-18in. F5-7. Z4-7.
A. tetraquetra. This is a cushion plant for gritty soil, with tiny, tight-angled leaves and stemless, white flowers which are seldom seen. H5cm/2in, W15cm/6in. F5-6. Z3-5.

ARISARUM Mouse plant

A. proboscideum. Mainly of curiosity value, its arrow-shaped leaves tend to conceal the charming, mouse-tail spathes, which usually appeal to children. The rhizomes do best in a cool, shady place in humus-rich, well-drained soil. H10cm/4in, W25cm/10in. F4-5. Z5-8.

ARMERIA Thrift

These very useful and showy evergreens have tufty mounds or mats of grassy leaves and rounded, pincushion flower heads. The sea thrift (*A. maritima*) is easy to grow and ideal as edging or in front of taller perennials. Thrifts need well-drained soil and prefer sun.
A. 'Bloodstone'. See under Perennials.
A. caespitosa (syn. *A. juniperifolia*). This is the best-known true alpine species. There is also an attractive white-flowered form, **'Alba'**. **'Bevan's Variety'** is the brightest form, with little pink flower heads. It needs very well-drained soil. All H10cm/4in, W15-25cm/6-10in. F5-7. Z4-8.
A. juniperifolia. See *A. caespitosa*.
A. maritima. See under Perennials.

ARTEMISIA Wormwood

Most are of value for foliage rather than flowers. They prefer full sun and dry to damp soil but will not tolerate winter wet. They have a fairly rapid spread.
A. lanata. See *A. pedemontana*.
A. pedemontana (syn. *A. lanata*). This is a smaller version of *A. schmidtiana*. The silver, filigree foliage hugs the ground, above which are carried white, button-type flowers. It becomes leggy after a year or two, but pegging down stems encourages rooting. H10cm/4in, W25cm/10in. F6-7. Z3-7.
A. schmidtiana 'Nana'. Its fine, silvery,

filigree foliage makes a pleasing foil to green or coloured leaves. H15cm/6in, W30cm/1ft. Z3-7.

A. stelleriana. See under Perennials.

ARUNCUS Goat's beard
A. aethusifolius. See under Perennials.

ASARINA
A. procumbens. The creamy yellow, snapdragon flowers appear on trailing stems with greyish, sticky, heart-shaped leaves. Moderately hardy, it prefers a cool, well-lit spot, where the soil is well drained. H15cm/6in, W45cm/18in. F6-9. Z6-8.

ASPERULA Woodruff
This genus includes two or three choice species for sun and gritty, well-drained soil.

A. hirta. Spreads moderately below ground, and produces pale pink flowers. H8cm/3in, W15cm/6in. F6-7. Z5-7.

A. lilaciflora caespitosa. Its filmy, green mat is set with short sprays of tiny, clear pink, tubular flowers for weeks, often with a second flush. H5cm/2in, W20cm/8in. F6-8. Z5-7.

A. nitida. The species has deep green hummocks bearing clusters of little, pink flowers. H5cm/2in, W15cm/6in. F6-7. Z5-8.

A. puberula. Somewhat similar to *A. nitida*, it is even more compact, needing almost scree conditions. H5cm/2in, W15cm/6in. F6-7. Z5-7.

A. suberosa. This treasure for very gritty soil has soft, grey-leaved stems and clusters of light pink, tubular flowers. Worth protecting from winter wet, it is one of my long-standing favourites. H5cm/2in, W15cm/6in. F5-7. Z6-8.

ASTER
A very few species in this large genus are dwarf enough to be classed as alpines. None is difficult to grow, given sun and good drainage.

A. alpinus. The alpine aster flowers in spring, in colours ranging from the rare white through mauve to lavender-blue and rosy lilac. Named varieties include **'Albus'**, white; **'Beechwood'**, lavender-blue; and **'Wargrave Variety'**, purpley pink; all with one flower per stem. Divide every three to four years. All H15-20cm/6-8in, W30-45cm/12-18in. F5-6. Z4-7.

A. farreri. See under Perennials.

A. natalensis (syn. *Felicia rosulata*). Dwarf but not compact. From its little rosettes emerge blue, golden-eyed flowers. Needs a warm spot. H13cm/5in, W30cm/1ft. F5-6. Z5-8.

A. sativus atrocaeruleus. A distinctive, very desirable but rare species, which has a light green, bushy habit set with small, sky-blue, yellow-eyed flowers for months. H15cm/6in, W15cm/6in. F5-9. Z5-8.

Artemisia schmidtiana 'Nana'

Asperula suberosa

ASTILBE
Those under 30cm/1ft high need humus-rich soil, shade and/or moisture. All Z4-8.

A. × crispa. See under Perennials.

A. glaberimma saxatilis. This has deeply dissected foliage and sprays of tiny, light pink flowers. H10cm/4in, W20cm/8in. F6-8.

A. simplicifolia. A variable species, with some forms over 30cm/1ft high, but the dwarfer ones are excellent alpines, with low mounds of attractive, shiny leaves and dainty sprays in mainly shell-pink. H20cm/8in, W25cm/10in. F6-8. There are several worthwhile hybrids derived from *A. simplicifolia*: see under Perennials. **'William Buchanan'** is of doubtful parentage, but grows compactly with creamy pink sprays. H15cm/6in, W20cm/8in. F6-8.

AUBRIETA
Commonly pronounced 'Orbreeshia', its value is in the spring display of its many

Asperula hirta

Aster alpinus 'Albus'

varieties, which have largely replaced the species. All prefer sun and well-drained, limy soil. Though easily raised from seed, they do not come true to colour and it is best to choose named varieties, segregating blues, pinks, purples and reds according to personal taste. Curb their fairly rapid surface spread by shearing back annually after flowering.

The range of varieties in cultivation is enormous, but my selection of the best would include the following. **'Alix Brett'**, double carmine-purple. **'Bob Saunders'**, close to red, double. **'Bressingham Pink'**, single pink. **'Bressingham Red'**, large, deep red, single. **'Dr Mules'**, an old favourite, single violet-purple. **'Joan Allen'**, double crimson. **'Maurice Prichard'**, single light pink. **'Red Carpet'**, the best single red. **'Silver Edge'** (syn. 'Silberrand'), blue with narrow, cream-edged leaves. Average H10-15cm/4-6in, W30-45cm/12-18in. F4-6. Z5-8.

Aubrieta 'Bressingham Pink'

AURINIA
A. saxitalis. See *Alyssum saxatile.*

AZORELLA
A. trifurcata (syn. *Bolax glebaria*). This fairly quickly makes a hard mat of shiny, evergreen rosettes with little, yellow flowers. Good for dry soil. H5cm/2in, W25cm/10in. F6-7. Z6-7. The dwarf 'Nana' makes a tighter, lower cushion. H2.5cm/1in, W15cm/6in. F6-7. Z6-7.

BELLIS Common daisy
Daisies are more often treated as weeds in the lawn, but the species listed below can be recommended. They dislike dry conditions.
B. perennis. The pink-flowered 'Dresden China', the dark red 'Pomponette', the red 'Rob Roy', 'White Pearl', as well as the curious 'Hen and Chickens', are double-flowered and dwarf enough for alpines, but must be divided and replanted annually to maintain vitality. All H10-15cm/4-6in, W15cm/6in. F5-8. Z3-8.
B. rotundifolia 'Caerulescens'. This cultivar has an almost blue, pale lavender flower and is truly perennial. H13cm/5in, W15cm/6in. F5-8. Z4-8.

BOLAX
B. glebaria. See *Azorella trifurcata.*

BORAGO
B. laxiflora. This produces sprays of small, gentian-blue flowers for months from a base

Calceolaria falklandica

of hairy, puckered leaves. Easy in sun or part shade, it dies after two seasons but more than amply reproduces itself from self-sown seeds. H20cm/8in, W20cm/8in. F5-9. Z5-9.

BRACHYCOME
Only two species are worth including, both easy and long-flowering, given sun and good drainage. Both Z6-9.
B. rigidula. This has lavender-blue, daisy flowers on arching sprays and small, divided leaves. H15cm/6in, W15cm/6in. F6-8.

Bellis perennis 'Pomponette' (top) and 'Dresden China'

Campanula carpatica 'Bressingham White'

B. scapiegera. A species with a more compact habit and white flowers. H15cm/6in, W15cm/6in. F6-8.

CALAMINTHA
C. alpina. This short-lived plant has a loose, semi-trailing habit with small, round leaves and a long season of little, lavender-mauve flowers. It prefers a sunny position and any soil of reasonable quality. H13cm/5in, W25cm/10in. F5-8. Z5-9.

CALCEOLARIA
These highly distinctive plants need annual attention to keep them happy, including regular lifting and dividing and protection in harsh winters. All are best in gritty, humus-rich, cool, damp soil.
C. acutifolia. See *C. polyrrhiza.*
C. darwinii. This choice rarity, which has rounded leaves and large, yellow, pouched flowers with maroon spots, is a connoisseur's plant for part shade. Often short-lived. H10cm/4in, W15cm/6in. F6-7. Z7-9.
C. falklandica. Deep green foliage, and bright yellow flowers for several months. H20cm/8in, W15cm/6in. F5-8. Z6-8.
C. 'John Innes'. This is an improved hybrid with large, yellow, crimson-spotted, pouched flowers. It needs annual replanting in enriched soil. H25cm/10in, W20cm/8in. F6-8. Z6-8.
C. polyrrhiza (syn. *C. acutifolia*). This species has yellow, purple-spotted, pouched flowers and spreads quickly at first, but is apt to die back after flowering. Replant each year in enriched soil. H25cm/10in, W20cm/8in. F6-8. Z6-8.
C. tenella. Roots as it creeps, with little, crimson-speckled, yellow, pouch-like flowers, and very small, oval leaves. H5cm/2in, W25cm/10in. F5-8. Z7-8.

CAMPANULA Bellflower
This large, varied genus contains many true alpines, some choice and difficult, but those listed below are both pleasing and reliable. Most flower after the spring and early summer flush of alpines, adding greatly to continuity of colour. Unless otherwise stated, sun or light shade are fine, and any well-drained soil.
C. allionii (syn. *C. alpestris*). This species creeps below ground and bears large, upturned bell flowers, purplish to lavender-blue. Rounded leaves. Needs lime-free, gritty soil or scree. Sometimes shy to flower. H8cm/3in, W15cm/6in. F6-8. Z4-7.
C. alpestris. See *C. allionii.*
C. arvatica. A mat-forming, narrow-leaved gem for gritty soil and sun, with starry, violet-blue flowers. H8cm/3in, W30cm/1ft. F6-8. Z4-7.
C. 'Birch Hybrid'. A valuable, long-flowering plant with evergreen, ivy-like

leaves and erect stems of lavender-blue flowers. H13cm/5in, W30cm/1ft. F6-8. Z4-7.
C. carpatica. All varieties of the tussock, or Carpathian, bellflower are long-lived, and make shapely summer growth, with wide open, cup- or saucer-shaped, upturned flowers on thin stems. Taller types are also useful in herbaceous borders. All Z4-7. **'Blue Moonlight'** has large, china-blue blooms. H10cm/4in, W20cm/8in. F6-8. **'Bressingham White'** is one of several whites. H20cm/8in, W20cm/8in. F6-8. **'Chewton Joy'** has small, smoky blue bells later than most. H13cm/5in, W20cm/8in. F6-8. **'Hannah'** has small, white flowers but it is prolific and long-flowering. H13cm/5in, W20cm/8in. F6-8. **'Isabel'** has rich blue, saucer flowers. H23cm/9in, W20cm/8in. F6-8. **'Karl Foerster'** has deep cobalt-blue, prolific blooms. H23cm/9in, W20cm/8in. F6-8. **'Snowsprite'** is the purest white and very free-flowering. H20cm/8in, W20cm/8in. F6-8. **'Wheatley Violet'** is a charming miniature. H10cm/4in, W20cm/8in. F6-8.
C. cochleariifolia (syn. *C. pusilla*). The aptly named fairy's thimble has small, nodding, dainty bells and easily controlled, tufted growth, spreading below ground. All Z6-7. **'Blue Tit'** has deep green mats and deep blue bells. I raised and named it in about 1932. H8cm/3in, W30cm/1ft. F6-8. Likewise, the lighter **'Cambridge Blue'**. H6cm/2¹⁄₂in, W30cm/1ft. F6-8. **'Elizabeth Oliver'** is a distinctive, double blue. H6cm/2¹⁄₂in, W30cm/1ft. F6-8. **'Oakington Blue'** is another deep blue form raised by me in about 1932. H8cm/3in, W30cm/1ft. F6-8.
C. **'Constellation'**. This outstanding hybrid has wide sprays of starry, lavender-blue flowers for a long time. It flowers again if cut back and can be used as a window plant inside or out. H25-30cm/10-12in, W30cm/1ft. F6-9. Z6-8.
C. **'G. F. Wilson'**. A worthy old hybrid, with profuse, large, violet-blue bells on tufty, light green foliage. H10cm/4in, W15-30cm/6-12in. F6-8. Z6-8.
C. garganica. The Adriatic bellflower forms compact, leafy tufts and lax sprays of starry flowers, good in crevices and walls. H8cm/3in, W15-30cm/6-12in. F6-8. Z6-8. **'Dickson's Gold'** has golden-green, almost evergreen leaves and sprays of mid-blue flowers. H13cm/5in, W15-30cm/6-12in. F6-8. Z6-8. The form *hirsuta* has greyish, hairy leaves and light blue flowers. H8cm/3in, W15-30cm/6-12in. F6-8. Z6-8. **'W. H. Paine'** is a more compact version of the species, with deep green leaves, and deep blue, white-eyed, starry flowers. H10cm/4in, W15-30cm/6-12in. F6-8. Z6-8.
C. **'Hallii'**. This hybrid is a good albino. H8cm/3in, W30cm/1ft. F6-8. Z6-7.
C. innesii. See *C.* 'John Innes'.
C. **'John Innes'** (syn. *C. innesii*). This is a

distinctive hybrid of tufty but fragile appearance, it gives a long display of light blue flowers. H15cm/6in, W30cm/1ft. Z4-7.
C. kemulariae. This spreading species carries small clusters of lilac-blue flowers. H25cm/10in, W25cm/10in. F6-7. Z6-7.
C. linifolia. See *C. rotundifolia*.
C. **'Molly Pinsent'**. Another oldie with bushy growth and profuse, lavender-blue bells. H15cm/6in, W20cm/8in. F6-8. Z4-7.
C. muralis (correctly, *C. portenschlagiana*). I prefer the older name for this very useful, adaptable plant, with its violet, bell-shaped flowers. It blooms for weeks and will inhabit crevices and walls. **'Resholt'** is the best form. Both H15cm/6in, W60cm/2ft. F6-9. Z4-8.
C. **'Norman Grove'**. This has golden-green foliage and masses of nodding, violet-blue bells. H10cm/4in, W20cm/8in. F6-8. Z4-8.
C. persicifolia planiflora (syn. *C. p. nitida*). This is a miniature form with rosettes of deep green, crinkled leaves and stumpy spikes of blue bells. Seedlings revert to full size. **'Alba'** is the white-flowered form. H15cm/6in, W10cm/4in. F6-8. Z3-8.
C. pilosa. Rosettes form from slowly creeping roots, each carrying light blue, upturned bells. H5-8cm/2-3in, W10-15cm/4-6in. F6-8. Z4-7.
C. portenschlagiana. See *C. muralis*.
C. poscharskyana. Makes a fine show with sprays of pale lavender, starry flowers, but is much too invasive to grow near weaker subjects. A good wall plant but impossible to control once established. H30cm/1ft, W60-90cm/2-3ft. F6-9. Z4-7. **'E. H. Frost'** has more upright and arching sprays than the species, from a vigorous clumpy plant, and carries small, nearly white blooms . H25cm/10in, W60-90cm/2-3ft. F6-9. Z6-8. **'Stella'** is similar to the hybrid *C.* 'Constellation'.
C. pulla. Dainty, nodding, tubular bells of deep violet on slowly spreading mats. Likes lime and shade; divide and replant regularly. H5cm/2in, W30cm/1ft. F6-8. Z4-7.
C. × pulloides. Larger than *C. pulla*, with slightly nodding, deep violet flowers. H10cm/4in, W20cm/8in. F6-8. Z4-7.
C. pusilla. See *C. cochleariifolia*.
C. raddeana. This is a spreader, but not a menace, with deep green mats, and stems carrying small clusters of violet-blue flowers. Likes lime. Lift, divide and replant regularly. H15cm/6in, W25cm/10in. F6-7. Z6-7.
C. rotundifolia (syn. *C. linifolia*). The best form of harebell for display is **'Olympica'**, with its profusion of large, deep blue flowers on thin stems. H20cm/8in, W30-45cm/12-18in. F6-9. Z2-7.
C. sarmatica. This compact plant has

Campanula carpatica 'Blue Moonlight'

greyish, hairy leaves and clusters of warm lavender-blue flowers. Needs sun. H20cm/8in, W30cm/1ft. F6-8. Z4-7.
C. × stansfieldii. This has a tufty habit, light green leaves and abundant lavender-blue flowers. H15cm/6in, W15cm/6in. F6-8. Z4-7.
C. × wockei. This makes a little, congested, deep green mound, set with many small, starry, blue flowers. Sun and gritty soil essential. H8cm/3in, W15cm/6in. F6-8. Z4-7. **'Puck'** has larger, deeper blue flowers. H8cm/3in, W15cm/6in. F7-9. Z4-7.

Campanula carpatica 'Karl Foerster'

Campanula × stansfieldii

Carduncellus rhaponticoides

Carlina acaulis caulescens

Cheiranthus 'Harpur Crewe'

CARDUNCELLUS
C. rhaponticoides. This stemless thistle is not at all weedy. It makes a large rosette from a central crown, topped by a blue, pincushion flower head. H8cm/3in, W30cm/1ft. F6-8. Z5-7.

CARLINA Stemless thistle
Dry, very well-drained soil and sun suit these ornamental thistles. All Z5-7.
C. acanthifolia. This species has a wide leaf spread, stemless, light blue flower heads and attractive, silvery bracts. H10cm/4in, W30cm/1ft. F6-8.
C. acaulis caulescens. This is smaller than the above species, with a slow spread below ground. It has ivory, tufty flowers and silvery bracts. H10cm/4in, W15-23cm/6-9in. F6-8.

CENTAUREA Knapweed
C. cana 'Rosea'. A non-invasive creeper with silvery rosettes and quite large pink cornflowers. Sun essential. H5cm/2in, W20cm/8in. F6-8. Z4-8.
C. simplicicaulis. See under Perennials.

CENTAURIUM
C. scilloides. With clear pink flowers above mats of bright green leaves, this little plant is best in troughs or a scree bed. H5cm/2in, W15cm/6in. F5-7. Z5-7.

CERASTIUM Snow in summer
This rampant genus has ruined many a choice collection of alpines, *C. tomentosum* being the worst offender, with its all-invading roots. Avoid all but the following.
C. columnae (syn. *C. tomentosum columnae*). Less invasive and no less pleasing as a year-round, silvery mat set with sprays of white flowers. H5cm/2in, W30-45cm/12-18in. F5-7. Z2-7.

CERATOSTIGMA Hardy plumbago
C. plumbaginoides. See under Perennials.

CHAMAEMELUM
C. nobile. See *Anthemis nobilis*.

Chiastophyllum oppositifolium

CHAENORRHINUM
C. glareosum. See *Linaria glareosa*.

CHEIRANTHUS Wallflower
C. 'Harpur Crewe'. Most perennial wallflowers are technically *Erysimum* but this old-fashioned, yellow, double form makes a pleasing, scented bush among lower-growing subjects. H30cm/1ft, W30cm/1ft. F5-7. Z8-9.

CHIASTOPHYLLUM Lamb's tail
C. oppositifolium (syn. *Cotyledon simplicifolia*). A first-rate plant for cool semi-shade. Abundant, succulent, basal greenery produces sprays of yellow, dangling flowers, like lamb's tails, from short stems. Creeping and self-rooting. H15cm/6in, W60cm/2ft. F6-7. Z5-7.

CHRYSANTHEMUM
Nomenclature is confusing but those below are worth noting regardless. Full sun and perfect soil drainage are essential; the silvery types dislike winter wet.
C. hosmariense (syn. *Leucanthemum hosmariense*). Given a warm, sheltered spot, this is seldom out of flower. Lacy, silvered bushlets carry white, golden-eyed flowers. H20cm/8in, W30-40cm/12-16in. F5-10. Z8-9.
C. nipponicum. See under Perennials.
C. weyrichii (syn. *Dendranthema weyrichii*). Fully hardy with white, pink-tinged daisies on quite vigorous clumps. H20-25cm/8-10in, W25-30cm/10-12in. F8-10. Z5-9.
C. yezoense (syn. *C. arcticum*). See under Perennials.

CHRYSOGONUM
C. virginianum. This low, leafy plant bears bright yellow flowers for months, the stems elongating late in the season. Needs well-drained, lime-free soil in sun or part shade. H15-23cm/6-9in, W10-15cm/4-6in. F5-9. Z5-9.

CODONOPSIS Bonnet bellflower
A genus with deep but non-spreading roots, which send up wiry stems of nodding, mostly light blue bells, delicately spotted within. Almost any species can be used among alpines to sprawl over a rock or wall.
C. clematidea. This is compact, with a semi-twining habit. Pale blue flowers, purple within. H30-45cm/12-18in, W30cm/1ft. F6-8. Z5-8.
C. ovata. Semi-erect, with pale blue bells, purple-veined inside. H30-45cm/12-18in, W23cm/9in. F6-8. Z5-8.

CORTUSA
C. matthioli. Its leaves are crinkly, soft and rounded, and umbels of magenta-crimson, primula-like flowers are carried on its leafless stems. Happy in humus-rich, dampish soil and shade. H13cm/5in, W25-30cm/10-12in. F5-6. Z5-8.

CORYDALIS
C. cashmeriana. For those able to meet its needs, this is a treasure. It has deeply cut, bluish leaves on low tufts and a marvellous display of intense ice-blue, tubular, spurred flowers. Given gritty, peaty, lime-free soil, it should succeed in cool semi-shade, but perseverance may be called for. H8cm/3in, W25cm/10in. F4-6. Z6-8.

COTYLEDON
C. simplicifolia. See *Chiastophyllum oppositifolium*.

CREPIS Hawkweed
C. aurea. An easy, rosette-forming plant, this has deep orange, dandelion flowers.

H20cm/8in, W25cm/10in. F5-7. Z5-7.
C. incana. This compact beauty is for well-drained soil and sun. Its soft pink flowers appear above hairy, greyish leaves. H20cm/8in, W30cm/1ft. F5-8. Z7-8.

CYANANTHUS Trailing bellflower
C. lobatus. This fleshy rooted mat-former has prostrate, leafy stems of solitary, large, mid-blue flowers for several weeks. It needs well-drained, peaty, acid soil. H8cm/3in, W40cm/16in. F6-8. Z6-7.
C. microphyllus. Similar to the above, but with smaller, heath-like leaves and purple-blue flowers. H5cm/2in, W30cm/1ft. F6-8. Z5-7.

DELPHINIUM
Only two or three species are sufficiently dwarf to be included here.
D. brunonianum. A plant with soft, hairy leaves and spikes of purple-blue flowers. H30cm/1ft, W30cm/1ft. F6-8. Z3-9.
D. cashmerianum. This has rich violet flowers. H30cm/1ft, W30cm/1ft. F6-8. Z3-9.
D. nudicaule. A short-lived species, this has loose panicles of orange-red flowers on slender stems, with little basal leafage. H25cm/10in, W20cm/8in. F6-8. Z5-7.

DENDRANTHEMA
D. weyrichii. See *Chrysanthemum weyrichii*.

DIANTHUS Rock pinks
An indispensable genus for the alpine gardener, but hybrids have largely overtaken the true species. They all like sun and free drainage and almost all prefer an alkaline soil. Most have mats or tufts of silvery or bluish green, evergreen foliage. Hummock-formers prefer scree or very gritty soil. For the connoisseur or collector the genus offers immense scope and much satisfaction.
D. alpinus. This and such hybrids as 'Spark', which derives from the species, are richly coloured, with deep green foliage. H10cm/4in, W15cm/6in. F5-7. Z3-7.
D. deltoides. Maiden pinks are distinctive trailing types with green or purplish foliage and small, red or pink flowers. Good for walls. H15-23cm/6-9in, W40cm/16in. F5-7. Z3-7.
D. freynii. This species is ideal for sinks or troughs. It makes a dense grey-green cushion, with masses of small pink flowers. H2.5-5cm/1-2in, W10cm/4in. F6-7. Z4-7.

Hybrids. There are literally hundreds of varieties which defy classification but which are suitable for the alpine garden. A short list of some of my favourite dianthus would have to include the following. All F6-8, Z4-8. '**Alderhouse**', deep red, single. H13cm/5in, W20cm/8in. '**Bombardier**', red. H13cm/5in, W30cm/1ft. '**Dubarry**',

Crepis incana

Delphinium nudicaule

Dianthus 'Pike's Pink'

Dianthus 'Garland'

double pink, crimson centred. H10cm/4in, W20cm/8in. '**Garland**', pure pink. H10cm/4in, W20cm/8in. '**Inshriach Dazzler**', vivid carmine-pink, green leaves. H10cm/4in, W20cm/8in. '**La Bourboule**' (syn. 'La Bourbille'), pink and white. H8cm/3in, W15cm/6in. '**Nellie Clark**', cerise, semi-double. H13cm/5in, W25cm/10in. '**Nyewood's Cream**', dwarf, cream flowers. H8cm/3in, W15cm/6in. '**Oakington**', a soft double pink, which I raised in 1928. H10cm/4in, W25cm/10in. '**Pike's Pink**', double, showy pink. H10cm/4in, W20cm/8in. '**Richard Gibbs**', double pink. H13cm/5in, W25cm/10in.

DIASCIA See under Perennials.

DODECATHEON See under Perennials.

DOUGLASIA
D. vitaliana. See *Vitaliana primuliflora*.

DRABA
This genus forms neat, tight, hard, little mounds. All are sun lovers and flower on wiry stems. Some are suitable only for scree or the alpine house. They are best grown in well-drained, gritty soil and should be protected from winter wet, or transferred to an alpine house. All Z4-6.
D. aizoides. This makes green cushions and bright yellow flowers. It is the easiest to grow from seed. H5cm/2in, W20cm/8in. F3-5.
D. bruniifolia. This has deep yellow flowers which appear on compact, green pads with hairy leaves. H8cm/3in, W20cm/8in. F3-5.
D. rigida bryoides. This makes dense cushions with small, sparse, yellow flowers on slender stems. H5cm/2in, W8cm/3in. F3-5. The form *bryoides imbricata* is even more diminutive, with miniscule, overlapping leaves. Ideal for scree, a trough or pan. H5cm/2in, W5cm/2in. F3-5.

Draba rigida bryoides imbricata

Epilobium glabellum

DRYAS Mountain avens

These somewhat shrubby sun lovers form bright green, evergreen mats of oak-like, leathery leaves, with a fairly rapid spread. All need well-drained soil. All Z3-6.

D. drummondii. This plant has nodding, yellow, cup-shaped flowers on short stems. H10cm/4in, W25cm/10in. F5-7.

D. octopetala. This is the best-known species. It has white flowers which are followed by silky seed heads. H8cm/3in, W30-45cm/12-18in. F5-7.

D. × suendermannii. A hybrid between the two previous species, its flower buds are yellow, opening to white. H8cm/3in, W60cm/2ft. F5-7.

EDRAIANTHUS Grassy bells

A choice but short-lived genus of mat-forming alpines for gritty, limy soil or limestone scree and usually growing from a central rootstock, they can only be propagated from seed. All Z4-7.

E. dalmaticus. This forms narrow-leaved rosettes, with violet-blue, bell-shaped flowers. H10cm/4in, W15cm/6in. F5-6.

E. dinaricus. A species with needle-like leaves and clusters of pale purple flowers. **E. graminifolius** is similar. Both H5cm/2in, W20cm/8in. F5-6.

E. pumilio. Makes grey-green, close-set hummocks, with clusters of upturned, violet-blue flowers. A real gem. It needs protection against winter wet. H2.5cm/1in, W10cm/4in. F5-6.

EPILOBIUM Willow herb

Only two or three species are worth growing. Easy in sun and moist but well-drained soil.

E. glabellum. This species has a late display of creamy white, funnel-shaped flowers above a mat of glossy, often bronzed leaves, and is attractive for months on end.

H20cm/8in, W45cm/18in. F6-9. Z8-9.

E. kaikourense. This has bronzy foliage and pinkish flowers. Short-lived, but self-sown seedlings often appear. H15cm/6in, W30cm/1ft. F6-8. Z6-8.

ERIGERON Dwarf fleabane

These daisy flowers are easy, though a few need gritty, free-draining soil.

E. aureus. This is a species that needs free-draining soil, especially disliking winter wet. It makes dense tufts of grey leaves and large, golden-yellow flowers. H5cm/2in, W10cm/4in. F5-7. Z5-8.

E. leiomerus. Forms a tufty mat of small, shiny leaves, with little, lavender-blue flowers. H8cm/3in, W15cm/6in. F5-7. Z4-7.

E. mucronatus. A long-lived profusion of pinkish daisies appears on the somewhat twiggy growth. It is liable to self-seeding freely but is still worthwhile. H15-20cm/6-8in, W30cm/1ft. F6-10. Z5-7.

ERINUS Fairy foxglove

E. alpinus. This is the only species in cultivation and, though short-lived, it makes a neat, evergreen mound. The flower sprays are either lilac, lavender, or pale pink, or, in the case of the well-known 'Dr Hähnle', deep pink. H5cm/2in, W15cm/6in. F5-7. Z4-7.

ERIOGONUM Wild buckwheat

Very few of these mat-forming or mounded evergreens are seen. They need full sun and well-drained, even poor, gritty soil, and dislike winter wet.

E. umbellatum. A fairly reliable species with leathery leaves, woolly beneath, and heads of creamy yellow, fluffy flowers. H20cm/8in, W30cm/1ft. F5-7. Z6-8.

ERIOPHYLLUM

E. caespitosum. See *E. lanatum*.

E. lanatum (syn. *E. caespitosum*). It makes an exuberant summer growth of divided, silvery foliage and a long display of deep yellow daisies. Apt to seed and need curbing, it is good on a wall, where it wants sun and well-drained soil. H20cm/8in, W30-45cm/12-18in. F5-9. Z6-8.

ERODIUM Storksbill

These mound-forming sun lovers, closely related to hardy geraniums, are long-flowering with dainty foliage, but some crowns become woody with age. They prefer sun and well-drained, preferably limy soil, and resent winter wet. For the connoisseur with scree conditions or an alpine house, there are several other long-flowering species and hybrids from which to choose.

E. chamaedryoides. See *E. reichardii*.

E. chrysanthum. Its filigree, silver foliage sets off the pale yellow, cup-shaped

Erinus alpinus

Eriophyllum lanatum

flowers. H25cm/10in, W30-40cm/12-16in. F6-9. Z7-8.

E. guttatum. A rather ugly name for a pretty sub-shrub, with purple-spotted, white flowers. H15cm/6in, W25cm/10in. F6-9. Z8.

E. macradenum. This species has pale violet and purple flowers on low, ferny mounds. H13cm/5in, W30cm/1ft. F6-9. Z7-8.

E. reichardii (syn. *E. chamaedryoides*). This little gem makes compact, deep green mounds set with white or pink flowers; and crimson-veined, pink, stemless flowers in the most popular form, '**Roseum**'. A double form, '**Flore Pleno**', also exists. All H2.5cm/1in, W25cm/10in. F5-8. Z8-9.

E. supracanum. The grey-green, finely cut leaves complement its clear pink flowers. H15cm/6in, W30cm/1ft. F6-9. Z7-8.

ERYSIMUM Dwarf wallflower

Still often placed under the wallflower genus, *Cheiranthus*, most in circulation are hybrids, some upright and bushy, others spreading mats. All prefer full sun and good drainage. They are short-lived but often self-seed. All Z5-8.

E. 'Constant Cheer'. Grows erectly and is seldom out of flower. Its blooms are violet-mauve, tinged amber. It needs poor soil. H30cm/1ft, W25cm/10in. F4-7.

E. 'Harpur Crewe'. See *Cheiranthus* 'Harpur Crewe'.

E. 'Jacob's Jacket'. This has multi-coloured flowers and a loosely upright habit. H20cm/8in, W25cm/10in. F4-7.

E. 'Moonlight'. Mat-forming, with clear, light yellow flowers. H15cm/6in, W25cm/10in. F4-7.

E. 'Orange Flame'. Rich orange flowers on spreading, green mats. H13cm/5in, W30cm/1ft. F6-7.

E. 'Sunbright'. Also a spreader, this has bright yellow flowers. H15cm/6in, W30cm/1ft. F4-7.

ERYTHRONIUM Dog's tooth violet

Also called adder's tongues and trout or fawn lilies, these bulbs, with their pretty foliage, mottled in some species, and charming, trumpet-like flowers, prefer light shade, moist but well-drained, humus-rich soil and cool summers. Either allot them their own space, or use them to underplant alpine shrubs. They resent disturbance. All Z5-8.

E. californicum. The Californian fawn lily has clusters of creamy yellow flowers and purple-mottled leaves. H25-30cm/10-12in, W15cm/6in. F4-5.

E. 'Pagoda'. This has pale yellow flowers. H30-45cm/12-18in, W20cm/8in. F4-5.

E. 'White Beauty'. This has white flowers, zoned yellow at the centre. H30cm/1ft, W20cm/8in. F4-5.

Erodium macradenum

Erythronium 'Pagoda'

Euryops acraeus

EURYOPS

E. acraeus (syn. *E. evansii*). This makes a neat, mounded, silvery leaved bushlet, carrying a long succession of yellow daisies. Prefers sun and gritty soil. Deadhead. H20cm/8in, W40cm/16in. F5-8. Z9-10.

E. evansii. See *E. acraeus*.

FELICIA

F. rosulata. See *Aster natalensis*.

FRANKENIA

A sun-loving and mat-forming genus, but patches are liable to die back in severe winters. Best grown in light, free-draining soil. Divide and replant every two or three years. All Z6-9.

F. laevis. Makes a thyme-like carpet bearing pale pink flowers. H2.5cm/1in, W20cm/8in. F6-8.

F. thymifolia. This has greyish, harmlessly spreading mats and clear pink flowers. H2.5cm/1in, W20cm/8in. F6-8.

FUCHSIA

A few dwarf kinds can be grown with alpines. They are not fully hardy, so plant deeply in a sunny, sheltered spot and protect in hard winters with a deep mulch of leaf litter or bark around the plants.

F. magellanica 'Pumila'. Grows erectly with tiny red and violet flowers. H15cm/6in, W15cm/6in. F7-9. Z7-8.

F. procumbens. This species has trailing summer growth of rounded leaves and petal-less, mainly purple flowers which are followed by large, magenta berries. H8cm/3in, W60cm/2ft. F7-9. Z8-9.

F. 'Tom Thumb'. This popular hybrid has large, pink and red flowers on neat, upright growth. H20cm/8in, W15cm/6in. F7-10. Z7-8.

Fuchsia 'Tom Thumb'

Gentiana × macaulayi 'Kingfisher'

Geranium cinereum 'Ballerina'

Gentiana verna

GENTIANA Gentian

A genus which is almost synonymous with the term 'alpine', these plants fall into three fairly distinct groups of spring-, summer- and autumn-flowering species. The first prefer some lime, the second are lime-tolerant and the third need an acid soil.

Most of the autumn-flowering species have narrow leaves on lax stems. They resent hot, dry conditions. The trumpet-shaped flowers range from pale ice-blue to rich violet. Their thong-like roots are apt to become congested after a few years, but they can be divided and replanted in spring or given a light annual mulch of sandy compost with a little organic fertilizer mixed in. Where suited, they make a brilliant late display.

G. acaulis. The trumpet, or stemless, gentian has large, upstanding, blue trumpets from low, slow-spreading mats. How freely it flowers seems to be a matter of chance. H10cm/4in, W30-45cm/12-18in. F4-5. Z4-7.

G. decumbens. Narrow-leaved rosettes and radiating sprays of purple-blue flowers. H15cm/6in, W20cm/8in. F7-9. Z4-7.

G. farreri. This favourite species has light blue flowers. H10-15cm/4-6in, W13cm/5in. F8-10. Z5-7.

G. freyniana. Upright, leafy stems and deep blue trumpets. H20cm/8in, W15cm/6in. F7-9. Z4-7.

G. lagodechiana. This species and its forms, **'Doeringiana'** and the fairly upright **'Hascombensis'**, are similar to *G. septemfida*. H13-25cm/5-10in, W30cm/1ft. F7-9. Z3-7.

G. × macaulayi **'Kingfisher'**. Large, brilliant blue blooms. H10cm/4in, W20cm/8in. F8-10. Z5-7.

G. septemfida. See under Perennials.

G. sino-ornata. This, the best-known species, has brilliant 'gentian' blue flowers. **'Alba'** is a white form. **'Angel's Wings'** is bright blue, feathered and striped white. **'Mary Lyle'** has attractive white flowers. All H10cm/4in, W20cm/8in. F8-10. Z5-7.

G. **'Susan Jane'**. A hybrid with deep blue, white-throated flowers which are tinged green inside. H10cm/4in, W20cm/8in. F8-10. Z5-7.

G. verna. A gem for humus-rich, gritty soil, with smaller but brighter blue flowers, abundant if not starved. H8cm/3in, W15cm/6in. F3-5. Z4-7.

GERANIUM Cranesbill

Most dwarf kinds make first-rate alpines, easy to grow in any well-drained soil and sun. They flower for a long time and are generally drought-resistant, with good, deeply cut, evergreen or semi-evergreen foliage to complement the five-petalled, saucer-shaped flowers.

G. cinereum. This has ash-grey foliage and pale pink, dark-centred flowers. The true species is seldom available but the clear, light pink hybrid **'Apple Blossom'**, which I introduced in 1972, is. Provide full sun and gritty soil. H10cm/4in, W25cm/10in. F5-8. Z5-8. **'Ballerina'** is ranked highly for its adaptability and long display of lilac-pink flowers, charmingly flecked and veined with crimson. It pleases me to see this so widely known and grown since I introduced it, also in 1972. H13cm/5in, W25cm/10in. F5-9. Z5-8. **'Laurence Flatman'**, named after one of my most likeable and enthusiastic helpers, was a later introduction, with green leaves and long sprays of larger flowers with heavy crimson markings, only slightly deeper in colour than 'Ballerina'. I have transferred the name to a more recent, more distinctive and vigorous plant, with even larger, deeper pink blooms. H15cm/6in, W30cm/1ft. F5-9. Z5-8.

G. dalmaticum. Makes glossy, leafy clumps, bright red in autumn, and dainty, soft pink, upstanding flowers. **'Album'** is a white form, tinged with pink. Both H8cm/3in, W45-60cm/18-24in. F5-7. Z4-8.

G. farreri. A species which may lack vigour, but not appeal, with its dense mat of deep green leaves and soft pink, black-centred flowers. It needs sharp drainage and grows best in humus-rich soil. H10cm/4in, W20cm/8in. F6-8. Z5-8.

G. pylzowianum. This spreads quickly below ground, producing mottled, feathery leaves and a short season of pink flowers. H10cm/4in, W25cm/10in. F6-7. Z4-8.

G. sanguineum. The compact form of bloody cranesbill, *lancastriense*, given the space, makes a wide, near evergreen mat set with clear pink flowers for several weeks. H10cm/4in, W20cm/8in. F6-8. Z4-8. **'Shepherd's Warning'** makes mounds dotted with deeper, brighter pink flowers. H15cm/6in, W30cm/1ft. F6-8. Z4-8. See also under Perennials.

G. sessiliflorum nigricans. This produces bronzy brown hummocks and almost stemless, whitish flowers. Not long-lived but seeds itself. H5cm/2in, W15cm/6in. F6-7. Z4-8.

G. subcaulescens. Mounds of grey-green leaves set off the vivid, magenta-purple

Geranium cinereum 'Apple Blossom'

Geranium subcaulescens 'Splendens'

flowers of this species. **'Giuseppii'** is similar. Both H13cm/5in, W23cm/9in. F6-8. Z5-8. **'Splendens'** is weaker but the flowers are an intense salmon-pink. H13cm/5in, W30cm/1ft. F6-8. Z5-8.

G. wallichianum. See under Perennials.

GLOBULARIA Globe daisy
This genus makes deep green mats or tufts and powder-puff flowers. Evergreen and reliable in well-drained soil and sun.

G. bellidifolia. See *G. meridionalis.*

G. cordifolia. Similar to *G. meridionalis* and sometimes listed incorrectly as *G. nudicaulis,* which is taller. H13cm/5in, W25cm/10in. F5-8. Z5-7.

G. incanescens. A rare beauty, with tight hummocks of stemless, light blue flowers. Needs very gritty soil. H2.5cm/1in, W15cm/6in. F5-6. Z5-7.

G. meridionalis (syn. *G. bellidifolia*). Tangled, woody mats carry nearly stemless, little, blue, fluffy flowers. H10cm/4in, W15cm/6in. F5-6. Z5-7.

G. nudicaulis. Deep green, slow-spreading mats carry blue puffs on erect stems. Easy, but not always free-flowering. H20cm/8in, W15cm/6in. F5-7. Z5-7.

G. trichosantha. This has toothed basal leaves and stems of bright blue flowers. H20cm/8in, W15cm/6in. F6-8. Z5-7.

GYPSOPHILA Baby's breath
These mostly trailing, narrow-leaved perennials make a fine summer display. All are sun lovers for well-drained soil; their deep roots are drought-resistant.

G. cerastioides. A non-trailer which makes neat, tufty mats of velvety leaves and white, purple-veined flowers. H5cm/2in, W30cm/1ft. F5-6. Z4-7.

G. repens. All varieties of this species have prostrate, glaucous, narrow leaves and tangled, wiry stems of small, clear pink flowers, and are excellent draped over a wall or rock. **'Dubia'** and *fratensis* are sometimes listed separately but belong here. **'Dorothy Teacher'** has slightly larger flowers than the species. **'Letchworth Rose'** is light pink with a more robust, mounded habit. **'Rosa Schönheit'** is the deepest pink. All H5-10cm/2-4in, W60cm/2ft. F5-7. Z3-8.

HABERLEA
There are only very slight differences between this genus and the better-known ramondas. The haberleas must have north-facing crevices and the crinkly, evergreen rosettes are not happy on a flat surface. Cool, peaty soil is ideal, dryish in winter. All Z5-7.

H. ferdinand-coburgii. This has dark green rosettes and tubular, open, pale lilac flowers, with pronounced, golden flecks. H13cm/5in, W20cm/8in. F4-5.

Globularia meridionalis

Gypsophila repens 'Dorothy Teacher'

H. rhodopensis. Rounded, hairy rosettes send up sprays of smaller, soft lavender-lilac flowers, less flecked with gold than *H. ferdinand-coburgii.* H8cm/3in, W20cm/8in. F4-6.

HACQUETIA See under Perennials.

HEBE Shrubby veronica
Only the dwarfest of this wide-ranging genus are included here; taller types are listed under Shrubs. All are of somewhat suspect hardiness but have a unique distinction. They need sun and good drainage. See also the low, semi-shrubby parahebes.

H. buchananii **'Minor'**. This makes a neat, little bush of glossy, olive-green leaves and sparse, white flowers. H13cm/5in, W15cm/6in. F6-7. Z9-10.

H. buxifolia **'Minima'**. 'Box-leaved' describes this miniature form with small, white flowers. H15cm/6in, W15cm/6in. F6-7. Z9-10.

HEDYOTIS (syn. HOUSTONIA) Bluet
H. caerulea. The only species in common cultivation forms loose mats of lance-shaped leaves and small, soft blue, yellow-eyed flowers. Best in a sandy, acid soil in part shade. H2.5cm/1in, W10cm/4in. F4-5. Z5-8.

HELIANTHEMUM Sun rose
Indispensable for a bright summer display, all are inclined towards shrubbiness, though some are prostrate. Most are quite robust hybrids and should be trimmed with shears

after flowering to keep them neat and tidy. All are sun lovers and can withstand dry, and even starved, soil. Colours range through white to pink, yellow, orange, brown and red, and several have double flowers.

H. lunulatum. This makes erect, little, grey cushions decked with yellow, orange-centred flowers. H15cm/6in, W20cm/8in. F6-8. Z6-7.

H. nummularium glabrum (syn. *H. serpyllifolium*). Shiny, prostrate, quick-spreading mats carry bright yellow flowers.

Helianthemum 'Raspberry Ripple'

H5cm/2in, W25cm/10in. F5-7. Z6-7.

H. scardicum. The species has grey, felty foliage and golden-yellow flowers. H20cm/8in, W30cm/1ft. F5-7. Z6-7.

H. serpyllifolium. See *H. nummularium glabrum.*

Hybrids. The following are some of the best. **'Annabel'**, soft pink, double. **'Boughton Double Primrose'**, light yellow, double. **'Cerise Queen'**, cherry-red, double. **'Fireball'**, deep red, double. **'Henfield Brilliant'**, deep orange, single. **'Jubilee'**, clear yellow, double. **'Raspberry Ripple'**, crimson to pink, single. **'Wisley Pink'**, pale pink, single. **'Wisley Primrose'**, pale yellow, single. **'Wisley White'**, white, single. All H15-30cm/6-12in, W60-90cm/2-3ft. F5-7. Z5-7.

Helianthemum 'Wisley White'

Helichrysum bellidioides

Hypericum olympicum 'Grandiflorum'

HELICHRYSUM

These sun-loving, drought-resistant plants vary quite considerably in habit. Some are shrubby but very adaptable. Provide full sun and well-drained, gritty soil, and protect from winter wet.

H. angustifolium. See under Perennials.
H. bellidioides. Mat-forming and vigorous, this has dark green and silver, woolly leaves and white, crispy flowers. H5cm/2in, W45cm/18in. F6-8. Z7-9.
H. milfordiae. Very compact with silver hummocks and red buds opening into white flowers, this needs a warm, well-drained spot. H5cm/2in, W25cm/10in. F6-8. Z8-9.
H. orientale. See under Perennials.
H. splendidum. See under Perennials.

HEPATICA See under Perennials.

HOUSTONIA See under HEDYOTIS.

HUTCHINSIA

H. alpina. A pretty mat-former with deep green, ferny leaves and dainty sprays of tiny, white flowers. H10cm/4in, W25cm/10in. F5-6. Z5-7.

HYLOMECON See under Perennials.

HYPERICUM St John's wort

A reliable source of summer colour, some are excellent in hot, dry walls, a few

Iberis 'Little Gem'

Iberis sempervirens

are tender, and all need well-drained soil and full sun.

H. coris. Neatly upright, this has narrow, evergreen, heather-like leaves and many small, bright yellow flowers. Likes limy soil. H13cm/5in, W20cm/8in. F6-9. Z7-9.
H. fragile. See *H. olympicum minus*.
H. olympicum (syn. *H. polyphyllum*). This and its forms are especially good in sunny crevices or on walls. Foliage is blue-grey and flowers have prominent stamens. Variations include the lemon-yellow 'Citrinum', the larger-flowered 'Grandiflorum', and the form *minus* (syn. *H. fragile*), which is not markedly different from the type. All H15-20cm/6-8in, W30cm/1ft. F6-8. Z6-8.
H. polyphyllum. See *H. olympicum*.

H. reptans. Prostrate, with leafy stems carrying scarlet buds opening into deep golden-yellow flowers, this needs a warm spot. Leaves turn yellow or red in autumn. H2.5cm/1in, W20cm/8in. F6-8. Z6-8.
H. trichocaulon. Prostrate with tiny leaves and golden flowers, red in bud. Short-lived in cold districts. H2.5cm/1in, W25cm/10in. F6-8. Z7-8.
H. yakushimanum. This is quite a minute creeper, with profuse, bright yellow, stemless flowers. Best in warm areas. H2.5cm/1in, W20cm/8in. F6-8. Z6-8.

IBERIS Candytuft

These are evergreen and generally long-lived perennials. Nomenclature is confused but only a few, all white-flowered, are usually offered. All need well-drained soil and sun.

I. commutata. See *I. sempervirens*.
I. 'Little Gem' (syn. 'Weisser Zwerg'). Though often listed under *I. sempervirens*, this is a quite distinct form, being bushy and upright, with intensely white flowers. H15cm/6in, W30cm/1ft. F5-7. Z3-9.
I. saxatilis. A choice dwarf, with a modest spread, needle-like leaves and white flowers. Needs gritty soil. H10cm/4in, W20cm/8in. F4-6. Z4-8.
I. sempervirens (syn. *I. commutata*). Excellent for walls, its trailing, dark foliage spreads steadily and flowers profusely. H15cm/6in, W50cm/20in. F4-6. Z3-9. The vigorous **'Snowflake'** (syn. 'Schneeflocke') is larger-leaved and flowered, but less spreading than the species. H20cm/8in, W23cm/9in. F4-6. Z4-8.

IRIS

Most non-bulbous iris are listed under Perennials. Bulbous types are not included here, but *I. reticulata* and *I. danfordiae* make a brave display in early spring.
I. barbata (syn. *I. pumila*). See under Perennials.
I. chamaeiris. This is an early, bearded species, with all too brief a display. Its yellow, white or purple flowers are carried singly or in pairs. H20cm/8in, W20cm/8in. F4. Z3-9.
I. cristata. A charming pygmy with branching rhizomes, fans of slender leaves and white-crested, lilac and orange flowers. It prefers cool, gritty, acid soil. H13cm/5in, W15cm/6in. F5-6. Z3-9.
I. gracilipes. Produces grassy leaves and branching stems of flat, gold-crested, lilac flowers. It needs light shade and humus-rich soil. Plant in spring. H20cm/8in, W20cm/8in. F5-6. Z7-9.
I. graminea. See under Perennials.
I. innominata. See under Perennials.
I. lacustris. Similar to *I. cristata*, this is an even dwarfer, crested species. H8cm/3in, W10cm/4in. F5-6. Z3-9.

ALPINES

ISOPYRUM

I. thalictroides. A choice plant for cool shade and damp, humus-rich soil, it has tiny, lobed foliage and pearl-white, starry flowers. H15cm/6in, W15cm/6in. F3-5. Z5-8.

JASIONE

J. jankae. An unusual plant with a tufted habit of thereabouts evergreen leaves. The rounded, pincushion-type flowers, unbranched, are bright blue. H25cm/10in, W23cm/9in. F5-7. Z5-8.

J. perennis. This is more readily available than the above and more reliably perennial. Otherwise, it is fairly similar. It is also good as a frontal border subject. H23cm/9in, W25cm/10in. F5-8. Z5-8.

JEFFERSONIA

J. dubia. This choice plant has lobed leaves, coppery purple when young, and cup-shaped, light blue flowers. Provide gritty soil, humus and light shade. H15cm/6in, W15cm/6in. F4-5. Z5-8.

LEONTOPODIUM Edelweiss

As well as the traditional *L. alpinum*, others, more curious than showy, are also worth growing. All need sun and well-drained soil. All Z4-7.

L. aloysiodorum (syn. *L. haplophylloides*). More reliably perennial than *L. alpinum* but with smaller flowers. The whole plant is lemon-scented. H25cm/10in, W25cm/10in. F5-7.

L. alpinum. Whitish, clustered flower heads appear above narrow-leaved tufts. There are one or two named forms. H13cm/5in, W25cm/10in. F5-6. Z4-7. The form *krasense* is prolific, with very white leaves and flowers. H15cm/6in, W25cm/10in. F5-6.

L. haplophylloides. See *L. aloysiodorum*.

LEUCANTHEMUM

L. hosmariense. See *Chrysanthemum hosmariense*.

LEWISIA

These somewhat tricky, short-lived plants have an unfailing appeal for their brilliant colours. They form rosettes from usually fleshy roots and most prefer a slope or crevice, in full sun for herbaceous types and light shade for evergreens. All need sharp drainage and humus-rich, ideally lime-free soil. Evergreen types cannot abide winter wet, and survive best in crevices. All are good in alpine houses.

L. columbiana. This has red-veined flowers in shades of pink on branching sprays. The roots are fleshy and thick. H20cm/8in, W15-25cm/6-10in. F5-6. Z4-7.

L. cotyledon. There are many named forms, ranging from white through pink and orange, tinged with red. The evergreen

rosettes are quite fleshy with saw-edged, radiating leaves. H20-25cm/8-10in, W15-25cm/6-10in. F5-7. Z4-7. **'Edithae'** has dark green rosettes and pink flowers. H15cm/6in, W10-15cm/4-6in. F5-6. Z4-7.

L. nevadensis. Deciduous and dormant from August to February, it produces tufty leaves followed by almost stemless, large, white flowers. H5cm/2in, W5cm/2in. F5-6. Z5-7.

L. rediviva. Commonly known as bitter root, the thick roots of this, another deciduous, species produce glaucous, fleshy leaves which wither as the large, many petalled, pink or white flowers open. H5cm/2in, W15cm/6in. F4-5. Z5-7.

L. tweedyi. The gem of the genus, this has large, fleshy leaves and large, open flowers

Leontopodium alpinum

of a striking, apricot-pink shade. Like so many lewisias, it prefers a drying-off period after flowering. Selected forms waver towards salmon or cerise. H15cm/6in, W15cm/6in. F4-5. Z6-9.

LIMONIUM Sea lavender

L. cosyrense. This has rosettes of almost evergreen, leathery leaves and sprays of tiny, pinkish flowers. It needs full sun and sharp drainage. H10cm/4in, W15cm/6in. F6-8. Z5-8.

LINARIA Toadflax

These are easy, sun-loving plants, but some are short-lived.

L. alpina. Alpine toadflax is pretty, but one of the short-lived forms. It has narrow, blue-green leaves and trailing stems of tiny, mauve, blue or pink snapdragon flowers. It is long-flowering and can be easily raised from seed. H10cm/4in, W25cm/10in. F5-8. Z3-8.

L. glareosa (syn. *Chaenorrhinum glareosum*). This has a similar habit but deep green leaves and violet-blue flowers. H10cm/4in, W25cm/10in. F5-7. Z3-8.

LINUM Flax

A large genus of sun-loving plants, some resent winter wet and frost; all need good drainage. Most are long-flowering, coming after the main flush of alpines.

Lewisia cotyledon

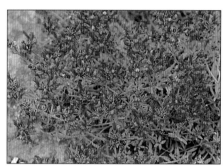

Linaria alpina

Linum arboreum

L. arboreum. Erect and shrubby, this has clusters of bright yellow, flat-petalled, funnel-shaped flowers. H25cm/10in, W25cm/10in. F6-8. Z3-8.

L. flavum. **'Compactum'**, with bright yellow flowers, is a good form of golden flax. H25cm/10in, W23cm/9in. F6-8. Z4-8. The best variety is **'Gemmell's Hybrid'**, which is domed, with grey-green leaves and many intense, deep yellow flowers. Provide full sun and sharp drainage. H20cm/8in, W20cm/8in. F6-8. Z4-8.

L. suffruticosum salsoloides **'Nanum'**. This has low, heathery growth and white flowers. H8cm/3in, W45cm/18in. F6-8. Z6-8.

L. **'Waterperry'**. A hybrid bearing small, yellow flowers with overlapping petals. H15cm/6in, W20cm/8in. F6-8. Z6-8.

Lithodora diffusum 'Alba'

Lithodora diffusum 'Heavenly Blue'

Lysimachia nummularia 'Aurea'

LITHODORA (syn. LITHOSPERMUM)
This is the correct generic name for the shrubby species known until recently as *Lithospermum*, except for some species which have been transferred to *Moltkia*. In common usage the name *Lithospermum* still prevails.
L. diffusum. Among the most popular of all alpines are the cultivars '**Alba**', white, '**Grace Ward**', blue, and '**Heavenly Blue**'. These are prostrate and semi-shrubby, with narrow, dark green leaves and small but intensely blue flowers over a long period. Lime-free soil is essential. Both H10cm/4in, W60cm/2ft. F5-8. Z6-8.
L. oleifolium. Spreading below ground, it produces grey-green, silky leaves and sky-

blue flowers. Provide a warm, sunny spot and gritty soil. Tolerates lime. H15cm/6in, W30cm/1ft. F5-7. Z6-8.

LITHOSPERMUM See under LITHODORA.

LOTUS Bird's foot trefoil
L. corniculatus '**Plenus**'. A dwarf, double-flowered form of the British wildflower, it has dense, purplish, clover-like foliage and orange-yellow flowers. It is a rampant carpeter. H8cm/3in, W30cm/1ft. F6-7. Z5-8.

LYCHNIS Campion
A genus which suffers from a multiplicity of alternative names. All forms are easy to grow in well-drained soil and sun, but some are short-lived.
L. alpina (syn. *Viscaria alpina*). This has compact, leafy rosettes and dense heads of light purple flowers. Pink and white forms exist. Short-lived but easy from seed. H8cm/3in, W8cm/3in. F5-7. Z4-7.
L. flos-jovis. See under Perennials.
L. lagascae (syn. *Petrocoptis glaucifolia*). This has bright pink, starry flowers above tufty, blue-green foliage, but it is rather short-lived. H10cm/4in, W15cm/6in. F6-7. Z4-7.
L. viscaria. See under Perennials.

LYSIMACHIA Loosestrife
This genus contains clump-forming plants of greatly contrasting heights. All are easy to grow in sun or light shade and moist soil.
L. japonica '**Minutissima**'. Makes tight, green carpets set with small, stemless, golden flowers. Provide cool soil and shade. H2.5cm/1in, W23cm/9in. F6-7. Z3-8.
L. nummularia '**Aurea**'. The golden-leaved form of creeping Jenny is useful as ground cover or crevice planting in shade, or in sun where not dry. Its yellow, buttercup flowers are sparse. H5cm/2in, W60cm/2ft. F6-7. Z3-8.

MARGYRICARPUS
M. setosus. An evergreen, low-growing shrub with tiny leaves and inconspicuous flowers, followed by numerous, pearl-like berries. For full sun. H20cm/8in, W30cm/1ft. F6-8. Z7-9.

MAZUS
These creeping, deciduous plants spread below ground. Provide shelter, sun and moist soil.
M. pumilio. This has dark green leaves set with stemless, blue and white flowers. H2.5cm/1in, W23cm/9in. F5-7. Z5-9.
M. reptans (syn. *M. rugosus*). A rapid carpeter with toothed leaves and tubular, deep blue flowers, flecked white and yellow. H5cm/2in, W30cm/1ft. F5-7. Z5-9.
M. rugosus. See *M. reptans*.

MENTHA
M. requienii. Corsican mint is the smallest mint, forming merely a green film on hard surfaces, but highly aromatic and with minute, mauve-blue flowers. Useful for cool, damp crevices and paving, though not entirely hardy. H1.5cm/¹/₂in, W30cm/1ft. F6-7. Z7-9.

MERTENSIA
M. asiatica. See under Perennials.
M. coventryana. This has spreading, deep green, deciduous tufts and little sprays of indigo-blue flowers. Best in shade. H8cm/3in, W15cm/6in. F4-5. Z5-7.
M. echioides. Lax growth, light green leaves and deep blue, forget-me-not flowers, sometimes repeating in autumn. Divide every two or three years, in autumn. H10cm/4in, W25cm/10in. F4-5. Z6-8.

MICROMERIA
These choice little semi-evergreen or evergreen, aromatic plants, closely related to thyme, need the warmest, sunniest spot and well-drained soil. All Z7-9.
M. corsica (syn. *Acinos corsicus*). A grey-leaved, strongly aromatic, prickly shrublet with tiny, lilac flowers. H8cm/3in, W15cm/6in. F6-7.
M. croatica. Varies from the above only in having spikes with more compact flower heads. H8cm/3in, W15cm/6in. F6-7.
M. microphylla. This deep green, little bush carries pink flowers. H23cm/9in, W23cm/9in. F6-8.
M. varia. See *Thymus ericifolius*.

MIMULUS Monkey flower
Most of these showy, mat-forming plants are shallow-rooting and rapid-spreading, and need frequent lifting, dividing and replanting. They prefer good, moist soil and are best in mainly sunny spots. If cut back and well treated, a number will flower a second time, later in the season. Some are short-lived.
M. '**Andean Nymph**'. Spreads quickly, producing a profusion of creamy pink, tubular flowers. H23cm/9in, W25cm/10in. F6-8. Z9-10.
M. '**A. T. Johnson**'. This has large, yellow flowers with copper-red spots. H20cm/8in, W20cm/8in. F6-7. Z8-10.
M. × burnetii. A reliable hybrid, with coppery orange flowers. H15cm/6in, W20cm/8in. F6-8. Z7-9.
M. '**Firedragon**'. Its large, flame-red trumpets are flecked inside with yellow spots. H20cm/8in, W25cm/10in. F6-8. Z7-9.
M. '**Mandarin**'. Bears bright orange, speckled red, large flowers. H15cm/6in, W20cm/8in. F6-8. Z7-9.
M. primuloides. Carries dainty, little, yellow flowers for weeks. It spreads well in summer, but makes only vestigial new

growth after a severe winter. H5cm/2in, W20cm/8in. F6-9. Z7-9.
M. 'Whitecroft Scarlet'. This is attractive but short-lived, as is the richly coloured **M. 'Wisley Red'.** Both H10cm/4in, W30cm/1ft. F6-8. Z9-10.

MINUARTIA
A genus now much confused by name changes involving *Arenaria* and *Sagina*, these mostly evergreen, cushion-forming, white-flowered plants need sun and good drainage. All Z4-7.
M. imbricata. This forms greyish cushions of congested rosettes and sizeable, white flowers. H5cm/2in, W15cm/6in. F5-7.
M. laricifolia (syn. *Arenaria laricifolia*). A useful little plant for crevices, with larch-like leaves and white flower sprays. H15cm/6in, W25cm/10in. F5-7.
M. stellata. Makes firm, green pads set with stemless, white flowers. H2.5cm/1in, W25cm/10in. F5-6.

MITELLA
M. breweri. Valuable ground cover in shade, this has shiny green, tidy rosettes and sprays of greenish flowers. Provide shade and moist, humus-rich soil. H15cm/6in, W15cm/6in. F6-7. Z5-7.

MOLTKIA
Some of these bushy sub-shrubs were formerly *Lithospermum*. All need full sun and very well-drained soil. All Z7-8.
M. petraea. This choice, beautiful little bush has grey-green foliage and abundant, funnel-shaped, soft blue flowers from pinkish buds. H13cm/5in, W30cm/1ft. F5-7.
M. speciosa. Another choice and rare species, this has silvery foliage and sprays of small, soft blue flowers. H15cm/6in, W23cm/9in. F5-7.
M. suffruticosa (formerly *Lithospermum graminifolium*). Splendid, though a little tender and slow to establish, with narrow leaves and a long season of bright blue flowers. H20cm/8in, W30cm/1ft. F5-8.

MORISIA
M. monanthos. A deep-rooting plant with rosettes of deeply toothed leaves and a cluster of stemless, yellow flowers, it makes but little spread and grows best in light sandy or gritty soil and sun. H5cm/2in, W15cm/6in. F5-6. Z5-7.

NIEREMBERGIA White cup
N. caerulea (syn. *N. hippomanica*). This is 90 per cent hardy and useful for continuity with its deep blue flowers on leafy stems. In cold climates, it is grown as an annual. H25cm/10in, W25cm/10in. F6-9. Z7-9.
N. hippomanica. See *N. caerulea*.
N. repens (syn. *N. rivularis*). Given full sun and gritty but moist soil, this spreads below

ground to give a long succession of large, white, golden-throated, cup-shaped flowers. The small leaves are oval in shape. H5cm/2in, W45cm/18in. F6-9. Z4-8.
N. rivularis. See *N. repens*.

OENOTHERA Evening primrose
The dwarf species are easy in sun and have a long flowering season. They are tufty and shallow-rooting.
O. acaulis. Makes dandelion-type rosettes and stemless, saucer-shaped, white to yellow flowers. Short-lived but it self-seeds.

Mimulus 'Andean Nymph'

Mimulus × burnetii

Nierembergia repens

Oenothera tetragona riparia

Omphalodes cappadocica

H8cm/3in, W20cm/8in. F6-8. Z5-9.
O. missouriensis. See under Perennials.
O. perennis (syn. *O. pumila*). Dwarf sundrops make neat, tufty growth, with tiny spikes of small, yellow flowers, opening in the daytime. It needs moist soil. H10cm/4in, W15-25cm/6-10in. F6-8. Z3-9.
O. pumila. See *O. perennis*.
O. tetragona riparia. Twiggy, rather lax and tangled, leafy growth provides a long succession of yellow cups. Prefers moist soil; cut back before dormancy to promote new basal growth. H20cm/8in, W25cm/10in. F6-9. Z3-9.

OMPHALODES Navelwort
These pretty, long-lived plants have forget-me-not type flowers and lush, oval-shaped foliage.
O. cappadocica. In cool shade this slowly makes a clump of near-evergreen leaves and short sprays of bright blue flowers. **'Anthea Bloom'** is sky-blue, with slightly greyish foliage. Both H13cm/5in, W30cm/1ft. F4-5. Z6-9.
O. luciliae. A choice species for a rock crevice or an alpine house, this has blue-grey leaves and sprays of sky-blue flowers. Full sun and gritty, alkaline soil. H15cm/6in, W45cm/18in. F4-5. Z6-7.
O. verna. Blue-eyed Mary and its white form, **'Alba'**, are easy plants which spread quickly by means of stolons, and are shade-tolerant. They are early but have a short season. H10cm/4in, W60cm/2ft. F3-4. Z6-9.

133

Origanum pulchellum

Oxalis adenophylla

ONOSMA

These are rare and distinctive plants, with dangling, tubular flowers. They need full sun and light soil. All Z7-9.
O. echioides. See *O. tauricum*.
O. tauricum (syn. *O. echioides*). Upright, with clusters of fragrant, light yellow flowers and narrow, hairy leaves, this is good for sunny walls and crevices. H25cm/10in, W30cm/1ft. F5-7.

OPHIOPOGON Lily turf

O. planiscapus 'Nigrescens'. This looks like near-black, gracefully arching grass.

Papaver alpinum

Parahebe catarractae

Moderately hardy and evergreen, it grows densely, spreads slowly, and has tiny spikes of white flowers followed by black berries. A striking subject for rich soil. H20cm/8in, W30cm/1ft. F7-8. Z6-10.

ORIGANUM

Mat-forming or sub-shrubby sun lovers, they are all aromatic relatives of the herb marjoram. All resent winter wet.
O. amanum. This makes tidy, light green bushes and bears clusters of pinkish, tubular flowers. Gritty soil essential. H10cm/4in, W15cm/6in. F6-8. Z5-8.
O. × hybridum. Carries dangling, pink flowers on arching, grey-leaved stems. H13cm/5in, W15cm/6in. F6-8. Z5-8.
O. laevigatum. See under Perennials.
O. pulchellum. Fairly vigorous, this has clusters of pink flowers. H20cm/8in, W15cm/6in. F6-8. Z5-8.
O. pulchrum. Spreading slowly in gritty soil, its pale greenery carries masses of lilac-pink, hop-like flowers on twiggy stems. H20cm/8in, W15cm/6in. F7-9. Z5-8.
O. vulgare 'Aureum'. See under Perennials.

OSTEOSPERMUM See under Perennials.

OXALIS

A large genus which includes pernicious weeds, among them *O. acetosella*, *O. corniculata* and *O. inops*, as well as choice, demanding species. Provide well-drained soil and sun or light shade.
O. adenophylla. Bulbous roots send up tufts of glaucous, finger-like, crinkled leaves and cup-shaped, pink flowers. H5cm/2in, W10cm/4in. F4-6. Z7-10.
O. enneaphylla. This gem for lime-free soil spreads slowly, producing silvery, crinkled leaves and quite large flowers, white to blush-pink. Best in crevices. H2.5cm/1in, W10cm/4in. F5-6. Z7-9.
O. lobata. An unusual and elusive, yellow-flowered beauty, often blooming twice a year, from tiny corms, but then quickly returning to dormancy. H5cm/2in, W8-10cm/3-4in. F7-9. Z7-9.
O. magellanica. This bronzy green, filmy

mat gives a profusion of white flowers. Best in damp shade. H2.5cm/1in, W25cm/10in. F7-8. Z8-9.

PAPAVER Poppy

Dwarf kinds are short-lived but come readily from seed. All are easy in sun and light soil.
P. alpinum. Like a miniature Iceland poppy, this grey-leaved plant has white, orange, pink or yellow flowers. It can also be grown as a hardy annual. H13cm/5in, W10cm/4in. F5-8. Z5-8.
P. miyabeanum. Also short-lived, it has soft yellow flowers above bluish green rosettes. Dislikes winter wet. H15cm/6in, W15cm/6in. F5-8. Z5-8.

PARAHEBE

The dwarf sub-shrubs listed below formerly came under the genus *Veronica*. They are useful and easy in sun and well-drained soil, but liable to suffer in severe winters.
P. × bidwillii. A minute hybrid, with white flowers, veined pink, on slender stems. H5cm/2in, W15cm/6in. F6-7. Z8-9.
P. catarractae. This and its variants have twiggy stems, round leaves and purple-veined, white or mauve flowers. H15cm/6in, W25cm/10in. F6-7. Z8-9. The form *diffusa* is prostrate. 'Tiny Cat' is similar, with pinkish flowers. Both H8cm/3in, W15cm/6in. F6-7. Z8-9.
P. hookeriana. Similar to *P. catarractae*, but the flowers are bluish. H15cm/6in, W25cm/10in. F6-7. Z8-9.
P. lyallii. This deep green, leafy, prostrate shrub has white flowers. H15cm/6in, W25cm/10in. F6-7. Z8-9.
P. 'Miss Willmott'. An old hybrid with lilac-mauve flowers. H15cm/6in, W25cm/10in. F6-7. Z4-7.

PARONYCHIA

These modest, evergreen, mat-forming perennials are best in dryish, sunny positions, and make good ground cover. All Z5-7.
P. capitata. Grey foliage with inconspicuous flowers surrounded by papery, white bracts. A steady but not invasive spread. H2.5cm/1in, W40cm/16in. F6-7.
P. serpyllifolia. More compact, this has minute, silvery leaves and bracts. H2.5cm/1in, W20cm/8in. F6-7.

PATRINIA

P. palmata. See *P. triloba*.
P. triloba (syn. *P. palmata*). A useful plant for late flowering, its upright, branching stems carry clusters of bright yellow flowers for many weeks above glossy, deeply cut greenery. In good, damp soil and semi-shade, it spreads well. H15cm/6in, W15cm/6in. F6-10. Z5-8.

PENSTEMON

The alpine forms have a wide colour range. Many need replanting deeply after a time to encourage new stem roots if they become straggly. Sun, shelter and well-drained soil are essential, and winter protection in very cold areas. Much confusion exists over nomenclature.

P. campanulatus. See under Perennials.
P. cardwellii. This has a low, shrubby habit, shiny green leaves and large pink flowers. H20cm/8in, W25cm/10in. F5-6. Z7-9.
P. fruticosus. Densely shrubby, this has profuse, purplish flowers. H20cm/8in, W40cm/16in. F5-6. Z6-8.
P. heterophyllus. See under Perennials.
P. menziesii. Variable species with low, shrubby growth and usually violet-purple flowers. The dwarfest, almost prostrate form is *microphyllus.* H8cm/3in, W25cm/10in. F5-6. Z7-9.
P. newberryi. Evergreen mats of small, leathery leaves bear rosy purple flowers. H15cm/6in, W30cm/1ft. F5-6. Z7-9.
P. pinifolius. This has finely cut leaves and loose spikes of bright red flowers. Reliably hardy in dry sun. H15cm/6in, W25cm/10in. F6-8. Z8-9.
P. roezlii. A possible hybrid (perhaps of *P. newberryi),* this form is low and shrubby, with rosy red flowers. H15-20cm/6-8in, W30cm/1ft. F5-6. Z8-9.
P. rupicola. Distinctive for its cherry-pink flowers on dense, nearly prostrate, mat-forming growth. H10cm/4in, W20cm/8in. F5-6. Z7-8.
P. scouleri. This sub-shrub comes in purple and white forms. H30cm/1ft, W45cm/18in. F5-6. Z6-8.
P. 'Six Hills'. Lavender-blue trumpets appear above glaucous, shrubby growth on this robust hybrid. H20cm/8in, W30cm/1ft. F5-6. Z8-9.
P. virens. A non-shrubby carpeter with deep green foliage and violet-blue flowers. Easy to grow. H15cm/6in, W30cm/1ft. F5-7. Z8-9.

PETROCOPTIS

P. glaucifolia. See *Lychnis lagascae.*

PETROPHYTON Rock spiraea

P. hendersonii. A good crevice plant, this forms compact, bronzy hummocks and stumpy, fluffy flower spikes. H15cm/6in, W60cm/2ft. F5-6. Z6-9.

PETRORHAGIA See under TUNICA.

PHLOX

The dwarf and creeping species are indispensable, making a fine show to follow early spring subjects. Most are easy in light soil and sun. A few are less adaptable but worth growing in an alpine house.
P. adsurgens. Somewhat straggly, with

Penstemon pinifolius

Penstemon roezlii

Penstemon 'Six Hills'

salmon-pink flower clusters, this is best in the form **'Waggon Wheel'**, with larger flowers and deeply cut petals, hence the name. Provide cool, humus-rich soil and light shade. Both H10cm/4in, W30cm/1ft. F5-6. Z7-9.
P. amoena (syn. *P. × procumbens).* This is an easy, mat-forming species with small heads of purplish pink flowers. The vigorous **'Millstream'** has round leaves and clear pink, red-eyed flowers. There is also a variegated form, **'Variegata'.** All H15cm/6in, W30cm/1ft. F5-6. Z7-8.
P. divaricata. See under Perennials.
P. douglasii. Popular for its fine spring display, this creeping evergreen is covered with almost stemless flowers. Good forms include the blue-mauve **'Eva'**, **'Kelly's Eye'**, pink with a red eye, **'Lilac Cloud'** and **'Lilac Queen'**, **'Red Admiral'** and **'Waterloo'**, an intense crimson-red. All H2.5cm/1in, W15-45cm/6-18in. F4-6. Z5-8.
P. × procumbens. See *P. amoena.*
P. stolonifera. Creeping phlox's short runners spread rapidly but are easy to curb. The small flowers are of soft blue colouring. The forms **'Blue Ridge'** and **'Pink Ridge'** are liable to die out in patches. All H10cm/4in, W30cm/1ft. F4-5. Z2-8.
P. subulata. Like *P. douglasii* but a little less compact, moss phlox, or moss pink, carries its flowers well above the mat. **'Alexander's Surprise'** is salmon-pink. **'Benita'** is lavender-blue with a purple eye. **'MacDaniel's Cushion'** is rose-pink. **'May Snow'** is white. **'Oakington Blue'**, which I raised and named in 1930, is an unsurpassed light blue. **'Red Wings'** is crimson. **'Scarlet Flame'** is scarlet. **'Temiskaming'** is rosy red. **'White Delight'** is self-descriptive. All H8-13cm/3-5in, W45cm/18in. F4-6. Z2-9.

Phlox subulata 'Alexander's Surprise' (left) and 'White Delight'

Potentilla nitida 'Rubra'

Potentilla tabernaemontani 'Nana'

PHUOPSIS See under Perennials.

POLYGALA Milkwort
P. calcarea. In light, limy soil or scree, the little, green mats send up sprays of bright blue flowers. Self seeding. H8cm/3in, W30cm/1ft. F5-6. Z5-7.

POLYGONUM
P. capitatum and *P. runciforma* are invasive, but the following are worthwhile and need only a fair share of sun.
P. affine. See under Perennials.
P. tenuicaule. A showy subject, this makes clumps of heart-shaped leaves and sprays of pinkish white flowers. H15cm/6in, W30cm/1ft. F3-4. Z4-8.
P. vacciniifolium. This is a good standby for late flowering. Its twiggy stems form a tough mat of small leaves and clear pink, poker-like spikes. H10cm/4in, W60cm/2ft. F9-10. Z4-8.

Potentilla × tonguei

Pratia pedunculata

POTENTILLA Cinquefoil
This large genus includes trouble-free, mat-forming or tufty plants for mid-season display. The former need annual or biennial replanting to encourage free-flowering. All have deeply divided or compound leaves and rose-like blooms. They are sun lovers, for any soil.
P. alba. See under Perennials.
P. alpestris. See *P. crantzii*.
P. aurea. This has close, green mats and rich yellow flowers. H5cm/2in, W30cm/1ft. F5-7. Z4-8. **'Aurantiaca'** has unusual, orange-buff flowers. H2.5cm/1in, W15cm/6in. F4-7. Z4-8. The form *chrysocraspeda* (syn. *P. ternata*) has bright yellow flowers. **'Plena'** is a double, yellow form. Both H5cm/2in, W13cm/5in. F6-7. Z5-8.
P. cinerea. See *P. tommasiniana*.
P. crantzii (syn. *P. alpestris*). This is similar to *P. aurea* but a little taller, with yellow flowers, blotched with orange. H8cm/3in, W30cm/1ft. F5-7. Z4-8.
P. eriocarpa. Compact and creeping, with a long season of yellow, stemless flowers. H5cm/2in, W20cm/8in. F5-8. Z5-7.
P. fragiformis. See under Perennials.
P. nitida. Makes silvery, tufty mats set with stemless, pink flowers. **'Rubra'** is deep pink. Both like lime and scree. Both H2.5cm/1in, W30cm/1ft. F5-7. Z5-8.
P. tabernaemontani **'Nana'** (syn. *P. verna* 'Nana'). This forms close, little, green hummocks set with bright yellow flowers. Excellent in a trough. H2cm/³/4in, W60cm/2ft. F5-7. Z4-8.
P. ternata. See *P. aurea chrysocraspeda*.
P. tommasiniana (syn. *P. cinerea*). Makes a rampant spread of silvery leaves, covered with yellow flowers. H2.5cm/1in, W30cm/1ft. F5-6. Z5-7.
P. × tonguei. A most valuable hybrid, it forms a bronzy green clump, sending out branching, prostrate sprays of apricot-yellow flowers, suffused crimson, for weeks on end. H10cm/4in, W45cm/18in. F6-10. Z5-7.
P. verna **'Nana'**. See *P. tabernaemontani* 'Nana'.

PRATIA
These fast-growing, mat-forming, self-rooting, evergreen plants romp away in good, moist soil and shade, but can be a nuisance. The flowers are lobelia-like.
P. angulata. A white-flowered form, it has trailing growth and purple-red berries in autumn. H1.5cm/¹/₂in, W60cm/2ft. F5-7. Z6-9.
P. pedunculata. This has little, pale blue flowers but is not easy to control. H1.5cm/¹/₂in, W60cm/2ft. F5-8. Z5-7.
P. treadwellii. Ground-hugging, with white flowers, it is similar to *P. angulata*, and ideal for planting between paving slabs. H1.5cm/¹/₂in, W60cm/2ft. F5-7. Z6-9.

PRIMULA
The following are sufficiently dwarf to include as alpines, but some are best in shade and/or humus-rich soil. *Primula* species are classified into thirty different sections, and enthusiasts can build impressive collections, based on informed choice, of this one genus. See also under Perennials.
P. capitata mooreana. Much-loved but short-lived, this forms tooth-leaved rosettes, white underneath, and round heads of soft lavender-blue on slender stems. For cool shade and humus-rich, light soil. H20cm/8in, W10cm/4in. F5-7. Z5-7.
P. cortusoides. A rarity, it has lobed, hairy leaves and umbels of reddish pink flowers. Needs light shade and humus-rich, light, well-drained soil. H20cm/8in, W15cm/6in. F5-6. Z6-8.
P. frondosa. A short-lived but pretty little plant with mealy leaves and sprays of yellow-eyed, lilac flowers. H13cm/5in, W10cm/4in. F4-5. Z5-7.
P. heucherifolia. The heuchera-like leaves are rounded and lobed; the flowers, deep pink. Needs cool shade. H13cm/5in, W15cm/6in. F4-5. Z6-8.
P. **'Johanna'**. This miniature primrose-like hybrid has small, bright pink flowers. Reliable, but lift, divide and replant every other year after flowering. H2.5cm/1in, W5cm/2in. F3-4. Z5-7.
P. lichiangensis. See *P. polyneura*.
P. nepalensis. See under Perennials.
P. nutans. This short-lived beauty has powdery, narrow leaves and clusters of drooping, deep blue flowers. Gritty, moist

soil in cool semi-shade is essential. H20cm/8in, W15cm/6in. F5-6. Z5-7.

P. petiolaris. A group of allied, early-flowering types which needs special care. Cool shade and a humid climate are essential. H15-20cm/6-8in, W15-20cm/6-8in. F2-4. Z5-7.

P. polyneura (syn. *P. lichiangensis*). Tufty habit, deeply lobed leaves, silvery beneath, and open heads of pink or magenta-purple flowers. H15cm/6in, W10cm/4in. F4-5. Z6-8.

P. rosea. See under Perennials.

P. sieboldii. This charming group in various colours should be more widely grown. They produce loose umbels of white-eyed flowers above soft green, lobed and toothed foliage. Fully hardy and neither invasive nor difficult, they need part shade in well-drained but moist, humus-rich soil. Often sold as a mixture but several good, named selections are available. **'Cherubim'**, light lavender-blue. **'Geisha Girl'**, clear light pink. **'Mikado'**, reddish pink. **'Seraphim'**, deep pink. **'Snowflake'**, pure white. All H15-25cm/6-10in, W10-20cm/4-8in. F4-5. Z4-8.

P. vulgaris. All are firm favourites as primroses. They prefer heavy soil, light shade and good living. Their one weakness is susceptibility to red spider after flowering: treat with preventative sprays or pellets. Named varieties, many of them hybrids, are too numerous to mention more than a few. The colour range is now very wide but the old favourites, such as the bronzy leaved, pink-flowered **'Garryarde Guinevere'**, purple-red **'Wanda'** and **'Wisley Red'**, are still in demand. The lesser-known, white **'Schneekissen'** and pink *sibthorpii* are free-flowering, often in autumn as well as spring. Double primroses have always appealed to, and often baffled, the plant growers, but in recent years tissue culture appears to have put new life into them. The following are worthy selections. **'Alan Robb'**, apricot. **'Dawn Ansell'**, double white. **'Easter Bonnet'**, prolific, lilac-blue, large flowers. **'Lillian Harvey'**, magenta. **'Miss Indigo'**, compact, purple-blue, edged white. **'Roy Cope'**, deep crimson-red. **'Red Velvet'**, ruby-red. **'Sue Jervis'**, pretty shell-pink. **'Sunshine Susie'**, golden-yellow. All H10-15cm/4-6in, W15-25cm/6-10in. F3-5. Z5-8.

P. yargongensis. This has rosettes of narrow leaves and small heads of pink, mauve or purple, white-eyed flowers. Conditions as for *P. sieboldii*. H20cm/8in, W15cm/6in. F4-5. Z4-8.

PRUNELLA See under Perennials.

PTEROCEPHALUS

P. parnassi. A spreading cushion of soft greenery set with pale pink, pincushion flowers, this close relative of *Scabiosa* is easy to grow. H10cm/4in, W15cm/6in. F6-8. Z5-7.

Primula 'Johanna'

Primula sieboldii 'Mikado'

PULSATILLA See under Perennials.

RAMONDA

A small genus of evergreen, rosette-forming plants which thrive only in north-facing crevices on a sheer face or steep slope. Where suited, they flourish for years, though they do not spread.

R. myconi (syn. *R. pyrenaica*). A popular species, with deep green, rounded, puckered leaves and sprays of violet-blue, open flowers with conspicuous stamens. *R. nathaliae* is similar, but has glossier leaves. Both H10cm/4in, W25cm/10in. F5-6. Z5-7.

R. pyrenaica. See *R. myconi*.

RANUNCULUS Alpine buttercup

Most dwarf species are clump-forming or tufted, with bowl-shaped flowers. The genus includes one or two with a rapid spread as well as rarities. All are fairly easy to grow in sun and good soil.

Primula 'Wisley Red'

R. amplexicaulis. See under Perennials.

R. calandrinioides. A choice species with large, pink-flushed, white flowers above spear-shaped leaves which die down in late summer. Best in an alpine house. H15cm/6in, W15cm/6in. F3-4. Z7-8.

R. ficaria. The more compact forms of lesser celandine are attractive, but have a long dormant period. **'Albus'**, white flowers. **'Aurantiacus'**, coppery orange flowers. **'Major'**, large, golden-yellow flowers. **'Primrose'**, creamy yellow flowers. All H10cm/4in, W20cm/8in. F4-5. Z4-8.

Ranunculus montanus 'Molten Gold'

R. gouanii. See under Perennials.

R. gramineus. See under Perennials.

R. montanus 'Molten Gold'. Dwarf, free-flowering and brilliant, with its yellow flowers above lobed leaves. H10cm/4in, W15cm/6in. F5-6. Z5-8.

RAOULIA

These filmy carpeters are grown for their evergreen foliage rather than their flowers. They thrive in sun, well-drained, gritty soil and a mild climate. Protect from winter wet.

R. australis. The best-known species, it makes silvery mats and has insignificant pale yellow flowers. H7mm/¼in, W30cm/1ft. F6-7. Z7-8.

R. hookeri. This is slightly larger and even more silvery than the above. H1.5cm/½in, W30cm/1ft. F6-7. Z8-9.

R. tenuicaulis. A quick-spreading, grey mat which makes excellent ground cover for bulbs. H7mm/¼in, W30cm/1ft. F6-7. Z7-8.

Raoulia australis

Sagina subulata 'Aurea'

Saponaria 'Bressingham'

SAGINA

S. subulata 'Aurea'. This golden form makes evergreen, spreading mats but needs frequent replanting to retain its vigour. Its tiny, white, star-shaped flowers are borne sparsely. Sun and moist, gritty soil are needed. H1.5cm/¹/₂in, W20cm/8in. F6-7. Z6-8.

SANGUINARIA See under Perennials.

SAPONARIA Soapwort

These sun-loving plants give a long display with few faults. Their trailing stems are excellent for covering banks.

S. 'Bressingham'. This is a slow-spreading, close mat, with stemless, bright pink flowers. As a choice little gem, it responds best to humus-rich, gritty soil. H2.5cm/1in, W15cm/6in. F5-6. Z4-8.

S. caespitosa. Slow-growing, congested hummocks produce small, flat, single pink

Saxifraga 'Jenkinsiae'

Saxifraga 'Salamonii'

flowers. H10cm/4in, W10cm/4in. F5-6. Z4-7.

S. ocymoides. This makes ample, but easily controllable, surface growth, with sheets of pink on dark greenery. Self seeding. H10cm/4in, W60cm/2ft. F5-7. Z2-7.

S. × olivana. Sturdy and long-lived, this makes compact cushions set with wide-open, light pink flowers. H5cm/2in, W20cm/8in. F5-7. Z4-7.

SATUREIA Winter savory

S. montana 'Pygmaea'. Low, bushy mounds carry a brave show of tiny, deep blue flowers in autumn. I consider this a much underrated plant. H20cm/8in, W15cm/6in. F9-10. Z6-9.

SAXIFRAGA Saxifrage

The range and variety of this genus is immense. Because of marked differences in both appearance and cultural needs, they are dealt with in sections, beginning with the first to flower.

Kabschia or cushion section

Cushion saxifrages make slow-growing rosettes of lime-encrusted, greenish, silvery or greyish leaves, forming evergreen mats or hummocks. These carry profuse, often large, saucer-shaped flowers, in small clusters or singly. Many are high alpines, needing well-drained, gritty, ideally limy, soil with some humus. Although best in sun, they are liable to suffer if they dry out under summer sun and heat, and they also dislike winter wet. Good for rock crevices and walls. Green types are generally more adaptable than grey or silvery kinds. In mild

winters flowering may begin in February. The following are just some of the many forms in existence, which only a few specialists now have on offer. All Z4-6.

S. × apiculata. Green-leaved and hummocky, both the primrose-yellow species and the white form *alba* are reliable and showy. H8cm/3in, W30cm/1ft. F2-4.

S. 'Boston Spa'. This free-flowering, yellow hybrid forms green cushions. H8cm/3in, W25cm/10in. F2-4.

S. 'Bridget'. Makes silvery rosettes and clusters of deep rose flowers. H10cm/4in, W15cm/6in. F2-4.

S. 'Cranbourne'. Its silvery blue cushions are studded with pink flowers. H2.5cm/1in, W20cm/8in. F2-4.

S. × elizabethae. This has soft yellow flower clusters and light green, spiny foliage. H8cm/3in, W15-20cm/6-8in. F2-4.

S. 'Gold Dust'. The green cushions bear profuse, deep yellow flowers. H8cm/3in, W15cm/6in. F2-4.

S. × irvingii. Very slow-growing, tight, grey hummocks of minute leaves in rosettes carry stemless, pink flowers. H2.5cm/1in, W8cm/3in. F2-4.

S. 'Jenkinsiae'. Slow-growing, tight, greeny grey cushions carry pink flowers. H8cm/3in, W25cm/10in. F2-4.

S. 'Riverslea'. Sprays of carmine flowers appear on tight, silvery cushions. H5cm/2in, W25cm/10in. F2-4.

S. 'Salamonii'. Grey-silver mats and white flowers. H5cm/2in, W13cm/5in. F2-4.

S. sancta. This is a strong-growing, green-leaved species with yellow flowers. H5cm/2in, W13cm/5in. F2-4.

Mossy section

A group which make low, green carpets or mounds of deeply divided leaves and sprays of open, starry or bell-shaped blossom. With one or two exceptions, they grow freely in damp shade. Lift, divide and replant deeply every two or three years if they become ragged. All Z5-6.

S. 'Cloth of Gold'. Striking golden leaves, but the white flowers are sparse. Colour is best in shade. H5cm/2in, W30cm/1ft. F4-5.

S. 'Dartington Double'. This is actually a semi-double, deep pink. H10cm/4in, W15cm/6in. F4-5.

S. 'Dubarry'. Gives a fine display of crimson flowers, relatively late. H20cm/8in, W20cm/8in. F4-5.

S. 'Flowers of Sulphur'. Its lemon-yellow flowers are an unusual colour for a mossy form. H15cm/6in, W20cm/8in. F4-5.

S. 'Four Winds'. This has crimson-red flowers. H25cm/10in, W20cm/8in. F4-5.

S. 'Gaiety'. A bright and early rose-pink. H10cm/4in, W25cm/10in. F4-5.

S. 'Hi-Ace'. Makes tight, variegated hummocks and reddish flowers. H8cm/3in, W20cm/8in. F4-5.

S. **'Findling'**. This forms a close, mossy carpet with tiny sprays of white. Both H2.5cm/1in, W15cm/6in. F4-5.

S. **'Pearly King'**. The best white: tidy, free-flowering and vigorous. H10cm/4in, W30cm/1ft. F4-5.

S. **'Peter Pan'**. Neat and dwarf, this has mossy, bright green hummocks and crimson stems carrying clear pink flowers with reflexed petals. H5cm/2in, W30cm/1ft. F4-5.

S. **'Pixie'**. This hybrid is very compact, with rose-pink flowers. H8cm/3in, W30cm/1ft. F4-5.

S. **'Triumph'**. This gives a bright display of large, blood-red flowers. H15cm/6in, W40cm/16in. F4-5.

S. **'Whitlavei Compacta'**. Makes dense, mossy growth but only a few white sprays. H5cm/2in, W15cm/6in. F4-5.

Aizoon or encrusted section

These are rosette-forming plants with narrow leaves, edged in silvery lime encrustations, and mostly long-lived. The starry flowers are carried in sprays. They need sun and gritty, well-drained soil that does not bake dry in summer. For simplicity, older, better-known names are used for a relatively short selection of the large number in existence.

S. aizoon. See *S. paniculata*.

S. × *burnatii*. This has silver rosettes and white flowers on purplish stems. H15cm/6in, W23cm/9in. F5-6. Z6-8.

S. callosa **'Albertii'**. A reliable white, its lime-encrusted leaves die after flowering and are replaced by new ones produced annually from stolons. H30cm/1ft, W20cm/8in. F5-6. Z4-7.

S. cochlearis **'Minor'**. Tight, silvery, encrusted hummocks and sparse, white flowers. H13cm/5in, W15cm/6in. F5-6. Z6-8.

S. cotyledon. A larger type, this forms silvery mounds, attractive all year round. Tall stems carry myriads of white flowers. H30cm/1ft, W25cm/10in. F5-6. Z4-7.

S. **'Esther'**. This is an appealing, soft yellow variety. H20cm/8in, W15cm/6in. F5-6. Z4-7.

S. **'Kathleen Pinsent'**. Very silvery, with delicate pink sprays. H20cm/8in, W15cm/6in. F5-6. Z4-7.

S. **'Norvegica'**. Makes a good, silvery mat with white flowers. H30cm/1ft, W20cm/8in. F5-6. Z4-7

S. paniculata (formerly *S. aizoon*). This very variable, evergreen, rosette-forming species makes hummocks or mats of greeny grey, narrow leaves and loose sprays of pink, yellow or white flowers. The form *baldensis* (syn. *minutifolia*) is very compact, forming a close mat of tiny, silvery rosettes with sparse, white flowers. H5cm/2in, W13cm/5in. F5-6. Z5-7. **'Lutea'** has sprays

Saxifraga 'Dubarry'

Saxifraga 'Triumph'

Saxifraga 'Cloth of Gold'

Saxifraga 'Tumbling Waters'

of soft yellow flowers and light green foliage. **'Rex'** is the best white-flowered form. **'Rosea'** has deep green, lime-encrusted leaves and sprays of soft pink flowers. All H15cm/6in, W40cm/16in. Z2-6.

S. **'Southside Seedling'**. Similar to *S. cotyledon* but with white flowers spotted pink. H30cm/1ft, W25cm/10in. F5-6. Z4-7.

S. **'Tumbling Waters'**. A hybrid with tight, lime-encrusted rosettes and, after some years, arching sprays of white flowers. After flowering, the main rosette dies, but small offsets survive. H60cm/2ft, W20cm/8in. F5-6. Z5-7.

S. **'Whitehill'**. A free-flowering white, this has silvered rosettes. H15cm/6in, W20cm/8in. F5-6. Z5-7.

S. **'Winifred Bevington'**. This makes a pleasing display of buff flowers on low, matted, green rosettes. H13cm/5in, W15cm/6in. F5-6. Z4-7.

Saxifraga 'Whitehill'

Saxifraga juniperifolia

Saxifraga oppositifolia 'Florissa'

Scutellaria alpina

Miscellaneous section

S. aizoides. Mat-forming, with narrow, deep green, fleshy foliage, these carry short sprays of red-spotted, yellow flowers, coppery red in the best-known *atrorubens* form. It needs rich, damp soil and cool conditions in sun or part shade. Both H5cm/2in, W30cm/1ft. F6-8. Z4-6.

S. cuneifolia. Deep green, fleshy rosettes make neat, evergreen mats, brightest in 'Variegata'. Grow in light shade. Both H8cm/3in, W20cm/8in. F4-5. Z4-6.

S. cuscutiformis. This species makes runners forming green or purplish, round-leaved rosettes and spreading quickly in all but dry places. It carries slender sprays

of white flowers. H20cm/8in, W20cm/8in. F5-6. Z5-7.

S. fortunei. See under Perennials.

S. granulata. Meadow saxifrage, or fair maids of France, is a European, including Britain, bulbous species, with white flowers and fleshy, kidney-shaped leaves that die back after flowering. The double 'Flore Pleno' is pretty but untidy. Provide moist but well-drained soil in full sun. Both H20cm/8in, W20cm/8in. F5-6. Z3-6.

S. juniperifolia. This makes a dense, green carpet, studded with yellow flowers. H5cm/2in, W15cm/6in. F3-4. Z5-7.

S. oppositifolia. Forms hard, dark green mats of tiny leaves studded with stemless, cup-shaped, lilac flowers. Best in cool, open positions, protected from summer heat, and in moist but well-drained soil. Cultivars include lilac-pink 'Florissa', deep rose pink *latina*, the large-flowered, rich red 'Ruth Draper' and 'Wetterhorn', another deep red form. All H5cm/2in, W45cm/18in. F3-4. Z2-6.

S. primuloides 'Elliott's Variety'. Like a miniature London pride, it makes mats of green rosettes, with erect, deep pink sprays. H15cm/6in, W15cm/6in. F4-5. Z5-8.

S. × *urbium*. See under Perennials.

SCABIOSA

S. alpina 'Nana'. The naming is confused but this usually denotes a dwarf species with a neat mound of greyish foliage and mauve-blue, pincushion flowers. It is happy in any sunny spot. H15cm/6in, W30cm/1ft. F5-9. Z5-7.

S. graminifolia. See under Perennials.

SCUTELLARIA Skullcap

These summer-flowering, sun-loving alpines have hooded, little flowers and pointed leaves.

S. alpina. Mounded, greyish foliage is set with cream and purple flowers on short spikes. H15cm/6in, W45cm/18in. F6-8. Z5-7.

S. hastifolia. A spreader and apt to invade, its light blue flowers on short spikes are, however, quite attractive. Lift, divide

Sedum lidakense

and replant every spring. H20cm/8in, W15cm/6in. F6-7. Z5-8.

S. indica japonica. A charming but rather tender little plant, it has soft, felted greenery and little spikes of lavender-purple flowers for a long time. Light soil is best. H10cm/4in, W25cm/10in. F6-9. Z7-8.

S. orientalis. Prostrate, hairy, rooting stems carry rosy cream flowers above grey-green foliage. H10cm/4in, W20cm/8in. F6-8. Z5-8.

S. scordiifolia. Violet-blue flowers with white, streaked lips, carried above oval, wrinkled leaves. Its quick-spreading roots resemble maggots. Lift, divide and replant every spring. H15cm/6in, W15cm/6in. F6-7. Z6-8.

SEDUM Stonecrop

This vast genus includes good, late-flowering alpines, but a few are weedy. Most are easy in well-drained, gritty soil and almost all prefer sun. *S. ellacombeanum*, *S. ewersii*, *S. floriferum* 'Weihenstephaner Gold', *S. rosea*, *S.* 'Ruby Glow' and *S.* 'Vera Jameson' are of equal value as alpines. See under Perennials.

S. acre. The true stonecrop, also called wall pepper and golden moss, can grow on rocks almost bare of soil. Its bright yellow flowers appear above an evergreen mat or mound. Can be invasive. H5cm/2in, W25cm/10in. F6-7. Z3-8.

S. album. The species is too invasive, but the form *murale* makes purplish mats and light pink flowers. H10cm/4in, W30cm/1ft. F6-7. Z3-8.

S. cauticolum. This has arching stems of profuse, rosy crimson flowers above bluish, deciduous foliage. H10cm/4in, W30cm/1ft. F8-10. Z4-8.

S. dasyphyllum. A variable species with pink flowers on minute, grey-blue, downy mats. 'Riffense' is superior. Both H5cm/2in, W20cm/8in. F6-7. Z4-8.

S. kamtschaticum. A trouble-free, deciduous species, this has dark green, spatula-shaped leaves and golden flowers. 'Variegatum' is equally attractive. Both H15cm/6in, W20cm/8in. F6-8. Z3-8.

S. lidakense. This is valuable for late-flowering, with bluish, deciduous foliage and glistening, rose-red heads. H10cm/4in, W15cm/6in. F8-10. Z4-8.

S. lydium. Bright green, bronzy leaf tufts, red in summer, and clustered, white flower heads. H10cm/4in, W20cm/8in. F6-7. Z5-7.

S. middendorfianum. This makes low, slow-spreading, bronzy green tufts of very narrow leaves and golden flowers. H10cm/4in, W20cm/8in. F6-8. Z3-8.

S. obtusatum. See *S. oreganum*.

S. oreganum (syn. *S. obtusatum*). Fleshy, little, rounded leaves, bronzy red in summer, and small, deep yellow flower heads. H5cm/2in, W15cm/6in. F6-8. Z5-9.

S. pulchellum. Unusual in preferring cool,

moist soil, its mats of light green, narrow leaves bear large, glistening pink, cockscomb heads. Flowers for a long time. H8cm/3in, W15cm/6in. F6-9. Z4-7.

S. rupestre. This makes upright, evergreen, bronzy growth and old gold flowers. **'Estelle'** is the best form. Both H20cm/8in, W20cm/8in. F6-8. Z4-8.

S. sexangulare. This is like a refined *S. acre*. H5cm/2in, W25cm/10in. F6-7. Z3-8.

S. spathulifolium. Powdery, bluish, fleshy leaves and yellow flowers. **'Cape Blanco'** is more compact, with low mounds of near white leaves, and **'Purpureum'** has larger, purplish leaves. All H5cm/2in, W25cm/10in. F6-7. Z4-7.

S. spurium. A rapid-growing, nearly ever-green mat-former, this has broad leaves and pale pink flowers on red stems. **'Erdblut'** has bright carmine-red flowers. **'Green Mantle'** seldom flowers but makes excellent ground cover. **'Purple Carpet'** has reddish leaves and flowers, and **'Variegatum'**, pale buff, variegated leaves. All are easy to curb. All H8cm/3in, W40cm/16in. F6-7. Z3-8.

S. tatarinowii. This quite choice species slowly makes clumps of arching, purplish stems carrying toothed, grey-green leaves and corymbs of light pink flowers. H13cm/5in, W20cm/8in. F7-8. Z5-7.

SEMPERVIVUM Houseleek

This large genus is of value mainly for its succulent rosettes, rather than for its flowers. The rosettes range from tiny, hoary cushions or mounds to large, purple, bronze or reddish leaved forms, including the so-called houseleek, once used to ward off lightning. Little, clustered spikes or sprays of white or pale to deep pink flowers appear, 5-20cm/2-8in tall, but some small forms scarcely flower. They thrive on a near starvation diet and can grow in the poorest soils as long as they are in sun. Hundreds of species and cultivars exist and though selection by sight is ideal, the following are a few outstanding choices. All F6-7, Z5-9.

S. arachnoideum **'Laggeri'**. One of the best silvered, 'cobwebby' types. H2.5-8cm/1-3in, W20-30cm/8-12in.

S. **'Blood Tip'**. These make compact rosettes with upturned, red tips. H2.5-8cm/1-3in, W20-30cm/8-12in.

S. **'Commander Hay'**. Large, flat rosettes with crimson markings. H2.5-8cm/1-3in, W20-30cm/8-12in.

S. **'Engle's Rubrum'**. Soft grey-green rosettes, edged with red, turning a deeper colour in winter. H15-20cm/6-8in, W20-30cm/8-12in.

S. **'Jubilee'**. This makes green and maroon foliage, and is compact and free-flowering. H2.5-8cm/1-3in, W20-30cm/8-12in.

S. **'Lavender and Old Lace'**. Its pinkish lavender rosettes are covered in silvery hairs. H2.5-8cm/1-3in, W20-30cm/8-12in.

Sedum spurium 'Purple Carpet'

Sedum kamtschaticum 'Variegatum'

S. montanum braunii. Little green, maroon-tipped rosettes. H2.5-8cm/1-3in, W20-30cm/8-12in.

S. **'Patrician'**. Green, bronze-tipped rosettes, red-centred in winter. H2.5-8cm/ 1-3in, W20-30cm/8-12in.

S. **'Royal Ruby'**. This is a rich ruby-red overall. H2.5-8cm/1-3in, W20-30cm/8-12in.

S. **'Rubrifolium'**. Makes extra-large, reddish rosettes. H2.5-8cm/1-3in, W20-30cm/8-12in.

S. **'Snowberger'**. Its jade-green rosettes have a silvery sheen. H2.5-8cm/1-3in, W20-30cm/8-12in.

S. tectorum tectorum **'Triste'**. Medium-sized, purplish rosettes. H2.5-8cm/1-3in, W20-30cm/8-12in.

SERRATULA See under Perennials.

Sempervivum arachnoideum 'Laggeri'

Sempervivum 'Lavender and Old Lace'

SILENE Campion

The low-growing species include early- and late-flowering kinds, all fault-free and reasonably easy to grow in sun.

S. acaulis pedunculata. Moss campion, or cushion pink, makes close, deep green mats set with profuse, small, bright pink flowers. H2.5cm/1in, W30-45cm/12-18in. F5-6. Z3-5.

S. alpestris. This has neat, tufty growth and white flowers; the double **'Flore Pleno'** is especially attractive. H15cm/6in, W15cm/6in. F5-7. Z4-7.

S. keiskii minor. Forms neat tufts of rose-pink flowers. H10cm/4in, W15cm/6in. F5-7. Z4-7.

S. maritima. Sea campion, a British native, has large, single, white or pale pink flowers on a grey-green base. **'Flore Pleno'** has double flowers. **'Rosea'** has small, pink flowers. **'Whitethroat'** is also a good selection. All H8cm/3in, W30cm/1ft. F6-8. Z4-7.

S. schafta. This has tufty growth and bright pink flowers. **'Robusta'** makes a display of deep green clumps and bright pink flowers. Both H10cm/4in, W10cm/4in. F7-9. Z4-8.

SISYRINCHIUM

These tufty, iris-like plants have narrow, grassy leaves, starry flowers and fibrous roots. Easy in ordinary soil and sun, they divide readily and actually flower better if divided and replanted every other year.

S. bellum. This has narrow leaves and sprays of violet-blue flowers. H10cm/4in, W10cm/4in. F5-8. Z8-9.

S. brachypus (syn. *S. californicum*). Golden-eyed grass has open, golden-yellow flowers on and off for months. H10cm/4in, W10cm/4in. F6-9. Z8-9.

S. californicum. See *S. brachypus*.

S. **'E. K. Balls'**. Produces fanned-out leaves and mauve flowers. H10cm/4in, W10cm/4in. F5-8. Z8-9.

S. idahoense. See under Perennials.

S. **'May Snow'** (syn. *S. idahoense* 'May Snow'). An excellent, free-flowering alpine, with an abundance of pure white, yellow-

Sisyrinchium 'May Snow'

Soldanella alpina

centred flowers for weeks. H10-15cm/4-6in, W15cm/6in. F5-7. Z7-8.

S. **'North Star'**. A white-flowered, upward-growing hybrid. H13cm/5in, W8cm/3in. F5-8. Z7-8.

SOLDANELLA Snowbell

Delightful evergreen, carpeting plants for damp, leafy soil in shade, these have rounded, densely packed, leathery leaves and fringed, nodding, bell-shaped flowers. Vulnerable to slugs and winter wet. All Z4-7.

S. alpina. The alpine snowbell has lavender-blue flowers with delicately laced petals. Grow in limy soil. H8cm/3in, W20cm/8in. F4-5.

S. pindicola. This has leathery leaves and mauve flowers. H8cm/3in, W15cm/6in. F4-5.

S. villosa. Reliable in most soils, it has lacy, mauve-blue flowers on hairy stems. H10cm/4in, W30cm/1ft. F4-5.

SOLIDAGO Goldenrod

These are easy in any open situation. All Z3-9.

S. brachystachys. Useful for late flowering, this makes clumps of narrow leaves and short, deep yellow plumes. H15cm/6in, W20cm/8in. F8-10.

S. **'Golden Dwarf'**. This is an early-flowering and compact hybrid, like a miniature goldenrod, but with upstanding plumes. H20cm/8in, W20cm/8in. F6-7.

STACHYS Betony

S. macrantha **'Spicata Nana'** (syn. *S. m.* 'Stricta'). This is neat and evergreen with heart-shaped, crinkled leaves and lilac or white flower spikes. H15cm/6in, W15cm/6in. F7-9. Z2-8.

SYNTHYRIS

These pretty but rare spring subjects prefer a cool, humus-rich soil and part shade.

S. reniformis (syn. *S. rotundifolia*). This has evergreen, rounded, deep green leaves and short sprays of small, blue, bell-shaped flowers. H10cm/4in, W15cm/6in. F4-5. Z5-8.

S. rotundifolia. See *S. reniformis*.

S. stellata. This slow-growing species has purple-blue flowers above deeply divided leaves. H10cm/4in, W10cm/4in. F4-5. Z5-7.

S. suendermannii. Bright green leaves and a good show of blue flowers. H25cm/10in, W23cm/9in. F4-6. Z5-7.

TANACETUM

A genus of aromatic, silvery leaved plants which are useful for dry, sunny places.

T. argenteum. See *Achillea argentea*.

T. densum amani. This sub-shrub makes a fairly rapid surface spread of soft, silvery, ferny foliage and deep yellow flowers, which are often pinched out for an all-foliage effect. Dislikes winter wet. H15cm/6in, W30-40cm/12-16in. F6-7. Z6-8.

T. herderi. See under Perennials.

TANAKAEA

T. radicans. This pretty, shade-loving evergreen has basal rosettes of delicate, round leaves and sprays of starry, white flowers. It spreads steadily below ground, given well-drained, humus-rich, sandy soil. H8cm/3in, W20cm/8in. F5-6. Z5-7.

TEUCRIUM Germander

This genus includes interesting plants for full sun and well-drained, even poor, soil.

T. aroanum. Makes congested mats of silvery, evergreen leaves and crowded racemes of small, light purple flowers. H8cm/3in, W30cm/1ft. F6-8. Z7-9.

Silene maritima 'Whitethroat'

Synthyris stellata

T. chamaedrys 'Nanum'. Wall germander has dark, shiny, evergreen leaves, grey beneath, and little spikes of pink flowers, spotted with red and white. H15cm/6in, W45cm/18in. F7-8. Z4-9.

T. pyrenaicum. A mat-forming species with cream and lavender, hooded flowers above rounded, hairy leaves. H10cm/4in, W30cm/1ft. F6-8. Z4-8.

T. subspinosum. This makes dense, prickly mounds of grey, minute, aromatic leaves, and cats find it irresistible. The flower spikes are deep pink. H5cm/2in, W15cm/6in. F6-8. Z5-8.

THALICTRUM Meadow rue

The dwarf species are choice plants and need shady, humus-rich soil; a peat bed is ideal. All Z5-8.

T. coreanum. This has delicate, deeply divided, bronze-tinted leaves on wiry stems and little, fluffy, lilac-pink flowers. H10cm/4in, W15cm/6in. F6-8.

T. kiusianum. Forms a mat of purplish, maidenhair-like leaves and little, puffy, mauve flowers. H2.5cm/1in, W20cm/8in. F6-8.

THYMUS Thyme

These much-loved aromatic plants have been subject to recent nomenclature changes but here common usage prevails. All are sun lovers and some have a rapid but not menacing spread which can be trodden upon with impunity, and trimmed, if necessary, every year or two to keep it compact.

T. 'Bressingham Pink'. A chance seedling from *T. doerfleri*. It forms grey-green mats and gives a bright display of clear pink flowers. H2.5cm/1in, W15cm/6in. F5-6. Z4-7.

T. × *citriodorus*. Makes lemon-scented little bushes, showier in the variegated forms, such as 'Archer's Gold'. 'Anderson's Gold'. See *T.* 'E. B. Anderson'. Both H15cm/6in, W30cm/1ft. F5-6. Z4-8. 'Silver Posie' and 'Silver Queen' are colourful but may revert in parts to green. Both H15cm/6in, W30cm/1ft. F5-6. Z4-8.

T. 'Doone Valley'. This has deep green foliage, speckled with gold. The lavender flowers are sparse. H15cm/6in, W30cm/1ft. F5-6. Z4-8.

T. 'E. B. Anderson' (syn. *T.* × *citriodorus* 'Anderson's Gold'). Low but bushy and evergreen, this gives good, green-gold ground cover but seldom flowers. H5cm/2in, W23cm/9in. F5-6. Z6-8.

T. ericifolius (correctly, *Micromeria varia*). Makes little, golden-green bushes but rarely flowers. H10cm/4in, W25cm/10in. F6-7. Z5-8.

T. herba-barona. This has dark green, caraway-scented mats which carry short sprays of pinkish flowers. H8cm/3in, W40cm/16in. F6-7. Z4-7.

T. lanuginosus. The soft, almost woolly, grey mats spread quickly, but the deep pink flowers are sparse. H2.5cm/1in, W20cm/8in. F5-6. Z6-8.

T. micans. A close-growing carpeter, this has purple-pink flowers. H5cm/2in, W20cm/8in. F6-7. Z5-8.

T. nitidus. Erect, twiggy growth carries grey leaves and profuse, small, clear pink flowers. Variable 'Peter Davis' is the best form. Both H20cm/8in, W30cm/1ft. F5-6. Z7-8.

T. serpyllum. There are now several named varieties, with white, light red, deep pink and rosy crimson flowers. All are carpeters, easy to grow, and quite quick to spread, making a good display. The form *albus* is white. 'Annie Hall' is light pink. The form *coccineus* is a deep pink. 'Elfin' makes tight, emerald-green hummocks but is shy to flower. 'Minor' forms little more than a film of deep green, with pink flowers. 'Russetings' has rosy red flowers and dark foliage. All H2.5-5cm/1-2in, W10-25cm/4-10in. F5-7. Z4-8.

TIARELLA See under Perennials.

TOFIELDIA

T. gracilis. Forms grassy, nearly evergreen leaves and tiny, buff flowers. H15cm/6in, W15cm/6in. F5-6. Z4-7.

Teucrium aroanum

Thymus 'E. B. Anderson'

Thymus 'Bressingham Pink'

Thymus 'Doone Valley'

TOLMIEA See under Perennials.

TOWNSENDIA

T. formosa. This miniature aster has large, violet-blue and yellow-eyed daisies and evergreen foliage. It lives longest in sun and gritty soil. Dislikes winter wet. H8cm/3in, W10cm/4in. F5-6. Z4-7.

TUNICA (syn. PETRORHAGIA)

T. saxifraga (correctly, *Petrorhagia saxifraga*). The tunic flower is a mat-former with tiny, pink flowers on very slender stems, and though not long-lived, it is self-seeding. The double, white form is rare. The pink double 'Rosette' is pretty and longer-lived. Full sun and very well-drained, poorish soil are needed. All H15cm/6in, W15cm/6in. F6-8. Z4-7.

Thymus serpyllum albus

Verbascum dumulosum

Viola biflora

Veronica prostrata

Zauschneria cana

VANCOUVERIA See under Perennials.

VERBASCUM Mullein
Two sub-shrubby mulleins are worth growing in gritty soil and full sun. All Z8-9.
V. dumulosum. This species has soft grey leaves and stumpy spikes of clear yellow, purple-eyed flowers. Protect from winter wet with glass. H25cm/10in, W25cm/10in. F5-7.
V. **'Letitia'**. A hybrid of real merit raised by the late Ken Aslet. It makes twiggy, little bushes and thin spikes of small, yellow flowers. H20cm/8in, W20cm/8in. F5-8.

VERONICA Speedwell
This is a large genus even after hebes and parahebes have been excluded. Those that remain are non-woody or bushy, generally hardy and easy to grow in mainly sunny positions. Their saucer-shaped flowers are carried in spikes.
V. armena. Finely cut foliage from a tough, central root forms a mat covered in short spikes of blue flowers. H10cm/4in, W13cm/5in. F5-7. Z5-8.
V. cinerea. Makes a fairly vigorous surface spread of small, ash-grey foliage, set with bright blue flowers. H10cm/4in, W40cm/16in. F5-7. Z5-8.
V. filifolia. This is rare, but interesting for its summer spread of rich green, finely cut foliage and light blue flowers. It should not be confused with the pretty but weedy *V. filiformis*, which roots as it spreads. H10cm/4in, W20cm/8in. F5-7. Z6-8.
V. **'Heidekind'**. This has a neat, tufty habit

and short spikes of deep pink. H15cm/6in, W20cm/8in. F5-8. Z5-8.
V. pectinata. Quickly makes a mat of soft, grey, hairy foliage and deep blue, white-eyed flowers, pink in **'Rosea'**. Both H5cm/2in, W40cm/16in. F5-6. Z2-7.
V. prostrata (syn. *V. rupestris*). Prostrate speedwell is a sturdy, moderately spreading mat-former with little, upright spikes of rich blue. **'Blue Sheen'** is a very profuse, pale blue. **'Mrs Holt'** is a deep pink. **'Rosea'** is lighter pink. **'Spode Blue'** is a china-blue. The golden-leaved **'Trehane'** prefers some shade. All H8-10cm/3-4in, W30-40cm/12-16in. F5-7. Z5-8.
V. rupestris. See *V. prostrata*.
V. saturejoides. Fairly vigorous mats of slightly fleshy leaves carry sprays of blue flowers, marked with red. H8cm/3in, W40cm/16in. F5-7. Z5-8.
V. selleri. This forms close, deep green mats and spikes of violet-purple. H10cm/4in, W20cm/8in. F5-7. Z4-8.
V. teucrium. See under Perennials.

VINCA See under Perennials.

VIOLA Violet, viola
Although hesitatingly listed as alpines, some are quite suitable in height and habit, and even bedding violas are good as gap fillers or in front of taller perennials. All are easy to grow, but only a few are reliably long-lived if left undivided for more than one or two years.
V. biflora. The twin-flowered violet has bright yellow flowers in pairs above slowly

creeping mats. It needs damp, gritty soil. H10cm/4in, W15cm/6in. F5-6. Z4-8.
V. cornuta. See under Perennials.
V. cucullata. See under Perennials.
V. gracilis. The true species might not now exist in gardens but hybrids, such as the dark violet **'Black Knight'**, the purple-black, long-stemmed **'Major'** and the pale yellow **'Moonlight'**, are good, long-flowering and fully perennial. All H10cm/4in, W20cm/8in. F4-8. Z5-8.
V. labradorica **'Purpurea'**. This is first-rate for shade, even dry shade. It has purplish, evergreen foliage and purplish violet flowers. It is self-seeding. H10cm/4in, W20cm/8in. F4-6. Z3-8.

Hybrids. Some have some *V. cornuta* blood, which gives a longer life but smaller flowers. **'Arkwright's Ruby'** is deep red, but short-lived. **'Maroon Picotee'** is yellow-maroon. **'Molly Sanderson'** is nearly black. **'Nellie Britton'** is lilac-pink. All H8-15cm/3-6in, W15-25cm/6-10in. F4-7. Z5-7. See also under Perennials.

VISCARIA
V. alpina. See *Lychnis alpina*.

VITALIANA
These are choice subjects for scree or gritty soil in sun. They slowly form pads of greenery, with androsace-like flowers.
V. primuliflora (syn. *Douglasia vitaliana*). This makes mat-forming rosettes of grey-green leaves and stemless, yellow, primrose-like flowers. The form *praetutiana* is even more compact, silvery and free-flowering. Both H5cm/2in, W30cm/1ft. F4-5. Z4-8.

WULFENIA
These tufty, evergreen plants are partial to some shade and humus-rich soil. They dislike hot, dry positions.
W. amherstiana. A charming species with deep green, overlapping leaves and spikes of small, deep blue flowers. H20cm/8in, W15cm/6in. F5-6. Z7-9.
W. carinthiaca. This has larger, lighter green leaves than the above, with arching sprays of small, blue flowers. H20cm/8in, W20cm/8in. F5-6. Z6-9.

ZAUSCHNERIA California fuchsia
In a hot, dry spot in light soil, these sub-shrubs produce a splash of late colour. Growth dies down to a woody root in autumn and is late to emerge again in spring. All Z8-10.
Z. californica **'Glasnevin'**. See under Perennials.
Z. cana. This has twiggy, branching stems, small, narrow, grey leaves and bright red flowers. H30cm/1ft, W60cm/2ft. F8-10.
Z. canescens. See under Perennials.

ALPINES FOR A SLOPING SITE

All these plants, with the exception of the dwarf *Berberis*, in time make carpets of foliage. They are easy to grow, though not all are evergreen, and can be allowed to run into each other to create a delightfully informal look. They are planted on a gently sloping site, but would still succeed on a much steeper incline. Growing best in sun and with reasonable drainage, they will provide a splash of colour from late spring to midsummer, although the flowers shown here will not always bloom at exactly the same time. The foliage will remain attractive throughout summer and autumn, requiring only a little tidying the following spring. The low retaining wall can be made of Norfolk flintstone, as here, or other stone, brick or suitable materials. The peak period of interest is late spring to midsummer.

1 *Dianthus* 'Garland' (× 5)
2 *Veronica prostrata* (× 5)
3 *Thymus* 'E. B. Anderson' (× 5)
4 *Armeria maritima* 'Dusseldorf Pride' (× 5)
5 *Iberis sempervirens* 'Snowflake' (× 5)
6 *Berberis* × *stenophylla* 'Corallina Compacta' (× 1)
7 *Ajuga reptans* 'Burgundy Glow' (× 7)
8 *Campanula* 'Birch Hybrid' (× 7)

Area required: approx. 5.5 sq. m/5½ sq. yd

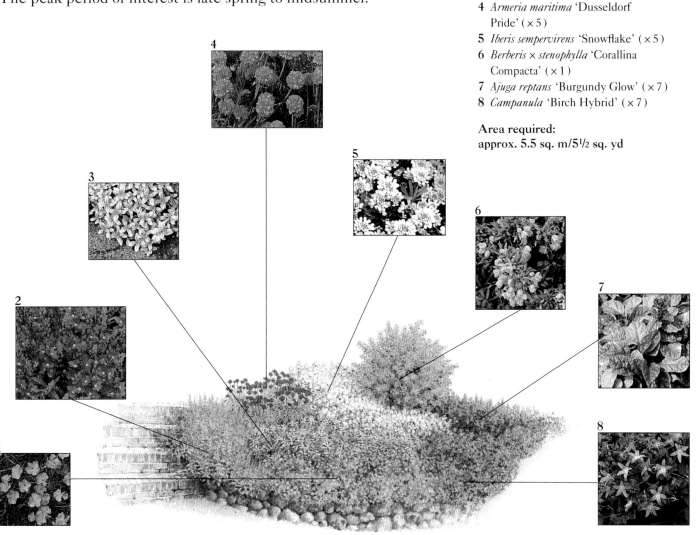

ALPINES FOR A SMALL RAISED BED OR TROUGH

A big advantage of alpines or rock plants is that they can be used in restricted areas and still look natural, whilst at the same time giving scope for variety in a small space. Many of the choice alpines prefer a gritty, well-drained compost, but they must not be allowed to dry out in summer. Here the surface of the planted area is covered with grit. This selection will make an attractive feature and will provide a long period of interest. Even in such a small area a couple of truly dwarf conifers or shrubs can provide a degree of structure and form throughout the summer and winter, whilst some miniature bulbs could produce a bonus of even earlier flowers. The peak period of interest is early spring to midsummer.

1 *Sempervivum arachnoideum* 'Laggeri' (× 1)
2 *Aubrieta* 'Silver Edge' (× 1)
3 *Achillea × lewisii* 'King Edward' (× 1)
4 *Juniperus communis* 'Compressa' (× 1)
5 *Campanula cochleariifolia* 'Elizabeth Oliver' (× 1)
6 *Salix* 'Boydii' (× 1)
7 *Sedum spathulifolium* 'Purpureum' (× 1)
8 *Dianthus* 'Pike's Pink' (× 1)

Area required:
approx. 60 × 90 cm/2 × 3 ft

ALPINES FOR EDGING AND PAVING

There is a wide range of low-growing, creeping or carpeting alpines suitable for planting along the edges of paving, although some are inclined to become invasive in the alpine garden if given too much freedom. Here alpines are used to edge a paved pathway and for growing between the slabs to soften their hard outlines. Most of these low-growing plants will grow in shallow soils or grit, preferring sun and good drainage. The alpines illustrated give an idea of the variety of foliage and flower colour that is available, but fewer species could be used if required. The taller plant, *Artemisia nutans*, is a pretty, feathery-leaved shrub which provides a good background for the lower-growing plants. The peak season of interest is mid-spring to late summer.

1 *Thymus* 'Bressingham Pink' (×3)
2 *Raoulia australis* (×3)
3 *Azorella trifurcata* (×3)
4 *Campanula muralis* 'Resholt' (×3)
5 *Artemisia nutans* (×6)
6 *Sagina subulata* 'Aurea' (×3)
7 *Acaena microphylla* (×3)
8 *Pratia pedunculata* (×3)

Area required:
approx. 60 × 210 cm/2 × 7 ft

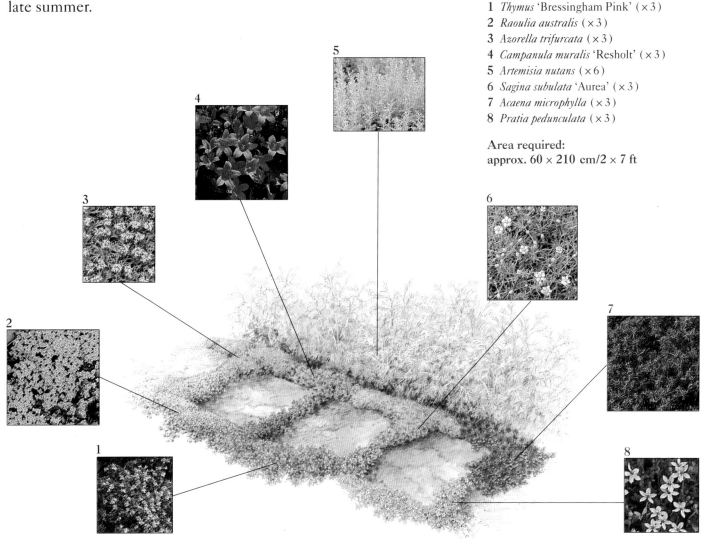

147

ADRIAN BLOOM'S INTRODUCTION

I had the opportunity to develop my 6-acre garden at Bressingham in 1967. Having created a heather and conifer garden next to my father's Dell garden, I was anxious to show how these plants could be used in a home garden setting. Though the area in question was less than half an acre, it still took me four years to fill it with plants.

The land was flat, so I created my own contours and then planted taller conifers for scale and vertical contrast. With heathers planted in groups of ten to fifteen of each variety, the garden soon filled up. Within six years I learned first-hand what constituted a dwarf, slow-growing or large conifer! Either I or the books had got it wrong, as most grew much quicker than suggested, though my soil was undeniably rich, fertile loam. The area began to look overcrowded, and I began to covet the adjacent, 5-acre meadow for a 'demonstration garden'.

So the fence came down and from 1973 to 1978 I gradually developed section by section. The soil pH varied from just above neutral 7 to acid 5.5, so I was able to try a wide range of plants. Heavy loam towards the garden's higher, north side gave way, further down, to fine-textured alluvial loam overlying soft sand, which had drainage problems, especially in winter. The garden was a frost pocket and winter temperatures were usually 2-3 degrees lower than in my father's garden; but few gardens are perfect, and I was basically happy with the site.

My initial obsession with dwarf conifers and heathers coincided with their rapid growth in popularity and our increasing nursery production, but gradually I introduced a much wider range of plants, including shrubs and perennials, to add variety and greater interest at other times of the year.

My garden continues to be a rewarding experience. The range of plants available is staggering, and it is fascinating to try new plants and to rediscover old ones, assessing them first-hand and deciding which plants to associate with them. I hope that my experience will be useful in giving others some ideas to follow.

Adrian Bloom in his garden at Foggy Bottom

CONIFERS

Conifers, especially dwarf and slow-growing types, have become increasingly popular in recent years. Though they are not universally 'fashionable' plants, the average gardener has recognized their potential, particularly for the smaller garden. Conifers provide an amazing range of forms and colours for year-round interest, yet most require little maintenance.

Since I first became interested in conifers twenty-five years ago, I have come to appreciate their worth fully, especially in my own garden at Foggy Bottom. As it gradually developed from an open, windswept field, the taller conifers grew to provide shelter for other plants. These conifers now give respite from cold winds, shade for woodland plants, a place for birds to nest and, in the long dull months of an English winter, a backcloth of continuous interest.

Twenty-five years ago there were few dwarf and slow-growing garden conifers available. Since then the range of new forms has increased enormously, to meet demand, and now we are almost spoilt for choice.

WHAT ARE CONIFERS?

'Conifer' comes from the Latin *conus*, meaning 'cone', and *ferre*, meaning 'to bear'; most mature species bear cones but some species and most dwarf conifers do not. Conifers are evergreen with the exception of *Larix*, *Ginkgo*, *Metasequoia* and *Taxodium*, which shed their leaves or needles in autumn.

Conifers grow wild in many parts of the world, with the greatest concentration in the Northern Hemisphere, where vast conifer forests still exist. In nature, most species reproduce from seed and these plants often vary considerably. The discovery and distribution over the last century of plants and seed from such far-flung outposts as New Zealand, Japan and China also added to the range of conifers available. Nurseries, private collections and botanical gardens have

The grace of a weeping larch is evident in this specimen of *Larix decidua* 'Pendula', prettily set off by violas, the white *Dicentra* 'Pearl Drops' and a drift of *Geranium* 'Johnson's Blue'

150

been sources of even more 'new' ornamental conifers. And chance seedlings often provide pleasant surprises, as with the many dwarf, golden, variegated and blue-foliaged forms of *Chamaecyparis lawsoniana*.

A gardener or nurseryman may find a golden or cream-coloured sport, or mutant shoot, on an otherwise green conifer. Rooting a cutting of this shoot creates a new plant. Pines and spruces can also mutate as witches' brooms, small congested growths of many-branched twigs on the crowns of trees, which, if propagated, provide other new dwarf conifers for cultivation.

As more people become interested in conifers the choice gets wider and wider, so the need for more selectivity becomes greater. There is always room for a *good* new conifer but it needs careful, professional assessment before being registered and marketed commercially. Over the years well over 1000 varieties have entered my collection at Bressingham, and many have been discarded, too.

HOW TO MAKE A SELECTION

For the first-time gardener, choosing conifers is probably more confusing than choosing almost any other group of plants. Unless conifers are clearly labelled it is difficult for the uninitiated to see or know the difference between similar-looking plants.

Rates of growth

Some eventually large conifers may grow 90cm/3ft a year, while miniature forms may grow less than 2.5cm/1in a year, so it is vital to consider rate of growth as well as appearance. I have seen amusing, and perhaps frightening, examples of conifers unwittingly purchased at 15cm/6in high, planted outside a living-room window, only to grow like the proverbial beanstalk, shutting out all light from the house!

As a guide, conifers officially classified as **large** might grow 4m/13ft or more in ten years and ultimately more than 15m/50ft; **medium** conifers might grow 1.8-3m/6-10ft in ten years and ultimately 8m/26ft or more; **slow-growing** conifers might grow 90-180cm/3-6ft in ten years and ultimately 5m/16ft or more; and **dwarf** conifers might grow less than 90cm/3ft in ten years and ultimately less than 3m/10ft. Do not let some of the figures frighten you, since many of the slow-growing and dwarf conifers take twenty-five to fifty years to become an embarrassment, and think what fun and enjoyment you can have in the meantime! Some conifers do not grow upright, but remain prostrate or semi-prostrate. Approximate growth rates and habits of growth for these are given in the descriptive directory.

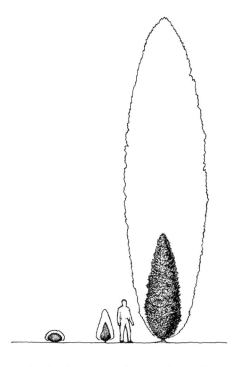

An indication of the sizes and growth rates of slow-growing, medium and large conifers after 5 years and 15 years

Little-known characteristics of some conifers

Many conifers have flowers, both male and female, but only the females develop into cones which ultimately drop their seeds. The flowers can be spectacular in spring before breaking up into clouds of pollen. *Chamaecyparis lawsoniana* 'Wissellii' and 'Little Spire' both have bright crimson flowers, as does *Abies procera*, the noble fir, and some others.

Adult and juvenile foliage is another interesting feature. Adult foliage is generally coarse and rough, juvenile usually more feathery. In the *Chamaecyparis* and *Thuja* genera some dwarf and slow-growing forms from seed have foliage fitting the description of juvenile: for example, *Chamaecyparis lawsoniana* 'Ellwoodii' and *Chamaecyparis pisifera* 'Squarrosa Sulphurea'. Occasionally such plants can revert, with older, coarser foliage taking over. The Chinese junipers, *Juniperus chinensis*, often have adult and juvenile foliage on the same plant, but in this case the juvenile foliage is sharp and prickly. *Juniperus chinensis* 'Aurea', for instance, has juvenile foliage which becomes more and more adult over a number of years.

An association of dwarf conifers with other plants in Adrian Bloom's garden. Most of these plants are over twenty years old and provide a year-round framework for deciduous shrubs, alpines and perennials

153

This prostrate Colorado blue spruce, *Picea pungens* 'Prostrata', allows itself to be invaded by a dwarf, spreading shrub, *Vaccinium vitis-idaea* 'Koralle', seen here in fruit in autumn

Conifers for every purpose

There are conifers to suit almost every site and purpose: for woodland, shelter belts, tall screens and hedges; shrub and mixed borders; to associate with heathers and dwarf shrubs; and for alpine gardens. There are conifers for specimens in lawns, ground cover on banks, raised beds, troughs, window boxes and tubs. For the devotee, dwarf and slow-growing conifers can be planted in a bed of their own.

The widest selection of conifers is available from specialist nurseries. Many of these will despatch by mail order, but plants thus sent must be limited in size, because of prohibitive mailing costs. Ensure that your source is reputable; this applies to garden centres, too, though here you can make the selection yourself and, if necessary, seek advice. Look for healthy plants with no signs of stress or pest damage and, in most cases, foliage well furnished to the base of the plant.

Most conifers for sale today are grown for some of their life in a container. Their roots should at least make growth to the side of the pot, preferably totally holding the rootball together. Rootballed plants from the open ground should have their roots, with ample soil attached, wrapped in cloth or hessian; again, roots and soil should hold firmly together. Pot- or container-grown conifers can be planted at any time of the year as long as soil and weather conditions allow. If the ground is frozen or you have no means of keeping plants watered in summer, or if soils are very wet or waterlogged, a delay may not only be advisable but also necessary. Rootballed conifers are best planted from early autumn to late spring, and later only with great care.

Large conifers are not necessarily old; small conifers are not necessarily young. A 1.8m/6ft Leyland cypress (× *Cupressocyparis leylandii*) may be two to three years old, while a *Pinus leucodermis* 'Schmidtii' 20cm/8in high and 30cm/1ft across may be ten years old. Both serve different purposes, and while you should expect to pay more for the pine, you *can* pop it on the seat of your car, while the Leyland cypress may need to be delivered.

No rule of thumb can be made as to price, but expect to pay extra according to the number of years a nurseryman has spent growing a plant, and for the cost of handling a large specimen. Another factor affecting the price of a conifer, even when purchasing a young one, is its method of propagation. Conifers grown from seed may be the cheapest, but most garden conifers are grown from cuttings, which ensures uniformity of offspring to the parent. Select forms of silver fir, cedar, spruce and pine, however, as well as some others, grow satisfactorily only if grafted onto a more vigorous seedling understock. A cutting, or scion, from a Colorado blue spruce cultivar such as *Picea pungens* 'Hoopsii' is grafted by making a long diagonal cut on the stem and matching it with a similar but opposite-angled cut on the two- to three-year-old seedling, probably a Norway spruce (*Picea abies*). Tied and sealed, this should slowly effect a union, which eventually produces a young blue spruce for sale. Success is less certain than with propagation from cuttings, so grafted plants are often twice the price, or more, of a similar-sized plant grown from cuttings.

Grafting conifers onto more vigorous rootstock

SOME CULTURAL ADVICE

When choosing conifers, select not only according to personal taste, but also for what you want to achieve. Keep habit and growth rates in mind when spacing. Most conifers prefer open situations and golden-leaved conifers need sunlight to colour well. Few conifers thrive happily in deep shade. Consider, too, how exposed your garden is to the elements, and protect newly planted conifers until established.

Soils and fertilizers
Most conifers are not fussy about soils but some have preferences. Few, except for common yew, most juniper and some pine species and varieties, thrive on thin, chalky soils. All soils can be improved by adding well-rotted compost or farmyard manure, leaf mould, or bark-based products. Excellent though it is, use peat only if no substitute is available. All these help aerate heavy soils and retain moisture on light ones. Ensure all planting areas are completely free from perennial weeds. This is especially important with permanent planting.

On reasonably fertile soils, fertilizer is generally not necessary. To the soil improvements mentioned above one can, according to

requirements, add bonemeal or an inorganic, slow-release, well-
balanced fertilizer. On poor and highly alkaline soils, iron chelate,
or flowers of sulphur, helps to reduce the pH.

Planting

Water plants well twenty-four hours before planting by immersing
the rootball, in its container, in water for an hour or so, then allowing
to drain. (If the plant is rootballed and wrapped, however, immerse
for only a few minutes.) A friable weed-free soil is ideal for conifers.
Make the hole 60cm/2ft larger in diameter than the rootball, to allow
the roots room to spread, and deep enough for the top of the rootball
to come *just* below the soil level. Mix moist peat or compost into the
hole; most conifers are now grown in peat-based compost, and their
roots more easily establish themselves in a similar medium. Remove
the pot or container. If the roots are congested, gently prise them
apart at the base with a fork, or, in extremes, cut away the 'corkscrew'
older roots. Place the conifer in the hole and return the soil, firming
but not jamming it in. Water thoroughly and repeat as necessary for
the first growing season. In hot weather, spray or syringe the foliage
each evening. Stake larger specimens to support them against strong
winds until their roots are established.

   If planting in a lawn, thoroughly prepare the planting area and
remove turf at least 30cm/1ft beyond the outermost part of the
conifer, whether rootball or foliage. Always keep grass clear of the
conifer base. Protect from cold winds and frosts by using an anti-
desiccant spray, or by surrounding the conifer with staked hessian or
shading material, kept clear of the foliage.

Pruning

Most conifers, except those grown as hedging, never require pruning,
but many can be kept in check or improved by careful removal of
branches or foliage. There are many reasons for initial pruning.
Nurserymen shape young plants to make them bushier or more
evenly branched so they appeal to eventual customers. Grafted plants
with upright habits need their main vertical shoot trained up and side
branches trimmed. Both practices should be continued by the gardener
on such plants as *Picea pungens* cultivars, the Colorado blue spruce.

   Prostrate and semi-prostrate conifers are often vigorous and need
their spreading branches pruned from quite a young age. This also
creates a bushier plant. With careful, regular trimming and pruning it
is possible to keep many large conifers looking natural, yet compact
enough for a small garden.

   Prune or trim in spring before new growth begins, which then covers
the cuts. More densely foliaged plants and hedges can also be pruned

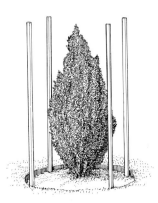

Surround the conifer with stakes,
keeping them well clear of the foliage

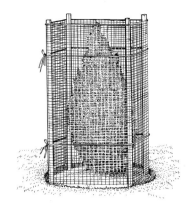

Nail hessian, shading material or
garden netting to the stakes. This will
protect exposed, newly planted conifers
from wind and frost

Pruning the lower, spreading branches
of prostrate or semi-prostrate conifers

in midsummer. For hedges and specimens with thin branches, use sharp shears, and sharp secateurs for thicker branches and those that need individual treatment. On spruces and pines, primarily, cut just in front of two side shoots or buds. If density is required, pines can be sheared as soft new shoots begin to harden in spring.

Hedges

Several conifers make ideal hedges, providing year-round protection and privacy, but the faster the growth, the more need there is for trimming, and the more difficult they are to control if left to get out of hand. Thus the rapid-growing × *Cupressocyparis leylandii* can be a menace in a small suburban garden; *Thuja occidentalis* 'Smaragd' is better. Whatever the hedge, decide your ultimate height and trim the sides lightly as it grows, and the top 15-30cm/6-12in below that ultimate height. This improves bushiness and promotes side growth.

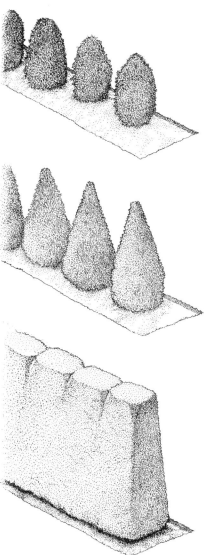

Conifer hedge in the first year (*top*), requiring no pruning; in the second and third years, prune the sides and top lightly with shears (*centre*); a regularly pruned hedge after five or six years (*bottom*)

The golden Scots pine, *Pinus sylvestris* 'Aurea', in February, proves the point that conifers need not be dull in winter

CONIFERS DIRECTORY

This is a personal selection and includes primarily dwarf and slow-growing types, introduced and used in Europe, North America, Japan and Australasia. An indication of the approximate size, after ten years, appears after each description; inevitably, this is an estimate, since growing conditions, soils and climate can differ widely.

Key

H: Approximate height after 10 years
W: Approximate width after 10 years
G: Propagated by grafting
Z: Relevant hardiness zone(s)

ABIES Silver fir

There are about forty wild species, many too large for the average garden, but the genus also includes attractive, smaller cultivars. The common name comes from the silvery leaf undersides. Most species are hardy and adapt to normal garden conditions, though some dislike shallow, chalky soils and industrial atmospheres. Silver firs generally prefer temperate zones, with cool winters. Their cones usually stand above the foliage, and on some species, such as *A. procera* and *A. koreana*, can be most impressive.

A. balsamea 'Nana'. A popular, hardy form of balsam fir discovered in the windswept New Hampshire mountains. Deep green needles, compact habit; relatively lime-tolerant. Plants listed as *A. balsamea* 'Hudsonia' are almost identical. H30cm/1ft, W30-45cm/12-18in. Z4-6.

A. cephalonica 'Meyer's Dwarf' (syn. 'Nana'). A compact form of Greek fir of

Abies lasiocarpa 'Compacta'

irregular habit with dark, rich green foliage, slightly pendulous branch tips and attractive winter buds. Starts into growth early, so avoid planting in frost pockets. H30-45cm/12-18in, W45-75cm/18-30in. G. Z5-6.

A. concolor 'Candicans' (syn. 'Argentea'). One of the best Colorado firs, with intense silver-grey foliage and an open, upright habit. Ideal tall specimen but needs adequate space. H1.8-3m/6-10ft, W3m/10ft. G. Z4-7. 'Compacta' has an irregular, rounded habit; inner needles dark green, new leaves silvery blue and in warm sun silvery blue throughout; best in full sun. H60-75cm/24-30in, W60-75cm/24-30in. G. Z4-7. 'Green Globe' (formerly *A. balsamea* 'Globosa') is a slow-to-establish, round bush of soft, light green foliage. It apparently arose as a seedling on a New Jersey nursery in the USA. H60cm/2ft, W45-60cm/18-24in. G. Z4-7.

A. koreana. The Korean fir carries deep blue cones from an early age. Most form narrow pyramids of rich green foliage, with bright silver undersides. H1.8-3m/6-10ft, W1.2-1.8m/4-6ft. G. Z6-7. 'Aurea' has pale golden leaves, prone to scorch in hot climates; eventually forms a small tree with bluish cones. H1.2-1.5m/4-5ft, W90-150cm/3-5ft. G. Z6-7. 'Brevifolia' has very short needles, and can be grown as a prostrate or upright form, with widely spaced branches. As an upright it will produce miniature cones. 'Piccolo' is a similar, usually prostrate plant. H60-90cm/2-3ft, W (if prostrate) 60-5cm/24-30in. G. Z6-7. 'Horstmann's Silberlocke' (syn. 'Horstmann's Silver Curls') was raised in Germany and its leaves twist outwards and upwards, looking like a silver tinselled bush. If required, the removal of the leading shoot keeps the plant as a bush, ensuring an effective display. H1.5-1.8m/5-6ft, W1.2m/4ft. Z6-7.

A. lasiocarpa 'Compacta'. A superb, compact form of Arizona cork bark fir; it slowly makes a broadly pyramidal, dense, silvery blue bush with light brown winter buds. The foliage turns intense silver in midsummer. H60-90cm/2-3ft, W45cm/18in. G. Z6-7.

A. nordmanniana 'Golden Spreader'. A form of Caucasian fir, excellent for winter colour; slow and prostrate when young, eventually forming an irregular, compact bush with light gold summer leaves turning glowing, deep gold in winter. In hot climates, best in part shade. May form a

Abies koreana 'Horstmann's Silberlocke'

Abies koreana cones

leader unless pruned. H45-60cm/18-24in, W45-60cm/18-24in. G. Z5-7.

A. pinsapo 'Horstmann's Nana'. One of the best forms of Spanish fir; spiky branches and short, blue-grey, rigid needles form a dense, irregular bush. Fine on chalk soils. H45-60cm/18-24in, W60-75cm/24-30in. G. Z6-7.

A. procera 'Glauca Prostrata'. A dwarf or prostrate form of noble fir, with bright, silver-blue foliage, impressive cylindrical cones, and deep crimson male flowers in spring, making a very irregular, spreading bush unless pruned, but ideal for the larger rockery or heather garden. Occasional upright shoots can be pruned, or left to make a small, controllable tree, as at Bressingham. Unsuitable for chalk. H30-45cm/12-18in, W75-120cm/30-48in. G. Z6-7. A more reliable compact form is 'Nobel', from the Nobel collection in Golden Gate Park, San Francisco.

ARAUCARIA Monkey puzzle

The twenty or so species of this genus are found only in the Southern Hemisphere. Only one, given below, is hardy.

A. araucana. Today slightly unfashionable, but, given space, this makes a fine, eventually huge tree, with well-spaced, spidery branches clothed in dark green, rigid, sharp-pointed leaves. Prefers moist, loamy soil; to retain lower branches it needs light, air and grass-free ground in early years. Produces large, coconut-like cones when older. H1.8-3m/6-10ft, W1.5m/5ft. Z7-8.

CALOCEDRUS Incense cedar

C. decurrens (syn. *Libocedrus decurrens*). Eventually tall-growing; most cultivars are narrow columns of rich green, fan-like sprays, effective as a single specimen or in group planting. Suitable for most soils. H3-5m/10-16ft, W60cm/2ft. Z5. 'Aureovariegata' is slow-growing but eventually forms a broadly conical tree with deep green foliage, irregularly splashed golden-yellow. Pruning branch tips in early years promotes density. H2.1-3m/7-10ft, W90cm/3ft. G. Z6-8.

CEDRUS Cedar

A genus of four species, originating from the Mediterranean to the Western Himalayas. Most become large trees, pyramidal in mid-life, some flat-topped with age, with needle-like leaves spirally arranged in clusters along the branches. The upright cones often take two or three years to ripen. Most species prefer deep, moist, but well-drained soil.

C. atlantica 'Glauca'. The blue cedar is spindly when young, but soon fills out, eventually becoming a statuesque, bright silver-blue specimen, 23m/75ft high, so site with care. I have seen specimens pruned to make a column or used against a wall – effective if not natural. H3-5m/10-16ft, W1.5-2.1m/5-7ft. G. Z7-8. 'Fastigiata' is not as glaucous but its narrow, columnar form is better suited to small spaces and makes an attractive specimen. H3-4m/10-13ft, W60-90cm/2-3ft. G. Z7-8. 'Glauca Pendula' is scruffy or magnificent, depending upon how it is grown. Naturally prostrate and sprawling, it can be trained as a tree with pendulous branches clothed with blue-grey needles. It can also be trained into an arch or along a fence. Prune, if required, in April or August. Growth rate normally 15-30cm/6-12in per annum, in whatever direction. G. Z7-8.

C. brevifolia (syn. *C. libani brevifolia*). Slow at first but eventually of some size, the Cyprian cedar has well-spaced, arching branches clothed in short, dark green needles; able to withstand heat and drought better than most cedars. H1.8-3m/6-10ft, W1.2-1.5m/4-5ft. Z6-7.

C. deodara. The Deodar cedar is the least

Abies procera 'Glauca Prostrata'

Cedrus atlantica 'Glauca' flowers

Calocedrus decurrens 'Aureovariegata'

hardy species, though forms in the wild spread from Afghanistan to the Himalayas. Typically producing luxuriant, blue-green foliage when young, it soon becomes pyramidal, with graceful, cascading, wide-spreading branches; so allow space. H3-5m/10-16ft, W2.1-3m/7-10ft. Z7-8.

'Albospica' was introduced in 1874, but is still rare. Eventually a large tree, with startling white tips on new growth in late spring. Best in full sun and more effective if pruned regularly. H1.5-2.4m/5-8ft, W1.2m/

Cedrus deodara 'Gold Mound'

4ft. Z7-8. 'Blue Dwarf' arose as a promising chance seedling in Holland, and is slow-growing initially, later making a wider-spreading bush with greyish blue foliage. Approximate H30-45cm/12-18in, W60-75cm/24-30in. Z7-8. 'Cream Puff' is a most attractive new conifer, one of many selected on Alan Goddard's nursery in Victoria, Vancouver Island, Canada. All are gradually entering wider cultivation and are worth looking out for. 'Cream Puff' is the most vigorous of the following, making a small pyramid with creamy white foliage, brighter in summer. Pruning will enhance density. H1.5-1.8m/5-6ft, W90cm/3ft. G.Z7-8. Dwarfer, white-needled forms include 'Silver Mist', 'Snowsprite' and 'White Imp', all worth a try, though prone to wind and frost damage, especially when young. Approximate H90cm/3ft, W90cm/3ft. G.Z7-8. 'Gold Mound' is broad in outline and deep yellow; a good replacement for 'Aurea', since it holds its colour better in winter. H3-5m/10-16ft, W1.8-3m/6-10ft. G. Z7-8.

'Golden Horizon' is a Dutch form with bright, golden-yellow needles in summer, golden-green in winter. It varies considerably in habit, perhaps according to grafting; in its best form low and prostrate, but can become semi-prostrate and sometimes throw up a leading shoot which, if not cut out, will develop into a large upright form. Approximate H45-60cm/18-24in, W1.5-1.8m/5-6ft. G. Z7-8. 'Karl Fuchs' is one of several seedlings grown, selected and introduced from Germany from seed collected in the Paktia Province, Afghanistan, all considerably hardier than the type. Time

Cedrus deodara 'Nana Aurea'

Cedrus libani 'Sargentii'

will tell but 'Karl Fuchs' is already distinctive, making a pyramid of striking, blue-grey foliage. If it proves hardy enough it can be grown in place of the more tender Deodar cedar. H3-5m/10-16ft, W1.5-2.1m/5-7ft. G. Z6-8. **'Nana Aurea'** is one of the best, though unexciting when young and perhaps prone to spring frost damage. It slowly develops into a dense, golden-yellow bush and keeps its colour throughout the year. If allowed to make a leading shoot, it forms a narrow, conical tree. For the smaller garden, prune the leading shoots for a dome of golden foliage which retains the pendulous branch tips typical of Deodar. H (unpruned) 1.8-3m/6-10ft, W1.5m/5ft. G. Z7-8.

C. libani. Seldom planted now, since *C. atlantica* 'Glauca' is considered more ornamental, the cedar of Lebanon forms a large, flat-topped tree in time. Mature trees exceed 30m/100ft in height and need a huge area to accommodate them. H3-5m/10-16ft, W2.1m/7ft. Z6-7. **'Aurea Prostrata'** (syn. 'Golden Dwarf') is a rare, slow-growing form, needing light shade in hot climates to prevent the golden-yellow foliage scorching. H60cm/2ft, W90-120cm/3-4ft. G. Z7. Var. *brevifolia*. See *C. brevifolia*.

'Nana' slowly makes an upright globe of dense, light green foliage and is a must for the collector. H60-90cm/2-3ft, W60-75cm/24-30in. G. Z6-7. **'Comte de Dijon'** is similar but with darker green needles and faster growth. H90-120cm/3-4ft, W60-90cm/2-3ft. Z6-9. **'Sargentii'** is a bluish green, weeping form with a prostrate, eventually mounded habit ideal for cascading down a bank or over a wall. H30-45cm/12-18in, W75-120cm/30-48in. G. Z6-7.

CEPHALOTAXUS

A genus with many similarities to yew (*Taxus*), though usually with larger leaves. Like yew, the species grow in sun or shade, even deep shade under other trees, and tolerate alkaline soils. They are native to China, Japan and Korea.

Cephalotaxus harringtonia 'Fastigiata'

C. fortunei. A large, spreading, somewhat untidy bush, with glossy green leaves on widely spaced branches, and male and female flowers on separate trees. Females often bear olive-like fruits, hence the common name Chinese plum yew. H1.8-3m/6-10ft, W1.8-3m/6-10ft. Z6-9.
C. harringtonia, or Japanese plum yew, is hardier, slower and more compact than *C. fortunei*. H1.5-1.8m/5-6ft, W1.8m/6ft. Z6-9. Best of all is the upright **'Fastigiata'**, an attractive, fastigiate or vase-shaped plant with deep green needles, like a coarse Irish

yew (*Taxus baccata* 'Fastigiata'). H1.5-1.8m/5-6ft, W60cm/2ft. Z6-9.

CHAMAECYPARIS False cypress

One of the most important conifer genera, it has contributed many excellent plants for garden use. The species originate from North America and Eastern Asia.

C. lawsoniana. In its natural habitat of northern California and Oregon, the Lawson cypress is a large forest tree, up to 45m/150ft high. In 1854 the first seed was sent to Europe, to Lawson's Nursery near Edinburgh, Scotland, and Lawson's name is forever associated with these valuable ornamental cultivars – in Britain, many are referred to as Lawsons rather than *Chamaecyparis*! In the past 100 years or so, hundreds of seedling selections have been made and introduced, in a wide range of shapes, colours and sizes. Seedling Lawsons are often sold as fairly cheap hedging, but they are liable to differ in habit, and are prone to windburn and scorch in exposed positions.

Most cultivars are hardy to Zone 6 but young golden- and cream-foliaged forms need shelter from cold winds and intense sunlight. Desiccation of foliage can occur in severe winters and some are prone to the fungal disease *Phytophthora*, which attacks roots, generally in wet, warm conditions. Ironically, one of the worst areas for growing *C. lawsoniana* cultivars in gardens is in Oregon, USA!

'Albospica' makes a slow-growing, conical tree with slightly pendulous branches, irregularly tipped creamy white. An old cultivar, and not spectacular, but still worth garden space. H1.5-1.8m/5-6ft, W60-75cm/24-30in. Z7. **'Aurea Densa'** and its sister plant, 'Minima Aurea' (see below), are two of the finest dwarf conifers. Both, and the similar but rare 'Lutea Nana', were seedlings selected before the Second World War at the Rogers' Nursery at Eastleigh in Hampshire, England. 'Aurea Densa' makes a very compact bush of stiff, golden-yellow foliage, eventually rounded in habit. Best in full sun. H30-45cm/12-18in, W30cm/1ft. Z7.

'Bleu Nantais', a French cultivar, and **'Chilworth Silver'**, raised in England, are two of many forms similar to the popular and ubiquitous 'Ellwoodii', with bright, silver-blue, soft, feathery juvenile foliage. Both are slower-growing than 'Ellwoodii'. H1.1-1.35m/43-53in, W60-75cm/24-30in. Z6-7. **'Columnaris'** (syn. 'Columnaris Glauca') is a true, column-shaped form, though often conical when young, and eventually quite large. It has deep blue-grey foliage, open in the vigorous top growth, but dense below. Grown on lighter, drier soils, it is often much thinner and more pillar-like than those grown on richer, heavier soils. **'Grayswood Pillar'** is similar. H1.8-3m/6-10ft, W60-90cm/2-3ft. Z6-7.

'Ellwoodii' makes a very neat bush of feathery blue-green foliage, appealing when young, and becoming steel-blue in winter. At first conical, it grows fastigiate with age. H1.5-1.8m/5-6ft, W45-75cm/18-30in. Z6-7. **'Ellwood's Gold'**, extremely popular in England where it was raised, is similar but slower-growing than 'Ellwoodii', with golden-yellow summer foliage, toning down in autumn and winter to lime-green. Again, the more exposed to sun, the brighter the colour. H1.2-1.5m/4-5ft, W30-45cm/12-18in. Z7. **'Ellwood's Pillar'** is a first-class French introduction, slow-growing and varying in habit according to soil and site. It normally makes a narrow column of tightly congested, dark blue-green foliage, but in exposed positions it assumes a dwarfer, squatter form. It and 'Ellwood's Gold' are more interesting plants than 'Ellwoodii'. H60-75cm/24-30in, W20-30cm/8-12in. Z6-7. **'Ellwood's White'** generally describes plants with blue-green foliage liberally variegated with creamy white, though some plants under this name have just the foliage tips white. The former are more prone to wind and sun damage, but more striking; the latter are less striking, but more reliable and slightly faster-growing. H90-120cm/3-4ft, W20-30cm/8-12in. Z7.

'Gimbornii'. From an undistinguished young stage, this soon becomes a neat, globe-like bush of dense, soft greyish green foliage, with mauve tips. Even at twenty years old, it is unlikely to outgrow its space. H45-60cm/18-24in, W45-60cm/18-24in. Z6-7. **'Gnome'** forms a tightly congested bun of dense, blue-green leaves, perfect for troughs or sink gardens, but may throw up reverting shoots, which should be cut away. I prefer the even more compact 'Green Globe'. H15-20cm/6-8in, W20-30cm/8-12in. Z6-7. **'Golden Pot'** is a sport from 'Pottenii', hence the name and the similar soft, feathery, upright branching foliage, but it is much slower-growing and maintains a bright yellow colour all year round. It is excellent with contrasting foliage shrubs or heathers. H90-120cm/3-4ft, W30-45cm/12-18in. Z7. **'Green Globe'**, a minute cultivar, was discovered as a seedling on a nursery in New Zealand some years ago. Its slow growth, rich green foliage and compact habit make it perfect for rock gardens, troughs and sinks. More rounded than 'Gnome'. H20-30cm/8-12in, W20-30cm/8-12in. Z6-7. **'Green Pillar'**, a rich green-foliaged conifer, is one of the best medium-growing Lawsons and a green counterpart to the blue-grey 'Columnaris'; its narrower form makes it a better plant than **'Erecta Viridis'**, which eventually gets large and open-branched. Ideal as a foil for both blue- and golden-foliaged forms. H1.8-2.4m/6-8ft, W60-90cm/2-3ft. Z6-7.

'Howarths Gold' has rich, golden-yellow foliage, and a nice, bushy habit from a young age, eventually forming a narrow pyramid. H2.4-3m/8-10ft, W90cm/3ft. Z6-7. **'Lane'**, a taller-growing Lawson, also known as 'Lanei', has golden-yellow summer foliage, turning brighter, clearer yellow in winter. It needs space, eventually making a broad pyramid, and can also make an effective and colourful screen. H2.4-3m/8-10ft, W1.2m/4ft. Z6-7. **'Little Spire'**, though distinct and useful, has hardly fulfilled its prophecy of 'little'. An interesting English cross between 'Fletcheri' and 'Wissellii', it is a smaller edition of the latter. Like 'Wissellii', it carries bright crimson male flowers on dark blue-green, congested, fern-like foliage in late spring. H1.5-2.4m/5-8ft, W30-60cm/1-2ft. Z6-7.

Chamaecyparis lawsoniana 'Pygmaea Argentea'

Chamaecyparis lawsoniana 'Rijnhof'

'Minima Aurea' is a very slow-growing conifer, selected as a seedling (see 'Aurea Densa' above) nearly fifty years ago. Its rigid branches carry dense sprays of bright golden-yellow leaves which appear brighter in winter. After many years, 'Minima Aurea' makes a dwarf pyramid; 'Aurea Densa' is more ovoid, but both are equally desirable. The rare **'Lutea Nana'** is like a slightly larger 'Minima Aurea'. H45-60cm/18-24in, W30cm/1ft. Z6-7. **'Minima Glauca'** makes a compact bush with fan-shaped sprays of bluish green foliage, closer to 'Aurea Densa'

Chamaecyparis lawsoniana 'Minima Aurea'

than 'Minima Aurea' in habit. The rigid branching system carries soft foliage. **'Minima'** has lighter green leaves with no hint of blue, but I prefer 'Minima Glauca'. H45-60cm/18-24in, W45-60cm/18-24in. Z6-7.

'Nana Albospica', at its best, is most attractive, with lime-green winter foliage turning a dramatic creamy white in summer. Unfortunately, this transformation cannot be relied on and in shade or on dry, poor soil the colour may remain dull green all year round. Very slow-growing, forming a broad cone of soft foliage. Give it light and plenty of fertilizer or well-rotted compost. H60-75cm/24-30in, W45-60cm/18-24in. Z7. **'Nidiformis'** is one of the most attractive prostrate or semi-prostrate Lawsons, gradually forming a spreading bush. Its arching branches carry horizontal sprays of bright green, fern-like foliage, drooping gracefully at the tips. H60-90cm/2-3ft, W90-120cm/3-4ft. Z7. Similar when young but eventually much taller and more vigorous is **'Tamariscifolia'**, a flat-topped bush of rich green, certainly needing space. H90-120cm/3-4ft, W1.2-1.5m/4-5ft. Z6-7. Also, with similar foliage, there is **'Rijnhof'**, a recent introduction from Holland which makes a low-growing, spreading carpet of overlapping, lacy green foliage. H20-30cm/8-12in, W60-75cm/24-30in. Z7.

'Pembury Blue' is one of the best taller Lawsons, with young open growth soon developing into a broad column of bright silver-blue, particularly in summer. Ideal as a screen plant with other tall golden and green cultivars. H2.4-3m/8-10ft, W1.2m/4ft. Z6-7. **'Pottenii'** is at its best when young, making a cone of dense, feathery green foliage. Later, it tends to open up and lose branches in snow and wind. Though not quite comparable, 'Green Pillar' is more satisfactory as a long-term garden plant. H2.4-3m/8-10ft, W60-90cm/2-3ft. Z6-7. **'Pygmaea Argentea'** is a favourite among British gardeners for its bright, year-round

Chamaecyparis lawsoniana 'Silver Threads'

Chamaecyparis obtusa 'Kosteri'

show. Similar in habit to the rounded, dome shape of 'Minima', it has bluish green inner foliage and almost completely creamy white outer foliage, as if stroked with a paintbrush. Prone to suffer from windburn and sunburn, and unsuitable for extreme climates, but an absolute gem at its best. Plants grown in shade may lose their colour. Extremely slow-growing. H30-45cm/12-18in, W30-45cm/12-18in. Z7. The excellent but rare **'Pygmy'** is a miniature replica of 'Minima' and 'Minima Glauca', a dome-shaped, grey-green bush. H30cm/1ft, W30cm/1ft. Z6-7. **'Romana'** (syn. 'Aurea Romana') starts as a narrow young plant, but soon fills out to become a neat, conical bush of soft, deep golden-yellow, turning greeny yellow in winter. H1.8-3m/6-10ft, W75-90cm/30-36in. Z6-7.

'Silver Threads', a sport or variegated shoot found on 'Ellwood's Gold', is a pleasing dwarf conifer which makes a column of soft, greenish yellow foliage, speckled creamy white. May need protection when small. H90-120cm/3-4ft, W30-45cm/12-18in. Z7. **'Wissellii'** is an old but distinctive cultivar, making a dark blue-green pillar. Its rigid vertical branches are open and twist upwards, with short branchlets carrying crowded tufts of fern-like foliage, creating a cockscomb appearance. Often produces a show of crimson strobili or flowers in late spring. Vigorous. H2.4-3m/8-10ft, W45-60cm/18-24in. Z6-7.

C. nootkatensis. The Nootka cypress is a very hardy native of the coast of western North America, from British Columbia to Alaska. The species will reach well over 30m/100ft, forming an open, conical shape, with upright branches and gently

pendulous, dull green aromatic foliage. It prefers deep, moist soils and dislikes chalk and very peaty types. H1.8-3m/6-10ft, W90-120cm/3-4ft. Z5-7. **'Aurea'** (syn. 'Lutea') is bright yellow in summer as a young plant, but seems to lose this colouring a few years later, becoming just lightly suffused with yellow in summer. Soil and site affect colour. H1.8-3m/6-10ft, W90-120cm/3-4ft. G. Z5-7. **'Aureovariegata'** is a rare but handsome plant with green foliage speckled golden-yellow. Similar growth rate to 'Aurea', both making excellent specimens especially where more colourful Lawsons may not be reliably hardy. H1.8-3m/6-10ft, W90-120cm/3-4ft. G. Z5-7. **'Pendula'** comes in several forms, some denser and less pendulous than others. The best, worthy of wider planting, makes a rather narrow pyramidal outline, with horizontal primary branches carrying long, weeping branchlets that hang like streamers. H1.8-3m/6-10ft, W90-120cm/3-4ft. G. Z5-7.

C. obtusa. The Hinoki cypress, from Japan and Taiwan, is considered sacred by the followers of the Shinto faith. Though reaching well over 30m/100ft in the wild, it has given rise to many extremely desirable dwarf and slow-growing garden forms. The species is seldom offered but makes initially a slow-growing, conical tree of dark green, glossy foliage. Alkaline soils are unsuitable, and on thin, poor soils growth is liable to be sparse. H1.8-3m/6-10ft, W60-90cm/2-3ft. Z5-8.

'Chabo-yadori' eventually forms a compact pyramid of twisted, irregular sprays of both adult and juvenile, light green foliage. Light pruning on richer soils may be needed to maintain bushiness. H1.2-1.5m/4-5ft, W45-60cm/18-24in. Z5-8. **'Crippsii'** is

unruly when young but, given time and pruning of side branches, is superbly elegant. Flattened horizontal branches are clothed with bright golden-yellow foliage having wispy, slightly pendulous tips. The foliage can scorch when young. **'Goldilocks'**, a recent Dutch selection, is slower and denser, and may prove best of all. H1.8-3m/6-10ft, W60-75cm/24-30in. Z5-8.

'Fernspray Gold' is popular in New Zealand, where it grows in full sun without scorching, sometimes a problem in harsher climates. A golden-leaved selection of fernspray cypress (*C. obtusa* 'Filicoides'), it is often straggly or open in habit unless trimmed from an early age. Fern-like foliage clothes the branches exposed to sunlight, whereas the inner branches are bare. The similar **'Tetragona Aurea'** is a deeper gold colour and less open in its habit of growth. 'Fernspray Gold': H1.5-1.8m/5-6ft, W90-120cm/3-4ft. Z6-8. **'Flabelliformis'** was one of several extremely dwarf seedlings selected many years ago at the Rogers' Nursery in England. It is similar to 'Nana', making a compact bush of dark green, slightly bloomy, fan-shaped sprays. H30cm/1ft, W30cm/1ft. Z5-8. Other dwarfs from this nursery worth looking for, perfect for troughs and sinks, include **'Bassett'**, **'Caespitosa'**, **'Chilworth'**, **'Intermedia'** and **'Juniperoides'**. Never expose these and other miniatures to too much sun, wind or frost when young. A cold frame or alpine house is sensible. **'Golden Sprite'** is one of many selected by Mr Spingarn, a private collector on Long Island, New York, but it takes years to assess these slow-growing new cultivars, which include **'Dainty Doll'**, **'Elf'**, **'Golden Nymph'** and **'Leprechaun'**. 'Golden Sprite' makes a perfect bun of congested, golden-yellow foliage. These plants, though frost-hardy, may burn in extreme heat, and are ideal for the cool British climate. 'Golden Sprite': H15cm/6in, W20cm/8in Z5-8. **'Graciosa'**, like many conifers, has an undistinguished early life that belies its potential when mature. Flattened sprays of light green summer foliage darken in winter. Best in an open spot in full sun. H1.2-1.5m/4-5ft, W90-120cm/3-4ft. Z5-8.

'Kosteri' is slow-growing but quick enough to make a nice plant within three or four years, and seldom becomes embarrassingly large. Often flat-topped with light green, horizontally held, fan-shaped, mossy sprays, its slightly irregular shape has considerable character. H45-60cm/18-24in, W30-5cm/12-18in. Z5-8. **'Mariesii'** is an extremely slow-growing dwarf, open in habit when young, with thin, light green foliage liberally suffused creamy white in summer, especially on new growth, and yellow-green in winter. Most spectacular variegated form of *C. obtusa*. Lightly pruning tips in late spring

Chamaecyparis obtusa 'Nana Lutea'

encourages density. H30-45cm/12-18in, W30-45cm/12-18in. Z5-8. **'Nana'** is a genuine dwarf (not to be confused with the much more vigorous 'Nana Gracilis'), slowly making a neat, flat-topped bush of minute, dark green, fan-shaped sprays, arranged in horizontal tiers. At least twice as wide as high, it is ideal for the rock garden. H10cm/4in, W20cm/8in. Z5-8. **'Nana Aurea'** has an open, irregular growth habit, and pendulous golden-yellow foliage that quickly loses its colour if not in full sun. H60-75cm/24-30in, W30cm/1ft. Z5-8. **'Nana Gracilis'**, the best-known form of Hinoki cypress, makes an irregular globe-shaped bush when young, eventually becoming more pyramidal with twisted, shell-like sprays of dark, rich green foliage. It is often grafted though it roots relatively easily from cuttings. Avoid plants propagated by grafting as they are liable to be less compact, often sending up long vigorous reverting shoots, which should be pruned off. H60-90cm/2-3ft, W45-60cm/18-24in. Z5-8. **'Nana Lutea'** is a valuable dwarf, golden-yellow in summer and clear yellow in winter in an open position. It gradually forms a broad, irregularly pyramidal bush. H45-60cm/18-24in, W30-45cm/12-18in. Z5-8.

'Pygmaea' is a vigorous cultivar, belying its name. Bronze-green, glossy foliage, becoming deeper bronze in winter, grows in flat tiers, ending in thin, twisted, whipcord shoots. H30-45cm/12-18in, W60-75cm/24-30in. Z5-8. The slower-growing **'Pygmaea Aurescens'** has finer foliage, suffused greeny yellow in summer and richer in winter. H20-30cm/8-12in, W30-45cm/12-18in. Z5-8. **'Repens'** is slow-growing and

shade-loving, with loose sprays of bright green, fan-shaped foliage tinged yellow in winter. H20-30cm/8-12in, W60-75cm/24-30in. Z5-8. **'Rigid Dwarf'** is an excellent if rare cultivar, its stiff, upright branches gradually forming a densely foliaged, narrow pyramid of rich green foliage, glaucous beneath. H45-60cm/18-24in, W20-30cm/8-12in. Z5-8. **'Tonia'**, seen at its best, is striking. A sport of 'Nana Gracilis', it has spasmodic white-tipped foliage, usually not showing until the plant is some age. The variegation may not appear every year, and the plant needs a sunny position to tempt it. H45-60cm/18-24in, W30-45cm/12-18in. Z5-8. The even slower-growing Canadian **'Snowkist'** is more reliable and may in time replace 'Tonia'. H30-45cm/12-18in, W30cm/ 1ft. Z5-8.

C. pisifera. The Sawara cypress is an enormous tree up to 45m/150ft high in the warm, moist climate of its native Japan. The species is seldom planted as an ornamental, but many fine cultivars have become popular garden plants. There is a considerable diversity, from those with rough-textured adult foliage, to the 'Filifera' group with feathery, semi-juvenile leaves. Some dwarf forms are prone to reversion, often sending up strong growths which should be cut away.

'Boulevard', introduced in the USA in 1934 by Boulevard Nurseries, is generally sold as a dwarf, though eventually it probably exceeds 4.5m/15ft. It is most attractive when young, with bright, silver-blue, feathery foliage, soft to the touch. In time it makes a broad pyramid. It dislikes dry, impoverished soils, heavy clay or waterlogged soils, and alkaline ones, and reacts by turning light grey, purplish or brown and dying in patches. Prune lightly every year, starting when the plant is quite young. It makes an effective dwarf hedge. H1.5-1.8m/5-6ft, W90cm/3ft. Z5-8. **'Devon Cream'**, a variegated sport of 'Boulevard', at its best looks like a creamy white beacon of brilliant summer foliage, but is unreliable and frost-tender – worth trying, however, if you want a challenge! H75-90cm/30-36in, W45-60cm/18-24in. Z7-8.

'Filifera Aurea' eventually grows large but is extremely slow in its early years. All 'Filifera' types have long, thin, thread-like foliage; on this plant it is bright yellow all year round. It may be slow to produce upright shoots and pruning side shoots may help – hardly natural but most effective pruned as a narrow pyramid. H90-120cm/3-4ft, W90-120cm/3-4ft. Z5-8. More reliable and almost identical is **'Golden Mop'**, which seldom throws up a leader and has bright yellow foliage, a little prone to sunscorch. **'Filifera Aureovariegata'** is sprawling and untidy when young but slowly forms a mounded bush of cascading, string-like, dark green foliage, irregularly splashed golden-yellow. H75-90cm/30-36in,

Chamaecyparis pisifera 'Filifera Aurea'

Chamaecyparis pisifera 'Filifera Aureovariegata'

Chamaecyparis obtusa 'Nana Gracilis'

W60-90cm/2-3ft. Z5-8. **'Filifera Nana'** is another attractive mop-head cypress, forming a broad bush of dark green foliage, wider than high. These forms lend themselves to training and trimming into all sorts of shapes. H60-75cm/24-30in, W60-90cm/2-3ft. Z5-8. **'Filifera Sungold'**. See 'Sungold'. **'Gold Spangle'**, a sport of 'Filifera Aurea', has coarser, more flattened adult foliage of brilliant yellow, but prone to sunscorch. It gradually forms a leading shoot, becoming pyramidal in shape. H90-120cm/3-4ft, W75-90cm/30-36in. Z7-8.

'Nana', a dwarf form, makes a neat bun of densely packed, slightly curved green foliage, silvery beneath, and eventually becomes a compact dome, sometimes with a smaller dome on top, of congested foliage. H15-20cm/6-8in, W23-30cm/9-12in. Z5-8. 'Nana Aureovariegata' is one of several variegated forms in cultivation – a cause of confusion to nurserymen as well as gardeners, since some apparently identical plants have different names. The plant generally offered under this name has light green foliage, flecked with golden-yellow. It seems identical to 'Gold Dust', recently introduced from Canada. Also sold as 'Nana Aureovariegata' is a form lacking variegation but light green in summer, and covered with a bright golden sheen in winter – a very desirable little plant and identical to 'Minima Aurea'. Make sure you know which you are getting! 'Nana Variegata' makes a similar compact bun, but with sparse flecks of white, and seems identical to 'Silver Lode'. All these varieties have much the same growth rate. H15-20cm/6-8in, W23-30cm/9-12in. Z5-8. Lastly, looser-growing forms of the above normally come under the name 'Compacta', 'Compacta Variegata', etc.

'Plumosa Aurea Nana' is well suited to a small garden. It makes a dense bush of feathery foliage, bright yellow all year round, but especially in spring. Slow to make a leading shoot, it eventually becomes a broad, pyramidal bush. Prune out any reversions; the whole plant stands light pruning. H90-120cm/3-4ft, W90-120cm/3-4ft. Z5-8. 'Plumosa Compressa' is a dwarf sport of 'Squarrosa', hence its diminutive, soft, parsley-like juvenile foliage. It slowly forms an irregularly shaped bush, but can be pruned to form a tight ball. The foliage is usually light sulphur-yellow in summer, yellow-green in winter, but it varies according to soil and site. H10-15cm/4-6in, W20-30cm/8-12in. Z6-8.

'Snow' puts on a brilliant summer show

Chamaecyparis pisifera 'Squarrosa Sulphurea'

of snow-white, feathery foliage that belies its hardiness – mine has survived temperatures to –21°C/–5.8°F. It still needs shelter from cold winds and hot sun, though, until well established. H23-30cm/9-12in, W30cm/1ft. Z6-8. 'Squarrosa Intermedia' has the soft, fully juvenile foliage that distinguishes the 'Squarrosa' group, though without annual pruning of reverting adult shoots it would soon lose its dwarf habit. Pruned, it can be kept as a tight, round bush of bright greyish blue, congested foliage and, thus treated, would make a growth of only 2.5cm/1in a year. H45-60cm/18-24in, W60-75cm/24-30in. Z5-8. 'Squarrosa Lombarts' shows no reversion from its soft, heather-like foliage, grey-blue in summer, turning deep purple in winter. It dislikes extremely heavy or alkaline soils and makes a large bush in time. H1.2-1.5m/4-5ft, W1.2-1.5m/4-5ft. Z5-8. 'Squarrosa Sulphurea' changes from a rather dull grey-green in winter to bright sulphur-yellow in summer flush, toning down again in autumn. Soft, feathery, juvenile foliage forms a tight pyramidal bush which takes well to trimming. H90-150cm/3-5ft, W75-90cm/30-36in. Z5-8. 'Sungold' (syn. 'Filifera Sungold') arose in Canada, and though less bright than most yellow-foliaged cultivars, is generally hardier and less prone to sunscorch. Its short, thread-like leaves held on overlapping branches are golden-yellow in summer, greeny yellow in winter. It is more compact and slower-growing than other 'Filifera' forms and needs full sun. H45-60cm/18-24in, W45-60cm/18-24in. Z5-8.

C. thyoides. The white cypress comes from eastern North America, spreading from Maine down to Florida, where it makes a tall tree. 'Andelyensis' makes a slow-growing column with erect branches bearing sprays of bluish green adult foliage, deeper bronze-green in winter, and often showing attractive male flowers in spring. Dislikes alkaline soils, particularly where dry. H90-120cm/3-4ft, W30cm/1ft. Z4-8. The dwarf 'Andelyensis Nana' is slower-growing, making an irregular bush with both juvenile and adult foliage, but it may eventually revert to its normal stronger habit. H30-45cm/12-18in, W30-45cm/12-18in. Z4-8. 'Ericoides' is a very old cultivar with all juvenile foliage, a bushy oval shape, greyish green in summer and plum-purple in winter. Larger plants are subject to snow damage. Prone to winter damage from frost and desiccating winds, a fault shared by other selections with juvenile foliage, such as 'Heather Bun', 'Purple Heather' and 'Rubicon', all with distinctive purple winter foliage, but more compact than 'Ericoides'. H1.2-1.5m/4-5ft, W60-75cm/24-30in. Z7-8.

CRYPTOMERIA Japanese cedar
C. japonica is the only species in the genus

Chamaecyparis thyoides 'Purple Heather'

and an important forest and timber tree in its native Japan, where it grows to 40m/130ft. It is less vigorous in cooler, drier climates, and though planted widely in Victorian Britain it is seldom planted now. It makes a narrow cone of light green foliage, its branchlets rope-like and as green as the leaves it is densely clothed with. H5-6m/16-20ft, W1.8-2.4m/6-8ft. Z6-8.

'Aurea' probably covers several different Japanese clones or selections, some resembling the species, but with golden-yellow foliage, brighter in winter than summer. 'Ogon', the Japanese for yellow, is particularly brilliant, but prone to sunscorch. 'Sekkan-sugi' (see below) looks similar in winter, but is creamy white in summer. Some are a little frost-tender in early years. H3-4m/10-13ft, W90-120cm/3-4ft. Z6-8. 'Bandai-sugi', like many of the dwarf forms of *C. japonica*, is odd rather than beautiful. It carries congested juvenile and adult foliage, with leaves of various lengths and forms. They form an irregular, bushy plant, bright green in summer, bronze in winter. H75-90cm/30-36in, W60-75cm/24-30in. Z6-8.

'Elegans' is a popular form with finely cut, feathery foliage, soft to the touch. It eventually becomes broadly conical, varying according to climate and situation. Fresh-green summer foliage turns deep purple-bronze in late autumn and winter. Ideal for the winter garden, though not hardy in very cold climates. H1.8-3m/6-10ft, W1.2-1.5m/4-5ft. Z7-8. 'Elegans Aurea' is a nice contrast to 'Elegans', with bright green juvenile foliage, yellow-green in winter. Some make an upright conical bush, others a broader spreading form. H1.5-1.8m/5-6ft, W1.2-1.5m/4-5ft. Z7-8.

'Globosa Nana' has typical foliage with pendulous, rope-like branchlets fully clothed in sharply pointed light green needles, turning blue-green in winter; it slowly makes a dense, broad, round bush, eventually covering a large area. H90-120cm/3-4ft, W90-120cm/3-4ft. Z6-8. 'Lobbii Nana' is a most attractive, slow-growing form, though eventually of some size. Its soft, juvenile foliage grows unevenly, with clusters or congested growths, light green in summer, touched with bronze in winter, interspersed through the plant. H60-90cm/2-3ft, W90-120cm/3-4ft. Z7-9. 'Nana' has an open growth habit, compared with the better-known 'Vilmoriniana', and narrow, pendulous-tipped branches carrying small, light green leaves. Both congested growths and extended shoots appear on the same plant. H45-60cm/18-24in, W75-90cm/30-36in. Z6-9.

'Sekkan-sugi', at its best, can only be described as superlative. It makes a broad column of upright branches from which hangs looser, pendulous green inner foliage, but those exposed to the light are sulphur-yellow in winter and the most startling creamy white in summer. As the nurseryman in me would say, 'sells on sight'! It needs shelter from strong sun and cold winds in early years. H1.5-1.8m/5-6ft, W90-120cm/3-4ft. Z6-9.

'Spiralis', commonly known as 'Granny's ringlets', has unusual, rope-like branches, its light green leaves adpressed to the stem and often twisted, particularly at the growth tips. It slowly builds a compact, irregular bush, often without a definite leader, but any vigorous shoots that occur can be cut away if they upset the balance of the plant. H45-60cm/18-24in, W60-75cm/24-30in. Z6-9.

'Tansu', originally called 'Yatsubusa', deserves to be more widely known. It makes a small, irregular pyramid of dark green, finely textured foliage, nodding at the tips, and is perfect for bonsai. H30-45cm/12-18in, W23-30cm/9-12in. Z6-9. 'Tenzan' is a collectors' item, making a perfect tiny bun of densely packed foliage in which you could hardly insert a pencil. It needs light shade, though is hardier than one might expect. H10-15cm/4-6in, W10-15cm/4-6in. Z7-9.

'Vilmoriniana' is deservedly one of the most popular dwarf conifers, making a very tight ball of dense, congested foliage, bright green in summer and bronze in winter, particularly in exposed situations. H30-45cm/12-18in, W30-45cm/12-18in. Z6-9. Similar but neater is 'Compressa', an even more startling reddish brown in winter.

Cryptomeria japonica 'Sekkan-sugi'

Cryptomeria japonica 'Spiralis'

× CUPRESSOCYPARIS
Leyland cypress

× *C. leylandii*. The Leyland cypress is the fastest-growing conifer, popular for hedges (for which it is often unsuitable) and screening. The first seedlings arose in England as natural hybrids between *Cupressus macrocarpa* and *Chamaecyparis nootkatensis* in the late nineteenth century but remained unknown until the late 1960s. The hybrids derived fast growth from the former species and grace and hardiness from the latter, and are chalk-tolerant. Crosses made with *Cupressus lusitanica* and *Chamaecyparis nootkatensis* produced × *Cupressocyparis ovensii*; *Cupressus macrocarpa* and *Chamaecyparis lawsoniana* resulted in *Cupressocyparis* 'Stapehill Hybrid'; and *Cupressus glabra* and *Chamaecyparis*

× *Cupressocyparis leylandii* 'Golconda'

nootkatensis produced × *Cupressocyparis notabilis*. Sold as garden plants, most are labelled as × *Cupressocyparis leylandii*, but all are fast-growing and best planted young without staking, to enable them to establish a root system before their rapid growth produces the abundant foliage, prey to wind. Ideal as shelter belts, but as a hedge can soon get out of hand without constant trimming. Average size of green forms of × *C. leylandii* at ten years: H8-10m/26-33ft, W1.8-3m/6-10ft. Z6.

'Castlewellan Gold' has a narrow, conical habit, bright golden-yellow foliage in summer, much less so in winter. It is one of the best golden conifers for hedging. H6-8m/20-26ft, W1.5-2.1m/5-7ft. Z6-10. 'Golconda', from Devon, England, is one of the brightest golden conifers, excellent in winter. Open in habit when young, it fills in nicely with age. H5-6m/16-20ft, W1.5-2.1m/5-7ft. Z6-10. 'Silver Dust' comes from the USA, though there are other selections with variegated foliage in cultivation. 'Silver Dust' is vigorous, with splashes of creamy white on dark green foliage. H5-6m/16-20ft, W2.4-3m/8-10ft. Z7-9.

CUPRESSUS Cypress

The cypresses differ from *Chamaecyparis*, or false cypress, in having much sparser, scale-like foliage, with leaves closely adpressed to the stem; and much larger cones, often very hard and lasting on the tree for years. Since many true cypresses have to endure heat and drought, they developed long taproots to reach available moisture. The faster-growing species, however, can be unstable on some soils and liable to 'blow' or topple over. They are not good transplanters, and many are only hardy in warmer climates, betraying their mostly Mediterranean, tropical or subtropical origins. The yellow-foliaged forms colour best in sun.

C. arizonica. See *C. glabra.*

C. glabra. This was formerly considered a form of *C. arizonica.* Whatever its name, the smooth Arizona cypress originates in the south-west USA, and it, its forms and cultivars are the hardiest *Cupressus*, thriving in hot, dry climates and poor soils, but also in colder regions. **'Compacta'** has slow, congested growth gradually forming a globe of blue-green, rigid foliage, ideal for a well-drained spot on the rock garden. H30-45cm/12-18in, W30-45cm/12-18in. G. Z7-9. A recent discovery in Australia, **'Crowborough'** is an equally attractive blue-grey, a little more vigorous and open in habit. **'Conica'**, **'Glauca'** and **'Pyramidalis'** are all attractive, slow-growing and eventually large conical or pyramidal forms of striking blue-grey foliage, enhanced with large, round 'nuts' or cones. **'Blue Ice'** and **'Silver Smoke'** are two new cultivars worth looking for. Ensure when planting that roots are not 'corkscrewed' around the pots. Often grafted. H3-5m/10-16ft, W1.2-1.5m/4-5ft. Z7-9. **'Sulphurea'**. I originally obtained plants of this from France and a marvellous conifer it has turned out to be. It forms a striking column of densely packed, sulphur-yellow foliage, brighter in summer, and as hardy as blue forms. Often grafted. H2.1-3m/7-10ft, W90-120cm/3-4ft. Z7-9.

C. macrocarpa. The fast-growing Monterey cypress is native to southern California, and will grow successfully close to the coast but not in cold climates. It is usually columnar

Cupressus glabra 'Sulphurea'

when young but broader and flat-topped with age. Old trees have reached 30-40m/100-130ft. Though too big for garden use, several dwarf and coloured-foliage forms have been introduced, some not reliably hardy in temperate climates.

'Goldcrest', perhaps the brightest yellow, fast-growing cultivar, starts as a compact cone of dense, shining yellow, juvenile foliage, broadening with age. Brightest in full sun but can scorch in exposed situations. H4-5m/13-16ft, W1.2-1.5m/4-5ft. Z7-10. The similar **'Donard Gold'** and **'Lutea'** are fast-growing selections, of a deeper golden-yellow colour; 'Lutea' is especially good near the sea. Both H4-5m/13-16ft, W1.2-1.5m/4-5ft. Z7-10. **'Golden Pillar'** seems the hardiest golden Monterey cypress, making a densely branched, narrow column of greeny yellow foliage in winter, bright golden-yellow in summer. Slow-growing. H1.5-1.8m/5-6ft, W60-75cm/24-30in. Z7-10. **'Greenstead Magnificent'**, perhaps tender in some temperate climates, is worth growing in a container which can be brought in for the winter, for its magnificent, brilliant silver-blue foliage. It has a spreading habit and grows vigorously in the Mediterranean climate it prefers. Mostly grafted. H60-90cm/2-3ft, W1.2-1.5m/4-5ft. Z7-10. **'Pygmaea'** is a dwarf form with adult, green, scale-like foliage, forming an irregular mounded bush. Needs shelter or cold greenhouse when young. H15-20cm/6-8in, W15-20cm/6-8in. Z8-10. **'Sulphur Tip'** has distinctive adult foliage, is slow to get started, but once established throws up vigorous shoots of bright sulphur-yellow. Untidy unless pruned annually. H45-60cm/18-24in, W45-60cm/18-24in. Z7-10.

C. sempervirens. The Italian or Mediterranean cypress is a feature of the Mediterranean landscape. The original species is an upright but spreading conifer of variable form, but over the centuries the form **'Stricta'**, or **'Fastigiata'**, with narrow, upright habit, has become the most widely planted, though seldom known in the wild. Clonal selection over many years means that seed from the columnar forms mostly comes true; several have been given cultivar names. Many are relatively hardy, but often suffer from frost and desiccating winds when young. H3-5m/10-16ft, W30-60cm/1-2ft. Z8-10. **'Swane's Golden'** arose as a seedling on the Swane's Nursery in New South Wales in about 1960. It soon became a best-seller in Australia and New Zealand, where it formed a narrow column of upright, golden-yellow foliage, brilliant in summer. It will grow in sheltered, sunny positions on well-drained soil in temperate climates, but suffers from frost and cold winds. It can be grown in a container, and kept in a cool greenhouse or conservatory over winter. H2.1-3m/7-10ft, W30cm/1ft. Z9-10.

Cupressus glabra 'Blue Ice'

Ginkgo biloba

GINKGO Maidenhair tree

G. biloba. Some authorities suggest that the maidenhair tree should not be classed as a conifer, being deciduous and broad-leaved. Originating in China, it is one of the most beautiful, and ancient, of trees, going back over 150 million years. The ginkgo has fan-shaped, pale green leaves and normally makes an upright-branching tree. Its leaves are especially striking in late autumn, when they often briefly turn butter-yellow before falling. A mature tree may reach 30m/100ft and male and female trees look similar. The female, when several years old, fruits readily in warmer climates, but the edible nuts have a fleshy, green, pungent-smelling covering and female trees are best avoided for planting. An excellent and adaptable tree for hot climates, but often disappointing in cooler ones. Several seedlings have been selected and named in countries where the ginkgo grows well, such as Australia, New Zealand and the USA, and are reproduced by grafting or budding. These include columnar and weeping forms. H3-5m/10-16ft, W75-120cm/30-48in. Z4-9.

JUNIPERUS Juniper

The junipers are among the most ornamental and adaptable conifers for garden use. The genus contains over forty species, native to the Northern Hemisphere, and from which have arisen hundreds of cultivars. Many are extremely hardy, surviving low and high temperatures, and thin and impoverished soils, including limy ones.

J. chinensis. The Chinese juniper is not only native to China but is also found in Mongolia and Japan. In the wild it varies considerably in habit from a shrubby to its more typical columnar form, often reaching 60m/195ft in height. The species, seldom listed by nurseries or seen in gardens, is well represented by selected cultivars. Most have both sharp, prickly juvenile leaves and coarser adult ones on the same plant. The world of horticulture does not seem to agree totally on the classification of many junipers which, in the USA in particular, are listed under *J. chinensis*, but which are listed else-where under *J. × media* (see also p.169).

'Aurea'. The golden Chinese juniper, or Young's golden juniper, was discovered as a sport or seedling on Mr Young's nursery in Surrey, England, in 1860. It is lovely but difficult to propagate and grow as a young plant, so destined to remain scarce. Both prickly whitish yellow juvenile foliage and non-prickly golden-yellow adult foliage combine to form eventually a narrow cone of deep golden-yellow, especially bright in winter. Hardy, but protect from cold winds and hot sun in early years. Often grafted. H1.2-1.5m/4-5ft, W60-75cm/24-30in. Z5-9.

'Blue Alps' (syn. *J. squamata* 'Blue Alps'), a recent introduction from Sweden, is vigorous, with an upright branching habit and outward-pointing, slightly nodding branch tips. Its bright steel-blue summer foliage, blue-green in winter, takes well to pruning. H1.5-1.8m/5-6ft, W60-90cm/2-3ft. Z5-8. 'Echiniformis', one of the slowest and dwarfest junipers, makes a prickly, hedgehog-like mound of light green, juvenile, pointed foliage. An ideal bun for rock gardens, troughs and sinks. H10-15cm/4-6in, W10-15cm/4-6in. Z5-9.

'Japonica Variegata' is often mistakenly sold as 'Kaizuka Variegata'. It can be semi-prostrate, almost vase-shaped, with juvenile foliage or, more commonly, an upright, irregular pyramid of mostly adult foliage, in each case splashed creamy white. H1.5-1.8m/5-6ft, W90-120cm/3-4ft. Z5-9. 'Kaizuka' (syn. 'Torulosa') is known as the Hollywood juniper because of its popularity in southern California, but it originated in Japan, where it was used for garden wall planting and bonsai. It makes an upward, spreading bush with several leading stems, forming a plant

Juniperus chinensis 'Aurea'

of great character. Excellent for specimen planting in a lawn or heather garden. To train it as a wall shrub or espalier, start early! H1.2-1.8m/4-6ft, W1.2-1.5m/4-5ft. Z4-9. 'Keteleeri' produces its annual autumn and winter display of bluish grey berries, long-lasting when cut. An upright grey-green columnar form. H2.1-3m/7-10ft, W90cm/3ft. Z5-9.

'Kuriwao Gold', from New Zealand, first makes a compact, spiky bush of golden-yellow foliage, but grows rapidly and becomes less gold with age. It expands in all directions, its upright, outward-reaching stems covered in dense foliage. Takes trimming well and

Juniperus chinensis 'Japonica Variegata'

Juniperus chinensis 'Kuriwao Gold'

might make a nice hedge. H1.5-1.8m/5-6ft, W1.2-1.5m/4-5ft. Z5-9. 'Obelisk' slowly forms a formal column of prickly, blue-green juvenile foliage. As it matures it often develops a distinctive bend to one side. H1.5-2.1m/5-7ft, W60-75cm/24-30in. Z5-9. 'Pyramidalis' is more columnar than pyramidal, with relatively soft, juvenile, blue-green foliage, and is attractive both as a young and older plant. Confusingly, a more recent introduction, 'Stricta', *is* pyramidal, but has more prickly foliage of a pleasant blue-grey. Both have erect branches forming compact bushes, though 'Stricta' with age is prone to go brown in the centre. (If nurserymen have mixed up conifer names over the years it is easy to see why!) Plant both in open positions. H1.5-1.8m/5-6ft, W60-75cm/24-30in. Z5-9. 'Robusta Green' is one of the most distinctive upright junipers, with often several twisted branches bearing juvenile and adult foliage of a bright, apple-green. Older plants bear clusters of light green fruit in autumn and winter. An excellent informal specimen plant, ideal with heathers. H1.5-1.8m/5-6ft, W90-120cm/3-4ft. Z5-9.

J. communis. This grows wild in Europe, Asia and North America, mostly as a shrub or, occasionally, small tree. Its shapes vary from prostrate and spreading to narrowly upright, some quite vigorous and others dwarf, hence so many good garden cultivars! All have juvenile, awl-shaped, generally prickly leaves with obvious silver-grey bands on the undersides. Female plants often produce greenish blue berries, the oil of which is used in medicines and for flavouring gin.

Juniperus communis 'Golden Showers'

Juniperus communis 'Sentinel'

'Berkshire' was discovered in the Arnold Arboretum in Massachusetts, USA. It slowly forms a prickly little bush of spiky dark green and silver needles, bright blue-green in summer. Ideal for miniature gardens and troughs. H15cm/6in, W20-30cm/8-12in. Z3-7. **'Compressa'**, or Noah's Ark juniper, makes a perfect miniature cone, like a diminutive Irish juniper. There are at least two types in cultivation, both with tiny, awl-shaped, green, silver-backed leaves closely pressed to upright branches, but one is narrower than the other. The broader form is sometimes called **'Suecica Nana'** and it may be hardier. Shelter both from cold winds, particularly when young. Perfect for troughs, sinks and association with dwarf alpine plants. H30-45cm/12-18in, W9-15cm/3½-6in. Z3-7. **'Depressa Aurea'** is an unusual semi-prostrate conifer, bronze-green in winter, changing to greeny yellow in spring, and transformed in early summer when golden-yellow new shoots appear. The whole bush becomes butter-yellow, toning down later in summer. Full sun essential. At its best superb; excellent for ground cover. H30-45cm/12-18in, W1.2-1.5m/4-5ft. Z3-7. **'Gold Cone'** was first introduced as 'Suecica Aurea', the golden Swedish juniper, and makes a conical bush of greenish yellow in winter, true gold in summer. Liable to suffer from windfrost or hot sun when small, but hardy once established. H90-120cm/3-4ft, W15-30cm/6-12in. Z4-7.

'Golden Showers' (syn. 'Schneverdinger Goldmachangel') is upright and fairly narrow, though broader than 'Gold Cone', with nodding branch tips which are a rich golden-yellow in summer, bronzed in winter. H1.2-1.5m/4-5ft, W30-45cm/12-18in. Z4-7. **'Green Carpet'**, one of the best dwarf conifers,

slowly makes a tight mat of dark, bronze-green foliage, brighter green in summer. Excellent in a container, or hanging over a rock or a wall. H5-10cm/2-4in, W75-90cm/30-36in. Z3-7. **'Hibernica'** (syn. 'Stricta'), or Irish juniper, forms a narrow, formal column of greyish green foliage. There are broader and less attractive clones, but all when established may need tying in to prevent snow damage. H1.8-2.1m/6-7ft, W20-45cm/8-18in. Z3-7.

'Horstmann' (syn. 'Horstmann's Pendula') needs training upwards when young or it will become a sprawling, ungainly bush. Thus trained, its main branches will trail long, pendulous, greyish green branchlets. Reasonably rapid-growing, perhaps 10-15cm/4-6in each year. **'Oblonga Pendula'** is similar but bushier, with darker green leaves, bronzing in winter. H1.5-1.8m/5-6ft, W90-120cm/3-4ft. Both Z3-7. **'Repanda'** is reliable ground cover but rather vigorous for general garden use. Dark green leaves turn bronze-green in winter. Excellent for sunny banks or in association with other spreading conifers. H30cm/1ft, W1.8-2.1m/6-7ft. Z3-7. **'Sentinel'**, or 'Pencil Point', is intermediate between 'Compressa' and 'Hibernica' and makes an excellent accent plant, as a narrow column of dense, green foliage. Cut away occasional stronger growths. H1.2-1.5m/4-5ft, W15-25cm/6-10in. Z3-7. **'Suecica'** is the Swedish equivalent of Irish juniper; several upright fastigiate selections may exist under this name. H1.8-2.1m/6-7ft, W30-45cm/12-18in. Z3-7. *J. conferta*. The shore juniper is a creeping native of the sandy coastal areas of Japan. It has bright, apple-green, prickly foliage, tolerant of salt but not of heavy wet soils. H15-30cm/6-12in, W1.8-2.1m/6-7ft. Z6-8.

'Blue Pacific' has only a hint of blue in its foliage, but makes a low-growing carpet, with striking, bright summer foliage. H15cm/6in, W1.5-1.8m/5-6ft. Z6-8. *J. davurica* **'Expansa'** (syn. *J. squamata* 'Parsonsii') is useful, very hardy ground cover, with coarse adult foliage mixed with finer juvenile foliage held just clear of the ground. None of these types should be planted too deeply. H30-45cm/12-18in, W1.5-1.8m/5-6ft. Z5-9. **'Expansa Aureospicata'** makes similar but less vigorous growth, with spreading branches carrying sea-green adult and juvenile foliage, irregularly splashed with butter-yellow. H15-30cm/6-12in, W90-120cm/3-4ft. Z5-9. **'Expansa Variegata'** has a growth rate similar to 'Expansa' but the white variegation tends to be damaged by winter frost. Striking at its best but can be disappointing. H30-45cm/12-18in, W1.5-1.8m/5-6ft. Z6-9. *J. horizontalis*. The creeping juniper is native to North American seashores, hillsides, rocky areas and even swamps! Many selections have been made, some too much like others. They are popular and effective ground cover, on banks and over rocks, making carpets of colour, and are used widely in North America in landscape and roadside plantings. They tolerate hot, dry sites and poor soils, but some are unfortunately prone to juniper blight, a fungus which attacks some prostrate junipers and for which there is little long-term control.

'Banff', one of the most striking carpet junipers, was introduced from Canada. It is prostrate, with upward-arching branches carrying juvenile feathery foliage, bluish purple in winter and a brilliant silver-blue in summer. H20-30cm/8-12in, W75-90cm/30-36in. Z4-9. **'Bar Harbor'** may cover several clones, but the original was selected from a plant growing by the sea in Maine, USA. It is vigorous, making a large, prostrate, deep blue-green mat with long, whipcord-like branches spreading outwards from the centre. It turns a distinctive mauve-purple in winter, particularly on exposed sites. Prune for density. H15-20cm/6-8in, W1.5-1.8m/5-6ft. Z4-9. **'Blue Chip'** (syn. 'Blue Moon') is an outstanding selection of *J. horizontalis*. Prostrate and spreading, with slightly raised, feathery foliage, it makes a dense carpet of blue-green winter foliage, brightest steel-blue in summer. H30cm/1ft, W1.2-1.5m/4-5ft. Z4-9. **'Emerald Spreader'**, a vigorous Californian selection, has long, snake-like branches hugging the ground, and emerald-green summer foliage, dull in winter. Prune leading shoots to improve density, though the long shoots add character. H10-15cm/4-6in, W1.5-1.8m/5-6ft. Z4-9.

'Grey Pearl' is perhaps related to the upright-growing **'Alpina'**. It is very slow with erect branches of soft, feathery foliage crowding the stems. The needles are bluish green, tinged purple in winter and bright steel-blue in summer. H20-30cm/8-12in, W45-60cm/18-24in. Z4-9. **'Hughes'**, a rapid grower, starts life almost prostrate but soon grows into a taller but horizontally spreading, light-textured bush with bright silver-grey foliage, duller in winter. Excellent ground cover on banks, or with other shrubs and conifers. H45-60cm/18-24in, W1.5-1.8m/5-6ft. Z4-9. **'Mother Lode'** was discovered by the late plantsman Jean Iseli in Oregon, USA. A large, wild *J. horizontalis* had apparently been struck by lightning, resulting in a sport, or mutation, which developed a golden-yellow shoot. This was propagated by Iseli Nurseries and is now being distributed. It has a compact, low-growing habit, and bright golden-yellow summer foliage, yellowish-tinged and bronze-purple in winter. A similar selection has been discovered in Germany. Estimated H10-15cm/4-6in, W60-90cm/2-3ft. Z5-9. **'Plumosa'**, or Andorra juniper, comes not from the Pyrenees, but was less romantically found in Maine, USA, and selected by Andorra Nurseries in Philadelphia in 1907. It and similar 'Plumosa' types are good ground cover, semi-prostrate, with abundant foliage rising at an angle of forty-five degrees. The blue-grey leaves are soft ('plumose' means feathery) and turn a distinct bronze-purple in winter, particularly in cold climates. H45-60cm/18-24in, W1.2-1.5m/4-5ft. Z4-9. More garden-worthy is **'Plumosa Compacta'**, slower-growing, shorter and denser. Similar to 'Youngstown' in growth rates. Z4-9.

'Prince of Wales', like 'Banff', comes from Banff National Park in the Canadian Rocky Mountains, so hardiness is guaranteed. Good for the small garden, very flat-growing with fine-textured, feathery foliage, bright green in summer, suffused purplish brown in winter. H10-15cm/4-6in, W90-120cm/3-4ft. Z4-9. **'Turquoise Spreader'** slowly makes a dense mat of turquoise-green, feathery foliage. An excellent ground cover, keeping its colour in winter better than most. H10-15cm/4-6in, W90-120cm/3-4ft. Z4-9. **'Wiltonii'**, or the blue rug juniper, was named after the nursery in Wilton, Connecticut, USA, which introduced it. It is the same as most plants sold in Europe as 'Glauca', a name that should now be discontinued. Impressive-looking 'lawns' can be made out of hundreds of plants of 'Wiltonii', though how much wear they would take is uncertain. Unless young plants have been pruned first by the nurseryman, they normally have a rather open habit, with long fingers of whipcord branches radiating from the centre. The plant gradually fills in to make a low, mounded carpet, blue-green, sometimes tinged purple in winter, bright steel-blue in summer. Very adaptable and popular. H10-15cm/4-6in, W1.5-1.8m/5-6ft. Z4-9. **'Youngstown'** is

Juniperus horizontalis 'Turquoise Spreader'

the most attractive of the 'Plumosa' types. It makes a dense, low-spreading bush, bright blue-green in summer, purple-bronze in winter. Good in association with variegated or golden-foliaged plants. H30-45cm/12-18in, W75-90cm/30-36in. Z4-9. *J.* × *media*. Most authorities on conifers in recent years include and describe hybrids between *Juniperus chinensis* and *Juniperus sabina* under *J.* × *media*, but most American books and catalogues still list many of the following forms and cultivars under *J. chinensis*. For them to accept the majority rule would initially cause problems among nurserymen and gardeners, but would eventually be a great benefit to all. Whatever their name, they include first-class, mostly semi-prostrate cultivars of great ornamental value. Most exhibit to a smaller or larger degree the pungent scent of *Juniperus sabina*, or savin juniper. Many are too vigorous for the average garden, but all can be pruned if necessary. Remember, though, that pruning to prevent a vigorous juniper spreading too wide will inevitably encourage it to grow taller.

'Blaauw', an attractive Japanese cultivar, has an upright, vase-shaped habit, and stiffly held branches clothed in deep blue-green, rough adult foliage. Sometimes grafted. H1.5-1.8m/5-6ft, W90-120cm/3-4ft. Z4-9. **'Blue and Gold'**, a new, semi-prostrate selection, is very striking at its best, with upright-spreading branches of blue-grey, scale-like foliage, irregularly and liberally scattered with creamy yellow. These can burn in hot sun or winter frost, spoiling the overall appearance. H1.2-1.5m/4-5ft, W1.5-1.8m/5-6ft. Z4-9. **'Gold Coast'**. Several golden-yellow, semi-prostrate cultivars have been introduced recently, some considerable

Juniperus horizontalis 'Prince of Wales'

Juniperus horizontalis 'Youngstown'

Juniperus × *media* 'Blue and Gold'

Juniperus scopulorum 'Blue Heaven'

improvements over the original 'Pfitzeriana Aurea', but 'Gold Coast', a selection from Monrovia Nurseries in the USA, is one of the best. It has a low-growing and wide-spreading habit with bright, mostly adult, golden-yellow foliage, less brilliant in winter. It takes pruning well. H60-90cm/2-3ft, W1.5-1.8m/5-6ft. Z4-9. **'Gold Sovereign'** is a selection made at Bressingham from a sport of 'Old Gold' and growing to only half its size. It is a very compact cultivar, ideally suited to the smaller garden, with brilliant golden-yellow juvenile and adult foliage in summer, and in a sunny situation remaining bright in winter. Can be kept quite dwarf with annual pruning. H45-60cm/18-24in, W75-90cm/30-36in. Z5-9. **'Gold Star'**, an introduction from Ontario, Canada, is low, spreading and, unusually for such a vigorous plant, has practically all juvenile, prickly foliage. Its almost layered branching system carries dense, bright yellow foliage in summer, gold and green in winter, the past season's stems conspicuously yellow-brown. H60-90cm/2-3ft, W1.8-2.1m/6-7ft. Z4-9.

'Hetzii' and the similar **'Pfitzeriana Glauca'** are too vigorous for the average garden, though attractive, tough, hardy and ideal for a long-term screen. 'Hetzii', which

may reach 6m/20ft, has upright, spreading branches, well covered with blue-grey juvenile and adult foliage, brighter in summer than winter. It can be pruned as a hedge, to cover a wall, or even, as I once saw in California, as a topiary steam engine! H1.8-2.1m/6-7ft, W1.8-2.1m/6-7ft. Z4-9. **'Mint Julep'**, a vigorous, spreading bush with arching branches clothed with rich green foliage, makes an ideal foil to other colours. Deservedly popular, but it needs pruning to keep it small. Maintains a good winter colour. H90-120cm/3-4ft, W1.5-1.8m/5-6ft. Z4-9. **'Old Gold'**, the first to supersede 'Pfitzeriana Aurea' as a brighter, slower-growing juniper, has now been superseded by 'Gold Coast', though it is still widely grown. Compact, semi-prostrate, bright golden-yellow foliage in summer, less so in winter. H90-120cm/3-4ft, W1.2-1.5m/4-5ft. Z4-9. **'Pfitzeriana'** and **'Pfitzeriana Aurea'** were first introduced many years ago but there are now better and more attractive conifers for the garden. 'Pfitzeriana', sometimes sold as a dwarf, may end up 10m/33ft across and 5m/16ft high in time. Both low-spreading and tall forms are in existence, but all have mid-green, semi-juvenile foliage, with arching

branches, slightly pendulous at the tips. Excellent for ground cover where space allows. H90-120cm/3-4ft, W1.8-2.1m/6-7ft. Z4-9. 'Pfitzeriana Aurea' is a vigorous, wide-spreading form, with semi-juvenile, prickly foliage, mostly green in winter with greenish yellow shoots becoming bright yellow in summer, toning down again in autumn. H60-90cm/2-3ft, W1.8-2.1m/6-7ft. Z4-9.

'Plumosa Aurea' belongs to the distinct 'Plumosa' group of junipers, to which 'Blaauw' also belongs. This group has mostly adult, scale-like foliage and spreading, semi-prostrate habits. 'Plumosa Aurea' has low, arching branches clothed in golden-yellow foliage, turning an attractive deep golden-bronze in winter. Often grafted. H60-90cm/2-3ft, W1.2-1.5m/4-5ft. Z5-9. **'Plumosa Aureovariegata'** is frustratingly slow-growing in early years, but worth the wait for its striking deep green and golden-yellow variegated foliage. H30cm/1ft, W60-90cm/2-3ft. Z5-9. **'Sulphur Spray'** was discovered in the 1960s as a sport on 'Hetzii' and propagated and introduced by the Konijn Nursery in Holland. It makes a vigorous, semi-prostrate bush of striking, sulphur-yellow adult foliage, particularly in summer. It is generally brighter as a young plant than when mature and needs sun to produce the best colour. Regular pruning will keep it within bounds. H90-120cm/3-4ft, W1.2-1.5m/4-5ft. Z4-9.

J. procumbens **'Nana'**. This makes an excellent ground-hugging carpet of prickly, apple-green foliage, closely following

Juniperus × media 'Gold Sovereign'

Juniperus × media 'Sulphur Spray'

contours of slopes and ideal to hang over a wall or rock. It can also be trained upwards or top-grafted on a stem, with branches sweeping down and tips typically turning up. There is confusion between this and 'Bonin Isles', which is considered more vigorous and also has green needles, but both are desirable. H15-23cm/6-9in, W1.2-1.5m/4-5ft. Z5-9.

J. recurva 'Coxii'. This is a form of coffin juniper, so called because the wood in its native Burma and China is used for making coffins. It is slow to form an elegant tree, with graceful pendulous branches bearing deep green leaves. Attractive red bark is a feature. H1.8-3m/6-10ft, W90-120cm/3-4ft. Z7-10. 'Densa' is a rare, low-spreading cultivar with semi-prostrate shoots of bright green feathery foliage, attractive the year round. H30-45cm/12-18in, W90-120cm/3-4ft. Z7-10. 'Embley Park' (syn. 'Viridis'), though not always easy to establish, has showy, mint-green, soft, feathery foliage throughout the year. Tolerates shade. H45-60cm/18-24in, W60-90cm/2-3ft. Z7-10.

J. sabina. The savin juniper grows wild, mostly as spreading shrubs, in the mountains of Southern and Eastern Europe and Siberia. Though all selected forms are hardy, shade-tolerant and adaptable ground cover, some are more valuable as space fillers than for their beauty. Most forms have extremely pungent foliage when bruised. Z4-7. 'Arcadia' is a vigorous, low-spreading cultivar, selected from seed imported from Russia over fifty years ago. It has long, overlapping branches, with lacy, fern-like foliage, bright green in summer, duller in winter. H30-45cm/12-18in, W1.2-1.5m/4-5ft. Z4-7. 'Buffalo', another form raised from seed collected in Russia, is possibly more attractive than 'Arcadia'. It has a lower, more prostrate habit, with bright green, semi-juvenile foliage and long, whipcord-like branches whose tips curve upwards as they creep along the ground. H20-30cm/8-12in, W1.2-1.5m/4-5ft. Z4-7. 'Tamariscifolia' is still one of the most popular junipers for ground cover, with spreading branches gradually building up to overlap each other in a picturesque way, particularly if grown on a bank or slope. Sometimes prone to juniper blight (see p.168). H30-45cm/12-18in, W1.2-1.5m/4-5ft. Z4-7.

J. scopulorum. The Rocky Mountain juniper grows wild from Canada to Texas, USA, usually at heights over 1500m/5000ft, and is well adapted to cold and hot, arid conditions. Several selections have been collected and provide excellent cultivars for the garden. They generally do well in drier climates with warm summers, but most are tolerant of cooler conditions.

'Blue Heaven', sometimes wrongly called 'Blue Haven', is a reliable, vigorous, upright, pyramidal form, with coarse, bright

Juniperus scopulorum 'Skyrocket'

Juniperus scopulorum 'Wichita Blue'

silver-blue summer foliage, blue-green in winter. Mostly grafted. H2.1-2.7m/7-9ft, W60-75cm/24-30in. Z4-7. 'Blue Pyramidal' is similar but less effective. 'Gray Gleam' is a stunning accent plant, making a dense column of silver-blue. Like most of the *J. scopulorum* cultivars, it has tiny, scale-like leaves. Best in an open position in full sun. Often grafted. H1.5-1.8m/5-6ft, W30cm/1ft. Z4-7. 'Skyrocket', sometimes listed under *J. virginiana*, has long been the most popular cultivar. It is a superb accent plant and very effective planted in groups of three or more, forming narrow pillars of dense, blue-green foliage, brighter in summer than winter. Vigorous. H1.8-2.4m/6-8ft, W30cm/1ft. Z4-7. 'Sparkling Skyrocket' describes a creamy white sport discovered on a 'Skyrocket' on a nursery in New Jersey, USA. It forms a pencil-shaped tree with blue-green foliage, dotted and splashed with cream. Other variegated selections of 'Skyrocket' have also been introduced. H1.8-2.1m/6-7ft, W15-30cm/6-12in. Z4-7. 'Table Top' is semi-prostrate, with brilliant, silver-blue summer foliage. The branches, however, grow upwards as well as outwards, not flat. An excellent plant nevertheless. Often grafted. H1.2-1.5m/4-5ft, W1.8-2.1m/6-7ft. Z4-7. 'Tollesons

Weeping' is an unusual, pendulous form, with irregular, conical-to-pyramidal habit and thin, drooping branchlets of silver-blue, scale-like leaves. Grafted and probably needs training and careful pruning in early years. H1.8-2.1m/6-7ft, W1.2-1.5m/4-5ft. Z4-9. 'Wichita Blue' is a distinctive cultivar of fairly narrow, pyramidal habit, with vivid, silver-grey foliage in summer, retained well in winter. Often grafted. H1.8-2.4m/6-8ft, W45-60cm/18-24in. Z4-7.

J. squamata. This native of mountains from Afghanistan to Eastern China is variable in the wild, but mostly shrubby. There are two main types of foliage: short branchlets and soft leaves, and long branchlets with larger, often prickly leaves.

'Blue Alps'. See *J. chinensis* 'Blue Alps'. 'Blue Carpet', a low-spreading, vigorous form, is not truly prostrate. Its long branches rise at a low angle from the centre, clothed with vivid, almost ice-blue summer foliage, steel-blue and often purple-tinged in winter. Dislikes wet conditions. One of the best for ground cover. Prune as necessary. H30-45cm/12-18in, W1.5-1.8m/5-6ft. Z5-8. 'Blue Star', found as a sport on 'Meyeri' on a nursery in Holland around 1950, has since become one of the most popular garden

Juniperus squamata 'Blue Swede'

Juniperus squamata 'Holger'

Larix kaempferi 'Nana'

conifers in the world. It quickly makes a compact bush, deep blue in winter, changing to a brilliant, silvery blue in summer. H30-45cm/12-18in, W45-60cm/18-24in. Z5-8. **'Blue Swede'** is a selection made in Sweden just after the Second World War. Eventually quite big, it is broadly vase-shaped with densely held foliage, metallic blue-grey in winter, rich blue in summer. H90-120cm/3-4ft, W1.2-1.5m/4-5ft. Z5-8.

'Holger', similar in habit to 'Blue Carpet' but denser, more prostrate and different in colour, has light bluish green winter foliage, with bright creamy yellow shoots in late spring, giving the whole plant a whitewashed appearance. Gradually tones down towards winter. H30cm/1ft, W1.2-1.5m/4-5ft. Z5-8. **'Loderi'**, a rare but worthwhile, slow-growing conifer, arose from seed collected in China over fifty years ago. It forms a narrow column of soft, dense, grey-green foliage, nodding at the tips. H1.2-1.5m/4-5ft, W30-45cm/12-18in. Z5-8. **'Meyeri'**, at its best marvellous, can sometimes be disappointing. Strong, erect, outward-arching branches are clothed in dense, rich, silver-blue summer foliage, purplish blue in winter. Older plants tend to turn unsightly brown in the centre. Best grown in an open position and given regular light pruning. H1.5-1.8m/5-6ft, W90-120cm/3-4ft. Z5-8. **'Parsonsii'**. See *J. davurica* 'Expansa'. **'Pygmaea'** makes a slow-spreading bush of short, semi-erect branches with feathery, grey-green foliage, gently nodding at the tips. H30-45cm/12-18in, W45-60cm/18-24in. Z5-8.

J. virginiana. This is native to eastern North America from Canada to Florida. Known as the eastern red cedar, or pencil cedar, because of its narrow form, it varies considerably in the wild. Most cultivars have thin, scale-like leaves, are generally very hardy and adaptable to a wide range of soil and climatic conditions. **'Burkii'** is a broad, columnar form with dense, blue-green summer foliage, blue or purple in winter. H1.8-2.1m/6-7ft, W60-90cm/2-3ft. Z3-9. **'Grey Owl'** is one of the best junipers for ground cover where little else will grow. Its thin, wide-spreading branches carry smoky grey, scale-like leaves, blue-grey in winter.

Its vigour and adaptability to sun, shade, flat ground, banks and heavy or light soils are remarkable! Lacy, overlapping foliage can be kept in check with regular trimming. H60-90cm/2-3ft, W1.8-2.4m/6-8ft. Z3-9. Similar but slower-growing is **'Blue Cloud'**, with curled and twisted branch tips. **'Helle'** slowly forms a broad column of rich green foliage, maintained well in winter. Distinct but considered by some authorities to be the same as *J. chinensis* 'Spartan'. H1.5-1.8m/5-6ft, W45-60cm/18-24in. Z3-9. **'Silver Spreader'** was introduced from California some years ago. There it creates a vigorous, low-growing carpet of bright silver-blue, but is less impressive in cooler, wetter climates. H30-45cm/12-18in, W1.2-1.5m/4-5ft. Z4-9.

LARIX

L. decidua. The European larch is native to the Alps but has been widely planted for forestry across Europe and elsewhere, where it makes a large tree up to 30m/100ft. One of the few deciduous conifers, along with *Ginkgo*, *Metasequoia* and *Taxodium*, in spring it bursts into clusters of bright green leaves, which darken through the summer before turning golden in late autumn. A beautiful tree, but rather large for average gardens, and not good on chalk soils. H8-10m/26-33ft, W3-5m/10-16ft. Z3-6. **'Corley'** was found as a witches' broom by conifer enthusiast Mr Ronald Corley many years ago. It makes a leaderless, prostrate, mounded bush of bright green leaves with good autumn colour and attractive tracery of winter branches. Like all larch cultivars, it must be propagated by grafting. H30-45cm/12-18in, W60-90cm/2-3ft. Z3-6. **'Pendula'** is a beautiful, if variable, tree with weeping branches. There are forms with extremely pendulous branches, some wider-spreading, and occasionally a specimen grows upwards and makes a tree. Often sold as a standard with shoots of 'Pendula' top-grafted onto the stem of a seedling of the species. Height is difficult to estimate, but growth can be vigorous, 30-45cm/12-18in a year. Pruning may be necessary. G. Z3-6.

L. kaempferi. The Japanese larch is as valuable a timber tree as its European cousin and equally vigorous, though more densely branched, growing to 30m/100ft or more. It has broader, almost sea-green leaves and reddish winter twigs. Several forms have been selected from witches' brooms. H6-8m/20-26ft, W3-4m/10-13ft. Z5-7. **'Blue Dwarf'** forms a semi-prostrate bush with striking, silver-blue leaves in first growth, blue-green in late summer. Likely to be popular, too, top-grafted onto a stem to form a standard. H60-75cm/24-30in, W60-90cm/2-3ft. G. Z5-7. **'Diana'**, a new and unusual cultivar, has peculiarly twisted and curly branches and long, light green leaves similarly curled. Estimated H90-

Larix kaempferi 'Diana' (standard)

Microbiota decussata

120cm/3-4ft, W90-120cm/3-4ft. G. Z5-7.
'Nana' is rare and several selections of this name might exist, but in its best form it is truly dwarf, with shortened and congested branches and bright fresh-green leaves. It does not appear to be long-lived. An even more compact selection, **'Varley'**, was named after the man who found it as a witches' broom. 'Nana': H30-45cm/12-18in, W45-60cm/18-24in. G. Z5-7. **'Pendula'**, the pendulous Japanese larch, shares many similarities with the European, *L. decidua* 'Pendula'. *L. kaempferi* 'Pendula' has the typical blue cast to its leaves and may be a more desirable form, but older specimens are variable in habit, with a growth rate of 15-30cm/6-12in a year. G. Z5-7.

LIBOCEDRUS
L. decurrens. See *Calocedrus decurrens*.

METASEQUOIA Dawn redwood
M. glyptostroboides. The ancient dawn redwood was first discovered only as recently as 1941 in the Chinese province of Szechwan, having been seen only in fossil form until then and thought to be extinct. Since its introduction to world botanic gardens in 1948, it has become widely distributed. It is a rapid-growing deciduous conifer which prefers moist, free-draining soils but tolerates a wide range of soils and climates. Conical in habit, it has delicate-looking, fresh-green feathery foliage clothing erect branching stems. In late autumn the dying leaves turn pink, russet or gold. H5-8m/16-26ft, W1.2-1.5m/4-5ft. Z5-10.

MICROBIOTA
M. decussata. The sole species of this genus was discovered in the early twentieth

Picea abies 'Acrocona'

century in Siberia, so its hardiness is assured! An excellent, adaptable ground cover, its lacy sprays of foliage gently overlap to form an attractive carpet. Bright green summer foliage changes to a deep rust-purple in winter, a good contrast to golden and variegated evergreens and excellent with heaths and heathers. It is adaptable to sun or shade. H15-30cm/6-12in, W1.2-1.5m/4-5ft. Z2-8.

PICEA Spruce
This large genus spreads across the Northern Hemisphere in mostly temperate forests, some containing among the tallest trees in the world. There are attractive ornamental species, but mainly the dwarf forms, usually arising from selected seedlings or witches' brooms, are grown in the smaller, modern-day garden. *Picea* and *Abies* can look confusingly alike, but firs hold their cones upright above the foliage and the cones tend to fall apart, dropping their seed, while spruces have pendant cones, which generally fall intact. Though fairly adaptable to a wide range of conditions, they are less happy on very dry or thin chalky soils.
P. abies. The Norway spruce, widely grown as a forest tree and popular as the traditional British Christmas tree, is not the best for gardens. Specimens can reach over 45m/150ft but left-over Christmas trees seldom thrive. H5-8m/16-26ft, W2.1-3m/7-10ft. Z3-8.

'Acrocona' is slow-growing, though eventually of some size, with upright, arching branches and dark green foliage, and mostly notable for a spectacular show of red male flowers, usually followed by attractive buff cones. H1.5-1.8m/5-6ft, W1.5-1.8m/5-6ft. G. Z3-7. **'Aurea Magnifica'** is an improvement on the more common **'Aurea'**. The latter is more vigorous, forming a pyramid of mid-green foliage, yellower on leaves exposed to sun, but except in areas of high light intensity, only golden-yellow for a short time in summer, while 'Aurea Magnifica' is brighter all year, light yellow in summer and much brighter in winter and spring. Both need sun to colour well. 'Aurea Magnifica': H2.1-3m/7-10ft, W1.5-2.4m/5-8ft. G. Z3-7. **'Clanbrassiliana'**, introduced in 1836, is one of the oldest dwarf conifer

173

cultivars, and is still distinct today. Very slow-growing, its congested branches grow in layers to form a compact bush, with short, dark green needles and striking brown buds. H30cm/1ft, W30-45cm/12-18in. Z3-8. **'Columnaris'**, eventually tall-growing, makes a narrow column of dark green, with bright, fresh-green new summer growth. Tie in where winter snowfall occurs. **'Cupressina'** is similar, but broader at the base. H1.8-2.4m/6-8ft, W15-30cm/6-12in. G. Z3-8. **'Frohburg'** is one of three selections made by Haller Nurseries in Switzerland, the others, **'Aarburg'** and **'Wartburg'**, equally distinctive. All make upright leading shoots

Picea abies 'Reflexa'

Picea bicolor

if trained, otherwise sweeping, pendulous branches form a carpet at the base. 'Frohburg' has the shortest, finest needles and is slowest, with a dense skirt at the base, often taking vigour from the leading stem. H1.5-1.8m/5-6ft, W1.5-1.8m/5-6ft. G. Z3-7.

   'Gregoryana' slowly develops its radially arranged branches into a round cushion of congested, light green, minute leaves. Not as prickly as the aptly named and similar **'Echiniformis'**, the hedgehog spruce. H15-20cm/6-8in, W20-30cm/8-12in. Z3-7. **'Inversa'** is totally prostrate, but training the main stem to 2.1-3m/7-10ft eventually produces a weeping form of long, dark green shoots cascading down. Darker green and broader leaves than 'Frohburg'. **'Reflexa'** is almost identical. Approximate annual growth rate 10-15cm/4-6in. G. Z3-7. **'Little Gem'**, one of the best dwarf conifers, was discovered as a witches' broom on another slow-growing spruce, 'Nidiformis', in Boskoop, Holland. Popular because it is easily propagated and has a neat, compact shape, the branches densely packed with small, light green leaves, bright fresh-green in summer. Vulnerable to red spider mites. H20-30cm/8-12in, W30-45cm/12-18in. Z3-7. **'Nidiformis'** is known as the bird's nest spruce because of the flat, indented centre that often develops. The branches radiate from the centre to build up tight horizontal layers of mid-green foliage, growing quite large in time. H30-45cm/12-18in, W60-90cm/2-3ft. Z3-7.

   'Procumbens' is one of several, similar prostrate forms. It is flat-topped and wide-spreading, mounding in layers with age, and with each shoot slightly raised at the tip. Annual shoot growth is 10-15cm/4-6in, with light, mid-green summer leaves, darkening in autumn. Effective on a slope, at the entrance to a driveway, or in the larger heather garden. **'Prostrata'** and **'Repens'** are similar. H30-45cm/12-18in, W1.2-1.5m/4-5ft. Z3-8. **'Pygmaea'**, the oldest dwarf cultivar, must have started life as a witches' broom. Its irregular, congested growths very, very slowly form a broadly pyramidal mid-green bush, sometimes making a strong leader but then slowing to let the rest catch up. Prominent orange-brown buds attractive in winter. H20-30cm/8-12in, W15-20cm/6-8in. Z3-7. **'Will's Dwarf'** (syn. 'Will's Zwerg') was first discovered in the Holstein area of Germany in 1936, but only introduced commercially in 1956. It makes a pyramid of short, rigid branches, clothed in rich green foliage, rather open at the top. Will probably get quite large in time. H1.2-1.5m/4-5ft, W60-90cm/2-3ft. Z3-7.
P. alcockiana. See *P. bicolor*.
P. bicolor (syn. *P. alcockiana*). A narrow pyramid with rigid, upward, open-spreading branches with dark green needles and distinct silvery undersides, this is an

admirable species for the larger garden. Cylindrical cones are crimson-purple, turning to brown as they ripen. Older plants often bear crimson flowers, fading to tan and scattering their pollen. H3-5m/10-16ft, W1.2-1.5m/4-5ft. Z4-8. The bushy, semi-prostrate form **'Howell's Dwarf'** may not stay dwarf for long, and any leading shoot should be pruned away. H90-120cm/3-4ft, W1.5-1.8m/5-6ft. Z4-7.
P. breweriana. Brewer's weeping spruce, native to the mountains of California and Oregon, USA, is beautiful if frustrating because it is so slow in forming its eventual shape. Seedlings can be slowest and variable. A good, grafted clone should be better and more vigorous. Plants reach 30m/100ft or more in the wild but seldom in 'captivity', since summer warmth and high rainfall are necessary. Once 3m/10ft or more high, it displays its graceful, weeping branchlets on wide-spreading branches and dark, almost sombre, green foliage. May need training as a young plant. H1.2-1.8m/4-6ft, W90-150cm/3-5ft. Z6-8.
P. engelmannii **'Glauca'**. This best selection from the Engelmann spruce is a superb specimen for the larger garden, vigorous, with a broad pyramidal habit and upward-angled side branches. The luxuriant, grey-green leaves, bright blue-grey in summer, densely cover the branches. Attractive brown winter buds and, on older plants, reddish green pendulous cones which turn light brown. Best on moist, heavy soils and unsuitable for dry, chalky ones. The slower-growing **'Compacta'** is worth seeking for the smaller garden. H2.7-3m/9-10ft, W1.5-1.8m/5-6ft. G. Z3-7.
P. glauca. The white spruce grows wild across Canada and north-east USA, and is grown extensively for forestry. Fairly slow-growing, it makes a narrow pyramid of blue-green foliage and has produced excellent, hardy garden forms.

   'Alberta Globe' is one of innumerable dwarf and compact forms arising as bud sports or witches' brooms on the dwarf Alberta spruce. This excellent dwarf slowly makes a dome of densely packed mid-green foliage, bright green in early summer. A better alternative to its parent for the small garden. H30-45cm/12-18in, W30-45cm/12-18in. Z3-7. **'Albertiana Conica'**, the dwarf Alberta spruce, was a seedling found in the early 1900s growing in the Canadian Rockies. It is now one of the most popular slow-growing conifers. It quickly forms a perfect, mid-green cone, its new growth fresh-green and smothering the plant in late spring. Unfortunately prone to red spider mites and aphids, it needs constant vigilance and adherence to a spraying routine with systemic insecticide. H90-120cm/3-4ft, W60cm/2ft. Z3-7. **'Coerulea'**, selected over 100 years ago, is slower-

Picea glauca 'Laurin'

Picea mariana 'Ericoides'

W60-90cm/2-3ft. Z3-6. **'Nana'** makes a delightful bun of congested, minute blue-green leaves, with shoots radially arranged around the branches. Cut off occasional stronger growths. Plants at Bressingham over thirty years old are still less than 30cm/1ft high and 60cm/2ft across. H10-15cm/4-6in, W15-20cm/6-8in. Z3-6.

P. omorika. The Serbian spruce is one of the most beautiful and adaptable conifers in cultivation. In its native Yugoslavia it makes a magnificent spire-like tree approaching 30m/100ft, though most plants in cultivation are conical or narrowly pyramidal. Its dark green foliage can look sombre en masse, but it is excellent in mixed planting. The leaves, silver underneath, densely cover the pendulous branches which turn up at the tips. Deep purple cones hang in clusters on older trees. H3-4m/10-13ft, W1.2-1.5m/4-5ft. Z5-8. **'Nana'** is small for the first ten years or so but eventually forms a broad pyramid 3-5m/10-16ft or more high. Slow to develop leading shoots, it is initially dome-shaped with dark green upper leaves, bright silver-blue beneath. H90-120cm/3-4ft, W60-75cm/24-30in. Z5-8. **'Pendula'** covers several forms, some broad and pendulous but not very distinct from the species. The best types are extremely narrow, making a slender spire with weeping branches. Beautiful as a specimen but seldom attractive when growing in early years and more compact than the species, making a narrow pyramid with upward-angled branches of short, soft, blue-grey needles. Small green cones appear on quite young trees on the branch tips, maturing to light brown. Eventually quite tall. H1.5-1.8m/5-6ft, W90cm/3ft. G. Z3-7. **'Echiniformis'** is rare, the one generally sold as such being a looser-growing form of *P. mariana* 'Nana'. The real 'Echiniformis' is a slow-growing, cushion-shaped plant with closely set branches and forward-pointing, thick, greyish green leaves covering shoot and terminal bud. The foliage is soft, not at all reminiscent of a hedgehog! H20-30cm/8-12in, W20-30cm/8-12in. Z3-7. **'Laurin'**, a miniature German bud mutation of 'Albertiana Conica', is almost a replica of its parent but grows much more slowly. Its minute, bright green leaves gradually form a tiny pyramid, ideal for a sink, trough or miniature rock garden. H20-30cm/8-12in, W10-15cm/4-6in. Z3-7.

P. mariana **'Ericoides'** is flat-topped and spreading, like *P. abies* 'Nidiformis'. Short, soft needles are blue-grey in winter, bluer in summer. H30-45cm/12-18in,

Picea omorika 'Nana'

Picea orientalis 'Skylands'

Picea pungens 'Hoto'

young, and the leading shoot often needs training up a cane until self-supporting. H1.8-2.4m/6-8ft, W90-120cm/3-4ft. Z5-8.

P. orientalis. The Oriental spruce is also named the Caucasian spruce, since it comes from the Caucasian mountains and Asia Minor. A tall, vigorous tree eventually becoming a narrow, dark green pyramid, its leaves and those of its cultivars are much shorter than most spruces. Probably too vigorous and uninteresting for most gardens. H4-5m/13-16ft, W1.8-2.1m/6-7ft. Z5-7.
'**Aurea**' (syn. 'Aureospicata') is initially fairly slow but grows strongly once established to form a broad, dark green pyramid with branches sweeping upwards. In late spring or early summer it is transformed by the bright yellow new shoots. These make a startling contrast to the deep green foliage for a few weeks before the yellow slowly fades so that by late summer all is sombre again. H2.4-3m/8-10ft, W1.5-2.1m/5-7ft. Z5-7. '**Skylands**' is beautiful when well grown but prone to sunscorch when young and slow to make a leading shoot, hence its other name, 'Aurea Compacta'; unless trained when young it is almost semi-prostrate. When established it grows strongly, as much as 30cm/1ft a year, into a narrow conical tree with a rather open branching system. The leaves are bright golden-yellow on the upper surface, but green underneath. Provide light shade for part of the day, and occasionally prune the more vigorous side shoots. H1.2-1.8m/4-6ft, W90-120cm/3-4ft. G. Z5-7.

P. pungens. The Colorado spruce provides some of the finest and most striking garden conifers. The species is native to Colorado and other mountainous regions in the USA, from Wyoming to New Mexico. There it

often grows to 30m/100ft, broadly conical with grey-green, sharply pointed leaves, silver-blue on fresh growth. Most cultivars are much more silver-blue than those raised from seed. Nearly all cultivars are propagated by grafting, often using side shoots from upright trees, so young plants generally need their main shoot trained upwards on a cane for several years. Pruning vigorous side shoots in early spring helps maintain a better form and removes competition from the leading shoot. Seedlings vary but species average: H2.1-3m/7-10ft, W1.2-1.5m/4-5ft. Z3-8.

'**Compacta**', introduced in 1863 and grown from seed collected from the 4000m/13,000ft Pikes Peak in Colorado, USA, is distinct from the better-known but similar 'Globosa'. It slowly makes a densely branched, flat-topped, blue-green bush, brighter silver-blue in summer. Grown widely in the USA but seldom seen in Europe. H45-60cm/18-24in, W45-60cm/18-24in. G. Z3-8. '**Endtz**' is a rare treasure, very slowly forming a compact pyramid with dense layers of horizontal branches, grey in winter, silvery blue in summer. H1.5-2.1m/5-7ft, W90-120cm/3-4ft. G. Z3-8. '**Fat Albert**'. This distinctively named selection from the Iseli Nurseries in Oregon, USA, is rooted from cuttings, which creates a neat, dense form even when young. Soft almost feathery blue foliage, eventually tall. H3m/10ft, W90-120cm/3-4ft. Z3-8. '**Globosa**' (syn. 'Glauca Globosa') has closely set, congested branches slightly angled up from the centre, gradually forming a neat but irregular bush. The stiff, prickly needles are grey-blue in winter; in late spring soft, bright blue new leaves transform the colour for the

whole summer. Unless grown from cuttings (not easy) grafted plants may, within four or five years of planting, make one or more leading shoots. Prune away in early spring, unless you want an equally desirable compact pyramid. Almost identical to 'Montgomery'. Mostly grafted. H45-60cm/18-24in, W45-60cm/18-24in. Z3-8.

'**Hoopsii**', one of the most popular blue spruces, can be reluctant to produce a respectable leading shoot. Stout, widely spaced branches turn up at the tips. Needles are soft, broad, bright silver-blue in summer and silver-grey in winter. Narrow pyramidal or broadly conical form, eventually large. Prune side shoots when young to improve habit. H1.8-2.4m/6-8ft, W90-120cm/3-4ft. G. Z3-8. '**Hoto**' soon makes a neat pyramid of horizontal, evenly spaced, dense branches, with needles remaining on the inner parts of the plant, an attribute not shared by all cultivars. A good blue the year round. H2.1-3m/7-10ft, W1.2-1.5m/4-5ft. G. Z3-8. '**Iseli Fastigiate**' is a truly fastigiate blue spruce, introduced from Iseli Nurseries in Oregon, USA. It slowly forms a very dense, narrow column, clothed in blue-green needles, bright blue in summer. With age it becomes somewhat broader. Mostly grafted. H1.8-2.4m/6-8ft, W45-60cm/18-24in. Z3-8. '**Koster**' is an old but popular cultivar. In early years it is difficult to train a leading shoot, and even later the main terminal tends to bend or snake. Side shoots are irregular and need annual pruning to make a balanced specimen. Branches are angled sharply upwards from the main stem. Good year-round silver-blue. Cones quite freely. H1.8-2.4m/6-8ft, W1.2-1.5m/4-5ft. G. Z3-8. '**Montgomery**', an American introduction,

Picea pungens 'Iseli Fastigiate'

Picea pungens 'Prostrata'

Picea pungens 'Thomsen'

is almost if not totally identical to the European 'Globosa', even to their reversion to a dense pyramidal form when unpruned. Mostly grafted. H45-60cm/18-24in, W45-60cm/18-24in. Z3-8.

'Oldenburg' was selected at the Jeddeloh Nurseries near Oldenburg, Germany, for its early ability to form a leading shoot and its regular habit, even from young grafted plants. Quite vigorous, making a narrow, dense, blue-grey pyramid. H2.1-3m/7-10ft, W1.2-1.5m/4-5ft. G. Z3-8. 'Pendula' (syn. 'Glauca Pendula'), a variable oddity, can be attractive but often forms a rather sprawling

Picea pungens 'Montgomery'

untidy bush, eventually of some size. Find and train up a leading shoot when young, since it will not do this of its own accord. All other branches are more or less pendulous and eventually may make a spectacular cascading sheet of silver-blue, often forming a broad skirt at the base. Not a nurserymen's favourite, so rare. Growth rate 15-20cm/6-8in a year. G. Z3-8. 'Prostrata' (syn. 'Glauca Prostrata' and 'Procumbens') covers any prostrate blue spruce but completely flat ones are rare, since most sooner or later try to make angled or vertical shoots. Cut these away to maintain a low-growing habit. Grafted side shoots from various cultivars are likely to be as prostrate as grafts from 'Prostrata'. With careful pruning these will make broad, spreading specimens, their bright silver-blue foliage showing brilliantly against golden heathers or conifers. Annual growth 15-30cm/6-12in. H30-45cm/12-18in, W1.5-1.8m/5-6ft. G. Z3-8. 'Thomsen', one of the best and most popular, is named after the Danish Thomsen Nursery, though discovered in Pennsylvania, USA, before the nursery moved back to Europe. It is narrow, with branches angled upwards and soft, thick needles, distinctive silver-grey in winter, bright silver-blue in summer. Difficult to propagate. H1.8-2.4m/6-8ft, W90-120cm/3-4ft. G. Z3-8.
P. sitchensis 'Papoose', and its almost identical twin, 'Tenas', were discovered as witches' brooms on the Sitka spruce, *P. sitchensis*, a northern North American timber tree now widely planted elsewhere. 'Papoose' eventually forms a dense, broadly conical bush whose blue-green leaves have showy silver undersides. H45-60cm/18-24in, W45-60cm/18-24in. G. Z4-8.

PINUS Pine

The pines are extremely varied and valuable, with over 100 species. A few are subtropical, but most are native to northerly climates, in a broad band across the globe up into the Arctic. Some grow 65m/200ft or more high, while others, usually from high mountains or tundra, are dwarf. Taller forms are mostly conical when young, often becoming craggy and flat-topped with age, many surviving or even thriving on the poorest soils, on sandy dunes, rocky hillsides and mountain crags. All have needles growing in bunches of two to five. In spring many have cone-like male flowers, or strobili, which shed pollen, whilst female flowers produce cones. Striking 'candles' of new shoots emerge each summer, often in a contrasting colour to the mature foliage. Unlike *Chamaecyparis*, *Juniperus* and *Thuja*, which continue growing through the summer, *Pinus*, *Abies* and *Picea* have one growth flush from a winter bud, then stop by July, in time for next year's bud to form. Most species have seed-bearing cones, some extremely large and attractive. The majority of species are eventually too large for the average garden, but there are many garden-worthy cultivars which arose as selections from the wild, seedlings, and sports, or mutations, such as witches' brooms. Some cultivars root readily from cuttings but most must be grafted.
P. aristata. The Bristlecone pine is the oldest living plant; gnarled specimens in the Californian White Mountains are known to be over 5000 years old, their longevity partly due to the arid mountainous climate. It is not as slow as one might think; my ten-year-old plants are 1.8m/6ft high and 1.5m/5ft

Pinus cembra 'Glauca'

Pinus densiflora 'Alice Verkade'

Pinus leucodermis ' Compact Gem'

wide, with several leaders growing outwards and upwards, the stems covered with dense clusters of five needles each. The whitish scales liberally dotting all the needles are resin droplets, not aphids! The cones also exude resin, with small black bristles protruding from the scales. H1.5-1.8m/5-6ft, W1.2-1.5m/4-5ft. Z4-7. **'Sherwood Compact'** is a compact replica of its parent, erect branches forming a tight, conical, blue-green bush, the needles' scales much less and sometimes not at all noticeable. H45-60cm/18-24in, W20-30cm/8-12in. G. Z4-7.

P. banksiana. The Jack pine is two-needled extremely hardy, growing wild further north than any other North American pine and, depending on locality, ranging from a shrub to a medium-sized tree. Of no great interest to the gardener except for dwarf selections. Most notable are seedlings raised by Alf Fordham of the Arnold Arboretum in Massachusetts, USA: **'Chippewa'**, **'Manomet'**, **'Neponset'**, **'Schoodic'**, the picturesquely named **'Uncle Fogy'**, and **'Wisconsin'**. All are tough plants for the alpine garden or dwarf conifer collection

with typical, short green needles. G. Z3-8.
P. bungeana. Introduced from China by Robert Fortune in 1846, the three-needled, lace-bark pine has the most beautiful bark of any in cultivation but is rarely grown. On mature trees, smooth, grey-green bark flakes away to reveal light yellow patches which turn green, red, brown and purple. Variable habit, often branching near the base, conical when young, broader and more open with age, with rather sharp, dark green needles. Very slow-growing though eventually 15m/50ft or more. H1.2-1.8m/4-6ft, W60-90cm/2-3ft. Z5-8.

P. cembra. The arolla pine, or Swiss stone pine, is excellent for garden and landscape use, forming a formal column of upright branches, densely clothed young shoots in sets of five blue-green needles, with bright bluish white insides, and covered with thick, orange-brown down. In spring, yellow-to-buff male flowers often form and, later, deep blue or purplish cones which seldom open. Though adaptable to a wide range of soils and climates, it prefers fairly open positions and good drainage. Most plants offered are from seed and may be variable. An attractive German selection with dark blue needles, **'Glauca'**, is grafted, as is the slower-growing **'Aurea'**, or 'Aureovariegata', which needs full sun, has paler foliage and gold-tipped needles, particularly in winter. *P. cembra* and 'Glauca': H1.5-1.8m/5-6ft, W75-90cm/30-36in. G. Z4-7.

P. contorta. The two-needled beach pine, or lodgepole pine, is variable and adaptable, with several geographical forms, spreading from the Californian shores to Canada and the Rocky Mountains. They have attractive, dark green needles, and are now widely used in other parts of the world for forestry, especially on poor, peaty soils. H3-5m/10-16ft, W2.1-3m/7-10ft. Z6-8. **'Frisian Gold'**, a remarkable dwarf, was discovered at the Jeddeloh Nurseries when a bright gold shoot appeared among the lustrous green; cuttings, or scions, were taken, and a striking

new conifer resulted. Very slow-growing, with golden-yellow needles all year round. Prone to sunscorch, so provide light shade. Difficult to propagate and therefore always in short supply. H45-60cm/18-24in, W60cm/2ft. G. Z6-8. **'Spaan's Dwarf'** has upward-sweeping, contorted branches, closely set with short, dark green needles and tipped with round, brown-purple winter buds. Thin the branches to make a picturesque form, and to let in air and light. Excellent for bonsai. H45-60cm/18-24in, W45-60cm/18-24in. G. Z6-8.

P. densiflora. The Japanese red pine, seldom grown as an ornamental in Europe, generally makes a medium-to-large tree, similar to the Scots pine, *P. sylvestris*. **'Alice Verkade'** is a flat-topped, bushy selection from the Verkade Nursery in New Jersey, USA. The long, deep green needles on upward-turning branches are so thick on young plants that the stems are hidden. H60-90cm/2-3ft, W60-90cm/2-3ft. G. Z4-7. **'Oculus Draconis'**, the dragon's eye pine, from late summer through to winter can be a striking oddity. The light green needles have alternate yellow bands and, viewed from above, with the brown central bud appear as circles or rings, hence the name. Rather poor and open grower. H1.5-1.8m/5-6ft, W90-120cm/3-4ft. G. Z4-7. **'Umbraculifera'** (syn. 'Tagyosho'), the Japanese umbrella pine, once established has branches dividing from the base, like an upturned umbrella, topped with sets of long, deep green needles, and carrying profuse tiny cones. Attractive when young but can look scruffy later. 'Alice Verkade' is a better plant. H1.2-1.5m/4-5ft, W1.2-1.5m/4-5ft. G. Z4-7.

P. excelsa. See *P. wallichiana*.
P. griffithi. See *P. wallichiana*.
P. heldreichii leucodermis. See *P. leucodermis*.
P. koraiensis 'Silveray' is the correct name for plants listed as *P.k.* 'Glauca'. A very attractive selection of the rare, five-needled Korean pine, the hardy, adaptable 'Silveray' is fairly slow when young, making a rather open column of grey-green branches with clusters of blue-green needles, bright silver-grey underneath. Red male and female flowers often appear in spring, later on older plants. Quite large olive-green cones hug the stems, ripening brown. A distinctive pine for garden and landscape. H1.5-1.8m/5-6ft, W60-75cm/24-30in. G. Z5-7.

P. leucodermis (syn. *P. heldreichii leucodermis*), the two-needled Bosnian pine, varies considerably in the wild from northern Italy through Yugoslavia to the Balkans, but mostly is a rather open, conical tree, distinctive for its long, dark green needles which in their first years press forward close to the branches. Bright blue cones ripen brown. Very useful on dry, poor and alkaline soils. Slow when young but eventually tall. H2.4-3m/8-10ft, W90-120cm/3-4ft. Z6-8.

'Compact Gem', introduced by the famous Hillier Nursery in Hampshire, England, in 1964, was first listed as 'Compacta'. Compact and quite slow-growing when young, with dense clusters of lustrous, deep green needles, it begins to pick up speed once established. My eighteen-year-old specimens are 3m/10ft tall and 1.8m/6ft across, so allow for its future development! H90-120cm/3-4ft, W60-90cm/2-3ft. G. Z6-8.

'Schmidtii' (syn. 'Pygmy'), found originally in 1926 by Mr Eugen Schmidt in the Bosnian Mountains near Sarajevo, Yugoslavia, this bush, over 100 years old, was less than 3m/10ft high. From a graft it develops into a perfect cushion of short, sharp, dark green needles, more compact on poor, thin soils than heavy, rich ones. Like most pines it dislikes poor drainage. H30cm/1ft, W30cm/1ft. G. Z5-8.

P. mugo. The two-needled mugo pine, or Swiss mountain pine, varies in its native central European mountains from dwarf compact bushes, usually found at higher altitudes, to trees 15m/50ft high. There are numerous selections, some very similar to each other; most succeed in inhospitable conditions, including alkaline soils, as long as good drainage exists. Mugo pines take kindly to pruning and many nurserymen prune them with shears just as they develop new shoots in early summer, still early enough for them to bush out and form buds for the following year. Mugo pines make no taproots, so transplant easily. Most dwarf selections are not sheared. Z3-7.

'Corley's Mat', named by Mr Ron Corley, an English conifer enthusiast who found this in a nursery seedling bed, is widespreading, with bright green, twisted leaves, remaining less than 30cm/1ft high after ten years. Similar but nearly twice as high in the same period is the German 'Jeddeloh' and the similar 'Prostrata'. Trim to keep low if required. Most cone freely and make good ground cover for inhospitable sites, including slopes and mounds. H30cm/1ft, W90-120cm/3-4ft. G. Z3-7. 'Humpy', one of the most compact and attractive dwarf pines, from the Dutch conifer nursery, Draijer, forms a neat cushion with branches densely clothed in short, dark green needles. Prominent brown-purple winter buds. H30cm/1ft, W60cm/2ft. G. Z3-7.

'Kissen', one of the shortest needled mountain pines, was formerly named *brevifolia*. Also a selected seedling, it eventually forms a round bun with dark green needles, only half as long as those of 'Humpy', exposing the spiky branching system and brown winter buds encrusted with whitish resin. Stronger growth may develop later which can be pruned to retain the compact form. Very similar is the American 'Glendale'. H30-45cm/12-18in, W45-60cm/18-24in. G. Z3-7.

'Mops', an attractive, popular dwarf, has a neat, mounded habit, light green needles and brown winter buds. It is better for a small garden than 'Gnome', which grows twice as fast in all directions, though 'Mops', too, will pick up speed with age. H60-75cm/24-30in, W60-75cm/24-30in. G. Z3-7.

'Ophir' is completely nondescript in summer, but in winter, with shorter days and colder nights, its green needles are gradually transformed to golden-yellow. An open, sunny position gives best colour. Immune to the severest frost. Plant with blue-flowered grape hyacinths, *Muscari armeniacum*. H60cm/2ft, W90cm/3ft. G. Z3-7.

'Wintergold' differs from 'Ophir' in that its needles turn completely golden-yellow, while 'Ophir' needles remain green where

Pinus mugo 'Humpy'

Pinus mugo 'Ophir'

light does not reach. Neither suffers sun– or frostburn. Both discovered in Holland. H60-75cm/24-30in, W90cm/3ft. G. Z3-7.

P. nigra. The black pine is variable, with several geographical forms spreading from the Pyrenees through the European Alps to Asia Minor. The typical form of *P. nigra*, the Austrian pine, is most popular as an ornamental. From seed it, too, varies but it is tough, adaptable, pyramidal when young and mop-headed when older. The dark green needles are long, often sharp; the trees make a good windbreak or shelter against which other colourful conifers can be contrasted. Does well by the sea and on chalk. H3-5m/10-16ft, W2.1-3m/7-10ft. Z5-8.

'Aurea', a striking if rare curiosity, slowly assumes an upright habit after patient training and pruning in early years. In late spring, new shoots are golden-yellow, in contrast to the older green foliage. They fade to green as summer continues, though in exposed sites the gold colour may persist until winter. Prune side shoots when young. H1.5-1.8m/5-6ft, W (unless pruned) 1.2-1.5m/4-5ft. G. Z5-8.

Pinus nigra 'Aurea'

Pinus nigra 'Hornibrookiana'

Pinus pumila 'Globe'

Pinus strobus 'Reinshaus'

'Columnaris' (syn. 'Fastigiata'), a rare but distinct column-shaped selection, makes a good accent plant. Long, dark green needles almost hide the erect branches. Attractive, white-tipped, prominent winter buds. H2.4-3m/8-10ft, W60cm/2ft. G. Z5-8.
'Hornibrookiana'. Named after an early dwarf conifer authority, Murray Hornibrook, this slow-growing pine was discovered as a witches' broom in New York State, USA. It is eventually broad-spreading, with many short, upright branches densely covered with very prickly, stiff, dark green needles. The reddish brown winter buds are tipped white and nestle in a cup-shaped circle of needles. H45-60cm/18-24in, W60-90cm/2-3ft. G. Z5-8. **'Pygmaea'**. See *P. sylvestris* 'Moseri'.
P. parviflora. The Japanese white pine is upright, conical, later round-topped and eventually reaching 15-25m/50-80ft. The forms usually grown and associated with Japanese gardens are cultivars, generally more open and wide-spreading, as broad as high. A five-needled pine, with long, blue-green needles, silvery beneath, borne in clusters at the end of branches and branchlets. Most cone freely when young, with as many as six cones clinging to the stem just behind the current season's growth. When more mature, branches tend to retain several of the previous years' opened cones rather than dropping them – a detraction rather than an attraction. Used widely for bonsai. Species and cultivars tolerate a wide range of soils and climates, but dislike poor drainage. H2.4-3m/8-10ft, W1.8-2.4m/6-8ft. Z5-8.
'Adcock's Dwarf' was named after Graham Adcock, who found it in a bed of seedlings at the Hillier Nursery in Hampshire, England. Its congested, spreading branches carry clusters of short green needles, silver-grey beneath. Must have good drainage. H30cm/1ft, W30-45cm/12-18in. G. Z5-8.
'Glauca', the most popular form, has distinctly blue-green needles with silver undersides, especially bright in summer, and an upright habit, more spreading with age. Eventually attains 6-10m/20-33ft or more, though often sold as a dwarf. Prune if

required to form a narrower outline, or for bonsai. Cones freely. H1.8-2.4m/6-8ft, W1.8-2.4m/6-8ft. G. Z5-8. **'Negishi'** is one of hundreds of selections catalogued by the Japanese, all slightly different, so confusion among Western names is understandable. 'Negishi' appears identical to a cultivar called **'Bonsai'** and is bushy, spreading and upright, with a dense branching habit and even denser blue-green needles. Picturesque but probably improved by careful thinning of some stems. Ideal in a Japanese garden. H1.5-1.8m/5-6ft, W1.8-2.4m/6-8ft. G. Z5-8.
P. pumila. The five-needled Japanese stone pine, or dwarf Siberian pine, is variable, but generally found as low-growing shrubs or genuine dwarfs. **'Dwarf Blue'** is low-growing but not prostrate, with short, nearly erect branches densely clothed in green needles, bright silver-white beneath. Dislikes poor drainage and lime. H45-60cm/18-24in, W90-120cm/3-4ft. G. Z4-7. **'Globe'**, one of the most attractive dwarf pines, makes a round, bright blue-green bush; the needles' green outer surface is silvery white beneath, resulting in the distinct blue cast. Occasional small cones. Ideal for a small garden. H45-60cm/18-24in, W45-60cm/18-24in. G. Z4-7.

'Jeddeloh'. A pine worth mentioning for its wide-spreading habit, with upward-arching branches clothed in bunches of curiously curved needles. Here the green top and silver reverse of the needles give more of a striped effect. Early into growth. Cones quite freely. H30-45cm/12-18in, W90-120cm/3-4ft. G. Z4-7.
P. strobus. Native from Newfoundland to Georgia, the eastern white pine, or Weymouth pine, can reach up to 50m/160ft. Extremely fast-growing and conical when young, it is slower and rounder with age. The blue-green needles, in groups of five, are up to 15cm/6in long. Generally unsuitable for small garden use, but many cultivars have been selected and introduced from seedlings and witches' brooms. The American pioneering spirit remains strong among conifer enthusiasts, who go out into the white pine woods with their rifles to shoot down witches' brooms found high up in the trees! Long cylindrical cones. Best on free-draining soils; can be prone to blister rust. H5-8m/16-26ft, W2.4-3m/8-10ft. Z4-9.
'Brevifolia' (syn. 'Densa'), very slow-growing with an upright, extremely compact, pyramidal habit, has short stems bearing clusters of dark blue-green needles, silvery beneath. A perfect rock garden conifer. H45-60cm/18-24in, W20-30cm/8-12in. G. Z4-9. **'Fastigiata'** (syn. 'Pyramidalis'), though almost as vigorous as the species, with its narrower conical habit is more suited to smaller gardens. Long, blue-grey needles are held close to the erect stems and long, cylindrical, pendulous cones appear on older plants. H2.4-3m/8-10ft, W75-90cm/30-36in. G. Z4-9. **'Minima'** makes a dense, low, neat, round bush of thin, blue-green needles. Similar but even slower are **'Horsford'** and the German **'Reinshaus'**. Many compact selections are listed under a 'Minima' group. Whilst this does help to identify them more closely, so many are now being introduced that it has become confusing to gardener and nurseryman alike. H30cm/1ft, W60-75cm/24-30in. G. Z4-9.
'Nana', like 'Minima', refers to a group of plants, generally slow-growing rather than dwarf but seldom exceeding 3m/10ft. To add to the confusion, the cultivar almost always sold as 'Nana' is **'Radiata'**, making a dense, broad bush, wider than it is high. The needles, up to 10cm/4in long, are green with bright silver-grey bands beneath and, except for the tufty shoot tips, lie forward against the stems. H90-120cm/3-4ft, W1.2-1.5m/4-5ft. G. Z4-9. **'Pendula'** is scrawny when young but with early training up a cane grows more robust and vigorous. Pendulous branches radiate from a central leading stem and end in 'brushes', or large clusters of blue-green needles. Needs space but is impressive when well grown, and can be trained in other shapes. Growth

rate 15-30cm/6-12in a year or more when established. G. Z4-9. **'Prostrata'**, discovered nearly 100 years ago in the Arnold Arboretum, Massachusetts, USA, and since widely distributed, makes a sprawling, open specimen, branches lying flat on the ground or forming a low mound, sparsely clothed in light blue-green needles. Effective on a bank or over rocks. Prune to improve density. H30cm/1ft, W1.5-1.8m/5-6ft. G. Z4-9. *P. sylvestris*. The Scots pine is two-needled and the only pine native to the British Isles, but it also spreads from northern Spain and across Scandinavia to Russia and Siberia. Some geographical forms differ in habit but all are hardy and adaptable, generally conical when young, more open and wide-spreading as they mature. Old specimens reach 30m/100ft or more, so it is hardly suitable for the smaller garden. Its needles are slightly twisted, dark blue in winter, brighter in summer. Small rounded cones. Grows well in most soils and sites, including acid and alkaline ones, but prefers good drainage. H3-5m/10-16ft, W2.1-3m/ 7-10ft. Z3-7.

'Albyns', a distinct, prostrate form, arose as a chance seedling on the Albyn Nursery in Ohio, USA. It has low, spreading branches and dense, blue-green needles. More of a carpet than **'Prostrata'**, as is the similar **'Hillside Creeper'**. H30-45cm/12-18in, W75-120cm/30-48in. G. Z3-7. **'Aurea'** covers several forms in cultivation, including a fairly rapid-growing one similar to the species, but with light grey-green leaves in summer changing to pale yellow in winter. Though grafted and starting a bit slower, estimated H3-4m/10-13ft, W2.1-3m/7-10ft. G. Z3-7. A much better and initially slower-growing form, sometimes referred to as **'Nisbets'**, has needles that turn a bright, deep golden-to-orange yellow in winter. Estimated H1.8-2.4m/6-8ft, W1.5-1.8m/5-6ft, developing more strongly each year. G. Z5. The so-called dwarf **'Gold Coin'** and **'Gold Medal'** have probably been grafted from small, secondary shoots or weak plants and, given time or rich, heavy soil, they soon want to become grown up, too! Unless continually pruned, with age they become much taller, with deep golden winter needles, exposure to sunlight producing the strongest colour. For a golden dwarf Scots pine, prune new growth with secateurs or shears each spring, just as the plant develops 5cm/2in or so of soft foliage. It will still bush out and make attractive winter buds by late summer, as though it had not been trimmed at all. Place against contrasting conifers and underplant with hardy cyclamen. Your plant could be kept for many years at, say, H60cm/2ft, W60-75cm/24-30in by this method. G. Z4-7.

'Doone Valley', one of the most attractive compact cultivars, was discovered by Jim Archer and Ron Corley, noted conifer

Pinus sylvestris 'Hibernia'

Pinus sylvestris 'Watereri'

Pinus sylvestris 'Doone Valley'

Pinus sylvestris 'Gold Coin'

enthusiasts, in Surrey, England, around 1960. It gradually forms a dense, conical bush with bunches of bright silver-grey needles, bluer in summer. Cut away stronger growths on older plants to maintain the compact habit. H30-45cm/12-18in, W20-30cm/8-12in. G. Z3-7. **'Fastigiata'**, an eventually taller-growing cultivar, remains narrow for some years, forming a column of erect branches, bright blue in summer, dark in winter. Unfortunately it tends to open up with age, wind and snowfall. Best in an open position. H1.8-2.4m/6-8ft, W30-45cm/12-18in. G. Z3-7. **'Hibernia'** (syn. 'Nana Hibernica'), a selection found as a witches' broom in Ireland by J. D. zu Jeddeloh, is one of the best for density and colour. It makes an irregular bush, with light greyish green needles in winter, startling grey-blue in summer. Prominent brown winter buds. Ideal for the heather garden. H60-75cm/24-30in, W75-90cm/30-36in. G. Z3-7.

'Moseri' (formerly *P. nigra* 'Pygmaea'), an old cultivar, has distinctive, long needles, twisted and congested around the top of the branches, and buds surrounded by a sheaf of short green leaves. The needles are nondescript green but turn green-gold in

winter, the colour in some winters more extreme than others. It is slow-growing, round and very bushy, sometimes confused with **'Globosa Viridis'**, which has darker green needles the year round. H75-90cm/30-36in, W60-75cm/24-30in. G. Z3-7. **'Repens'**, very slow-growing and unlikely to reach higher than 30cm/1ft after thirty years, gradually forms a dense, prostrate, blue-green bush. Ideal for the rock garden. H15cm/6in, W30-45cm/12-18in. G. Z3-7. **'Watereri'**, like many eventually large conifers, is often sold as a dwarf. Discovered as a seedling on a heath in Surrey, England, in 1865 and named after the owner of the nursery that introduced it, 'Watereri' is slow-growing, conical when young, but eventually becomes a much wider-spreading, small tree. Good blue-green needles. H1.5-1.8m/5-6ft, W1.2-1.5m/4-5ft. G. Z3-7. *P. thunbergii* **'Sayonara'**. This dwarf form of the Japanese black pine, almost the equivalent of the more familiar Austrian pine, forms a squat bush with rigid branches, its stiff, dark green needles short and sharp. Prominent winter buds are tipped white. Excellent on poor, sandy soils. H45-60cm/18-24in, W45-60cm/18-24in. G. Z5-8.

P. wallichiana (syn. *P. griffithi* and *P. excelsa*). A beautiful conifer, the five-needled Himalayan pine originates in the Himalayas from Bhutan to Afghanistan, where it grows to 45m/150ft. Once established, it grows as much as 90cm/3ft a year, becoming broadly pyramidal when young, wider with age. Its clusters of long, blue-grey needles droop from the end of the stems and long, cylindrical, pendulous cones start shiny green, turning to purple then brown towards winter. It makes a magnificent specimen where space allows, retaining its branches to the ground in the open. In cool temperate climates it prefers shelter and moist, well-drained soils; unsuitable for alkaline types, and can suffer in severe frost and drying winds. H5-8m/16-26ft, W3-4m/10-13ft. Z6-8. **'Nana'**, one of the few slow-growing forms, has a broad, bushy habit, its semi-erect branches bearing dense clusters of blue needles, slightly drooping like an upturned mop, bright silver-blue in summer. A rather neglected though worthwhile pine. H60-90cm/2-3ft, W90-120cm/3-4ft. G. Z6-8.

PODOCARPUS

This large genus is mostly native to the Southern Hemisphere, from South America, Africa, Asia and Australasia. The species vary from true dwarfs to large trees, but are more adapted to warmer, even tropical, climates than temperate ones. The Australasian species, however, offer some interesting hardier types. The few dwarfs of note are similar to yews in appearance. Male and female plants must be in close proximity for the females to produce attractive, berry-like, brightly coloured, seed-holding receptacles, similar to *Taxus*.

P. alpinus. Originating from the hills and mountains of south-east Australia and Tasmania, this slowly forms a prostrate bush of dark green needles, a few leading branches spreading beyond the mass of foliage. With age it becomes a larger shrub. Provide shelter in early years from severe frosts. Excellent as ground cover or in a rock garden. H20-30cm/8-12in, W60-90cm/2-3ft. Z8-11.

PSEUDOTSUGA

P. menziesii. The Douglas fir, or Oregon Douglas fir, is one of five species in the genus and the only one with interesting dwarf and slow-growing forms. It is widely used for timber, making an enormous tree in its native north-western USA and British Columbia, some 90m/300ft high. There it gets the moisture, summer warmth and acid soils on which it thrives best; it is unsuitable for alkaline soil. It makes a tall pyramid, flat-topped with age, when lower branches characteristically sweep downwards. The leaves vary from yellow-green and bluish green to dark, shiny green, all with silver-white bands beneath. The attractive cones hang below the branches and are narrowly cylindrical with green overlapping scales,

Sciadopitys verticillata

Sequoia sempervirens 'Adpressa'

Taxodium distichum

each with a pointed 'flag' protruding, ripening to a light brown. H5-8m/16-26ft, W2.1-3m/7-10ft. Z5-7. **'Blue Wonder'** is a rare but striking, slow-growing conifer with beautiful, luxuriant blue-grey leaves, brighter in summer. Some authorities describe it as upright, but my plants always tend to lean to one side, adding to its character rather than its beauty. H1.5-1.8m/5-6ft, W1.2-1.5m/4-5ft. G. Z5-7.

SCIADOPITYS

S. verticillata. The Japanese umbrella pine, native to two small areas in Japan, is a unique, slow-growing but eventually quite tall conifer. It needs lime-free soil and patience, since it is often frustratingly slow when young. Its stiff-looking needles are held in unique clusters, or whorls, around the stems where the year's growth begins and ends, each whorl resembling the spokes of an upturned umbrella. Glossy, bright or olive-green, the 'single' needles are actually two fused together. It grows in full sun or part shade, on warm, acid soils which are not too dry, gradually assuming a pyramidal shape. When grown well, whether 1.8m/6ft or 18m/60ft (though the latter could take sixty or seventy years to achieve), it is a beautiful sight indeed. H90-120cm/3-4ft, W60cm/2ft. Z5-8.

SEQUOIA Giant redwood, Californian redwood

S. sempervirens. This can hardly be considered a conifer for today's small gardens, growing in its native habitat to 90m/300ft and vigorous elsewhere, too. **'Adpressa'**, if treated properly, is excellent for small and large gardens alike. Normally rooted from cuttings, it makes an untidy bush unless trimmed when young, its flexible branches covered with small, light green leaves, silvery beneath and held close to the branches. Leading branches have small clusters of shoots, and in late spring, when new growth appears, the whole plant, particularly if regularly trimmed, looks as though it is covered in snow. Trimming is the secret with 'Adpressa', since a plant that is not trimmed eventually makes a tree some 18m/60ft or more high. The redwood and its cultivars take well to hard pruning, breaking into growth even from a stump. It can be kept to 60-90cm/2-3ft without difficulty, pruned annually or biennially. Left untrimmed, it grows 15-30cm/6-12in a year or more. Z7-9.

SEQUOIADENDRON Wellingtonia

S. giganteum **'Pendulum'**. This oddity is an unusual form of the mammoth tree, or Wellingtonia, which with the Californian redwood is among the tallest and oldest trees on earth. 'Pendulum' has blue-green foliage, with coarse, scale-like leaves closely pointed forward along the stems. Unless trained when young it tends to twist and turn into unusual shapes, but if trained it eventually makes a narrow column with side branches sweeping down close to the stem. It could, like *Cedrus atlantica* 'Glauca Pendula', be trained to form an arch. Easily controlled by secateurs. Annual growth rate 15-30cm/6-12in. Sometimes grafted. Z6-9.

TAXODIUM

An interesting genus of deciduous conifers for the larger garden, originating from the southern USA through to Mexico, and thriving in moist and swampy soils. When growing in or beside water they develop picturesque 'knees' or stumps, which are thought to assist breathing. Unsuitable for alkaline soils; plant on mounds in waterlogged soil.

T. ascendens. The pond cypress is a narrow, columnar species with short, upward-spreading branches holding erect branchlets, the colour of the bright green shoots in spring well maintained, with good red-brown autumn colour before leaf fall. **'Nutans'** has thinner, bright green, erect shoots which later nod at the tips. H4-5m/13-16ft, W90-210cm/3-7ft. Z5-10.

T. distichum. The better-known swamp cypress, or common bald cypress, has a more pyramidal habit, with wide-spreading or ascending branches, usually very congested when young. The picturesque outline of the bare winter stems is broken when new, bright green shoots appear along the branches in spring, the foliage soon hiding the branches. In late autumn the leaves turn a deep reddish brown, staying on the stems for several weeks. Older trees have attractive, reddish brown bark. A beautiful tree to plant beside a pond. H4-6m/13-20ft, W1.5-2.4m/5-8ft. Z5-10.

TAXUS Yew

Yews are among the most useful conifers because of their adaptability to a wide range of soil, cultural and climatic conditions. They grow wild in western and eastern North America, Europe, Asia Minor, and from the Himalayas to China, Japan and Korea. The species are similar but vary considerably from seed, and while some are not as hardy as others, all tolerate alkaline and acid soils, and succeed in dry, dense shade. The cultivars come in all shapes and sizes, like yews in nature, which can be bushy, spreading, upright and tree-like. All withstand clipping well and are widely used as hedging. Normally dark, sombre green and often seen in churchyards and cemeteries, there are many introductions with colourful foliage.

T. baccata. The common yew, known outside Britain as the English yew, is part of the British heritage and trees centuries old can still be found. Variable from seed but

leaves are glossy dark green, lighter green beneath; male and female flowers on separate plants but red-capsuled fruits borne only on females. The berries and foliage are poisonous, and one should be aware of possible dangers if children use the garden; also avoid yew on boundaries accessible to livestock. It makes an excellent hedge, quicker than imagined, but buy a selected clone or inspect plants first; a mixed batch of spreading and upright seedlings makes unsatisfactory hedging material and very young plants may not show true characteristics. Yew is also ideal for topiary, taking pruning, even hard pruning, well. Growth rate per annum once established 15-30cm/6-12in. Z6-7.

'**Adpressa**' covers several selections with different leaf colour but all possess needles about half the length of those of the species, pointing forward along the stem. 'Adpressa' itself is dark green and wide-spreading, eventually a small tree. H90-120cm/3-4ft, W90-120cm/3-4ft. Z6. '**Adpressa Aurea**' is much slower and rare, with bright golden-yellow shoots and yellow variegated foliage. H45-60cm/18-24in, W45-60cm/18-24in. Z7. '**Adpressa Variegata**' is very slow when young, making a densely foliaged, gradually spreading bush. New spring shoots are golden, developing into yellow variegated leaves with a central band of green. Older leaves may be variegated creamy white. Prune, if wished, to keep it small. H60-75cm/24-30in, W60-75cm/24-30in. Z6-7. '**Dovastoniana**', with dark green leaves, makes a broad-spreading shrub, its branches elegantly tiered, but too large for the small garden. H90-120cm/3-4ft, W1.8-2.4m/6-8ft. Z6. '**Dovastonii Aurea Pendula**', often wrongly listed as 'Dovastonii Aurea', is propagated from upright shoots, which later develop side branches with graceful pendulous tips and branchlets. Foliage is identical to the larger and wider-spreading '**Dovastonii Aurea**', similar in size to 'Dovastoniana', with golden young shoots becoming variegated. The upright form becomes a small tree in time and also wide-spreading, so prune when young to keep it manageable. H1.8-2.4m/6-8ft, W90-120cm/3-4ft. G. Z6-7.

'**Dwarf White**' (syn. 'Argentea Minor'), slow-growing, spreading, and eventually quite large, has young leaves variegated white. Prune to keep dwarf. H30-45cm/12-18in, W60-75cm/24-30in. Z6-7. '**Fastigiata Aurea**', the golden Irish yew, makes a dense column of erect branches, the new shoots golden-yellow, paling as summer progresses but in a sunny site always tinged light yellow. Other similar forms with golden or yellow-margined leaves exist. Large in time. H1.8-2.4m/6-8ft, W45-60cm/18-24in. Z6-7. '**Fastigiata Robusta**', an outstanding accent plant, is narrower than 'Fastigiata', the

Taxus baccata 'Fastigiata Robusta'

Taxus baccata 'Dovastonii Aurea Pendula'

more common Irish yew, and possesses dark green foliage which remains untouched by severe frosts. It is perfect for a spot where formality is required. H1.5-1.8m/5-6ft, W20-30cm/8-12in. Z6-7.

'Repandens', low-growing and ideal ground cover, succeeds in shade where few other conifers would. Black-green leaves are densely held on spreading, semi-prostrate branches. Dislikes poor drainage. H60-90cm/2-3ft, W90-120cm/3-4ft. Z6-7. 'Repens Aurea'. Slow and low-growing when young, with wide-spreading branches close to the ground though raised at the tips, this eventually, sometimes helped by pruning, builds up height. Orange-yellow shoots turn golden-yellow in spring, the foliage gracefully drooping along the outer branches. Older leaves are golden variegated with a green central stripe, almost identical to 'Dovastonii Aurea Pendula', leading some authorities to suggest this is a 'cultivariant' from that plant. Colours best in sun. H45-60cm/18-24in, W1.2-1.5m/4-5ft. Z6-7.

'Semperaurea', like many yews, seems very slow-growing for several years until you notice how large it has suddenly become! It has an erect semi-spreading habit, with intense orange-gold shoots in spring, and bright golden-yellow leaves the rest of the year. Excellent winter colour. Prune as necessary. H1.2-1.5m/4-5ft, W1.2-1.5m/4-5ft. Z6-7. 'Standishii' (syn. 'Fastigiata Standishii') is the best upright golden yew for the British climate. Much slower and narrower than the golden-leaved 'Fastigiata' types, it is also much brighter in summer and winter. In open, sunny positions the needle tips are a bright, deep old-gold. H1.2-1.5m/4-5ft, W30cm/1ft. Z6-7. 'Summergold', an excellent, semi-prostrate Dutch selection, makes robust, ornamental ground cover. Upward-spreading branches of dark green leaves, with a narrow yellow margin in winter, are followed by bright yellow summer shoots which cover the plant with golden-yellow leaves. H45-60cm/18-24in, W1.2-1.5m/4-5ft. Z6-7.

T. cuspidata. The Japanese yew is similar to the English yew, but considerably hardier and more adapted to areas in Canada and the USA where *T. baccata* and its cultivars would not survive. It is variable in the wild, forming shrubs or small trees, with deep green leaves, yellowish green beneath. Z4. 'Densa', an old cultivar much used in the USA, makes a low, dense shrub with very dark green leaves on crowded, erect stems. A female fruiting form. H60-90cm/2-3ft, W90-120cm/3-4ft. Z5-7. 'Minima', an old and attractive but rare miniature, forms an irregular bush of congested branches with minute, dark green leaves. Ideal for sinks or troughs. H20-30cm/8-12in, W15-20cm/6-8in. Z5-7. 'Nana', the most popular Japanese yew, is

Taxus baccata 'Summergold'

semi-prostrate, eventually large and wide-spreading, with an open branching system, the leaves on short side branches dark dull green and congested. A male non-fruiting form. Very hardy, but not particularly ornamental. H45-75cm/18-30in, W90-120cm/3-4ft. Z4-7.

T. × media. This is a hybrid between *T. cuspidata* and *T. baccata* from which arose several selections or cultivars. Hardy and strong-growing, they form the backbone of traditional landscaping or foundation planting in American gardens. Innumerable cultivars have been introduced, several almost identical, leading to confusion in naming and identification. Most end up severely trimmed, so their originality is often, sadly, lost. Z5-7.

'Beanpole', introduced in 1970 by John Vermeulen on his nursery in New Jersey, USA, is a self-descriptive, female form, with bright crimson arils, or capsules, surrounding the seeds. Often grafted. H90-120cm/3-4ft, W15-20cm/6-8in. Z5-7. 'Hicksii', one of the most widely used cultivars for hedging, makes a dark green vase-shaped bush. 'Brownii' and 'Hillii' are similar and all are useful as specimens or hedging. H1.8-2.4m/6-8ft, W90-120cm/3-4ft. Z5-7. 'Kelseyi', an upright, globe-shaped, dense shrub with large, dark green leaves, is a reliable fruiting form. H1.5-1.8m/5-6ft, W90cm/3ft. Z5-7. 'Nidiformis' maintains its very slow growth rate and low, semi-prostrate habit with a nest-like centre for many years without pruning. Dark green leaves. H20-30cm/8-12in, W60-75cm/24-30in. Z5-7. 'Sentinalis'. Until the later addition of 'Beanpole', John Vermeulen, who introduced 'Sentinalis' in 1947, considered this the best narrow fastigiate yew. It is still widely used as such, proving a popular and hardy form. H1.8-2.4m/6-8ft, W45-60cm/18-24in. Z5-7.

THUJA Arbor-vitae

The thujas, related to the chamaecyparis which they closely resemble, are among the most important ornamental conifers. The six species are native to North America and Asia; *T. orientalis, T. plicata* and *T. occidentalis* have produced many valuable garden forms. Most form conical trees with flattened foliage sprays bearing scale-like foliage, noticeably aromatic on certain species and cultivars. Most are hardy, though *T. orientalis* and some of its cultivars are much less so. Adaptable to a wide range of soils, including alkaline types, but most dislike poor drainage. *T. occidentalis.* The eastern arbor-vitae, American arbor-vitae or white cedar, is native to the eastern USA and Canada. Variable in the wild and generally very hardy, it seldom reaches more than 20m/65ft, with a pyramidal habit. Its bright green summer foliage turns dull brown in winter, a trait unfortunately copied by some green-foliaged cultivars. It is less good for hedging than *T. plicata* but hardier, and succeeds where the latter would perish from cold. Most of the cultivars have pleasantly aromatic foliage. Z3-8.

'Danica', a popular, attractive dwarf from Jensen's Nursery in Denmark, makes a neat, compact globe with erect, flattened sprays of bright green foliage, bronze-tinged in winter. Better for a small garden than the similar 'Woodwardii', which grows at least twice as fast. H30-45cm/12-18in, W45-60cm/18-24in. Z3-8. 'Hetz Midget' is one of the dwarfest forms, slowly making a tight bush of lacy, mid-green foliage, bronze or brown in winter. H20-30cm/8-12in,

Taxus baccata 'Standishii'

W20-30cm/8-12in. Z3-8. **'Holmstrup'** was the most popular, slow-growing, columnar form before 'Smaragd' became well known. It has compact, narrowly pyramidal habit, and bright green, flattened sprays of summer foliage, slightly bronzing in winter. H1.2-1.5cm/4-5ft, W45-60cm/18-24in. Z3-8. **'Holmstrup Yellow'**, also from Holmstrup, Denmark, but much harder to come by, is more open in habit than 'Holmstrup', forming a broad column of yellow-green summer foliage, bright yellow in winter, perhaps the brightest of any thuja. H1.5-1.8m/5-6ft, W90-120cm/3-4ft. Z4-8.

'Lutea Nana', contrary to its name, probably grows to 8m/26ft or more, but is better than the taller-growing **'Lutea'** (formerly named 'George Peabody'), being quite slow in early years. It makes a broad column of loose foliage sprays, bright yellow in summer, deep golden-yellow in winter. **'Europe Gold'**, which forms a narrower column, is smaller still. H1.8-2.4m/6-8ft, W90-120cm/3-4ft. Z3-8. **'Malonyana'**, found in a Hungarian count's garden in 1913 (now in Czechoslovakia), has taken time to get recognition. It makes a distinct, narrow column of compact, glossy green foliage, eventually 10-15m/33-50ft high. Excellent for avenue planting. H1.8-2.4m/6-8ft, W45-60cm/18-24in. Z3-8. **'Marrison Sulphur'** is slow-growing and broadly pyramidal with delicate, lacy, creamy yellow foliage, even in winter. H1.5-1.8m/5-6ft, W90-120cm/3-4ft. Z3-8.

'Rheingold', long one of the most popular garden conifers, is also a source of confusion and mystery. Plants propagated

Thuja occidentalis 'Smaragd' hedge

Thuja occidentalis 'Rheingold'

by cuttings from the softer, juvenile foliage at the base of the mother plant will be reliable dwarfs for some years, making broad bushes of soft, feathery foliage. Cuttings taken from the top of the plant, where growth is stronger and more open with coarser adult foliage, produce stronger, faster-growing, more open plants; and cuttings propagated from the area in between have half-way characteristics. **'Ellwangeriana Aurea'** is supposed to represent the faster-growing form, with the name 'Rheingold' being used for the slower, dwarfer type, which also eventually produces much more open and stronger foliage. Prune 'Rheingold' as necessary, since with age it often gets too broad and untidy. The plant makes an attractive bush of lacy, bright golden yellow summer foliage, rich coppery bronze in winter. Excellent with heathers but colours best in an exposed spot. Variable size but approximate H90-120cm/3-4ft, W90-120cm/3-4ft. Z3-8.

'Smaragd', a Danish cultivar, becomes 'Emeraude' in French and 'Emerald' in English. It is excellent as a specimen or for hedges, forming a narrow column of bright, rich green foliage, loose, soft and, rare among the green-foliaged cultivars, maintaining its rich colour through winter. An ideal hedge for suburban gardens, needing only occasional clipping. H1.8-2.4m/6-8ft, W60-75cm/24-30in. Z3-8. **'Sunkist'**, slower-growing and more densely pyramidal than 'Lutea Nana', is a popular Dutch selection that soon forms a bush with several leading shoots, the flattened foliage sprays golden-yellow in summer, bronze-gold in winter. H1.2-1.5m/4-5ft, W90-120cm/3-4ft. Z3-8. A more recent Dutch introduction of similar growth rate, **'Yellow Ribbon'**, is much narrower but not quite as bright. **'Trompenburg'**, from Trompenburg Arboretum, near Rotterdam, Holland, is

Thuja occidentalis 'Sunkist'

Thuja occidentalis 'Trompenburg'

very slow-growing when young, making an irregular mound of congested foliage. In time it forms a conical bush of sprays of scale-like foliage, with a golden sheen in spring, light green in summer, and copper-tipped shoots in winter, when grown in a sunny, exposed spot. H45-60cm/18-24in, W45-60cm/18-24in. Z3-8. **'Wansdyke Silver'**, selected at Wansdyke Nursery in Devizes, Wiltshire, England, some years ago, slowly forms a broad pyramid of light green foliage, splashed and variegated white, well coloured the year round. The older **'Beaufort'** is similar. H90-120cm/3-4ft, W60-90cm/2-3ft. Z3-8.

T. orientalis. The Chinese arbor-vitae, or Oriental arbor-vitae, grows wild in northern China, Manchuria and Korea. It makes a small, usually conical tree, seldom exceeding 12m/39ft, with vertical, many-branched stems, holding flattened sprays of scale-like foliage. It is the only species with scentless foliage. Though considerably less hardy than the others, it provides attractive, colourful cultivars, most of which prefer sun and good drainage, but which vary in hardiness. Z6-9.

Thuja orientalis 'Aurea Nana'

'Aurea Nana', one of the most colourful, popular dwarf conifers, under 1.8m/6ft high even after fifty years, makes a neat, round-to-oval bush, with many erect branches carrying flattened sprays of soft, feathery foliage. In spring, light yellow-green leaves become bright golden-yellow, a colour held until autumn, when it is tinged with brown. Often wrongly listed by American nurserymen as Berckman's golden arbor-vitae, a name which correctly applies to 'Conspicua'. **'Semperaurea'** seems identical, though reputedly taller-growing. H60-75cm/24-30in, W30-45cm/12-18in. Z6-9. **'Blue Cone'** provides a change from golden-foliaged cultivars but 'blue' is somewhat exaggerated. Originally an American seedling, it makes a neat cone of upright, flattened sprays of deep green foliage described by Monrovia Nurseries, who introduced it, as having a 'bluish cast'. A New Zealand nursery catalogue suggests it has blue cones, giving quite a different meaning to the name. H75-90cm/30-36in, W45-60cm/18-24in. Z6-9. The similar American **'Fruitlandii'** has rich green leaves and eventually a more pyramidal shape. H60-90cm/2-3ft, W30-45cm/12-18in. Z6-9. **'Collen's Gold'** forms a narrow column of open foliage, bright golden-yellow in summer, well maintained in winter. H1.5-1.8m/5-6ft, W30-45cm/12-18in. Z6-9.

'Conspicua', not 'Aurea Nana', should bear the common name Berckman's golden arbor-vitae. It is quite distinct from 'Aurea Nana', making a broad cone or pyramid with vertical planes of soft, loosely held foliage, golden-yellow in summer, slightly

Thuja orientalis 'Conspicua', with *Aubrieta* and *Cytisus*

less so in winter. With age, on heavier soils, the foliage tends to open in wet weather, wind and snow, and should be tied in. 'Pyramidalis Aurea' (see below), tighter in form, is a better garden conifer. H1.5-1.8m/5-6ft, W60-90cm/2-3ft. Z6-9. **'Elegantissima'** has a much stiffer, more upright habit than 'Conspicua', its flat foliage sprays held on curving branchlets. The leaves are deep golden-yellow in summer, deep bronze in winter, particularly in an open sunny spot. Though slow when young, may eventually reach 5m/16ft or more. H1.2-1.5m/4-5ft, W60-75cm/24-30in. Z6-9.

'Juniperoides', a juvenile-leaved form and consequently one of the least hardy, quickly forms a dense, oval bush of feathery foliage, grey-green in summer, rich plum-purple in winter. Prone to wind, frost and snow damage. H45-60cm/18-24in, W30-45cm/12-18in. Z7-9. **'Meldensis'** makes one

of the tightest, neatest oval bushes, with coarse, though juvenile, foliage, light green in summer, purple-tinged in winter. So unbelievably dense and perfect in shape, you'll want to stroke it! H60-75cm/24-30in, W45-60cm/18-24in. Z6-9. **'Pyramidalis Aurea'**, introduced into northern Europe by the Italian nursery trade, is fairly slow when young, but in time makes an imposing specimen, perhaps to 8m/26ft. Conical when young with vertical, flattened branchlets, its bright yellow summer foliage turns light yellow-green in winter. Excellent in a formal garden or as an accent plant. H1.8-2.4m/6-8ft, W60-90cm/2-3ft. Z6-9. **'Rosedalis'** (syn. 'Rosedalis Compacta'), a bright, popular form with soft, juvenile foliage and a compact, bushy habit, changes colour three times a year. It is usually brownish purple in winter, bright creamy yellow in spring, and light green in summer. H45-60cm/18-24in,

W30-45cm/12-18in. Z7-9.

T. plicata. The western red cedar is native to north-western North America, from northern California, Oregon and Washington to the Canadian Rockies and Alaska. It grows 50m/160ft or more, an invaluable forest and timber tree, also widely planted elsewhere as an ornamental. The trunks were a favourite with the American Indians for carving totem poles and making hollowed-out canoes. Fast-growing, it forms a tall, eventually broad-based pyramid, the foliage flattened in fern-like sprays, from mid- to dark green, the scale-like leaves glossy above and pale green beneath with silver markings. Prefers moist conditions and areas of high rainfall, but tolerates shade and alkaline soils. Excellent for hedges and screens, stands clipping well, and is one of the few conifers to produce new growth from its centre. The species has a most pleasant, fruity odour when the foliage is brushed or rubbed. H5-8m/16-26ft, W2.1-3m/7-10ft. Z6-8.

'**Atrovirens**', the selection most often offered by nurserymen in place of the species, has a more formal, conical shape, with erect branches clothed in deep, rich, glossy green foliage all year round. H4-5m/13-16ft, W90-120cm/3-4ft. Z6-8. '**Irish Gold**', though prone to sunscorch when young, is one of the brightest conifers in winter. Pyramidal, its foliage is creamy white lightly flecked with green if grown in full sun. Shelter from cold, desiccating winds, and grow in full sun. '**Zebrina**' is much denser and more yellow-green. H1.5-2.4m/5-8ft, W90-120cm/3-4ft. Z7-8. '**Rogersii**' (syn. 'Aurea Rogersii') and the somewhat similar '**Cuprea**' were raised at the Rogers' Nursery in Hampshire, England, as seedlings from 'Aurea'. 'Cuprea' has creamy yellow and coppery leaves and a more open, broader habit than 'Rogersii'. The latter slowly forms a dense, round bush of congested foliage, dark green inside, deep golden yellow-to-bronze at the tips. Longer growths occasionally break the surface and should be cut away if they begin to grow too strongly. Good, year-round colour, ideal for the rock garden. H30-45cm/12-18in, W30cm/1ft. Z6-8. '**Stoneham Gold**', introduced in 1948, is one of the best plants in the winter garden. It is slow-growing, often with several leading shoots to start with. The stems are reddish brown, especially in winter, the foliage dark green inside, golden-yellow and green where exposed to sunlight, and orange-yellow, often bronze, at the tips. Excellent winter colour in exposed spots. Trim occasionally. H60-90cm/2-3ft, W45-60cm/18-24in. Z6-8.

THUJOPSIS

T. dolabrata. Native to Japan and closely related to thujas, this is the only species in

Thuja plicata 'Stoneham Gold'

Tsuga canadensis 'Bennett'

the genus. Though slow when young, it eventually reaches 18m/60ft or more and in an open position becomes broad at the base. It is similar to *T. plicata*, but with larger, rounder and thicker branchlets, the outer stems sheathed in green overlapping leaves, or scales. The foliage sprays are flattened, the leaves glossy green above, bright silver in the centre, with green margins below. A good background ornamental for a large garden. H1.5-1.8m/5-6ft, W1.2-1.5m/4-5ft. Z6-8. '**Aurea**', slower-growing than the species, gradually forms a wide bush reluctant to develop a leading shoot. The foliage is flattened and scale-like, light green suffused yellow, coppery in winter. H1.2-1.5m/4-5ft, W1.2-1.5m/4-5ft. Z6-8.

TSUGA Hemlock

The hemlocks are a genus of ten species confined to North America and South-east

Thuja plicata 'Rogersii'

Asia. In the wild they are mostly medium or tall, graceful, stately trees, pyramidal in habit. The branches and branchlets are slender and mostly arching or pendulous, the leaves and cones quite small. They are not always easy to grow or establish, requiring a moist but freely drained, preferably acid soil. They succeed well in full or part shade where moist and need shelter from wind when young, even though the species listed here are perfectly frost-hardy.

T. canadensis. The Canadian hemlock, or eastern hemlock, provides numerous cultivars, mostly raised in the USA, but the species is also a valuable ornamental. A tall, graceful tree, often forked at the base into two main stems, it has spreading branches with thin, pendulous branchlets, each with a spaced row of glossy green leaves, silvery banded beneath, either side. Remarks for *Tsuga* apply, though this species and its cultivars tolerate lime, as long as general soil and cultural needs are met. H4-6m/13-20ft, W2.1-3m/7-10ft. Z5.

Cultivars vary from miniatures to slow-growing types, upright, spreading and tall, most but not all with green foliage. Many are improved by pruning, important in small gardens. Most Z4-8. '**Albospica**' slowly makes a pyramid of arching branches, the new shoots white, retaining colour well into winter. Pruning medium-growing, white-tipped forms creates more shoots and a more compact, much brighter bush. Best in light shade. H1.5-1.8m/5-6ft, W60-90cm/2-3ft. Z4-8. '**Armistice**', one of the most attractive selections, starts dense and low-growing, later forming a conical outline with stiff,

Tsuga canadensis 'Cole's Prostrate'

Tsuga canadensis 'Minuta'

Tsuga canadensis 'Jeddeloh'

horizontally tiered branches. Glossy green leaves. H30-45cm/12-18in, W45-60cm/18-24in. Z4-8. **'Bennett'** (syn. 'Bennett's Minima' and 'Minima'), an older variety, makes a low, dark green bush, wider than it is high, the branchlet tips gracefully pendulous. H30-45cm/12-18in, W60-90cm/2-3ft. Z4-8. **'Cappy's Choice'** is a compact, ground-hugging form, at least when young, with thin, pendulous branch tips, the leaves light green, reputedly with a hint of gold. Best in light shade. H10-15cm/4-6in, W45-60cm/18-24in. Z4-8. **'Cole's Prostrate'**, a ground-hugging selection, makes a dense carpet before gradually forming a low mound, the bare central stems or trunk often picturesque later. Ideal for a bank, slope or over a rock, or a patio container in shade. Dark green leaves. Barely distinct from **'Prostrata'**, which is flatter, and older specimens of which do not form the central bare branches. H10-15cm/4-6in, W60-90cm/2-3ft. Z4-8.

'Everitt Golden' (syn. 'Aurea Compacta') very slowly forms an upright bush, and eventually a small tree, with upright, stiff branches, the small leaves golden-yellow all year round. Colours best in full sun but prone to damage from drying winds. H45-60cm/18-24in, W30cm/1ft. Z4-8. **'Gentsch White'**, slow-growing and bushy, has dark green foliage at its centre but the new season's brown stems bear startling white leaves. Trim annually once well established. **'Dwarf Whitetip'** is similar. H60-90cm/2-3ft, W60-90cm/2-3ft. Z4-8. **'Hussii'** is very slow when young but eventually forms a small tree of irregular, open, upright habit, with no leading shoot. Sturdy, light brown branches, short and twiggy branchlets, dark green leaves, silvery beneath. H60-75cm/24-30in, W30cm/1ft. Z4-8. **'Jeddeloh'**, the most popular form in Europe, is dwarf and spreading, with a nest-like centre. It has light, fresh-green foliage, slightly raised branches and branchlets gracefully drooping at the tips. H30-45cm/12-18in, W45-60cm /18-24in. Z4-8. **'Lewis'** slowly forms an irregular, eventually pyramidal bush, with rigid, twisting branches. Dark green, glossy leaves, bright silvery blue beneath. H60-90cm/2-3ft, W30-45cm/12-18in. Z4-8. **'Minuta'**, one of the slowest hemlocks, grows 2cm/³/4in or so a year, forming a congested,

globe-shaped bush, with rigid branches and branchlets, clothed in clusters of minute, deep green leaves. Prominent, light brown buds. Perfect for troughs and sinks. H10-15cm/4-6in, W10-15cm/4-6in. Z4-8.

'Pendula' eventually assumes large proportions but, unless trained up when young, begins as a prostrate spreader, gradually building height, with long, overlapping branches. Impressive on a bank, over a rock or wall, or as a large specimen in a lawn, with branches cascading down from any height provided. Annual growth rate 15-20cm/6-8in or more when established. Takes pruning well. Z4-8. **'Rugg's Washington Dwarf'** is cushion-shaped and very slow-growing, with dense, soft foliage. Its mid-green leaves are tinged bronze-yellow and it has distinctive, cinnamon-brown curved winter shoots. H10-15cm/4-6in, W15-30cm/6-12in. Z4-8. **'Verkade's Recurved'** is similar to **'Curly'**, though the latter is apparently more vigorous. Both have upward-spreading, twisted, rigid branches, very brittle and easily damaged. The terminal shoot and rows of deep glossy green leaves, brightly silver underneath, curve downwards. H60-75cm/24-30in, W30-45cm/12-18in. Z4-8.

T. mertensiana. The mountain hemlock originates in western North America and, unlike other species, which have leaves in two rows either side of the branchlets, has narrower leaves radially arranged around the stems, and larger cones. It is very hardy, growing high in the Oregon Cascade Mountains, but in cultivation prefers moist, lowland conditions. Slow-growing when young, it attains 18m/60ft or more, making a narrow spire with short, weeping side branches. H1.5-1.8m/5-6ft, W60-75cm/24-30in. Z6-8. **'Blue Star'**, raised in Holland, has bright silver-blue foliage, particularly in summer, and gradually forms a narrow pyramid of gently pendulous branches. **'Glauca'** is similar but may be more variable, with nurserymen perhaps offering selected seedlings with glaucous foliage rather than a distinct cultivar. Whatever its parentage, if you can grow a glaucous form well, it will be a continuing source of enjoyment. 'Blue Star': H75-120cm/30-48in, W30-60cm/1-2ft. Z6-8. **'Elizabeth'**, an American form, is low and spreading, its branches arching gracefully upwards at a slight angle, the branchlets densely clothed in soft blue-grey leaves, brighter in summer than winter. Regrettably hard to propagate. H30-45cm/12-18in, W60-90cm/2-3ft. Z6-8.

SMALL BED OF DWARF CONIFERS

Dwarf conifers can make attractive features planted on their own, with their different colours and shapes providing year-round interest. This planting includes a few dwarf conifers with this in mind, but some dwarf shrubs and alpines are also added to create variety and provide extra colour through the seasons. The lower-growing alpines contrast in both colour and foliage with the conifers and the coppery foliaged dwarf *Berberis*. Dwarf bulbs could also be planted to give early colour. The combinations and possibilities are almost endless, but the bed shown here might be ideal for an open, well-drained situation, perhaps on a slight slope. The conifers may need pruning after a few years to restrict their size, and this is best done in late spring. The peak period of interest is spring to midsummer, but this bed will never be dull.

1 *Campanula carpatica* 'Blue Moonlight' (×5)
2 *Berberis thunbergii* 'Bagatelle' (×1)
3 *Pinus contorta* 'Spaan's Dwarf' (×1)
4 *Artemisia schmidtiana* 'Nana' (×3)
5 *Picea pungens* 'Globosa' (×1)
6 *Chamaecyparis obtusa* 'Nana Lutea' (×1)
7 *Geranium sanguineum* 'Shepherd's Warning' (×3)
8 *Juniperus communis* 'Green Carpet' (×1)

Area required:
approx. 2.5 sq. m/2½ sq. yd

Conifers for Seasonal Colour

This relatively mature planting of conifers shows the versatility and range of colours and textures of this group of plants. Shapes vary from upright to prostrate and semi-prostrate, and the colours range from blue and green to gold. The conifers are shown here in their winter colours, but they can change considerably in the summer. The *Pinus*, for example, becomes green in summer; the semi-prostrate *Juniper* × *media* 'Gold Coast' remains bright all year; and the *Microbiota* turns bright green in summer. These conifers are shown at about six to seven years old, the plants having knitted together since they were put in three or four years earlier. This is an easy-to-maintain border, although some pruning may be necessary to keep the balance. All the plants prefer sun and good drainage. This bed is equally effective all year round.

1 *Microbiota decussata* (× 5)
2 *Juniperus × media* 'Gold Coast' (× 1)
3 *Picea pungens* 'Thomsen' (× 1)
4 *Juniperus horizontalis* 'Blue Chip' (× 5)
5 *Thuja occidentalis* 'Smaragd' (× 1)
6 *Pinus mugo* 'Wintergold' (× 1)
7 *Juniperus procumbens* 'Nana' (× 3)

Area required:
approx. 5 sq. m/5 sq. yd

CONIFER WINDBREAK FOR YEAR-ROUND INTEREST

Given the wide range of taller-growing conifers available, it seems a pity to see so many hedges and screens of only one type. A screen, of course, requires much more space than a hedge, and certainly space would be needed for this planting to allow full development of the individual specimens. Those shown here are about ten years old, and the space between each one varies from 1 to 2 metres. These conifers will provide a marvellous variety of colour, form and texture the year round and, once established, will act as an effective windbreak. They can also be used as a backcloth to the garden, planted in grass, or as a background to other plants. They will grow well in most reasonable soils. The peak period of interest is spring, but these will be attractive all year.

1 *Pinus sylvestris* 'Aurea' (× 1)
2 *Picea omorika* (× 1)
3 *Thuja plicata* 'Atrovirens' (× 3)
4 *Picea pungens* 'Hoopsii' (× 1)
5 *Chamaecyparis lawsoniana* 'Howarths Gold' (× 1)
6 *Picea engelmannii* 'Glauca' (× 1)
7 *Abies koreana* (× 1)

Area required:
approx. 7 × 20 m/23 × 65 ft

CONIFERS

191

HEATHS
& HEATHERS

For those who can grow them successfully, heaths and heathers are excellent evergreen shrubs with year-round foliage colour and a flowering period of practically twelve months. They also combine admirably with conifers, ideal for a relatively trouble-free garden with year-round appeal. Lastly, for those living in countries with long and often miserable winters, heathers can be the delightful unifying ingredient in a winter garden.

It has been said that heathers and dwarf conifers are rather static plants, whose appearance is much the same the year round, and that having a garden with heathers and dwarf conifers is not 'gardening' in the true sense of the word. My answer is that while 10-20 per cent of those who garden may be keen, most people would be only too glad to have a garden which looked equally attractive summer and winter. Nor am I suggesting that one should plant *only* heaths, heathers and dwarf conifers – there are so many other good plants that can make a more interesting seasonal garden – but where heathers can be successfully grown, any garden is poorer without them.

The botanical name for heath is *Erica*; the closely related *Calluna vulgaris* is the heather. It can get confusing, but for the ordinary gardener it does not really matter. The heaths are a much larger genus, and though most of the several hundred species originate from South Africa, and are tender, the fifteen or so European species offer a varied choice. The European species range from *Erica arborea*, the tree heath, which surrounds the Mediterranean, to *E. cinerea*, the bell heather, native to Britain and north-west Europe and found often on cliffs and near the sea, to *E. carnea*, the winter heath, the hardiest of all, from the European Alps. The common ling, or heather, *Calluna vulgaris*, grows wild all over Europe, from Iceland to Norway, the British Isles and the northern Mediterranean. It is an adaptable, hardy shrub, surviving severe frosts, salt spray and even recovering when burnt to the ground by fires. For simplification from now on I shall refer to both *Erica* and *Calluna* as heathers.

This view of Adrian Bloom's garden in March shows two drifts of contrasting heaths – the white *Erica erigena* 'W.T. Rackliff' in the foreground with *Erica carnea* 'Myretoun Ruby' behind. *Thuja occidentalis* 'Holmstrup' provides the vertical balance

HEATHERS AS GARDEN PLANTS

As with most plants, it was not until selections were made in the wild and adapted for gardens that most people became aware of the possibilities of heathers. Self-sown seedlings with different form or colour from the common species were discovered in the mountains or moorlands. Once brought into cultivation, more seedlings or shoot mutations were discovered in nurseries and gardens, leading to an even wider selection. The absolute explosion of new *Calluna vulgaris* cultivars started in the 1950s and during the past thirty years hundreds of new varieties have been introduced, with the inevitable result that far too many similar cultivars were named and distributed.

But what an amazing variety there is! We have now not only an extremely broad range of flower colours but a tremendous selection of colourful foliage – shades of green, bronze, yellow, gold, orange, red, grey and silver, which often change with the seasons and in sunny situations light up the winter garden. They look best planted in groups or drifts, though for small gardens one plant each of a few varieties could become a feature. Though generally best planted in open, sunny spots, most tolerate shade where not too dry, although they will not produce such a profusion of bloom nor such colourful foliage. Heathers can be used as ground cover, in the open, on banks or under trees, but again where not too dry. They are useful as frontal groups to shrub beds or borders, or as edging for paths. Smaller-growing cultivars are ideal in rock gardens with alpines or other dwarf shrubs. They can even be used in window boxes and, of course, in raised beds.

One of the most effective associations is with slower-growing conifers, whose various forms, textures and colours contrast dramatically with heathers. Shrubs, such as rhododendrons, azaleas, pieris, potentillas or spireas, give extra variety as well as height to the mostly low-growing heathers. Ornamental grasses associate well, too, providing height, movement, contrast and texture. Heathers can provide almost twelve months of continuous flower: *Erica carnea* and *E.* × *darleyensis* types during the winter, *E. erigena* and *E. arborea* in the spring, then a short lull before *E. cinerea*, *Calluna vulgaris* and *E. vagans* carry right through from early summer until late autumn.

Heathers can succeed for many years in suitable conditions: twenty years or more is not uncommon.

Some heather problems

Nearly all summer-flowering heathers, including *Calluna vulgaris* cultivars, require acid soil. The only summer-flowering species which tolerates some alkalinity is *Erica vagans*, the Cornish heath, although most winter- and spring-flowering heathers, among the most

A group of lings, *Calluna vulgaris*, creates colourful ground cover between conifers, backed by taller shrubs and more conifers. The pink *Calluna* in the centre is *C. vulgaris* 'H. E. Beale'

valuable, tolerate some lime. An ideal pH for growing most acid-loving plants is 5.5 to 6.5 (neutral being pH 7, and alkaline above that). It would be a big task to reduce the pH or soil alkalinity for a large area but worth doing on a small scale (see below). You could also use an acid compost in a raised bed for growing summer-flowering heathers and other acid-loving plants.

Other fairly basic problems, less easily overcome, are summer heat and winter cold. Those that adapt well to the former, such as *E. australis* and *E. lusitanica*, are likely to suffer under the latter, and those that are winter-hardy, such as *E. carnea*, suffer in extreme heat, high humidity and drought. All suffer from dry, desiccating winds, especially during severe frosts with no snow cover. Occasionally these conditions occur in Britain, but in the north-eastern USA they occur readily. I have seen good collections in Pennsylvania and Long Island, where severe winters occur, but there it is customary to cover heathers during the worst of the winter with bracken, pine branches or a light scattering of hay. The term 'trouble-free' is relative, and with heathers it is a combination of careful planning, selection, commitment and perhaps luck that determines your success.

Conifers and heathers in close-up. The Cornish heath, *Erica vagans* 'Mrs D. F. Maxwell', and *Erica carnea* 'Westwood Yellow' create a pleasing combination with the needles of *Picea pungens* 'Globosa', the dwarf Colorado blue spruce

SOME CULTURAL ADVICE

Know whether your garden soil is acid or alkaline. Alkaline soils restrict the range of plants that can be grown, since summer-flowering heathers do not tolerate lime.

Reducing the alkalinity of soil

An efficient, relatively inexpensive method of reducing the alkalinity or high pH level in your soil is to incorporate flowers of sulphur. This is commonly used as a fungicide and is available from some garden centres and chemists. It is not a fertilizer or soil conditioner; if these are needed, they can be added at the same time or separately.

You must first find out the pH of your soil, either by seeking professional advice from a garden centre or horticultural specialist, or by using a simple pH soil tester. If the pH is a neutral 7 or above, reduce the pH by at least 1 to make it acid. To reduce the pH by 1, use 60g of flowers of sulphur per square metre/2oz per square yard; and by 2, use 120g per square metre/4oz per square yard. If the original pH is higher, increase the application as required.

Thoroughly dig and prepare the area to a depth of 30cm/1ft and rake to a reasonable tilth. Mark out the area in square metres or yards, using string or canes. Weigh out the correct amount of flowers of sulphur to cover 1 square metre or yard at a time into a large pepperpot or a tin or jar with holes in the top. On a windless day, shake the powder to cover the square metre or yard evenly and rake into the surface. Water in thoroughly. It is safe to plant in the soil within a few days if required. Remember to wear gloves when handling the product and avoid breathing the dust.

Within a year the pH should be reduced to the required level and should remain so for some time, though if the alkaline soil surrounding the plot raises the pH, the process can be repeated around the plant roots. If your plant has roots which reach 60cm/2ft into the ground, you may have to add more flowers of sulphur into well-prepared soil, to the depth required. Continue to mulch with acid compost and, if necessary, more flowers of sulphur in later years.

Planting

Thorough soil preparation is essential. Perennial weeds must be eradicated by spraying, digging, or both. In the case of clay or heavy soils, add sharp sand and well-rotted compost, leaf mould or composted bark to the soil; use peat only if there is no substitute available. These materials assist water retention on sandy soils, too. Heathers dislike their fine roots compacted, so good aeration is essential.

A planting distance of 30-45cm/12-18in suits most heathers, though the stronger-growing *E. × darleyensis* and *E. erigena* types might need 60-75cm/24-30in. Leave at least 60cm/2ft around conifers or shrubs. This spacing should give complete ground cover within three years.

Plant whenever soil conditions are reasonable, though early autumn or late spring is ideal. Most heathers are container-grown so thoroughly soak them, then drain immediately before planting. Most are grown in non-soil composts, so add a handful or two of moist, peaty or similar material to surround the roots. Firm gently. Ideally, mulch with sterile leaf mould or composted bark, both of which are acid, to assist root development and keep down annual weeds. Water during extended dry spells in the first summer at least.

Aftercare and pruning

After planting, water and hand weed as necessary. After the first year's growth, consider pruning. Do not prune winter-flowering heathers for a few years, until they get untidy, but summer-flowering types need annual pruning with secateurs or shears. Prune in early to mid-spring, at the first signs of growth; pruning in autumn and winter may cause weather damage to the severed shoots, and the dead flower heads on many summer-flowering heathers are attractive through the winter.

Trim dead flowering stems by between a third and a half. Better to prune too little than too much, since pruning too low into old wood may prevent the plant making new shoots. Pruning keeps plants looking young, healthy and vigorous, and produces better flowers and foliage.

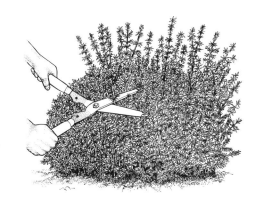

Pruning summer-flowering heathers

HEATHS & HEATHERS DIRECTORY

As a guide to planting densities, the approximate widths of heathers after only 3-4 years are given, this being the period within which plants will have matted together.

Key

H: Approximate height after 8-10 years
W: Approximate width after 3-4 years
F: Months in flower
Z: Relevant hardiness zone(s)

CALLUNA Common heather, ling
C. vulgaris. This grows wild throughout Britain and many parts of Europe, on open moorlands, in hilly and mountainous regions, and on heathland and breckland, on acid soils whether peat, clay or sand. Hundreds of cultivars have been selected and introduced in recent years, with an amazing range of colours, shapes and sizes. Prune all except the dwarfest and very prostrate types in early to mid-spring, before growth really begins. All flowers are single unless otherwise stated. All Z5-7.

Var. *alba.* Almost any wild white form with single flowers could be called 'lucky white heather', though this is normally associated with plants in Scotland. They can be variable in habit. The cultivars

'**Alba Carlton**', '**Alba Elata**' and '**Alba Elegans**' are all fine for garden use. H45-60cm/18-24in, W50cm/20in. F8-9. '**Alba Minor**' is low-growing, with bright green foliage and a profusion of small sprays of white flowers. H15cm/6in, W25cm/10in. F7-9. '**Alba Plena**', the first double-flowered white, can be unreliable, often producing single flowers and sometimes reverting completely to single when old. Long spikes of pure white flowers, fresh-green foliage. H30-45cm/12-18in, W30cm/1ft. F8-10. '**Alba Rigida**', a distinct dwarf form, has bright green foliage. H15cm/6in, W25cm/10in. F8-9. '**Allegro**', recently introduced from Germany, has a profusion of deep red flowers and dark green foliage. H45-60cm/18-24in, W45cm/18in. F8-10. '**Alportii**', going back to 1838, has deep crimson-purple flowers on deep green, upright foliage. Perhaps now superseded by 'Darkness' and 'Allegro'. H60-75cm/24-30in, W50cm/20in. F8-9.

'**Anne Marie**', from Germany, has a bushy habit and dark green foliage. Flowers open bright pink, gradually deepening to brilliant carmine-rose. H23-30cm/9-12in, W45cm/18in. F8-11. More compact than the similar '**Schurig's Sensation**', a first-

class heather with a long flowering period. F8-11. The light, grey-green foliage of '**Anthony Davis**' provides an unusual background to masses of white flowers. H30-45cm/12-18in, W45cm/18in. F8-9. '**Barnett Anley**', with its compact, bushy habit, has long spikes densely packed with soft purple flowers. A robust grower. H45cm/18in, W40cm/16in. F8-10. '**Beoley Gold**', one of the best yellow-foliaged cultivars, was introduced by J. W. Sparkes from Birmingham, England, who was responsible for many outstanding heather introductions in the 1950s and 1960s. 'Beoley Gold' makes a bushy plant with bright yellow, year-round foliage, and contrasting white flowers. H30-45cm/12-18in, W45cm/18in. F8-9. '**Gold Haze**' is similar but duller in winter. '**Blazeaway**' is a robust cultivar with bronze-yellow summer foliage, bright bronze-red in winter, colouring in an exposed sunny spot. Freely produced but modest light lilac-purple flowers. H45cm/18in, W45cm/18in. F8-9. '**Boskoop**' was raised on and named after the famous Dutch nursery centre. Has superb, dense, feathery foliage, golden-orange in summer, bronze-red in winter. Light mauve-purple flowers. H30-45cm/12-18in, W45cm/18in. F8-9.

'**County Wicklow**' is an old but worthwhile cultivar, with a compact, mounded habit, and dainty spikes of fully double, bright shell-pink flowers. H23-30cm/9-12in, W35cm/14in. F8-9. '**Darkness**' has erect stems of dark green foliage and bright crimson flowers. Compact habit. H30-45cm/12-18in, W40cm/16in. F8-10. '**Foxii Nana**', a real miniature, is grown more for its bun shape than for the occasional, sparse purple flowers. Ideal for the rock garden. H10-15cm/4-6in, W20cm/8in. F8-9. '**Golden Carpet**' was introduced by Mr and Mrs John F. Letts, who owned a magnificent garden in Surrey, England, the source of several first-class heather cultivars. 'Golden Carpet', a seedling discovery, makes a low, prostrate mat of golden-yellow foliage, tinged bronze and red in winter. Mauve flowers often sparse. H10cm/4in, W40cm/16in. F8-9. The very similar '**John F. Letts**' was introduced later.

'**Golden Feather**', a first-class foliage form, has bright gold, feathery summer foliage, turning reddish orange in winter. Needs an open, well-drained position. Occasional mauve flowers. H30-45cm/12-18in, W45cm/18in. F8-10. '**H. E. Beale**', introduced by the heather specialists Maxwell and Beale Nurseries in England in about 1926, soon became one of the most popular flowering heathers. Vigorous, with strong, erect spikes of soft, double, silver-pink flowers lasting for weeks. H30-45cm/12-18in, W50cm/20in. F9-11. '**Elsie Purnell**' is similar but flowers a little later.

Calluna vulgaris 'Anne Marie'

Calluna vulgaris 'Golden Feather'

Calluna vulgaris 'H.E. Beale' (top) and 'My Dream' (bottom)

Excellent for cutting and drying. H45-60cm/18-24in, W50cm/20in. F9-11.
'Humpty Dumpty', a curiosity, makes a dense, irregular, miniature bush with bright moss-green foliage. Very occasional white flowers on old plants. H15-20cm/6-8in, W20cm/8in. F8-9. **'J. H. Hamilton'**, introduced in 1935, remains distinct, with its compact habit, thin foliage and masses of early, double pink flowers. H20-30cm/8-12in, W30cm/1ft. F7-9. **'Kinlochruel'**, discovered in Argyll, Scotland, as a sport on 'County Wicklow', is bushy, with short spikes of white, double flowers. H20-30cm/8-12in, W30cm/1ft. F8-9.

'Mair's Variety', a free-flowering, taller cultivar, has long spikes of white flowers. Good for cutting and flower arranging. Trim regularly. H60-75cm/24-30in, W50cm/20in. F8-9. **'Mrs Pat'**, though weak, is a great foliage plant, with delicate shoots brightly tipped pink most of the year and sometimes deeper coral or red. Insignificant lavender flowers. H20-30cm/8-12in, W30cm/1ft. F9-10. **'Mrs Ronald Gray'**, of slow-growing, prostrate habit, hugs the ground. Dark green foliage, twiggy shoots bearing purple flowers. Ideal for the rock garden, but needs good drainage. H5cm/2in, W25cm/10in. F8-9. **'Mullion'**, like the preceding cultivar, was introduced over fifty years ago by Maxwell and Beale in Dorset, England. Dense, compact, semi-prostrate habit with short, sturdy spikes of deep mauve-purple flowers. **'Roma'** is similar. H20-30cm/8-12in, W35cm/14in. F8-9. **'Multicolor'** (syn. 'Prairie Fire'), of American origin, has orange, yellow, bronze and red foliage at different times of the year. Cut away any shoots reverting to green. Modest purple flowers, which if allowed to seed produce green-foliaged plants. H15-20cm/6-8in, W35cm/14in. F8-9. **'My Dream'** is an ideal counterpart to 'H. E. Beale', from which it originated as a sport in a garden in Warwickshire, England. Erect spikes bear masses of brilliant white flowers, often tinged pink in autumn. Attractive winter stems. Can be unreliable. H45-60cm/18-24in, W45cm/18in. F9-10.

'Orange Queen' has bushy growth, golden-yellow in spring, more orange in summer, deeper in winter. Lavender flowers. H30-45cm/12-18in, W40cm/16in. F8-9. **'Peter Sparkes'** is similar to 'H. E. Beale', but with much deeper, double pink flowers on sturdy erect spikes. H45-60cm/18-24in, W45cm/18in. F9-10. **'Robert Chapman'**, one of the most popular foliage cultivars, changes from gold to yellow, orange to bronze and red. Lower winter temperatures enhance the colour intensity. Purple flowers. H30-45cm/12-18in, W45cm/18in. F8-9. **'Silver Knight'** provides ideal contrast to greens, yellows and golds, making an erectly branched bush

Calluna vulgaris 'Robert Chapman'

with silvery grey, woolly foliage, and lavender-pink flowers. H30cm/1ft, W40cm/16in. F8-9. **'Silver Queen'** has bushy, hairy, spreading foliage, distinctly silver-grey, making a fine contrast to its purple flowers. Not easy to grow, but beautiful at its best. H30-45cm/12-18in, W45cm/18in. F8-9.

The upright stems of **'Silver Rose'** are covered with silver, grey-green foliage and bright rose-pink flowers. H45cm/18in, W50cm/20in. F8-9. **'Sir John Charrington'**, arguably the best foliage cultivar and named after the first president of the British Heather Society, is compact and bushy with golden-yellow foliage, orange with bright red and crimson tips in winter. Excellent in bloom, with short spikes of crimson flowers. H30-45cm/12-18in, W40cm/16in. F8-9. **'Sister Anne'** (syn. 'Hirsuta Compacta') is dwarfish, with woolly, grey-green foliage, almost prostrate, though building up with age. Mauve-pink flowers. Similar to **'Dainty Bess'**. Both need good drainage. H10-15cm/4-6in, W25cm/10in. F8-9. The green foliage of **'Spring Cream'** is tipped cream in spring and is followed by white flowers. H45cm/18in, W30cm/1ft. F8-10. Two other selections made for their spring foliage colour, and like 'Spring Cream' needing full sun and regular pruning, are **'Spring Glow'** and **'Spring Torch'**. 'Spring Glow' has pink and red tips but dull lilac flowers; 'Spring Torch' is similar but more compact. Both H45-60cm/18-24in, W30cm/1ft. F8-10. **'Sunset'**, an excellent foliage cultivar, makes a broad, spreading bush of golden-yellow in spring, orange in summer and bronze-red in winter. Lilac-pink flowers. H30cm/1ft, W40cm/16in. F8-9. **'White Lawn'** has a flat, ground-hugging

habit, bright green foliage and masses of white flowers. H5-8cm/2-3in, W35cm/14in. F8-9. **'Wickwar Flame'**, with bright orange-yellow foliage in summer, turns bright crimson-red in winter. Lavender flowers. H30cm/1ft, W40cm/16in. F8-10.

DABOECIA Irish bell heather

D. cantabrica. Though commonly called Irish bell heather (and also known as St Dabeoc's heath), this is native to northern Spain and Portugal as well as north-west Ireland. Some of the selected cultivars are

Calluna vulgaris 'Kinlochruel'

Calluna vulgaris 'Silver Rose'

Daboecia × *scotica* 'Jack Drake'

Daboecia × *scotica* 'William Buchanan'

Erica carnea 'Eileen Porter'

reasonably hardy, surviving temperatures as low as –15°C/5°F for short periods, but generally these plants prefer a mild, moist climate, resenting drought almost as much as severe frost. Where they can be grown they offer a contrast to other heathers, with their long flowering period, glossy green leaves and bell-shaped flowers. Though best in sun, they tolerate light shade as long as sufficient moisture is available to the roots. Stronger-growing cultivars can get straggly with age and should be pruned each year. Either lightly prune once the flowers have finished in late autumn, then more severely in spring, or, preferably, leave it all until spring. All Z7.

'Alba' may cover more than one form but all have bright, glossy green foliage and almost continuous white bell flowers from midsummer to winter. May self-seed pink. H45-60cm/18-24in, W45cm/18in. F6-11. 'Alba Globosa' is similar but dwarfer and more spreading, with rounded flowers. One of the hardiest and most reliable is 'Atropurpurea', with bronze-green leaves and rich purple flowers. H60cm/2ft, W50cm/20in. F6-10. 'Donard Pink' is actually white, washed with pale pink, but still distinct and very

free-flowering. H60cm/2ft, W40cm/16in. F6-10. 'Hookstone Purple' is strong-growing, with profuse, large, bright purple flowers. H60cm/2ft, W40cm/16in. F6-11. 'Snowdrift' has bright green foliage and masses of white bell flowers. H45cm/18in, W45cm/18in. F6-10. A recent Spanish introduction, 'White Carpet', is only 15cm/6in high and 30cm/1ft wide. F8-9.

D. × *scotica*. 'Jack Drake' is a dwarf, with small, dark green glossy leaves and deep ruby-red bell flowers. H10-15cm/4-6in, W25cm/10in. F5-8. Z7. 'William Buchanan', one of several dwarf hybrids between *D. azorica*, the Azores heath, and *D. cantabrica*, bears glossy green leaves and masses of crimson flowers. One of the hardiest of the *Daboecia* cultivars. H30cm/1ft, W30cm/1ft. F5-10. Z7.

ERICA Heath

E. carnea (syn. *E. herbacea*). The winter heaths are among the most valuable garden plants. Native to the European Alps, they are hardy and adapt to a wide range of conditions, growing successfully on alkaline and acid soils. Most cultivars are low-growing with a bushy or spreading habit,

and flower from late autumn to late spring, some lasting several months. Flowers often appear gradually before the plant is at its peak. Flowering is usually more profuse and foliage colour brightest in full sun, but many cultivars grow reasonably well in shade. Like most heathers, they dislike compacted, badly drained soils. The many new introductions allow gardeners on alkaline soils to enjoy brightly coloured foliage previously only provided by summer-flowering types. Very few of the winter heaths need pruning, except to prevent them spreading into other plants or to tidy them occasionally. All Z5-7.

'Ann Sparkes', a superb foliage sport of 'Vivellii', slowly makes a compact bush of deep orange-yellow foliage, tipped bronze-red. Deep carmine-red flowers. Similar to 'Vivellii Aurea'. H15cm/6in, W25cm/10in. F2-4. 'Aurea', though perhaps surpassed by 'Foxhollow' as a foliage plant, is a good all-rounder, with golden-yellow leaves, bronze-tinted in winter, and deep pink flowers. H23-30cm/9-12in, W35cm/14in. F2-4. 'Carnea'. One of the best for ground cover under trees, though fewer flowers produced there than in full sun. Bright green foliage and masses of bright pink flowers. H25-30cm/10-12in, W35cm/14in. F2-4. 'Eileen Porter', though reputedly less hardy than some, has endured temperatures of –20°C/–4°F in my garden. For length of flowering period it still out-performs all others. Rich carmine flowers, producing a bicoloured effect. H15-20cm/6-8in, W25cm/10in. F10-5. 'Foxhollow' has a low-growing, spreading habit. It is one of the finest foliage heathers, with brilliant golden-yellow foliage in late spring and summer, deep gold in winter, often flecked with red. In low-lying areas new growth can be caught by late spring frost. The foliage would probably scorch in hot climates. Pale pink flowers rarely borne. H15-25cm/6-10in, W45cm/18in. F2-4. **'Westwood Yellow'** has similar foliage but is more compact and flowers more freely. H15cm/6in, W40cm/16in. F2-4.

'**January Sun**', a recently introduced sport of 'Winter Beauty', and perhaps the most compact winter heath, slowly forms a low mound of bright golden-yellow foliage with occasional pink flowers. Ideal for the alpine garden. H10cm/4in, W25cm/10in. F2-4. '**King George**', an old English cultivar but still one of the best, has a compact, bushy habit, dark green leaves and bright pink flowers, rose-red with age. Always reliable. '**John Kampa**', a recent introduction, has slightly darker flowers. Both H20-25cm/8-10in, W30cm/1ft. F12-3. '**Myretoun Ruby**' produces a magnificent display of deep ruby-red flowers which smother the plant. Dark green foliage. H30cm/1ft, W35cm/14in. F3-4. '**Pink Spangles**', a first-class spreader, carries large, bicoloured, pink and cream flowers, deepening to rose-pink. H20-30cm/8-12in, W35cm/14in. F1-3. '**Praecox Rubra**' has dark green foliage and deep rose-red flowers. Exceptionally early. '**Queen Mary**' is similar. H20-30cm/8-12in, W30cm/1ft. F11-3.

'**Ruby Glow**', though now surpassed perhaps by 'Myretoun Ruby', has a neat, bushy habit, dark green foliage, rich red flowers. H20-30cm/8-12in, W30cm/1ft. F3-4. '**Springwood Pink**', a popular, low-growing, spreading plant, is good ground cover. Pale pink flowers, deepening with age. 'Pink Spangles' may arguably be an improvement. H15-20cm/6-8in, W40cm/16in. F2-3. '**Springwood White**' has never been surpassed since its introduction in 1930, following its discovery on Monte Careggio in Italy by Mrs Ralph Walker from Springwood, Stirling, Scotland. An excellent ground cover with spreading, bright apple-green foliage, rooting as it goes, though it may need curbing next to weaker plants. A mass of pure white blooms smother the plant, hiding the foliage. H20-30cm/8-12in, W60cm/2ft. F2-4. '**Vivellii**' (syn. 'Urville'), attractive for both foliage and flower, has dark, bronze-green foliage, ideal against gold, silver or blue evergreen plants. Deep carmine-red flowers. Found and introduced in Switzerland before 1910. H10cm/4in, W35cm/14in. F2-3.

E. ciliaris. Growing wild in south-west England, western Ireland, western France, Spain and Portugal, the Dorset heath is one of the least hardy European species. It is lime-hating and summer-flowering, preferring moist conditions, though often succeeding

Erica carnea 'Myretoun Ruby'

in drier gardens. Best in sun, but tolerates light shade and has a long flowering period of relatively large, bell-shaped blooms. Most tend to be straggly but with careful pruning of the brittle wood each spring they can be kept in shape. Plants often break from the base following frost damage. All Z8.

'**Aurea**', for a sunny, moist spot protected from cold winds, has golden-yellow foliage often tinted red, brighter in summer. Occasional pink flowers. Can be tricky. H30cm/1ft, W35cm/14in. F7-9. '**Camla**', hardier than some, has coarse green foliage and large purple-pink flowers. H30cm/1ft, W35cm/14in. F7-10. '**Corfe Castle**', one of the best and most reliable, has compact green foliage, bronze-tinged in winter, and clear, salmon-pink flowers. H23-30cm/9-12in, W35cm/14in. F7-10. '**David McClintock**', named after the discoverer, who found it growing wild in Brittany, has bicoloured flowers of white-tipped purple-pink, turning all-pink with age, and grey-green foliage. H30-45cm/12-18in, W35cm/14in. F7-10. '**Stoborough**' is a taller plant with vigorous, erect growth, bright green leaves and large white flowers. H45-60cm/18-24in, W40cm/16in. F7-10. '**White Wings**', with darker green leaves and dwarfer habit, is similar.
E. cinerea. The bell heather is native to the British Isles and Europe, from western Norway to northern Italy, Spain and Portugal. It grows on cliffs by the sea, on moorlands and mountains, surviving with less moisture than most species. Best in sun and needing acid soil, it possesses a long flowering period, as do some of the cultivars. Prune in spring, just as new growth

Erica carnea 'Springwood White'

Erica carnea 'Vivellii'

begins. Most bell heathers resent heavy, compacted and poorly drained soils. All Z7.

'**Alba Minor**' is a compact, bright green plant with short spikes of white flowers. H15cm/6in, W25cm/10in. F6-10. '**Ann Berry**', though less brilliant than some golden-foliaged cultivars, is reliable, with greeny yellow summer foliage, bronzing in winter. Abundant mauve-pink flowers. H20-30cm/8-12in, W35cm/14in. F7-10.

Erica cinerea 'Eden Valley'

Erica cinerea 'Hookstone White'

'Atrosanguinea Smith's Variety', an excellent, free-flowering form, has dark green foliage and intense scarlet flowers, but lacks vigour. H15-20cm/6-8in, W25cm/10in. F6-9. **'C. D. Eason'**, an old but reliable cultivar, is still among the showiest. Erect spikes of dark green leaves and glowing, red-pink flowers. H23-30cm/9-12in, W30cm/1ft. F7-9. **'C. G. Best'**. Introduced by Maxwell and Beale Nurseries in 1931, this popular cultivar is vigorous, producing long spikes of clear salmon-pink flowers. Prune back at least by half each spring. H30cm/1ft, W40cm/16in. F7-8. **'Cindy'** has dark green foliage and large purple flowers. H20-30cm/8-12in, W35cm/14in. F7-10.

'Eden Valley', found near Penzance in Cornwall, England, over fifty years ago, is bushy and compact, with soft lavender and white bicoloured flowers. H15-20cm/6-8in, W25cm/10in. F7-10. **'Foxhollow Mahogany'** has deep green foliage and an abundant show of unusual, rich mahogany-red flowers. H25-30cm/10-12in, W35cm/14in. F7-9. **'Golden Drop'**, perhaps the first introduced with golden foliage, has been overtaken by more easily grown cultivars. Slow to make a compact mound of foliage. Copper-orange in spring and summer, reddish orange in winter. Occasional mauve-pink flowers. Needs good drainage. H15-20cm/6-8in, W25cm/10in. F7-8. **'Hookstone White'**, vigorous and reliable, has light green, straggly foliage, but a profusion of white flowers. Prune well in spring. **'Hookstone Lavender'** is similar but with pale lavender flowers. H30-45cm/12-18in, W40cm/16in.

F7-10. **'Lavender Lady'** has light green foliage and delicate, pale lavender flowers. Compact. H20-30cm/8-12in, W25cm/10in. F7-9. **'My Love'**. A striking selection with dark green leaves and luminous blue-mauve flowers. **'Vivienne Patricia'** has similar, slightly softer coloured flowers. H23-30cm/9-12in, W30cm/1ft. F7-9.

'Pink Ice' makes a low, compact mound of dark green foliage, bronze in winter, with masses of large, bright pink flowers. Light prune only. H23-30cm/9-12in, W25cm/10in. F6-9. **'Purple Beauty'**, one of my favourites, is easy and reliable, with a bushy, spreading habit, dark green foliage and large, bright purple flowers. H30cm/1ft, W40cm/16in. F6-10. **'Rock Pool'**. Low, spreading form, with deep golden-yellow foliage in summer, rich copper-bronze, often with red tints, in winter. Occasional purple-red flowers. Excellent contrast to blue spruce. H15cm/6in, W25cm/10in. F7-9. **'Stephen Davis'** makes a compact bush, with short flower spikes of glowing magenta flowers. H15cm/6in, W25cm/10in. F6-9. **'Velvet Night'**. One of the darkest-flowered bell heathers, its almost black-green foliage and long spikes of deep maroon-purple flowers make a vivid show. Similar and equally striking is **'Katinka'**. H30cm/1ft, W30cm/1ft. F6-9. **'White Dale'**, less vigorous than 'Hookstone White', is a more tidy, delicate-looking plant, with white flowers. H25-30cm/10-12in, W30cm/1ft. F7-9. **'Windlebrooke'** differs from 'Rock Pool' in having brighter yellow foliage in summer, orange-yellow in winter. Purple flowers. H25-30cm/10-12in, W30cm/1ft. F7-9.

Erica × darleyensis 'Furzey'

E. × darleyensis. These first-class cultivars all came from an original cross between *E. carnea* and *E. erigena*. This hybrid, a chance seedling, arose around 1890 on the nursery of James Smith and Sons, Darley Dale, Derbyshire, England, and was named *E. × darleyensis*, later changed to 'Darley Dale'. All cultivars tolerate alkaline soils and are excellent ground cover, in broad drifts or on banks. The group inherited from *E. erigena* taller and more vigorous growth than most *E. carnea* cultivars, but also its lower hardiness tolerance. Prune only to tidy up any unkempt growth, if necessary. New growth often begins while plants are giving a last burst of spring bloom, so you may have to sacrifice some flowers. Many cultivars have attractively coloured spring growths of pink, cream or red. All Z7-8.

'Arthur Johnson', reputedly a hybrid between *E. erigena* 'Glauca' and *E. carnea*, is taller than others, making a looser plant with long, narrow stems, dark green foliage and pink flowers. A superb garden plant and useful for cutting. H60-75cm/24-30in, W60cm/2ft. F11-4. **'Darley Dale'** is still good value, making a robust, spreading bush of dark green with profuse pale mauve-pink flowers, untroubled except by severe frosts. **'George Rendall'** is similar but with darker foliage, bright cream and pink new shoots in spring. H30-45cm/12-18in, W50cm/20in. F12-3. **'Furzey'**. Notable for its very dark, black-green foliage and bright rose-pink flowers. H30-45cm/12-18in, W45cm/18in. F1-4. **'Ghost Hills'** is extremely floriferous, with rose-pink flowers deepening almost to red. Vigorous spreading habit, deep green foliage. H30-45cm/12-18in, W50cm/20in. F11-4. **'J. W. Porter'** quickly makes a dark green, rounded bush topped with bright purple flowers. New spring shoots are bright cream and red. H30-45cm/12-18in, W45cm/18in. F1-4. **'Jack H. Brummage'**, named after its discoverer, has bright golden-yellow foliage in summer in full sun, orange-gold in winter. Foliage colour and bright pink flowers are less good in shade. H30-45cm/12-18in, W40cm/16in. F1-4. **'Silberschmelze'** (syn. 'Molten Silver'), until given this English synonym, appeared under various names such as 'Silver Beads', 'Silver Bells' and 'Silver Mist'. Introduced in 1937 by the famous German nursery of George Arends, its name perhaps reflecting the atmosphere of the Ruhr industrial area! It is similar to 'Darley Dale' but has silvery white, sweetly scented flowers beginning well before Christmas and lasting until after Easter. H30-45cm/12-18in, W50cm/20in. F12-4.

E. erigena. The Irish heath was formerly known as *E. mediterranea*, a misnomer since it originates from western Ireland, the northern Iberian peninsula and south-west France around the Bay of Biscay. Though less hardy than some winter-flowering species, they are useful garden plants, being lime-tolerant and having a long flowering period, with honey-scented blooms. The species varies in height from 60cm/2ft to 2.4m/8ft, though most modern cultivars are compact and bushy. The species can be damaged in severe frosts, and the brittle branches break under the weight of snow, but new growth generally sprouts from the base in spring. Prune away any damaged or dead stems, but if severe damage occurs, start again with fresh stock. All Z8.

'Alba' has bright green foliage and white flowers, but is much less showy than the denser-growing 'W. T. Rackliff'. H75-90cm/30-36in, W35cm/14in. F2-4. **'Brightness'**, with dark green foliage, tinged bronze in winter, has bronze-red winter buds, opening bright purple-red. H60-90cm/2-3ft,

Erica cinerea 'Stephen Davis'

Erica erigena 'Golden Lady'

Erica erigena 'Irish Dusk'

W40cm/16in. F3-5. **'Golden Lady'**, a sport of 'W. T. Rackliff', makes a dense bush of bright yellow, all year round, but is prone to sunscorch in exposed situations. Colours well in light shade. Sparse white flowers. Shoots can revert to green. H45-60cm/18-24in, W35cm/14in. F4-5. **'Irish Dusk'** is compact and bushy with erect branches of dark to mid-green foliage and deep salmon-pink flowers. Older plants can get open and woody. H45-60cm/18-24in, W40cm/16in. F12-5. **'Superba'**, a taller heather, has dark green foliage smothered in honey-scented, rose-pink flowers, though free flowering cannot always be relied on. H1.2-1.8m/4-6ft, W40cm/16in. F3-5. **'W. T. Rackliff'** forms a dense, rounded bush of rich green foliage and white flowers. H60-75cm/24-30in, W40cm/16in. F3-5.

E. herbacea. See *E. carnea*.

E. mackaiana. This acid-loving, dwarf

Erica tetralix 'Pink Star'

species from western Ireland and northern Spain requires moist conditions. It is fairly hardy. Cultivars include **'Dr Ronald Gray'**, white; **'Plena'**, double magenta; and **'William M'Calla'**, deep mauve-pink, the latter having long been grown as the species. All H15cm/6in, W25cm/10in. F7-10. Z8.

E. tetralix. The cross-leaved heath grows wild across northern Europe from Spain to Norway, including the British Isles, and is much hardier than supposed. Its leaves are arranged in fours to make a 'cross' around the stem, hence the name. It prefers reasonable moisture, often inhabiting moors and wet peatlands, but tolerates much drier conditions. It is intolerant of lime. The flowers are held in terminal clusters on erect shoots. Prune in spring by removing old flower heads and a third or so of the stem. On acid soils, it contrasts well with other heathers. All Z6-8.

'Alba Mollis' has silver-grey downy foliage and white flowers. H20-25cm/8-10in, W35cm/14in. F6-9. **'Con Underwood'** forms grey-green hummocks contrasting well with its large crimson flowers. H20-25cm/8-10in, W30cm/1ft. F6-10. The erect stems of **'Hookstone Pink'** bear silver-grey foliage and red flower buds opening to soft pink. H30cm/1ft, W30cm/1ft. F6-10. **'Pink Star'**, perhaps the most impressive cultivar, has soft pink, star-like flowers on compact, silver-grey bushes. H20-25cm/8-10in, W25cm/10in. F6-9.

E. vagans. The Cornish heath is not only a British native but grows wild in western France, Spain and Portugal. Also called wandering heath, from its spreading habit, although most of the cultivars form neat, symmetrical bushes. It tolerates some lime in the soil and prefers sun, though the species and its cultivars will grow in light shade. Old flower heads remain attractive through the winter and though frost damage can occur plants usually sprout from the base in spring. Prune in spring just as new growth begins. All Z7-8.

'Cream' makes a dense bush of bright green foliage and has creamy white flowers. **'Cornish Cream'** is similar but has longer flower spikes. H45cm/18in, W50cm/20in. F8-10. **'Lyonesse'**, introduced by Maxwell

Erica vagans 'Mrs D.F. Maxwell'

Erica arborea 'Albert's Gold'

Erica arborea 'Alpina'

and Beale Nurseries, England, in 1923, continues to be the most popular white. It has light green leaves, with a reliable annual show of white flowers with golden anthers. The buff faded heads are equally attractive. H45cm/18in, W45cm/18in. F8-10. **'Mrs D. F. Maxwell'** has proved itself perhaps the most outstanding of all the cultivars, with a neat, mounded habit, and sprays of deep cerise-pink flowers. H45-60cm/18-24in, W40cm/16in. F8-10. **'St Keverne'**, another old yet still popular cultivar, has clear rose-pink flowers. **'Holden Pink'**, also dwarf, is similar. H30cm/1ft, W35cm/14in. F8-10. **'Valerie Proudley'**, slow-growing, makes a compact, bright yellow bush. Good in light shade; it can scorch in exposed positions. Flowers white but seldom occur. H15-20cm/6-8in, W35cm/14in. F8-9.

ERICA HYBRIDS
I have already described the important *E.* × *darleyensis* and its cultivars, which are among the most popular heaths. Other hybrids are all from summer-flowering species and although some are of garden value, they are mostly of interest to the enthusiast and are probably available only from specialist heather nurseries. *E.* × *praegeri* is a cross

between *E. mackaiana* and *E. tetralix*. There are a few interesting cultivars all 30cm/1ft or less in height. *E.* × *watsonii* is a hybrid between *E. ciliaris* and *E. tetralix*. Most cultivars have lilac-pink flowers and some have bright foliage, particularly in spring. All are 30cm/1ft or less. *E.* × *williamsii* is represented by two interesting hybrids between *E. vagans* and *E. tetralix*, which are tolerant of slightly alkaline soils. Both 'Gwavas' and **'P. D. Williams'** have light yellow-green foliage, bright in spring, with pink flowers. H30cm/1ft, W35cm/14in. F7-10. Z8.

TREE HEATHS
The tree heaths provide the height lacking in most other heathers, and have a flowering period that knits together the late winter- and spring-flowering types with the earliest summer ones. They are generally hardy but in exposed spots and colder regions can suffer damaged or broken foliage. At their best in sunny or partly shaded, sheltered positions, they make magnificent, free-flowering plants, useful for cutting. Some are sweetly scented. Most species are adaptable to acid or alkaline soils.
E. arborea. Native to North Africa and

Mediterranean Europe, this species grows naturally on alkaline soils, in full sun, and can eventually reach 5m/16ft or more, though it rarely does so in cooler climates, where it often suffers winter damage. The species has light green foliage, bushy if trimmed, with white, sweetly scented flowers beloved by bees. All Z8. **'Albert's Gold'**, recently introduced in England, is remarkably hardy, with upright branches and bright golden-yellow foliage, tolerant of cold winds and frost. White flowers a bonus and the ultimate height perhaps 1.5-1.8m/5-6ft, W60-75cm/24-30in. F3-5. It is much brighter than **'Estrella Gold'**, a slow-growing bush with greeny yellow foliage and white flowers. H90-120cm/3-4ft, W60-75cm/24-30in. F3-5. **'Alpina'**, discovered high in the mountains of central Spain in 1872, makes an upright bush with strong, rigid branches, dark green leaves and white, honey-scented flowers, though flowering is not entirely reliable. The hardiest form. H1.5-2.4m/5-8ft, W45cm/18in. F4-5.
E. australis. The southern tree heath, or Spanish heath, originates not in Australia but in Spain, Portugal and Morocco. Best in a warm, sunny, sheltered situation on all but highly alkaline soils. Prone to wind and frost damage but generally recovers from the base. The white-flowered **'Mr Robert'** has light green leaves. Also look for the rare but superb **'Riverslea'**, with larger, deeper rosy red flowers than the species. Except in mild, sheltered areas, they both seldom exceed 1.8m/6ft in height and 40cm/16in in width. Prune away thin, open branches to create a more compact bush, if frost does not do it for you! F4-6. Z9.
E. lusitanica. The tall-growing Portuguese heath, or Spanish heath in the USA, is useful where climate allows, though once established it tolerates –10°C/14°F for short periods. It has an affinity for alkaline soils and flowers from mid-winter to spring, producing tubular, slightly scented blossom, pinkish in bud, opening white, on long spikes. Without frost damage may reach 2.4-3m/8-10ft, W90-120cm/3-4ft. The bright golden foliage of **'George Hunt'** provides a focal point in a sunny, sheltered spot, but it can be as frost-tender as the species. H1.5m/5ft, W60-90cm/2-3ft. F12-4. Z8-9.
E. × *veitchi* **'Exeter'** was discovered on the famous Veitch Nursery at Exeter, England, at the end of the nineteenth century, a hybrid between *E. arborea* and *E. lusitanica*. It has inherited a greater hardiness from the former and the scented flowers from the latter, borne in great profusion. It still requires shelter in early years, but succeeds on acid or alkaline soils. **'Gold Tips'** has few flowers but new growth is orange and yellow. Both make compact bushes. H90-150cm/3-5ft, W45cm/18in. F3-5. Z8-9.

HEATHS AND HEATHERS WITH SHRUBS AND CONIFERS

Where they can be grown successfully, few other plants can give such a long period of interest for so little maintenance as heaths and heathers. Generally they are low-growing plants and need some taller shrubs or conifers to provide structure and contrast. This association combines not only colour and texture in foliage and flower, but also creates variation in height, spread, shape and form. Heaths and heathers mostly require a soil that is free-draining, but neither too wet nor too dry, and the summer-flowering types must have a lime-free soil. All benefit from a generous mulch of weed-free material, such as composted bark. Full sun is best for the plants featured here. The peak period of interest is late summer and spring, but this bed will look good all year round.

1 *Erica carnea* 'Myretoun Ruby' (×5)
2 *Erica vagans* 'Mrs D. F. Maxwell' (×5)
3 *Thuja occidentalis* 'Sunkist' (×1)
4 *Potentilla fruticosa* 'Abbotswood' (×1)
5 *Juniperus chinensis* 'Blue Alps' (×1)
6 *Erica × darleyensis* 'Silberschmelze' (×5)
7 *Calluna vulgaris* 'Boskoop' (×5)
8 *Festuca glauca* (×5)

**Area required:
approx. 4.5 sq. m/4½ sq. yd**

SHRUBS

With the modern trend towards smaller gardens, there is an increasing demand for small or dwarf plants and especially those with a long period of interest. Shrubs can play an indispensable role in providing year-round interest in any garden, however small. Whatever the space you wish to fill, this chapter will help you answer the vital questions of which shrubs to choose and how to grow them.

There is enormous diversity of shape, height, width, flower, foliage and bark among the thousands of species and cultivars available; a bewildering range from which to choose. Shrubs are deciduous or evergreen, multi-stemmed woody plants. Some, such as *Fuchsia*, remain green and shrubby in warm climates, but behave like herbaceous perennials in cold ones. Others, such as *Hypericum*, comprise both choice alpines and hardy vigorous shrubs, whereas hollies include evergreen and deciduous species, as well as dwarf and tree forms. Many species eventually reach tree height, some more quickly than others, depending on climate as much as age. Some grow as little as 10cm/4in high.

Numerous introductions from native species and cultivated forms, plus a tremendous influx of new genera and species from China, Japan and South America during the last 200 years, have formed the basis for the plants we grow today. The great plant hunters of the past risked life and limb to send back plants and seed from far-flung places, for private and public benefactors to grow in botanical gardens and on great estates. Knowing a plant's origins can reveal its needs and hardiness, though continual selection and breeding can produce hardier forms and an even wider range for garden use. In Britain and many parts of Europe and North America, an equable climate allows many exotic plants to grow, if not always thrive. That said, some northern European plants will not tolerate the extremes of temperature or humidity found in much of North America, and many North American plants often flower and fruit less freely in British climates. The hardiness zones in the directory provide a guide to such plants.

This grouping illustrates the importance of foliage in the garden, with the reddish purple *Acer palmatum* 'Garnet' contrasting with *Acer japonicum* 'Aureum', whilst in the distance pink rhododendrons are highlighted against the creamy leaves of *Cornus alternifolia* 'Argentea'

SELECTING SHRUBS AND CLIMBERS

When planning a new garden or changes to an existing plan you can seek advice from a nursery or garden designer, but it is equally possible to draft the planting scheme yourself, perhaps after studying books. Begin by measuring your garden, including the house, and, using graph paper, draw to scale a diagram of the available space. Indicate north, east, south and west, and the direction of the prevailing winds and the coldest, driest winds. Mark the present position of any existing trees, shelter belts, fences or walls, plus areas of sun or shade. Then test your soil to determine the pH value: 7 is neutral, above is alkaline and below acid. A pH of 5.5 to 6.5 accommodates the widest range of plants but there is still an enormous variety of plants for extremely acid or alkaline soils. With heavy clay or dry, sandy soil, certain plants are likely to be unsuitable, but nearly all soils can be improved.

Now the process of selection can begin. First, consider the permanent framework of trees, conifers and shrubs, for feature and background planting. Read books, browse through catalogues, look round gardens and garden centres, concentrating on what suits your garden and tastes. Unless you want and can afford an instant landscape, take your time. It is all too easy to select reliable, familiar shrubs, such as *Forsythia*, rather than unusual, possibly more interesting ones, and there is often an understandable reluctance to part with established shrubs, even if they have become too large for a site or an eyesore.

List options according to defined areas in your garden. Fit plants to the space available, creating focal points with striking plants or plant associations. Informal design offers the most flexibility. Plan shelter for smaller and more tender plants, and shade for both plants and people. Be clear about what space you have, now and in the future. Some magnolias, dogwoods, hazels and hollies can grow large and need careful siting so they can become well-shaped specimens. Plant short-term shrubs or perennials as infill. Balance deciduous and evergreen shrubs to give year-round interest, including some for coloured or variegated foliage and others for flowers. Include climbers, winter-flowering shrubs, those with coloured bark and with scented flowers, and reserve more tender plants for sheltered positions.

Climbing plants

This heading covers mostly woody shrubs which are either natural climbers, such as the vines (*Vitis*) and ivies (*Hedera*), which attach themselves to any support they can find by aerial roots, or twiners,

The winter stems of some of the dogwoods show up particularly well against snow and a blue spruce, *Picea pungens* 'Hoopsii'. The black stems are those of *Cornus alba* 'Kesselringii', the red ones are *Cornus alba* 'Sibirica' and the yellow stems are those of *Cornus stolonifera* 'Flaviramea'

such as *Clematis* and *Wisteria*. The range can be extended by considering shrubs which grow well against walls but which need support, such as *Ceanothus* and *Fremontodendron*. Of course, both climbers and twiners can be used as ground-covering ramblers or scramblers, too, growing not only up walls, pergolas and fences but also up trees and through shrubs. Some of these climbers are indispensable for covering vertical surfaces and for creating a garden with wall-to-wall plants.

However, there are a few basic rules to remember when planting near walls and buildings. If a roof has an overhang, plant roots far enough away from the building to avoid both the underground footing and the narrow strip of ground that might not receive sufficient moisture. Then lean the plant towards the wall and train it in the direction you require. Contrary to popular belief, very few climbers will damage foundations or walls of houses.

Dwarf foliage shrubs provide a long period of interest on this sheltered patio. On the left is *Artemisia* 'Powis Castle', in the centre is *Choisya ternata* 'Sundance', and on the right is *Salvia officinalis* 'Purpurascens'. In the terracotta container is the variegated ground elder, *Aegopodium podagraria* 'Variegatum', here kept in captivity

Buying shrubs

If shrubs are to succeed, you must start with healthy plants. Use a reputable nursery or garden centre. Choose clearly labelled, well-grown, bushy or evenly branched plants, in pots free of weeds. The leaves, if any, should be a healthy colour. You can buy good plants by mail order and sometimes the more unusual are available only by mail from specialists; but again, deal only with reputable firms. Larger, older specimens are of course more expensive than younger equivalents. As with conifers, there are dwarf, slow-growing and large shrubs, an indication of eventual size giving a clue to the plant's age.

SOME CULTURAL ADVICE

Always eradicate perennial weeds and prepare soil as for conifers (see pp. 155-6), although ericaceous shrubs need acid soil with humus, leaf mould or composted bark added, to lighten heavy soils and retain moisture on lighter types. Most shrubs benefit from a generous mulch of composted bark, pine needles or leaf mould to keep roots cool and moist, so that plants can withstand heat and drought. Sun-loving shrubs generally prefer good drainage, so add sharp sand or grit to heavy clay soils and slightly raise the bed for good drainage.

Planting

Most shrubs are sold in containers, though in some countries root-balled (balled and burlapped) plants are available and if well prepared can be established equally successfully. Avoid planting during frosty periods or in waterlogged soil. Depending upon the species, plant in early autumn or from mid-spring onwards, but the later you plant the more aftercare is needed. With few exceptions, plant at the same depth as the top of the soil in the container or rootball. Mix composted bark, well-rotted weed-free compost or leaf mould with soil prior to planting. Water thoroughly after planting, and regularly in hot or dry periods during the first summer, in the evening.

Aftercare

Mulch after planting, particularly shallow- or fibrous-rooted shrubs, thereafter annually or every two years. If shrubs lack colour or vigour, apply a general slow-release fertilizer in early spring at approved rates. Seek advice on this from a garden centre which knows your local conditions. Avoid staking unless necessary, since a healthy plant is best left to establish its own stabilizing root system. If staking, use tree ties, broad hessian (burlap) strips or tape which will not cut into the bark. Some evergreens need protection in their first winter from

Mulching with composted bark

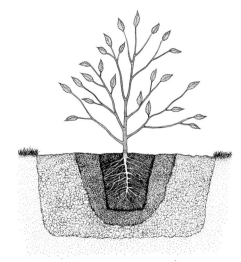

Planting shrubs to the correct depth

SHRUBS

211

Autumn foliage and fruit are provided here by the golden leaves of *Cornus alba* 'Aurea' and *Cotoneaster* 'Hybridus Pendulus', in fruit and creeping over the prostrate conifer *Juniperus squamata* 'Blue Carpet'

cold, drying winds. Drive four sturdy stakes into the ground, and then surround with hessian (burlap), polythene, or close-woven or meshed shade netting to the required height. Though this will not be the prettiest of sights, if you invest in a specimen shrub it pays to give it every chance of success.

OPPOSITE: Few shrubs are more spectacular than the rhododendrons at their peak in late spring and early summer. The colour here is provided in the foreground by deciduous azaleas and in the background by a large-flowered hybrid rhododendron

Pruning

Space allows only guidelines to be offered here. Individual pruning needs are also given under each genus in the directory.

It is, of course, important to have the right tools: at least a reliable pair of shears, sturdy secateurs, and perhaps a pruning saw for larger branches. Wear a thick pair of gloves for protection against thorns.

Shrubs such as *Euonymus*, *Potentilla fruticosa*, *Lavandula*, *Hypericum*, *Santolina* and *Spiraea* should be pruned every two or three years to prevent them becoming untidy or to improve flowering. Shrubs grown for their winter stems, such as *Rubus*, *Cornus* and some *Salix*, need to be pruned annually or biannually in late spring to produce strong shoots for the following winter. Generally, spring-flowering shrubs, such as *Ribes sanguineum* and *Forsythia*, should be pruned back immediately after flowering, enabling them to produce new flowering wood for the following spring. Late-flowering shrubs, such as *Caryopteris*, *Buddleia* and *Perovskia*, should be pruned hard in mid-spring to produce more flowering wood by autumn. Some shrubs, such as *Deutzia*, *Philadelphus* and *Hydrangea*, are pruned by thinning out old wood, while others, such as *Acer negundo* cultivars, can be kept bushy and suitable for the smaller garden by annual shortening of stems in late spring.

Pruning *Buddleia* close to the ground with secateurs

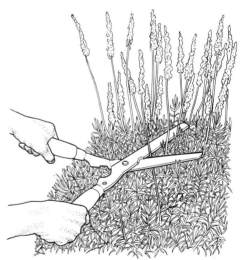

Using a pruning saw to prune *Sambucus*

Removing *Lavender* flower heads with shears

SHRUBS DIRECTORY

The approximate size of each shrub after ten years is given at the end of its description. Remember that geographical situation, climate, soil conditions and pruning affect size, flowering times and sometimes even a plant's appearance. The hardiness zones allocated to each shrub are even more approximate, with local micro-climates, as well as protection provided by sunny walls, providing an exception to every rule.

Key

H: Approximate height after 10 years
W: Approximate width after 10 years
F: Months in flower
Z: Relevant hardiness zone(s)

ABELIA

These deciduous or evergreen flowering shrubs are mostly tender, though some are hardier than supposed. Adaptable to most soils, they tolerate sun or part shade. Those below are evergreen in mild climates, semi-evergreen or deciduous in cold areas. Hot summers and warm autumns increase hardiness, so abelias thrive better in colder areas in the USA where such conditions exist than in cooler temperate areas of Britain. In spring lightly prune or thin out old branches, and cut away all dead branches.

A. chinensis. Less hardy than *A. × grandiflora*, this bushy but generally deciduous species carries small, fragrant, bell-like, white flowers, flushed pink. H1.2-1.5m/4-5ft, W1.2-1.5m/4-5ft. F7-8. Z7-9.

A. 'Edward Goucher'. A strong, American hybrid with purple-pink flowers. H1.2-1.5m/4-5ft, W1.2-1.5m/4-5ft. F6-8. Z7-9.

A. × grandiflora. The glossy abelia has oval, shiny leaves and pale pink flowers. H1.2-1.5m/4-5ft, W90-120cm/3-4ft. F7-8. Z6-9. **'Francis Mason'** has yellow-variegated leaves, brightest in full sun, and blush-pink flowers. **'Gold Sport'** has bright golden-yellow leaves and pink flowers, and needs sun and shelter. All H1.2-1.5m/4-5ft, W1.2-1.5m/4-5ft. F7-10. Z7-9.

A. schumannii. This dwarf, tender Chinese species has light green leaves, often tinted red, and rosy lilac flowers. H90-120cm/3-4ft, W90-120cm/3-4ft. F7-9. Z7-9.

ABELIOPHYLLUM
White forsythia

A. distichum. This rare, underrated Korean shrub is slow-growing, twiggy and rather untidy, but exciting in early spring when mature, the bare stems carrying masses of small, blush white, almond-scented flowers. It flowers better with regular summer heat and cold winters. Happy on any well-drained soil and in sun or light shade. Prune, once established, after flowering, as for *Forsythia*. Old plants can have their old wood cut back to the base, to encourage new shoots. Grow against a south-facing wall in cool climates. H90-150cm/3-5ft, W90-150cm/3-5ft. F3; occ. F8-9. Z5-9.

ACANTHOPANAX See under ELEUTHEROCOCCUS.

ACER Maple

Most are trees but some species, especially the Japanese maples, *A. japonicum* and *A. palmatum*, are so slow-growing that they can be considered shrubs. Others, such as *A. negundo* and its cultivars can be kept shrubby by annual pruning.

A. circinatum. The rare vine maple from western North America forms a broad, wide-spreading shrub or small tree, with brilliant orange-red autumn colour and clusters of white flowers with ruby-red sepals. Prune to keep compact. Needs fertile, not too dry, soil; good in light shade. H1.8-2.4m/6-8ft, W1.8-2.1m/6-7ft. F4. Z6-9.

A. ginnala. The Amur maple, an oriental slow-growing, large shrub or small bushy tree, succeeds on alkaline and acid soils. Its large, three-lobed, bright green leaves assume red colouring in autumn and its white flowers are fragrant. Prune if required to keep compact. H4-5m/13-16ft, W4-5m/13-16ft. F5. Z3-8.

A. japonicum. The Japanese maple or full-moon maple includes excellent garden shrubs or small trees, most with attractive coloured foliage, finely textured leaves and on many, good autumn colour. Most mature plants carry pendulous clusters of purple-red flowers on bare stems, followed by winged fruits. The species varies from seed but is cheaper to purchase than cultivars, which must be rooted from cuttings or grafted. Preferring moist but well-drained acid or neutral soils, most will succeed on alkaline types if correct conditions are provided.

These comments apply to the other Japanese maples, *A. palmatum*, and since both are desirable and expensive, it is worth providing the right conditions. Add large amounts of leaf mould and peat to planting holes, especially on heavy soils, and flowers of sulphur to reduce pH on highly alkaline soils (see p. 196). Good drainage in winter and regular summer moisture is ideal, but

Abelia × *grandiflora* 'Francis Mason'

Abeliophyllum distichum

most are quite tolerant. Mulch with composted bark, peat or leaf mould in spring. Grow in full sun or, better, part shade, sheltered from cold winds by conifers or other tall trees and avoiding frost pockets. Late spring frosts have killed plants in my garden, though they generally stand winter temperatures as low as -20°C/-4°F. In full sun, high temperatures and drying winds, leaves can scorch; some cultivars suffer occasional stem dieback. Prune in late spring before leaves appear, and remove soft branch tips in summer. Always use clean tools, disinfected between each tree, because wilt and other diseases can be carried on tools from one to another. Average H2.1-3m/7-10ft, W2.1-3m/7-10ft. F5. Z6-8. **'Aconitifolium'** (syn. 'Filicifolium', 'Laciniatum'), strong, upright habit, deeply dissected leaves, crimson-scarlet in autumn, maroon and white flowers. H1.5-1.8m/5-6ft, W1.2-1.5m/4-5ft. F5. Z6-8. **'Aureum'**, one of my favourite trees, gradually forms a beautiful, broad-spreading bush with short, much divided branches, more upright in shade; yellow, broad-lobed leaves remain a good colour, though can scorch in open positions in hot climates. Orange and red autumn colour not reliable. Crimson-purple flowers on older plants. H1.2-1.5m/4-5ft, W90-120cm/3-4ft. F4-5. Z6-8.

A. negundo. The box elder, a vigorous, deciduous, North American tree, is grown in its coloured foliage forms and frequently sold as standards, but more effective if maintained as shrubs by regular pruning. The species adapts to a wide range of soils. Cultivars are less vigorous; most are grafted onto species understocks or seedlings, hence the occasional reversion. Cut away all-green shoots as soon as seen, otherwise they gradually take over. Cultivars may root from cuttings but these plants often lack vigour. Prune in late spring, and twice during the growing season nip out the soft short tips between thumb and forefinger. **'Auratum'**, bright golden leaves all summer, but may scorch in warm climates. **'Elegans'**, leaves have an irregular golden-yellow margin. **'Flamingo'**, slow to colour but by summer shoots and leaves are pink, cream and green. **'Variegatum'**, leaves irregularly margined creamy white. All (unpruned) H5-7m/16-23ft, W4-6m/13-20ft. Z3-9.

A. palmatum. The 'Japanese' maple comes from China, Korea and Japan, and makes a shrub or small tree no more than 8m/26ft in height but often wider. The species varies considerably, with an array of shapes, sizes and coloured-leaved forms selected for garden and landscape use. All have lobed or deeply cut leaves, colouring well in autumn, and most produce small purple flowers, followed by fruit in winged capsules. Cultural needs as for *A. japonicum*. Just a few selections can be described here, and an indication only of the average size of this variable species would be H1.2-1.8m/4-6ft or more, W1.2-1.5m/4-5ft. F4-5. Z5-8. **'Atropurpureum'**, like other purple- or red-leaved cultivars, turns almost green in deep shade, and in hot climates may bronze or burn in sun. Best in light shade. Variable from seed but at its best, a graceful, open, small, upward-spreading tree with lobed, red-purple leaves. H1.8-3m/6-10ft, W1.5-1.8m/5-6ft. F4-5. Z5-8. **'Aureum'**, finely cut, greeny gold leaves in shade, bright yellow, often tinged red, in sun; graceful, upright growth, with long, thin, red-tipped stems. H1.8-3m/6-10ft, W1.5-1.8m/5-6ft. F4-5. Z5-8. **'Bloodgood'** is more vigorous, healthy and adaptable, with deep reddish-purple, almost black leaves. H1.8-3m/6-10ft, W1.5-1.8m/5-6ft. F4-5. Z5-8.

Those in the **Dissectum Group** are the most shrub-like of all Japanese maples. Most make low, spreading mounds with cascading branches. The fern-like leaves are seven-, nine- or eleven-lobed, each lobe finely and deeply cut. The following seven varieties are just a few of the innumerable cultivars, some as tall as 4m/13ft, more across, after many years.

'Atropurpureum', gracefully downward-sweeping branches, deep purple leaves; variable, since some are selected seedlings. More reliable are **'Crimson Queen'** and **'Garnet'**, both with redder leaves which seldom fade. **'Filigree Lace'**, widely

Acer palmatum 'Garnet'

Acer negundo 'Flamingo'

Acer japonicum 'Aureum'

Acer palmatum 'Senkaki'

Actinidia kolomikta

Osakazuki'), small tree, with large, green leaves and consistently brilliant crimson autumn colour, though quickly over in wet autumns. Clusters of red flowers on mature plants. H2.1-3m/7-10ft, W1.8-2.1m/6-7ft. F4-5. Z5-8. **'Red Pygmy'**, dwarf, spreading habit, narrow, maroon-red leaves. H1.5-1.8m/5-6ft, W1.5-1.8m/5-6ft. Z5-8. **'Senkaki'** (syn. 'Sango Kaku'), upright, dense form, coral-red stems, hence the name coral-bark maple, and light, airy, finely toothed leaves, reddy green in spring, light green in summer, golden in autumn. Small red flowers. H1.8-2.4m/6-8ft, W1.2-1.5m/4-5ft. F4-5. Z5-8. **'Shishigashira'** (syn. 'Ribesifolium'), shrub or small, erect tree; dense clusters of green leaves, golden-yellow with red tints in autumn. Popular for Japanese gardens and bonsai. H90-150cm/3-5ft, W60-90cm/2-3ft. Z5-8.

ACTINIDIA

This genus of deciduous, twining climbers comes from India, China and Japan. Most are very vigorous with large leaves and are suitable for walls, pergolas or even over shrubs and trees.

A. chinensis. The fruit of the Chinese gooseberry is now widely popular as Kiwi fruit, due to the amazingly successful recent marketing campaign by the New Zealanders for a plant originating in China but grown commercially in their country. On walls and pergolas it makes rapid growth, with broad, heart-shaped leaves soon creating summer shade. Plant male and female plants close together to ensure fruiting. Fragrant creamy white flowers in midsummer mature to buff-yellow, followed by large, oval, furry brown fruit. Grow in free-draining soil and a warm, sheltered spot, and train and tie in as necessary. Look for named male and female plants. H5-6m/16-20ft, W5-6m/16-20ft. F7. Z8-9.

A. kolomikta. A striking foliage climber for walls, pergolas or through shrubs. The variegated lower halves of the oval to heart-shaped, green leaves are irregularly splashed with white and pink in summer. Brightest in sun but will colour in light shade. It has scented white flowers and yellow fruits which are edible but tasteless. Train slender stems and prune as required. H3-4m/10-13ft, W3-4m/10-13ft. F6. Z5-9.

AESCULUS Horse chestnut

Most horse chestnuts are eventually too large for small gardens, but the buckeyes could certainly be used more.

A. parviflora. The North American bottlebrush buckeye is impressive, but too large and spreading for a small garden. Adaptable to most soils and sun or light shade if not too dry, it forms a thicket of slender, erect stems, eventually creating a

spaced lobes, finely cut, narrow leaves of unchanging purple-red, slender pendulous branches. **'Inaba Shidare'**, deep purple leaves, umbrella-like form, good autumn colour. **'Viridis'** covers many green-leaved selections arising from seedlings raised in seed beds, with deeply dissected foliage; a broad-spreading, pendulous form with yellow, orange or red autumn colour. **'Variegatum'**, white-margined leaves, needs shelter. Average H1.2-1.5m/4-5ft, W1.5-2.1m/5-7ft. Z5-8.

'Linearilobum', green leaves with widely spaced, long, finger-like lobes. The purple-leaved **'Linearilobum Atropurpureum'** slowly form broad shrubs with good autumn colour. Both H1.5-1.8m/5-6ft, W1.5-1.8m/5-6ft. Z5-8. **'Osakazuki'** (syn. 'Heptalobum

round dome with deciduous horse-chestnut leaves and candle-like, white flower heads for several weeks. Remove suckers to control spread; ideal as a lawn specimen. H2.4-3m/8-10ft, W2.4-3m/8-10ft. F7-8. Z5-9.

A. pavia. The North American red buckeye is rare in European gardens, yet is an unusual and adaptable shrub or small tree. Deep green chestnut leaves and erectly held panicles of bright red flowers create a striking effect. Most are grown from seed; selections such as **'Atrosanguinea'**, with deep red blooms, the red **'Humilis'**, with a slightly more spreading habit, and the pink-flowered **'Rosea'**, are grafted. H1.5-2.1m/5-7ft, W1.5-2.1m/5-7ft. F6. Z6-9.

AKEBIA

A. quinata. A vigorous, semi-evergreen, twining climber from Japan and China, for walls, pergolas, growing through trees and shrubs or over stumps. The five-fingered leaves are purple when young and become blue-green when mature. Hanging clusters of small, scented chocolate-purple flowers appear in early spring, half-hidden by the leaves. Unusual, sausage-shaped purplish fruits in autumn after hot summers. Requires sun to light shade and tolerates most soils. Train and prune, as necessary, after flowering. H6-7m/20-23ft, W6-7m/20-23ft. F3-4. Z5-9.

AMPELOPSIS

A. brevipedunculata (syn. *Vitis heterophylla*). This vigorous, deciduous, vine-like climber is grown for its bright, porcelain-blue fruit in autumn, occurring most reliably in warm, sunny sites and climates. Self-clinging on rougher surfaces, but train when young. Its lobed, hop-like green leaves turn yellow in most autumns. Good for walls, fences and pergolas. H4-5m/13-16ft, W4-5m/13-16ft. F8-9. Z6. The form **'Elegans'**, also sold as 'Variegata' or 'Tricolor', is much less vigorous but worth attempting for its irregularly splashed white, pink and green leaves. Young stems are red and pink. It seldom fruits. Best in damp shade. Good patio container plant. H2.1-3m/7-10ft, W2.1-3m/7-10ft. F8-9. Z4-8.

ANDROMEDA

A small group of dwarf, evergreen, acid-loving plants for peaty gardens, thriving in moist, humus-rich soils in sun or shade.
A. polifolia **'Compacta'**. This compact form of bog rosemary is a selection from the wild, with tiny, grey-green leaves and delicate, bell-shaped, pink flowers which last for many weeks. **'Compacta Alba'**, which has creamy flowers, is rarer. Both H15-25cm/6-10in, W45-60cm/18-24in. F5-6. Z2-7.

ARBUTUS Strawberry tree

A. × andrachnoides. This hybrid is similar to *A. unedo*, but with striking, cinnamon-red, peeling bark on old trees. H2.1-2.4m/7-8ft, W1.8-2.1m/6-7ft. F10. Z8-9.
A. unedo. This evergreen shrub or small tree is a native of the Mediterranean and south-west Ireland. Though ericaceous, it tolerates alkaline and seaside conditions, and is hardier than supposed. It has small, dark green leaves and, in autumn, clusters of pendulous white or pink bell flowers at the same time as round, orange-red, edible but insipid fruit, which ripens from the previous year's flowers. Old stems develop attractive, reddish brown bark. Very slow-growing at first. Sun or light shade. H2.1-2.4m/7-8ft, W1.8-2.1m/6-7ft. F10. Z7-9.

Aesculus pavia 'Humilis'

Aronia melanocarpa 'Brilliant'

ARCTOSTAPHYLOS

A. uva-ursi. The red bearberry or kinnikinick makes effective, low, evergreen ground cover and is surprisingly lime-tolerant. From cooler temperate zones of the Northern Hemisphere, it prefers sunny, well-drained soils, or even sand. It makes wide-spreading mats of dark green leaves, and its pendulous white or pink flowers are followed by red fruit. There are several named cultivars planted widely in North America for landscape use. H30cm/1ft, W60-90cm/2-3ft. F4-5. Z2-8.

ARONIA Chokeberry

These useful, easily grown fruiting and flowering shrubs from eastern North America need neutral to acid soil; they tolerate shade but flower, fruit and produce better autumn colour in sun. The erect, supple stems spread by suckers; control size by hard pruning in late winter.
A. arbutifolia. This has round, red, edible fruit in autumn. **'Erecta'**, an upright, narrower form, has rich red autumn leaf colour. Both have small white flowers. H1.8-2.1m/6-7ft, W2.1-3m/7-10ft. F4-5. Z5-9.
A. melanocarpa. This species, with inconspicuous, black fruits and wine-red autumn leaf colour, is surpassed by the form **'Brilliant'**, which has larger leaves and more decorative fruits. H1.2-1.5m/4-5ft, W2.1m/7ft. F4-5. Z4-9.

ARTEMISIA

Mostly aromatic grey or silver-leaved shrubs or perennials, these are adaptable plants but

Akebia quinata

Artemisia 'Powis Castle'

revel in hot sun and good drainage. The foliage is ideal in silver and grey borders, or as contrast to other colours.
A. abrotanum. Southernwood has a shrubby base, soft, erect, delicately dissected foliage, and yellow flowers which are best removed. Prune hard in late spring. Often dies back in severe winters but usually puts out new growth again in late spring. H75-90cm/30-36in, W75-90cm/30-36in. F8. Z5-8.
A. absinthium. Wormwood or absinth is best in the form **'Lambrook Silver'**, raised by Margery Fish. It is neater, brighter and denser than the species. H75cm/30in, W60cm/2ft. F7-8. Z4-9.
A. **'Powis Castle'** makes a non-flowering mound of bright silver-grey, finely cut foliage; also dies back in severe winters. H90-120cm/3-4ft, W90-120cm/3-4ft. Z5-8.

AUCUBA Spotted laurel

A. japonica. The Japanese aucuba is one of many in this genus of leathery leaved evergreens and the most popular, particularly its green and coloured-leaved forms. They adapt to a wide range of soil conditions, and will tolerate either sun or deep, even dense, shade, though shade is necessary in very hot climates. Introduced from Japan in 1783, plantsmen and gardeners were slow to realize that there

Aucuba japonica 'Picturata'

Azara serrata

were both male and female plants and that both were necessary for females to set fruit. Plant both sexes together and in good light for profuse red fruits. Male plants bear panicles of purple-petalled flowers in spring. Slow-growing initially, they can easily be pruned.

There have been many introductions with coloured or variegated foliage, not all stable, and some confusion of names exists. **'Crassifolia'** is male and slow-growing, with glossy green leaves. **'Crotonifolia'** has

large, green leaves blotched and speckled with gold, considered by some authorities to be male, by others, female! **'Longifolia'** is female with narrow, lance-shaped leaves. **'Mr Goldstrike'** is similar to 'Crotonifolia' but definitely male! **'Nana Rotundifolia'** is a dwarf female with small leaves. **'Picturata'** is a large, free-fruiting female cultivar with broad leaves bearing bold central golden markings. **'Rozannie'**, a Dutch dwarf introduction, is hermaphrodite, and therefore self-fertilizing. **'Salicifolia'** is another female with narrow, lance-shaped leaves. **'Variegata'** is similar to 'Picturata' but the leaves are delicately splashed and dotted in yellow. All H2.1-3m/7-10ft, W2.1-3m/7-10ft. F4-5. Z7-11.

AZARA

A. serrata. One of the hardier species of this evergreen genus from Chile, but for most cool temperate zones it still needs the protection of a sunny wall, where it makes a spectacular late spring or summer show of

Berberidopsis corallina

golden-yellow flowers, contrasting with bright green, serrated leaves. Can be grown freely or trained as a wall shrub. H2.1-3m/7-10ft, W2.1-3m/7-10ft. F5-7. Z8-10.

BERBERIDOPSIS
Coral plant

B. corallina. A distinctive, evergreen, Chilean scandent shrub, the coral plant is the only species in the genus. Ideal trained up shady walls. The glossy, leathery, slightly spiny leaves are enhanced by clusters of

pendent crimson flowers on red stalks. Needs moist, acid, open, sandy soil and shelter in cold areas. H2.1-3m/7-10ft, W2.1-3m/7-10ft. F7-8. Z8-9.

BERBERIS Barberry

This large genus of deciduous and evergreen shrubs provides many easily grown, adaptable plants. Some are dwarf, others large; some have beautiful, usually yellow or orange flowers in spring, others striking berries, and a great many have colourful foliage and autumn colour. Very thorny types make effective hedges or barriers against animals or vandals. Most thrive in sun or part shade in almost any soil that is not waterlogged. Most withstand pruning, but use protective gloves and clothing when doing so. Most species come freely from seed but often vary considerably, which has led to the introduction of innumerable named cultivars, thereafter propagated by cuttings. Hardiness varies.
B. aggregata. Introduced from China by plant hunter Ernest Wilson in 1908, this has parented many hybrids. Deciduous, sharply spiny, pale yellow flowers, burnt-red leaves and red fruit in autumn. Makes a low, protective, informal hedge. H1.2-1.5m/4-5ft, W90-120cm/3-4ft. F5-6. Z6-9.
B. calliantha. This rare, dwarf evergreen was discovered by plant hunter Frank Kingdon Ward in Tibet in 1924. It has glossy, holly-like leaves, with white undersides, large, creamy yellow flowers, blue-black berries and sharp spines. H60-90cm/2-3ft, W90-120cm/3-4ft. F5. Z7-9.
B. candidula. From western China, this is a low, round, prickly bush. Glossy, evergreen leaves with blue undersides. Yellow flowers and purple berries, with a distinct bloom, somewhat hidden by foliage. H90cm/3ft, W90-120cm/3-4ft. F4-5. Z6-9.
B. × carminea. This group of selected cultivars originated some years ago at the Royal Horticultural Society gardens at Wisley, Surrey, in England. They are deciduous shrubs, valuable for autumn foliage and startlingly colourful fruits, at first pale apple-green and so abundant that they weigh the branches down. Easily grown, they slowly create impenetrable, thorny thickets. Sun or part shade. Some of the selections described below may not be true to name any more, due to seed-raised plants being mixed in with the original selections by the nursery trade over the years. However, seed-raised plants will create similar effects. All F4-5, Z6-9.
'Barbarossa' has bright red fruit. H1.5-1.8m/5-6ft, W1.5-1.8m/5-6ft. **'Bountiful'** has coral fruit. H90cm/3ft, W90cm/3ft. **'Buccaneer'** is upright, with long-lasting carmine berries. H1.2-1.5m/4-5ft, W1.2-1.5m/4-5ft. **'Pirate King'** has orange-red fruits. H1.2-1.5m/4-5ft, W1.2-1.5m/4-5ft.

SHRUBS

B. darwinii. This beautiful Chilean shrub was discovered by Charles Darwin on the voyage of the HMS *Beagle* in 1835. A dense evergreen with spiny, dark leaves, arching branches and racemes of orange-yellow flowers followed by plum-coloured fruit, and often another flush of flowers. It needs shelter and reasonably fertile, not-too-dry soil. Prune, if required, after flowering. H1.5-2.1m/5-7ft, W1.2-1.5m/4-5ft. F4-5. Z7-9.

B. julianae. This eventually large, tough, spiny evergreen is useful for a thick hedge or screen. Large, holly-like leaves, yellow flowers and oval black fruit with a blue bloom. Sun or shade and not too dry. H2.1-3m/7-10ft, W1.8-2.4m/6-8ft. F5-6. Z6-8.

B. koreana. Vigorous, erect and thorny, with deciduous, pale leaves, yellow flowers and clusters of bright red fruit. Usually good autumn foliage colour. **'Harvest Fire'**, deep, almost purple-black leaves, slow to establish but eventually vigorous. **'Red Tears'**, tear-shaped fruit, performs best in open positions. All H1.5-1.8m/5-6ft, W90-120cm/3-4ft. F5-6. Z4-7.

B. linearifolia. This Chilean evergreen is spectacular in flower but can be straggly with sparse foliage. Hanging clusters of bright apricot and orange flowers; prune after flowering to keep compact. Grows in shade where not too dry and needs shelter from cold winds. **'Orange King'**, larger orange flowers. Both H1.5-1.8m/5-6ft, W90-120cm/3-4ft. F5. Z6-9.

B. × lologensis. This bushy hybrid has dark, evergreen leaves and superb, large, orange and apricot flowers. Sun or light shade where not too dry; prune after flowering. **'Apricot Queen'** has apricot blooms. **'Gertrude Hardijzer'** is a Dutch introduction with larger, darker blooms. All H1.8-2.4m/6-8ft, W1.5-1.8m/5-6ft. F4-5. Z6-9.

B. × media 'Red Jewel'. This dense, deciduous or semi-evergreen shrub has thorny stems and bronze-purple leaves, with brilliant autumn colours. H90-120cm/3-4ft, W90-120cm/3-4ft. F4-5. Z6-8.

B. × ottawensis 'Superba' (syn. 'Atropurpurea Superba'). A vigorous, deciduous shrub, with large, deep purple leaves with a distinctly metallic sheen, it needs sun for best colour. Yellow flowers, sparse red fruit. Prune to the ground every few years to rejuvenate. H1.5-1.8m/5-6ft, W1.2-1.5m/4-5ft. F5. Z5-9.

B. × stenophylla. A popular, evergreen hybrid for garden and landscape planting, and also useful for hedges, in time it makes a tall, suckering, dark green bush, with arching branches briefly massed with small, orange-yellow flowers, then blue-black berries. Sun or light shade; prune after flowering. H1.8-2.4m/6-8ft, W1.5-1.8m/5-6ft. F4-5. Z6-9. **'Claret Cascade'** is a low, spreading form with wine-purple new shoots and green-maroon foliage. Its rich

orange flowers are stained purple. H90-120cm/3-4ft, W90-120cm/3-4ft. F4-5. Z6-9. **'Corallina Compacta'** is a dwarf plant with dark green leaves, coral-red buds and deep orange flowers. Can be tender. H30-45cm/12-18in, W60-75cm/24-30in. F4-5. Z6-9. **'Cream Showers'** is a vigorous plant with strong, arching branches, dark green leaves and creamy white, bell-like flowers. Prune long shoots after flowering to keep compact. H1.5-1.8m/5-6ft, W1.5-1.8m/5-6ft.

Berberis × media 'Red Jewel'

Berberis darwinii

F4-5. Z6-9. **'Etna'** is slow-growing and bears greeny bronze leaves with fiery red buds and orange flowers. **'Irwinii'**, slow-growing, upright, slightly pendulous; yellow flowers. Both H90-120cm/3-4ft, W90cm/3ft. F4-5. Z6-9.

B. thunbergii. This variable, very hardy, deciduous Chinese species has many excellent cultivars. Its spiny branches bear tufts of leaves with excellent autumn colour, yellow flowers and, later, bright red fruit. Purple-leaved forms need sun to

colour well, otherwise happy on most soils and sites. Lightly prune taller cultivars every few years, or prune to the ground in early spring to rejuvenate. H90-240cm/3-8ft, W90-240cm/3-8ft. F3-5. Z5-8. **'Atropurpurea'** has erect, arching branches, reddy purple leaves, abundant fruit and good autumn colour. H1.5-1.8m/5-6ft, W1.2-1.5m/4-5ft. F3-5. Z5-8. **'Atropurpurea Nana'** (syn. 'Crimson Pygmy', 'Little Favourite'), has congested,

Berberis × stenophylla 'Etna'

Berberis thunbergii 'Aurea'

Berberis thunbergii 'Bagatelle'

contorted branches, reddy purple leaves and good autumn colour. **'Kobold'** is similar, with green leaves and yellow flowers. Both H30-45cm/12-18in, W45-60cm/18-24in. F4-5. Z5-8. **'Aurea'**, soft yellow foliage, bright yellow in sun, with reddy shoots. Hardy but needs shade in hot climates and shelter from cold winds. Can look tired but eye-catching at best. H60-75cm/24-30in, W60-75cm/24-30in. F4-5. Z6-8. **'Bagatelle'** is a dwarf Dutch introduction. Compact with small, purple

Berberis thunbergii 'Dart's Red Lady' (centre) and *Juniperus × media* 'Gold Sovereign' (front)

Betula 'Trost's Dwarf'

Buddleia davidii 'Nanho Blue'

leaves and copper-red new shoots. Ideal with dwarf shrubs or alpines. H30cm/1ft, W30-45cm/12-18in. F4-5. Z5-8. **'Dart's Red Lady'** is tall and spreading with black-purple leaves. Ideal with grey, green or golden foliage, it has excellent autumn colour. H60-75cm/24-30in, W75-90cm/30-36in. F4-5. Z5-8.

'Golden Ring' has reddy purple leaves, with a gold margin. H1.5-1.8m/5-6ft, W1.2-1.5m/4-5ft. F4-5. Z5-8. **'Helmond Pillar'**, erect, but widening with age, has purple leaves, good autumn colour and profuse red fruit. H1.2-1.5m/4-5ft, W30cm/1ft, wider at the top. F4-5. Z5-8. **'Red Chief'** is a vigorous, thorny shrub with strongly arching branches. It has crimson-red young shoots, shiny, reddish purple leaves, good autumn colour and red fruits. H1.5-1.8m/5-6ft, W1.2-1.5m/4-5ft. F4-5. Z5-8. **'Red Pillar'** is erect with reddy purple leaves. H1.2-1.5m/4-5ft, W30-45cm/12-18in, wider at the top. F4-5. Z5-8. **'Rose Glow'**, new shoots purple, foliage splashed cream and silver-pink, in sun and light shade. Variegations last all summer and look perfect against a green background. Prune fairly hard in early spring, to encourage new growth. (**'Pink Queen'** and **'Harlequin'** are similar.) All H1.5-1.8m/5-6ft, W1.2-1.5m/4-5ft. F4-5. Z5-8. **'Silver Beauty'**, light green leaves, young foliage splashed silvery white and pink; colours enhanced in late summer and good autumn colour. Prune regularly to renew new growth. **'Kelleriis'** is similar. Both H90-120cm/3-4ft, W90-120cm/3-4ft. F4-5. Z5-8.

B. verruculosa. Dense, dark, leathery foliage and arching, spiny stems make this a useful background plant. Pale yellow flowers, blue-black fruit. H1.2-1.5m/4-5ft, W90-120cm/3-4ft. F4-5. Z6-9.

B. wilsoniae. This variable deciduous species, discovered by plant hunter Ernest Wilson in 1904 in western China, has adapted successfully to cultivation. It is a low shrub with arching, thorny branches, grey-green leaves and pale yellow flowers, followed by profuse, translucent coral-red berries. Good autumn colour. Roy Lancaster has introduced a clone with very blue-grey leaves, closer to the original Wilson plants. H1.2-1.5m/4-5ft, W1.2-1.5m/4-5ft. F4-5. Z6-9.

BETULA Birch
Though mostly trees, a few species are shrubs, and others can be kept as shrubs by annual pruning. All are deciduous and adaptable, though they prefer northern, cooler climates.

B. nana. This remarkable dwarf from bog- or marshland in the northern USA and Britain grows less than 1.2m/4ft high. Erect, spreading branches carry small, shiny, toothed leaves and occasional yellow catkins. If growth becomes congested, occasional thinning helps. Perfect in a rock garden or with other dwarf shrubs and heathers. H60-90cm/2-3ft, W45-60cm/18-24in. Z2-5.

B. **'Trost's Dwarf'**, from Oregon, USA, makes a dense, spreading mound, branching in all directions at once. The leaves are thread-like, and could be mistaken for a Dissectum maple. Vigorous once established, it can be pruned in mild weather in winter, to form a stem, or thinned out. H1.5-1.8m/5-6ft, W1.5-1.8m/5-6ft. Z2-5.

BUDDLEIA Butterfly bush
Named after the Reverend Adam Buddle, the various species form shrubs or small trees preferring sun and reasonable soil (neither extremely wet nor dry), though some seed freely and colonize derelict ground and stone walls. Most need pruning annually or every few years to create new growth because it is on new growth that they flower. Flowers are often scented and attract bees and butterflies. Originating from Asia, South America and South Africa, they vary in form and hardiness.

B. alternifolia. A vigorous, hardy Chinese shrub or small tree, with narrow, alternate leaves on long, pendulous branches. Untidy when young unless trained to form a dense, weeping-willow-like tree. Profuse, fragrant, lilac flowers appear along cascading stems on established plants. Prune stems after flowering by a third. **'Argentea'**, slower, less hardy, with silver leaves. Both eventually need space. Both H2.4-3m/8-10ft, W2.4-3m/8-10ft. F7-9. Z5-9.

B. davidii. A variable species named after

the French missionary Abbé Armand David, who discovered it in China in 1869, it now provides a wide choice of cultivars. All have fragrant flowers, 10-60cm/4-24in long, attractive to insects, in mid- to late summer. Some form low-spreading shrubs, others are more vigorous and upright. Prune in late winter or spring as new shoots start into growth, to within 15-30cm/6-12in of the ground. Stronger cultivars often grow 2.4m/8ft or more in one season. All F7-9. Z5-9.

'Black Knight', deep violet-blue trusses, vigorous, erect and hardy. H2.4m/8ft, W2.4m/8ft. 'Border Beauty', more compact and spreading, violet-purple flowers. H1.5m-5ft, W1.5m/5ft. 'Empire Blue', erect, blue flowers with a touch of violet. H2.4m/8ft, W2.4m/8ft. 'Fascinating', lilac-pink flowers. H2.1m/7ft, W2.1m/7ft. 'Harlequin', less vigorous, with creamy variegated leaves and purple-red flowers. H1.2-1.5m/4-5ft, W1.2-1.5m/4-5ft. 'Lochinch' needs sun, good soil and protection from cold winds and frosts. Broadly speaking, with large, orange-scented, lavender flowers. H1.8-2.4m/6-8ft, W1.8-2.4m/6-8ft. The form *nanhoensis*, introduced from China by plant hunter Reginald Farrer, has a dwarf, spreading habit and scaled-down leaves and flowers which are ideal for a small garden, though perhaps less hardy than others. The flowers are lilac. The form *nanhoensis alba* has white flowers on arching stems, and silver-grey leaves. 'Nanho Blue', deep blue flowers. 'Nanho Purple', deep purple flowers. All H1.2-1.5m/4-5ft, W1.2-1.5m/4-5ft.

'Orchid Beauty', less vigorous, mauve flowers. H1.5m/5ft, W1.5m/5ft. 'Pink Delight', lilac-pink flowers. H2.1m/7ft, W2.1m/7ft. 'Royal Red', rich purple-red flowers and compact, arching habit. H1.8m/6ft, W1.8m/6ft. 'White Profusion', large, silver-white flowers and broad habit. H1.5-1.8m/5-6ft, W1.5-1.8m/5-6ft. *B.* × *weyeriana* 'Sungold'. This deciduous, in mild climates evergreen, shrub is a most unusual buddleia. It has large, orange-yellow, scented, globe-shaped flower heads. Prune lightly to tidy in spring. H1.8-2.4m/6-8ft, W1.8-2.4m/6-8ft. F8-10. Z6-9.

BUXUS Box, boxwood

These very slow-growing, evergreen shrubs and small trees are returning to popularity after years of neglect. Most have small leaves, brightly coloured or variegated in some forms. They are mostly very hardy, though some can brown in winter or scorch in summer, and all adapt to a wide range of well-drained soils, including thin chalk. Sun to deep shade, though golden and variegated types lose colour in deep shade. Prune in July for hedge or topiary work.

B. microphylla. A very slow-growing Japanese species, with small leaves and round, bushy habit. H90-120cm/3-4ft, W90-120cm/3-4ft. Z6-9. 'Compacta' forms a very dwarf hummock of minute leaves. H30-45cm/12-18in, W90-120cm/3-4ft. Z6-9. 'Green Pillow' has leaves which are larger and brighter green. H30-45cm/12-18in, W90-120cm/3-4ft. Z6-9. The form *koreana* is very hardy, low, spreading and open, making useful ground cover in shade and dry soils. Its leaves can brown in winter, a fault not shared by the American 'Wintergreen'. H30-45cm/12-18in, W60-90cm/2-3ft. Z5-9.

B. sempervirens. The common box, it has been used for centuries for low hedging, edging and topiary, and has produced numerous selections, some rare and others indistinguishable from one another. Mostly Z6-8. 'Aurea Pendula' (syn. 'Aurea Maculata Pendula') is a slow, eventually large shrub with pendulous branches. Leaves are splashed creamy yellow. H90-120cm/3-4ft, W90cm/3ft. Z7-8. 'Aureovariegata' (syn. 'Aurea Maculata'), a bushy form with leaves mottled golden-yellow. New shoots are bright yellow. H60-90cm/2-3ft, W60-75cm/24-30in. Z7-8. 'Elegantissima' is dwarf with a dense, round habit. Leaves are margined creamy white. H30-45cm/12-18in, W30-45cm/12-18in. Z7-8.

'Handsworthensis' (syn. 'Handsworthii'), initially upright, later spreading shrub which makes a good hedge or screening plant. Broad, leathery leaves. H1.2-1.5m/4-5ft, W90cm/3ft. 'Latifolia Maculata', slow-growing, round habit. Large leaves splashed golden-yellow; bright yellow new shoots. H45-60cm/18-24in, W30-45cm/12-18in. 'Suffruticosa', most useful for formal edging but extremely slow. H15-30cm/6-12in, W15cm/6in.

Buddleia davidii 'Pink Delight'

Buddleia davidii 'Nanho Purple'

Buddleia davidii 'White Profusion'

Buxus sempervirens 'Latifolia Maculata'

Callicarpa bodinieri 'Profusion'

CALLICARPA

These deciduous shrubs from Japan, China and Korea are grown for their startling. mostly lilac or purple, glossy fruit, abundant when three or more shrubs are planted together. They have small, pinkish flowers. The leaves often turn yellow or pink before dropping, leaving clusters of fruit on naked branches. They prefer well-drained, not too alkaline soil and sun or part shade. Fruiting occurs more readily after hot summers. Lightly trim to tidy; prune to 15cm/6in above ground every few years to induce more vigour, the plants flowering and fruiting on year-old wood.

C. bodinieri **'Profusion'**. The best for cool climates, this upright shrub regularly fruits as a single specimen, with profuse, pale violet fruits. H1.5-1.8m/5-6ft, W90-120cm/3-4ft. F6-8. Z6-9.

C. dichotoma (syn. *C. koreana*). Its pink flowers are followed by profuse, lilac-violet fruit along leafy stems, which arch from the weight of it. There is a white-fruiting form, *albifructus*. H90-120cm/3-4ft, W1.2-1.5m/4-5ft. F6-8. Z5-9.

C. japonica. A compact shrub with violet fruits. The white-berried **'Leucocarpa'** is attractive next to violet-fruited forms. H1.2m/4ft, W1.2m/4ft. F6-8. Z6-9.

C. koreana. See *C. dichotoma*.

CAMELLIA

The camellias are among the elite of evergreen shrubs, with attractive, glossy green leaves and exotic flowers. Most of the more than 200 species, including *C. sinensis*, the tea plant, are of no ornamental value or are too tender to succeed in temperate zones, but *C. japonica* and *C. × williamsii* have produced thousands of garden-worthy hybrids. In northern climates camellias generally bloom in late winter and spring, but they flower earlier under glass, where their flowers are also protected from weathering. Established plants carry

Camellia × williamsii 'Donation'

Campsis radicans

hundreds of blooms over several weeks, in a variety of colours and combinations, singles and doubles.

Camellias need acid soil, though may succeed on neutral soil with peat or flowers of sulphur added to reduce the pH (see p.196). You can grow them in containers of acid compost, but pots must be plunged in peat in winter or brought under glass. Ideally, soil should be well-drained but not dry, with peat, composted bark or leaf mould added to allow aeration for the roots, and a similar mulch 5cm/2in deep every spring. Camellias dislike cold winds and severe frost, so grow them in light shade beneath trees, or in more open positions protected from cold winds and early-morning sun; frosted flowers caught by the sun can be disfigured by bursting cells. If plants are untidy or misshapen, prune back stems by up to one third after flowering. Choose from cultivars offered by local

garden centres and nurseries. The following species and hybrids have given rise to the hardier cultivars.

C. japonica. The Japanese camellia, or common camellia. H1.5-1.8m/5-6ft, W90-120cm/3-4ft, but eventually, according to cultivar, much larger. F2-3. Most Z8-9.

C. sasanqua. More sun-loving, requiring hot summers and warm autumns to provide a good show of mostly scented flowers in autumn and winter. Grown as wall shrubs or in a cold glasshouse in cool climates, flowers are less likely to get damaged. Eventually larger and more spreading than *C. japonica*. F10-2. Z7-9.

C. × williamsii. This has produced a first-class range of hardy, free-flowering cultivars which bloom from an early age. The best camellia for the beginner, **'Donation'**, is hardy, trouble-free and smothered in double, rich pink flowers. Both H1.8-2.1m/6-7ft, W1.5m/5ft. F2-5. Z7-9.

CAMPSIS Trumpet vine

At their best, these are some of the showiest climbers, but they need hot summers to flower well, and in cool temperate zones, including Britain, require full sun. Train against or over walls, low buildings, pergolas, or up sunlit trees. Grow on fertile, well-drained loam. Slow to establish but once the required space is filled, prune the previous season's growth in late autumn to within 5cm/2in of the older wood.

C. grandiflora. The Chinese trumpet creeper has pinnate green leaves, often appearing late in the season, and clusters of exotic orange-red trumpet flowers. H4-5m/13-16ft, W4-5m/13-16ft. F8-9. Z7-9.

C. radicans. This species, from the eastern USA, is usually freer-flowering in cool climates than *C. grandiflora*. Tendrils help it cling, but it may require extra support. Clusters of orange to red trumpet flowers appear at the end of the stems. Selected forms are propagated by cuttings. **'Flava'** has yellow flowers but **'Yellow Trumpet'** is bolder and better. All H5-6m/16-20ft, W5-6m/16-20ft. F8. Z4-9.

C. × tagliabuana **'Madame Galen'**. This hybrid, with spectacular salmon-red flowers, is perhaps the hardiest and most reliable. H5-6m/16-20ft, W5-6m/16-20ft. F8. Z5-9.

CARAGANA

These deciduous shrubs and small trees are generally thorny or prickly, the cultivars less so than the species. Small leaves are mostly arranged in clusters; flowers, also small, are usually yellow. All prefer sun and good drainage, and thrive on quite poor soils. They are becoming better known as patio or small-garden plants, top-grafted on a stem.

C. arborescens **'Lorbergii'**. This has upright stems and bright green, ferny

Caragana arborescens 'Lorbergii'

Carpenteria californica

leaves. Prune every two or three years to keep shrubby and dense. H1.8-2.4m/6-8ft, W1.2-1.5m/4-5ft. F5-6. Z3-8. **'Nana'** is slow-growing, with rigid, contorted branches; good in a rock garden or among low-growing shrubs. Mostly grafted. H90-120cm/3-4ft, W45-60cm/18-24in. F5-6. Z3-8. **'Pendula'** has very weeping, graceful branches and greyish stems. **'Walker'**, a Canadian cross between 'Pendula' and 'Lorbergii', has the former's weeping habit and the latter's fern-like leaves. Mostly top-grafted onto the species; cut away any suckers from the base. Both H according to height of stem, W2.1-3m/7-10ft. F4-5. Z3-8.
C. frutex **'Globosa'**. This dwarf and the larger-growing species are thornless; 'Globosa' gradually makes a neat, multi-branched bush with grey-green leaves, flowering best in sunny situations. H15-30cm/6-12in, W10-20cm/4-8in. F5. Z2-7.
C. pygmaea. The pygmy peashrub is small,

spreading and pendulous, with thin, arching stems and profuse orange-yellow blooms. Often top-grafted on *C. arborescens*. H60-75cm/24-30in, W60-90cm/2-3ft. F5-6. Z3-8.

CARPENTERIA
C. californica. A wonderful flowering, rounded evergreen shrub for mild districts, usually grown against a warm, protected wall. It has pure white, saucer-shaped flowers in summer on old wood. Can be fan-trained against a wall. Plants cut to the ground by frost generally shoot again from the base, but may not flower for two or three years. H2.1m/7ft, W1.8m/6ft. F7. Z8-9.

CARYOPTERIS Bluebeard, blue spiraea
These aromatic, deciduous shrubs provide late-season bright blue flowers. Mostly dwarf or low-growing, they prefer sun and any well-drained soil. They flower on year-

old wood, so prune back each spring to 10-15cm/4-6in from the ground. In cold climates, grow against a south-facing wall. Plant in spring.
C. × clandonensis **'Arthur Simmonds'**. This hybrid has wide-spreading, erect branches bearing grey-green leaves and profuse, bright blue flower clusters. **'Ferndown'** has dark green leaves and violet-blue flowers. **'Heavenly Blue'** is compact, with deep blue flowers. **'Kew Blue'** also has dark flowers. **'Worcester Gold'** is an attractive variation with greeny gold leaves contrasting with bright blue flowers. All H60-75cm/24-30in, W60-75cm/24-30in. F8-9. Z6-9.
C. incana. Californian lilac. This strong-growing species has grey, felted, aromatic leaves, strong, erect stems and violet-blue flowers which last for several weeks. Prune to 15-30cm/6-12in in spring. Unpruned H1.2-1.5m/4-5ft, W90-120cm/3-4ft. F8-9. Z6-9.

Caryopteris × clandonensis 'Heavenly Blue'

CEANOTHUS

Most gardens have a sheltered, sunny spot in which these frustratingly tender shrubs can grow. Both the deciduous and evergreen species mostly originate from the west coast of North America, hence the hardiness problem. The innumerable cultivars offer a wide choice and perhaps greater hardiness. The evergreens are generally spring-flowering and less hardy, the deciduous species mostly summer-flowering, though in warm climates some are evergreen. They are good seaside

Ceanothus thyrsiflorus repens

Ceanothus impressus 'Puget Blue'

shrubs. All prefer sun, well-drained, acid to slightly alkaline soils, and shelter from cold winds and frost. Plant in spring next to a south- or west-facing wall, shrubbery or hedge; autumn plantings risk winter fatalities. Compact cultivars need no pruning but vigorous types, especially when wall-trained, can become untidy and top-heavy. Prune established spring-flowering types after flowering, not cutting into old wood. Prune summer-flowering types in late spring, to 5-10cm/2-4in of the previous year's growth.

C. arboreus 'Trewithen Blue'. This evergreen is a showy, if tender, plant; in mild climates it grows to tree size. Glossy leaves, large panicles of cobalt-blue flowers. Best against a high wall. H3m/10ft, W3m/10ft. F5-6. Z9-10.

Ceratostigma willmottianum

C. 'A. T. Johnson'. Evergreen and vigorous, with profuse, deep blue flowers. H3m/10ft, W3m/10ft. F3-5; occ. F9. Z8-10.
C. 'Autumnal Blue'. One of the hardiest evergreens, with luxuriant, glossy foliage and dark blue flowers. H1.5-1.8m/5-6ft, W1.5-1.8m/5-6ft. F8-9. Z8-10.
C. 'Blue Mound'. Quite hardy, but needs shelter. Evergreen mound of small, shiny leaves, with profuse light blue flowers. H60-75cm/24-30in, W60-90cm/2-3ft. F5. Z8-10.
C. 'Burkwoodii'. This is a dense, bushy, evergreen hybrid with panicles of bright blue flowers. H90-150cm/3-5ft, W90-150cm/3-5ft. F7-10. Z8-10.
C. 'Cascade'. Evergreen, with long, arching branches and powder-blue flowers. Can be tender; grow against a wall. Prune immediately flowering has finished. H2.4-3m/8-10ft, W2.4-3m/8-10ft. F5-6. Z9-10.
C. × *delileanus*. The French hybrids are a little slow to establish and tend to 'blow' in exposed, windy positions. They have flower panicles on growth made earlier in the year, so prune in late spring. 'Gloire de Versailles', very popular, with large, powder-blue heads, blooms for many weeks. 'Henri Desfossé', deep blue flowers. 'Marie Simon', large panicles of rose-pink flowers, reddish stems. 'Topaz', deep cobalt-blue flowers. All H1.5-1.8m/5-6ft, W1.2-1.5m/4-5ft. F8-9. Z8-10.
C. dentatus. This densely branched evergreen is best against a wall except in mild spots. Small, serrated, dark green leaves, gentian-blue flowers. H1.5-1.8m/5-6ft, W1.5-1.8m/5-6ft. F6. Z9-10.
C. impressus. This broad, dense shrub with

rigid branches carries clusters of rich blue flowers. 'Puget Blue' is more upright, flowering for a longer period. Both H90-120cm/3-4ft, W90-120cm/3-4ft. F5. Z9-10.
C. prostratus. The squaw carpet makes a prostrate mat of prickly leaves; unreliable flowering in cool climates. H15-30cm/6-12in, W90-120cm/3-4ft. F4-5. Z8-10.
C. thyrsiflorus. One of the hardiest evergreen species, forming a large shrub or small tree, with clusters of pale blue flowers. H2.4-3m/8-10ft, W2.4-3m/8-10ft. F4-6. Z7-10. The form *repens* makes vigorous, spreading, excellent, mounded ground cover with deep blue, bottlebrush flowers. H60-90cm/2-3ft, W1.5-1.8m/5-6ft. F4-6. Z8-10.

CERATOSTIGMA
Hardy plumbago

Only two or three species are shrubs, the remainder being perennials. All are sun-loving, deciduous plants needing good drainage.
C. griffithii. This leafy, upright, spreading shrub has bright blue flowers and good autumn colour. H30-45cm/12-18in, W60-75cm/24-30in. F8. Z9-11.
C. willmottianum. Hardier and taller, with twiggy, upright stems, this has bright, deep blue flowers. Prune to the ground in late spring. H60-75cm/24-30in, W60-75cm/24-30in. F8-10. Z5-9.

CERCIS Redbud

These shrubs or small trees are interesting for their pea-like flowers and attractive leaves. All do best in full sun and well-drained soil.

C. canadensis. This large, spreading shrub or small tree, the North American redbud, has big leaves and red shoots; the flowers, red in bud, open to pink. **'Forest Pansy'**, like the species, seldom flowers in cool climates but the large leaves open a bright red-purple, deepening in summer; the undersides are crimson-purple, giving the shrub a lighter touch than *Cotinus coggygria* 'Royal Purple'. Needs sun and well-drained soil. Prune in late spring as required. H1.5-2.4m/5-8ft, W1.8-2.4m/6-8ft. F4-5. Z4-9.
C. siliquastrum. The Judas tree in full bloom just before leaves appear can be spectacular, the branches clothed in a mass of small, purple-lilac pea flowers. A native of the eastern Mediterranean, it needs full sun or light shade. It has attractive glaucous green leaves and in hot summers reddish brown seed pods. H2.1-3m/7-10ft, W1.5-2.1m/5-7ft. F5-6. Z7-9.

CHAENOMELES Japonica, flowering quince
Sometimes listed under *Cydonia*, these deciduous Chinese and Japanese shrubs are mostly very hardy and adaptable to acid or fairly alkaline soil, sun or shade. With their dense, congested, often sharply thorned branches, they are used widely as ground cover and wall shrubs, where their early flowers are often carried on bare branches. Apple-blossom-type flowers, in crimson, pink, orange or white, are often followed by quinces — bitter, apple-like fruits used for making jelly — and these shrubs are sometimes confused with the true quince, *Cydonia oblonga*. Prune as required immediately after flowering. For wall shrubs, cut back all the previous season's growth to the original shoot; late-summer pruning of fresh growth helps flower buds swell and exposes flowers more clearly.
C. japonica. The Japanese quince is a low-growing, spreading shrub, with dense, thorny stems and profuse flowers, bright scarlet, orange or red, appearing before leaves on year-old wood. Yellow-green fruit. This species is mostly raised from seed; the cultivars have been selected from seedlings of *C. speciosa* or from *C.* × *superba*, a hybrid between *C. japonica* and *C. speciosa*. H60-90cm/2-3ft, W1.2-1.8m/4-6ft. F3-4. Z5-9.
C. speciosa. The common flowering quince, more upright than *C. japonica*, is a broad, spreading bush of densely congested, thorny branches. Its scarlet flowers appear often in late autumn, especially if grown against a sunny wall, and continue through winter, becoming more plentiful in spring and some even appearing in summer. Good at the back of a border, against a high wall or as an effective hedge. Prefers sun. **'Cardinalis'**, large, crimson flowers. **'Geisha Girl'**, low-growing, with large, peach-pink flowers. **'Moerloosei'**

Cercis canadensis 'Forest Pansy'

(syn. 'Apple Blossom'), white, flushed-pink flowers. **'Nivalis'**, white flowers, ideal in shade. **'Simonii'** (60-90cm/2-3ft high), spreading, blood-red, semi-double flowers. **'Umbilicata'**, deep salmon-pink. All H1.2-1.8m/4-6ft, W90-120cm/3-4ft. F11-4. Z5-9.
C. × *superba*. The hybrids between *C. japonica* and *C. speciosa* are mounded or prostrate. Vigorous and showy, some are excellent ground cover, others good in borders or against walls. **'Boule de Feu'**, orange-red flowers. **'Cameo'**, double, peach-pink flowers. **'Coral Sea'**, coral-pink flowers, good fruit. **'Crimson and Gold'**, blood-red flowers, prominent golden anthers. **'Fascination'**, deep scarlet, flat flowers. **'Fire Dance'**, low, spreading habit, brilliant red flowers. **'Jet Trail'**, profuse, white flowers, spreading habit. **'Nicoline'**, scarlet flowers. **'Pink Lady'**, red flower buds, opening bright rose-pink. **'Rowallane'**, brilliant scarlet-red flowers. **'Texas Scarlet'**, dense, low, spreading habit, bright red flowers. **'Vermilion'**, bright scarlet-red flowers. All H1.2-1.5m/4-5ft, W1.5-1.8m/5-6ft. F12-4. Z5-9.

CHIMONANTHUS Wintersweet
C. fragrans. See *C. praecox*.
C. praecox (syn. *C. fragrans*). Tucked up against a wall or close to a pathway, this rather dull, upright, twiggy bush is transformed by the yellow, purple-centred, sweetly fragrant, waxy, bell-like flowers which appear on mature plants. Excellent for cutting. Best in sun, where wood ripens. Tolerates most soils. Can be trained as a wall shrub. Prune to tidy in late winter, after

Chaenomeles speciosa 'Nivalis'

Chaenomeles × *superba* 'Crimson and Gold'

Chionanthus virginicus

flowering. **'Grandiflorus'** has less fragrant but larger, clear yellow flowers. **'Luteus'** has clear yellow, waxy flowers. All H1.5-1.8m/5-6ft, W1.2-1.5m/4-5ft. F12-1. Z6-9.

CHIONANTHUS Fringe tree
The common name comes from the white, wispy flower panicles on mature plants. Both flower best where summers are reliably hot, in moist, acid soil, and have purple, plum-like fruits.
C. retusus. The Chinese fringe tree has small, erect flower panicles on current year's growth. H3m/10ft, W3m/10ft. F6-7. Z6-9.
C. virginicus. The North American fringe tree has large heads of drooping, narrow-petalled, fragrant white flowers on wood made the previous year. H1.8-2.4m/6-8ft, W1.8-2.4m/6-8ft. F6. Z4-9.

Choisya ternata

Choisya ternata 'Sundance'

Cistus × *purpureus*

CHOISYA Mexican orange blossom
C. 'Aztec Pearl'. A recent very garden-worthy hybrid between *C. arizonica* and *C. ternata*. In late spring clusters of pink buds open to fragrant white flowers lasting for several weeks, with usually another show in late summer. H1.5-1.8m/5-6ft, W1.2-1.5m/4-5ft. F5-6; occ. F8. Z7-9.
C. ternata. A surprisingly hardy evergreen, given its Mexican origins. It forms a dense, slow-growing bush of glossy leaves and, eventually, fragrant, white flower clusters. Young plants can be tender, so plant in

spring or early summer in any well-drained soil, sheltered from cold winds or frost pockets. Best in sun, but tolerates shade. Good as a patio or wall plant. Prune lightly after flowering, but cut back almost to ground level in late spring plants damaged by severe frosts, and untidy or old and woody plants. H1.5-1.8m/5-6ft, W1.2-1.5m/4-5ft. F5-6; occ. F9. Z7-9.
'Sundance', compact, with bright yellow, year-round foliage. Needs sun; occasional scorch on new growth but otherwise hardy. H1.2-1.5m/4-5ft, W90-120cm/3-4ft. F5-6; occ. F9. Z7-9.

CISTUS Sun rose, rock rose
These colourful, semi-hardy evergreens look like *Helianthemum* in flower and confusingly share the common name, rock rose. From southern Europe and North Africa, they need sun and good drainage, disliking winter wet and prolonged or severe frost.

The single rose- or poppy-like flowers are individually brief, but appear over several weeks. Mostly white, pink, rose or purple, they often have contrasting patches on the inside of the papery petals, and yellow stamens. Most have grey or grey-green leaves, which cool the 'hot' summer flowers. They are often short-lived and, unlike the hardier helianthemums, do not freely break into new growth from the centre. Plant in late spring or early summer

Cistus 'Silver Pink'

in any soil, including chalk. Lightly trim in spring, but not into old wood. The following are just a few of the many species and varieties available. All F6, Z7-9.
C. × *aguilari* 'Maculutus'. A strong-growing form with glossy dark green leaves and large white flowers, with a central ring of crimson blotches. H90-120cm/3-4ft, W90-120cm/3-4ft.
C. × *cyprius*. This has large flowers, white with crimson blotches in the centre, and is vigorous. H1.8-2.1m/6-7ft, W1.8-2.1m/6-7ft.
C. formosus. See *Halimium lasianthum*.

C. 'Grayswood Pink'. An excellent plant, with grey-green leaves and masses of pink flowers. H90cm/3ft, W90cm/3ft.
C. laurifolius. This is considered the hardiest species, with dark bluish green leaves and white yellow-centred flowers. H1.8-2.1m/6-7ft, W1.8-2.1m/6-7ft.
C. 'Peggy Sammons'. This has grey-green leaves and an erect habit, with light pink flowers. H1.2m/4ft, W90-120cm/3-4ft.
C. × *pulverulentus* (syn. *C.* 'Warley Rose'). Compact spreading habit, with dark green leaves and bright rose-cerise flowers. H60cm/2ft, W60-90cm/2-3ft.
C. × *purpureus*. Upright habit, with narrow, dark green leaves and rosy crimson flowers with a chocolate blotch at the base. H1.2-1.5m/4-5ft, W90-120cm/3-4ft.
C. 'Silver Pink'. An outstanding and popular plant, with grey leaves and clusters of silver-pink flowers. H60-75cm/24-30in, W90-120cm/3-4ft.
C. 'Warley Rose'. See *C.* × *pulverulentus*.

CLEMATIS
Perhaps the most important, varied and indispensable garden climbers, these are still much underused. Among the species and cultivars are a tremendous range of flower shapes and colours to provide interest from spring until autumn, and one or two flower in winter. They can be used for training up walls, pergolas, fences and trees, or allowed to scramble over shrubs or other low-growing plants. They are excellent for patios, in containers. Most clematis are easy to please, given a moist but well-drained soil. The majority flower best in full sun, but the roots prefer shade, which can be provided by mulching after initially enriching the planting hole with well-rotted compost. Plant with the surface of the rootball 5-10cm/2-4in below the surface of the soil and place 45-60cm/18-24in away from dry walls and the main stem of shrubs or trees. Clematis grow up and through supports, whether artificial or living, but need assistance or they become unruly. Some species are vigorous and may need controlling.

Prune immediately after flowering those that flower in mid- to late spring (denoted in the entries that follow as Group 1); most are small-flowered species and hybrids that may not need pruning for some years, and then only to control growth. Those in Group 2, comprised mostly of large-flowered hybrids flowering from early to midsummer, should be allowed to build a framework, then the stems should be pruned back halfway from the previous year's growth as soon as buds swell in mid-spring. Those in Group 3 flower on the new season's growth, in mid- to late summer, and are pruned hard each early spring to within 30cm/1ft of the base of the plant or,

SHRUBS

on established plants, to just above the previous year's main pruning. Any exceptions to the above are given in the following descriptions, and heights are only approximate.

C. alpina. This species, from northern Europe and northern Asia, is one of the most charming. It has masses of pendent flowers, the slender sepals blue or purple with white centres, followed by glistening, silky seed heads. It is a steady but not rapid grower, perfect for covering fences, walls, shrubs and small trees. Named forms include **'Columbine'**, pale blue, **'Pamela Jackman'**, mid-blue, **'Ruby'**, purple-pink, and **'White Moth'**, double white. Group 1. All H2.4m/8ft, W1.8-2.4m/6-8ft. F4-5. Z5-9.

C. armandii. A superb, evergreen, Chinese species with leathery, glossy green leaves and a mass of creamy white flowers. Vigorous, but ideal for walls, pergolas and trees. Needs the protection of a sunny, sheltered wall or fence in cold areas. Prune only every few years to restrict growth. **'Apple Blossom'** has flushed pink sepals. **'Snowdrift'** has white flowers. Group 1. All H5m/16ft, W5m/16ft. F4. Z7-9.

C. cirrhosa. Pendent, bell-shaped, creamy yellow flowers appear on slender, leafy stems in late autumn, winter and early spring during mild spells. Use among deciduous shrubs. The form *balearica* has more attractive foliage and purple-spotted yellow flowers, but is a little less hardy. **'Freckles'** has large, crimson-purple splashed flowers. Provide shelter in cold areas; a perfect conservatory plant. Group 1. All H3m/10ft, W3m/10ft. F10-3. Z8-9.

C. flammula. A European native, especially useful for covering large walls, or contrasting with dark foliage. Strong-growing, with abundant, fragrant, small, starry white flowers. Group 3. H5m/16ft, W5m/16ft. F8-10. Z7-9.

C. florida **'Bicolor'** (syn. 'Sieboldii'). At its best, this is the most spectacular clematis and is often mistaken for passion flower. Creamy white sepals surround the prominently raised violet-purple, petal-like stamens. **'Alba Plena'** is white-centred. Both are weak garden plants, but excellent container plants if overwintered under glass. Group 3. Both H3m/10ft, W3m/10ft. F7-8. Z7-9.

C. macropetala. An attractive, easy, hardy species from China and Siberia, closely related to but generally more vigorous than *C. alpina.* Light green, divided leaves make a pretty background to nodding, semi-double lavender-blue flowers, followed by attractive seed heads. Suited to sun or shade. Good for walls or fences. **'Markham's Pink'**, rose-pink, and **'White Swan'**, white, widen the choice. Group 1. Both H3m/10ft, W3m/10ft. F5-6. Z5-9.

Clematis alpina

Clematis florida 'Bicolor'

Clematis armandii

Clematis macropetala 'Markham's Pink'

Clematis *montana* 'Elizabeth'

Clematis 'Daniel Deronda'

Clematis *orientalis*

Clematis 'Mrs N. Thompson'

C. montana. This indispensable, vigorous Himalayan species is excellent for walls, fences or climbing up trees, with long-lasting flowers ranging from white to deep pink. Happy in sun or shade, its roots prefer moisture. Forms include **'Alexander'**, with good foliage and scented white flowers with prominent yellow stamens, and **'Elizabeth'**, with pale pink flowers and a heady fragrance. The form *grandiflora* has profuse, large, scented white flowers and is excellent for north walls. **'Marjorie'** has creamy pink, semi-double flowers. The Chinese form *rubens* has bronze-purple shoots and young leaves, with pink flowers. **'Tetrarose'** has bronze foliage, with large, rose-pink flowers. Group 1. All (unpruned) H10m/33ft, W10m/33ft. F5-6. Z6-9.
C. orientalis. An Asian climber and scrambler with light green, finely dissected leaves and yellow, pendent, subtly fragrant flowers, like golden lanterns. Long-lasting flowers are followed by attractive fluffy seed heads. H2.1-3m/7-10ft, W2.1-3m/7-10ft. F8-9. Z6-9. Larger-flowered and considerably

more vigorous is **'Bill Mackenzie'**. At Bressingham this climbs a purple-leaved birch, where its yellow flowers and silvery seed heads make a striking contrast. Group 3. Both H5-6m/16-20ft, W5-6m/16-20ft. F8-9. Z6-9.
C. tangutica. So closely related to *C. orientalis* that it is often listed as a form of that species, this is more vigorous, with similar, yellow, lantern-like flowers with thick sepals and silky, silvery seed heads. Effective on fences or climbing up trees. Group 3. H5-6m/16-20ft, W5-6m/16-20ft. F7-9. Z6-9.
C. viticella. This southern European, semi-woody species has been grown for 400 years. The species is variable, with rosy pink, blue or purple flowers. Its vigorous cultivars, with small, nodding, bell-shaped flowers, are ideal for scrambling up trees, through shrubs or over fences, and are seemingly unaffected by clematis wilt. **'Abundance'** has profuse, nodding, wine-red, dark-veined flowers. **'Alba Luxurians'** is white, flushed mauve and with green

markings. **'Etoile Violette'** has violet, open flowers and yellow anthers. **'Kermesina'** is deep red-purple. **'Minuet'** is delicate-looking, with white flowers edged mauve-pink. **'Polish Spirit'**, a new Polish selection, has outstanding velvety, purple-violet open flowers, good against gold or variegated foliage. **'Purpurea Plena Elegans'**, an old variety recently rediscovered, has nodding, double, violet-purple flowers. Group 3. All H3m/10ft, W3m/10ft. F7-9. Z5-9.

Large-flowered hybrids
These spectacular clematis include a wide range of colours with single, double and semi-double flowers as much as 18cm/7in across. Support and train them against a fence or wall, grow them through wall shrubs or conifers, through shrubs or trees in open beds, or as an up-market ground cover! The following are a few of the many excellent cultivars. In general, the spread is roughly the same as the height. All Z4-9.
  'Asao', rose-pink, darker edges, attractive seed heads. Group 2. H2.4m/8ft. F6. **'Ascotiensis'**, bright blue, green stamens. Group 3. H3m/10ft. F8. **'Barbara Jackman'**, mauve-blue, deep pink bar, yellow anthers, good seed heads. Group 2. H2.4m/8ft. F6. **'Beauty of Worcester'**, deep blue double and single, creamy yellow anthers. Group 2. H2.4m/8ft. F6. **'Carnaby'**, deep pink, central darker bar, free-flowering, attractive seed heads. Group 2. H2.4m/8ft. F6. **'Daniel Deronda'**, large, purple-blue semi-double and single, free-flowering, good seed heads. Group 2. H2.4m/8ft. F6. **'Dr Ruppel'**, deep rose-pink, darker bar. Group 2. H2.4m/8ft. F6. **'Duchess of Edinburgh'**, fully double white, long season. Group 2. H2.4m/8ft. F6. **'Duchess of Sutherland'**, carmine-red, yellow anthers. Group 2. H3m/10ft. F7. **'Edith'**, white, compact habit, good seed heads. Group 2. H2.1m/7ft. F6. **'Elsa Spath'**, mid-blue, free-flowering, long season. Group 2. H2.4m/8ft. F6-8. **'Ernest Markham'**, vigorous old favourite, magenta. Group 3. H4m/13ft. F8. **'Etoiles de Paris'**, mauve-blue, good seed heads. Group 2. H2.1m/7ft. F6. **'General Sikorski'**, striking deep blue, free-flowering. Group 2. H3m/10ft. F7. **'Gipsy Queen'**, rich violet-purple, velvety flowers. Group 3. H3m/10ft. F8. **'H.F. Young'**, Wedgwood-blue, free-flowering. Group 2. H2.4m/8ft. F6. **'Jackmannii Superba'**, rich purple, larger than **'Jackmannii'**. Group 3. H3m/10ft. F8. **'Lady Huxtable'**, free-flowering white. Group 3. H2.4m/8ft. F8. **'Lady Lousborough'**, pale blue, free-flowering. Group 2. H2.1m/7ft. F6. **'Marie Boisselot'**, excellent large white, long season. Group 2. H3m/10ft. F6-7. **'Maureen'**, rich purple-red. Group 2. H3m/10ft. F7. **'Mrs Cholmondeley'**,

SHRUBS

lavender-blue, free-flowering, good seed heads. Group 2. H2.4m/8ft. F6. **'Mrs N. Thompson'**, blue with red bar, striking, free-flowering. Group 2. H2.4m/8ft. F6-7. **'Niobe'**, ruby-red velvety flowers, yellow anthers, long season. Group 2. H3m/10ft. F6-8. **'Perle D'Azur'**, distinctive azure blue, free-flowering. Group 3. H3.6m/12ft. F8. **'Proteus'**, mauve-pink double and semi-double flowers, long season. Group 2. H2.4m/8ft. F6-7. **'Richard Pennell'**, large, rich purple-blue, yellow anthers, good seed heads. Group 2. H3m/10ft. F6. **'Rouge Cardinal'**, crimson velvety flowers. Group 3. H3m/10ft. F8. **'Royalty'**, good purple-mauve, semi-double and single flowers. Group 2. H2.1m/7ft. F7. **'Serenata'**, deep purple, darker bar, yellow anthers. Group 2. H3m/10ft. F7. **'Silver Moon'**, pale silvery lilac, free-flowering. Group 2. H2.4m/8ft. F6. **'Sylvia Denny'**, white, semi-double and single. Group 2. H3m/10ft. F7. **'Ville de Lyon'**, reliable, single crimson-red, yellow anthers. Group 2. H3m/10ft. F6. **'Will Goodwin'**, attractive pale blue, long season. Group 2. H3m/10ft. F6-8.

CLERODENDRUM
In this large genus of mostly tropical shrubs and climbers only three Chinese species are hardy enough for temperate-climate garden use.
C. bungei. Almost herbaceous, its fleshy stems are cut to the ground by frost. New purple shoots emerge in spring. Large, heart-shaped, purple leaves, turning purple-green, have a pungent odour when crushed. Round heads of rose-pink, scented flowers. Best in warm, sheltered spots, in sun or part shade. Can be invasive. H1.2-1.8m/4-6ft, W1.2-1.8m/4-6ft. F8-9. Z7-9.
C. trichotomum. Beautiful at its best, but in cool climates can suffer from winter dieback. It is grown for its clusters of fragrant, white, starry flowers with maroon-red calyces. The calyces contrast strikingly with turquoise autumn fruit. Suckers if roots are damaged. Prune in spring if required. H1.5-1.8m/5-6ft, W1.5-1.8m/5-6ft. F8. Z7-9.

CLETHRA
These acid-loving, mostly deciduous shrubs provide a late summer show of fragrant, white or pink flowers. They are best in hot summers, and in sun or light shade where not too dry.
C. alnifolia. The sweet pepper bush from eastern North America is erect and branching, with bottlebrush heads of fragrant, white flowers. **'Paniculata'** has larger panicles. **'Pink Spire'** has pink panicles which fade. **'Rosea'**, pink in bud, produces pink flowers fading to white. All H1.5-1.8m/5-6ft, W90-120cm/3-4ft. F8. Z4-9.

Clerodendrum bungei

COLUTEA Bladder senna
C. arborescens. Once planted widely, now seldom seen, this member of the pea family tolerates all but wet, heavy soils, otherwise adapting to acid or alkaline types, sun or shade and even poor conditions. It bears small, yellow, pea flowers. The large, light green, bladder-like pods hang among the foliage with the flowers. Prune the previous year's growth to old wood in spring.
'Copper Beauty' has bluish green leaves and copper-orange flowers. Both H1.8-2.4m/6-8ft, W1.8-2.4m/6-8ft. F7-9. Z6-8.

CORNUS Cornel, dogwood
These indispensable deciduous shrubs and small trees are grown for their spectacular flowers, brightly coloured foliage and colourful winter stems.
C. alba. The red-twigged, or Siberian, dogwood has so many good cultivars and selected forms that one would use the species only in wild gardens. Vigorous and spreading, with erect, flexible, dark red branches, its oval leaves colour well in autumn. Clusters or umbels of white flowers appear on old wood, followed by small, bluish white fruit. It and its cultivars are extremely hardy, growing in most soils, moist or dry. Most are vigorous and, if grown for winter stems, best cut to the ground every year or two in late spring just before new growth begins, to produce the brightest stems. Grow in an open position. Good beside water. Unpruned H2.4-3m/8-10ft, W2.4-3m/8-10ft. F5-6. Z2-8. **'Aurea'**, golden-yellow leaves, reddish in autumn, crimson stems. H1.5-1.8m/5-6ft, W1.5-1.8m/5-6ft. F5-6. Z3-8. **'Elegantissima'**, grey-green leaves broadly splashed silvery white, turning pink in autumn, maroon stems. Similar to 'Sibirica Variegata'. H1.5-1.8m/5-6ft, W1.5-1.8m/5-6ft. F5-6. Z3-8. **'Kesselringii'**, vigorous, upright, shiny, black-purple stems, effective with red and

Clethra alnifolia 'Paniculata'

Colutea arborescens 'Copper Beauty'

Cornus alba 'Sibirica Variegata'

Cornus canadensis

Cornus alternifolia 'Argentea'

Cornus kousa 'Gold Star'

yellow forms; purple-green shoots, dark green leaves, crimson-purple in autumn. H1.8-2.4m/6-8ft, W1.2-1.5m/4-5ft. F5-6. Z3-8. **'Sibirica'**, shorter and less vigorous than *C. alba*. Coral-red bark, brilliant in winter, effective against water; bluish fruits, good autumn colour; prefers moist soils. H1.2-1.5m/4-5ft, W1.2-1.5m/4-5ft. F5-6. Z2-8. **'Sibirica Variegata'**, small, dark green leaves with cream margins, deep red stems; flowers and fruits freely. H1.2-1.5m/4-5ft, W1.2-1.5m/4-5ft. F5-6. Z2-8. **'Spaethii'**, golden-yellow splashed leaves, deep red winter stems. H1.5-1.8m/5-6ft, W1.5-1.8m/5-6ft. F5-6. Z3-9.

C. alternifolia **'Argentea'**. This form, at its best, is a graceful bush with layered, purplish, twiggy branches and small, variegated, light green and white leaves. Needs shelter. Generally grafted. H1.5-2.4m/5-8ft, W1.5-2.4m/5-8ft. F5-6. Z5-7.

C. canadensis. The creeping dogwood, or bunchberry, is an acid-loving, almost herbaceous, mat-forming species, spreading by runners in moist, peaty or sandy soil. White flower bracts, then vivid red fruit in autumn. Prefers shade. H5-10cm/2-4in, W60-90cm/2-3ft. F6-7. Z2-6.

C. florida. At their best in the USA, flowering dogwoods create a breathtaking spectacle. Britain generally lacks the hot summers and warm autumns needed to ripen their wood; spring frosts do not help either. They make slow-growing shrubs or small trees, with four showy bracts, usually white but can be pink or red, surrounding small, insignificant, green-yellow flowers. Pleasing bark on older trees. Provide

neutral to acid soil, sun or part shade where not too dry. Foliage turns reddish purple towards autumn and in North America there is usually a superb show of scarlet fruit. **'Rainbow'** has golden-yellow and green leaf variegations. Both H1.8-2.4m/6-8ft, W1.8-2.4m/6-8ft. F5. Z5-9.

C. kousa chinensis. This Chinese selection is a finer form, with larger flower bracts and stronger than the species, though plants sold as *chinensis* do vary. Slow-growing and bushy, shy to flower when young, but white flower bracts, carried above the green leaves, almost weigh down the spreading branches of the mature plant. The bracts fade to pink, often followed by edible, red, strawberry-like fruits, and good autumn colour. It prefers full sun or part shade on well-drained, reasonable, acid to slightly alkaline soils where not too dry. Plants vary from seed; reliable flowering selections such as **'China Girl'** and **'Milky Way'** are propagated by grafting or cuttings, and thus cost more. **'Gold Star'** has green leaves with a yellow central splash. All H1.8-2.4m/6-8ft, W1.5-1.8m/5-6ft. F7. Z5-9.

C. mas. The cornelian cherry has a broad, bushy habit and congested branches, with small, yellow flowers along the bare stems. Sometimes has good autumn colour and edible crimson fruit, often hidden among the foliage. Good against a dark background. Likes most soils, sun or part shade. Prune as required after flowering. **'Aurea'** has leaves suffused yellow in spring, greening in summer. Both H2.4-3m/8-10ft, W2.4-3m/8-10ft. F2. Z4-8. **'Elegantissima'** is slow-growing and needs shade and shelter when young. Leaves variegated cream, yellow and pink. H1.8-2.4m/6-8ft, W1.2-1.5m/4-5ft. F3. Z6-8. **'Variegata'**, slow-growing, also needs shade, and has grey-green leaves with creamy white margins. H1.5-1.8m/5-6ft, W.1.2-1.5m/4-5ft. F2. Z6-9.

C. sanguinea **'Winter Flame'** (syn. 'Winter Beauty'). This Dutch introduction has soft green leaves, golden-yellow in autumn, and breathtaking stems of bright gold, yellow and pink. Prune as for *C. alba* cultivars. Needs well-drained soil. H1.5-1.8m/5-6ft, W1.5-1.8m/5-6ft. F5-6. Z4-8.

C. stolonifera (syn. *C. sericea*). **'Flaviramea'** is similar to *C. alba* and needs the same treatment. Requires moist soil. Vigorous erect branches, green leaves, and in open situations yellow stems, excellent with red- and black-stemmed dogwoods. H2.4-3m/8-10ft, W1.8-2.4m/6-8ft. F6-7. Z3-8. **'Kelsey's Dwarf'** is low-growing, with narrow, upright stems and bright green, finely ribbed leaves. Good autumn colour. H60-75cm/24-30in, W60-90cm/2-3ft. Z3-8. A new variety, **'White Gold'**, has variegated gold leaves which turn creamy white. H1.5m/5ft, W1.5m/5ft. F6-7. Z3-8.

Cornus alba 'Sibirica'

Cornus sanguinea 'Winter Flame'

CORONILLA
This little-appreciated genus includes many herbaceous plants and a few shrubs, all sun-loving, for any well-drained soil, and providing a succession of small yellow pea flowers from early summer on.

C. emerus. This trouble-free, vigorous plant has bushy, upright stems and yellow flowers, reddish brown on the outside. Narrow green pea pods. To maintain as a dwarf, prune annually or less often to the ground in late winter; otherwise, remove old stems to let air and light into the plant. H1.8-2.4m/6-8ft, W1.5-1.8m/5-6ft. F5-9. Z7-9.

C. emeroides. This scaled-down version of the above grows 90cm/3ft or so high, less across. F5-9. Z7-9.

CORYLOPSIS
Fragrant winterhazel
Related to witch hazels, these Japanese and Chinese shrubs have an upright, spreading habit and delicate, pendent yellow flowers on bare stems in early spring. They prefer acid to neutral, moist but well-drained soil, but will grow on alkaline loam with peat or leaf mould added. Provide shelter from cold winds and spring frosts by planting under or near trees, against a hedge, wall or tall conifers in light shade where protected from early-morning sun. Prune only to thin congested branches, immediately after flowering.

C. pauciflora. Known in the USA as the buttercup hazel, this dwarf form has a bushy, spreading habit, and pendulous racemes of scented primrose-yellow flowers. Provide shelter from summer sun and severe frost. H1.2-1.5m/4-5ft, W1.2-1.5m/4-5ft. F3. Z6-8.

C. spicata. This beautiful species slowly forms a spreading, irregularly branched shrub with long spikes of pale yellow, cowslip-scented flowers. H1.2-1.8m/4-6ft, W1.5-1.8m/5-6ft. F3. Z6-8.

C. willmottiae. Vigorous and upright, with pendulous racemes of greenish yellow, fragrant flowers. **'Spring Purple'** has a longer show of plum-purple shoots and young leaves, later turning to green. H1.5-2.1m/5-7ft, W1.5-2.1m/5-7ft. F3-4. Z6-8.

CORYLUS Hazel, filbert
These large deciduous shrubs or small trees are easy to grow in most soils. To maintain *C. avellana* 'Aurea' and *C. maxima* 'Purpurea' as shrubs, prune to the ground every few years. For a more open, tree-like form, thin out stems and any excess annual regrowth of shoots from the base. Prune in mid- to late winter.

C. avellana '**Aurea**'. A dense bush with large, round or oval yellow leaves, brighter in open positions, deepening later in summer. Older plants usually carry long, yellow, male catkins in late winter and

Coronilla emerus

Corylopsis spicata

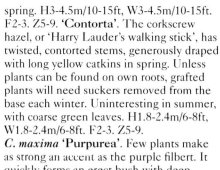

Corylus avellana 'Contorta'

spring. H3-4.5m/10-15ft, W3-4.5m/10-15ft. F2-3. Z5-9. '**Contorta**'. The corkscrew hazel, or 'Harry Lauder's walking stick', has twisted, contorted stems, generously draped with long yellow catkins in spring. Unless plants can be found on own roots, grafted plants will need suckers removed from the base each winter. Uninteresting in summer, with coarse green leaves. H1.8-2.4m/6-8ft, W1.8-2.4m/6-8ft. F2-3. Z5-9.

C. maxima '**Purpurea**'. Few plants make as strong an accent as the purple filbert. It quickly forms an erect bush with deep purple leaves all summer, fading to green in hot climates. Purplish buds and catkins. Prune as above. H3-4.5m/10-15ft, W3-4.5m/10-15ft. Z5-8.

Corylus avellana 'Aurea'

Cotinus coggygria 'Royal Purple'

Cotinus 'Grace'

COTINUS Smoke bush, Venetian sumach

Formerly *Rhus cotinus*, the common name smoke bush comes from the fluffy, plumed beige-pink panicles which turn smoky grey in late summer. They are happy on most well-drained soils, flowering more freely in hot, dry spots than heavy, rich soils, where foliage is often produced at the expense of flowers. Good autumn colours most years. Prune in late spring just before new growth appears. To keep plants compact, prune annually to within 15-60cm/6-24in of the ground. Strong stems and large, oval leaves result, but no flowers. Flowers occur on two- to three-year-old wood, so prune only to thin out a few older stems, for rejuvenation.

C. americanus. See *C. obovatus*.

C. coggygria. The Venetian sumach is often underrated against its colourful, purple-leaved progeny, but is more natural-looking in a garden or landscape. It has a bushy habit and oval, light green leaves, which turn yellow or red in autumn. Older plants, especially in open situations, are smothered in fluffy, beige-pink panicles in late summer, fading to beige or grey. H2.4-3m/8-10ft, W2.4-3m/8-10ft. F8. Z5-9.

'**Foliis Purpureis**', '**Notcutt's Variety**' and '**Royal Purple**' all have dark purple, oval leaves, and colour best in full sun, going green in shade. 'Foliis Purpureis' has leaves which fade to purple-green, and pink panicles; 'Notcutt's Variety' has larger, dark maroon-purple leaves, with pinkish purple inflorescences; 'Royal Purple' has the deepest purple leaves, and pinkish purple heads. Place against soft-toned, contrasting plants. Reddish purple and crimson autumn tints. All H2.4-3m/8-10ft, W2.4-3m/8-10ft. F8. Z5-9.

C. '**Grace**'. This beautiful new hybrid from the Hillier Nursery in Hampshire, England, is a tall, open bush with distinct, soft red-purple leaves through which the sun glows. Imposing pinkish inflorescences. H3-3.6m/10-12ft, W2.4-3m/8-10ft. F8. Z5-9.

C. obovatus (syn. *C. americanus*). The strong-growing, upright American smoke tree is primarily grown for its spectacular yellow, orange and red autumn colour. Best in sun and well-drained, poor soil. Large, wispy, brown-pink inflorescences. H3-3.6m/10-12ft, W2.4-3m/8-10ft. F8. Z4-8.

COTONEASTER

This is one of the largest and most invaluable genera of deciduous and evergreen shrubs, ranging from dwarf forms to shrubs of tree-like proportions. Most have white flowers followed by often spectacular displays of various coloured fruit in late summer and autumn. These are naturally attractive to birds, though some species and cultivars seem less so,

Cotoneaster congestus

depending on the birds' hunger and the winter's severity. Cotoneasters grow on most soils, and in sun or shade. Many vigorous ground-covering types are used extensively in landscape planting. Prune only to shape or control vigour, ideally in early spring. Many so-called evergreen forms retain their leaves in mild climates but become deciduous in cold regions.

C. adpressus praecox. This has compact, spreading, rigid branches, with small green leaves, white flowers, and large orange-red fruit. Good autumn colour. '**Boer**', with dark green leaves, has larger red fruit. Deciduous. Both H30-45cm/12-18in, W90-120cm/3-4ft. F6-7. Z5-8.

C. apiculatus. A dense, deciduous, Chinese species with arching branches, shiny green leaves and pink-tinged flowers followed by single red fruits. Crimson-purple autumn leaves. H1.5-1.8m/5-6ft, W1.8-2.4m/6-8ft. F6-7. Z5-8.

C. bullatus. A deciduous species with open and arching branches; large, dark green ribbed or puckered leaves; and heavy clusters of large, brilliant red berries. Good autumn foliage. H1.8-2.4m/6-8ft, W1.8-2.4m/6-8ft. F6-7. Z6-8.

C. buxifolius. The box-leaved cotoneaster is a low-growing, slow-spreading evergreen, with spiky, angled branches. It has small, dark green leaves, white flowers flushed with pink, and small red fruit. H30-45cm/12-18in, W60-90cm/2-3ft. F6-7. Z6-8.

C. congestus. This is a small creeping evergreen shrub with tiny, round-to-oval leaves, pinkish white flowers, and occasional red fruit. If pruned, it forms hummocks. H10-30cm/4-12in, W90cm/3ft. F6-7. Z7-8.

C. conspicuus '**Decorus**'. A selected evergreen form with a low, arching and spreading habit. It has small, grey-green leaves and profuse white flowers, followed by brilliant red berries. Good for ground cover and banks. H90-120cm/3-4ft, W1.2-1.8m/4-6ft. F6. Z7-8.

C. '**Coral Beauty**'. One of the best ground covers, taller in shade than in sun, with dark, dense evergreen leaves, white flowers, and coral-red fruit. H30-60cm/1-2ft, W1.5-1.8m/5-6ft. F5. Z6-8.

C. '**Cornubia**'. A vigorous deciduous or semi-evergreen shrub, eventually a small tree. It has large, dark green leaves, and reliable, profuse bright scarlet fruit weighing branches down in autumn and winter. H3-4.5m/10-15ft, W2.4-3m/8-10ft. F6-7. Z7-8.

C. dammeri. Prostrate evergreen ground cover, useful in sun or shade. It has long stems which hug the ground, dark green leaves, and crimson-red fruits. '**Oakwood**' (syn. 'Eicholz') is denser and less vigorous. Both H10-15cm/4-6in, W1.8-2.4m/6-8ft. F6-7. Z6-8.

C. distichus. Seldom touched by birds, this slow-growing deciduous or semi-evergreen has erect branches clothed in scarlet-red fruit well into winter. Pinkish flowers and glossy green leaves. H1.5-1.8m/5-6ft, W1.2-1.5m/4-5ft. F6-7. Z6-8.

C. divaricatus. Dense, multi-stemmed, deciduous, spreading bush. The small, dark green, glossy leaves turn crimson-red in autumn. Deep red fruit. Good as hedging. H1.5-1.8m/5-6ft, W1.5-1.8m/5-6ft. F6-7. Z5-8.

C. 'Exburiensis'. A tall, wide-spreading, semi-evergreen shrub or small tree with arching branches and profuse, pendulous clusters of pale yellow fruit well into winter. Very similar is *C.* 'Rothschildianus'. Both were raised at Exbury Gardens, family home of the Rothschilds, in Hampshire, England. H2.4-3m/8-10ft, W2.4-3m/8-10ft. F6-7. Z6-8.

C. franchetii. A graceful, semi-evergreen shrub with arching branches, glossy sage-green leaves, and ovoid, orange-scarlet fruit. The form *sternianus* is similar but with round fruit and green foliage, silvery grey beneath. Good autumn colour. Both H1.8-2.4m/6-8ft, W1.8-2.4m/6-8ft. F6-7. Z7-9.

C. horizontalis. Probably the most used cotoneaster in British gardens, it is a low, spreading shrub which is more often wall-trained, where its herringbone branching pattern looks very effective. It has dark green leaves, red in autumn, and bright red fruits. 'Variegatus' is similar but slower-growing, with creamy white leaf margins, bright in summer, brighter in autumn with reddish tinges, and less plentiful red fruit. Both H60-75cm/24-30in, W1.2-1.5m/4-5ft. F6-7. Z5-8.

C. 'Hybridus Pendulus'. A free-fruiting shrub with large, glossy green deciduous leaves and a graceful, open habit. Mostly trained up or grafted onto a stem, from which long branches sweep to the ground. In autumn it is laden with bright red fruit. Non-grafted. H45-60cm/18-24in, W1.5-1.8m/5-6ft. F6-7. Z6-8.

C. lacteus. This has distinct evergreen foliage, dark green above, milky white beneath. The clusters of white flowers in midsummer are followed by heavy, dark red fruit in autumn and well into winter. H1.8-2.4m/6-8ft, W1.8-2.4m/6-8ft. F7. Z6-8.

C. microphyllus. An evergreen shrub, with rigid, spiky branches and glossy leaves. White flowers and large scarlet-red berries are borne along the stems. Excellent for the front of the border or against walls. H45-60cm/18-24in, W1.2-1.5m/4-5ft. F6-7. Z6-8.

C. salicifolius. The willowleaf cotoneaster is a variable Chinese evergreen, the parent of many ground-cover hybrids. The species, eventually 5m/16ft or more, has slender arching stems, willow-like leaves and bright red fruit. H1.8-3m/6-10ft, W1.8-2.4m/6-8ft. F6-7. Z6-8. The form *floccosus* is evergreen, with small, narrow leaves, silvery beneath. It has white flowers, and glossy red berries in autumn, weighing down the arching branches well into winter. H1.8-2.4m/6-8ft, W1.8-2.4m/6-8ft. F6-7. Z6-8. 'Parkteppich' makes evergreen, semi-prostrate ground cover, growing strongly in sun or shade: a congested thicket of low, arching branches. Narrow leaves, small red fruit. 'Repens' (syn. 'Avondrood') and 'Gnome' are lower but not always free-fruiting. All H90-120cm/3-4ft, W1.8-2.4m/6-8ft. F6-7. Z6-8.

C. simonsii. Used for hedging, this vigorous, erect semi-evergreen has glossy leaves, white flowers and large scarlet fruit well into winter. H1.8-2.4m/6-8ft, W1.5-1.8m/5-6ft. F6-7. Z6-9.

C. 'Skogholm'. A vigorous Swedish ground cover with small, dark green leaves and orange-red fruit, although this is not always plentiful. H30-45cm/12-18in, W1.8-2.4m/6-8ft. F6-7. Z6-8.

C. 'Streibs Findling'. A small-leaved German selection with a controllable creeping habit and red fruit in autumn. Try on a bank, over a rock or a wall. H10-15cm/4-6in, W90-120cm/3-4ft. F6-7. Z6-8.

CRATAEGUS Hawthorn

C. monogyna 'Compacta' (syn. 'Inermis Compacta'). This dwarf form of common hawthorn is a thornless, miniature replica of a much older tree, with sturdy, forked, greyish white branches, pretty if unspectacular white flowers and deeply cut, bright green leaves. Sometimes it has good autumn colour, but except in hot summers little or no fruit. Needs an open position, ideally among alpines or dwarf shrubs. Must be grafted. H90-120cm/3-4ft, W60-90cm/2-3ft. F3-5. Z5-7.

Cotoneaster 'Exburiensis'

Cotoneaster 'Hybridus Pendulus'

Crataegus monogyna 'Compacta'

Crinodendron hookerianum

Cytisus × *praecox* 'Allgold'

Cytisus battandieri

CRINODENDRON

C. hookerianum. This Chilean native is the hardiest species but still needs shelter in all but the mildest districts. It is an upright bush with narrow, dark leaves, whitish beneath, and striking, narrow, heart-shaped, pendent crimson flowers on long red stalks. The stalks appear in autumn but the flowers emerge in late spring or early summer on mature wood. Needs shade, acid soil, and shelter from cold winds and frost. Try on a sheltered north wall. Once established, even if cut back or damaged by winter it often recovers in time, and in warm climates makes a large tree. Prune only after winter damage. H1.5-1.8m/5-6ft, W90-120cm/3-4ft. F5-6. Z9-11.

CYTISUS Broom

These sun-loving members of the pea family are easily grown, mostly evergreen shrubs adapting to any well-drained soil, except extremely acid or alkaline ones. Most have narrow, pithy green stems, insignificant leaves and pea flowers in late spring or early summer, usually yellow in the species but hybrids provide a multitude of single and mixed colours. Brooms can be untidy and sometimes short-lived, so prune occasionally, immediately after flowering, especially since taller plants can get top-heavy and flop. Secateurs are slow and not

Cytisus × *praecox* 'Frisia'

Cytisus purpureus

as good as a sharp knife. Do not prune into old wood.

C. albus. See *C. multiflorus*.

C. ardoinii. This rare alpine species forms a low carpet smothered with creamy yellow flowers. H10-15cm/4-6in, W60-90cm/2-3ft. F6. Z6-8.

C. battandieri. Few gardeners would recognize this striking, temperamental tall shrub as a member of the broom family, with its broad, oval, silvery grey, laburnum-like leaves. The Morocco broom carries erect, bottlebrush heads of golden-yellow, pineapple-scented flowers. Plants often get leggy and untidy; prune occasionally, immediately after flowering, to thin out old wood. Provide sun, good drainage and shelter; excellent against a high wall. H3-5m/10-16ft, W2.4-3m/8-10ft. F7. Z8-9.

C. × *beanii*. A pleasing prostrate dwarf, forming a low mound of dark green shoots covered with golden-yellow flowers. H30-45cm/12-18in, W60-75cm/24-30in. F6. Z7-8.

C. demissus. A deciduous species ideal in a rock garden. Prostrate, with bright green leaves, yellow flowers with rich brown keels, or markings. H5-10cm/2-4in, W45-60cm/18-24in. F5. Z6-8.

C. × *kewensis*. A deservedly popular hybrid with a vigorous, prostrate, open habit, ideal for a border, larger rock garden or over a wall. Long, tangled stems carry masses of large creamy white flowers. 'Niki', a yellow-flowered Dutch cultivar, is quickly winning equal popularity. Both H30cm/1ft, W60-90cm/2-3ft. F6. Z7-8.

C. multiflorus (syn. *C. albus*). The white Spanish broom is a light, airy, tall shrub, its long, upright branches studded with small, white flowers, often followed by a heavy crop of grey-green seed pods. H1.8-2.4m/6-8ft, W1.2-1.8m/4-6ft. F6. Z6-8.

C. × *praecox*. The Warminster broom is a magnificent garden hybrid, its dense, narrow, green, upright stems so laden with creamy-yellow flowers they are often weighed down to the ground. 'Albus' is taller, with equally spectacular white flowers. 'Allgold' and 'Canary Bird' are almost replicas of *C.* × *praecox* but with rich, deep gold blooms. Closely related are 'Frisia', tallish with white, pink, lilac, yellow and brown flowers, which somehow seems to look alright; 'Hollandia', with abundant cream and cerise blooms; and 'Zeelandia', with creamy-white and lilac-pink flowers. All H1.2-1.5m/4-5ft, W1.2-1.5m/4-5ft. F4-5. Z6-9.

C. purpureus. This deciduous dwarf broom is unassuming-looking until its striking, lilac-purple flowers cover the arching branches. 'Albus' is white. 'Atropurpureus' has deep purple flowers, perhaps more outstanding than the species. All H30-45cm/12-18in, W45-60cm/18-24in. F6. Z6-9.

C. prostratus 'Golden Carpet'. Covers a distinct selection of the prostrate golden form of *C. scoparius*. It makes a wide-spreading carpet of deep green, angled stems covered with large, golden-yellow flowers. H30-45cm/12-18in, W90-120cm/3-4ft. F6. Z7-9.

C. scoparius. Though its erect green stems give the impression of being evergreen, the common broom is actually deciduous, with rich, golden-yellow flowers. It has given rise to come colourful forms and hybrids. **'Andreanus'** has striking, large, yellow and brown pea flowers. The vigorous **'Burkwoodii'** has deep red, brown and yellow blooms. **'Cornish Cream'** has fresh creamy white and yellow blooms. The compact **'Goldfinch'** has crimson, pink and yellow blooms. The compact **'Killiney Red'** has one of the brightest reds. The early, strong-growing **'Luna'** has light and dark yellow blooms. The vigorous **'Palette'** has yellow, white, red and lilac blooms. **'Windlesham Ruby'** has deep carmine-red flowers. All H1.5-1.8m/5-6ft, W1.2-1.5m/4-5ft. F6. Z7-9.

Hybrids. Those of special interest for the smaller garden include **'Compact Crimson'**, which has startling, rich crimson flowers. H90-120cm/3-4ft, W90-120cm/3-4ft. F5-6. Z7-9. **'Dukaat'** has bushy, rigid, upright stems wreathed in gold and creamy white, bicoloured flowers. H30-45cm/12-18in, W30-45cm/12-18in. F5-6. Z7-9. **'Lena'** has brilliant crimson and yellow flowers and contrasting, dark green foliage. H90-120cm/3-4ft, W60-90cm/2-3ft. F5-6. Z7-9.

DANAE

D. racemosa. The Alexandrian laurel is the only species in the genus. Its glossy green, bamboo-like, arching stems carry evergreen 'leaves' that are technically part of the stem. Flowers insignificant but attractive, if sparsely borne; red fruit, produced following hot summers. Clump-forming, slowly spreading and growing well in damp shade. Stems useful for winter decoration. Cut away old untidy branches at the base in spring. H60-90cm/2-3ft, W60-90cm/2-3ft. Z7-9.

DAPHNE

The slow-growing daphnes include deciduous and evergreen shrubs, nearly all with sweetly fragrant flowers. Though reputed to be difficult, daphnes are often easier than supposed, and require little or no pruning. According to species, flowers are borne in clusters or around the stem, from late winter until autumn, though most are spring- and summer-flowering. The berries, which range from golden-yellow to red and black, are poisonous. Some

Cytisus 'Lena'

daphnes prefer sun, others part shade, but most need good drainage without extremes of wet or dry. Adding well-rotted leaf mould or peat when planting always helps, whatever the soil type. Some are easy to come by; others resent propagation or require grafting and are both expensive and rare. Admittedly, a few are temperamental and can be short-lived. Such is the challenge of gardening!

D. arbuscula. A dwarf evergreen with shiny, narrow leaves and dense, mounded habit, bearing on branch tips clusters of

Cytisus 'Compact Crimson'

Danae racemosa

fragrant, rose-pink flowers which last for several weeks. H15-20cm/6-8in, W20-30cm/8-12in. F6. Z5-8.

D. blagayana. Terminal clusters of highly scented, creamy white flowers and an open, spreading habit. A woodland plant, best in light shade with moist, peaty soil. Not the easiest species but worth the effort. H30-45cm/12-18in, W45-60cm/18-24in. F3-5. Z7-9.

D. × burkwoodii 'Somerset'. One of the easiest and most rewarding daphnes, it makes a vigorous, semi-evergreen bush with large terminal clusters of white, suffused pink, scented flowers. Almost as vigorous are **'Carol Mackie'**, a form from

Daphne retusa

Daphne × *burkwoodii* 'Somerset Gold Edge'

Daphne blagayana

the USA with leaves edged creamy white, and **'Somerset Gold Edge'** (syn. 'Variegata'), with light yellow margins. All H90-120cm/ 3-4ft, W90-120cm/3-4ft. F5-6. Z5-9.

D. cneorum. The garland flower is a trailing, dwarf evergreen, with narrow, dark green leaves, which slowly forms a prostrate mat. It has clear pink, fragrant flowers. The white-flowered form **'Alba'** is rare but beautiful. **'Eximia'** has larger, deeper green leaves and rose-pink flowers. **'Variegata'** has creamy yellow-margined

leaves. All H20-30cm/8-12in, W60-75cm/ 24-30in. F5-6. Z5-8.

D. collina. A dwarf evergreen native to Italy, with small, deep green leaves on erect branches, and rosy red, fragrant flowers. Excellent for rock gardens. H20-30cm/8-12in, W45-60cm/18-24in. F5-6. Z7-8.

D. laureola. The native English spurge laurel is an easily grown evergreen, with shining, dark green leaves and greenish yellow, subtly fragrant flowers, followed by black fruits. Best in part or full shade. **'Phillipii'** is more compact, with smaller leaves and flowers. Both H60-90cm/2-3ft, W75-90cm/30-36in. F3. Z7-9.

D. mezereum. Perhaps the best-known species, a striking deciduous shrub with stiff, upright branches and fragrant, rosy purple flowers carried on naked stems. Can get leggy, colour varies from seed and often short-lived, but valuable nonetheless. **'Alba'** has white flowers and yellow fruits. **'Rubra'** has deep purple-red flowers. All H75-90cm/30-36in, W60-75cm/24-30in. F2-3. Z5-8.

D. × napolitana. An attractive, easy-growing, dwarf evergreen considered a hybrid between *D. collina* and *D. cneorum*. Forms a compact, green-leaved, rounded bush with deep pink flowers. H1m/39in, W1m/39in. F5-6. Z7-8.

D. odora. The winter daphne is a bushy evergreen, with large, dark green leaves and terminal clusters of scented, rosy pink flowers. Needs shelter from frosts and cold winds. **'Aureomarginata'** is hardier, its petals pale in the centre, rosy purple outside and leaves margined creamy yellow. Both H60-90cm/2-3ft, W60-90cm/2-3ft. F2-5. Z7-9.

D. retusa. A charming, dwarf evergreen with short, rigid branches, thick, glossy green leaves and deliciously fragrant flowers, purple outside, pinky white inside. H20-30cm/8-12in, W20-30cm/8-12in. F5. Z7-9.

D. tangutica is similar to *D. retusa*, but taller, with more pointed leaves and flowers earlier. H20-30cm/8-12in, W20-30cm/8-12in. F5. Z7-9.

DECAISNEA

D. fargesii. A large, deciduous Chinese shrub whose strong, upright branches bear pinnate leaves up to 90cm/3ft long! These have up to twelve pairs of leaflets, light green above, greyish blue beneath. Pendulous clusters of unusual, greeny yellow flowers, followed by striking, long, blue, sausage-shaped pods. Best in good, moist loam and sun or light shade. Not always free to fruit in cool climates and new foliage can be damaged by spring frosts. Prune only to cut out any old and dead wood. H2.4-3m/8-10ft, W2.4-3m/8-10ft. F6. Z7-9.

Decaisnea fargesii

DECUMARIA

The two species in this genus are self-clinging climbers related to the climbing hydrangea, *H. petiolaris*.

D. barbara. A native of south-eastern USA, this has attractive, oval pointed leaves and erect clusters of small white flowers. In cool climates it needs a warm, sheltered site. Slow to establish. H10m/33ft, W10m/33ft. F6-7. Z7-9.

D. sinensis. From China, this is less vigorous and rarer than the above, but it deserves wider usage. It has glossy, light green, ever-green leaves and white, honey-scented flowers. H5m/16ft, W5m/16ft. F5. Z7-9.

DESFONTAINIA

D. spinosa. This tender but beautiful Chilean evergreen is worth trying if you can provide the right conditions. Bushy, with dark, glossy green, prickly, holly-like leaves, it provides a lengthy show of single, dangling scarlet and yellow tubular flowers. It needs moist air and rich, moist but well-drained soil, and resents drying winds, alkalinity and low temperatures. Happy in sun where the conditions described can be provided but in dry climates try in shade against a sheltered north wall or protected by other evergreens. H1.2-1.8m/4-6ft, W1.2-1.8m/4-6ft. F7-11. Z9-10.

DESMODIUM

D. penduliflorum. See *Lespedeza thunbergii*.

DEUTZIA

Garden centres usually carry a limited range of this very popular shrub, but there are more worth trying. Though rather dull out of flower, they are among the showiest summer-flowering shrubs, varying from low, spreading forms to upright, eventually large ones. Most species have undergone considerable breeding, notably earlier this century by the French Lemoine Nursery. The majority have serrated leaves and star-like, sometimes scented flowers, though in hot weather flowering is short-lived. All are easy, given fertile, well-drained soil and sun or part shade. Generally very hardy, but flowering can be ruined by late spring frosts. Established deutzias benefit from occasional pruning. Flowers appear on previous year's growth, so prune immediately after flowering; winter pruning removes flowering wood. Cut back some branches to the start of the previous year's growth to promote new flowering shoots, or completely remove older woody or congested stems to the ground, to allow new stems to develop.

D. chunii. Beautiful if well-grown, but can look untidy. Grey-green leaves contrast with short sprays of pink, bell-shaped flowers, white inside, with golden anthers. 'Pink Charm' has completely pink flowers. Both

H1.2-1.5m/4-5ft, W1.2-1.5m/4-5ft. F8. Z6-9.

D. compacta. Mound-forming, with clusters of pink buds opening to white. Fragrant. 'Lavender Time', with lavender flowers, fading to white. Both H60-90cm/2-3ft, W90-120cm/3-4ft. F7. Z6-9.

D. discolor 'Major'. Rare, but worth growing for its large terminal clusters of white flowers, flushed pink outside. H90-120cm/3-4ft, W90-120cm/3-4ft. F6. Z6.

D. × elegantissima. Medium-sized deutzia, broadly spreading with thin, arching branches and rose-pink, fragrant flowers. 'Rosealind', perhaps the best medium-sized deutzia, laden with deep carmine and pink, scented flowers. Both H90-120cm/3-4ft, W1.2-1.5m/4-5ft. F6-7. Z6-8.

D. × hybrida. This covers a group of hybrids bred by Lemoine over fifty years ago, and still among the best and most colourful. All Z6-9. 'Contraste' has arching branches, with large clusters of pink flowers, red-purple outside. H90-120cm/3-4ft, W1.2-1.5m/4-5ft. F6. 'Magicien', vigorous and upright, has terminal clusters of purple-red buds opening to reveal carmine-pink, white-edged petals. H1.8-2.4m/6-8ft, W1.5-1.8m/5-6ft. F6. 'Mont Rose', the most common, is free-flowering and upright, with clear pink, starry flowers and yellow anthers. H1.8-2.4m/6-8ft, W1.2-1.5m/4-5ft. F6. 'Pink Pompom' is slow-growing, initially compact, but developing arching branches which in midsummer are covered with dense, rounded clusters of double pink flowers fading to white. H1.8-2.4m/6-8ft, W1.5-1.8m/5-6ft. F7.

D. × kalmiiflora. Densely branched, with masses of purple buds and small, purple-flushed, white flowers along arching stems. H1.2-1.5m/4-5ft, W90-120cm/3-4ft. F6. Z6-9.

D. × magnifica. Strong-growing, upright with dense heads of showy, double, white flowers. One for the taller shrub border. There are several cultivars in this group, all extremely vigorous and with white flowers. H1.8-2.4m/6-8ft, W1.5-1.8m/5-6ft. F6. Z6-9.

D. 'Nikko'. One of the best for small gardens. Low, spreading habit, with arching branches wreathed in clusters of white flowers for some weeks. H45-60cm/18-24in, W60-90cm/2-3ft. F5-6. Z5-8.

D. × rosea 'Carminea'. Another Lemoine hybrid and still one of the best. Dwarf, spreading habit, flower clusters on arching branch tips; purple-red in bud, opening to rosy pink. H90-120cm/3-4ft, W1.2-1.5m/4-5ft. F6. Z6-9.

D. scabra. Easily grown, vigorous species from which several cultivars have been selected. Ideal for large gardens. Strong, upright habit, older stems with peeling bark, erect, white flower clusters on narrow spikes. 'Candidissima', clear double white flowers. 'Flore Pleno', purple-tinged

Desfontainia spinosa

Deutzia × hybrida 'Pink Pompom'

Deutzia × kalmiiflora

outside, white inside, double. 'Pride of Rochester', similar to 'Flore Pleno', with rosy pink outer petals. All H1.8-2.4m/6-8ft, W1.5-1.8m/5-6ft. F6. Z5-8.

D. 'Strawberry Fields' (syn. *D. × hybrida* and *D. × magnifica* 'Rubra'). This is sometimes confused with *D. × hybrida* 'Magicien' (strong upright habit). It is perhaps the closest to red of any form, the large flowers having petals which are crimson on the outside, white suffused pink on the inside. H1.8-2.4m/6-8ft, W1.5-1.8m/5-6ft. F6-7. Z6-9.

DICENTRA

D. macrocapnos. This remarkable herbaceous perennial is included in this chapter for its climbing ability and value of flower and foliage. It originates from the Himalayas, as does the similar **D. scandens**, and from a fleshy rootstock it produces vigorous shoots, clothed in glaucous green leaves which are followed by pendent yellow flowers. It climbs by means of self-clinging tendrils, and can be treated as an annual, but is hardy once established to -10°C/14°F. Grow in reasonably moist, well-drained soil. In winter, mulch roots with hay, straw or bracken. H3m/10ft, W3m/10ft. F6-8. Z8-9.

DIERVILLA Bush honeysuckle

Members of this genus of easily grown, deciduous, suckering shrubs resemble the popular and better-known weigelas in leaf and habit. Hardly spectacular, but useful ground cover for sun or shade, some with ornamental foliage.

D. sessilifolia. Low-growing, spreading habit, making a mound of dark green, dense foliage with clusters of tubular, sulphur-yellow flowers, and good autumn colour. Prune by half immediately after flowering or back to the ground in late winter. In light soil suckers can be vigorous, so remove as required. H90-150cm/3-5ft,

Diervilla × splendens

Dipelta floribunda

Disanthus cercidifolius

W1.2-1.5m/4-5ft. F7-8. Z5-8.

D. × splendens. An underrated plant, its spreading branches clothed in light green leaves, becoming dark green and bronze. It has small, yellow tubular flowers. Prune as for *D. sessilifolia*. H90-150cm/3-5ft, W1.2-1.5m/4-5ft. F7-8. Z5-8.

DIPELTA

A small group of rare, Chinese deciduous shrubs, hard to propagate, so unlikely to become popular until nurserymen improve the success rate. The three species grown have weigela-like flowers. Unusual flower bracts of thin, papery, green discs follow, fading to rosy pink. Grow in reasonably fertile, not dry, soil, in sun or part shade. Established plants can look untidy; if so, prune flowering shoots back to previous year's growth immediately after flowering, and occasionally cut a few stems back to the ground to allow light and air into the centre.

D. floribunda. The best-known and most desirable, with strong, upright, arching stems, and clusters of fragrant pink, yellow-throated, bell-shaped flowers. Attractive peeling bark on older stems. H1.8-2.4m/6-8ft, W1.2-1.5m/4-5ft. F5. Z6-9.

D. ventricosa. Similar to *D. floribunda*, but slower-growing, and its deep pink, orange-throated flowers appear a little later. H1.5-1.8m/5-6ft, W1.2-1.5m/4-5ft. F5-6. Z6-9.

D. yunnanensis. This is more spreading, with large, pink-flushed, white flowers, followed by distinctively shaped bracts. H1.5-1.8m/5-6ft, W1.2-1.5m/4-5ft. F5. Z7-9.

DISANTHUS

D. cercidifolius. This choice, Japanese shrub's main attribute is its autumn colour. It needs moist, well-drained, humus-rich, acid soil, protection from spring frosts and cold winds, and shade in hot climates to thrive. It makes an upright, spreading shrub with shiny, heart-shaped, blue-green leaves which turn rich wine-purple and orange in autumn, given an open position. Insignificant purple flowers. H1.5-1.8m/5-6ft, W1.5-1.8m/5-6ft. F10. Z6-8.

DRIMYS

D. winteri. Winter's bark, a South American evergreen shrub or small tree, is best grown against a sheltered, sunny wall in all but the mildest areas. The glossy green, silver-backed leaves are a good background to its jasmine-scented clusters of creamy white flowers. Bark and leaves are both aromatic. Prune only to remove untidy or winter-damaged stems. Main stems may need supporting against a wall. H8m/26ft, W2.1-3m/7-10ft. F5. Z8-10.

ECCREMOCARPUS
Chilean glory flower

E. scaber. This semi-woody climber is hardy in only the mildest localities in cool temperate climates, but is worth growing as an annual or conservatory plant for its succession of striking, pendulous, tubular, orange-yellow flowers. Stems carry finely divided, light green leaves, each leaf stalk ending in a tendril. **'Aureus'**, with yellow flowers, and **'Rubra'** (syn. 'Carmineus'), with scarlet flowers, are rare. In mild areas plants may overwinter, with new growth breaking from the base, but in one year from seed, growth may be as much as H2.1m/7ft, W2.1m/7ft. F6-10. Z9-10.

ELAEAGNUS Oleaster
This genus contains many worthwhile deciduous and evergreen shrubs and small trees, mostly tough, sun-loving plants more resistant to heat and drought than to cold and wet. Most have attractive, leathery foliage, green or variegated above, silver or gold and scaly beneath. Some make excellent, quick-growing maritime hedges and windbreaks. Adaptable to acid, neutral or alkaline soil, but not to thin chalk. Small, insignificant but highly fragrant flowers, sometimes followed by fruits. Evergreen foliage excellent cut for winter decoration.
E. argentea. See *E. commutata.*
E. commutata (syn. *E. argentea*). The deciduous silverberry is the only species native to North America and undoubtedly hardy. A suckering shrub with upright, slender branches and narrow, vivid silver leaves and silvery yellow, fragrant flowers, followed by ovoid, silver fruits, ripening in autumn. Resents wet, heavy soils. Prune to keep tidy and remove old wood; new growth shoots readily from the base. H90-120cm/3-4ft, W1.5-1.8m/5-6ft. F5-6. Z2-6.
E. × ebbingei. This evergreen hybrid is deservedly popular, if sometimes over-used for hedging and screening. Fast-growing, it is wind-resistant, excellent near the sea, and a useful background evergreen, with dark, glossy green leaves, silver underneath, fragrant flowers in autumn and orange fruits in spring. The hybrid and cultivars listed can suffer defoliation in bad winters, but usually recover in spring. Prune any dead wood and also to encourage bushiness, cutting back by a third or a half in spring. Slow-growing, variegated sports include **'Gilt Edge'**, sometimes slow to establish, with deep green leaves irregularly margined golden-yellow, and **'Limelight'** with central splashes of greeny yellow and gold. Both are excellent for winter colour. All H1.8-2.4m/6-8ft, W1.5-1.8m/5-6ft. F10-11. Z6-9.
E. pungens. Its cultivars include some of the best evergreens for winter colour, and the species itself is a reliable if modest background shrub useful for hedging and screening, forming a vigorous, wide-spreading, often thorny, dense bush. Its wavy-edged leaves, smaller than *E. × ebbingei* types, are dark green above, dull white beneath and spotted with brown scales. Fragrant, silvery white flowers; seldom fruiting in cool climates. Prune as required in spring. Variegated forms tend to revert back to green; cut these shoots away at once. Generally, the more gold or cream

Elaeagnus × ebbingei 'Limelight'

in the leaf, the less vigorous the variety. H1.8-2.4m/6-8ft, W1.8-2.4m/6-8ft. F9-11. Z6-10. **'Dicksonii'** (syn. 'Aurea') is slow, with mostly yellow leaves, the rest margined irregularly golden-yellow. H1.2-1.5m/4-5ft, W90-150cm/3-5ft. F9-11. Z7-10. The Dutch **'Goldrim'** is more reliable, with dark green leaves banded with gold. **'Maculata'**, with dark green leaves splashed liberally with gold, is the best-known and most widely planted, excellent for winter colour. **'Variegata'** is similar to the species but with a thin, pale yellow leaf margin. All H1.8-2.4m/6-8ft, W1.8-2.4m/6-8ft. F9-11. Z7-10.

ELEUTHEROCOCCUS
E. sieboldianus (formerly *Acanthopanax sieboldianus*). The adaptable, deciduous, five-leaved aralia is mostly grown for its

Elaeagnus pungens 'Maculata'

foliage. From China, it is multi-branched, with arching, thorny stems densely covered with light green leaves. Inconspicuous greenish white flowers and black fruits are rare in cooler climates. It accepts any well drained soil, in sun or shade. **'Variegatus'** has light green and cream leaves, but needs sun and shelter to look its brightest. Good in urban gardens. Prune in spring to keep plants bushy. Both H1.8-2.1m/6-7ft, W1.5-1.8m/5-6ft. F5-6. Z4-9.

ELSHOLTZIA See under Perennials.

EMBOTHRIUM Chilean fire bush
E. coccineum. Given the right conditions, this South American shrub or small tree is a marvellous feature. Semi-tender, and needing lime-free, moist soil and shelter from cold, drying winds, it can eventually grow 9m/29ft or more, but I have been unsuccessful in dry, cold Bressingham, in spite of ideal light woodland shade. An erect, narrow shrub with mostly long, oval, glossy evergreen leaves, and spectacular, orange-scarlet flowers in terminal clusters, hence its common name. The form *lanceolatum* is hardier and less evergreen, and its flowers are more scarlet than orange. **'Norquinco Valley'** is the one most often offered by nurserymen. All H2.4-3m/8-10ft, W90-120cm/3-4ft. F5-6. Z9-10.

Embothrium coccineum lanceolatum

Enkianthus campanulatus

Enkianthus perulatus

ENKIANTHUS

These acid-loving, slow-growing, deciduous shrubs are lovely but can disappoint, unless given moist, acid soil in sun or part shade – similar conditions to rhododendrons. The few species all originate in China and Japan, most becoming bushy, with round, green leaves, sometimes turning a beautiful autumn colour. Clusters of dangling, bell-shaped flowers. Little pruning needed.

E. campanulatus. A reliably free-flowering species which makes an upright, twiggy bush with layered branches. The flowers are cream or yellow, delicately veined pink or red, lasting several weeks. Leaves often turn yellow, orange and red in the autumn. Easiest species to grow. **'Albiflorus'** has white flowers. Both H1.2m-1.8m/4-6ft, W90-120cm/3-4ft. F5-6. Z5-8.

E. cernuus rubens. Also known as red bells, for its masses of hanging, cup-shaped, deep red, fringed flowers. Sturdy, upright branches gradually form broad tiers. *E. cernuus* has large, white flowers but is rarer than the red form. Both have good autumn colour. Both H1.2m-1.8m/4-6ft, W90-120cm/3-4ft. F6. Z6-8.

E. chinensis. More vigorous and less hardy than *E. campanulatus*, and variable from seed, but can make a small tree. Bright green leaves appear with the pendulous clusters of large, yellow, red-striped flowers. H1.8-2.4m/6-8ft, W1.2-1.5m/4-5ft. F5. Z7-8.

E. perulatus. A distinct, Japanese dwarf species, slowly forming tiers of branches, with red branchlets and white, urn-shaped

flowers just before or with the new leaves. Reliable autumn leaf colour. A choice but rare plant. H75-90cm/30-36in, W60-75cm/24-30in. F4. Z6-8.

ESCALLONIA

All escallonia species are South American but many showier and hardier hybrids have been selected from cultivated plants. They are easily grown, somewhat tender, evergreen shrubs but can, like fuchsias, be semi-evergreen or deciduous in cold areas. Some are upright, with strong-growing, arching stems, others lower, more compact and bushy. Most have glossy green leaves and tubular, white, pink or red flowers, borne singly or in clusters, from early summer onwards. They grow in sun or part shade, well-drained acid and reasonably alkaline soils and are excellent, drought-tolerant coastal plants.

They make lovely flowering hedges or wall shrubs; but because of their tenderness, plant in spring or early summer except in mild climates. Some vigorous forms may need annual pruning after flowering, usually in late summer when untidy branches and long stems can be cut by a third to a half. Plants damaged by frosts usually break from the base, though sometimes not until the early summer. Cut away old or dead branches in late spring or just as new shoots appear. Most cultivars flower on growth made in the previous year, though sometimes strong growths flower in the same year. Most F6-8. All Z8-9.

Escallonia 'Red Elf'

E. **'Apple Blossom'**. This hybrid, one of the most floriferous, has large, glossy, green leaves and mostly single, pink, white-eyed flowers. H1.2-1.5m/4-5ft, W1.2-1.5m/4-5ft. F7-9.

E. **'C. F. Ball'**. This is a taller, vigorous evergreen, with an open, arching habit. A good hedge or background shrub in mild areas, best against a wall in colder regions. Scarlet-crimson flowers. H1.5-2.1m/5-7ft, W1.5-1.8m/5-6ft. F7-9.

E. **'Donard Beauty'**. One of many selections from the Donard Nursery in Northern Ireland, this has arching, pendulous branches and clusters of rose-red flowers. H1.2-1.5m/4-5ft, W1.5-1.8m/5-6ft.

E. **'Donard Brilliance'**. This is larger-leaved and more vigorous, and has profuse, rich crimson flowers. H1.2-1.5m/4-5ft, W1.5-1.8m/5-6ft.

E. **'Donard Radiance'**. One of the best, with its bushy, upright habit, shining leaves and large, rosy pink flowers. H1.2-1.5m/4-5ft, W1.5-1.8m/5-6ft.

E. **'Donard Seedling'**. This is taller than *E.* 'Donard Beauty', with pink buds and pink and white flowers. H1.2-1.5m/4-5ft, W1.5-1.8m/5-6ft.

E. **'Edinensis'**. This was raised in Edinburgh Botanic Gardens before the First World War and makes a dense, upright bush with crimson flower buds, opening pink, along the narrow, arching stems. H1.5-1.8m/5-6ft, W1.5-1.8m/5-6ft.

E. **'Gwendolyn Anley'**. One of the hardiest hybrids, this has a low, dense,

Escallonia 'Iveyi'

spreading habit, small leaves and a mass of small, shell-pink flowers. H60-90cm/2-3ft, W90-120cm/3-4ft.

E. 'Iveyi'. A distinct, somewhat tender hybrid with large, glossy leaves and bold heads of scented, white flowers. Provide shelter in cold areas. H1.8m/6ft, W1.2-1.5m/4-5ft.

E. 'Langleyensis'. A hardy hybrid which arose in the famous old Veitch Nursery in Langley, Buckinghamshire, England, at the end of the last century. A tall, bushy shrub with narrow, arching branches, it bears bright, rosy red flowers. It was used in the breeding of the Donard cultivars. H1.5-1.8m/5-6ft, W1.5-1.8m/5-6ft. F7-9.

E. 'Peach Blossom'. Similar to *E.* 'Apple Blossom', with pure pink flowers. H1.2m-1.5m/4-5ft, W1.2-1.5m/4-5ft.

E. 'Red Elf'. Perfect for small gardens, this makes an open bush with singly borne, crimson flowers. H90-120cm/3-4ft, W90-120cm/3-4ft. F6-9.

E. rubra 'Crimson Spire'. Ideal for hedges, this has large, glossy, dark green leaves, a strong, upright habit and deep crimson flowers. H1.8m/6ft, W1.2-1.5m/4-5ft. The form *macrantha* is less hardy than most, but vigorous and excellent for seaside hedges and shelter in mild areas, where it may exceed 3m/10ft. Large, glossy, green, aromatic leaves on strong, dense bushes and rosy red flowers on terminal clusters. H1.8-2.4m/6-8ft, W1.5-1.8m/5-6ft.

E. 'Slieve Donard'. A medium-sized, bushy shrub, which has narrow, arching branches, glossy leaves and pale shell-pink flowers. H1.2-1.5m/4-5ft, W1.5-1.8m/5-6ft.

EUCRYPHIA

These eventually tall, multi-stemmed shrubs or trees need moist, neutral or acid soil and a mild climate. They thrive in Ireland, and west and south-west England, where the Gulf Stream creates moist air currents, but are less happy in cold, eastern parts, where sheltered woodland conditions are best.

E. glutinosa. The only deciduous species, this makes an upright shrub or small tree carrying, when mature, a fine show of large, white flowers with prominent, yellow stamens, followed by glorious autumn foliage colour. If grown in sun, shade the roots with a deep mulch of compost, peat or bark. H1.8-3m/6-10ft, W90-120cm/3-4ft. F7-8. Z8-9.

EUONYMUS

These useful, variable shrubs and small trees are seldom grown for their insignificant flowers, but for the colourful foliage of the evergreen forms and for the attractive fruits and autumn leaf colour of the deciduous types. They generally thrive in any well-drained soil, especially chalk, and sun or shade; most are extremely hardy.

Escallonia 'Apple Blossom'

Euonymus alatus

Planting several plants together helps ensure cross-pollination.

E. alatus. The winged euonymus, so-called from the narrow, flanged wings extending along each four-cornered branchlet, is a deciduous native of China and Japan. It has an upright, later spreading habit and dark green leaves, in favourable climates brilliant crimson in autumn. Autumn colour is usually less spectacular in northern Europe than most of North America. The tiny flowers form purple-red fruits, though in cooler climates neither is reliable. H1.8-2.4m/6-8ft, W1.5-1.8m/5-6ft. F5. Z4-9.

'Compactus' is smaller but colours equally brilliantly, making an ideal low hedge. H1.2-1.5m/4-5ft, W1.5m/5ft. F5. Z4-9.

E. europaeus. The common spindle is native to Europe and the British Isles, where it makes a large, often untidy, shrub or small tree, unnoticed until its red fruits surrounded by fleshy, yellow arils dangle from the branches in autumn. The species is raised from seed and may vary. Prune only to tidy plants in late winter. If attacked by caterpillars or other insects, use systemic insecticide, but ask advice about scale insect from your local nursery. The white-fruited, less robust 'Albus' is occasionally seen in the wild. 'Atropurpureus' has purple leaves in spring. A reliably free-fruiting form is 'Red Cascade'. Autumn foliage colour on the above forms varies from yellow to reddish purple and can be quite spectacular. All H2.4-3m/8-10ft, W1.5-1.8m/5-6ft. Z4-8.

Euonymus europaeus 'Red Cascade'

E. fortunei. The winter-creeper euonymus is a low-growing, Chinese evergreen with oval leaves and trailing stems, which root as they grow. It is parent to numerous hardy, adaptable forms, many with coloured foliage, most excellent for ground cover in sun or shade, some making self-clinging climbers against walls or trees. Tiny flowers and occasional orange fruits in pink capsules, but coloured-foliage forms seldom flower or fruit. Prune occasionally in early spring to tidy bushes. As ground cover: H30-45cm/12-18in, W1.8-2.4m/6-8ft. Z5-9.

'Dart's Blanket' has dark green leaves turning bronze and purple in autumn and winter and quickly forming a dense carpet. H30-45cm/12-18in, W1.5-1.8m/5-6ft. Z5-9.

'Emerald Gaiety' can be ground cover, a low hedge or a bushy specimen shrub. Round leaves, broadly margined in creamy white, sometimes tinged pink in winter. H90-120cm/3-4ft, W90cm/3ft. Z5-9.

Euonymus fortunei 'Emerald Gaiety'

Euonymus fortunei 'Sheridan Gold'

Euonymus fortunei 'Sunspot'

Euonymus planipes

Euonymus fortunei 'Emerald 'n' Gold'

'Emerald 'n' Gold' has small, glossy green leaves, edged gold, tinged pink and cream in winter, especially in exposed sites. Climbs trees, walls and other plants. Several, slightly different sports exist. H45-60cm/18-24in, W60-90cm/2-3ft. Z5-9. **'Golden Prince'** (syn. 'Gold Tip') has dark green leaves and golden new growth. Best in full sun. H45-60cm/18-24in, W60-90cm/2-3ft. Z5-9. The Canadian **'Sheridan Gold'** has dark green leaves and golden-yellow new growth, remaining bright through the year in open sites. H60-90cm/2-3ft, W90-120cm/3-4ft. Z4-9. **'Silver Queen'** is similar to 'Emerald Gaiety' but less hardy, with creamy yellow new shoots and winter foliage. H90-120cm/3-4ft, W90cm/3ft. Z5-9. **'Sunspot'** has cream-to-yellow leaves, with deep green margins. H30-45cm/12-18in, W60-90cm/2-3ft. Z5-9. **'Variegatus'**, a variable form, climbs up walls or through other shrubs, its mostly small, creamy white and green leaves often tinged pink in winter. H45-60cm/18-24in, W1.5-1.8m/5-6ft. Z5-9.
E. japonicus. The evergreen Japanese euonymus is upright, densely clothed with large, oval, dark leaves, eventually reaching 5m/16ft or more. Once mature, greenish white flowers precede orange seeds in pink

capsules in autumn. Though happy on most soils in sun or shade, it is more tender than *E. fortunei*, but excellent as a hedge in coastal districts. It is subject to mildew and caterpillars; use fungicide or systemic insecticide as necessary. There are several golden and variegated forms; cut out any branches that revert to green. H1.8-2.4m/6-8ft, W1.8-2.4m/6-8ft. F6. Z7-9.
'Albomarginatus' has dark green leaves, edged white. H1.5-1.8m/5-6ft, W1.2-1.5m/4-5ft. Z8-9. **'Aureopictus'** (syn. 'Aureus') has bright gold leaves, irregularly edged with green. H1.5m-1.8m/5-6ft, W1.2-1.5m/4-5ft. Z8-9. **'Macrophyllus'**, with large, leathery leaves, is a good background shrub in mild areas. **'Macrophyllus Albus'** has creamy white leaf margins. Both H1.8-2.4m/6-8ft, W1.8-2.4m/6-8ft. Z8-9.

The slightly tender **'Microphyllus'** is a miniature, box-like bush, with small leaves clinging to erect stems. **'Microphyllus Pulchellus'**, with gold-variegated leaves, and **'Microphyllus Variegatus'**, with green leaves edged silvery white, are pretty, if tender, dwarf shrubs. All H60-90cm/2-3ft, W60-75cm/24-30in. Z8-9. The slow-growing, compact **'Ovatus Aureus'** has oval leaves margined or suffused yellow, some new shoots fading to creamy yellow, other shoots

and leaves yellow throughout. Rather brash and variable. H1.5-1.8m/5-6ft, W1.5-1.8m/5-6ft. Z8-9.
E. planipes (syn. *E. sachalinensis*). This seldom seen deciduous species is a large, upright, eventually spreading shrub or small tree. Purple winter buds open to light green leaves, usually turning crimson in autumn; yellowish green flowers and rosy red fruits in autumn. H3m/10ft, W2.4-3m/8-10ft. F4-5. Z6-9.
E. sachalinensis. See *E. planipes*.

EXOCHORDA Pearlbush
These deciduous Asian shrubs are outstandingly beautiful when covered in white blossom, in late spring or early summer, but are otherwise dull. If space allows, worth growing for the element of surprise when they burst into flower, especially when seen against contrasting plants. Most make large, untidy, upright or mounded bushes with cascading or pendulous branches. Best in full sun or part shade on good, moist loam, but will grow on all but highly alkaline and shallow chalk soils. Prune to tidy wayward branches and keep large plants a reasonable size immediately after flowering, since flowers appear on the previous year's growth.

E. giraldii. This robust, spreading shrub has salmon-pink shoots, oval, grey-green leaves and profuse terminal heads of white flowers. H1.5-1.8m/5-6ft, W1.8-2.4m/6-8ft. F5. Z5-8.

E. korolkowii. Distinct, erect habit with racemes of large, white flowers. Relatively lime-tolerant. H1.8-2.4m/6-8ft, W1.5-1.8m/5-6ft. F6. Z5-8.

E. × macrantha* 'The Bride'.** The best for a small garden, it slowly forms an uneven mound of cascading branches, covered with white flowers. The hybrid ***E. × macrantha is equally beautiful in flower but much larger. H1.2-1.5m/4-5ft, W1.5-1.8m/5-6ft. F5. Z5-8.

E. racemosa. The common pearlbush, rare in cultivation, is a round shrub with white flowers on terminal racemes. It dislikes highly alkaline and especially chalky soils. H1.5-1.8m/5-6ft, W1.5-1.8m/5-6ft. F5-6. Z5-8.

× FATSHEDERA

× *F. lizei.* This adaptable, useful evergreen shrub is reputedly a hybrid of *Fatsia japonica* 'Moseri' and *Hedera helix* 'Hibernica'. Better known as a house plant, it makes a sprawling, rambling, wall shrub with large, glossy, palmate leaves. It is excellent in deep shade, and thrives in most soils. Tolerant of urban pollution and coastal areas. Well-trained, it needs tying in and regular pruning. **'Variegata'** has greyish green leaves, margined white. Both H6m/20ft, W4m/13ft. F9. Z8-11.

FATSIA

F. japonica. This versatile Japanese evergreen shrub is used as a house plant, but in gardens it adapts to shade, urban and seaside conditions. Its large, leathery, lustrous, deep green leaves, lighter in sun, are palmate. Erect clusters of creamy white flowers are produced outside in autumn, followed by small black fruit. Grow in sheltered semi-shade. Prune in spring to keep in shape and reduce size; hard pruning of old shrubs produces new basal growth. H2.1-4m/7-13ft, W2.1-4m/7-13ft. F7-8. Z8-11.

FORSYTHIA

Almost everyone knows *Forsythia*, the harbinger of spring, but few gardeners can name more than one or two species. All are hardy, trouble-free, deciduous shrubs with yellow flowers on bare stems in early spring, thriving in most soils and sun or light shade. They can be too large and overpowering in small gardens, but larger forms make fine background shrubs whose early show is admired before smaller shrubs and perennials bloom against the bright green summer foliage. Many can be wall trained. To tidy if required, prune back some or all

Exochorda × macrantha 'The Bride'

Forsythia × intermedia 'Minigold'

flowering stems in late spring just as the last flowers fade, or on mature plants remove a few older stems from the base to allow new vigorous young shoots to develop. Buds can be damaged by severe frost in late winter.

***F.* 'Beatrix Farrand'.** The plant usually sold may differ from the original seedling selected at the Arnold Arboretum in Boston, Massachusetts, but it is good enough to include. Vigorous, with strong, upright branches densely clothed in deep yellow flowers, followed by coarse leaves. H1.8-2.4m/6-8ft, W1.5-1.8m/5-6ft. F3-4. Z5-9.

***F.* 'Golden Nugget'.** A compact, densely branched form with large, bright yellow flowers. Excellent for a small garden. H1.5-1.8m/5-6ft, W90-120cm/3-4ft. F3-4. Z5-9.

***F. × intermedia* 'Karl Sax'.** Like *F.* 'Beatrix Farrand', this originates from the Arnold Arboretum and is a good, bushier alternative to it. H1.8m-2.1m/6-7ft, W1.2-1.5m/4-5ft. F3-4. Z6-9. **'Lynwood'** (syn. 'Lynwood Gold'). A sport discovered in a Northern Ireland garden over fifty years ago, deservedly popular and widely planted. Erect, branching habit. H1.8-2.4m/6-8ft, W1.2-1.5m/4-5ft. F3-4. Z5-9. **'Minigold'** is compact, with large, pale yellow flowers. H1.2-1.5m/4-5ft, W90-120cm/3-4ft. F3-4.

Z5-9. **'Spectabilis'**, introduced in 1906 and still one of the best, most popular and floriferous, its profuse flowers hide the branches. Excellent for cutting. H1.8-2.4m/6-8ft, W1.2-1.5m/4-5ft. F3-4. Z5-9. **'Spring Glory'**, densely branched with masses of sulphur-yellow flowers, good for cutting. H1.5-1.8m/5-6ft, W1.5-1.8m/5-6ft. F3-4. Z4-8.

F. ovata. A Korean dwarf species, very hardy and early but yellow flowers not always freely produced. The more vigorous, twiggy, Canadian **'Ottawa'** has buds that survive intense frost. **'Tetragold'** has deeper yellow and more plentiful flowers than the species. All H90-150cm/3-5ft, W90-150cm/3-5ft. F2-4. Z5-9.

F. suspensa. This and its forms are graceful and informal, but difficult to control. The species makes a rambling mound, excellent on or over a wall, with long, slender branches. Wall-trained, it can reach 10m/33ft. Flowers appear on the previous year's shoots, often lasting for several weeks. The form *atrocaulis* has dark purple young stems. **'Nymans'** is more erect with browny purple, arching branches and large, lemon-yellow flowers. All H1.5-1.8m/5-6ft, W1.8-2.4m/6-8ft. F3-4. Z5-8.

***F. viridissima* 'Bronxensis'.** This chance dwarf seedling, with its short, stubby branches, would be very popular if it flowered more reliably. Best in full sun with good drainage. H30-45cm/12-18in, W45-60cm/18-24in. F3-4. Z6-8.

Forsythia 'Golden Nugget'

243

FOTHERGILLA

These acid-loving, North American deciduous shrubs, related to witch hazel, have honey-scented flowers on bare branches and good autumn colour. Slow-growing and under-utilized, they prefer an open, sunny position but succeed in part shade, and need well-drained, acid soil which does not dry out – conditions similar to those for rhododendrons, with which they associate well.

F. alnifolia. See *F. gardenii*.

F. gardenii (syn. *F. alnifolia*). The choice but rare, dwarf fothergilla seldom exceeds 1m/39in, even after thirty years. Its twiggy stems bear small, bottlebrush heads of white, fragrant flowers. The oval leaves are dull green in summer, yellow, orange and fiery red in autumn. H45-60cm/18-24in, W45-60cm/18-24in. F5. Z5-9. **'Blue Mist'**,

Fothergilla major

Fremontodendron californicum 'California Glory'

Fuchsia magellanica 'Aurea'

discovered in the Morris Arboretum in Pennsylvania, has bright, powder-blue leaves, which darken during summer. H90-120cm/3-4ft, W75-90cm/30-36in. F5. Z5-9.

F. major (syn. *F. monticola*). This erect, picturesque shrub can reach 3m/10ft, its congested branches carrying small, white, honey-scented, cylindrical flowers. Variable in habit, but nearly all provide excellent autumn colour of yellow, orange and crimson, sometimes on the same leaf. H90-120cm/3-4ft, W75-90cm/30-36in. F5. Z5-9.

F. monticola. See *F. major*.

FREMONTODENDRON

F. californicum. Often listed as a climber, this spectacular, evergreen or semi-evergreen Californian shrub needs a sunny south wall, except in the mildest localities, and well-drained, poorish soil. Excellent on chalk. Severe winters can be fatal, but spring-planted replacements grow quickly and soon cover any loss. Once established

for two or three winters, hardiness increases. Strong, upright branches are light brown and woolly; the shiny green, lobed leaves have a brown indumentum or hairy covering beneath. The large, golden-yellow, saucer-shaped flowers continue, on and off, for months. Tie in and train against a wall, and prune to keep vigorous shoots growing in the right direction. Improved hybrids include **'California Glory'** and **'Pacific Sunset'**. All H3-5m/10-16ft, W2.1-3m/7-10ft. F6-9. Z8-10.

FUCHSIA

This is a vast group of shrubs, small trees and climbers, the hardy forms listed here surviving in cooler temperate regions under garden conditions, to perhaps -10°C/14°F or Zone 8 once established. These are excellent against walls, in mixed borders and in containers, giving a continuous display of pendulous flowers for several months. In mild and coastal districts they form flowering hedges. Hardy fuchsias grow 30-180cm/1-6ft, the latter only if not cut to the ground by frost. Severe winters can be fatal, but most shoot again from beneath the ground in late spring. In cold areas, plant the crown 1.5-2.5cm/1-2in deeper than the level of the pot and cover with sharp, gritty soil or peat; protect the crown with leaves, straw, peat or bracken after the first frost. In mild areas plants may be evergreen or semi-evergreen.

Fuchsias prefer sun and any fairly moist, well-drained soil. Plants untouched by severe frost shoot all the way up the stem and flower in early summer, those breaking from the base flower from midsummer on. Prune the latter's dead stems away just as new growth appears. All Z8-10.

F. magellanica. A South American native with several good forms, most with long, narrow flowers, with scarlet sepals and purple petals, and slender, arching stems. **'Alba'** (syn. var. *molinae*), slightly tender, has pink-tinged, white blooms, sometimes shy to flower. **'Aurea'** is bushy and spreading, with bright yellow leaves and striking red flowers. The floriferous form *gracilis* has slender stems and serrated leaves. All H90-120cm/3-4ft, W90-120cm/3-4ft. F5-10. **'Pumila'** has crimson and purple flowers. H30cm/1ft, W30cm/1ft. F5-10. **'Variegata'**, less hardy, has bright, creamy, white-edged leaves, suffused pink. The distinct **'Versicolor'** has grey-green leaves flushed pink and creamy white. Both H90-120cm/3-4ft, W90-120cm/3-4ft. F5-10.

Hybrids. There are innumerable hardy hybrids. **'Alice Hoffman'** has bushy, purple-tinged foliage, white and rosy red flowers. H90-120cm/3-4ft, W90-120cm/3-4ft. F5-10. **'Chillerton Beauty'**, popular since 1847, has pale pink and purple flowers. H1.2-1.5m/4-5ft, W90-120cm/3-4ft. F5-10. The upright 'Dr Foster' has large, scarlet and violet-purple flowers. H90-120cm/3-4ft, W90-120cm/3-4ft. F5-10. 'Eva Boerg' has pale pink and purple-pink flowers. H75-90cm/30-36in, W75-90cm/30-36in. F5-10. The bushy 'Genii' has yellow leaves in sun and small, red and purple flowers. H90-120cm/3-4ft, W90-120cm/3-4ft. F5-10. The vintage 'Madame Cornelissen' is upright and bushy, with semi-double, white and scarlet blooms. H1.2-1.5m/4-5ft, W1.2-1.5m/4-5ft. F5-10. 'Mrs Popple', one of the hardiest, carries masses of crimson and violet blooms. H1.2-1.5m/4-5ft, W1.2-1.5m/4-5ft. F5-10. 'Mrs. W. P. Wood' has long, narrow, white and pale pink flowers. H90-120cm/3-4ft, W90-120cm/3-4ft. F5-10. 'Riccartonii', one of the strongest and commonly used as a hedge; its flowers are crimson and purple. H1.8-2.4m/6-8ft, W1.8-2.4m/6-8ft. F5-10. The free-flowering 'Tom Thumb' also has crimson and purple flowers. H30-45cm/12-18in, W30-45cm/12-18in. F5-10.

GARRYA

G. elliptica. The silk-tassel bush, from California and Oregon, quickly forms a broad bush with glossy, evergreen, leathery leaves. Established male plants carry clusters of long, silvery, grey-green, pendulous catkins which can, on 'James Roof', reach 30-40cm (12-16in). The female is far less showy. Happy on most well-drained soils, including dry, poor ones, and sun or part shade. They dislike cold, desiccating winds, especially when young, and leaves easily scorch. I have had plants killed in one part of my garden but a ten-year-old specimen elsewhere survived -20°C/-4°F. In cold regions, best as a wall shrub. Prune in late spring, removing unruly branches or to keep it within bounds. Both H3-4m/10-13ft, W3m/10ft. F11-2. Z8-10.

× GAULNETTYA

Apparently it is not uncommon to have the two evergreen acid-loving genera *Gaultheria* and *Pernettya* hybridize themselves. The following selections arose as hybrids between *G. shallon* and *P. mucronata*. All are evergreen with deep green, leathery, heavily veined leaves, growing happily in sun or shade in acid soils, once established, and spreading by underground suckering shoots. Pendulous clusters of bell-shaped flowers in late spring are followed by autumn fruits. Of the three I prefer 'Pink Pixie', raised by Peter Dummer by back crossing 'Wisley Pearl' with *G. shallon*. It has larger leaves, pretty pinky white flowers, and purple-red berries. 'Ruby' and 'Wisley Pearl', the latter arising at the Royal Horticultural Gardens, Wisley, Surrey, in

England, have attractive white flowers, but rather sombre deep red fruits. All H45-60cm/18-24in, W1.2-1.5m/4-5ft. F5-6. Z7-9.

GAULTHERIA

This genus comprises over 200 evergreen species, from Australia, New Zealand, Japan, India and North and South America. In cool temperate climates only a few are worth growing, all of them low-growing and needing moist, acid soils and preferring part shade. Gaultherias are very effective en masse, as ground cover, with pendulous, bell-shaped flowers followed by coloured fruit. Most spread by underground stems and can be invasive.

G. cuneata. This dense Chinese species has glossy leaves, racemes of small, white flowers and white fruits, but can be shy to flower. H30-45cm/12-18in, W60-90cm/2-3ft. F6. Z6-8.

G. miqueliana. Similar to *G. cuneata* but more compact, with white or pink edible fruits. H30cm/1ft, W60-90cm/2-3ft. F5-6. Z6-8.

G. procumbens. The North American checkerberry, or creeping wintergreen, forms a prostrate carpet, slowly spreading by underground shoots. The leaves turn an attractive reddish purple in winter, followed by white, urn-shaped flowers and numerous, bright red fruit, from late summer often lasting through winter. When crushed they emit a wintergreen odour. H10-15cm/4-6in, W60-75cm/24-30in. F5-6. Z3-8.

G. shallon. From western North America, with large, leathery leaves and vigorous suckering habit; racemes of pale pink bell-flowers, followed by clusters of succulent purple fruits. Ideal ground cover in shade, but can be invasive. H90-150cm/3-5ft, W1.5-1.8m/5-6ft. F6. Z6-8.

Fuchsia 'Mrs Popple'

Garrya elliptica

× *Gaulnettya* 'Pink Pixie'

Gaultheria procumbens

Genista aetnensis

Genista tinctoria 'Royal Gold'

Genista hispanica

Genista pilosa 'Lemon Spreader'

GENISTA Broom

This large range of sun-loving species, closely related to *Cytisus*, are mostly all native to Europe. Small to medium-sized, mostly deciduous, late-spring and early-summer flowering shrubs, with yellow, pea-like blooms, they tolerate a wide range of soils, including acid, alkaline, sun-baked, dry and poor ones. There are dwarf forms for an alpine garden, ground-cover types and small trees. Prune, if necessary, immediately after flowering.

G. aetnensis. The Mount Etna broom eventually makes a large shrub or small tree with wispy, pendulous, almost leafless branches. Tiny, golden flowers cover the branchlets. Long-lived and lovely at the back of a border, but, like many taller brooms, may need support in later years in exposed sites. Best not pruned, but if necessary cut back only young stems. H3m/10ft, W3m/10ft. F7-8. Z9-10.

G. delphinensis. A dwarf form similar to *G. sagittalis*. A gem for the alpine garden but can be shy to flower. H15-20cm/6-8in, W45-60cm/18-24in. F7. Z6-8.

G. hispanica. The Spanish broom is a very prickly, deciduous shrub, like a compact gorse, slowly forming a round, spreading bush, with masses of deep golden-yellow flowers. Best on well-drained soil in sun; excellent for dry banks. H45-60cm/18-24in, W60-75cm/24-30in. F4-6. Z7-9.

G. lydia. This forms a woody central stem and many intertwining, arching or pendulous, dark green, slender branches, covered in bright yellow flowers. Prune lightly, if necessary, immediately after flowering, removing only green stems. Excellent over a wall or sunny bank. H45-60cm/18-24in, W90-150cm/3-5ft. F6. Z7-9.

G. pilosa. This prostrate British native is deciduous but its congested, densely branched stems look evergreen. The dark green foliage is hidden by a sheet of golden-yellow flowers. This and the similar 'Lemon Spreader' and 'Vancouver

× Halimiocistus wintonensis

Gold' from Canada are good for ground cover or hanging over a wall, the latter more compact when young. All H15-30cm/6-12in, W1.2-1.5m/4-5ft. F6. Z6-8.

G. sagittalis. Its odd-looking, evergreen, prostrate stems are flat and jointed, with terminal clusters of yellow flowers in midsummer. Makes good ground cover, but not always free to flower. H15-20cm/6-8in, W60-90cm/2-3ft. F6-7. Z6.

G. tenera. A native of Madeira that seems quite hardy and a good alternative to *G. aetnensis*. H3m/10ft, W3m/10ft. F7. Z8-11.

G. tinctoria. Common woadwaxen or dyer's greenwood is prostrate or low-growing with congested branches and a continuous, if unspectacular, show of yellow flowers. H30-60cm/1-2ft, W60-90cm/2-3ft. F6-8. Z5-7. 'Plena', with larger, more profuse, double, golden-yellow flowers, is worth garden space, as is the similar 'Golden Plate'. Both H30-45cm/12-18in, W60-90cm/2-3ft. F6-8. Z5-7. The distinctive 'Royal Gold' has an upright habit, its spikes adorned with bright yellow flowers in midsummer, often again in autumn. H75-90cm/30-36in, W1.2-1.5m/4-5ft. Z5-7.

HALESIA Snowdrop tree

In their native south-eastern USA these large trees are called silver bells. In northern Europe and Britain, most are shrubs but with age may reach tree-like proportions. Pendulous, white, bell-like flowers appear just before the leaves. Moist, lime-free soil, sun or part shade and shelter from cold wind are ideal. Prune, if necessary, immediately after flowering.

H. carolina. This has a bushy habit, its tiered branches briefly hung with graceful flower clusters, usually followed by pear-shaped, winged fruits. H3-4.5m/10-15ft, W3-4.5m/10-15ft. F4-5. Z5-8.

H. monticola. The mountain snowdrop is more tree-like, with attractive, peeling bark, larger flowers, often flushed pink, and larger fruits. 'Rosea' has pink flowers, but 'Vestita' is better, with larger, rose-pink flowers and downy leaves. All H3-4.5m/10-15ft, W3-4.5m/10-15ft. F4-5. Z5-8.

× HALIMIOCISTUS

This is an intergeneric cross between *Cistus* and *Halimium*. The species and cultivars are inclined to be tender, requiring similar conditions to *Cistus*, and provide often spectacular, saucer-shaped, rose-like flowers, with mostly grey-green evergreen foliage.

× *H. sahucii*. This has long, narrow, deep green leaves, a spreading habit and white flowers for months. H30-45cm/12-18in, W90-120cm/3-4ft. F6-9. Z8-9.

× *H. wintonensis*. A large-flowered hybrid with pearly white flowers marked deep crimson with a yellow base, and grey-green leaves. The form **'Merrist Wood Cream'**, a sport of × *H. wintonensis*, has creamy yellow flowers. Both H30-45cm/12-18in, W60-90cm/2-3ft. F5-6. Z8-9.

HALIMIUM

This small genus is closely related to *Cistus* and *Helianthemum*. Species require sun and good drainage.

H. lasianthum (syn. *Cistus formosus*). This has grey leaves and bright golden-yellow flowers, the base of each petal blotched dark purple. **'Concolor'** has yellow flowers with no blotches. **'Sandling'** is striking for its larger crimson-maroon basal markings. All H60-90cm/2-3ft, W90-120cm/3-4ft. F5-7. Z9.

H. ocymoides. A dwarf shrub with small grey leaves and a mass of bright golden-yellow flowers, each with dark brown basal blotches. The selection **'Susan'** is more bushy but equally showy. Both H60-90cm/2-3ft, W90-120cm/3-4ft. F6-7. Z9.

HAMAMELIS Witch hazel

Renowned for autumn colour and winter flowers, most are upright or spreading, with irregularly twisting branches. Slow to start, they eventually form large, deciduous shrubs with broadly oval, hazel-like leaves. Their mostly fragrant flowers have narrow, wavy, strap-like petals, resistant to frost and appearing on naked stems, depending on type chosen, from autumn until well into spring. Stems can be cut for indoor decoration.

Adaptable to most soils except thin chalk, they prefer full sun or part shade, moisture-retentive soil with humus, leaf mould, composted bark or peat added, and a similar mulch every two or three years. They can be trained as wall shrubs. Named selections are usually propagated by grafting the cultivar onto an understock of the vigorous *H. virginiana*, hence their relative scarcity and high price. Remove any suckers from the base of this union as seen. Prune only to reduce size, straight after flowering and before growth begins.

H. × *intermedia*. This group of hybrids between Chinese witch hazel, *H. mollis*, and Japanese witch hazel, *H. japonica*, includes some of the most colourful and varied forms. Many come from the famous Kalmthout Arboretum in Belgium, where Robert and Jelena de Belder have, for over thirty years, selected forms from more than 25,000 seedlings. **'Arnold Promise'**, from Arnold Arboretum in Boston, USA, is free-flowering, with upright, later spreading, branches and deep yellow, fragrant flowers and red sepals. Yellow autumn leaves. F2-3. **'Diane'**, a de Belder selection, has crimson-red flowers which are outstanding against sky or a light background, and orange-red autumn colour. F2-3. **'Feuerzauber'** (syn.

Halimium ocymoides 'Susan'

'Magic Fire') has bronze-red flowers and the most brilliant autumn leaves of all. F1-2. **'Jelena'** (syn. 'Copper Beauty') has large, coppery orange flowers, lasting sometimes for months, and orange-yellow autumn leaves. F12-2. **'Orange Beauty'** has profuse, orange-yellow flowers, lasting for several weeks. F2-3. For pale canary-yellow flowers and yellow-orange autumn colour, **'Primavera'**, with its upright habit, is good for a small garden. F1-2. Flowering slightly later is the canary-yellow, large-flowered **'Westerstede'**, from Germany. F2-3. All H2.4-3m/8-10ft, W2.4-3m/8-10ft. Z5-9.

H. japonica. The Japanese witch hazel is variable, but usually makes a wide-spreading, thinly branched shrub, its shiny leaves reliably providing rich autumn colours. Small, slightly fragrant, crinkled flowers. Eventual H3-5m/10-16ft, W4-6m/13-20ft. F2-3. Z5-9. **'Arborea'**, with fragrant clusters of small, yellow flowers, eventually makes a horizontally branched tree. H2.1-3m/7-10ft, W2.1-3m/7-10ft. F2-3. Z5-9. Smaller, erect and free-flowering is **'Zuccariniana'**, with small but profuse, bright sulphur-yellow flowers and yellow autumn leaves. H2.1-3m/7-10ft, W1.5-1.8m/5-6ft. F3-4. Z5-9.

H. mollis. The very popular Chinese witch hazel slowly forms an upright, later spreading, bush. Its downy, grey-green leaves turn butter-yellow in autumn. Clusters of deep yellow, fragrant flowers with bronze-red sepals appear for several months. The species is desirable, but the selection **'Pallida'**, raised at the Royal Horticultural Society's gardens at Wisley, England, from seed thought to have originated from Belgium's Kalmthout Arboretum, has copious, large, deliciously scented, bright sulphur-yellow flowers with bronze-red sepals. Site both against dark backgrounds to highlight their winter beauty. Both H1.5-2.4m/5-8ft, W1.5m-1.8m/5-6ft. F12-1. Z5-9.

Hamamelis × *intermedia* 'Feuerzauber'

Hamamelis × *intermedia* 'Jelena'

H. vernalis. From the southern and central USA, the variable Ozark witch hazel is rare in gardens, but tolerates a higher alkalinity and wetter soils than other species. Usually a multi-stemmed, compact bush, it has yellow autumn colour and yellow-through-red flowers, lasting for several weeks, which are pungent rather than fragrant. **'Sandra'**, selected at the Hillier Nursery, Hampshire, England, has purple young leaves, green in summer and rich flame-orange in autumn. Its small, yellow flowers are not always freely produced. Both H1.8-2.4m/6-8ft, W1.5-1.8m/5-6ft. F2-3. Z4-9.

Hamamelis mollis 'Pallida'

SHRUBS

Hebe pimeleoides 'Quicksilver'

Hebe brachysiphon

Hebe 'Margret'

H. virginiana. The common witch hazel is a very hardy and vigorous North American species, making a broad, spreading shrub or small tree with ascending branches. Medicinal witch hazel is extracted from its roots and branches. Though used for grafting selected forms, it is seldom grown as a shrub in its own right, a pity since it is an outstanding, large background shrub, with good autumn colour. Small, fragrant,

Hebe cupressoides 'Boughton Dome'

yellow flowers appear as the leaves change colour, and last several weeks. No selected named forms are available. H3m/10ft, W3m/10ft. F10-11. Z3-9.

HEBE

This genus has over 100 species of ever-green shrubs and small trees, all native to the Southern Hemisphere, mostly from New Zealand. Many are valuable garden plants, others are borderline hardy in cold northern temperate zones, and in the USA hebes are virtually restricted to the less humid West Coast. Many hardier hybrids and cultivars, dwarf or medium-sized, have proved adaptable plants for any well-drained soil, in full sun or part shade.

Taller ones are less hardy but thrive in warm regions and are excellent by the sea, flowering on and off all summer. According to type, they can be used as specimen shrubs, in mixed borders or as ground cover. Some, especially the conifer-like whipcord types, with scale-like leaves hugging the stems, are grown for foliage effects, with flowers as a bonus. If cut back by frost, hebes often shoot from the base in late spring or early summer. Prune in late spring to tidy straggly bushes and remove faded

flowers; rejuvenate old, woody shrubs by cutting back to 15cm/6in above ground.

H. albicans. This has glaucous, oblong leaves and white flowers. **'Red Edge'**, with red-margined leaves, is especially striking in late summer and winter. Both H45cm/18in, W60cm/2ft. F6-8. Z8-11.

H. 'Autumn Glory'. An old favourite with purple-tinged foliage and short spikes of bluish purple flowers. H60cm/2ft, W90cm/3ft. F8. Z8-11.

H. brachysiphon (formerly *H. traversii*). This dense, round bush of dark green, box-like foliage with white flowers is quite hardy, and a good lawn specimen. H1.5m/5ft, W1.5m/5ft. F6-8. Z9-10.

H. 'Carl Teschner'. A rather tender, compact, small-leaved shrub which carries profuse, deep blue flowers. Excellent ground cover. H30-45cm/12-18in, W45-60cm/18-24in. F7. Z8-11.

H. cupressoides. This upright, multi-branched shrub has grey-green, scale-like leaves; its terminal clusters of pale blue flowers appear only in warm seasons. **'Nana'** seems identical. H60-120cm/2-4ft, W60-120cm/2-4ft. F7. Z8-10. The grey-green **'Boughton Dome'** is a truly compact, rounded dwarf, ideal with alpines. It seldom flowers. H45-60cm/18-24in, W45-60cm/18-24in. Z8-10.

H. 'Diamonte'. See *H.* 'La Seduisante'.

H. 'Emerald Gem' (syn. *H.* 'Green Globe'). This makes an almost perfect mound of small, green leaves but may not survive severe frost. White flowers but grown more for foliage. H30-45cm/12-18in, W45-60cm/18-24in. F6-8. Z8-10.

H. × franciscana 'Blue Gem'. Small and dome-shaped, with green leaves and bright blue flowers. Hardier than **'Variegata'**, with leaves broadly margined creamy white. Both H1.2m/4ft, W1.2m/4ft. F6-8. Z8-10.

H. 'Great Orme'. A compact shrub, with lance-shaped leaves and tapering racemes of bright pink flowers. H90cm/3ft, W90cm/3ft. F6-9. Z8-10.

H. 'Green Globe'. See *H.* 'Emerald Gem'.

H. 'La Seduisante' (syn. *H.* 'Diamonte'). This old favourite is semi-hardy, with leathery leaves and dense spikes of bright crimson flowers. H1.5m/5ft. W1.5m/5ft. F6-9. Z9-10.

H. 'Margret'. A promising, quite hardy dwarf hybrid with deep green leaves and bright blue flowers, fading to white. Low, bushy habit. H30-45cm/12-18in, W45-60cm/18-24in. F6-9. Z8-10.

H. 'Marjorie'. Hardy, this forms a neat bush with rounded leaves and pale violet and white flowers. H90cm/3ft, W90cm/3ft. F7-9. Z8-10.

H. 'Midsummer Beauty'. Large leaves, red beneath, and profuse, lavender-purple flowers, on and off, for many months. H1.2m/4ft, W1.5m/5ft. F7-1. Z8-10.

SHRUBS

H. ochracea. This has a dwarf, spreading habit and cypress-like, whipcord foliage, old gold in summer, bronzing in winter. White flowers, less in cool climates. Often confused with *H. armstrongii*, which has olive-green foliage. H75cm/30in, W75cm/30in. F7-8. Z8-10. **'James Stirling'** is tidy and flat-topped, bright green in summer, bronze in winter. White flowers, rarely in cool climates. H30cm/18in, W75cm/30in. F7-8. Z8-10.

H. pimeleoides **'Quicksilver'**. This twiggy, narrow, spreading shrub has purple-black stems, brilliant silver-blue leaves and purple-lilac flowers. H30-45cm/12-18in, W45-60cm/18-24in. F6-8. Z8-10.

H. pinguifolia **'Pagei'**. An almost prostrate bush with small, round, blue-grey leaves and white flowers. H15cm/6in, W30-45cm/12-18in. F6-7. Z8-10.

H. rakaiensis. Ideal ground cover, this robust, compact bush has light green leaves and profuse white flowers. Often seen wrongly labelled as *H. subalpina*, but the latter has longer leaves. H45-60cm/18-24in, W45-60cm/18-24in. F6-7. Z8-10.

H. salicifolia. This elegant, tall shrub has light green, willow-like leaves and long heads of white, lavender-tinted flowers. **'Variegata'** has creamy-edged leaves. Both H1.5m/5ft, W1.5m/5ft. F6-8. Z9-10.

H. **'Wingletye'**. A low-spreading bush with blue-grey leaves and mauve flowers. H15cm/6in, W30-45cm/12-18in. F6-7. Z8-10.

HEDERA Ivy

Often listed as climbers, most are well-adapted to climb, if often slow to put out aerial roots. Contrary to common perception, the ivies will not damage trees if growth is kept to the main branches, nor brickwork on houses. Old ivy on walls can be pruned hard back in late spring. Some are excellent ground cover in dry shade, or can ramble over stumps; most are attractive in containers. Large-leaved types are very effective ground cover, their thick, overlapping leaves smothering weeds. Adaptable to a wide range of soils except those that are wet or badly drained.

H. canariensis **'Gloire de Marengo'**. Though used as a house plant, it is quite hardy in shelter and poor, dry soil, against a sunny or shady wall. Variegation greener in shade. Its grey, green and creamy white variegated leaves are smaller than *H. colchica*. Excellent as a patio plant in a container. H30cm/1ft, W2.4-3m/8-10ft. Z9-11.

H. colchica. The Persian ivy and its variegated forms are often reluctant to climb a wall without help, but eventually grow up trees unaided; the species has dark green leathery leaves. Variegated or coloured leaf forms are brighter in good light. **'Arborescens'** is a shrubby form, making a mound of broad green leaves,

Hebe 'Midsummer Beauty'

free-flowering and fruiting, both appearing at the same time. H90-120cm/3-4ft, W1.2-1.5m/4-5ft. Z6-9. **'Dentata'** has lighter, larger green leaves. **'Dentata Variegata'** has broad, grey-green leaves, margined creamy yellow. **'Sulphur Heart'** (syn. 'Paddy's Pride') has an irregular central splash. On older plants heads of rounded green flowers are usually followed by black fruits. All H30cm/1ft, W1.8-3m/6-10ft. Z6-9.

Hedera colchica 'Arborescens'

Hedera colchica

Hedera helix 'Arborescens'

Hedera helix 'Sagittaefolia Variegata'

Heptacodium jasminioides

Hibiscus syriacus 'Pink Giant'

H. helix. Common ivy grows wild throughout Europe, as ground cover in woods, and up trees. There are innumerable selections, with variously shaped, coloured, marbled or variegated leaves. Most climb, putting out aerial roots as they search for support. If no support is found, the upper stems eventually become shrubby, losing their wish to climb. Greenish flowers produced only on older shrubby arborescent stems, the leaves becoming rhomboid rather than lobed. These appear in autumn followed by black fruits. All below F9-11. Green forms Z4-9, variegated Z6-9, depending on site.

Classed as a shrub is **'Arborescens'** which slowly forms a mound of dark green leaves, yellow flowers and black fruits. H90-120cm/3-4ft, W90-120cm/3-4ft. **'Congesta'** forms a twiggy, irregular bush, with erect, stiffly held branches, and small, dark green leaves. H45-60cm/18-24in, W60-90cm/2-3ft. **'Conglomerata'** makes a low, mounded plant with dark green, prominently veined leaves, ideal for the rock garden. H30-45cm/12-18in, W60-75cm/24-30in. **'Erecta'**, with stiffly erect branches and handsome, dark green leaves, makes an excellent evergreen shrub for the smaller garden. H75-90cm/30-36in, W60-75cm/24-30in.

There are innumerable selections for ground cover, climbing and containers, but only a few can be mentioned here. **'Buttercup'** has pale yellow leaves in summer turning to pale green. H15cm/6in, W3-5m/10-16ft. **'Chicago'**, dense habit good for both purposes, dark green bronzy leaves. H15cm/6in, W3-5m/10-16ft. **'Glacier'**, one of the best white variegated forms, grey-green, diamond-shaped leaves margined white. H10-15cm/4-6in, W2.1-3m/7-10ft. **'Green Ripple'**, good ground cover, mid-green, finely veined, distinctly pointed leaves. H15cm/6in, W3-5m/10-16ft. **'Hibernica'**, the Irish Ivy, one of the best for ground cover, larger, dark green, glossy leaves. H15-25cm/6-10in, W4-5m/13-16ft. **'Sagittaefolia'** has deeply cut and lobed leaves, marbled silver. H15cm/6in, W3-4m/10-13ft. The leaves of **'Sagittaefolia Variegata'** are similar, but brightly margined creamy white. H10-15cm/4-6in, W2.1-3m/7-10ft. **'Spetchley'** has small, spear-shaped, dark green leaves and twiggy shoots, and is mat-forming. H6-10cm/3-4in, W1-2.1m/39-84in.

HELIANTHEMUM See under Alpines.

HELICHRYSUM
H. angustifolium. See under Perennials.
H. splendidum (syn. *H. alveolatum*). See under Perennials.

HEPTACODIUM
H. jasminioides. The common name, 'The Seven Son Flower of Zhejiang', is as uncommon as this fascinating deciduous shrub, originating from eastern China. It makes a large, erect shrub clothed in deep green ribbed leaves and, on established plants in late summer, large panicles of small, fragrant, white flowers, continuing until autumn. In warm climates the sepals turn bright crimson when the flowers have finished. Sun or part shade. An excellent back-of-the-border shrub worth looking for. H3-5m/10-16ft, W2.1-3m/7-10ft. F8-10. Z5-9.

HIBISCUS Mallow
H. syriacus. The shrub althaea, or tree hollyhock, is one of the few hardy hibiscus. Introduced from eastern Asia in the sixteenth century, its cultivars, with trumpet-like, single or double flowers, make spectacular late-flowering shrubs. Most slowly make upright, later round, large, grey-stemmed bushes; light green leaves appear in late spring or early summer. They have a long flowering period, but in cool, northerly regions flowering, especially of the double-flowered forms, can be disappointing. These hibiscus grow in most well-drained soils in full sun, but can be slow to establish. Hard pruning established plants in spring induces vigorous new flowering growth. **'Admiral Dewey'**, white, double. **'Ardens'** (syn. 'Caeruleus Plenus'), lilac-purple, double. **'Blue Bird'** (syn. 'Oiseau Bleu'), deep violet-blue, darker centres, single. **'Diane'**, white, single. **'Duc de Brabant'**, reddish purple, double. **'Hamabo'**, white or pink-flushed white, crimson eye, single. **'Pink Giant'**, bright rose-pink, dark centre, single. **'Red Heart'**, white, red-centred, single. **'Russian Violet'**, vigorous, leafy habit, violet, single. **'Violet Clair'**, double, violet-blue. **'William R. Smith'**, white, single. **'Woodbridge'**, pink, red centre, single. All H1.5-1.8m/5-6ft, W1.2-1.5m/4-5ft. F7-10. Z6-9.

HOLODISCUS
H. discolor. A rare North American native, this upright, large deciduous bush has small, grey-green leaves and creamy white panicles of pendulous flowers, reminiscent of *Spiraea* or *Astilbe*, and striking against a dark background. Full sun or part shade, any soil. Prune some old or congested stems almost to the base on older plants after flowering. H3m/10ft, W3m/10ft. F7. Z6-9.

HUMULUS
H. lupulus 'Aureus'. The golden hop is a hardy, herbaceous, perennial climber, useful for quickly covering large areas of wall, low roof or fence, or for growing up trees – wherever its clinging tendrils can reach.

The coarse, hairy leaves are bright yellow in full sun, less so in shade, and soon create a dense, eye-catching screen. Its flowers are insignificant, but its attractive autumn fruit, or hops, are light green, ageing to gold or brown, and can be used for making beer. Cut away old foliage after winter dieback. H5-6m/16-20ft, W5-6m/16-20ft. F7-8. Z6-9.

HYDRANGEA

Hydrangeas contain a much wider range of forms than is generally imagined. From dwarf to large shrubs with varying types of flowers and foliage, they offer much to the gardener. Large-flowered mopheads are striking, if unnatural-looking and sometimes overused; lacecaps and other species and hybrids are more graceful and subtle. All are deciduous. Some species need full sun or light shade, others need shade, but most grow successfully given moist, acid or reasonably alkaline soils. Some are excellent for containers.

H. arborescens. All the cultivars below are easy in any soil, sun or shade. All flower on the same year's growth; prune by half or to the ground in early spring. **'Grandiflora'**, a selection of this North American species, has large, round heads of creamy white, sterile flowers, or florets fading to green. It makes a broad bush, the upright stems a little lax, often weighed down by flowers which remain attractive even when dead in winter. Light green leaves. H1.2-1.5m/4-5ft, W1.5-1.8m/5-6ft. F7-9. Z3-9. The similar, but more compact **'Annabelle'** has enormous, domed flower heads, up to 30cm/1ft across, often weighing down slender branches. H90-120cm/3-4ft, W1.2-1.5m/4-5ft. F7-9. Z3-9. **'Sterilis'**. This makes a neat shrub with grey-green leaves and domes of small, white, sterile, natural-looking flowers, able to stand without support. H90-120cm/3-4ft, W90-120cm/3-4ft. F7-9. Z3-9.

H. aspera villosa. The species *H. aspera* is variable in type and habit, *villosa* being a good representative of the species. It is a shade-loving, slow-growing, woody shrub, erect in habit, sometimes tender when young, so protect with a wall or overhanging tree against spring frost. Soft, dark green, felted leaves; flat, large flower heads of tiny, bluish purple flowers and lilac florets. Attractive bark on older plants. Any reasonably moist soil. Prune to tidy or remove dieback. H1.5-1.8m/5-6ft, W1.5-1.8m/5-6ft. F8-9. Z7-9.

H. involucrata. This dwarf Japanese species has grey-green, downy foliage and dainty, small flower clusters surrounded by large, sterile ray flowers, pink on alkaline soils, pale blue on very acid ones. H75-90cm/30-36in, W75-90cm/30-36in. F7-9. Z7-9.

H. macrophylla. This Japanese species includes the self-descriptive mopheads and

Holodiscus discolor

Hydrangea aspera villosa

lacecaps, both dense bushes with erect branches, often weighed down by flowers. They need sun or light shade and humus-rich soil. Buds can be damaged by winter or spring frost; mature plants are more resistant but an autumn mulch of composted bark, leaf mould or rotted manure helps. Prune these and *H. serrata* types in spring, removing only the previous year's dead flower heads and, on older plants, a few woody stems from the base if congested. Both mopheads and lacecaps make good container plants for patios.

Some *macrophylla* and *serrata* types can change colour; very acid soils produce real blue, the same plant on neutral or alkaline soil can be pink or red. For blue flowers on neutral or alkaline soils, add aluminium sulphate: consult your local garden centre.

Lacecaps have small flowers surrounded by large, showy, flat ray florets. Most H1.2-1.5m/4-5ft, W1.2-1.5m/4-5ft. F6-9. Z6-9. The popular **'Blue Wave'** needs shade; blue fertile flowers, pink ray florets on alkaline soils, blue on acid soils. **'Geoffrey Chadbund'**, deep crimson, purple on acid

Hydrangea arborescens 'Sterilis'

H. m. 'Générale Vicomtesse de Vibraye'

Hydrangea paniculata 'Kyushu'

Hydrangea paniculata 'Pink Diamond'

Hydrangea quercifolia 'Snow Queen'

soils. **'Lanarth White'** and **'Mariesii'**, dwarf (H90cm/3ft), the former pink or blue with white ray florets; the latter, rose-pink ray florets, blue on acid soils. **'Tricolor'**, flowers like 'Mariesii', leaves splashed green, grey and pale yellow. **'White Wave'** (syn. 'Mariesii Alba'), large heads, pink on lime, blue on acid soils, white ray florets.

Mopheads or Hortensias have round heads of sterile florets of various colours, some changing according to pH. Sun or very light shade; dried flower heads attractive in arrangements. Most H1.2-1.5m/4-5ft, W1.2-1.5m/4-5ft. F6-9. Z7-9. **'Altona'**, rose-pink, deep blue on acid soils. **'Ami Pasquier'**, dwarf, crimson turning purple. **'Europe'**, vigorous, deep pink, changing to mid-blue. **'Générale Vicomtesse de Vibraye'**, pink, clear blue on acid soil; needs shade. **'Madame Emile Mouillère'**, slightly tender, serrated white florets with a pink or blue central spot according to soil. **'Masja'** has deep crimson heads. For patio containers or sheltered gardens, **'Pia'**, pink, and **'Tovelit'**, bright pink (both H30-45cm/12-18in).

H. paniculata. This has been superseded by many selections, all erect, dense shrubs, with large, usually pyramidal, flower panicles, first light green, then white or cream, later often pink. The panicles usually contain fertile and sterile flowers, and grow on current season's wood, so they escape spring frosts, can be regularly pruned to keep compact, and flower reliably in late summer and autumn. Any moist soil, sun or shade. Pruning not absolutely necessary, but to restrict size, improve flowering and keep bushier habit, prune branches back in spring to just above where previous year's growth started – usually half the height of the shrub.

'Grandiflora' with large, sterile flower heads, is very common; pruned as a standard, its panicles are grotesquely huge. **'Kyushu'** has glossy leaves and profuse, long panicles of creamy white flowers. The following all come from the Belgian Kalmthout Arboretum. **'Pink Diamond'**, large, creamy white heads, then pink, finally red-brown. **'Unique'**, with large, erect heads, rosy-pink in autumn. **'White Moth'**, with huge, round, nodding, green heads, turning creamy white. All, unpruned H2.4-3m/8-10ft, W2.4-3m/8-10ft. F7-10. Z4-8.

H. petiolaris. The climbing hydrangea, in its native Japan and Korea, climbs trees by means of aerial roots, like ivy, to heights of more than 20m/65ft. In cultivation it is slow to establish, but can be trained up trees, walls or fences, or used as ground cover. It may be a few years before it forms creamy yellow flower clusters surrounded by white bracts fading to pink. Easy on any reasonably moist, fertile soil, in sun or shade including north walls. Provide initial tying in to supports; thereafter it becomes self-clinging. H2.4-3m/8-10ft, W2.4-3m/8-10ft. F6. Z4-8.

H. quercifolia. The oak-leaf hydrangea, from the south-eastern USA, grows only half its natural height of 1.8m/6ft in climates with cool summers. Dark green 'oak' leaves turn bronze to purple in autumn. Small, erect, long-lasting, greeny white panicles which flop with age. **'Snowflake'** is double-flowered, the heavy panicles inclined to flop. Provide warmth and shelter. Both H90-150cm/3-5ft, W1.2-1.5m/4-5ft. F6-8. Z5-9. **'Snow Queen'**, more vigorous, has large, erect, white heads, later tinged pink. Needs a hot summer. Large, oak-shaped leaves turn bronze in autumn. Prune back only if stems damaged in winter or if required as foliage shrub. H1.2-1.5m/4-5ft, W1.2-1.5m/4-5ft. F6-8. Z5-9.

H. serrata. A variable species, rarely exceeding 90cm/3ft high, with clusters of blue or white flowers and blue, white or pink florets. Grow as for *H. macrophylla.* **'Bluebird'**, dense, erect habit; deep blue flowers, large ray florets, crimson-purple on alkaline soils, deep blue on acid ones. **'Blue Deckle'** and **'Diadem'** are dwarf forms from plant breeder and author Michael Haworth-Booth, pink on alkaline soils, blue on acid soils. **'Grayswood'** has blue flowers, white florets turning pink, then crimson. **'Miranda'** is another dwarf form from Michael Haworth-Booth, pink on alkaline soils, blue on acid soils. The floriferous German hybrid **'Preziosa'**, perhaps the best garden hydrangea, has deep green, later bronze, foliage and domed, pink flower heads, turning crimson. Sun or part shade. All H75-120cm/30-48in, W60-120cm/2-4ft. F6-9. Z6-8.

HYPERICUM

This large genus contains herbaceous plants, semi-shrubby alpines (see under Alpines) and easily grown, deciduous shrubs, evergreen in mild winters, all with yellow flowers. Most grow 60-150cm/2-5ft high in any well-drained soil, in sun or part shade and flower from midsummer onwards, some with colourful fruits in late summer. Prune for tidiness and flowering; cut back previous year's stems by a third, and every three to five years to the base, in early spring, to rejuvenate old plants. Some, unfortunately, are prone to rust, which is difficult to eradicate.

H. androsaemum. The Tutsan hypericum is adaptable ground cover, forming a dense, low-spreading bush with dark green leaves and small yellow flowers with prominent stamens. Red-brown fruits turn black in autumn. **'Gladys Brabazon'** is a form from Ireland with new shoots mottled cream and pink, yellow flowers, and bright red berries. **'Gold Penny'**, a free-flowering and fruiting Dutch selection, has maroon fruits, and the very hardy Danish **'Hysan'** has maroon fruits turning black and staying on erect branches all winter, excellent for cutting. All H90cm/3ft, W90-120cm/3-4ft. F7-9. Z6-8.

H. calycinum. The rose of Sharon, often considered a weed, spreads rapidly by underground stems, but is useful in shade and dry or poor soil. Its large, charming flowers with long, yellow stamens appear for months. Prune dead or semi-evergreen stems to the ground annually in spring to tidy and rejuvenate. H30cm/1ft, W1.2-1.8m/4-6ft. F7-10. Z6-8.

H. **'Hidcote'**. Deservedly popular, it makes a dense thicket of erect branches, producing large, saucer-shaped flowers. Non-fruiting. H1.5m/5ft, W1.5-1.8m/5-6ft. F7-10. Z6-9.

H. × *inodorum* **'Albury Purple'**. Noted for its striking purple leaves, especially when young, but prone to rust, as is **'Elstead'**, which is renowned for spectacular clusters of succulent, red fruit above the foliage in late summer and autumn. **'Summergold'** has dark yellow leaves, prone to sunscorch but effective in light shade. All H60-90cm/2-3ft, W90cm/3ft. F7-9. Z6-8.

H. kouytchense (syn. *H. patulum* 'Sungold'). Compact, lax and floriferous, this has flowers with reflexed, floppy petals and prominent clusters of erect stamens, then scarlet fruit. H90cm/3ft, W90-120cm/3-4ft. F7-10. Z7-9.

Hydrangea serrata 'Preziosa'

Hypericum androsaemum 'Hysan'

Hypericum 'Hidcote'

H. × *moserianum*. A low, dense shrub with spreading, red stems and large flowers with red anthers, this can be cut back to the ground by frost. H45-60cm/18-24in, W60-90cm/2-3ft. F7-10. Z7-8. **'Tricolor'** is hardy only in the mildest, sheltered localities, its leaves rose, pink and cream. H45-60cm/18-24in, W60-90cm/2-3ft. F7-10. Z9-10.

H. patulum **'Sungold'**. See *H. kouytchense*.

H. prolificum. Rare but excellent for a sunny spot, this densely branched North American species has slender, upright stems and profuse, small, tufted, bright yellow flowers. Adaptable and very hardy, as is the similar *H. kalmianum*. H90cm/3ft, W90-120cm/3-4ft. F7-9. Z5-8.

IBERIS See under Alpines.

ILEX Holly

Hollies include deciduous and evergreen species, miniatures under 60cm/2ft high after twenty-five years as well as trees 20m/65ft tall or more. Usually male and female flowers are on separate plants, the females bearing fruit but usually requiring a male nearby for pollination. Most are easy to care for but often slow to establish, and

Hypericum androsaemum 'Gladys Brabazon'

253

Ilex × altaclerensis 'Belgica Aurea'

Ilex aquifolium 'Flavescens'

Ilex aquifolium 'Ferox Argentea'

tolerant of most soils and sun or shade. Select and site larger-growing types with care because they eventually take a lot of space; they are good alternatives to conifers as background plants, many with colourful leaves. Most take well to pruning and are often improved by shaping early growth to increase density. Many make excellent hedges, tolerant of pollution and maritime exposure; prune in early spring or late summer.

I. × altaclerensis. Several selections have been made, mostly forming tall, pyramidal shrubs or trees with large leaves, small, white flowers and large fruit, excellent for hedging. Some leaf drop may occur in severe winters. **'Belgica Aurea'** (syn. 'Silver Sentinel') has lightly spined, green-grey leaves edged with creamy white to yellow, and orange-red fruits. **'Camelliifolia'** has glossy, camellia-like, almost spineless leaves, purple when young, and crimson fruit. **'Golden King'** is actually female, with spineless leaves edged yellow, and abundant red fruit. **'Lawsoniana'** has golden-centred, green-edged leaves, which can revert, and bright red fruit. The free-fruiting **'Purple Shaft'** has purple stems. All H3-4.5m/10-15ft, W1.8-2.4m/6-8ft. F5-6. Z7-9.

I. aquifolium. The English or common holly is native to Europe and western Asia, and there are numerous foliage and fruiting garden forms, all hardier than *I. × altaclerensis*, with mostly spiny leaves, small, white flowers, making large shrubs and eventually pyramidal trees. **'Amber'** has bronze-yellow fruit. **'Argentea Marginata'** is bushy and free-fruiting, with broad, silvery-white edged leaves. **'Atlas'** is a hardy male, with green young stems and

spiny leaves. **'Bacciflava'** (syn. 'Fructu-luteo') has bright yellow fruit.

'Ferox', the hedgehog holly, is a slow, low-growing male with crinkled, fiercely spiny leaves. Variegated forms include **'Ferox Argentea'**, with yellow and white leaf margins, and **'Ferox Aurea'**, with a central gold splash. Growth rate of all 'Ferox' forms about a third of that given below. The female **'Flavescens'**, the moonlight holly, needs sun to show its golden-yellow leaves best; young spring growth also very striking. **'Handsworth New Silver'** is striking, with purple shoots, dark green leaves edged white, and red fruit. The male **'J. C. Van Tol'**, with yellow-edged leaves, is popular for hedging. The prickly **'Madame Briot'** has purple young stems, with leaves broadly edged, and sometimes all golden-yellow, and orange-red fruit. **'Silver Milkmaid'**, a striking female, has dark green, spiny leaves splashed with creamy white, but can revert. **'Silver Queen'** has green and grey leaves edged creamy white. Average H3-4.5m/10-15ft, W1.8-2.4m/6-8ft. F5-6. Z7-9.

I. crenata. These small-leaved, Japanese and Korean hollies may seem dull at first sight. Much used for formal, low hedges in Japan, they could be used more in western gardens as a dwarf, clipped hedge or container plant. The species is rarely seen since, especially in the USA, hundreds of selections are in garden use, many almost identical. Most are compact, evergreen shrubs with rigid branches, dense, small, dark, glossy, spineless leaves, inconspicuous white flowers, and black fruit on the

Ilex × meserveae 'Blue Angel'

females. They prefer moist, well-drained, neutral or acid soils. Most below, F5-6, Z5-8. **'Buxifolia'** is pyramidal and ideal as a specimen or for a medium hedge. H1.5-1.8m/5-6ft, W90-120cm/3-4ft. **'Convexa'** is free-fruiting and broadly vase-shaped, good for a low hedge. H60-90cm/2-3ft, W1.2-1.5m/4-5ft. **'Dwarf Pagoda'**, a male clone, makes a miniature, irregular mound. H30-45cm/12-18in, W30-45cm/12-18in. **'Golden Gem'**, low and spreading, has golden-yellow leaves in sun; female, but seldom flowers or fruits. H45-60cm/18-24in, W60-75cm/24-30in. **'Helleri'**, female, slowly makes a dense, flatted hummock. H20-30cm/8-12in, W30-45cm/12-18in. **'Mariesii'**, also female and free-fruiting, is erect, with box-like leaves, ideal for troughs or bonsai. H45-60cm/18-24in, W30-45cm/12-18in.
I. × *meserveae*. This group of hybrids, between *I. aquifolium* and *I. rugosa*, from Mrs Meserve on Long Island, New York, are hardier and more adaptable than *I. aquifolium* and the first selections were originally offered as 'Blue Hollies', named after the glaucous bloom on the foliage at certain times of the year. The following varieties are dense and bushy in habit. Fruiting is less than spectacular in cool climates. All F4-5, Z4-5. **'Blue Angel'**, dark green leaves, red fruits. H1.2-1.5m/4-5ft, W1.2-1.5m/4-5ft. **'Blue Princess'**, blue-green leaves, free-fruiting. H1.5-1.8m/5-6ft, W1.2-1.5m/4-5ft. **'Blue Prince'**, shining dark green leaves, abundant flowers. H1.5-1.8m/5-6ft, W1.2-1.5m/4-5ft.
I. verticillata. The common winterberry is deciduous, mostly forming a broad, upright or spreading shrub or small tree with dark green leaves, yellow in autumn. Small clusters of creamy white flowers in the leaf axils in spring. A male must pollinate the female if bright red, long-lasting fruit is to appear. From swampy, acid soils in eastern North America, it adapts well to similar or drier sites, in sun or part shade. Unsuitable for chalk. Often used for flower arranging in autumn and winter. **'Aurantiaca'** has orange fruit and **'Chrysocarpa'** yellow fruit. **'Red Sprite'** is dwarfer than dimensions below. **'Winter Red'** and **'Xmas Cheer'** have bright red berries from autumn until well into winter, depending on the appetites of local birds. All H1.5-1.8m/5-6ft, W1.5-1.8m/5-6ft. F3-4. Z4-9.

INDIGOFERA
Some shrubby members of this large genus, part of the pea family, make worthwhile if rare garden plants. They have pinnate leaves and racemes of pink, white or purple flowers, usually for many weeks. Heights vary, species making 45-300cm/18-120in; in mild winters stems remain alive and shoot along their full length in spring, but in cold climates they die back to the ground, new

Indigofera decora

shoots emerging late in spring or early summer. Climate also affects flowering, with early-flowering forms blooming much later in cold areas. All prefer sun, heat and good drainage but tolerate some shade and drought. Prune semi-evergreen shoots back by a third in late spring, otherwise prune dead or poorly shaped stems away as soon as new shoots appear.
I. decora (syn. *I. incarnata)*. This rare Chinese and Japanese species is a beautiful, dwarf shrub, with low, arching stems freely producing racemes of large, pink flowers. **'Alba'** is white-flowered. Both H45-60cm/18-24in, W45-60cm/18-24in. F7. Z7-9.
I. gerardiana. See *I. heterantha*.
I. heterantha (syn. *I. gerardiana*). The most popular indigo, it makes a twiggy, upright bush with small, grey-green leaves and purple-pink flowers. H1.8-2.4m/6-8ft, W1.2-1.5m/4-5ft. F7-9. Z7-9.
I. incarnata. See *I. decora*.
I. kirilowii. Hardy and vigorous, this slowly spreads by underground suckers. Luxuriant, leafy stems almost hide the rose-pink flowers. Good in shade and dry areas. H90-120cm/3-4ft, W1.2-1.5m/4-5ft. F7-9. Z5-8.
I. potaninii. This and the almost identical *I. amblyantha* make erect, later arching, dense, multi-stemmed shrubs with bright green leaves and a continuous show of rose-pink flowers. H1.5-1.8m/5-6ft, W1.5-1.8m/5-6ft. F7-9. Z6-9.

ITEA
All but one of these deciduous and evergreen flowering shrubs originate from eastern Asia, *I. virginica* being North American.
I. ilicifolia. A tender but handsome, evergreen shrub, with glossy, holly-like

Indigofera heterantha

Itea ilicifolia

Itea virginica

Jasminum nudiflorum

Jasminum officinale

Kalmia angustifolia 'Rubra'

leaves, for milder climates or protected sites in cold areas. It grows well on most soils, acid or alkaline, preferring sun or light shade. Mature plants carry spectacular tassels, often over 30cm/1ft long, of greenish white, scented flowers. As a wall plant, tie to prevent wind damage, and wherever planted, protect from cold, desiccating winds. Prune only to control size, either in late spring or just after flowering. H1.8-2.4m/6-8ft, W1.8-2.4m/6-8ft. F8. Z8-10.

I. virginica. The deciduous Virginia sweetspire can, especially in cold climates, take time to make an impression. It has bright green leaves and pendulous, cylindrical racemes of small, white, fragrant flowers. Climate also affects autumn colour, which can vary from yellow to crimson. Happiest in part shade in good, moist acid to slightly alkaline soil. Little or no pruning is needed, except, perhaps, to thin older stems on mature plants. H1.5-1.8m/5-6ft, W1.2-1.5m/4-5ft. F6-7. Z6-9.

JASMINUM Jasmine
Popular as wall plants and climbers, many species also make adaptable free-standing or sprawling shrubs. The more vigorous can sprawl over a wall, rock, tree stump or low fence, their wiry, overlapping stems making a dense cover. Most are deciduous in cold winters, but their green stems create an evergreen effect. The yellow, trumpet-like flowers are sweetly fragrant. Provide an open, sunny position in any well-drained soil. As climbers or wall shrubs they require careful tying in and training against firm supports.

J. nudiflorum. The winter-flowering jasmine from China has a sprawling, eventually mounded habit, and congested branches wreathed in flowers. Tie in wall plants closely and prune regularly after flowering, or the centre becomes woody and unsightly. H90-120cm/3-4ft, W2.1-3m/7-10ft. F11-3. Z6-9. Trained as a wall shrub, H2.1-3m/7-10ft, W2.1-3m/7-10ft.

J. officinale. The well-known and vigorous

true, or common white, jasmine is mostly trained as a wall climber, where it can reach 10m/33ft in mild areas. It can also be grown as a semi-evergreen shrub, trained over a support and kept bushy by annual spring pruning. Deliciously fragrant, white flowers. 'Aureum', with gold-splashed leaves, is much slower than 'Grandiflorum'. H60-90cm/2-3ft, W1.8-2.4m/6-8ft. Trained as a wall shrub it can reach H1.8-2.4m/6-8ft, W1.8-2.4m/6-8ft. F7-9. Z8-11.
'Grandiflorum', with larger flowers, pink in bud, is similar to the species. H90-120cm/3-4ft, W5-6m/16-20ft. Trained as a wall shrub it can reach H5-6m/16-20ft, W5-6m/16-20ft. F7-9. Z8-11.

KALMIA
There are eight or so species of this North American, mainly evergreen, acid-loving genus with saucer-shaped flowers. One, *K. latifolia*, the mountain laurel or 'calico bush', provides a wonderful range of selections found in the wild or created by recent plant breeding. Acid, moist but well-drained soil and sun or light shade are best – conditions suited to rhododendrons. Prune only to tidy, if necessary.

K. angustifolia. The sheep laurel forms a thicket of small, bright green leaves, grey-green when mature, with dense clusters of deep rose-red flowers. The rare 'Candida' has white flowers. 'Rubra', more compact, with darker red flowers carried over a longer period, is most commonly offered. All H60-75cm/24-30in, W60-75cm/24-30in. F5-6. Z2-7.

K. latifolia. Richard Jaynes, a geneticist at the Connecticut Agricultural Experimental Station, did much experimental and breeding work in the 1960s and 1970s on this genus, forming the basis of the wide choice we have today. Formerly difficult to propagate, kalmias can now be multiplied by micro-propagation, so new selections are available more quickly.

The species grows wild in central and north-eastern USA, making a slow-growing shrub, eventually 1.8-3m/6-10ft high and as much or more across. Similar to rhododendrons, but less compact and tidy, they often take three to five years to flower. Flowers, usually pink, are often red or pink in bud, with prominent stamens once open. Pink and red selections have been made; other hybrids have purple, banded, striped or spotted blooms. H1-1.5m/39-60in, W1-1.5m/39-60in. F5-6. Z5-9.

Seedlings of various sizes and colours may be available, but all those below will be propagated by vegetative means. 'Alba', an old cultivar, has white flowers. 'Bullseye' has white, purple-banded flowers and reddish foliage. 'Candy' has white flowers, striped pink and red. 'Carousel', pink in bud, opens white with vivid purple-cinnamon banding. The dwarf **'Elf'** has pink buds opening to pale pink. **'Freckles'** has pink, burgundy-spotted flowers. **'Olympic Fire'** has deep crimson buds and light pink, white-centred flowers. **'Ostbo Red'** has red buds, opening pink. **'Richard Jaynes'** has red buds, deep pink blooms. The unusual **'Shooting Star'** has open, reflexed, white flowers. **'Silver Dollar'** has profuse, large, white flowers. Average H1.2-1.5m/4-5ft, W90-120cm/3-4ft. F5-6. Z5-9.

KERRIA

K. japonica. Sometimes easily grown and common shrubs are taken for granted or even despised. The deciduous Japanese kerria, popular during and since Victorian times, falls into that category. Though the only species in this genus, it has produced several forms, all extremely adaptable, growing on almost any soil, however poor, acid or alkaline, and happy in sun or part shade. They can be used free-standing, massed or against a wall, a favourite Victorian use. Growth is upright; the green-leaved forms are suckering, with graceful, arching branches, light green, serrated leaves and yellow, saucer-shaped flowers. All have distinctive green stems, attractive in winter, but in time these become congested; prune older branches from the base immediately after flowering. **'Golden Guinea'** is similar to the species but has larger, single, golden-yellow flowers. Both H1.5-1.8m/5-6ft, W1.5-1.8m/5-6ft. F3-5. Z5-9. The vigorous **'Pleniflora'**, a showy, taller form, has more upright stems and fully double, yellow flowers, and needs regular pruning. H1.8-2.4m/6-8ft, W1.8-2.4m/6-8ft. F3-5. Z5-9. **'Variegata'** (syn. 'Picta') is slower-growing and more spreading, with green leaves irregularly edged creamy white and single yellow flowers. H1.2-1.5m/4-5ft, W1.5-1.8m/5-6ft. F3-5. Z5-9.

KOLKWITZIA

K. amabilis. The deciduous beauty bush is a trouble-free, hardy, flowering shrub from China. It has densely erect, later arching, branches, light green leaves and freely borne clusters of trumpet-shaped, pale pink flowers with yellow throats. It makes a good specimen or background plant where space permits. Grows in almost any soil, acid or alkaline, sun or part shade. Very little pruning needed, but remove some older stems of specimen shrubs to the base, thinning out congested branches, immediately after flowering. **'Pink Cloud'** has deeper pink flowers. Both H1.8-2.4m/6-8ft, W1.8-2.4m/6-8ft. F5-6. Z5-8.

LAGERSTROEMIA

L. indica. The crape myrtle, from China and Korea, is a shrub or small tree for warm temperate zones, but even in Zone 7 or 8 the species and cultivars usually require long, hot summers to flower. Excellent breeding work was carried out by the late Don Egolf at the United States National Arboretum in Washington DC for colour, form, free-flowering, hardiness and ornamental bark, but the selections are unlikely to be as successful in cooler temperate regions of Europe as they are in the USA or southern Europe. The main stem has attractively mottled bark, and branches are usually arching, with shiny leaves and terminal racemes of white, pink, red or purple flowers, according to selection, on current season's growth. The species prior to breeding work was mostly pink to deep red. Pruning not necessary, but plants can be cut back nearly to the ground in spring, to induce flowering shoots. Good against south-facing walls. H1.8-3m/6-10ft, W1.8-3m/6-10ft. F7-9. Z7-9.

Kalmia latifolia 'Ostbo Red'

Kerria japonica 'Golden Guinea'

Kolkwitzia amabilis

Lagerstroemia indica

Lavandula stoechas pedunculata

Lavatera thuringiaca 'Barnsley'

Lavandula angustifolia 'Munstead'

Lavatera thuringiaca 'Rosea'

LAURUS Laurel

L. nobilis. The bay laurel or sweet bay is Mediterranean in origin and half hardy in cooler temperate climates, but thrives in milder ones. It makes a dense, pyramidal shrub or small tree with dark, glossy, evergreen, wavy-edged leaves, aromatic when crushed and much used in cooking. It can be grown as a wall or conservatory plant, and is often container grown, clipped into standards or formal pyramids. Small, yellow flowers, but black fruits appear only on females, if pollinated by a male. Provide sun or part shade, shelter and well-drained soil. The golden-leaved **'Aurea'** is

attractive in winter and early spring, best colour in sun, but the colour deteriorates in late spring and summer to look rather dirty. Prune from late spring on as required, established shrubs breaking well from old wood. Good for coastal planting. Both H1.8-2.4m/6-8ft, W1.2-1.5m/4-5ft. F4-5. Z8-11.

LAVANDULA Lavender

Everyone knows lavender, grown as specimens, low hedges or for edging, for its foliage, flowers and fragrance. The selections have silver-grey foliage and a lengthy display of mostly blue or violet flowers. Grow in any well-drained soil, acid or alkaline, and full sun or light shade. Though generally long-lived, longevity and flowering are improved by regular pruning every year or every two or three years. Remove faded flowers in autumn; prune old stems by at least half to just above the new shoots which appear inside the plant in mid-spring. Most of the following species and cultivars are long-lived, but some other species are less hardy.

L. angustifolia (syn. *L. spica*). The old English or common lavender, from which most garden lavenders derive. Excellent for seaside, herb, silver and grey gardens and mixed planting. H60-75cm/24-30in, W60-75cm/24-30in. F6-8. Z6-9.

The following, all F6-8, Z6-9. **'Alba'** is a robust, white-flowered form. **'Grappenhall'**, equally robust, is lavender-blue. Both H90-120cm/3-4ft, W90-120cm/3-4ft. The best and most popular, **'Hidcote'**, is compact, with violet-blue spikes. H60-75cm/24-30in, W60-75cm/24-30in. **'Hidcote Pink'**, **'Loddon Pink'** and **'Rosea'** are tinged pink, quickly fading. All H60-75cm/24-30in, W60-75cm/24-30in. The compact **'Munstead'** has grey-green foliage and blue flowers. H60-75cm/24-30in, W60-75cm/24-30in. **'Nana Alba'** makes a compact bush of grey leaves and white flowers. H30cm/1ft, W30-45cm/12-18in. **'Vera'**, the Dutch lavender, has large grey leaves and long spikes of lavender-blue flowers. H90-120cm/3-4ft, W90-120cm/3-4ft.

L. spica. See *L. angustifolia*.

L. stoechas pedunculata. This form of the French lavender seems hardier than the species and has deservedly become a very popular flowering shrub. Requiring similar conditions to the other lavenders, it has grey-green leaves and aromatic foliage with, usually, a spectacular show of flowers. Dense ovoid heads of purple are topped by wispy, lilac-blue bracts. H45-60cm/18-24in, W45-60cm/18-24in. F6-7. Z7-9.

LAVATERA

L. thuringiaca (syn. *L. olbia*). The tree mallow is a fast-growing, deciduous shrub for a warm, sunny climate. In colder regions, where not completely hardy, it could be grown almost as an annual. In spring it produces erect, pithy, semi-woody stems and grey, downy leaves; the large, cup-shaped, bright pink mallow flowers last until the first frost. Plants cut to the ground in winter generally shoot, as late as early summer, from the base. For those killed by frost, replacements soon make a good show; plant in spring or early summer. Prune dead or untidy stems in spring, if necessary almost to the ground. Good near the sea. H2.4-3m/8-10ft, W1.8-2.4m/6-8ft. F7-10. Z8-11.

Cultivars include the following. All F6-10, Z8-10. **'Barnsley'**, a sport of 'Rosea', makes a vigorous bush with white, red-centred flowers fading to a delicate pink. Flowers occasionally revert to pink, and these should be cut out. H2.4-3m/8-10ft, W1.8-2.4m/6-8ft. **'Burgundy Wine'** has wine-red flowers, a compact habit, and is free-flowering. H1.8m/6ft, W1.5-1.8m/5-6ft. **'Candy Floss'**, with its large pale pink flowers, has a fairly open habit. H1.8-2.1m/6-7ft, W1.5-1.8m/5-6ft. **'Ice Cool'**. An apt name for this pure white form with a green eye. H1.8-2.1m/6-7ft, W1.5-1.8m/5-6ft. **'Rosea'** is the most common form, with large pale pink flowers very freely borne. H2.1-2.4m/7-8ft, W1.8m/6ft.

LEDUM
L. groenlandicum. The Labrador tea is a rare, dwarf, evergreen shrub from swampy, northerly regions in North America, including Greenland. It needs moist, acid soil and sun or part shade, forming a low-spreading bush with dark green leaves, reddish brown beneath. Round clusters of white flowers are carried for weeks. **'Compactum'** is lower and denser, growing to about half the size of the species. Both deserve wider use as first-class ericaceous plants. H60-90cm/2-3ft, W60-90cm/2-3ft. Both F5-6, Z2-6.

LEPTOSPERMUM
Though tender in cool temperate climates, many of these Australasian evergreen shrubs can be grown in mild, coastal and sheltered locales or in cold areas against sunny, south- or west-facing walls, in acid or neutral, well-drained, but not really dry, soil. Some are upright, others spreading, with narrow stems, small leaves and profuse, small flowers. They can be pot-grown in a greenhouse or conservatory. Prune only on younger wood in early spring to encourage bushiness. Though a few species are in cultivation, the majority of cultivars are forms of **L. scoparium**, the manuka or tea tree of New Zealand. **'Kiwi'** is a bushy form with single, deep pink flowers. H90-120cm/3-4ft, W90-120cm/3-4ft. Others come in both single and double

Ledum groenlandicum 'Compactum'

flowers from white, pink, red and purple-red, the darker colours often matched by purple or bronze foliage. Expect growth rates in ten years to vary, depending on variety, between H1-3m/39-120in, W1-3m/39-120in. Mostly F5-6, Z9-11.

LESPEDEZA Bush clover
Closely related to *Indigofera*, this genus is both leguminous and needs sun, tolerating any well-drained soil. The species have profuse racemes of pea-like, pink to purple flowers along the stems in late summer and autumn on new growth. In cold climates, plants are herbaceous, dying to the ground with new shoots growing from the base in late spring, when old and dead stems should be pruned. Even in warmer climates untidy bushes can be cut to the ground in spring, flowering on new season's growth. In cool climates and summers, flowers can appear very late, but at their best they are extremely showy.
L. bicolor. Long, arching branches carry rosy purple flowers lasting for several weeks. In colder areas annual growth from the base can be 1.5-1.8m/5-6ft. H2.1-3m/7-10ft, W1.8-2.4m/6-8ft. F8-10. Z5-8.
'Yakushima' (syn. *L. kiusiana*), a dwarf Japanese form, makes a compact clump of short, erect stems, with clover-like leaves

Leptospermum scoparium 'Kiwi'

Lespedeza thunbergii

and a long show of small, purple flowers. H30-45cm/12-18in, W45-60cm/18-24in. F8-10. Z5-8.
L. kiusiana. See *L. bicolor* 'Yakushima'.
L. thunbergii (syn. *Desmodium penduliflorum*). Semi-herbaceous, with spring growth breaking late and quickly forming arching branches of 1.2-1.8m/4-6ft in one season, depending on climate; gradually make spreading clumps. Showy reddish purple flowers on stem tips often weigh down branches. Rarer, with white flowers, is **'Albiflora'** (syn. *L. japonica* 'Albiflora'). Both H1.2-1.8m/4-6ft, W1.5-1.8m/5-6ft. F8-10. Z5-8.

Leucothoe fontanesiana 'Scarletta'

LEUCOTHOE

These mostly evergreen, acid-loving shrubs originate from North and South America and Japan, and vary in hardiness. Most hardier types have leathery leaves and racemes of tubular or bell-shaped, often fragrant, flowers. Moist, peaty soil and light shade are best.

L. catesbaei. See *L. fontanesiana*.

L. davisiae. Attractive but rare, this forms a compact bush of glossy, evergreen leaves. Red spring shoots, followed by erect clusters of white, pitcher-shaped flowers. H30-60cm/1-2ft, W60-90cm/2-3ft. F6. Z8-9.

L. fontanesiana (syn. *L. catesbaei*). This suckering, North American species is the most commonly grown, with long, arching stems, glossy leaves and dangling, pitcher-shaped, fragrant, white flowers. The foliage, bright green or red in spring, turns glossy green in summer and purple-brown in winter. Ideal ground cover on acid soil. **'Rainbow'** has creamy yellow and pink new leaves, especially on young plants. Occasionally prune old stems to the base in early spring to promote new shoots; reduce stem length to improve density. Both H1.2-1.5m/4-5ft, W1.5-1.8m/5-6ft. F4-5. Z5-8. The American introduction **'Scarletta'**, considered a hybrid between *L. fontanesiana* and *L. axillaris*, is compact, with bright, glossy, small red leaves from early summer, turning bronze-red in autumn and winter. H30-60cm/1-2ft, W60-75cm/24-30in. Z5-8.

LEYCESTERIA

L. formosa. The Himalayan honeysuckle is an easily grown, vigorous, deciduous shrub, with unusual flowers. It quickly forms a mass of upright, hollow, green stems, large, lush leaves and white, funnel-shaped, terminal flowers with claret-red bracts, forming hanging panicles. Purple fruits follow and can freely seed in warm climates. Sun or part shade where not too dry. Prune away older stems to base in late spring or if the bush is untidy and needs rejuvenation

Leycesteria formosa

every few years all to the ground as new growth begins. H1.8-2.4m/6-8ft, W1.5-1.8m/5-6ft. F8. Z7-9.

LIGUSTRUM Privet

Most gardeners reject these fast-growing, evergreen or semi-evergreen shrubs as too common! Highly adaptable, they have their uses, most growing in any soil, sun or dry shade. Some have colourful, variegated foliage and most, if unpruned, produce heads, sometimes large, of white, tubular flowers, then black fruits. Many people find the scent unpleasant.

They are hungry, thirsty plants, so site with care. Prune free-standing shrubs only to help establish newly planted, bare-rooted specimens; cut back to 10-15cm/4-6in from the ground after planting. For hedges, do the same, and then trim two or three times in the growing season. Most privets break freely from the base, so rejuvenate older plants or hedges by pruning hard in spring.

L. japonicum. The Japanese privet, upright and evergreen, has large, glossy, olive-green leaves and terminal flower panicles which last for many weeks. **'Macrophyllum'** is similar, but has dark green leaves. H1.5-1.8m/5-6ft, W90-120cm/3-4ft. F7-8. Z7-11.

L. lucidum. The Chinese, or waxleaf, privet is more vigorous and open than *L. japonicum*, but less hardy, in mild regions making a small tree, with glossy leaves and large, erect, scented flower panicles. Provide shelter from frost and cold winds. **'Excelsum Superbum'**, free-flowering, has variegated white and yellow leaves. **'Tricolor'** has leaves margined white, flushed pink when young. All H3m/10ft, W3m/10ft. F8. Z8-11.

L. ovalifolium. The oval-leaved privet is the most common for hedging, though the glossy dark green leaves are not evergreen in cold areas. Panicles of dullish white flowers, rather pungent, will only appear on unpruned plants. Plant hedging 45-60cm/18-24in apart; prune hard the first year and trim regularly thereafter. H4m/13ft, W4m/13ft. F6-7. Z6-11. **'Argenteum'** has grey-green leaves, variegated creamy white. **'Aureum'**, the golden privet, is yellow with a green splash, but reverts to green or goes completely yellow. Both H2.1-3m/7-10ft, W2.1-3m/7-10ft. F6-7. Z6-11.

L. sinense. The Chinese privet is deciduous

or semi-evergreen, with showy, drooping flower panicles and later a good show of black-purple fruits. In hot climates, it fruits and scatters seeds freely, often becoming a weed. H4m/13ft, W4-5m/13-16ft. F7-8. Z7-11. **'Variegatum'** is less vigorous, with leaves margined creamy white. Both H3m/10ft, W3-4.5m/10-15ft. F7. Z7-11.

L. **'Vicaryi'**. A semi-evergreen golden privet of some attraction, considered a cross between *L. ovalifolium* 'Aureum' and *L. vulgare*. The leaves are yellow-green in early summer, becoming brighter gold, with panicles of creamy white flowers in late midsummer on mature plants, followed by black fruits. Deciduous in cold areas but otherwise leaves are purplish in winter. Needs sun for brightest colour. Prune in early spring to maintain bushiness; new young growth has the best colour. H3-4m/10-13ft, W3-5m/10-16ft. F7-8. Z6-8.

L. vulgare. The hardy common privet is undeniably adaptable, growing in the poorest, driest soil, even under dripping trees. A deciduous, broad, loose shrub with dullish white flower plumes, followed by black fruits, often persisting long after leaf drop. **'Aureum'** has dull yellow leaves, brighter in early summer. Both H3m/10ft, W3m/10ft. F7-8. Z5-7.

LITHODORA See under Alpines.

LONICERA Honeysuckle
Honeysuckles are best known as fragrant climbers and ramblers, but the genus includes worthwhile shrubs – the best of which are included below. Among these are unusual, hardy foliage and winter-flowering shrubs. Many also have attractive foliage, and the evergreen *L. pileata* is ideal for a compact hedge. The climbers are really scramblers, mostly trained against or over walls, up fences, pergolas, trees or large shrubs, but be aware that mature stems can eventually strangle weak plants. Most honeysuckles adapt to a wide range of soils and conditions, but the climbers generally prefer their roots in shade. Pruning of shrubby types generally only required to keep in shape or to restrict size. Prune after flowering. Climbers can have old stems thinned out and any general pruning to restrict size after flowering has finished. The fragrance is most noticeable at night and in the early morning.

L. × *americana*. One of the finest climbing honeysuckles, this has glossy green leaves and showy clusters of erect flowers, purple in bud, opening to yellow then fading to cream. Small, red fruits in autumn in warm climates. Grows well in sun or shade, where not too dry. Train and prune in early spring. H5m/16ft, W5m/16ft. F7-9. Z5-9.

L. × *amoena*. A robust shrub with arching branches and profuse, small, very fragrant,

Ligustrum sinense 'Variegatum'

Ligustrum 'Vicaryi'

Lonicera × *americana*

tubular, pink flowers. **'Rosea'** has deep pink flowers, fading to yellow. Prune flowering stems by a third after flowering, if necessary; occasionally remove old stems from the base of old shrubs. Both H2.4-3m/8-10ft, W2.4-3m/8-10ft. F6. Z5-9.

L. × *brownii*. The scarlet trumpet climbing honeysuckle, a North American native, has bluish green leaves and a succession of scarlet, orange-throated, scentless flowers. **'Dropmore Scarlet'** is the best form, with scarlet-red flowers. Sun or light shade where not too dry. Both H4m/13ft, W4m/13ft. F6-9. Z3-9.

L. chaetocarpa. An unusual shrubby honeysuckle, upright, with large, oval, hairy leaves and stems, and fragrant, yellow flowers, emerging from showy bracts. Orange-red fruits follow. H1.5-1.8m/5-6ft, W1.2-1.5m/4-5ft. F5-6. Z6-9.

L. fragrantissima. Scarcely attractive in summer when in leaf, this and similar forms, including *L.* × *purpusii*, provide winter interest. Depending on climate, its lemon-scented, creamy white flowers can last for many months. It is usually deciduous, semi-evergreen in mild areas. Prune as for *L.* × *amoena*, if necessary. H1.8-2.4m/6-8ft, W2.4-3m/8-10ft. F12-4. Z5-9.

L. × *heckrottii* (syn. 'Goldflame'). A handsome but rather untidy scrambling climber, this needs ongoing training. It has bluish green leaves, many encircling the stem, and clusters of fragrant flowers, purple in bud, opening pink, yellow inside. Sun or shade where not too dry. H2.4m/8ft, W1.8m/6ft. F6-7. Z5-9.

Lonicera chaetocarpa

Lonicera periclymenum 'Serotina'

L. involucrata. A little-known but worthwhile deciduous shrub of easy disposition from western North America. it has an upright habit, with leaves similar in appearance to the related genus *Weigela*. Bronze-green foliage provides a good contrast to the red bracts and small yellow flowers which are produced in succession from early to late summer and which later mature to black fruits. Sun or part shade in almost any soil. Prune in early spring if it is necessary to restrict size; this will not limit flowering as this occurs on new growth. The form *ledebourii* is almost identical. H2.1-3m/7-10ft, W2.1-3m/8-10ft. F6-8. Z5-9.

L. japonica 'Halliana'. The best and most common form of this vigorous, twining, evergreen, Asian climber, it is now a

Lonicera × tellmanniana

nuisance in parts of the USA. It has fast-growing, light green, semi-evergreen leaves and clusters of fragrant, white flowers, fading to yellow. Sun or shade; best where not too dry. Train and tie in as a wall climber, or allow to scramble. H5m/16ft, W5m/16ft. F6-9. Z5-9. **'Aureoreticulata'** has pleasing, light green, yellow-veined, oval leaves, its fragrant yellow flowers hidden among the foliage. H3m/10ft, W3m/10ft. F6-9. Z7-8.

L. korolkowii. The blue-leaf honeysuckle is a good foliage shrub with intensely blue leaves in early summer, and small, pink flowers on the shoot tips, followed by red fruits. Flowers and fruits best in hot climates. Trim after flowering to keep compact. H3m/10ft, W2.4-3m/8-10ft. F6-7. Z5-7.

L. microphylla 'Blue Haze'. A Dutch form, with slender, arching stems, small, blue-green leaves and tiny, creamy white flowers, then orange-red fruit. H90-120cm/3-4ft, W90-120cm/3-4ft. F6-7. Z5-8.

L. nitida. The evergreen box-leaf honeysuckle is compact, with arching branches, small, dark green leaves, modest, fragrant, yellow flowers and blue-purple fruit. It and most of its cultivars are used as foliage plants and for hedging. The species is variable and seldom sold; selected forms are, rooted easily from cuttings. All tolerate acid and alkaline soil, sun, shade and salt spray, but not very dry or wet soil. Plant hedging 30-45cm/12-18in apart, trim regularly through early summer. Unless supported, keep at 90cm/3ft or less, or it may flop. **'Baggesen's Gold'**, bright yellow

Lonicera involucrata

in full sun, especially in early summer, but colours less well in shade. **'Elegant'**, with dull green leaves, and **'Ernest Wilson'**, with glossy leaves (and often offered for *L. nitida*), are graceful if allowed to grow naturally. **'Fertilis'** and **'Yunnan'** have large, glossy leaves and erect habits, ideal for a taller hedge. All H1.5-1.8m/5-6ft, W2.4-3m/8-10ft. F5-6. Z7-9.

L. periclymenum. Common honeysuckle, or woodbine, from Europe, North Africa and western Asia, grows wild in British hedgerows, whence excellent selections have been made. A deciduous, scrambling, twining climber, it grows in most soils where not too dry. It has very fragrant, mostly white-centred flowers, yellow or purplish outside in early summer, followed by red fruits. **'Belgica'**, the early Dutch honeysuckle, has purple-red buds opening yellow in late spring for several weeks. **'Graham Thomas'**, found in a Warwickshire hedgerow and named after the distinguished English plantsman, has large, yellow flowers. There may be several forms of **'Serotina'**, the late Dutch honeysuckle, but the best has purple-tinged leaves, deep purple-red, budded, fragrant flowers, opening creamy white. All H3-4m/10-13ft, W3-4m/10-13ft. F5-9. Z5-9.

L. pileata. A Chinese evergreen or semi-evergreen, this excellent ground cover forms a low, spreading bush, with leaves like *L. nitida*, but larger, and needing similar conditions. Creamy yellow flowers, violet fruits, not freely produced in cooler climates. H45-60cm/18-24in, W1.5-1.8m/5-6ft. F5-6. Z7-8.

L. × purpusii. This little-known but easy, hardy deciduous shrub has considerable merit for winter interest. It is a hybrid between *L. fragrantissima* and *L. standishii*, and both it and the cultivar **'Winter Beauty'** are free-flowering plants with upright, spreading habits and fragrant, creamy white flowers. Both H1.8-2.4m/6-8ft, W2.4-3m/8-10ft. F12-4. Z5-9.

L. tatarica. Upright, dense and vigorous, hardy and drought-resistant, prolific in flower and fruit, the Tatarican honeysuckle and its forms are widely used for mass planting. The species carries small, pink, unscented flowers, then red berries. Prune stems back by as much as a third immediately after flowering, to control growth and improve flowering. Inclined to suffer from mildew and aphid attacks, **'Alba'** has white flowers. **'Arnold Red'**, purple-red flowers. **'Hack's Red'**, rose-pink flowers and bright red fruits. **'Lutea'**, pink flowers and yellow fruits. **'Morden Orange'**, pink flowers and orange fruits. All H3m/10ft, W3m/10ft. F5-6. Z4-8.

L. × tellmanniana. A deciduous hybrid climber with large, bright green leaves and spectacular, but unscented, orange-red

tipped yellow flowers. Blooms equally well in sun or shade. Best in cool, moist, fertile soil. H3m/10ft, W3m/10ft. F7-8. Z6-8.
L. tragophylla. Chinese woodbine is a beautiful deciduous climber with large, grey-green leaves and clusters of up to twenty large, bright yellow, unscented flowers. Roots are best in shade and moist soil. H6m/20ft, W6m/20ft. F7-8. Z6-9.

MAGNOLIA

These aristocratic trees and shrubs are mostly native to south-east Asia, the rest from North America. Many are tropical and unsuited to cool climates, but the range of hardy magnolias is still very wide. Flowers, some fragrant, vary from the small, star-shaped *M. stellata*, to the goblet-like *M. × soulangeana* or the open saucers of *M. sinensis*. Magnolias are relatively trouble-free, if chosen to match the site and soil. They like any good, moist but well-drained loam, but not thin, dry or chalky soils. Adding masses of enriched humus may help; mulch annually with composted bark, acid leaf mould or well-rotted compost. Some species are susceptible to frost damage on buds and new shoots; early-

Magnolia × kewensis 'Wada's Memory'

flowering types may be hit by spring frosts, especially in northern Europe. Site near a tree or wall, to protect plants from early-morning sun. Prune only to shape young plants or thin, congested branches. Light pruning is best after flowering; leave severe pruning until July or August, painting large cuts with a suitable dressing.
M. conspicua. See *M. denudata*.
M. cylindrica. Likely to become more popular when more available, this broad, spreading bush flowers when young, producing candle-like blooms on bare branches, then cylindrical fruits. H2.4-3m/8-10ft, W2.4-3m/8-10ft. F4-5. Z6-9.
M. denudata (syn. *M. conspicua*). The Chinese yulan or lily tree was the first species to be cultivated and is still among the finest flowering shrubs or small trees. Its early, free-flowering display of erect, cup-shaped, creamy white, fragrant flowers on naked branches appears even on young plants. Hardy, but protect from cold spring winds and frost, which damage the flowers. H3m/10ft, W3m/10ft. F3-5. Z6-8.
M. discolor. See *M. liliiflora*.
M. grandiflora. This magnificent evergreen eventually makes a large tree in warm climates, but can be grown as a wall shrub in cool ones. From south-eastern USA, it likes full sun and good, moist soil. Protect from cold, drying winds. Dark green, leathery leaves have cinnamon-brown felt beneath; the large, cup-shaped, creamy white flowers are deliciously fragrant. Plants from seed take years to flower, but many forms, such as **'Exmouth'** and **'Goliath'**, flower when young. All H2.4-3m/8-10ft, W1.5-1.8m/5-6ft. F7-9. Z7-9.
M. × kewensis **'Wada's Memory'**. Named after a famous Japanese plantsman, this erect bush has fragrant, white flowers before the leaves. Good for a small garden. H3m/10ft, W1.2-1.5m/4-5ft. F4-5. Z4-8.
M. liliiflora (syn. *M. discolor*). The lily magnolia is ideal, if untidy, for a small garden, its tulip-like flowers appearing with

Magnolia denudata

Magnolia grandiflora

Magnolia liliiflora × stellata 'Jane'

Magnolia stellata

Magnolia × soulangeana 'Rustica Rubra'

the leaves, thus avoiding frost damage, and continuing for several months. Flower petals are wine-purple outside, white inside. **'Nigra'** has larger, darker, scented flowers, flushed rose-purple inside. H1.5-1.8m/5-6ft, W1.5-1.8m/5-6ft. F5-7. Z6-8.

M. liliiflora × stellata. Several good selections were made from various crosses between *M. liliiflora* and *M. stellata* at the United States Arboretum in Washington DC in the late 1950s, all with girls' names. Most resemble *M. liliiflora* in flower, some fragrant, but generally bushier and freer-flowering. These include **'Ann'**, **'Betty'**, **'Jane'**, **'Judy'**, **'Pinkie'**, **'Randy'**, **'Ricki'** and **'Susan'**. All

H1.5-1.8m/5-6ft, W90-120cm/3-4ft. F5-6. Z5-8.
M. × loebneri. These hybrids between *M. kobus* and *M. stellata* include beautiful, free-flowering garden forms for all soils, including chalk. They flower young, each year becoming more floriferous, the multi-petalled, star-like, fragrant flowers appearing before the leaves. All eventually make large, broad shrubs or small trees. **'Leonard Messel'**, a chance seedling, has magnificent purple-pink flowers. **'Merrill'** and **'Snowdrift'** are white. All H2.4-3m/8-10ft, W2.4-3m/8-10ft. F3-4. Z5-8.
M. salicifolia. An upright, slender shrub or small tree, with fragrant, white flowers

before the willow-like leaves appear. **'Jermyns'**, from the Hillier Nursery, Hampshire, is slower and more compact with larger flowers, which appear later, less harmed by spring frosts. Both H3-4.5m/10-15ft, W1.8-2.4m/6-8ft. F4-5. Z5-8.
M. sinensis. Given space and shelter, this broad, leafy bush or small tree has large, nodding, creamy white, fragrant, saucer-like blooms, with central cones of crimson stamens, when in leaf, and crimson fruits in late summer. New shoots are vulnerable to late frosts. Two other worthwhile species, *M. sieboldii* and *M. wilsonii*, are somewhat similar. All H2.4-3m/8-10ft, W2.4-3m/8-10ft. F6. Z7-8.
M. × soulangeana. Among the most popular magnolias, most of these cultivars make tall, eventually wide-spreading shrubs or small trees, their goblet-shaped flowers appearing on bare branches. They prefer heavy, moist, lime-free soil but are otherwise easy. The species has profuse, large, creamy white, globe-shaped flowers stained rose-purple outside, flowering sometimes interrupted by spring frost. **'Alba Superba'**, fragrant, white flowers. **'Alexandrina'**, narrow, upright form, flowers rose-purple outside, white inside. **'Brozzonii'**, latest to flower, large, white, pink-flushed 'candles'. **'Lennei'**, vigorous, large leaves, broad, goblet-shaped flowers, wine-purple outside, white inside. **'Lennei Alba'**, white flowers. **'Rustica Rubra'**, rose-red flowers similar to 'Lennei'. All between H3-4m/10-13ft, W2.4-4m/8-13ft. F3-5. Z5-9.
M. stellata. The automatic choice for a small garden, the star magnolia is free-flowering, rarely over 4.5m/15ft high even after many years, but eventually wide-spreading; pruning can control size. A broad, round bush, it carries a cloud of starry, white, multi-petalled, fragrant blooms, unfortunately, like many magnolias, vulnerable to spring frost. Several clones may exist of the pink-flowered **'Rosea'**. Other selections include **'Royal Star'**, hardy, floriferous, late-flowering, with large, white flowers, and the fragrant **'Water Lily'**, larger flowers, pink in bud, opening pinkish white. All H1.5-1.8m/5-6ft, W1.5-1.8m/5-6ft. F3-4. Z5-9.

MAHONIA
The hardier forms provide shape and substance in a winter garden, and flower and fragrance from autumn until spring. All have erect clusters or graceful racemes of yellow flowers, and glossy, generally prickly, evergreen leaves. They vary from low-growing, dwarf shrubs to large shrubs or small trees, all preferring shelter from strong, cold, desiccating winds. Most grow in sun or shade in any reasonable garden soil, where not too dry. Prune only to tidy, but straggly old plants, especially

M. aquifolium and *M. pinnata*, can be cut to within 10cm/4in of the ground in spring to rejuvenate. Leaf drop may occur after severe frost, though new growth will follow, but if leaves drop as a result of poor drainage, move plants.

M. aquifolium. The Oregon grape, from western North America, so named for its clusters of blue-black fruits in summer and autumn. Its glossy, green leaves are tinged purple in winter and tight clusters of barely scented flowers appear on terminal shoots. It can be used as a specimen or ground-cover plant, good in shade. **'Apollo'**, a Dutch, free-flowering form, has large, rich yellow flowers. The old **'Atropurpurea'** has yet to be bettered, for its red-purple winter foliage and deep yellow flowers. Both H90-120cm/3-4ft, W1.2-1.5m/4-5ft. F3-5. Z5-8. **'Moseri'**, striking but rare, has copper-red young leaves, turning orange, then yellow, and later green as summer progresses. H1.2-1.5m/4-5ft, W90-120cm/3-4ft. F3-5. Z5-8. The tall, Danish **'Smaragd'** is hardy and reliable, with bright yellow flowers and deep green leaves, tinged purple in winter. H1.2-1.5m/4-5ft, W1.2-1.5m/4-5ft. F3-5. Z5-8.

M. japonica. Few plants emit such fragrance as this eventually large, erect shrub. Its long leaves are divided into glossy, spiny leaflets. Terminal racemes of soft yellow, scented flowers continue for many weeks. Purple fruits in summer. This and the similar **'Bealii'**, with shorter, more erect racemes, need shelter from cold winds. Both H1.8-2.4m/6-8ft, W1.8-2.4m/6-8ft. F11-4. Z7-9.

M. × media. A collective name for hybrids between *M. japonica* and *M. lomariifolia*, all with deeply divided leaves and erect, later pendulous, racemes of dark yellow, lightly fragrant flowers. Less hardy than some, the flowers can be damaged by early frost but a canopy of light shade or the shelter of a wall helps. **'Charity'**, **'Winter Sun'** and the rarer **'Buckland'**, **'Lionel Fortescue'** and **'Underway'** are all good. All H2.4-3m/8-10ft, W1.5-1.8m/5-6ft. F10-2. Z8-9.

M. nervosa. Slow to establish, this low-growing, suckering species has glossy green leaves, reddish in winter in good light, and erect racemes of flowers. H30cm/1ft, W90-120cm/3-4ft. F5. Z6-8.

M. pinnata. Similar to *M. aquifolium*, but taller with more plentiful clusters of light yellow flowers borne up the stems. Can become scrawny, in which case, prune back stems severely after flowering. Often used for mass planting. H1.5-1.8m/5-6ft, W1.2-1.5m/4-5ft. F2-4. Z5-8.

M. pumila. Even slower and more compact than *M. nervosa*, with small, bluish green leaves and clusters of yellow flowers. H20-30cm/8-12in, W30-45cm/12-18in. F3-4. Z6-8.

M. × wagneri **'Undulata'**. A garden-

Mahonia × media 'Winter Sun'

Mahonia aquifolium 'Smaragd'

Menziesia ciliicalyx purpurea

worthy form with bronze-red young growth, later glossy green, and large, deep yellow flower clusters. H1.5-1.8m/5-6ft, W1.5-1.8m/5-6ft. F3-5. Z6-8.

MENZIESIA

M. ciliicalyx. Though hardy, these slow-growing, deciduous shrubs are vulnerable to spring frost. They require moist, well-drained, acid soil in sun or part shade. The twiggy, upright bushes have clusters of dangling, pink and purple bells. The form *purpurea* is bluish in bud, opening to large, purple-pink flowers. Both H60-75cm/24-30in, W60-75cm/24-30in. F5-6. Z6-9.

MYRICA

A group of acid-loving, deciduous shrubs with aromatic foliage, some growing in extremes of dry and wet which few other plants would tolerate.

M. gale. The bog myrtle, or sweetgale, is a native of North America, Europe and north-east Asia. Could be more widely grown as an ornamental. All parts of the plant are aromatic, the erect stems clothed in small blue-grey leaves in summer and golden-brown catkins in spring appearing on naked branches. Tolerant of very boggy conditions but succeeds in drier, acid soils too. H90-120cm/3-4ft, W90-120cm/3-4ft. F4-5. Z1-8.

Nandina domestica 'Firepower'

Of the dwarf forms, **'Firepower'** is particularly colourful. **'Nana'** makes low, green, leafy, non-flowering hummocks, pink, red, orange and purple through autumn and winter. The shorter **'Nana Purpurea'** has purple-tinged foliage in summer. These colour better in sun. All H30-45cm/12-18in, W30-45cm/12-18in. Z7-9.

NEILLIA
Trouble-free and easy, if not spectacular, these are related to *Spiraea* and form dense, erect bushes, with toothed leaves and racemes of delicate, rose-pink flowers. Any soil but very dry, in sun or light shade. Thin congested branches by pruning old stems to the ground, in winter or immediately after flowering, when stems can be shortened by a third if necessary.
N. affinis and *N. thibetica* (syn. *N. longiracemosa*). Almost identical, matching the description for the genus. Both H1.8m/6ft, W1.5-1.8m/5-6ft. F6. Z6-9.
N. thyrsiflora. Rare and distinct, of lower and more spreading habit, the small, white flowers cluster along arching branches. H90-120cm/3-4ft, W1.2-1.5m/4-5ft. F6. Z6-9.

OLEARIA Daisy bush
A large family of Australasian evergreen shrubs and small trees, also called tree asters or tree daisies, these seldom make trees in cool temperate climates. Their panicles or clusters of daisy-like flowers are mostly white or cream. Most are tender but some thrive in mild coastal districts, withstanding gales and salt spray. In cold, inland regions, grow against a sunny, south-facing wall or near larger plants, to protect from frost, in any well-drained soil, especially chalk. Cut back hard old, untidy or frost-damaged bushes in spring as new growth begins, since they break freely from old wood.
O. × haastii. One of the hardiest species, this round bush has sage-green, leathery leaves, silver-grey beneath, and clusters of fragrant, white flowers. H1.2-1.5m/4-5ft, W1.2-1.5m/4-5ft. F7-9. Z8-10.

OSMANTHUS
More like holly than the olive, to which they are related, these evergreen trees and shrubs of varying hardiness usually have small, white, fragrant flowers, though some are grown for their foliage. Any well-drained soil is fine. To shape or control large plants, prune just after flowering or as new growth begins, according to species.
O. × burkwoodii (syn. *Osmarea burkwoodii*). This chance evergreen hybrid between *Phillyrea decora* and *Osmanthus delavayi* is often confused with the latter, but has stiffer, stronger branches, larger, smoother-edged leaves and clusters of small, white, fragrant, trumpet-shaped flowers on

NANDINA
N. domestica. Heavenly, or sacred, bamboo is not, as its common name suggests, a member of the bamboo family, but related to *Berberis*. The species, from India, China and Japan, is tall, multi-stemmed but unbranched, with divided, compound leaves, red or purple in autumn and winter. It needs hot summers to produce large, erect, white flower plumes, followed by red fruit, again if climate allows. Tall and dwarf forms prefer moist soil and need warmth and shelter in cool climates. May be cut to the ground in severe winters but usually recover, if late. **'Moyers Red'** and **'Richmond'** have crimson autumn and winter foliage and bright red fruit. H1.5-2.4m/5-8ft, W90-120cm/3-4ft. F6-8. Z7-9.

Neillia affinis

Olearia × haastii

SHRUBS

terminal shoots. A robust evergreen shrub, more tolerant of cold than *O. delavayi*. H1.8-2.4m/6-8ft, W1.8-2.4m/6-8ft. F3-4. Z7-9.

O. decorus. See *Phillyrea decora*.

O. delavayi. This dense, twiggy bush, eventually large in mild climates, has small, oval, glossy, toothed leaves and profuse, small, creamy white, scented, tubular flowers. Needs shelter. H2.4-3m/8-10ft, W2.4-3m/8-10ft. F3-4. Z8-10.

O. × fortunei. This little-known hybrid is relatively hardy, vigorous and handsome, with broad, leathery, extremely glossy, evergreen leaves, heavily spined. Small, fragrant white flowers. **'Variegatus'** has leaves widely margined creamy white. Growth rate is two-thirds that of the species which, at ten years, may be H1.8-2.4m/6-8ft, W1.8-2.4m/6-8ft. F9-11. Z7-9.

O. heterophyllus (syn. *O. ilicifolius*). The false holly or holly osmanthus, from Japan, is a large, round, dense shrub or small tree in mild climates, with shining, holly-like leaves, some spined, but mature leaves smooth-edged and oval. Small clusters of fragrant, white flowers appear on mature plants in hot climates, followed by blue berries. All selections can be tender, especially when young or exposed to severe frost or cold, desiccating winds. H1.8-2.4m/6-8ft, W1.8-2.4m/6-8ft. F9-11. Z7-9. **'Aureomarginatus'** has leaves edged in yellow. The Japanese **'Aureus'** has bright gold leaves in summer, greeny yellow in winter. **'Gulftide'** is compact, with heavily spined leaves and fragrant autumn flowers. **'Latifolius Variegatus'** has wide leaves edged silvery white (considered by some as identical to *O. × fortunei* 'Variegatus'). **'Purpureus'** has striking, purple young shoots and leaves in spring. **'Tricolor'** (syn. 'Goshiki') has dark green, white and pink leaves. **'Variegatus'** has creamy white margins. Average H1.2-1.8m/4-6ft, W1.2-1.8m/4-6ft. F9-11. Z8-9.

O. ilicifolius. See *O. heterophyllus*.

OSMAREA

O. burkwoodii. See *Osmanthus × burkwoodii*.

OXYDENDRUM

O. arboreum. In its native eastern USA the sorrel tree may reach 15m/50ft but seldom is more than a large shrub in climates with cool summers. Open, erect branches carry long, narrow, graceful leaves, turning yellow or crimson in autumn, given an open situation. Seldom as vigorous or spectacular in northern Europe as in the USA, the long, pendulous racemes of white, fragrant flowers create at their best a cascading shower of white streamers. Grow in sun or light shade and lime-free soil. H1.5-2.4m/5-8ft, W1.2-1.5m/4-5ft. F7-8. Z5-9.

Osmanthus heterophyllus 'Tricolor'

Osmanthus delavayi

Oxydendrum arboreum

PACHYSANDRA

Often classed as perennials, these carpet-forming evergreens are technically shrubs. They are excellent in dense shade under trees (spread by underground running), preferring moist soil, but when established tolerating dry soil. White or cream flowers. Unsuitable for chalk.

P. terminalis. Japanese spurge, the most common, has broad leaf clusters on short, upright stems, gradually forming an undulating mat. Plant 15-20cm/6-8in apart. **'Green Carpet'** is neater and lower (10-20cm/4-8in high), once established. **'Variegata'** has light green and white leaves. All H15-30cm/6-12in, W30-60cm/1-2ft. F2-4. Z4-8.

Pachysandra terminalis

Paeonia suffruticosa 'Godaishu'

Paeonia suffruticosa 'Hanakisoi'

PAEONIA Tree peony

The woody plants of this genus seldom reach tree size, mostly forming irregular, gaunt, often untidy, deciduous shrubs but spectacular in leaf and flower. They include species, hybrids and numerous Japanese and Chinese 'Moutans', selected and highly bred *P. suffruticosa* cultivars. All are frost-hardy in winter, but some, the 'Moutans' especially, may have leaves and flowers damaged during spring frosts, so avoid planting in frost pockets, and protect from early-morning sun. All prefer full sun but tolerate some shade if grown in any rich, well-drained loam that stays moist in summer. Add well-rotted compost to the soil, and mulch in spring.

P. delavayi. This suckering Chinese species has red-tinged, deeply divided new leaves and deep crimson, cup-shaped flowers with golden anthers. H1.2-1.5m/4-5ft, W90-120cm/3-4ft. F6. Z5-8.

P. × lemoinei. A French hybrid between *P. lutea* and *P. suffruticosa*, with several selections from the early 1900s, most with large, yellow, often double flowers above the foliage. Intensive breeding in the USA

Paeonia suffruticosa 'Kinkaku'

by Professor A. P. Saunders, produced the spectacular Saunders Hybrids. Most are propagated by grafting, so are likely to remain in short supply and expensive. H90-120cm/3-4ft, W90-120cm/3-4ft. F5-6. Z5-8.

P. lutea. Variable from seed and similar in leaf to *P. delavayi*, this grows 90-180cm/3-6 ft high. The small, saucer-shaped, often semi-double, canary-yellow flowers are frequently hidden by foliage. Can be shy to flower but the luxuriant foliage is outstanding. The selection usually offered, reasonably true from seed, is *ludlowii*, a superior, more vigorous form with larger, slightly earlier flowers, but still shy to flower. Both H1.5-1.8m/5-6ft, W1.2-1.5m/4-5ft. F5-6. Z5-8.

P. suffruticosa. The mystique surrounding 'Moutans' goes back to sixth-century China. Since then, innumerable cultivars have been introduced in China and Japan, many

later discarded, but most garden forms today have Japanese names. Nearly all are grown in Japan, grafted onto the herbaceous *P. lactiflora*. Plant bare root or container plants deeply, with the grafting union, if visible, at least 10cm/4in below the soil surface. The cultivar eventually forms its own roots; an annual mulch of well-rotted compost helps. 'Moutans' can be slow to build their gaunt branch framework, but even young plants produce a few flowers. Thriving plants increase in size and number of blooms annually. Little or no pruning needed. Remove dead leaves, branches or foliage as soon as seen, to prevent botrytis.

Single and double flowers have attractive, golden stamens, though hidden in fully double forms, and are up to an ungainly 30cm/1ft across; 15cm/6in is more usual and even these can weigh branches down when wet. Colours range from white through pink, carmine-red, purple, orange and yellow. Buy named varieties from reliable sources, not plants sold by colour. Translation of the names is tricky, but the following were checked with five contacts in Japan! **'Godaishu'** ('The Five Continents'), large, double, frilly white. **'Hanadaijin'** ('Flowers of a Potentate'), semi-double, purple-red. **'Hanakisoi'** ('Floral Rivalry'), semi-double, shell-pink, rose centre. **'Kaoh'** ('King of Flowers'), double, rich carmine. **'Kinkaku'** ('Golden Temple'), fully double, deep orange, begonia-like flowers. **'Renkaku'** ('Flight of Cranes'), semi-double, fragrant, white. All H1.2-1.5m/4-5ft, W90-120cm/3-4ft. F6. Z5-8.

PARTHENOCISSUS
Ornamental vine

A useful group of ten or so deciduous species of Asian and North American climbers which attach themselves by tendrils. Their leaves often colour well in autumn, and their usually insignificant flowers may be followed by small, grape-like fruits, particularly in warm summers. All are easy to grow in sun or shade in most well-drained, preferably not acid soils; like *Vitis*, they may need controlling during the growing season as most are vigorous – and just as happy to cover windows as walls!

P. henryana. Named after Augustine Henry, who discovered it in China around 1855, this is perhaps the most beautiful species, its small, deep green leaves veined with silver, occasionally flushed with pink and turning bright red in autumn. Blue-black fruit in autumn after hot summers. Leaves show most variegation in shade. Tying in and training necessary. H6-8m/20-26ft, W6-8m/20-26ft. F5-7. Z7-8.

P. tricuspidata (syn. *Vitis inconstans*). This vigorous, self-clinging climber, originating from Japan, China and Korea, is, ironically,

Parthenocissus quinquefolia

known as Boston ivy, having become so widely cultivated in New England. It is also often wrongly called Virginia creeper, which is the similar *P. quinquefolia*, a true native of the eastern USA. *P. tricuspidata* has glossy, dark green, variable, but maple-like leaves, which turn bright fiery crimson in autumn. The form **'Veitchii'** has smaller leaves, purplish green when young and crimson-purple in autumn. Both H5m/16ft, W5m/16ft. F5-7. Z4-8.

PASSIFLORA Passion flower

P. caerulea. This Brazilian species is the hardiest and most popular of an enormous genus of 500 species of woody and herbaceous climbers, most native to South America. Evergreen and woody in areas with little winter frost, elsewhere herbaceous, it is extremely vigorous and clings by means of tendrils. It is renowned for its spectacular, flat, star-shaped, white or pink flowers, with their raised circular crown of blue or purple and white filaments. These are followed, after hot summers, by orange-yellow fruits. Grow in well-drained soil and sun or light shade. Protect from cold winds. **'Constance Elliott'** has white flowers. Both H5m/16ft, W5m/16ft. F7-8. Z8-9.

PERNETTYA

P. mucronata. Known for its colourful berries, this is the showiest of the many species of evergreen, low-growing, acid-loving shrubs, most from the Southern Hemisphere. A vigorous, dense shrub, it spreads by underground suckers, with stiff, upright stems and small, prickly leaves. The small, white, bell-shaped flowers, carried on shoot tips, are showy en masse. Except for the hermaphrodite **'Bell's Seedling'**, with deep red fruits, plant at least two or three named female fruiting forms with a male, usually the non-fruiting 'Mascula', to ensure a free display of marbled, round, white, red, pink, lilac or purple berries in late summer and autumn. They last well into winter but may be hidden by new growth. This can be cut away, but it may effect next season's flowering. Cut two-year-old or older stems to the ground in spring, to produce new, young, vigorous growth. There are many cultivars, including **'Crimsonia'**, large deep crimson berries. **'Lilian'**, lilac-pink. **'Mother of Pearl'**, light pink. **'Mulberry Wine'**, magenta to purple. **'Signal'**, deep red, large fruits. **'Wintertime'**, free-fruiting white. All H75-120cm/30-48in, W90-120cm/3-4ft. F5-6. Z8-9.

PEROVSKIA Russian sage

Few shrubs provide as much late season colour, with their long display of shimmering blue flower spikes. Though

Passiflora caerulea and 'Constance Elliott'

Pernettya mucronata 'Bell's Seedling'

quite hardy, young stems can die back in cold winters, new shoots appearing from the base. Provide full sun and any well-drained soil. Prune to 15-30cm/6-12in from the ground in spring to promote new flowering growth. Perovskias are perfect with perennials and shrubs, and every garden should have one!

P. atriplicifolia. This, and especially its cultivar **'Blue Spire'**, are most common. The species has aromatic, downy, grey-green, serrated leaves, white stems and hazy panicles of lavender-blue flowers. 'Blue Spire' has more deeply cut leaves and larger flower heads. H90-120cm/3-4ft, W90-120cm/3-4ft. F8-10. Z6-8.

Pernettya mucronata 'Lilian'

Perovskia atriplicifolia 'Blue Spire'

Philadelphus 'Beauclerk'

Philadelphus coronarius 'Aureus'

Philadelphus 'Manteau d'Hermine'

PHILADELPHUS Mock orange

This is one of the most popular hardy shrubs, with new cultivars being continually introduced, so choosing a philadelphus is difficult, especially since most gardens have room for only one or two. Though beautiful for two or three weeks in flower, the rest of the year they look dull, which makes selection even more important. There are small, medium and large types, all deciduous, mostly densely branched, with outer branches arching with age. Most have light green leaves, becoming dark green, and white, fragrant, single or double flowers with yellow stamens, the centres sometimes stained purple. They prefer any reasonable, moist loam and sun, though they tolerate light shade and chalky soil. Mulch and feed occasionally. Susceptible to blackfly; spray with systemic insecticide, at the first sign of trouble. Immediately after flowering, thin out as much as a third of old woody stems on older plants, to the base, and shorten other branches, if desirable.

P. argyrocalyx. This rare, New Mexican native is worth mentioning, if only to prompt its wider acceptance. A gracefully spreading shrub, its arching branches carry flowers supported by downy, silver-grey sepals. H1.8m/6ft, W1.8m/6ft. F6-7. Z7-9.

P. coronarius. The name sweet mock-orange aptly describes the heavy scent of this species. Cultivated in Europe for centuries, it has now been surpassed by modern hybrids. Coloured foliage forms include '**Aureus**', with bright yellow leaves, turning yellow-green and even green in hot climates, and '**Variegatus**', with grey-green leaves irregularly edged creamy white, and single or semi-double, scented flowers. Both are slower than the species, and best in part shade. H1.8-2.4m/6-8ft, W1.8-2.4m/6-8ft. F6. Z5-8.

P. delavayi '**Nyman's Variety**'. The best selection of this vigorous species is for the larger garden. It has large, dark green leaves and fragrant flowers in short racemes along spreading branches, the calyces a striking wine-purple. H2.4-3m/8-10ft, W2.4-3m/8-10ft. F6-7. Z6-8.

Hybrids. All F6-7, Z5-8 unless otherwise indicated. '**Albâtre**' (or '**Alabaster**'), large clusters, white, fragrant, double or semi-double flowers. H1.5m/5ft, W1.5m/5ft. '**Atlas**', leaves sometimes splashed yellow, large, single, subtly fragrant, white flowers. H1.8m/6ft, W1.8m/6ft. '**Avalanche**', profuse, small, single, heavily fragrant, white flowers on arching branches. H1.5m/5ft, W1.5m/5ft. '**Beauclerk**', creamy white, single, saucer-shaped, fragrant, rose-stained flowers. H1.8m/6ft, W1.8m/6ft. '**Belle Etoile**', large, single, sweetly scented, carmine-centred white flowers. H1.8m/6ft, W1.8m/6ft. '**Buckley's Quill**', double, fragrant, white flowers. H2.1m/7ft, W2.1m/7ft. Z4-8. '**Enchantment**', arching branches, fully double, richly fragrant, white flowers. H2.4m/8ft, W2.4m/8ft. '**Etoile Rose**', dwarf habit, single, scented, rose-stained white flowers. H1.2-1.5m/4-5ft, W1.2-1.5m/4-5ft. '**Manteau d'Hermine**', small leaves, masses of small, double or semi-double, fragrant, white flowers. H90-120cm/3-4ft, W90-120cm/3-4ft. '**Minnesota**

Snowflake**', vigorous, fully double, sweetly scented, white flowers in clusters. H2.4m/8ft, W2.4m/8ft. Z4-8. '**Silver Showers**' (syn. 'Silberregen'), compact habit, large, single, fragrant, white flowers. H1.2m/4ft, W1.2m/4ft. '**Virginal**', vigorous, free-flowering, large, cup-shaped, semi-double, strongly fragrant, white flowers. H2.4m/8ft, W2.4m/8ft.

PHILLYREA

This is a relatively little-known genus of evergreen shrubs (originating from North Africa, the Mediterranean and south-west Asia). They are useful for their adaptability to a wide range of soils, situations and climatic conditions. Unprepossessing when young, given time they make pleasing shrubs for sun or some shade, and can be grown for hedging, too. They have glossy green leaves and mostly small, fragrant flowers in late spring or early summer.

P. angustifolia. This is excellent for seaside planting, with its narrowly ovate, small, dark green leaves and, on mature plants in early summer, clusters of small, fragrant, creamy yellow flowers. H1.8-2.4m/6-8ft, W1.8-2.4m/6-8ft. F6. Z7-9.

P. decora (syn. *Osmanthus decorus*). A hardy, broad-spreading evergreen with quite large, shiny, dark green, leathery leaves, which eventually forms a dense bush. It has small, fragrant, white flowers in spring, followed by black fruits. Should be more widely used. H3m/10ft, W3-4m/10-13ft. F3-5. Z7-9.

PHLOMIS

This huge genus includes shrubs and sub-shrubs, the latter with soft woody growth. Both have woolly, grey or grey-green leaves and lax spikes with tiers of flowers in whorls, or circles, around the stem. As Mediterranean plants, they prefer sun and good drainage, thriving against hot, dry walls or banks. Prune back a third or half of old, woody stems as needed in spring, as new growth starts.

P. chrysophylla. An attractive Lebanese species, with grey-green, sage-like foliage and, in hot summers, golden-yellow flowers. H90-120cm/3-4ft, W1.2m/4ft. F7-8. Z8-10.

P. fruticosa. The Jerusalem sage is the hardiest with grey-green, woolly leaves and spikes of bright yellow whorled flowers. H90cm/3ft, W90-120cm/3-4ft. F7-8. Z8-11.

PHORMIUM New Zealand flax

The introduction from New Zealand in the late 1970s of many new selections with colourful foliage has made these plants very popular. Most are attractive but not hardy in cold climates with severe or prolonged frost or drying winds. Older plants have a central, almost woody base; the strap- or sword-like leaves are flexible and pithy. They grow in most moist soils, but vary in hardiness and adaptability. In warm climates *P. tenax* and tall selections make good accent or specimen plants. Small forms are ideal for sheltered patios or tub plants, taken under cover in winter.

P. colensoi. See *P. cookianum.*

P. cookianum. (syn *P. colensoi*). The mountain flax inhabits hilly regions and sea cliffs in its native New Zealand, forming variable sized clumps of shining green, wavy, lax leaves. Older plants bear exotic yellow and red flowers on spikes which vary from 90cm/3ft to 1.8m/6ft in height. Foliage H60-90cm/2-3ft, W90-120cm/3-4ft. F7-8. Z9-11. The selection **'Tricolor'** is considered a form of *P. cookianum* and has bright green, strap-like leaves striped white and margined red. H45-75cm/18-30in, W75-90cm/30-36in. F7-8. Z9-11.

P. tenax. This imposing, architectural plant eventually needs a lot of space. Broad, erect, grey-green, sword-like leaves form a large clump. Older plants produce spectacular flower spikes up to 4.5m/15ft high, with panicles of bronze-red flowers, followed by reddish seed heads. Variable from seed. H1.8-3m/6-10ft, W1.5-3m/5-10ft. F7-8. Z8-11.

Expect some of the following selections with coloured foliage to flower once established. All F7-8, Z9-11. **'Purpureum'**, similar to the species, with broad blades of bronze-purple leaves. H1.5-1.8m/5-6ft, W1.2-1.5m/4-5ft. **'Radiance'**, narrow, upright habit, creamy yellow stripes. H1.5m/5ft, W90-120cm/3-4ft. **'Sundowner'**, an outstanding cultivar with leaves striped grey, coppery red and pink. H1.5-1.8m/5-6ft, W1.2-1.5m/4-5ft. **'Variegatum'**, broad, green leaves edged creamy white. H1.5-1.8m/5-6ft, W1.2-1.5m/4-5ft.

Hybrids. There are an increasing number of hybrids between the two species, not all of which can be relied upon to flower. The following, where flowering, F7-8. All Z9-11. **'Bronze Baby'**, narrow, bronze-purple leaves. H60-90cm/2-3ft, W45-60cm/18-24in. **'Cream Delight'**, sometimes listed under *P. cookianum*, has broad green, arching leaves with a central band of creamy yellow. H60-90cm/2-3ft, W90-120cm/3-4ft. **'Dark Delight'**, broad, erect, glossy red-purple leaves, pendulous tips. H90-120cm/3-4ft, W90-120cm/3-4ft. **'Dazzler'**, brightest of all but a weak grower, maroon with luminous carmine bands. H75-90cm/30-36in, W75-90cm/30-36in. **'Maori Chief'**, robust, clump-forming, erect leaves striped bright red, with maroon and bronze drooping tips. H90-120cm/3-4ft, W60-90cm/2-3ft. **'Tom Thumb'**, dwarf with narrow green leaves margined bronze. H30-45cm/12-18in, W30-45cm/12-18in. **'Yellow Wave'**, striking, bright yellow arching leaves, some edged green. H75-90cm/30-36in, W90-120cm/3-4ft.

Phlomis fruticosa

Phormium tenax 'Purpureum'

(Clockwise from bottom) *Phormium* 'Dazzler', 'Yellow Wave' and *P. tenax* 'Sundowner'

PHOTINIA

Mostly south-east Asian in origin, these make large shrubs or trees, usually depending on climate. Deciduous types dislike lime but the evergreens thrive in it, even on chalky soil. Both types prefer reasonably moist but free-draining, warm soil, sun or light shade. In cool summers,

Photinia × fraseri 'Red Robin'

Photinia davidiana

the evergreens are shy to flower, but still make excellent foliage plants. The flowers are white, hawthorn-like and borne in clusters or panicles, followed by red fruits. The evergreens need shelter in cold regions from freezing winds and severe frost. If leaf drop occurs they normally shoot again in spring. For compact, dense growth and ample new colourful shoots, prune leading shoots back by 30-60cm/1-2ft in spring, as new growth commences; hedges or screens might also need a summer trim.

P. davidiana (syn. *Stranvaesia davidiana*). This species makes an attractive, if ungainly, background shrub or small tree with irregular, erect branches, glossy, lance-shaped, evergreen leaves, a few turning red in autumn and winter, and small clusters of white flowers, usually followed by bright red fruit. Unfortunately it and some of its varieties are susceptible to fireblight, a serious fungal disease which also affects

other members of the rose family. H2.4-3m/8-10ft, W1.8-2.4m/6-8ft. F7. Z7-9. **'Fructu Luteo'**, with succulent, yellow fruits, is less vigorous and narrower. H2.1-2.4m/7-8ft, W1.2-1.5m/4-5ft. F6-7. Z7-9. **'Prostrata'**, with red fruits, needs room to spread since it is extremely vigorous once established; throws up occasional erect shoots, otherwise prostrate. H30-60cm/1-2ft, W1.8-2.4m/6-8ft. F6-7. Z7-9. **'Palette'** is variable, but relatively bushy with leaves irregularly splashed and variegated white, pink and green, new shoots flushed reddish pink. White flowers not always developing into impressive red fruit. H1.5-1.8m/5-6ft, W1.2-1.5m/4-5ft. F6-7. Z7-9.

P. × fraseri **'Birmingham'**. Raised on the Fraser Nurseries, Birmingham, Alabama, this is a robust evergreen, with dark, glossy green leaves, copper-red when young. It is denser and hardier than the closely related, more colourful **'Red Robin'**, a New Zealand introduction with an almost continuous show of brilliant red new growths all summer. Both make outstanding focal points. Both H2.4-3m/8-10ft, W1.8-2.4m/6-8ft. F6. Z8-9.

P. glabra. This native of Japan and China makes a broad bush with bronze young

× *Phylliopsis hillieri* 'Pinocchio'

growths developing to shiny green leaves, and white, hawthorn-scented flowers. H1.8-3m/6-10ft, W1.8-2.4m/6-8ft. F6. Z8-10. **'Parfait'** (syn. 'Variegata' and 'Rosea Marginata') is a pretty, slow-growing shrub, its new growth vivid pink, becoming grey-green, pink and white. Rather tender and slow to establish. **'Rubens'** has bronze-red, new spring foliage and a rather lax growth habit. Both H1.5-1.8m/5-6ft, W1.5-1.8m/5-6ft. F6. Z8-10.

PHYGELIUS See under Perennials.

× PHYLLIOPSIS

× *P. hillieri* **'Pinocchio'**. Makes a round bush with short spikes of bright green leaves and a long display of startling, deep pink, bell flowers. **'Coppelia'** is slightly more vigorous with profuse lavender-pink flowers. Both need acid, humus-rich soil, and sun or part shade and are ideal for rock gardens or peat beds. Trim after flowering to maintain compact growth habit. Both H30cm/1ft, W38cm/15in. F5-6. Z5-8.

PHYLLODOCE

These rare, dwarf, heather-like shrubs are only happy in cool, moist, northerly latitudes and damp, acid, peaty soil. Native to high altitudes and northern tundra, none grows above 60cm/2ft, most much lower. They have narrow leaves and clusters of hanging or nodding, bell-shaped flowers in white, cream, purple, pink and crimson. Most are extremely hardy. All below, F5-6, Z3-7.

P. aleutica. Creamy white flowers on low mats. H20-30cm/8-12in, W30-45cm/12-18in.

P. breweri. Notable Californian species with pinkish purple bells on erect terminal shoots. H20-30cm/8-12in, W30-45cm/12-18in.

Physocarpus opulifolius 'Dart's Gold'

P. × intermedia **'Fred Stoker'**. Bushy, dwarf shrub with pitcher-shaped flowers of light purple. H30cm/1ft, W60-90cm/2-3ft.

PHYSOCARPUS

P. opulifolius **'Dart's Gold'**. It was not until this cultivar became widely distributed that most gardeners took notice of these hardy, deciduous shrubs. This dwarfer form of the 3m/10ft high **'Luteus'**, itself a useful back-of-the-border shrub, has brighter leaves, which retain their yellow colour longer into the season. Its upright stems, clothed in light brown peeling bark, break freely into bright yellow shoots in spring. These develop into broad-lobed, serrated leaves of vivid yellow, later fading to a softer tone. The species and its cultivars carry round clusters of pink-tinged, white flowers on or towards the end of the previous year's stems. If 'Dart's Gold' is grown as a foliage plant, prune in early spring, removing flowering stems to within 30-60cm/1-2ft of the ground. Rejuvenate old plants in a similar manner. All grow in acid or alkaline soils in sun or part shade where not too dry; the yellow leaves can scorch in full sun. H1.5-1.8m/5-6ft, W1.5-1.8m/5-6ft. F6. Z3-7.

PIERIS

These acid-loving evergreens are so attractive in flower and foliage that they are often bought regardless of their needs; moist but well-drained, acid or neutral soil and sun or part shade. You can add flowers of sulphur to reduce soil pH (see p.196), adding composted bark or peat, or plant in a raised bed or tub with acid compost. Most make slow-growing, mounded bushes, with lance-shaped, glossy leaves. Racemes often develop in autumn, opening in spring, with mostly pendulous, fragrant, bell-shaped, white flowers. New growth can be vulnerable to spring frosts. Prune only to tidy up bushes or remove old flower heads as new growth begins. A mulch of leaf mould or composted bark is appreciated every two or three years.

P. **'Bert Chandler'**. This Australian foliage hybrid deserves wider usage. It has new leaves which are first shrimp-pink, then white, later pale green. Shy to flower. H1.2m/4ft, W1.2m/4ft. F4-5. Z6-8.

P. **'Flaming Silver'**. There seem to be several selections of *Pieris* with variegated foliage, which have new growths of scarlet or crimson, all appearing at about the same time. 'Flaming Silver', probably like most others, is a sport of *P.* 'Forest Flame'. It arose on a nursery in Holland and has leaves edged silvery white, a striking contrast to bright red shoots in late spring. H1.2m/4ft, W1.2-1.5m/4-5ft. F3-5. Z5-8.

P. floribunda. A hardy North American species, rarer than Asian types, which is dense and stiffly branched, erect spikes

Pieris 'Forest Flame'

bearing short racemes of white flowers. **'Brouwer's Beauty'** has light green foliage, red flower stalks and pitcher-shaped flowers. **'Elongata'** has larger flower heads. All H90-150cm/3-5ft, W90-150cm/3-5ft. F4-5. Z5-7.

P. **'Forest Flame'**. One of the best hybrids, it has dense flower sprays; its scarlet young growths turn pink and white, then green. H1.5m/5ft, W1.5m/5ft. F4-5. Z6-8.

P. formosa forrestii **'Wakehurst'**. The best form of the large-growing, leathery leaved *P. formosa* was probably one of several seedlings collected by George Forrest in China in the early 1900s and raised at Wakehurst Place in Sussex, England. It forms a broad, dense bush, its brilliant crimson new shoots and leaves fading to pink. Needs shelter from winter and spring frost. H1.5-1.8m/5-6ft, W1.5-1.8m/5-6ft. F4-5. Z7-8.

Pieris floribunda 'Brouwer's Beauty'

Pieris japonica 'Flamingo'

P. japonica. The Japanese pieris provides most of the new European and North American cultivars. They usually have glossy leaves and pendulous flower racemes, with waxy, often fragrant, bell-like flowers, showy even in winter as flowering racemes develop. Most prefer an open, sheltered spot in moist soil. All F3-5. Most Z6-8.

Pieris japonica 'Red Mill'

Pileostegia viburnoides

Piptanthus nepalensis

'**Debutante**', Dutch, dense trusses of white flowers. H75cm/30in, W75-90cm/30-36in. '**Dorothy Wyckoff**', red-tinged leaves, crimson stalks, pink-tinged flowers. H90cm/3ft, W90-120cm/3-4ft. '**Flamingo**', carmine-rose and white flowers, coppery young growth. H1.2m/4ft, W1.2-1.5m/4-5ft. '**Little Heath**', dwarf, variegated form, compact, seldom flowers; small white, pink and copper leaves. H60cm/2ft, W60cm/2ft. '**Little Heath Green**', neat, spreading habit, glossy leaves, seldom flowers. H60cm/2ft, W90cm/3ft. '**Mountain Fire**', coppery-red new leaves, sparse, white flowers. H90cm/3ft, W90-120cm/3-4ft. '**Pink Delight**', profuse, fragrant, rose-pink flowers on red stalks. H1.2m/4ft, W1.2m/4ft. '**Purity**', dense, dark green leaves, late-flowering, large trusses of white flowers. H60cm/2ft, W90cm/3ft. '**Red Mill**', glossy wine-red leaves, white flowers. H1.2m/4ft, W1.2m/4ft. '**Valley Valentine**', American, deepest red flowers, free-flowering. H1.5m/

Pittosporum 'Garnettii'

5ft, W1.5m/5ft. '**Variegata**' covers a fast-growing form with white margins, also called '**White Rim**' (H90cm/3ft, W90cm/3ft), and a compact form, with creamy yellow variegations, which needs shelter. H45-60cm/18-24in, W45-60cm/18-24in.

PILEOSTEGIA

P. viburnoides. This self-clinging, slow-growing, evergreen climber has leathery, deep green, ribbed leaves and panicles of small, creamy white flowers. Grow against a sunny or lightly shaded wall, where not too dry. Little or no pruning required. H2.1-3m/7-10ft, W2.1-3m/7-10ft. F8-9. Z7-9.

PIPTANTHUS

P. nepalensis. This Himalayan species is one of perhaps two or three evergreen or semi-evergreen shrubs in this genus which have trifoliate leaves and golden-yellow pea flowers. It varies somewhat from seed, but will usually form an open bush of flexible stems bearing dark green leaves, with flowers appearing throughout the plant. It makes a good wall plant, but can also be used in the same situations as brooms, enjoying sun and good drainage. There is a form from Bhutan, *P. tomentosus*, with silvery leaves which promises to be even more showy. If bushes get untidy, prune stems back after flowering. H3-4m/10-13ft, W2.1-3m/7-10ft. F5-6. Z9-10.

PITTOSPORUM

These mainly Australasian evergreen shrubs or small trees are grown for foliage and are useful for cutting. Few are hardy in cool temperate zones, but for mild and seaside areas there are good species and cultivars, the latter mostly belonging to *P. tenuifolium*. Leaves are rounded and undulating, pale or olive green with more recent variations purple, silver, gold or variegated. Purple or brown flowers, often small and fragrant, only appear on mature plants in warmer climates. Any well-drained soil and full sun; in cold, inland areas, grow against a south wall. Wet soil and cold, desiccating winds are fatal. If cut back by frost, most make new growth from old wood. Plant in late spring. If grown as patio plants in tubs, overwinter in a greenhouse or conservatory. All below, F4-5, Z9-11. **P. 'Garnettii'.** This hybrid has grey-green leaves, edged white and tinged pink. H3m/10ft, W1.5m/5ft. **P. tenuifolium.** This bushy tree, columnar when young, has glossy, pale, wavy-edged leaves and black stems. Good for hedging. There are innumerable cultivars. H3m/10ft, W1.5m/5ft. '**Purpureum**' has red-purple leaves. '**Silver Queen**' has white-edged leaves. Both H1.8-2.1m/6-7ft, W1.5-1.8m/5-6ft. '**Tom Thumb**' is a dwarf, purple-leaved form. H1m/39in, W1m/39in.

POLYGALA

P. chamaebuxus. This European, dwarf, creeping evergreen has bright, pointed leaves and profuse, large, creamy white and yellow flowers only a few centimetres/inches above the ground, lasting for many weeks. Any continually moist soil but chalk, sun or part shade. Good with alpines or in a peat bed. H10cm/4in, W30-45cm/12-18in. F3-4. Z4-7. The form *grandiflora* (syn. *rhodoptera*) is rather taller and more lax in growth with deep green leaves and red and yellow, pea-like flowers. H15cm/6in, W30-45cm/12-18in. F2-3. Z5-7.

P. vayredae. A charming, creeping shrub with glossy green leaves and bright purple and yellow flowers, makes a dense mat for moist positions. H2.5-5cm/1-2in, W30-45cm/12-18in. F3-4. Z8-10.

POTENTILLA Cinquefoil, shrubby cinquefoil

P. fruticosa. Among the most adaptable hardy shrubs, these often have a very long flowering period. Recent breeding and selection has introduced orange, red and pink cultivars to the range of yellows and white in dwarf, medium and low-spreading types. These new colours can fade badly in heat, but in a cool spring, autumn or even summer some are stunning in full flower, and breeders are trying to identify and control the gene which prevents fading. In winter, their crowded, twiggy stems are dull, but in spring their small, divided leaves appear, then single, usually five-petalled flowers, with central clusters of yellow stamens. The first flush is often best, but flowering usually continues for many months with rests in between.

They grow on all but very wet or dry soil, preferring full sun but tolerating some shade, where coloured forms may retain deeper hues. Prune established plants annually, using secateurs or shears, as new shoots appear. Cut back by a third each year to improve vigour and flowering; older wood can be cut to the ground every few years but very old plants may rejuvenate slowly.

The following are hybrids mostly listed at one time under *fruticosa*, which is the parent of many. All F4-10. Most Z3-8. **'Abbotswood'**, the best white, profuse-flowering, blue-green leaves. H1.2m/4ft, W1.6m/63in. **'Abbotswood Silver'**, small, white-edged leaves; slower, fewer white flowers. H75cm/30in, W1m/39in. **'Beesii'** (syn. 'Nana Argentea'), silvery-grey leaves, dense, mounded habit, deep yellow flowers. H45cm/18in, W60cm/2ft. Z6-8. **'Coronation Triumph'**, good for hot climates, bright yellow. H1.2m/4ft, W1.6m/63in. **'Dart's Goldigger'**, low, spreading, grey-green leaves, golden-yellow flowers. H60cm/2ft, W90cm/3ft. **'Daydawn'**, for cool climates, peachy flowers, fading yellow or white.

Polygala vayredae

H75cm/30in, W1m/39in. **'Elizabeth'**, bushy, grey-green leaves, golden-yellow flowers, long-flowering. H90cm/3ft, W1.2m/4ft. **'Goldfinger'**, bright green leaves, golden flowers. H90cm/3ft, W1.2m/4ft. **'Goldstar'**, erect, open habit, huge, yellow flowers. H90cm/3ft, W1.2m/4ft. **'Hopleys Orange'**, orange flowers. H75cm/30in, W1m/39in.

Potentilla fruticosa 'Goldstar'

'Katherine Dykes', an old favourite, primrose-yellow flowers, grey-green leaves. H1.2m/4ft, W1.6m/63in. **'Kobold'**, dense, dwarf, small, yellow flowers. H30-45cm/12-18in, W40-60cm/16-24in. **'Manchu'** (formerly 'Mandschurica'), blue-green leaves, white flowers, can be difficult. H45cm/18in, W60cm/2ft. **'Moonlight'** (syn. Maanelys'), grey-green leaves, long display of smallish, pale yellow flowers. H1.2m/4ft, W1.2m/4ft. **'Pretty Polly'**, dwarf, low-growing, with light rose-pink flowers. H35-50cm/14-20in, W45-65cm/18-26in. **'Primrose Beauty'**, blue-grey leaves, erect, spreading habit, primrose with deep yellow centres. H90cm/3ft, W1.2m/4ft. **'Princess'**, long-flowering; pale-pink, then paler, fading to white in heat. H75cm/30in, W1m/39in. **'Red Ace'**, bright vermilion-flame at best, fading to yellow in heat. **'Red Robin'** is similar but deeper red. Both H60cm/2ft, W80cm/32in. **'Royal Flush'**, slow, can be awkward, rose-pink, fading. H45cm/18in, W60cm/2ft. **'Sunset'**, compact orange-yellow flowers, fades in heat. H75cm/30in, W75cm/30in. **'Tilford Cream'**, low habit, rigid branches, white flowers, can look scruffy. H60cm/2ft, W60cm/2ft.

Potentilla fruticosa 'Princess'

Potentilla fruticosa 'Red Ace'

Prostanthera cuneata 'Alpine Gold'

Prunus laurocerasus 'Otto Luyken'

PROSTANTHERA

P. cuneata. This is considered the hardiest of the mint bushes, a group of aromatic Australasian shrubs. It forms a wide-spreading bush of small, dark, glossy green 'minty' leaves and pretty, white, lilac-centred flowers. **'Alpine Gold'** is an attractive variation, with leaves in sun suffused gold. Best in sun with good drainage, given shelter from frosty winds. Both H60-75cm/24-30in, W90-120cm/3-4ft. F5-6. Z9-10.

PRUNUS

This large family of trees and shrubs, nearly all from the Northern Hemisphere, contains many favourites, including deciduous ornamental plums, cherries, apricots, almonds and peaches, but also evergreen, broadleaf cherry laurels. Most deciduous forms prefer sun or light shade and any well-drained soil; evergreen forms are more shade-tolerant. Though spectacular in flower, some, like *Philadelphus*, flower only briefly – a drawback in a small garden.

P. cerasifera **'Pissardii'**. The purple-leaved plum, a form of the myrobalan, or cherry plum, is widely used as a foliage plant and for hedging. White, pink-budded flowers wreathe the naked branches in spring, followed by red young shoots and leaves, which turn purple in summer. Shy to fruit. As a hedge, prune immediately after flowering. H2.4-3m/8-10ft, W2.4-3m/8-10ft. F3-4. Z5-8.

P.* × *cistena (syn. 'Crimson Dwarf'). The purple-leaf sand cherry is valued for its white flowers and reddish purple foliage, best in full sun. Good for hedging: to keep low, prune after flowering, then regularly through the summer. H1.5-1.8m/5-6ft, W1.2-1.5m/4-5ft. F3-4. Z2-8.

P. glandulosa. The Chinese bush cherry, or, in the USA, Chinese dwarf flowering almond, has erect, branched stems with single, white or pink flowers, which appear before and with the leaves. Best in warm sun; hard prune previous year's growth immediately after flowering. There are several ornamental, double-flowered forms, including **'Alba Plena'**, white, and the densely petalled, pink **'Sinensis'** (syn. 'Flore Roseoplena'). All H1.2-1.5m/4-5ft, W1.2m/4ft. F3-4. Z5-8.

P. incisa. Many shrubby forms of Fuji cherry eventually make small trees, with small leaves, turning lovely autumn shades. Small, white flowers, pink in bud, cluster on leafless stems. Small, purple fruits. Flowers only briefly. The species varies widely from seed; best to look for named selections. **'Kojo nomai'**, a slow-growing form, has contorted branches, ideal for bonsai, with profuse flowers and year-round interest. H1.2-1.5m/4-5ft, W90cm/3ft. F3. Z4-7.

P. laurocerasus. The evergreen cherry laurels have variously shaped, glossy, leathery leaves. The taller types make excellent background shrubs, windbreaks, screening and hedging. The lower-growing, compact forms are good ground cover. The species, having produced many forms, is seldom seen or listed. Most have erect, bottle brush spikes of white flowers, often followed by purple fruit. Generally vigorous and accommodating, they grow on almost any well-drained soil but chalk, in sun or quite deep shade if not too dry. Prune only to control growth immediately after flowering; then trim hedges at regular intervals until late summer. Old, bare-stemmed plants rejuvenated if cut to the ground in mid spring. All F4-5. Most Z6-8. **'Cherry Brandy'**, broad, spreading; copper-bronze new foliage, later green.

Prunus glandulosa 'Alba Plena'

Prunus × *cistena*

H90cm/3ft, W1.8m/6ft. '**Herbergii**', good for hedging, upright, dense foliage, free-flowering. H2.4m/8ft, W1.5m/5ft. '**Low and Green**', low, free-flowering, glossy green leaves. H90cm/3ft, W2.1-3m/7-10ft. '**Magnoliifolia**', enormous, glossy leaves. H4.5m/15ft, W4.5m/15ft. Z7-8. '**Marbled White**', broad, spreading; leaves green, grey and cream. H2.4m/8ft, W2.4m/8ft. '**Otto Luyken**', broad, semi-prostrate; narrow, shiny leaves, white flowers, often again in autumn, good hedging. H1.5m/5ft, W1.5m/5ft. '**Reynvaanii**', erectly branched, good hedging. H1.8m/6ft, W1.5-1.8m/5-6ft. '**Rotundifolia**', used in Britain for hedges, rounded leaves, slightly tender. H2.4m/8ft, W2.4m/8ft. Z7-8. '**Schipkaensis**', narrow-leaved, spreading, very hardy ground cover. H2.1m/7ft, W2.1m/7ft. '**Zabeliana**', low, spreading, ground cover, narrow leaves. H1.2m/4ft, W1.8m/6ft.

P. lusitanica. The Portugal laurel is a dense bush or small tree, with glossy, evergreen leaves and usually profuse, small, white, fragrant flower spikes. Use as a background shrub, screening or hedging. Any well-drained soil, even chalk. Prune as for *P. laurocerasus*, if required. '**Variegata**' has red young stalks, white-edged leaves, tinted rose-pink in winter in a sunny spot. Both H3m/10ft, W3m/10ft. F6. Z7-9.

P. mume. Japanese apricots are worth space, even in a small garden. Slender, erect or spreading branches carry winter blossom for several weeks. Need well-drained soil, shelter and sun or light shade. Prune just after flowering. The white, semi-double '**Alba Plena**', and the semi-double, pink '**Alphandii**' are lovely, but the profuse Japanese '**Beni-shidare**', with carmine, fragrant, saucer-shaped flowers, and the similar, but white '**Omoi no Mama**' are superb. All H3m/10ft, W3m/10ft. F2-4. F7-9.

P. tenella. Very hardy, the dwarf Russian almond, with bright pink flowers as the leaves appear, is beautiful at its best, but can be shy to flower. Twiggy, upright and slow-spreading, it is dull out of flower. Sun and good drainage required. No pruning. '**Fire Hill**' has rose-red flowers. Both H1.2m/4ft, W1.2m/4ft. F4-5. Z2-6.

P. triloba '**Multiplex**'. This, the most often offered selection of the single-flowered Chinese species, is breathtaking in full bloom, its erect, leafless branches smothered in rose-pink, semi-double flowers. Not of great attraction for the rest of the year. Prune flowering stems hard after flowering. Best in a warm, sunny spot; can be grown against a wall. H1.5-2.4m/5-8ft, W1.2-1.8m/4-6ft. F3-4. Z3-7.

PYRACANTHA Firethorn

Species are found from south-east Europe, through the Himalayas and central China as far as Formosa. Most have been superseded

Prunus mume 'Beni-shidare'

by hybrids, some chance, others from breeding programmes. The late Don Egolf of the United States National Arboretum in Washington DC and Dr Elwin Orton of Rutgers University both made outstanding selections, many reputedly resistant to fireblight and scab, to which these shrubs are prone. Most are vigorous, evergreen or semi-evergreen, upright or spreading, thorny bushes with small, glossy leaves and clusters of white flowers, followed by showy, round, 'fiery' yellow, red or orange fruit, attractive to birds. They grow on most well-drained soils, fruiting better in sun than shade. They can be used as specimens, or as a hedge, a screen or a wall shrub, even on north-facing walls.

Informal shrubs need no pruning, though large ones carry most fruit above eye level, at 3m/10ft or more. Flowers and fruit appear mostly on previous year's growth, so prune after flowering, to remove any extended, non-flowering shoots and repeat in early autumn on any subsequent new growths. About every five years, remove extended stems to within 10cm/4in of main branches; this results in vigorous new growth, no flowering for a year, but a reborn plant!

P. coccinea '**Lalandei**'. Introduced over 100 years ago, and still popular. Erect habit, red fruits freely borne. H3m/10ft, W2.4m/8ft. F6. Z5-9.

P. rogersiana. Densely foliaged, abundant orange-red fruits, one of the best for hedging. H3m/10ft, W2.4m/8ft. F6. Z7-9.

Hybrids. The following are of complex parentage. All F5-6. '**Alexander Pendula**', ground-covering, undulating French form, but not free-fruiting, red fruits. H60cm/2ft, W2.4m/8ft. Z7. '**Golden Charmer**', vigorous, open habit, yellow-orange fruits less attractive to birds. H3m/10ft, W3m/10ft. Z7. '**Harlequin**', pinkish, creamy variegated leaves, occasional small, orange-red fruits. H2.4m/8ft, W1.2-1.5m/4-5ft. Z8-9. '**Kasan**', or '**Orange Giant**', broad,

Pyracantha 'Orange Glow'

pyramidal habit, free-flowering, orange-red fruits. H3m/10ft, W2.4m/8ft. Z5. '**Mohave**', vigorous, upright, free-flowering and fruiting, red-orange fruits. H3m/10ft, W2.4m/8ft. Z6-9. '**Orange Glow**', reliable, erect, dense habit, orange fruits. H3m/10ft, W2.4m/8ft. Z6-9. '**Red Cushion**', low, dense, spreading ground cover, red fruits. H60-90cm/2-3ft, W1.8m/6ft. Z6-9. '**Rutgers**', free-fruiting, orange-red fruits, disease-resistant, very hardy. H90cm/3ft, W2.4m/8ft. Z6-9. '**Santa Cruz**', from the USA, prostrate, free-fruiting, red fruits. H60cm/2ft, W2.4m/8ft. Z7. '**Soleil D'Or**' ('Golden Sun'), broad, upright habit, spreading, large clusters deep yellow fruits. H2.4m/8ft, W3m/10ft. Z7. '**Sparkler**', grey-green leaves, white margins, needs warm, sheltered spot, shy to fruit. H90-120cm/3-4ft, W1.2m/4ft. Z8-9. '**Teton**', strong, narrow, upright, yellow berries, disease-resistant. H3.6m/12ft, W2.4m/8ft. Z6-9.

Pyracantha 'Soleil D'Or'

Rhamnus alaternus 'Argenteovariegata'

Rhododendron bureavii

Rhododendron augustinii

Rhododendron davidsonianum

RHAMNUS Buckthorn

There are over 150 species in this widely spread genus of deciduous and evergreen trees and shrubs.

R. alaternus. This Mediterranean, pyramidal evergreen has small, dark, shiny leaves and modest, yellow flowers, followed in warm climates by abundant red, later black, fruit. Prefers sun and well-drained soil, and is suited to mild coastal districts; dislikes wet, heavy soils, low temperatures and winds. In cold or exposed gardens, plant in a sunny spot, sheltered by tall trees or a high wall. H3-4m/10-13ft, W3-4m/10-13ft. F3-5. Z8-9. Much showier but slightly more tender is **'Argenteovariegata'**, with marbled-grey leaves, margined creamy white. H3m/10ft, W3m/10ft. F5-6. Z9-10.

RHODODENDRON

This is a vast group of over 900 species of deciduous and evergreen shrubs and trees, including those commonly known as azaleas. They grow wild throughout the Northern Hemisphere, particularly in North America and Eastern Asia, spreading from Northern Siberia down to the tropics, edging into the Southern Hemisphere as far as the Philippines. They range from tough, hardy miniatures, surviving in almost tundra conditions, to exotic tropical trees. Over the years thousands of hybrids have been raised, by chance or by design, from plants collected in the wild. The genus contains some of the most spectacular flowering plants, and their popularity has led in recent years to more refined breeding and selection, with much regional variation in hardiness. Hybrids raised in Britain, for example, may not be hardy or necessarily desirable in Germany or the USA and vice versa, but gardeners in the cool temperate zones have more than an ample choice.

Their glorious flowering may be followed by a long gap of little interest for the next twelve months or so though, if space allows, the season can be extended by selecting varieties to give a succession of flowers from early spring through to late summer. That said, many rhododendrons have attractive foliage the year round. When selecting, consider their growth rate and your garden's size and suitability. Taller forms are ideal background plants, bright in flower and providing an evergreen backcloth for the rest of the year. It is useful to know that as a general rule, the larger the leaf the more shade is required. Site rhododendrons with similar-sized plants: medium-sized with shrubs or small trees, smaller types at the front of borders or with heathers and dwarf conifers, and true dwarfs with alpines. If a rhododendron outgrows its site, it can easily be moved to a more suitable position, even as a relatively large plant.

Most rhododendrons grow more compactly and flower more freely in sun, but light shade is often adequate. In climates with cold winters and hot summers, protection from extreme temperatures may be necessary. Spring frost can create havoc with flower buds, especially with early forms. According to flowering period and hardiness, protect plants from early morning sun by planting in areas shaded for at least the first half of the morning. This is less critical with late-flowering types, but in Britain frosts can occur until well into May! If spring frosts are severe, even shade may not prevent damage to blooms.

Moist but well-drained, acid soil is ideal. Some rhododendrons tolerate neutral soil, but none tolerates lime. If plants grow well nearby, you can probably grow them successfully; if not, have your soil tested to determine its pH. You can either increase its acidity (see p.196) or plant your rhododendrons in raised beds or tubs filled with ericaceous compost.

Like heaths and heathers, rhododendrons have fine, fibrous roots, most active near the surface. When preparing the soil, add peat or composted bark, or other fine, acid compost, to open up the soil and help it to retain moisture. Plant the rootball level with the surrounding soil or potting compost and then cover with 5cm/2in of acid leaf mould or composted bark. This helps retain moisture, keeps down weeds, protects roots from frost and creates an attractive appearance. Water if dry.

Large-flowered types look nicer and produce more flowers if dead-headed, the flower stalk being carefully snapped off at the base, but dead-heading is time-consuming and not absolutely necessary. Shorten or remove straggly branches; if an old plant needs drastic treatment, prune back old stems over two or three seasons to promote new shoots. More drastic still, you can cut back all stems to 15cm/6in from the ground, promoting strong new growth, but not all plants respond to this treatment. Prune in early spring or just after flowering.

Advice on selecting rhododendrons must of necessity be limited here, but always

Rhododendron oreodoxa

Rhododendron thomsonii

choose those that are recommended for your country or region, for the best chance of success. Most authorities classify rhododendrons under a number of different headings: species, with these sometimes divided into large and small forms; hybrids, also grouped into large and dwarf types; and azaleas, usually treated separately though now classed as rhododendrons, with these split into evergreen and deciduous types.

Larger species
R. arboreum. This large, Himalayan, evergreen shrub or small tree has white, pink or red flowers, the latter colour being most susceptible to frost. H1.5-1.8m/5-6ft, W90-120cm/3-4ft. F2-4. Z7-8.
R. augustinii. A bushy, small-leaved evergreen, it has clusters of lilac to violet-blue flowers, and is striking as a group. Provide shelter. H1.5-1.8m/5-6ft, W1.2-1.5m/4-5ft. F5-6. Z7-8.
R. bureavii. This has evergreen, glossy leaves, russet beneath, colourful new shoots,

Rhododendron lutescens

and pale pink, bell-shaped flowers. H1.2-1.5m/4-5ft, W1.2-1.5m/4-5ft. F4-5. Z6-8.
R. campanulatum. This has large, dark, glossy evergreen leaves, rusty brown beneath, and lavender, bell-shaped flowers. '**Knap Hill**', with deep lavender-blue blooms, is worth looking for. Both H1.2-1.8m/4-6ft, W1.2-1.5m/4-5ft. F4-5. Z7-8.
R. cinnabarinum. Evergreen, with an upright habit, blue-green leaves, and pendulous bell-shaped, waxy, red flowers. H1.5-1.8m/5-6ft, W90-120cm/3-4ft. F5-6. Z7-8.
R. davidsonianum. A free-flowering, Chinese, evergreen species with lance-shaped leaves and funnel-shaped flowers varying from pink to purple. '**Caerhays**' is a select pink form. Both H1.5-1.8m/5-6ft, W90-120cm/3-4ft. F4-5. Z7-8.
R. fortunei. A large, evergreen shrub or small tree, this has elliptic leaves, matt green above, blue-green beneath, and loose trusses of fragrant, pale pink flowers. H1.2-1.8m/4-6ft, W1.2-1.8m/4-6ft. F5. Z7-8.
R. lutescens. A charming, lax-growing, Chinese, semi-evergreen, but variable species, this has primrose-yellow flowers and bronze-red new leaves. H1.2-1.5m/4-5ft, W90-150cm/3-5ft. F3-4. Z7-9.
R. oreodoxa. A sterling evergreen shrub or small tree, this has narrow leaves, bluish beneath, and clusters of funnel-shaped, light pink flowers, red in bud. H1.2-1.5m/4-5ft, W90-120cm/3-4ft. F3-4. Z7-8.
R. thomsonii. This fine Himalayan, evergreen species has rounded, glossy green leaves, blue-green on new growth, and bell-shaped, blood-red, waxy flowers on older plants, which also develop peeling, cinnamon-brown bark. Needs shelter. H1.2-1.5m/4-5ft, W1.2-1.5m/4-5ft. F4-5. Z7-8.
R. wardii. A broad, evergreen shrub, with dark green leaves, bluish beneath, and loose clusters of saucer-shaped, yellow flowers, sometimes with crimson basal markings. Best in shelter. H90-150cm/3-5ft, W90-150cm/3-5ft. F5. Z7-8.

SHRUBS

Rhododendron impeditum

Rhododendron 'Anna Rose Whitney'

Dwarf species

R. calostrotum. An evergreen, compact, very free-flowering shrub, with grey-green leaves and clusters of saucer-shaped or flat, magenta-crimson flowers. H30-45cm/12-18in, W30-45cm/12-18in. F5-6. Z7-9.

R. campylogynum. A pretty dwarf, this has evergreen, glossy leaves, blue beneath, and small, purple-red, pendulous flowers on long stems carried from a young age. Also in pink, red and white. H15-20cm/6-8in, W20-30cm/8-12in. F5-6. Z6-8.

R. haematodes. An attractive, slow-growing, Chinese species with dark, evergreen, leathery leaves, woolly reddish brown beneath, and trusses of scarlet to crimson bells. H45-60cm/18-24in, W60-90cm/2-3ft. F5-6. Z6-8.

R. impeditum. This favourite evergreen dwarf makes a tangled mound of small, dark green leaves and mauve to purplish blue flowers. Ideal for rock gardens. H20-30cm/8-12in, W30-40cm/12-16in. F4-5. Z6-8.

R. keiskei. A variable, semi-evergreen, Japanese species with lance-shaped leaves and profuse clusters of lemon-yellow flowers. **'Yaku Fairy'** is a prostrate dwarf,

less than half the size. Species: H30-60cm/1-2ft, W30-60cm/1-2ft. F3-5. Z6-8.

R. neriiflorum. Not very dwarf, but a worthwhile species, this has oval, dark green leaves, pale bluish white beneath, and waxy, bright scarlet to crimson, bell-shaped flowers. H60-90cm/2-3ft, W60-90cm/2-3ft. F4-5. Z7-8.

R. pseudochrysanthum. A Taiwanese, evergreen, slow-growing species of note, this has a rounded habit, dark green, leathery leaves, woolly when young, and flowers dark pink in bud opening to pink or white, lined and spotted rose-pink. H60-90cm/2-3ft, W60-90cm/2-3ft. F4-5. Z7-8.

R. racemosum. A variable, Chinese evergreen. Good forms are compact, with dark green leaves, bluish green beneath, and tight clusters of rose-pink to white flowers along the branches. H60-120cm/2-4ft, W60-90cm/2-3ft. F3-4. Z6-8.

R. williamsianum. The parent of many excellent hybrids, this compact, Chinese evergreen has rounded, bright green leaves, bronze-red new growth, and tubular, clear pink flowers. H45-60cm/18-24in, W60-90cm/2-3ft. F4-5. Z7-8.

R. yakushimanum. A wonderful, hardy, Japanese, evergreen dwarf, which forms a dome of dark, glossy green, leathery leaves, beige beneath, and profuse, deep rose-pink buds, opening into light pink blooms fading to white. Many hybrids have been raised from this sterling species. H45-60cm/18-24in, W60-90cm/2-3ft. F5-6. Z5-8.

Medium to large, evergreen hybrids

R. **'Anna Rose Whitney'**. A medium-sized, American selection, with large, leathery, matt green leaves and trusses of deep rose-pink flowers. H1.5-1.8m/5-6ft, W1.2-1.8m/4-6ft. F5-6. Z7-8.

R. **'Betty Wormald'**. An old but reliable Dutch cultivar, with dark green leaves and enormous conical trusses of tubular, rose-pink flowers, crimson in bud. H1.5-1.8m/5-6ft, W1.5-1.8m/5-6ft. F5-6. Z6-8.

R. **'Fabia'**. There are various forms, with medium-sized, widely dome-shaped, dark green leaves with a light beige woolly coating, and loose trusses of orange-red or salmon, bell-shaped flowers. H90-120cm/3-4ft, W1.2-1.5m/4-5ft. F4-5. Z7-8.

R. **'Hotei'**. This has a dense habit, small, mid-green leaves and deep yellow flowers. A magnificent plant at its best. H90-120cm/3-4ft, W1.2-1.5m/4-5ft. F5-6. Z7-8.

R. **'Lady Chamberlain'**. A free-flowering favourite, with stiff branches, dark bluish green leaves and pendulous trusses of waxy, orange-salmon flowers. Rewarding but not always easy to please. Several clones available. H1.2-1.8m/4-6ft, W1.2-1.5m/4-5ft. F5-6. Z7-8.

R. **'Lady Roseberry'**. Similar to the above but with pink to rose flowers. H1.2-1.8m/4-6ft, W1.2-1.5m/4-5ft. F5-6. Z7-8.

R. **'Lem's Cameo'**. This has outstanding foliage and flowers; rounded leaves, bronze-red when young, and rounded heads of purple-pink buds which open to frilled flowers changing from apricot to pink and cream. H1.5-1.8m/5-6ft, W90-120cm/3-4ft. F5-6. Z7-8.

R. **'May Day'**. A British-raised hybrid with dark green leaves, woolly white beneath, broad habit and lax trusses of scarlet-red flowers. H1.2-1.5m/4-5ft, W90-120cm/3-4ft. F5-6. Z7-8.

R. **'Mrs Lionel de Rothschild'**. Compact habit, glossy green leaves, and large trusses of white flowers, flushed with pink, crimson in the throat. In the USA often wrongly sold as 'Lady de Rothschild'. H1.2-1.8m/4-6ft, W1.2-1.8m/4-6ft. F5-6. Z7-8.

Dwarf hybrids

R. **'Anna Baldsiefen'**. This has an upright habit, small leaves and masses of bright pink, tubular flowers. H60-90cm/2-3ft, W45-60cm/18-24in. F4-5. Z6-9.

R. **'Blue Diamond'**. Fragrant, deep green foliage, compact, slow-growing habit and

Rhododendron keiskei

Rhododendron 'May Day'

rich lavender-blue, funnel-shaped flowers. H60-75cm/24-30in, W60-75cm/24-30in. F4-5. Z6-8.

R. **'Bow Bells'**. An outstanding dwarf shrub with a rounded, compact habit, coppery young leaves and loose trusses of red-budded flowers opening to silvery pink bells. H60-75cm/24-30in, W60-75cm/24-30in. F4-5. Z7-8.

R. **'Carmen'**. A tough dwarf with a spreading, prostrate habit, this has mid-green, dense foliage and waxy, trumpet flowers of deep crimson. H45-60cm/18-24in, W60-75cm/24-30in. F4-5. Z6-8.

R. **'Curlew'**. A superb Scottish dwarf hybrid with small, dark green leaves and masses of yellow, bell-shaped flowers. H30-45cm/12-18in, W45-60cm/18-24in. F4-5. Z6-8.

R. **'Dora Amateis'**. This is a larger, free-flowering bush, with dark, glossy green leaves and clusters of bell-shaped flowers, pink in bud, opening white. H60-90cm/2-3ft, W60-90cm/2-3ft. F4-5. Z6-8.

R. **'Elizabeth'**. One of the most popular cultivars. It has mid-green leaves and profuse clusters of trumpet-shaped, scarlet flowers. H60-75cm/24-30in, W60-75cm/24-30in. F4-5. Z7-8.

R. **'P. J. Mezitt'**. A hardy, free-flowering, American form, with small, dark green leaves, purplish in winter, and striking, rosy purple flowers with darker spots. H90-120cm/3-4ft, W60-90cm/2-3ft. F3-4. Z5-8.

R. **'Pink Cherub'**. This is broad and spreading, with dark green leaves and erect trusses of fifteen to twenty deep pink buds, opening to light pink, fading white. H60-90cm/2-3ft, W60-90cm/2-3ft. F5-6. Z6-8.

R. **'Too Bee'**. An American introduction, with a dwarf, spreading habit, deep green leaves and red buds opening to frilled, deep pink, bell-shaped flowers, paler inside. H20-30cm/8-12in, W30-45cm/12-18in. F4-5. Z6-8.

Dwarf evergreen azaleas (rhododendrons)

Also called Japanese azaleas, these are actually semi-evergreen. They are ideal for massed planting, but come in a limited colour range. Most appreciate shelter and light shade. Most F4-5. Z6-8.

'Addy Wery', old, reliable, compact cultivar, with profuse vermilion flowers. H45-60cm/18-24in, W60-75cm/24-30in. **'Blue Danube'** (syn. 'Blaue Donau'), more mauve than blue, striking colour. H45-60cm/18-24in, W60-75cm/24-30in. **'Chippewa'**, low, spreading, free-flowering, late pink. H30-45cm/12-18in, W60-75cm/24-30in. F5-6. **'Hinomayo'**, famous Japanese Kurume azalea with a mass of small, bright pink flowers, small green leaves. H45-60cm/18-24in, W45-60cm/18-24in. **'Kermesina'**, hardy, free-flowering, Dutch cultivar, glossy green leaves, rich

pink flowers, deeper pink in **'Kermesina Rose'** and white in **'Kermesina White'**. H45-60cm/18-24in, W60-90cm/2-3ft. **'Panda'**, compact bush, glossy green leaves, brilliant white flowers. H30-45cm/12-18in, W45-60cm/18-24in. **'Rosebud'**, striking form, hose-in-hose, double, rose-pink flowers, quite late. H30-45cm/12-18in, W60-90cm/2-3ft. F5-6. **'Squirrel'**, startling late-flowering cultivar, with profuse, bright scarlet flowers. H30-45cm/12-18in, W45-60cm/18-24in.

Deciduous azaleas (rhododendrons)

There are several groups of these hybrids, many with brilliantly coloured spring and autumn leaves and fragrant flowers, but only a few can be mentioned. Unless

Rhododendron 'Curlew'

Rhododendron 'Pink Cherub'

otherwise indicated, all in ten years approximately H90-120cm/3-4ft, W90-120cm/3-4ft. F5-6. Z6-8. **'Berryrose'**, young coppery foliage, rose-pink, trumpet flowers with a yellow flash. **'Brazil'**, brilliant orange-red, frilled lobes. **'Exquisitum'**, fragrant pink, deeper pink outside, marked by an orange flare, frilled margins. **'Fireball'**, deep orange-red. **'Gibraltar'**, popular, frilled, glowing orange with a yellow flash. **'Golden Sunset'**, orange-tinged buds, bright yellow flowers with orange flare. **'Homebush'**, rounded heads of semi-double, rose-pink. **'Klondyke'**, fragrant, vivid orange-gold, red-tinted on back, coppery young growths. **'Persil'**, white with orange flare. **'Satan'**, deep geranium-red. **'Sunset Pink'**, pink with a yellow blotch.

R. azalea 'Persil'

Rhus typhina 'Dissecta'

Rhus glabra 'Laciniata'

Ribes laurifolium

Ribes odoratum

RHUS Sumach

This large group of deciduous and evergreen shrubs and trees contains few species of notable garden value. These are grown more for their summer and autumn foliage than for flowering, though some have striking fruit. Generally easy to grow in any well-drained soil, many spread by underground suckers, and can be invasive, so use with care. Their sap can be an irritant: always wear gloves and avoid touching cut stems with bare skin.

R. aromatica. The fragrant sumach is a good, if potentially invasive, ground cover for sun or part shade. Its bright green, lobed and toothed, glossy leaves are pleasantly fragrant when crushed, and turn orange and red in autumn, on light soils in full sun. Small, yellow flower clusters are followed by hairy red fruit in late summer. H90-120cm/3-4ft, W1.8-2.4m/6-8ft. F3-4. Z4-9.

R. glabra. The smooth sumach is an erect, spreading, deciduous shrub, with smooth, purplish stems and bright green, pinnate leaves turning glorious orange and red in autumn. Most often grown is **'Laciniata'**, with deeply dissected leaflets and brilliant autumn colour. The dense, erect panicles of greenish flowers are followed, on female plants, by bright crimson seed heads in

autumn, often remaining long after leaf fall. Both are shrubbier than the more vigorous *R. typhina*, and can either be left to develop a somewhat irregular, woody habit or can be treated as a foliage plant and cut to within 30cm/1ft of the ground in spring, then reaching 1.2-1.8m/4-6ft in the year. H2.4-3m/8-10ft, W2.4-4m/8-13ft. F6-8. Z3-9.

R. typhina. The stag's-horn sumach is a striking, if unruly, shrub or small, flat-topped tree, with erect, spreading stems,

gaunt in winter. Large, pinnate leaves usually turn bright orange and scarlet in autumn. Modest, greeny male and female flowers are borne on separate plants, the female flowers followed, if a male is present, by hairy, crimson seed heads. **'Dissecta'** (syn. 'Laciniata'), with deeply cut leaves and orange and yellow autumn colours, is arguably more garden-worthy. Both H3-4.5m/10-15ft, W3m/10ft. F6-8. Z3-9.

RIBES Flowering currant

Though the ribes are often overused and overgrown in gardens, one should not despise these showy flowering plants for being so popular, but rather consider them for their merits. Like *Forsythia*, they are deciduous and among the first to flower, just before or as the new leaves appear. Most have pendulous, graceful flower racemes, though the broadly lobed leaves often detract, as does the pungent aroma emitted by *R. sanguineum*. Generally easy, they grow in any not extremely wet or dry soil. Most prefer sun but tolerate light shade. Prune back older stems, at the same time shortening unruly stems as required. Pruning can be formal, but I prefer their more irregular, natural shape.

R. alpinum. The mountain currant is a tough, hardy, densely branched, deciduous shrub, with small, yellow flowers. Red fruit are only produced on female plants pollinated by males, but are not produced freely. It grows wild in woodlands, so adapts well to dry shade, and can be used for hedging. H1.5-1.8m/5-6ft, W1.2-1.5m/4-5ft. F4-5. Z3-7. If grown in sun, **'Aureum'** has vivid yellow leaves in early spring, turning green by late summer. Rarely flowers. **'Green Mound'** is uniformly compact, with bright green foliage. Both H60-90cm/2-3ft, W60-90cm/2-3ft. Z2-7.

R. laurifolium. This lax Chinese evergreen has glossy, dark green, leathery leaves and small, pendulous clusters of greenish white flowers. Prune after flowering to improve density. H90-120cm/3-4ft, W1.2-1.5m/4-5ft. F3-4. Z7-8.

R. odoratum. This central North American native is an upright, irregular, open-branched shrub with glossy leaves and short racemes of clear yellow, fragrant, clove-scented flowers, often followed by purple-black fruits. Good autumn leaf colour. Prune as required after flowering. H1.8-2.4m/6-8ft, W1.5-1.8m/5-6ft. F4-5. Z5-8.

R. sanguineum. The flowering currant, a shrub from western North America, was first introduced to Britain by plant hunter David Douglas in 1826. Since then, many selections have been made, most very similar, with a fairly stiff, upright habit; pendulous flower clusters on naked stems are quickly joined by emerging, downy, bright green leaves, and often followed by black fruit. Coloured forms are brightest in bud before flowers open, gradually becoming paler. Unless otherwise indicated, all below H1.8-2.4m/6-8ft, W1.5-1.8m/5-6ft. F4-5. Z5-7.

'**Albescens**' is white, flushed pink. '**Atrorubens Select**', a Dutch improvement on '**Atrorubens**', has larger, maroon-red flowers. The distinctly attractive '**Brocklebankii**' is slower-growing, with bright golden-yellow leaves and reddish-pink flowers, the leaves maintaining their colour all year, even in shade. H1.2-1.5m/4-5ft, W1.5-1.8m/5-6ft. '**Carneum**' is the best pink, with softly coloured blooms. The best red for the smaller garden is still the compact '**King Edward VII**', with large racemes of deep crimson flowers. '**Porky's Pink**', a distinctive name, is similar to '**Albescens**'. '**Pulborough Scarlet**' is more vigorous (eventually up to 3m/10ft), with rose-red, white-centred flowers. '**Red Pimpernel**', long-flowering, has dense racemes of rose-red flowers. '**Tydeman's White**' has pinkish buds and masses of silver-white flowers on long trusses. The Canadian introduction, '**White Icicle**', has large, white flowers flushed pink with age.
R. speciosum. The flowering gooseberry is a garden-worthy shrub from California. It is often used as a wall shrub where it can be fan-trained, but it is attractive, too, free-standing in a sheltered spot. It has an erect, vase-shaped, branching habit, the fuschia-like bright red flowers dangling from the reddish stems as bright green leaves appear in mid- to late spring. Little or no pruning required. H1.8-2.1m/6-7ft, W2.1-3m/7-10ft. F4-5. Z8-9.

ROSA Rose

All roses are shrubs, but this simple statement hides the tremendous variety within the genus and the range of uses possible. Here, with such limited space, only general guidelines can be given and a few selections in each main group listed. Shrub, ground cover, and climbing and rambling roses are included below, as they fit within the scope of this book. Detailed advice and lists of bush roses (Hybrid Teas and Floribundas), patio roses (Dwarf Cluster Roses) and miniature types must be sought elsewhere.

There are roses for floral colour, fragrance and beauty; for autumn and winter fruits; and for handsome foliage. Some are for climbing walls and fences; others for rambling over banks and other shrubs; for ground cover, hedges, window boxes and tubs; and a few are used as short-lived, indoor flowering plants. On the minus side, some are extremely vigorous and most are thorny, although this can sometimes be an advantage! Some flower briefly or intermittently, whilst others are prone to

Ribes sanguineum 'Red Pimpernel'

pests and diseases, and many need spraying and pruning. Most are unattractive in winter.

Roses succeed best in sun on rich, loamy soil, and dislike extremes of wet or dry. For best results, add well-rotted compost when planting, and give an annual dressing of fertilizer. Most roses also benefit from mulching with well-rotted compost. Prune as new buds swell in early spring, firstly any thin or dead stems, then to balance the shape. Prune just above the bud at an angle of 45 degrees away from it. Brief individual pruning notes are given with each group.

Gardeners now expect plants, roses included, to provide ongoing interest. Rose breeders are aware of changing needs and have done much in recent years to produce more natural-looking, compact and long-flowering forms, ideal for growing with other plants. Roses are now bred, too, for adaptability to different climates, but quite often those which thrive in southern France may not be as happy in northern Europe or cooler areas of the USA, and vice versa. Local experts know what succeeds best in their region, but keep in mind, if they are nurserymen, their possible prejudices!

Shrub roses

Shrub roses can be species or cultivars, tall specimen plants or low, ground-covering types, recent introductions of which provide colour from summer until well into autumn. Prune only to shape or to control size. If the stems of ground-cover types become old or untidy they can be pruned hard to 15cm/6in above the ground every two or three years.
R. '**Ballerina**'. Outstanding, with bold trusses of recurrent, soft pink, white-centred, weather-resistant flowers. Bushy, spreading habit and glossy green leaves. Good ground cover. H1.2m/4ft, W1.2m/4ft. F7-10. Z6-8.

Ribes sanguineum 'White Icicle'

Rosa 'Ballerina'

Rosa 'Canary Bird'

R. '**Bonica**'. Popular and versatile, with arching branches and masses of small pink flowers for months. Good ground cover. H90cm/3ft, W90cm/3ft. F7-10. Z4-9.
R. '**Canary Bird**'. An early-flowering, modern shrub rose, which mixes well with shrubs or perennials. Long, arching stems clothed with daintily cut leaves, and freely borne, single, canary-yellow, scented flowers. H1.8-2.1m/6-7ft, W1.5-2.1m/5-7ft. F5-6. Z5-9.

Rosa glauca

Rosa moyesii 'Geranium'

Rosa 'Iceberg, Climbing'

R. 'Eye Opener'. Bright red, yellow-centred, single flowers on bold clusters. Repeat-flowering ground cover. H60-75cm/ 24-30in, W90-120cm/3-4ft. F6-9. Z5-8.
R. 'Frühlingsgold'. Large, modern shrub with grey-green foliage, arching branches and profuse, large, semi-double, fragrant yellow flowers. H2.1-2.4m/7-8ft, W2.1-2.4m/7-8ft. F5-6. Z5-9.
R. glauca (syn. *R. rubrifolia*). An excellent, very hardy species for foliage, flower and fruit. Greyish purple young shoots and leaves on slender arching branches, single, cerise-pink flowers with white centres, and rounded, bright red hips in autumn. H1.8-2.1m/6-7ft, W1.5-1.8m/5-6ft. F6-7. Z4-8.
R. 'Graham Thomas'. A modern English shrub rose of note, with yellow, cup-shaped, fragrant flowers for a long period. H1.2m/4ft, W1.2m/4ft. F6-10. Z4-9.

R. 'Heritage'. Similar to the above and equally attractive, with blush-pink flowers. H1.2m/4ft, W1.2m/4ft. F6-10. Z4-9.
R. 'Kent'. An award-winning, repeat-blooming, ground-cover shrub with pure white, semi-double flowers. Weathers well. H45cm/18in, W60-90cm/2-3ft. F7-10. Z5-8.
R. 'Marjorie Fair'. Similar to its parent, *R.* 'Ballerina', but with fragrant, striking carmine-red, white-eyed flowers. H1.2m/4ft, W1.2m/4ft. F7-10. Z6-8.
R. moyesii 'Geranium'. At its peak a glorious sight, the tall, arching, thorny

Rosa 'Mermaid'

branches ablaze with single, bright scarlet flowers and yellow stamens. Flask-shaped, orange-red hips in autumn. H2.4-3m/8-10ft, W2.4m/8ft. F6-7. Z6-8.
R. 'Roseraie de l'Hay'. A thorny, dense, vigorous rugosa shrub rose, with crinkled, disease-resistant foliage and fragrant, wine-red, double blooms for months. Good for vandal-proof hedging. H2.1m/7ft, W1.8m/6ft. F7-10. Z5-8.
R. rubrifolia. See *R. glauca*.
R. 'Surrey'. Outstanding ground-cover rose with beautiful, soft, double, pink flowers. H90cm/3ft, W1.2m/4ft. F7-10. Z6-8.
R. virginiana. A suckering but ornamental species with bright green foliage turning russet-purple to crimson and then yellow in autumn, and large, single, pink flowers followed by shining, round, scarlet-red fruits. Good on drier soils. H1.5-1.8m/5-6ft, W1.8-2.1m/6-7ft. F6-8. Z4-8.

Climbing and rambling roses
Use climbing and rambling roses for walls, over fences, pergolas, trellises and arches, or up trees. Most need tying in and training. Plant as for other climbers, ideally at least 45cm/18in away from a wall, so they can more easily obtain moisture. To prune, reduce side shoots by two thirds in autumn, but only reduce main leading stems if they are too tall. If plants become bare at the base, severely prune one main stem to 30-60cm/1-2ft above ground to encourage

new growth. Ramblers can have old stems cut away in late summer as soon as flowering has finished.
R. 'Albéric Barbier'. An old favourite rambler with vigorous, semi-evergreen, glossy, dark green foliage and fragrant, creamy white, double flowers opening from creamy yellow buds. Good for a tree or an arch. H3-5m/10-16ft, W3-5m/10-16ft. F6-8. Z5-8.
R. 'Cécile Brunner, Climbing'. An old climbing China sport, the small, fully double, fragrant flowers are light pink with deeper pink centres. Often repeat-blooming in autumn. H5-6m/16-20ft, W5-6m/16-20ft. F6-10. Z5-8.
R. 'Compassion'. Very fragrant, repeat-blooming climber with shapely, salmon-pink, apricot-orange shaded blooms and dark, glossy green foliage. Good for pillars and fences. H3m/10ft, W1.8-3m/6-10ft. F7-10. Z5-8.
R. 'Dublin Bay'. Long-flowering climber with clusters of slightly fragrant, crimson flowers and glossy, dark green leaves. H1.8-2.4m/6-8ft, W1.8-2.4m/6-8ft. F7-10. Z6-8.
R. 'Golden Showers'. Modern shrub climber with glossy, dark green foliage, clusters of recurrent, large, fragrant, single, bright yellow flowers, fading to cream. Popular, upright grower. Good for pillars. H2.4-3m/8-10ft, W2.4m/8ft. F6-9. Z5-8.
R. 'Handel'. Climber, with deep green, bronze-tinted leaves, distinctive semi-double, recurrent, cream flowers edged rosy red, slightly fragrant. H3m/10ft, W3m/10ft. F7-9. Z5-8.
R. 'Iceberg, Climbing'. A climbing Floribunda sport with profuse, semi-double, sweetly scented, white flowers, sometimes tinged with pale pink. Repeat-bloomer. H3-4m/10-13ft, W3-4m/10-13ft. F7-10. Z4-8.
R. 'Madame Grégoire Staechelin'. Outstanding, vigorous climber with richly fragrant, large, semi-double, coral-pink blooms, the outer petals splashed with carmine. H5-6m/16-20ft, W3.6-5m/12-16ft. F6-7. Z4-8.
R. 'Mermaid'. At its best a superb old climber, producing a succession of soft, primrose-yellow, single flowers with amber stamens. Can be difficult to establish, and best against a warm, sunny wall, but worth the effort. H5-6m/16-20ft, W5-6m/16-20ft. F6-11. Z6-8.
R. 'New Dawn'. Introduced in 1930, a superb, free-flowering climber, with glossy green foliage and bold clusters of fragrant, blush-pink, semi-double flowers. H4.5m/ 15ft, W3.6-4.5m/12-15ft. F7-10. Z5-8.

ROSMARINUS Rosemary
R. officinalis. This aromatic evergreen is known to all. Its narrow, dark green leaves, silver beneath, are used extensively in cooking, but it is no mean foliage or

Rubus biflorus

Rosmarinus officinalis 'Sissinghurst Blue'

Rubus microphyllus 'Variegatus'

flowering plant either. A Mediterranean native, it revels in hot sun, but adapts surprisingly well. Even when damaged by frost and wind, it usually breaks freely from the base. Light blue flowers appear on growth made the previous year, so unless plants are severely damaged, prune after flowering, usually in midsummer. It makes an irregular, spreading bush, providing good contrast to silver, sun-loving shrubs. H90-150cm/3-5ft, W1.2-1.8m/4-6ft. F4-6. Z7-9.

'Alba' is tender, with white flowers. H90-120cm/3-4ft, W90-120cm/3-4ft. F4-6. Z8-9. 'McConnell's Blue' makes a prostrate mound, useful for tumbling over a path or sunny wall, and hardier than the similar 'Prostratus' (syn. *R. lavandulaceus*). H45cm/18in, W1.2m/4ft. F4-6. Z7-9. The most popular and hardiest cultivar, **'Miss Jessopp's Upright'** (syn. 'Fastigiatus')

makes good hedging, with an erect but informal habit. H1.2-1.5m/4-5ft, W90-120cm/3-4ft. F4-6. Z7-9. **'Sissinghurst Blue'**, a chance seedling raised at Sissinghurst Castle, Kent, England, has an erect habit and rich blue flowers. H90-120cm/3-4ft, W90-120cm/3-4ft. F5-6. Z7-8.

RUBUS Ornamental bramble
This enormous genus of over 400 species is mostly native to the Northern Hemisphere. It includes wild 'brambles' and cultivated raspberries and blackberries, as well as useful ground-cover plants, plants grown for ornamental flowers and fruit and a few for their attractive winter stems, displaying a silver-white 'bloom'. Nearly all are easy to grow in almost any soil, and in sun or quite deep shade. Most have spines or thorns, some vicious, so take care when pruning.

R. 'Benenden'. See *R.* Tridel 'Benenden'.
R. biflorus. An architecturally interesting species with twisted, spreading branches and thick stems covered in white 'bloom'. White flowers only appear on previous season's stems, followed by edible yellow fruits. It needs a lot of space. H1.8-2.4m/6-8ft, W3-4m/10-13ft. F5-6. Z5-9.
R. calycinoides. This prostrate species has light green leaves, downy white beneath, and furry stems. It forms a dense, seldom flowering mat, with white flowers and red fruits in favourable locations. Makes excellent ground cover. H10cm/4in, W1.2m/4ft. F6-7. Z7-8.
R. cockburnianus. This has a spreading habit and thorny, erect stems, dark, fern-like leaves and insignificant white flowers and yellow fruits, which only appear on previous season's stems. In winter, its purple stems are overlaid with a brilliant white 'bloom'. Needs plenty of space. Old flowering stems lose their glaucous bloom, so prune them to the base in late summer, leaving younger, showier ones for winter display, or prune all to the ground in late spring, just before new leaves appear. H2.4-3m/8-10ft, W2.1-3m/7-10ft. F6-7. Z5-9.
R. microphyllus 'Variegatus'. Though untidy, its bright new foliage is spectacularly variegated green, white, purple and pink. Insignificant flowers. Cut to the ground in winter. H60cm/2ft, W1.8m/6ft. F4-5. Z6-9.

Rubus odoratus

Rubus thibetanus 'Silver Fern'

R. odoratus. This suckering, spreading shrub has erect, thornless stems, large-lobed leaves and attractive, purple-pink, fragrant flowers, often followed by edible red berries. Prune any surplus older stems to the ground after flowering. Good in shade. H1.8-2.4m/6-8ft, W1.2-1.8m/4-6ft. F6-8. Z4-9.

R. thibetanus 'Silver Fern'. This easily controllable, first-class suckering shrub, has grey-green, finely cut leaves and arching bright white stems in winter. Prune annually in late spring, to maintain a height of 90-120cm/3-4ft. Purple flowers generally only on two-year wood. Unpruned H1.8-2.4m/6-8ft, W1.5-1.8m/5-6ft. F6-7. Z6-9.

R. tricolor. This fast grower has shiny, evergreen, slightly bronzed leaves, furry, bristly stems, sparse, white flowers and red fruits. It can be tender, but good for banks

Ruscus aculeatus

and under trees. H20-30cm/8-12in, W3m/10ft. F7-8. Z7-9.

R. Tridel 'Benenden' (syn. *R.* 'Benenden'). Though impressive, this hybrid is too enormous for all but the largest garden. Its arching, thornless branches carry single, white, scented flowers with prominent yellow stamens. Prune or thin old wood to the base after flowering, shortening other shoots at the same time, if wished. H3m/10ft, W3m/10ft. F5-6. Z5-9.

RUSCUS

These unusual evergreens, attractive in fruit, are otherwise rather dark and sombre, but being adaptable to almost any soil and deep shade, have a place in the garden.

R. aculeatus. Butcher's broom, the most common species, forms a slow-spreading clump of rigid, green, erect stems clothed in dark green cladodes, which resemble leaves. Tiny, white flowers appear in the centre of the cladodes, followed on females, if males are present, by bright red fruit, excellent for winter decoration. There are rare, self-fertilizing, hermaphrodite forms in cultivation. H60-75cm/24-30in, W60-90cm/2-3ft. F3-4. Z7-8.

RUTA Rue

R. graveolens 'Jackman's Blue'. This selected form of the well-known herb, native of the Mediterranean and southern Europe, is a striking foliage shrub or sub-shrub for full sun and any well-drained soil. Like the species, its deeply divided foliage is aromatic, but more compact and a more vivid ice blue. Both bear clusters of sulphur-yellow flowers held above the foliage, which generally detract from their effectiveness as ornamentals, and are best pinched out. Prune old plants regularly in spring down to new shoots at, or near the base. Handle rues with care since they can irritate skin. H60-90cm/2-3ft, W60-90cm/2-3ft. F7-8. Z6-8.

SALIX Willow

Willows as a group have the reputation of being fast-growing, thirsty trees that eventually take over a garden. While many

Ruta graveolens 'Jackman's Blue'

such trees exist among the 500 or so, largely deciduous, species which grow wild in nearly every continent, willows also include some of the most versatile and attractive shrubs, from dwarf alpines to large shrubs or small trees. Some are grown for foliage, others for spring catkins and a few for bright winter stems which rival dogwoods in impact.

Most are easy to grow in any reasonable, and sometimes poor, soil which is not too dry; many thrive in damp, waterlogged conditions few other shrubs would tolerate. Most grow and look well beside water; low, creeping forms are ideal for hanging over a wall. Willows are dioecious, with male and female flowers or catkins on separate plants; often one or the other, usually the male, is showier.

Prune prostrate forms to control spread as required when catkins finish. Tall, shrubby types need little pruning but you can remove some old stems to allow rejuvenation from ground level, or reduce stems by half in early spring as new growth appears.

S. alba. Not much to look at in summer, but very rewarding in winter, few plants show up brighter in the winter sun than **'Britzensis'** (syn. 'Chermesina') and **'Vitellina'**, both trees which if unpruned would reach 10m/33ft or more. The former has shining, orange-red stems, the latter bright yellow ones. Prune both hard each year when new leaves appear, to the ground for a multi-stemmed shrub, or allow them to make a trunk. Prune back to the same point each spring. They make annual stems of 1.8-2.4m/6-8ft. W1.8-2.4m/6-8ft.

S. apoda. This rare, prostrate, creeping species has bare stems and erect, woolly, silver catkins which gradually reveal golden anthers, followed by glossy young leaves. Choose the male clone. Excellent for rock gardens. H15-30cm/6-12in, W90-120cm/3-4ft. F3. Z4-7.

S. arbuscula. This vigorous ground cover has dense, shiny green leaves, but unspectacular catkins. H30-60cm/1-2ft, W1.5-1.8m/5-6ft. F4-5. Z4-8.

S. 'Boydii'. A chance hybrid, this is a gem for troughs or alpine gardens, its stubby, erect branches forming a miniature tree. Shy to show grey, woolly catkins, but oval, silver-grey new leaves are attractive. H30cm/1ft, W20-30cm/8-12in. F5. Z4-7.

S. caprea 'Kilmarnock'. The popular Kilmarnock willow has an unnatural form, top-grafted onto a stem, from which its branches weep almost vertically. It is briefly eye-catching when the branches break into silver catkins, with golden-yellow anthers on males. It fits only into the most formal schemes, though as prostrate ground cover it looks far more natural. Thin out congested branches as specimens age. The female **'Weeping Sally'** also has silver catkins. For both, height depends on height of stem on which grafted, usually 1.8-2.4m/6-8ft. W1.8-2.4m/6-8ft. F3-4. Z5-8.

S. erythroflexuosa. See *S. × sepulcralis* 'Erythroflexuosa'.

S. exigua. The coyote willow is a graceful, tall shrub or small tree with slender branches and branchlets clothed in narrow, silver leaves. A superb background foliage plant. Can be pruned hard every few years to rejuvenate. H3-4m/10-13ft, W2.1-3m/7-10ft. F4-5. Z6-8.

S. fargesii. This slow-growing bush has stout, erect branching stems, the previous year's growth like polished mahogany, with maroon winter buds. Catkins appear with the large leaves. H1.2-1.5m/4-5ft, W90-120cm/3-4ft. F4-5. Z6-8.

S. gracilistyla 'Melanostachys' (syn. *S*. 'Kurome'). A striking shrub, with shiny, deep purple stems and black catkins. Prune every other year when catkins have finished. H1.8-2.4m/6-8ft, W1.5-1.8m/5-6ft. F3. Z5-8.

S. hastata 'Wehrhahnii'. Tall, erect, purplish stems contrast with bright silver catkins, the bright green leaves later becoming dark, glossy green. H1.5m/5ft, W1.5-1.8m/5-6ft. F3. Z6-9.

S. helvetica. One of the brightest dwarf willows, the Swiss willow is a multi-branched shrub with greyish white catkins and bright silvery-grey leaves, white beneath. H60-75cm/24-30in, W60-90cm/2-3ft. F4-5. Z6-7.

S. integra 'Hakuro-nishiki' (syn. 'Albomaculata'). This Japanese, loose, twiggy shrub has bright shrimp-pink shoots opening to mottled, variegated cream and white leaves. Most effective pruned back in early spring. Best in sun or light shade where not too dry. Can be slow to establish. H1.8m/6ft, W1.2-1.5m/4-5ft. F4. Z6-7.

S. irrorata. Its winter stems are blackish purple with a distinctly whitish bloom, the small catkins appearing before the bright green leaves, blue-grey beneath. Prune annually in late spring for best stem colour. Height then 1.2-1.8m/4-6ft. Unpruned H3m/10ft, W3-5m/10-16ft. F4. Z5-9.

S. lanata. The deservedly popular woolly willow forms a low, spreading bush of rigid branches, its silver-yellow catkins followed by soft, grey-green, downy leaves. H60-90cm/2-3ft, W60-90cm/2-3ft. F4-5. Z4-6.

S. purpurea 'Gracilis' (syn. 'Nana'). For waterside planting, the dwarf purple osier is ideal, its narrow, willowy, purplish stems carrying small, purplish catkins, followed by slender, grey-green leaves. Prune only to improve density. H1.2-1.5m/4-5ft, W90-120cm/3-4ft. F3-4. Z4-7.

S. repens. This variable species has produced many ground-cover forms, including the semi-prostrate 'Argentea', with long, spreading and arching stems,

Salix irrorata

Salix hastata 'Wehrhahnii'

Salix reticulata

Salix integra 'Hakuro-nishiki'

small, yellow catkins and silvery leaves, and 'Voorthuizen', an equally vigorous Dutch form, densely branched, with silver-grey, later grey-green, leaves. Both H60-90cm/2-3ft, W1.5-2.4m/5-8ft. F3-4. Z4-8.

S. reticulata. This native of the Northern Hemisphere forms a ground-hugging mat of branches with round, dark, shiny, heavily veined leaves, greyish white beneath. Its small catkins appear after the leaves. Ideal for the alpine garden where not too dry. H5-10cm/2-4in, W90cm/3ft. F4-5. Z2-5.

S. × sepulcralis 'Erythroflexuosa' (syn. *S. erythroflexuosa*). An Argentinian hybrid making a small tree with curiously twisted branches and leaves. In winter orange-yellow, contorted stems are very striking. Pruned to the ground each spring it forms a fascinating dwarfer shrub for winter colour. H10m/33ft, W5-6m/16-20ft. F4. Z6-9.

Salix × sepulcralis 'Erythroflexuosa'

Salvia officinalis 'Purpurascens'

SALVIA Sage

S. officinalis. Common sage, an indispensable evergreen or semi-evergreen culinary herb, native to southern Europe, has also produced pleasing, if unreliably hardy, forms with attractive foliage. They are easy, low-growing shrubs for any well-drained soil in full sun or part shade, but foliage colour is most effective in sun. The species has grey-green leaves and violet-blue flower spikes above the foliage. Young plants grow rapidly but quickly become

Sambucus racemosa 'Plumosa Aurea'

Sambucus racemosa 'Sutherland'

Sambucus nigra 'Guincho Purple'

woody; prune back in spring into older wood at least every two years to rejuvenate. Dieback can occur due to excessively wet conditions or frosts; remove dead growth as necessary. Cuttings root easily, and a few taken in autumn provide replacements for late spring. There are various coloured-foliage forms, but they are shy to flower in cool climates. **'Icterina'** (syn. 'Variegata') has leaves splashed and variegated with creamy yellow, golden-yellow and light green. **'Purpurascens'** has purple younger

Santolina chamaecyparissus

shoots, older leaves turning soft grey-green. The most tender but colourful **'Tricolor'** has grey-green leaves boldly marked white and pink, its new shoots purple-tinged red. All H60-75cm/24-30in, W75-90cm/30-36in. F6-7. Z7-9.

SAMBUCUS Elder

Among the elders are attractive garden forms as well as coarse, weedy types. All hardy elders are deciduous, usually forming vigorous, medium to large shrubs or small trees with hollow, pithy stems and flat heads or erect panicles of white flowers, often followed by red, black or purple fruit, sometimes used in making jelly or wine.

Elders are very adaptable, growing in acid or alkaline soils, ranging from very wet to dry, though a moist loam is ideal. They tolerate shade, but sun or light shade is needed by coloured-foliage forms. With these types, prune in late winter to a 90-120cm/3-4ft framework or, if required, more drastically, to 30cm/1ft, to produce strong stems and bright new foliage. If pruned the flowers will be lost on the spring-flowering *S. racemosa*, but *S. nigra* and *S. canadensis* flower in midsummer and, if similarly pruned, flowers often still appear, but some weeks later.

S. canadensis. The American elder is a vigorous, variable shrub with pinnate leaves and large, slightly domed, white flower heads, followed by purple-black fruit. **'Aurea'** has bright gold leaves all summer, followed by red fruit. **'Maxima'**, a robust curiosity, has impressive leaves and huge flower heads, up to 40cm/16in across. All H2.4-3m/8-10ft, W3m/10ft. F7-8. Z4-9.

S. nigra. The common or European elder, a large shrub or small tree, grows wild all over Europe, and is seldom used as a garden shrub. There are several interesting foliage forms. All respond well to regular annual pruning. **'Albovariegata'**, with dark green, white-edged leaves. **'Aurea'**, the golden elder, with bright yellow foliage, dulling with age. **'Aureo-marginata'**, with gold-edged leaves. **'Guincho Purple'** (syn. 'Purpurea'), with black-purple leaves, in vivid contrast to its white flowers. **'Laciniata'**, with graceful, deeply cut, green leaves. **'Pulverulenta'**, less vigorous, with leaves striped and splashed white. All tend to dislike high humidity. All H2.4-3m/8-10ft, W2.4-3m/8-10ft. F6-7. Z5-7.

S. racemosa. The red-berried elder, native to Europe, Siberia and western Asia, is an erect shrub with arching branches and clusters or panicles of relatively small, creamy white flowers. Red fruits appear in favourable climates in mid- to late summer. Attractive garden forms with striking, golden-yellow foliage include **'Plumosa Aurea'** and **'Sutherland'** (syn. 'Sutherland Gold'), with finely cut, coppery yellow leaves, brighter yellow in summer. Primrose-yellow flowers are sometimes followed by red fruit, but neither appear if plants are severely pruned. 'Plumosa Aurea' leaves can scorch, less likely with 'Sutherland'. All H3m/10ft, W2.4-3m/8-10ft. F3. Z3-6. Much less vigorous is the graceful **'Tenuifolia'**, an attractive, slow-growing dwarf with finely cut, lacy, dark green foliage, purplish when young. H90-150cm/3-5ft, W90-120cm/3-4ft. F3-4. Z3-5.

SANTOLINA Cotton lavender
These sun-loving, dwarf, evergreen shrubs from southern Europe and the Mediterranean have cypress-like, grey or green foliage on soft, semi-woody stems, and make low, spreading mounds. Most have profuse, yellow button flowers, given full sun and well-drained soil. They grow quickly and can soon look untidy unless pruned annually or every other year in mid-spring. Prune all branches away to just above newly developing shoots.

S. chamaecyparissus (syn. *S. incana*). Still the most popular species, perhaps because it is reliably hardy and vigorous, with bright silver-grey, woolly foliage in summer, dull grey in winter, and yellow flowers which last for several weeks. H45-60cm/18-24in, W60-90cm/2-3ft. F7. Z6-9. **'Nana'**, a compact, dense bush with smaller leaves and flowers than the species but similarly attractive. There may be more than one form under this name. H30-45cm/12-18in, W45-60cm/18-24in. F6-8. Z6-9.

S. incana. See *S. chamaecyparissus*.

S. virens. This distinct alternative to the grey-leaved forms has bright green foliage, in vivid contrast to its deep yellow flowers. H45-60cm/18-24in, W45-60cm/18-24in. F7-8. Z7-9.

SARCOCOCCA Sweet box
Related to box, this small group of glossy, evergreen shrubs from southern and eastern Asia, has flowers which, if insignificant to the eye, provide a heady winter and spring fragrance, commending them for garden use and indoor decoration. They grow well in sun but are best in light shade and tolerate even deep shade, slowly spreading as clumps or suckers. Trim back tall forms which get untidy immediately after flowering.

S. confusa. A clump-forming, dense shrub with erect branches, pointed, dark, glossy leaves, clusters of fragrant, creamy white flowers and, often, black, shiny fruit. H1.5-1.8m/5-6ft, W1.5-1.8m/5-6ft. F2-3. Z7-8.

S. hookeriana digyna. This selected form of the species from western China has an untidy habit, spreading by suckers, with lance-shaped leaves, but worth garden space for its fragrance. Its pinkish flowers appear over several months, followed by

Sarcococca humilis

black berries. **'Purple Stem'** gets its name from its purple young stems. Both 1.2m/4ft, W1.2m/4ft. F12-3. Z6-8.

S. humilis. Few would give this low-growing, dense shrub a second glance in summer, but in winter its small, creamy white flowers fill a garden with their lovely fragrance. The black fruits are not always freely produced. Grows well in deep shade and is excellent near a door. H30-45cm/12-18in, W45-60cm/18-24in. F1-2. Z6-8.

S. ruscifolia chinensis. This form is more widely grown than the species, having narrower leaves and reputedly being more vigorous. It has fragrant white flowers, with crimson fruits following. H75-120cm/30-48in, W75-90cm/30-36in. F11-3. Z7-8.

SCHISANDRA Magnolia vine
A genus of about twenty-five species of twining, mostly Asian, climbers. Those described are all deciduous, thriving in moist, fertile, acid or alkaline loam, and sun or part shade. Their dangling, bell flowers appear on short stalks from the leaf axils and are often followed by attractive, long spikes of red fruit.

S. chinensis. From China, Japan and Korea, this has clusters of fragrant, pale pink or white flowers, followed by red fruit. H4-5m/13-16ft, W4-5m/13-16ft. F4-5. Z6-9.

S. rubriflora. A Himalayan species, sometimes sold as *S. grandiflora rubriflora*. Large leaves and solitary deep crimson flowers. H3-4m/10-13ft, W3-4m/10-13ft. F6. Z7-10.

S. sphenanthera. This Chinese species makes a good wall shrub, with ovate leaves and small, orange-red flowers borne on slender, drooping stalks. H3-4m/10-13ft, W3-4m/10-13ft. F5-6. Z7-10.

Schisandra sphenanthera

289

Schizophragma hydrangeoides 'Roseum'

Senecio 'Sunshine'

Skimmia × confusa 'Kew Green'

Skimmia reevesiana

SCHIZOPHRAGMA

S. hydrangeoides. This rare, deciduous Japanese and Korean climber is closely allied and similar to climbing hydrangea, *Hydrangea petiolaris*. It may take some encouragement initially but then attaches itself by aerial roots to trees, stumps, walls or fences, its deep green, oval, toothed leaves making a dense cover. When mature, wispy beige flowers are produced, terminating in showier cream bracts. The form **'Roseum'**, with rose-pink bracts, is even rarer. Both thrive in most moist soils in half sun or shade. Both H3m/10ft, W3-4m/10-13ft. F8. Z5-9.

SENECIO

Among this enormous genus of ornamental and weedy perennials are sun-loving but rather tender shrubs, mostly native to New Zealand, providing attractive foliage and flowers. They thrive in seaside locations, withstanding strong, salt-laden winds, but are less hardy in lower temperature areas, where they need sun and good drainage. Some authorities now list the woody types under *Brachyglottis*.

S. **'Sunshine'**. Widely grown and deservedly popular, it was formerly and often still is listed as *S. greyi* or *S. laxifolius*. The true *S. greyi* is tender, with soft grey, felted leaves. 'Sunshine' is hardier, making a compact, later spreading, bush, its white, woolly stems clothed with grey-green, leathery leaves, white beneath. In a warm, sunny position it has masses of golden-yellow, daisy-like flowers. In spring, prune established shrubs lightly annually and older, woody plants to 10cm/4in of the ground every few years for rejuvenation. H90-120cm/3-4ft, W1.2-1.5m/4-5ft. F6-8. Z9-11.

SKIMMIA

Skimmias are slow-growing, dwarf to medium-sized shrubs, valued for their evergreen leaves, mostly fragrant flowers and bright red fruit. Except for the hermaphrodite, or self-fertilizing, *S. reevesiana*, a male form is needed to fertilize the fruiting female, though one male is enough for several females. Female flowers are usually less showy than those of males.

Skimmias have attractive, year-round foliage, spring flowers and fruits which develop in late summer and last through winter. They prefer moist, acid, fertile soil, but on heavy soils, they tolerate some lime. Light shade is best but they tolerate sun if moisture is available, and succeed in deep shade if not too dry, though compactness, flowering, foliage colour and fruiting may be affected. They benefit from fertilizer and an annual mulch of well-rotted compost. Little or no pruning is needed, though old plants usually rejuvenate if cut close to the ground in spring.

Skimmias often seem to grow well in containers, and look tempting when grown by expert nurserymen, but they can be difficult to sustain in garden conditions.

***S. × confusa* 'Kew Green'**. A first-class evergreen shrub, one of several selections made from a cross between *S. japonica* and *S. anquetilia*. A male form which makes an attractive, mounded bush of glossy, bright green leaves, pungent when crushed, becoming darker with age and in shade. Its large, pyramidal, freely produced heads of sweetly fragrant, creamy white flowers with golden anthers rival any spring-flowering evergreen. Relatively easy to please, it is ideal for a moist, shady spot. H90-120cm/3-4ft, W90-120cm/3-4ft. F2-4. Z7-9.

S. japonica. The Japanese skimmia is the most common species grown, but is variable in the wild and equally so in cultivation, so choose named selections. Unless otherwise indicated, all H60-90cm/2-3ft, W60-90cm/2-3ft. F3-5. Z7-8. The male **'Bronze Knight'** is similar to 'Rubella'. **'Emerald King'** is a bushy, male form with pyramidal heads of bronze-green winter buds opening to fragrant white. **'Fructo Albo'** has dense clusters of white flowers and, if fertilized by a male, white fruit, but can be difficult. **'Nana Femina'**, a popular female, has dark green leaves and large heads of bright red fruit. **'Nana Mascula'** (formerly 'Rogersii Nana'), a male, with prominent, white winter buds and white flowers, is smaller. H30-60cm/1-2ft, W30-60cm/1-2ft. One of the best is a free-fruiting female, **'Nymans'**, with narrow leaves, an open habit, and bright red fruit. **'Rubella'**, one of the best male forms, is often seen as a pot plant. It makes a dense bush of dark green leaves, reddish-brown in winter, as are the leaf stalks and flower spikes. Bronze-red buds in winter open to reveal pink-flushed petals and yellow anthers; very fragrant flowers.

S. reevesiana. The well-known hermaphrodite species, seen containerized, laden with bright red fruit in garden centres, is not always so satisfying in the garden. It forms a low, spreading, open plant with panicles of fragrant, white flowers but is seldom free-fruiting in garden conditions. Dislikes lime. H45-60cm/18-24in, W60-90cm/2-3ft. F4-5. Z7-8.

SOLANUM Potato vine

There are some useful, South American wall shrubs and climbers in this vast genus, which also includes the potato. Those below are best on sheltered sunny walls in any dryish soil.

S. crispum 'Glasnevin'. This is the best and hardiest form of the climbing potato, or Chilean potato tree, *S. crispum*. 'Glasnevin', also sold as 'Autumnale', is semi-evergreen in mild districts, making vigorous growth from pithy stems. It has oval green leaves and profuse clusters of potato-like, lightly fragrant, purplish blue flowers, followed by creamy white, poisonous fruit. It is inclined to flower at the top of the plant, becoming bare at the base, so prune back by half in spring every season or two. H3-4m/10-13ft, W3-4m/10-13ft. F7-9. Z7-9.

S. jasminoides. The potato vine, or jasmine nightshade, is a fairly tender, semi-evergreen, rather woody, twining species with successive clusters of fragrant, pale blue, yellow-centred flowers, followed by insignificant fruit. **'Album'** has white, fragrant flowers. Prune as for *S. crispum* 'Glasnevin'. H5m/16ft, W5m/16ft. F6-8. Z9.

SORBARIA

These strong-growing, deciduous, suckering shrubs, though attractive in foliage and flower, must be selected and sited with care. Native to Asia, they have light green, pinnate leaves and white flowers on fluffy terminal panicles, borne on current season's growth. They prefer good, fairly moist soil and sun or light shade, but are adaptable. Some tall species can be invasive and may need curbing. Unpruned old plants can form a congested thicket, so prune some older stems to the ground each year in late winter, and shorten others to promote new vigorous flowering stems.

S. aitchisonii. This graceful plant has reddish young branches and foliage, and pyramidal heads of white flowers, lasting for some weeks. H2.4-3m/8-10ft, W1.8-2.4m/6-8ft. F8. Z6-8.

S. sorbifolia. Hardier and more useful in the smaller garden, but making less height on dry soil, this forms an erectly branched, suckering shrub, producing early reddish pink shoots and sorbus-like leaves, later becoming green, its stems topped by cloud-like, white flowers. Under control and in the right spot, a shrub of merit. H1.5-2.4m/5-8ft, W1.5-1.8m/5-6ft. F8. Z2-8.

SORBUS Rowan, mountain ash

Most species and cultivars in this large genus are trees, but there are excellent shrubs worthy of wider use, for their attractive foliage, often with good autumn colour, and late summer and autumn fruit, even though birds often strip them bare. Most are happy in any reasonable soil which

Solanum crispum 'Glasnevin'

Sorbaria sorbifolia

does not dry out, and prefer an open site, though they will tolerate some shade. The majority are grafted onto a stem, but many shrubby species, including the first two described below, are best raised from seed and allowed to develop naturally as a multi-branched bush.

S. cashmiriana. This beautiful, slow-growing species from the western Himalayas is of open, shrubby habit, with graceful, deeply divided leaves. Panicles of pink buds open white and, on older plants, reliably produce clusters of large, succulent, white fruit in late summer. H2.4-3m/8-10ft, W1.8-2.4m/6-8ft. F5. Z5-7.

S. koehneana. This easy-going shrub or small tree has dark green leaves, crimson-purple in autumn, clusters of pure white flowers, and bunches of small, porcelain-white fruit in late summer, even on young plants. H1.8-2.4m/6-8ft, W1.8-2.4m/6-8ft. F5-6. Z6-7.

S. poteriifolia (syn. *S. pygmaea*). Sometimes confused with *S. reducta*, this is a miniature, creeping species, with dark green leaves, pink flowers and deep pink fruit. H20-30cm/8-12in, W30-45cm/12-18in. F5. Z6-7.

S. pygmaea. See *S. poteriifolia*.

S. reducta. This dwarf, suckering, oriental species varies considerably in height according to situation. It grows best with ample moisture, though it looks picturesque as an alpine garden shrub. It has erect stems and short, deeply divided leaflets, dark green in summer and often coppery orange in autumn. White flowers and round, rose-pink fruit, often sparsely borne. H30-60cm/1-2ft, W30-120cm/1-4ft. F5. Z5-7.

Sorbus cashmiriana

SPARTIUM Spanish broom

S. junceum. This Mediterranean native and the only species in the genus is closely related to *Cytisus* and *Genista*, with similar requirements of sun and good drainage. It makes a tall, upright shrub, often bare at the base on older plants, with young, slender stems a deep green. Growing in any well-drained soil, it thrives on chalk and in coastal areas, with large, deep yellow, pea-like flowers. Prune green shoots when quite young to prevent plants becoming leggy, gathering several stems together and cutting with a sharp knife. It flowers on growth made in the same year, so prune to within 2.5cm/1in of the previous year's growth, just as shoots begin to appear in spring. Never prune into old wood. New shoots will form rapidly, giving a bright display within a few weeks. H2.4-3m/8-10ft, W1.8-2.4m/6-8ft. F7-8. Z7-11.

SPIRAEA

Spiraeas are some of the most useful and ornamental hardy shrubs, particularly for a small garden. Some tall species may not be worth garden space, however, since, like *Deutzia* and *Philadelphus*, once their brief, if spectacular, flowering period is over, they look dull for the rest of the year.

They are all deciduous, flowering shrubs, varying in size and shape, from reliably dwarf forms to those which are over 1.8m/6ft high, and flowering from late spring until early autumn, depending on type. Most grow in any reasonable, even poor,

soil, though not on thin chalk or very dry soil, and in sun or light shade.

S. albiflora. See *S. japonica* 'Alba'.

S. × arguta (syn. *S.* 'Arguta'). This popular hybrid, commonly known as bridal wreath, was introduced over 100 years ago, but is still popular. Its arching branches carry a mass of dazzling white flowers. Vigorous and tall, it makes an effective hedge. Prune some old stems to the base and shorten others, if required, immediately after flowering. H1.8-2.4m/6-8ft, W1.8-2.4m/6-8ft. F4-5. Z5-8.

S. betulifolia aemeliana. This dwarf forms a

Spiraea betulifolia aemeliana

twiggy shrub of reddish brown stems, oval, bright green leaves which darken, with excellent autumn colour, and flat heads of white flowers. Prune in late winter as for *S. japonica*, if necessary. H60-75cm/24-30in, W60-75cm/24-30in. F6. Z5-8.

S. × billiardii 'Triumphans'. This tall, suckering shrub has sturdy, upright stems, serrated, oval leaves and conical heads of purple-pink flowers. Can be invasive, but is easily controlled. Strong growth results if occasionally pruned to the ground in early spring. H1.8-2.4m/6-8ft, W1.8-2.4m/6-8ft. F7-8. Z4-8.

S. × bumalda 'Anthony Waterer' and **'Goldflame'.** See under *S. japonica*.

S. × cinerea 'Grefsheim'. This Norwegian shrub is attractive, even if the flowering period is short. It forms a dense bush with arching branches, wreathed in masses of white flowers. Prune as for *S. × arguta*. H1.2m/4ft, W1.2-1.5m/4-5ft. F5. Z5-8.

S. japonica. The Japanese spiraea cultivars are some of the best garden shrubs, easy to grow, generally dwarf and with flowers that continue for many weeks. The recent addition of coloured-foliage forms provides added interest, from early spring until autumn leaf-fall. Many of these make excellent dwarf hedges. All benefit from annual pruning in late winter, at least by half the length of the previous year's growth, or even to within 15cm/6in of the ground. Best in sun or light shade; new shoots, especially golden-leaved forms, may be damaged by spring frost but soon recover. Can be prone to mildew. All Z4-8.

'**Alba**' (syn. *S. albiflora*) is a pleasing, if sometimes weak, shrub with light green leaves and white flowers. H60cm/2ft, W60cm/2ft. F6-8. The ever popular '**Anthony Waterer**' (syn. *S. × bumalda* 'Anthony Waterer') is perhaps the most vigorous, strong and bushy of the coloured-foliage forms. Its leaves are sometimes yellow or variegated and its large, flat heads of bright carmine flowers are borne over a long period. H90-120cm/3-4ft, W90-120cm/3-4ft. F7-9. '**Bullata**' (its former name, *S. crispifolia*, describes its crinkled, green leaves) is a dwarf, round bush with rosy crimson flowers. H30-45cm/12-18in, W30-45cm/12-18in. F6-8.

'**Dart's Red**' is a coloured foliage form similar to 'Anthony Waterer' but has deeper carmine-red flowers. H90-120cm/3-4ft, W90-120cm/3-4ft. F7-9. '**Gold Mound**' and '**Golden Princess**' are considerably more colourful than 'Goldflame'; their early shoots are more yellow and bronze respectively, their summer leaves brighter, with no hint of reversion. 'Golden Princess' is round and compact, with golden-yellow leaves and pink flowers. H60-90cm/2-3ft, W60-75cm/24-30in. F7-8. 'Gold Mound' is low and more spreading, its leaves

Spartium junceum

Spiraea prunifolia 'Plena'

brighter yellow and its flowers a brighter pink. H60-90cm/2-3ft, W75-90cm/30-36in. F6-8. The Canadian **'Goldflame'** (syn. *S. × bumalda* 'Goldflame') has coppery crimson young shoots and deep golden-yellow leaves in early summer, fading by the time rose-pink flowers appear; prone to reversion to green. H60-90cm/2-3ft, W60-90cm/2-3ft. F6-7. The green-leaved **'Little Princess'** forms a broad dome of densely congested stems with free-flowering, pretty, pink flowers. H45-60cm/18-24in, W60-75cm/24-30in. F6-7.

'Nana' (syn. 'Alpina') forms a dense, round, later spreading, bush with green leaves and deep pink flowers, fading with age. Light prune only. H30-45cm/12-18in, W60-75cm/24-30in. F6. **'Shirobana'** (syn. 'Shibori'), a popular, green-leaved, Japanese introduction, carries both white and red flowers on the same plant. H90-120cm/3-4ft, W90-120cm/3-4ft. F7-8.

S. nipponica. This spiraea has produced some outstanding forms. The species and cultivars have erect, arching branches clothed at the ends with clusters of small, white flowers, creating the appearance of a snow-laden shrub. Prune out old and congested branches after flowering or in late winter. The most popular variety, of similar size to the species, is aptly named **'Snowmound'**. Both H1.8-2.4m/6-8ft, W1.8-2.4m/6-8ft. F5-6. Z4-8.

S. prunifolia 'Plena'. This attractive shrub has arching stems, serrated, oval leaves, a brilliant orange-red in autumn, and white, densely petalled, double flowers. Prune as for *S. × arguta*. H1.5-1.8m/5-6ft, W1.5m/5ft. F4-5. Z5-8.

S. thunbergii. A Chinese, free-flowering, dense, twiggy bush with arching branches; profuse, white flowers display along the stems before the leaves. On established plants, prune away older and weakest stems after flowering. A form with leaves edged with white and pink shoots, **'Mt. Fuji'**, gives a longer period of interest. Both H90-120cm/3-4ft, W1.2m/4ft. F5. Z5-8.

STACHYURUS

There are only two, similar species in this small genus of deciduous shrubs that are hardy. Both are beautiful, with erect, later spreading, branches and pale yellow, cup-shaped flowers on short, gracefully pendulous racemes formed the previous autumn. They flower on two-year-old wood; the younger, more vigorous stems are reddish purple. Humus-rich, moist but well-drained, acid loam is best, though they tolerate some lime. Place in light shade or sun, protected from spring frosts, for new growth can be damaged, though flowers seem immune. If necessary to restrict size, prune only recently flowered stems down to the base immediately after flowering,

Spiraea japonica 'Golden Princess'

Spiraea japonica 'Shirobana'

to encourage stronger shoots to develop.

S. chinensis. This has narrow, lance-shaped, dull green leaves, paler beneath. **'Magpie'** offers summer interest, too, with grey-green leaves edged with white and suffused reddish pink. Both H1.5-1.8m/5-6ft, W1.8-2.4m/6-8ft. F3-4. Z6-8.

S. praecox. This flowers a week or two earlier than *S. chinensis*, and has larger leaves and shorter racemes. H1.8-2.4m/6-8ft, W1.8-2.4m/6-8ft. F3-4. Z6-8.

STAPHYLEA Bladder nut

These large, deciduous shrubs or small trees have erect or pendulous panicles of white or pink flowers, followed by conspicuous, papery, bladder-like seed vessels. Most are easily grown in sun or light shade and moist but well-drained, acid to neutral soils, though they tolerate some lime.

S. colchica. The most common species, this has an erect, suckering habit and fragrant, white, lilac-like flowers, followed by inflated capsules. On older plants prune old and dead wood and suckers to base in winter. H1.8-2.4m/6-8ft, W1.2-1.5m/4-5ft. F5-6. Z6-8.

S. holocarpa. This pleasing Chinese species forms a shrub or small tree with spreading branches, trifoliate leaves and pendulous clusters of white flowers, pink in bud. The form **'Rosea'**, with bronze young leaves and blush-pink flowers, is even more desirable. Quite rare in cultivation. Both H1.8-2.4m/6-8ft, W1.5-1.8m/5-6ft. F6. Z6-8.

Stachyurus praecox

Stephanandra tanakae

Symphoricarpos × *doorenbosii* 'Magic Berry'

STEPHANANDRA

Spiraea-like in habit, leaf and flower, these shrubs have less garden value, but are easy to grow in most not too dry soils.

S. incisa. Vigorous and spreading, its branches root as they sweep along the ground, making a dense mass of congested stems. It has deeply cut leaves and clusters of small, creamy flowers on older stems. Excellent ground cover in sun or light shade, but not in a small garden. H90-120cm/3-4ft, W1.5-1.8m/5-6ft. F6-7. Z4-8. 'Crispa', most widely grown, makes a dense, low-growing mound with attractively crinkled leaves. Both can be pruned hard in early spring if too large or unruly. H60-90cm/

2-3ft, W1.2-1.5m/4-5ft. F6-7. Z4-8.

S. tanakae. This has large, oval leaves with good autumn colour and dull, creamy yellow flowers on widely arching, pendulous branches. Its rich brown stems are of great value in winter. Prune oldest wood to the base in late winter or early spring, making room for new growth. H1.5-1.8m/5-6ft, W1.5-1.8m/5-6ft. F7. Z6-8.

STRANVAESIA See under PHOTINIA.

SYMPHORICARPOS Snowberry

Widely planted as large-scale ground cover because of their ease in colonizing and often spectacular autumn fruits, but should be used with care in the garden. The common name refers only to *S. albus*, a tall, suckering shrub, used for game coverts and ground cover, but not in gardens. Recent selections and hybrids are less invasive and provide late-season interest. Most are easy to grow on almost any, not too dry soil. Once established, they tolerate dryish shade, but sun or light shade gives best results. Many are vigorous so growth may need to be restricted. Remove spreading suckers, prune old stems to the base and shorten others by half in winter; flowering or fruiting are unaffected, since both are produced on growth made in the same year.

S. × *chenaultii* 'Hancock'. This low-growing, dense hybrid has pinkish flowers and purple-pink fruit when exposed to the light, white-flushed pink elsewhere. Widely used for ground cover in shade, especially under trees. H45-60cm/18-24in, W90-150cm/3-5ft. F7. Z5-7.

S. × *doorenbosii*. Another hybrid, its selections spread relatively slowly. All below, F6-7, Z4-7. 'Magic Berry' has rose-pink fruits. H1.2m/4ft, W1.2m/4ft. 'Mother of Pearl' has white fruit, suffused pink.

H1.5m/5ft, W1.5m/5ft. 'White Hedge', dense, vigorous and upright, freely produces marble-like, white fruit. H1.5-1.8m/5-6ft, W1.5-1.8m/5-6ft.

SYRINGA Lilac

To most people, lilac means only the tall, suckering bushes of common lilac, *S. vulgaris*, and its cultivars, with sweetly fragrant flowers that you usually have to look up to. But there is a much wider range of less well-known species and cultivars, many more suited to the scale of the modern garden.

Some large-flowered forms are undoubtedly spectacular, but are unsuitable for small or natural-looking gardens, and do not give value for space. Most lilacs have a brief flowering period, and the large types look dull the rest of the year. They can be hungry and often suckering, drawing moisture from the surrounding soil, so plant at least the more vigorous types with care. It is worth looking for micro-propagated lilacs which are grown on their own roots. These make bushier plants without the suckering that often occurs with grafted plants.

Most soils will do, though heavy, well-drained alkaline soils are better than acid or peaty types. Lilacs are best in full sun and some demand it to flower well. Pruning varies according to type, the slow-growing forms needing little or none, the tall, vigorous types needing more attention.

Young plants may take time to establish but, with more established plants which need tidying or restricting in size, shorten some stems and branches by half the previous season's growth immediately after flowering. Avoid cutting back too hard because flowers normally appear on two-year-old wood. Ideally, deadhead large-flowered types as soon as they have finished blooming to enhance next season's flowering. If you inherit an old, unruly clump, rejuvenate by pruning all stems to within 15cm/6in of the ground in mid-winter, feeding it with well-rotted compost. Feed all *S. vulgaris* forms to retain vigour.

S. × *chinensis*. The hybrid Rouen lilac arose in France nearly 200 years ago. It forms a compact bush with pendulous branches and hanging clusters of fragrant, pale-lavender flowers. 'Saugeana' (syn. 'Rubra'), is deeper lilac-red. Both H1.5-1.8m/5-6ft, W1.5-1.8m/5-6ft. F5-6. Z4-7.

S. × *hyacinthiflora*. From this hybrid raised by the Lemoine Nursery in France have come many early-flowering selections, mostly upright, with lightly fragrant flowers. 'Alice Eastwood' has double flowers, deep wine-purple in bud, opening pale blue. The popular, vigorous 'Esther Staley' has carmine-red buds, opening pink. All H1.8-2.4m/6-8ft, W1.5-1.8m/5-6ft. F4-5. Z4-7.

Symphoricarpos × *chenaultii* 'Hancock'

Symphoricarpos × *doorenbosii* 'White Hedge'

S. × *josiflexa* 'Bellicent'. One of several Canadian selections from the original hybrid between *S. josikaea* and *S. reflexa*. Outstanding, though of considerable vigour, 'Bellicent' has large, open, pyramidal panicles of fragrant, rose-pink flowers. Prune some stems back by half to control size. H3m/10ft, W1.8m/6ft. F5-6. Z4-7.

S. *meyeri* 'Palibin' (syn. *S. palibiniana*). Often described as dwarf, but growth depends on conditions, plants can eventually exceed 2.4m/8ft. It is a dense shrub, smothered in small panicles of very fragrant, pale pink flowers, even when young. It remains reasonably attractive all year. H1.2-1.5m/4-5ft, W90-120cm/3-4ft. F6. Z4-8.

S. *microphylla*. This compact species is ideal for a small garden. Dense, upright and spreading, it has profuse, short panicles of fragrant, lilac-pink flowers, often with a second flush later in summer. The large-flowering selection **'Superba'** is especially attractive with deep rose-pink flowers, continuing on and off for weeks. Both H90-120cm/3-4ft, W90-120cm/3-4ft. F7 and 8; 'Superba' F7-9. Z4-8.

S. 'Miss Kim'. This fine, slow-growing lilac apparently originated in Korea of uncertain parentage. Freely branching and upright, its pink flower buds open deep lilac, fading to blue. Very floriferous and fragrant. H1.5-1.8m/5-6ft, W90-120cm/3-4ft. F5-6. Z3-8.

S. *palibiniana*. See *S. meyeri* 'Palibin'.

S. × *persica*. The Persian lilac is a small to medium-sized shrub of natural, bushy appearance, with small panicles of sweetly fragrant lilac flowers. Both this and the off-white **'Alba'** have been with us for centuries, though not widely available. Both H1.5-1.8m/5-6ft, W1.2-1.5m/4-5ft. F5 or 6. Z4-7.

S. × *prestoniae*. The Canadian hybrids were bred originally by Isabella Preston in Canada in the early 1900s, and noted for their hardiness and abundant flowers. The large, open panicles are only slightly less fragrant than the common lilac. **'Audrey'**, an older cultivar, has deep pink flowers. **'Elinor'**, deep wine-red in bud, opens to pale lavender-pink. **'Isabella'** has large panicles of lilac-pink. A wider range of vigorous cultivars is now available in Canada and the USA. All H2.4-3m/8-10ft, W2.4-3m/8-10ft. F5-6. Z3-7.

S. *vulgaris*. The species itself is seldom offered but there are numerous cultivars. Lilacs are often unhappy in a container, so these may not look their best at garden centres. *S. vulgaris* types used to be propagated by grafting, but are now much better on their own roots from cuttings or micro-propagation.

They slowly make erect, eventually bushy shrubs, but young plants may not flower for a few years. The single or double flowers are borne in dense panicles in

Syringa meyeri 'Palibin'

Syringa 'Miss Kim'

white, violet, blue, lilac, pink, purple and yellow. All cultivars listed below are scented. **'Charles Joly'**, deep purple, double. **'Congo'**, lilac-red, small heads. **'Firmament'**, free-flowering, blue. **'Katherine Havemeyer'**, dense trusses of deep lavender-purple, fading to lilac-pink. **'Madame Lemoine'**, popular double, white, cream in bud. **'Maud Notcutt'**, large, white panicles. **'Michel Buchner'**, lilac-blue, double. **'Primrose'**, small, pale primrose heads. **'Sensation'**, purple-red flowers, margined white. **'Souvenir de Louis Späth'**, an old cultivar, deep wine-red. All H2.4-3m/8-10ft, W1.5-1.8m/5-6ft. F6. Z4-7/8.

Syringa vulgaris 'Primrose'

Syringa vulgaris 'Souvenir de Louis Späth'

Tamarix ramosissima 'Pink Cascade'

Tamarix tetrandra

Ulex europaeus 'Aureus'

Vaccinium vitis-idaea 'Koralle'

TAMARIX Tamarisk

These distinctive shrubs are often seen in coastal areas but are hardier in colder, inland districts than often thought. Only a few of the fifty or so species are cultivated, most with narrow, upright, later arching branches, feathery, scale-like leaves and plumes of wispy, pink flowers. They grow in almost any well-drained soil, tolerating salt-laden winds, and ideally sun, or light shade. Plants can become unkempt and straggly, so trim every year or two. Prune late summer- and autumn-flowering species to within 2.5cm/1in of old wood in spring before new growth begins; prune spring-flowering species just after flowering.

T. parviflora (syn. *T. tetrandra purpurea*). This very hardy species has purplish stems, bright green leaves and pretty rose-pink flowers. H1.8-2.4m/6-8ft, W1.8-2.4m/6-8ft. F5 or 6. Z5-8.

T. pentandra. See *T. ramosissima*.

T. ramosissima (syn. *T. pentandra*). This has reddy brown branches, bluish-green foliage and clouds of rose-pink flowers. 'Pink Cascade', shell-pink. 'Rosea', rosy pink, very hardy. 'Rubra', deeper pink. All H2.4-3m/8-10ft, W2.4-3m/8-10ft. F8-9. Z3-8.

T. tetrandra. Hardy, early-flowering and rather open and straggly in habit, with arching branches and light pink flowers. H2.4-3m/8-10ft, W2.4-3m/8-10ft. F5-6. Z6-8. Var. *purpurea*. See *T. parviflora*.

ULEX Gorse

U. europaeus. Some forms are certainly ornamental, and were it not so often seen in the wild, the prickly common gorse would

Vaccinium corymbosum

be considered garden-worthy, growing easily on most soils where not too wet and particularly suited to dry, sandy, acid soils, especially near the sea. It has profuse, golden-yellow, pea-shaped flowers, and in mild weather some flower at Christmas, and often on and off almost all year. Gorse is always more compact on poorer, drier soils. To restrict size, prune immediately after flowering on younger, softer wood with shears, but older, straggly plants can be cut to the ground in spring as growth begins. H1.2-1.5m/4-5ft, W1.5-1.8m/5-6ft. F3-6. Z8-9. 'Aureus' has greeny yellow stems; spines and leaves turn clear yellow in summer. H1.2-1.5m/4-5ft, W1.5-1.8m/5-6ft. F4-5. Z8-9. 'Plenus' is denser, with double flowers, ideal with heathers. H60-90cm/2-3ft, W90-120cm/3-4ft. F4-6. Z8-9.

VACCINIUM

This large genus of acid-loving, evergreen and deciduous shrubs includes ornamentals and others, like blueberry (*V. corymbosum*), of considerable economic importance. Cranberry, blueberry and whortleberry are individual species, though the names are sometimes used to refer to the genus as a whole. Most grow wild through the Northern Hemisphere, from the Arctic to higher equatorial regions, and vary widely in type and hardiness. The ornamentals are mostly grown for fruit and foliage, not the modest flowers. Deciduous types have good autumn leaf-colour; the evergreens, often showy, mostly edible berries. Most prefer (and need) moist, acid, peaty soil in sun or part shade; many spread by underground stems.

V. corymbosum. The highbush blueberry provides many fruiting cultivars of blueberry, popular in North America and parts of Europe, but not yet in Britain. The species is also ornamental. Only happy in moist, acid soils, it makes an upright, multi-stemmed shrub with dark bluish-green leaves, turning scarlet and bronze in autumn. Clusters of white-tinged pink, urn-shaped flowers appear before the leaves in spring, followed in summer by blue-black fruits covered in a blue 'bloom'. The tasty fruits are much loved by birds. H1.5-1.8m/5-6ft, W1.2-1.5m/4-5ft. F4-5. Z4-8.

V. floribundum. This evergreen from the Andes is one of the showiest. New shoots are red and new leaves wine-purple, later becoming glossy green. The pink flowers are partly hidden by foliage, but followed by edible, red berries. Provide shelter from severe frost and cold, and desiccating winds. H60-90cm/2-3ft, W60-90cm/2-3ft. F6-7. Z8-9.

V. glauco-album. Native to the Himalayas, this suckering, thicket-forming shrub has large, leathery, evergreen leaves, blue-green in winter, and brilliant, ice-blue new shoots in spring and summer. Flowers are pinkish white, with attractive silvery bracts; berries black with a blue-white bloom. Not quite hardy, so protect from severe frosts. H60-90cm/2-3ft, W60-90cm/2-3ft. F5-6. Z8-9.

V. oxycoccos. The European cranberry spreads widely across all three continents in cooler, damper regions of the Northern Hemisphere. It makes a low, spreading, evergreen bush with small, deep green leaves, silver-blue beneath. Long-lasting, pink flowers with striking, yellow stamens appear on wiry stems, followed by red, edible fruits. Needs moist, peaty soil. H15cm/6in, W60-90cm/2-3ft. F5-6. Z2-5.

V. vitis-idaea. The cowberry is also widespread in northern, cooler latitudes, including the British Isles, forming a dense, creeping shrub of dark, glossy green leaves, with pinkish white, bell-shaped flowers, followed by abundant, shiny red, edible fruit. H15-20cm/6-8in, W60-90cm/2-3ft. F6-8. Z4-7. **'Koralle'** has pink, bell-shaped flowers and larger, if sparser, fruit than the species. It is slightly more vigorous, making a carpet of small leaves; excellent ground cover in shade. H10-15cm/4-6in, W60-90cm/2-3ft. F6-8. Z4-7.

VIBURNUM

Few woody plants are as valuable or varied as viburnums. Evergreen and deciduous shrubs and small trees, most come from a wide area of the Northern Hemisphere, but some of the 200 or so species are from tropical Asia and South America. A few are coarse, but there are garden-worthy viburnums almost all year round, some winter-flowering, most in spring or early summer, early types often fragrant. Some are grown for foliage; many, for their late summer and autumn fruits, or brilliant autumn leaf-colour. Generally easy, most grow in any soil, including chalk. Some need moist soil; others, especially evergreens, may need shelter from cold, desiccating winds.

V. alnifolium (syn. *V. lantanoides*). The hobblebush, from eastern North America, is large, open-growing and excellent in damp shade. Its broad, heart-shaped, downy, ribbed leaves are grey-green in summer, red and purple in autumn. Flat, lace-cap, sterile, white flowers, followed by red fruit, turning black in autumn. H1.8-2.4m/6-8ft, W1.8-2.4m/6-8ft. F6. Z4-6.

V. × bodnantense. These erect, eventually large, bushes produce fragrant flower clusters along the stems, even before the last leaves fall. Pink in bud, they open light pink, fading to white, and being frost-resistant, they last for many weeks. Perhaps the most striking is **'Charles Lamont'**, with deep rose-pink flowers. **'Dawn'** is the most popular form, deeper pink in bud. **'Deben'** is pink in bud, opening white

flushed with pink. All H1.8-2.4m/6-8ft, W1.5-1.8m/5-6ft. F10-3. Z5-8.

V. × burkwoodii. This fragrant, spring-flowering hybrid is now only one of many similar forms, most upright, eventually round, semi-evergreen, often with good autumn colour, the original hybrid nearly deciduous. In winter, round heads of tight, pink buds form, opening white and continuing for many weeks, their fragrance spreading some distance on warm days. Good for cutting. H1.5-1.8m/5-6ft, W1.5-1.8m/5-6ft. F3-5. Z5-8. **'Chenaultii'**, pale pink flowers, fading white. **'Fulbrook'** and **'Park Farm'** are more evergreen, spreading and slightly later flowering.

V. × carlcephalum. This is similar to *V. carlesii*, one of its parents, but has larger, fragrant flower clusters, pink in bud, opening white. H1.5-1.8m/5-6ft, W1.5-1.8m/5-6ft. F5-6. Z6-8.

V. carlesii. From Korea and Japan, this fragrant, deciduous shrub forms tight clusters of flower buds in autumn, becoming pink before opening to white in spring. From Slieve Donard Nursery in Northern Ireland come three fragrant cultivars. **'Aurora'**, red flower buds, opening pink, slow-growing. **'Charis'**, more vigorous, flowers fading to white. **'Diana'**, compact, with red buds, opening pink. All H1.2-1.5m/4-5ft, W1.2-1.5m/4-5ft. F5-6. Z4-8.

V. cassinoides. The witherwood viburnum is a North American species. It is a dense, round, deciduous shrub, with cinnamon-brown, later dark green shoots. Flat, cream flowers, followed by green fruit, turning pink, red and finally deep blue or black;

Viburnum davidii

Viburnum carlesii 'Diana'

Viburnum × bodnantense 'Dawn'

red or crimson autumn leaf colour. H1.2-1.8m/4-6ft, W1.2-1.8m/4-6ft. F6-7. Z5-9.

V. davidii. A popular, evergreen, low, spreading shrub, with leathery, narrow, corrugated leaves, dull flowers, but bright metallic-blue fruit in autumn and winter, not always freely produced. Plant several to ensure cross-pollination – many nurserymen offer fruiting female plants with an identifiable male. Best in light shade and moist soil; protect from severe frost and wind. H60-75cm/24-30in, W90-120cm/3-4ft. F6-7. Z8-9.

V. dilatatum. Improved selections, recently introduced from the United States National Arboretum in Washington DC, are finer than the species, from Japan and China, a large, coarse shrub with white flowers and bright red fruit, if cross-pollinated. **'Catskill'**, compact, good autumn leaf colour, creamy white flowers; long-lasting, red fruit. **'Erie'**, red fruit, turned pink by frost. **'Iroquois'**, dark green leaves, creamy white flowers, shiny red fruit, good autumn colour. **'Xanthocarpum'**, yellow fruit, rare. Average H1.2-1.5m/4-5ft, W1.8-2.4m/6-8ft. F5-6. Z5-8.

Viburnum opulus 'Compactum'

Viburnum opulus 'Xanthocarpum'

Viburnum plicatum 'Mariesii'

Viburnum plicatum 'Watanabe'

V. 'Eskimo'. One of many improved forms bred by the late Don Egolf of the National Arboretum in Washington DC. It is a deciduous or semi-evergreen dwarf shrub, with glossy, dark green leaves and a succession of snowball-white flowers from late spring. Prune after the main flowering to keep density. H1.2-1.5m/4-5ft, W1.2-1.5m/4-5ft. F4-6. Z6-8.

V. farreri (syn. *V. fragrans*). This large, deciduous, erect, Chinese shrub has been superseded by the similar *V.* × *bodnantense* and its forms. Several clones are in cultivation, some looser in habit. It has bronze young leaves and fragrant flower clusters, pink in bud and opening white, continuing spasmodically through all but severe winters. **'Candidissimum'** has light green leaves and white flowers. Both H1.5-1.8m/5-6ft, W1.2-1.5m/4-5ft. F11-3. Z5-8.

V. fragrans. See *V. farreri*.

V. lantanoides. See *V. alnifolium*.

V. opulus. This European native is called guelder rose in Britain, and the European cranberry-bush viburnum in the USA. An easy, deciduous shrub, often found in country hedgerows, it is outstanding in late summer when hung with clusters of succulent, bright red fruit. It prefers moist soil but adapts to drier ones. All selections have maple-like leaves and flat, white, lacecap flowers in early summer. Some have good autumn leaf colour, but fruit appears when leaves are green. **'Aureum'** has bright yellow leaves which can scorch in full sun, but which stay yellow well through summer. Red fruit and reddish brown autumn tints. H1.5-1.8m/5-6ft, W1.2-1.5m/

4-5ft. F6-7. Z3-8. **'Compactum'** is dwarf, free-flowering, with red fruit persisting after leaves have dropped. H90-120cm/3-4ft, W90-120cm/3-4ft. F6-7. Z4-8. **'Nanum'**, a rounded, dwarf bush, seldom flowers but usually has good autumn colour. H60-90cm/2-3ft, W60-90cm/2-3ft. F6-7. Z4-8. **'Notcutt's Variety'** has large, red fruit, and often purple autumn leaves. H2.4-3m/8-10ft, W1.8-2.4m/6-8ft. F6-7. Z4-8. **'Roseum'** (syn. 'Sterile'), the snowball tree, has light green leaves and masses of round, green flower heads, opening white. Non-fruiting. H2.4-3m/8-10ft, W1.8-2.4m/6-8ft. F6. Z4-8. **'Xanthocarpum'** has bright green leaves which contrast with white flowers and golden-yellow fruits, becoming translucent with age. H2.4-3m/8-10ft, W1.8-2.4m/6-8ft. F6-7. Z4-8.

V. plicatum. These include snowball and lacecap types, the latter with central flowers surrounded by larger, sterile florets; both often with fruit following. From Japan and China, they are less hardy than others, but undeniably showy. Best in moist soil, sun or light shade. The species is now rare, but many fine cultivars are sold. Most Z6-8. **'Cascade'**, dense, bushy habit; large, lacecap flowers, often abundant red fruit. H1.5m/5ft, W1.8m/6ft. F5-6. The choice **'Grandiflorum'** needs shade and moist soil, forming an erect shrub with large, pale green, sterile, snowball heads, turning white. H1.5-1.8m/5-6ft, W1.2-1.5m/4-5ft. F5-6. **'Lanarth'** and **'Mariesii'**, wide-spreading, horizontally tiered branches with rows of flat, white florets raised above the branches. Both H1.8m/6ft, W2.4m/8ft. F5-6.

Slower and slightly more tender is **'Pink Beauty'**, with white florets, turning pink. H1.2-1.5m/4-5ft, W1.2-1.5m/4-5ft. F5-6. **'Shasta'**, raised by the late Don Egolf at the United States National Arboretum in Washington DC, is free-flowering, with red fruit, turning black. H1.8m/6ft, W2.4m/8ft. F5-6. **'Watanabe'** (syn. 'Nanum Semperflorens'), from Japan, is narrow and upright, its small, lacecap flowers appearing on young plants, and continuing, in a small way, to bloom through summer. Provide shelter; excellent for small gardens. H1.2-1.5m/4-5ft, W60-90cm/2-3ft. F5-8.

V. × rhytidophylloides. These vigorous hybrids have handsome, deciduous or semi-evergreen, dark green, shiny leaves, ribbed or corrugated above, brownish grey felted beneath. They have large, creamy white, flat flower heads, usually followed by red, later black, fruit. **'Alleghany'** and **'Willowood'**, both free-flowering, are only for a large garden, though useful as background shrubs. Prune after flowering to keep small, if necessary. All H2.4-3m/8-10ft, W1.8-2.4m/6-8ft. F6. Z5-8.

V. rhytidophyllum. The leather-leaf viburnum is an evergreen or semi-evergreen shrub, with large, glossy, ribbed leaves, the lower surfaces covered with grey-brown felt; new stems and flower buds brown. Yellowish white flowers, but unless several plants present, seldom free-fruiting. **'Roseum'**, pink in bud, opens yellowish white. **'Variegatum'**, with some leaves splashed yellow, but unstable. Trim after flowering to improve density, if necessary. All H2.4-3m/8-10ft, W1.8-2.4m/6-8ft. F5-6. Z6-8.

V. sargentii. This Asian species, closely resembling *V. opulus*, is rarely grown, but **'Susquehanna'**, wide-spreading, with lacecap flowers and bright red fruit, is good if space allows. Both H2.4-3m/8-10ft, W2.4-3m/8-10ft. F6-7. Z3. A real gem, **'Onondaga'**, like 'Susquehanna', is from the United States National Arboretum in Washington DC. Narrow and upright, its bronze shoots open to maroon-purple leaves, the flower buds purple, surrounded by white florets. Shoots break freely from the base, given hard pruning in early spring, but flowers will be lost. H1.5-1.8m/5-6ft, W90-120cm/3-4ft. F6-7. Z4-7.

V. tinus. Though sometimes overused, laurustinus and its cultivars are valuable evergreens, providing winter form and fragrant flowers over a long period. Mediterranean in origin, it has dark, glossy leaves, and adapts well to cool climates, especially by the sea, but can be damaged in severe winters inland, especially when young. Exposed foliage is vulnerable to frost and freezing winds, though even if apparently killed, new shoots often break from the base in late spring. It grows in any well-drained soil, sun or light shade, but flowers less in shade.

Flower clusters can continue on and off for months, but the bright blue fruit are rare except in warm climates. For hedging or to retain density, prune immediately after flowering; to rejuvenate old, woody or open plants, prune to the ground in mid- to late spring when hard frosts are finished. The species varies, most plants sold being selected clones. H1.8-2.4m/6-8ft, W1.8-2.4m/6-8ft. F10-4. Z8-10.

'Eve Price', lower and more spreading, smaller leaves and rose-red flower buds, opening white, fragrant. **'Gwenllian'**, compact habit, small leaves, pinkish white flowers, deep pink in bud, free-fruiting. Both H1.2-1.5m/4-5ft, W1.2-1.5m/4-5ft. F11-4. Z7-8. **'Purpureum'**, purple-tinged leaves, particularly in winter, white flowers but not free-flowering. Young growth is purple. H1.5-1.8m/5-6ft, W1.5-1.8m/5-6ft. F12-4. Z9-10. **'Variegatum'**, leaves irregularly splashed and edged creamy yellow; less hardy. H1.2-1.5m/4-5ft, W1.2-1.5m/4-5ft. F12-4. Z9-10.

VITIS

The ornamental grape vines support themselves by tendrils and most are vigorous, ideal for covering walls, climbing up trees or training over pergolas, creating leafy shade. Most have maple-like leaves which colour spectacularly in autumn, and panicles of insignificant greenish white flowers followed by bunches of grapes, varying in ornamental and edible value.

V. coignetiae. This vigorous Japanese and Korean species is probably the most spectacular ornamental vine for autumn leaf colour. The large green leaves are broad and only slightly lobed, and in autumn turn from purple-bronze to bright crimson and scarlet, the best colour on poor, dry soil. In early years it needs tying in before it becomes self-supporting, and later it requires considerable space, though it can be pruned. Purple-black grapes. H5-6m/16-20ft, W5-6m/16-20ft. F6-7. Z5-9.

V. inconstans. See *Parthenocissus tricuspidata*.

V. vinifera. There are three good forms of this species. **'Brant'** is a well-tried hybrid with three- or five-lobed, maple-like leaves, bronze, purple and red in autumn with contrasting green veins. Small grapes are purple-black and quite sweet. H8-10m/26-33ft, W8-10m/26-33ft. F6-7. Z5-9. **'Incana'**, the dusty miller grape, is slow to start and has greyish green, downy leaves as though covered in dust, and black grapes.

'Purpurea', also known as the teinturier grape, is again quite slow to establish, but eventually makes a striking display of reddish purple leaves and, on older plants, deep purple, bloomy grapes. Both H3-4m/10-13ft, W3-4m/10-13ft. F6-7. Z6-9.

Viburnum sargentii 'Onondaga'

Viburnum tinus 'Eve Price'

Vitis vinifera 'Purpurea'

Vitis coignetiae

SHRUBS

299

Weigela middendorffiana

Weigela florida 'Variegata'

Weigela florida 'Foliis Purpureis'

WEIGELA

Recent developments in breeding and selection have highlighted this ornamental group of easily grown flowering shrubs, reminding us of their value as garden plants. New forms from Holland, France and Canada include dwarf, coloured-foliage and long-flowering types. Once listed under *Diervilla*, weigelas flower only on last year's stems, the former genus flowering on new season's growth. The trumpet-like flowers, often with prominent stamens, are sometimes so profuse that they weigh down the outer branches. They prefer full sun but tolerate some shade, and grow in any well-drained soil. Prune after flowering, thinning congested, old stems to the base and shortening untidy shoots by half, keeping the general habit of the plant. Old plants can be cut to the ground in early spring to rejuvenate, thinning the resulting stems in midsummer, but flowers will not be produced until the following year. Most are very hardy, though some can be tender and vulnerable to spring frosts. Those offering a longer season of interest than the flowers alone are best value for space.

W. florida. From northern China and Korea, and first introduced in 1844 by the famous plant hunter Robert Fortune, it soon became popular in Victorian England. A parent to many hybrids but rarely grown, it and most hybrids have an upright, arching habit, dark green leaves and rosy pink flowers, paler inside. H1.5-1.8m/5-6ft, W1.2-1.5m/4-5ft. F5-6. Z5-8. **'Foliis Purpureis'** has purple-green leaves and purplish pink flowers. The Canadian **'Minuet'**, similar in habit and leaf, has clusters of rosy purple flowers, with prominent, creamy white stamens. **'Rumba'** is similar again, but with red flowers. **'Tango'** has purplish foliage and red flowers. All H75-90cm/30-36in, W90cm/3ft. F5-6. Z5-8. **'Variegata'**, similar to the species, has coarse leaves with creamy yellow margins, pinkish in autumn, and pink flowers; more erect, with coarser, yellower leaves than *W. praecox* 'Variegata'. H1.5-1.8m/5-6ft, W1.2-1.5m/4-5ft. F5-6. Z5-8.

W. middendorffiana. Rare and striking, this has foxglove-like, sulphur-yellow flowers with orange markings. Needs shelter, light shade and protection from spring frost. H1.2-1.5m/4-5ft, W1.2-1.5m/4-5ft. F4-5. Z5.

W. praecox **'Variegata'**. This has white-edged, wavy leaves in sun, golden-yellow in shade, and fragrant, rose-pink flowers with a yellow throat. Can suffer from spring frost; best in shelter, in sun or light shade. H1.2-1.5m/4-5ft, W1.2-1.5m/4-5ft. F5-6. Z6-8.

Hybrids. Most flower from midsummer. Unless otherwise indicated, all H1.5-2.4m/5-8ft, W1.5-1.8m/5-6ft. F5-6. Z5-8. **'Abel Carrière'**, over 100 years old, is still one of the best; red buds opening carmine-rose, large and free-flowering. **'Boskoop Glory'**, large, satin-pink flowers. **'Bristol Ruby'**, large, deep red flowers, good foliage. **'Candida'**, white-flowered. The French **'Carnival'**, salmon-pink, white and dark pink. **'Dropmore Pink'**, deep pink, very hardy. **'Eva Supreme'**, vigorous, profuse, deep red flowers. **'Evita'**, a Dutch dwarf which lacks vigour. Excellent at its best; deep red flowers on and off all summer, after midsummer flush. H60-90cm/2-3ft, W90-120cm/3-4ft. F5-8. Z6-8.

'Looymansii Aurea', open and graceful, golden-yellow leaves and pink flowers all summer; lovely in part shade. **'Mont Blanc'**, fragrant, white flowers. **'Rosabella'**, large, deep pink, lighter-rimmed flowers. **'Rubigold'** (syn. 'Briant Rubidor'), French sport of 'Bristol Ruby', golden-yellow leaves prone to sunscorch, occasional green variegations, deep red flowers. **'Snowflake'**, pale foliage, robust white flowers. **'Victoria'**, dwarf, black-purple leaves, rose-pink flowers, often recurring. H90-120cm/3-4ft, W90-120cm/3-4ft. F5-8. Z6-8.

WISTERIA

One of the most aristocratic members of *Leguminosae*, the pea family, wisterias are a small group of ornamental, Asian and North American twiners, with pinnate leaves and often spectacular, pendulous racemes of white, blue, purple or pink flowers. Most named forms are grafted and usually flower within two or three years of purchase, but cheaper, seed-raised plants can take several years to flower. Wisterias can be trained and tied against walls and fences and over pergolas. They can also be trained up stakes and carefully pruned to form small trees, or grown as patio specimens in containers, as long as they are regularly fertilized. Plant in a sunny, sheltered spot and well-drained, fertile soil.

In climates with late spring frosts, grow against a west-facing wall, to protect the flower buds. Prune to control size and improve flowering. Train new growth to form a framework for two or three years, longer if necessary. On established plants, prune long shoots in late summer back to about 15cm/6in of the season's new growth, and in midwinter, prune a few more centimetres/inches back to two or three flowering buds which should have formed. Once out of reach, wisterias can be allowed to go their own way.

W. floribunda. The Japanese wisteria has stems which twine in a clockwise direction, while the Chinese wisteria, *W. sinensis*, goes anti-clockwise – one of the small wonders of nature! The Japanese wisteria has dark green leaves which unfurl as the 15-25cm/6-10in pendulous racemes of fragrant, bluish

Weigela 'Bristol Ruby'

Wisteria floribunda 'Alba'

Wisteria sinensis

purple flowers appear in succession. Pale yellow autumn leaf colour. **'Alba'** has 60cm/2ft long racemes on established specimens, the white flowers often tinged lilac. **'Macrobotrys'** (syn. 'Multijuga') is the most impressive of all, with racemes sometimes reaching 90cm/3ft or more in length; a specimen draped with numerous flowers, quite breathtaking. **'Rosea'**, pale rose-pink and purple. **'Violacea'**, violet-blue. **'Violacea Plena'**, unusual, double violet-blue. All H5-6m/16-20ft, W5-6m/16-20ft. F5-6. Z4-9.

W. sinensis. The Chinese wisteria is the most widely grown form. Unfortunately, it is often sold as a seed-raised plant, liable to have inferior flowers and take up to ten years to flower, so be sure to look for grafted plants. The species has mauve-lilac, fading to pale lilac, fragrant flowers on pendulous racemes to 30cm/1ft long, all opening at once and before the leaves appear. **'Alba'** has white flowers. **'Black Dragon'**, double, dark purple, long trusses. **'Peaches and Cream'** (syn. 'Kuchibeni'), pink buds opening creamy white. **'Pink Ice'** (syn. 'Hond Beni'), rose-pink, long racemes. **'Plena'**, lilac double flowers. **'Purple Patches'** (syn. 'Murasaki Naga Fuji'), long trusses, deep violet-purple flowers. **'Snow Showers'** (syn. 'Shiro Naga Fuji'), pure white. All H6-8m/20-26ft, W6-8m/20-26ft. F5. Z5-9.

ZENOBIA

Z. pulverulenta. This deciduous or semi-evergreen, acid-loving shrub is ideal for a woodland garden or a bed with acid compost. Its wiry, arching stems carry grey-green or striking, blue-green leaves and hanging, fragrant, white, bell-like flowers. From the south-eastern USA, it grows in sun or light shade, given reasonable soil moisture. Prune a few old stems to the base after flowering, shortening others if necessary. H60-90cm/2-3ft, W60-90cm/2-3ft. F6-7. Z6-9.

Zenobia pulverulenta

Shrubs for All Seasons

Shrubs are among the first plants to be considered for the garden, as they provide permanent structure and eventually stature. Too often, however, the majority flower for only a limited period and have little else to commend them for the rest of the year. Whilst a combination of shrubs and perennials is more common, a planting using only shrubs, as here, can be most attractive and will give a long period of flower and foliage interest. In the winter the frontal dwarf evergreen shrubs will provide flower and foliage, and some of the stems and bark are also colourful. Spring pruning will help to create a dense patchwork of foliage and flower colour for spring, summer and autumn. This bed would be best in sun in any reasonable soil. The peak period of interest is mid- to late summer.

1 *Hebe pimeleoides* 'Quicksilver' (×1)
2 *Euonymus fortunei* 'Emerald Gaiety' (×1)
3 *Rosa* 'Bonica' (×1)
4 *Perovskia atriplicifolia* 'Blue Spire' (×1)
5 *Viburnum sargentii* 'Onondaga' (×1)
6 *Cornus alba* 'Sibirica Variegata' (×1)
7 *Potentilla fruticosa* 'Goldfinger' (×1)
8 *Erica carnea* 'Springwood White' (×3)

Area required:
approx. 3.5 sq. m/3½ sq. yd

Shrubs and Perennials for Summer Colour

This carefully balanced planting will have considerable appeal all year round. The *Hydrangea*, an easy-growing type which does not suffer from frost as it flowers on the new year's growth, provides the height, supported by lower-growing foliage or flowering shrubs and, in the case of the lavender and the *Spiraea*, shrubs with both foliage and flower. The black-leaved *Ophiopogon* and golden-leaved *Acorus* are both 'evergreen' and as effective in winter as summer, but the *Bergenia*, shown here in its summer foliage, turns a deep ruby-red in winter. All are low-growing. This bed would be best for a sunny position in any reasonable soil. It is easy to maintain, requiring only some tidying and pruning each spring. The peak period of interest is probably early to late summer, but winter has its attractions, too.

1 *Acorus gramineus* 'Ogon' (×5)
2 *Ophiopogon planiscapus* 'Nigrescens' (×5)
3 *Lavandula angustifolia* 'Hidcote' (×3)
4 *Artemisia* 'Powis Castle' (×1)
5 *Hydrangea paniculata* 'Kyushu' (×1)
6 *Bergenia* 'Bressingham Ruby' (×5)
7 *Spiraea japonica* 'Golden Princess' (×1)
8 *Geranium* × *cantabrigiense* 'Cambridge' (×3)

Area required:
approx. 3 sq. m/3 sq. yd

SHRUBS

303

MIXED BED FOR SHADE

Shady areas in the garden offer many possibilities for growing some of the choicest plants – as long as the conditions are not too dry. This planting, which blends foliage, flower and form, would be suitable for such a situation, either in the shade provided by overhanging trees or the wall of a building, the latter probably more likely to be moist. The shrubs provide some structure, as does the Japanese maple, which eventually becomes a small tree. The *Geranium*, *Dicentra* and *Alchemilla* are as happy in sun as shade, and the latter two in particular provide a long period of interest and colour, complementing the foliage of the *Hosta* and the *Matteuccia*. The soft, golden leaves of the *Ribes* maintain their colour in shade. Spring bulbs could give earlier colour. The peak season of interest is mid-spring to late summer.

1 *Dicentra* 'Luxuriant' (× 5)
2 *Geranium* 'Johnson's Blue' (× 7)
3 *Viburnum plicatum* 'Cascade' (× 1)
4 *Ribes sanguineum* 'Brocklebankii' (× 1)
5 *Matteuccia struthiopteris* (× 3)
6 *Acer palmatum* 'Senkaki' (× 1)
7 *Alchemilla mollis* (× 5)
8 *Hosta* 'Halcyon' (× 7)

Area required:
approx. 6 sq. m/6 sq. yd

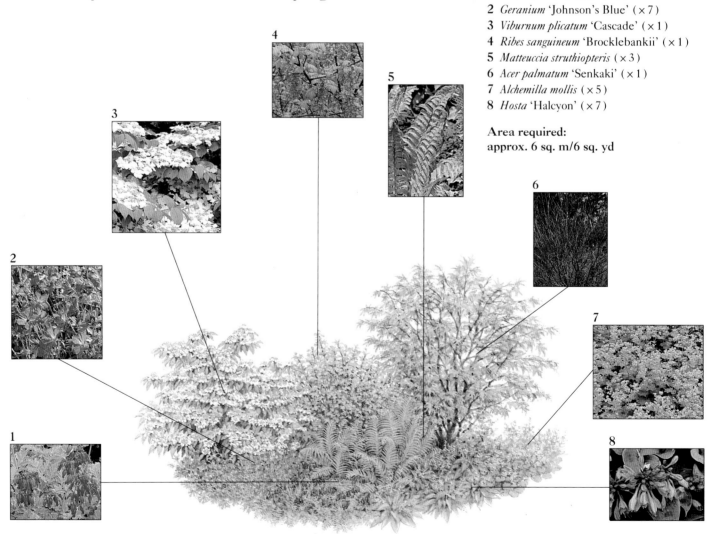

SHRUBS FOR CONTAINERS

Container gardening, for terrace, patio or balcony, is becoming increasingly popular, and the choice of plants being used even wider. Here are a few ideas using shrubs as the main ingredients, but complemented by other plants which extend the season of interest. *Acer negundo* 'Flamingo', for instance, is underplanted by *Viola*, which flowers in late winter and early spring before the leaves appear on the *Acer*. The *Choisya* is made even more striking by planting with it the *Houttuynia*. Plants in containers need constant watering and feeding during the growing season. In cold climates frost-resistant terracotta containers should be used, though many plants may still need winter protection. The peak period of interest is mainly early to late summer, although the *Clematis* finishes flowering in June.

1 *Clematis macropetala* (×1)
2 *Philadelphus coronarius* 'Variegatus' (×1)
3 *Acer negundo* 'Flamingo' (×1)
4 *Viola* 'Clementina' (×3)
5 *Acer palmatum* 'Garnet' (×1)
6 *Lamium maculatum* 'White Nancy' (×3)
7 *Choisya ternata* 'Sundance' (×1)
8 *Houttuynia cordata* 'Chameleon' (×3)
9 *Hydrangea macrophylla* 'Tovelit' (×1)

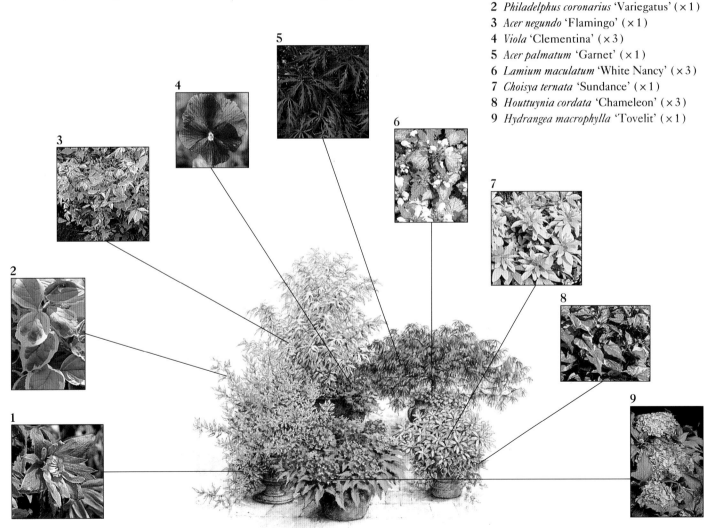

PLANTS FOR YOUR GARDEN

These lists are intended purely as a guide to assist those with special conditions or requirements to fulfil. Neither the categories nor the number of plants in each are exhaustive, but it is hoped the suggestions will be helpful in providing a few ideas. The allocation of a plant to a specific list does not necessarily preclude its use in other circumstances or under different conditions, as appropriate. Individual descriptions of the plants listed can be found in the relevant directory.

PLANTS FOR ACID SOILS

Perennials
Cautleya
Chelone
Dodecatheon
Epimedium
Hosta
Iris ensata
Kirengeshoma
Lupinus
Meconopsis
Primula
Thalictrum
Tricyrtis

Grasses
Carex
Deschampsia
Luzula sylvatica
Molinia

Hardy Ferns
Adiantum
Athyrium
Blechnum
Dryopteris
Matteuccia
Osmunda
Polypodium

Alpines
Corydalis
Gentiana sino-ornata
Lewisia
Sedum spathulifolium
Sempervivum
    arachnoideum
Soldanella

Heaths & Heathers
Calluna
Daboecia
Erica cinerea
Erica mackaiana
Erica tetralix

Shrubs
Acer japonicum types
Acer palmatum types
Andromeda
Arctostaphylos
Aronia
Camellia
Cercis siliquastrum
Cornus florida
Corylopsis
Crinodendron
    hookerianum
Cytisus
Enkianthus campanulatus
Fothergilla
× Gaulnettya
Gaultheria
Ilex
Kalmia
Leucothoe
Myrica
Pernettya
Pieris
Rhododendron
Vaccinium

PLANTS FOR ALKALINE (LIMY) SOILS

Perennials
Acanthus
Anthemis
Aster amellus
Campanula persicifolia
Centranthus
Dictamnus
Digitalis
Eryngium
Gypsophila
Helleborus
Iris germanica
Limonium
Linum
Origanum
Physalis
Polygonatum
Pulsatilla
Scabiosa
Stachys byzantina
Vinca
Yucca

Grasses
Avena
Bouteloua
Stipa

Alpines
Ajuga
Alyssum
Asperula
Aubrieta
Campanula carpatica
Campanula
    poscharskyana
Cerastium
Chiastophyllum
Dianthus (most)
Draba
Gentiana acaulis
Gentiana verna
Geranium subcaulescens
Helianthemum
Iberis
Leontopodium
Phlox subulata
Silene
Veronica

Conifers
Juniperus communis
Pinus sylvestris
Taxus baccata

Shrubs
Aucuba
Berberis
Buddleia
Buxus
Caragana
Ceanothus
Cistus
Cotoneaster
Deutzia
Euonymus
Forsythia
Fuchsia
Hebe
Hypericum
Laurus
Ligustrum
Lonicera
Olearia
Philadelphus
Photinia
Rosmarinus
Sambucus
Sarcococca
Senecio
Spiraea japonica
Symphoricarpos
Syringa
Weigela

PLANTS FOR MOIST LIGHT SHADE

Perennials
Aconitum
Alchemilla
Anemone
Astilbe
Bergenia
Brunnera
Cardiocrinum
Cimicifuga
Dicentra
Epimedium
Filipendula
Gentiana asclepiadea
Helleborus
Hosta
Lamium
Lysimachia
Meconopsis
Polygonum (some)
Primula
Pulmonaria
Rodgersia
Schizostylis
Smilacena
Thalictrum
Tiarella
Tricyrtis
Veratrum
Vinca
Viola (some)

Grasses
Carex elata
Glyceria

Hardy Ferns
Adiantum
Asplenium
Athyrium
Matteuccia
Onoclea
Osmunda

Alpines
Ajuga

Shrubs
Cornus alba
Cornus mas
Danae racemosa
× Fatshedera
Fatsia japonica
× Gaulnettya
Gaultheria
Leucothoe
Neillia
Sambucus
Symphoricarpos
Vaccinium
Viburnum (some)

PLANTS FOR GROUND COVER

Perennials
Alchemilla mollis
Bergenia
Epimedium
Geranium (many)
Hosta
Lamium
Polygonum affine
Pulmonaria
Sedum (some)
Stachys byzantina
Symphytum
Vinca
Waldsteinia

Grasses
Carex
Festuca
Luzula

Alpines
Acaena
Ajuga reptans
Aubrieta
Helianthemum
Lithodora
Mazus
Omphalodes
Phlox subulata
Thymus

Conifers
Chamaecyparis lawsoniana 'Rijnhof'
Juniperus (many)
Microbiota decussata
Picea abies (some)
Pinus (some)
Taxus (some)
Tsuga (some)

Heaths & Heathers
Calluna vulgaris
Daboecia
Erica carnea (some)
Erica cinerea (some)
Erica × darleyensis
Erica vagans

Shrubs
Arctostaphylos uva-ursi
Ceanothus prostratus
Cornus canadensis
Cotoneaster
Gaultheria
Genista pilosa
Hebe (some)
Hedera
Lavandula
Pachysandra
Photinia davidiana 'Prostrata'
Potentilla fruticosa (some)
Rosa (some)
Rubus calycinoides
Salix (some)
Vaccinium (some)

PLANTS WITH ORNAMENTAL STEMS OR BARK

Shrubs
Acer (some)
Arbutus
Cornus alba
Cornus sanguinea 'Winter Flame'
Cornus stolonifera
Corylus avellana 'Contorta'
Danae racemosa
Dipelta floribunda
Euonymus alatus
Kerria japonica
Kolkwitzia
Perovskia
Prunus (some)
Rhus (some)
Rosa virginiana
Rubus (some)

Ruscus aculeatus
Salix (some)
Spartium junceum
Stephanandra tanakae

PLANTS WITH FRAGRANT FLOWERS

Perennials
Asphodeline
Cardiocrinum giganteum
Cimicifuga
Clematis (some)
Crinum × powellii
Dianthus
Galtonia
Hemerocallis (some)
Hesperis matronalis
Hosta plantaginea grandiflora
Iris (some)
Lathyrus
Paeonia lactiflora (some)
Phlox (some)
Smilacena racemosa
Yucca

Alpines
Cheiranthus

Shrubs
Abelia chinensis
Abeliophyllum
Azara
Berberis × stenophylla
Buddleia (most)
Ceanothus (some)
Chimonanthus
Chionanthus
Choisya
Clerodendrum
Clethra
Corylopsis spicata
Cytisus (some)
Daphne
Drimys winteri
Elaeagnus
Genista (some)
Hamamelis (most)
Jasminum
Ligustrum
Lonicera (many)
Magnolia (some)
Mahonia (most)
Olearia
Osmanthus
Philadelphus (most)
Prunus (some)

Ribes
Rosa (some)
Sambucus
Sarcococca
Skimmia
Syringa
Viburnum (many)
Wisteria sinensis
Zenobia

EVERGREEN PLANTS

One has to qualify the term evergreen, since many plants are evergreen in warm temperate climates and coastal areas, but may not retain foliage in colder areas.

Perennials
Bergenia
Dianthus
Epimedium (some)
Eryngium (some)
Euphorbia (some)
Geranium (some)
Helleborus
Heuchera
Iris foetidissima
Kniphofia caulescens
Libertia
Limonium
Morina
Pulmonaria (most)
Stachys byzantina
Tellima
Vinca
Yucca

Grasses
Acorus
Carex
Cortaderia
Festuca
Luzula

Hardy Ferns
Asplenium
Blechnum
Polystichum

Alpines
Iberis
Ophiopogon planiscapus 'Nigrescens'
Sempervivum

Conifers
Most

Heaths & Heathers
All

Shrubs
Andromeda
Arctostaphylos
Aucuba
Azara
Buxus sempervirens
Ceanothus (some)
Choisya
Danae racemosa
Daphne
Elaeagnus (most)
Euonymus fortunei
× Fatshedera
Garrya elliptica
× Gaulnettya
Gaultheria
Hebe
Hedera
Ilex (most)
Leucothoe
Mahonia
Pachysandra
Pernettya
Phormium
Photinia (some)
Pieris
Prunus laurocerasus
Rhododendron (and some azaleas)
Ruscus aculeatus
Sarcococca
Skimmia
Vaccinium
Viburnum (some)

PLANTS FOR MOIST SOILS

Perennials
Aconitum
Alchemilla
Astilbe
Caltha
Cautleya
Cimicifuga
Dicentra (some)
Epimedium
Eupatorium
Filipendula
Fritillaria
Geum (some)
Gunnera
Heliopsis

Helleborus (some)
Hemerocallis
Hosta
Iris ensata
Iris laevigata
Iris pseudacorus
Iris sibirica
Lamium
Ligularia
Lysichiton
Lysimachia
Lythrum
Mimulus
Monarda
Peltiphyllum
Polygonum (some)
Primula (some)
Rheum
Rodgersia
Schizostylis coccinea
Thalictrum
Tiarella
Tradescantia
Trollius
Zantedeschia

Grasses
Carex
Deschampsia
Glyceria aquatica
Miscanthus
Phalaris
Scirpus

Alpines
Ajuga

Shrubs
Aronia
Clethra
Cornus alba
Cornus stolonifera
Ilex verticillata
Magnolia grandiflora
Myrica gale
Neillia
Physocarpus opulifolius
Salix (most)
Sambucus
Vaccinium (most)
Viburnum opulus

PLANTS WITH AUTUMN FOLIAGE COLOUR

Perennials
Agapanthus
Amsonia

Euphorbia (some)
Geranium (some)
Hemerocallis
Hosta
Peltiphyllum
Podophyllum
Polygonum affine

Grasses
Arundo donax
Calamagrostis
Carex
Deschampsia
Miscanthus
Panicum
Pennisetum
Stipa

Conifers
Cryptomeria japonica
　‘Elegans’
Ginkgo
Larix
Metasequoia
Taxodium
Thuja orientalis (some)

Shrubs
Acer ginnala
Acer japonicum
Acer palmatum
Aesculus parviflora
Berberis (many)
Cornus (many)
Cotinus
Cotoneaster (some)
Diervilla
Disanthus
Enkianthus
Euonymus (some)
Fothergilla
Hamamelis
Mahonia (some)
Nandina
Oxydendrum
Parthenocissus
Photinia davidiana
Rhododendron (azalea)
Rhus
Ribes
Sorbus reducta
Spiraea (some)
Stephanandra tanakae
Vaccinium
Viburnum (some)
Vitis

PLANTS WITH AROMATIC FOLIAGE

Perennials
Allium
Artemisia
Dictamnus
Elsholtzia
Geranium (some)
Helichrysum
Hyssopus
Mentha
Monarda
Nepeta
Origanum
Salvia (some)
Satureia

Alpines
Thymus

Shrubs
Artemisia
Caryopteris
Chimonanthus
Choisya
Cistus
Clerodendrum
Escallonia
Laurus
Lavandula
Magnolia
Myrica
Olearia
Perovskia
Ribes
Rosmarinus
Ruta
Salvia
Santolina

PLANTS FOR DRY SOILS

Perennials
Acanthus
Achillea
Anemone
Anthemis
Aquilegia
Aster
Campanula
Coreopsis
Dictamnus
Echinops
Erigeron
Eryngium
Euphorbia (some)
Filipendula (some)

Gaillardia
Inula
Iris (most)
Kniphofia
Lamium
Lupinus
Macleaya
Oenothera (some)
Papaver
Phlox (some)
Physalis
Pulsatilla
Solidago
Vinca
Yucca

Grasses
Calamagrostis
Festuca
Panicum
Pennisetum
Stipa

Alpines
Acaena
Alyssum
Arabis
Armeria
Aubrieta
Campanula
Cerastium
Dianthus
Draba
Gypsophila
Helianthemum
Iberis
Phlox
Saxifraga (most)
Scutellaria
Sedum
Sempervivum
Thymus

Shrubs
Abelia
Berberis
Buddleia
Caragana
Ceanothus
Cistus
Cornus (some)
Cotinus
Cotoneaster
Cytisus
Elaeagnus
Fremontodendron
Genista
Hebe
Hedera
Ilex

Indigofera
Kerria
Lavandula
Lavatera
Lespedeza
Lonicera
Mahonia aquifolium
Olearia
Perovskia
Philadelphus
Phlomis
Potentilla
Rhus
Ribes
Rosmarinus
Rubus
Ruscus
Santolina
Senecio
Spartium
Tamarix
Ulex

PLANTS FOR DRY SHADE

Perennials
Alchemilla mollis
Asarum europaeum
Bergenia cordifolia
Brunnera macrophylla
Epimedium
Euphorbia robbiae
Geranium macrorrhizum
Geranium procurrens
Iris foetidissima
Lamium galeobdolon
　‘Florentinum’
Lamium maculatum
Polygonatum
Saxifraga × *urbium*
Symphytum
　grandiflorum
Tiarella cordifolia
Vinca
Waldsteinia

Grasses
Carex (some)
Luzula
Milium

Hardy Ferns
Dryopteris
Polypodium
Polystichum

Alpines
Ajuga reptans
Omphalodes verna
Sedum spurium

Shrubs
Aucuba
Buxus sempervirens
Cotoneaster (some)
Danae racemosa
Elaeagnus × *ebbingei*
Euonymus europaeus
Euonymus fortunei
× *Fatshedera lizei*
Fatsia japonica
× *Gaulnettya*
Gaultheria
Hedera
Hypericum
　androsaemum
Hypericum calycinum
Ilex aquifolium
Ligustrum
Lonicera nitida
Lonicera pileata
Mahonia (some)
Osmanthus (some)
Pachysandra
Prunus laurocerasus
Rubus
Ruscus
Sarcococca
Symphoricarpos

WINTER-FLOWERING PLANTS

Perennials
Adonis amurensis
Helleborus (most)
Pulmonaria (some)

Heaths & Heathers
Erica carnea (and
　varieties)
Erica × *darleyensis* (and
　varieties)
Erica erigena (and
　varieties)

Shrubs
Abeliophyllum
　distichum
Arbutus unedo
Camellia
Chaenomeles speciosa
Chaenomeles × *superba*
Chimonanthus

Clematis cirrhosa
Cornus mas
Corylopsis
Corylus (catkins)
Daphne blagayana
Daphne mezereum
Daphne odora
Drimys winteri
Elaeagnus × ebbingei
Forsythia (some)
Garrya elliptica
Hamamelis (most)
Jasminum nudiflorum
Lonicera fragrantissima
Lonicera × purpusii
Mahonia japonica
Mahonia × media
Mahonia pinnata
Osmanthus × burkwoodii
Osmanthus delavayi
Pachysandra terminalis
Polygala chamaebuxus grandiflora
Prunus mume
Ribes laurifolium
Sarcococca
Stachyurus
Viburnum × bodnantense
Viburnum farreri
Viburnum tinus

PLANTS SUITABLE FOR HEDGING

This list includes some low-growing plants suitable for edging, as well as some plants which can be used for screening.

Conifers
Chamaecyparis lawsoniana (taller varieties)
Chamaecyparis nootkatensis
Chamaecyparis pisifera (taller varieties)
× *Cupressocyparis leylandii* (and varieties)
Cupressus glabra (taller varieties)
Cupressus macrocarpa (taller varieties)
Juniperus chinensis (some)
Juniperus × media (vigorous semi-prostrate types)

Picea omorika
Pinus (some)
Sequoia sempervirens 'Adpressa'
Taxus (most upright or semi-upright forms)
Thuja occidentalis (many)
Thuja plicata
Thuja plicata 'Atrovirens'
Tsuga canadensis (upright cultivars)

Shrubs: deciduous
Abelia
Aronia arbutifolia 'Erecta'
Berberis (many taller upright forms)
Caryopteris
Ceanothus (some)
Forsythia (some)
Lonicera (some)
Neillia
Physocarpus
Potentilla fruticosa
Prunus cerasifera 'Pissardii'
Prunus × cistena
Rosa (some)
Ruta
Spiraea (many)
Viburnum (some)

Shrubs: evergreen
Aucuba
Buxus sempervirens
Choisya
Cotoneaster (many upright types)
Elaeagnus × ebbingei
Elaeagnus pungens
Escallonia (mild areas only)
Euonymus japonicus
Hebe (some)
Ilex aquifolium (most)
Ilex × meserveae (some)
Lavandula (many)
Ligustrum (many)
Osmanthus (some)
Phillyrea
Photinia
Pittosporum
Prunus laurocerasus (many)
Prunus lusitanica
Pyracantha (also semi-evergreen)
Rosmarinus (some)

Salvia officinalis
Santolina
Viburnum (some)

PLANTS FOR COASTAL DISTRICTS

Perennials
Achillea
Agapanthus
Anemone
Anthemis
Armeria
Artemisia
Aster
Bergenia
Campanula
Centranthus
Chrysanthemum
Crocosmia
Dianthus
Dierama
Echinops
Erigeron
Eryngium
Euphorbia
Filipendula (some)
Geranium
Gypsophila
Heuchera
Iris
Kniphofia
Melissa
Morina
Nerine
Oenothera
Origanum
Penstemon
Phygelius
Polygonum
Romneya
Salvia
Scabiosa
Sedum
Sisyrinchium
Stachys
Veronica
Yucca
Zantedeschia

Grasses
Most

Conifers
Araucaria
Cupressus (most)
Juniperus (some)
Pinus (some)

Heaths & Heathers
Erica arborea
Erica erigena

Shrubs
Arbutus unedo
Choisya
Cistus
Colutea
Cotoneaster (most)
Crataegus
Cytisus scoparius
Elaeagnus
Escallonia
Euonymus fortunei
Euonymus japonicus
Fuchsia
Garrya
Genista (most)
Halimium
Hebe
Hydrangea macrophylla
Ilex aquifolium
Lavandula
Lavatera
Leptospermum
Leycesteria
Lonicera (many)
Olearia
Phillyrea
Phlomis (most)
Phormium
Pittosporum
Pyracantha
Rhamnus alaternus
Rosa (many)
Rosmarinus
Salix (many)
Santolina
Senecio (most)
Spartium
Tamarix
Ulex
Viburnum tinus

PLANTS ATTRACTIVE TO BEES

Perennials
Allium
Anchusa
Anemone
Asclepias
Aster
Calamintha
Campanula
Centaurea
Coreopsis

Cynara
Delphinium
Echinacea
Echinops
Eryngium
Helenium
Helianthus
Hyssopus
Inula
Ligularia
Lythrum
Monarda
Nepeta
Origanum
Polemonium
Rudbeckia
Salvia
Scabiosa
Sedum
Verbascum

Heaths & Heathers
All

Shrubs
Buddleia
Caryopteris
Ceanothus
Ceratostigma
Clematis
Cytisus
Escallonia
Genista
Hamamelis
Hebe
Hypericum (some)
Jasminum
Lavandula
Lavatera
Leycesteria
Lonicera
Mahonia
Perovskia
Philadelphus
Pieris
Pyracantha
Rhododendron
Ribes
Rosa
Rosmarinus
Weigela

INDEX

313

HARDINESS ZONES

The plant hardiness zones given in this chart are determined by the United States Department of Agriculture, and are based on the average annual minimum winter temperature for each zone. Hardiness zones are of particular relevance in the USA, where considerable variation in climate occurs across the country. In the British Isles, such variation is much less: Zone 7 covers the eastern Scottish Highlands; Zone 8 includes most of inland and eastern Britain and Ireland; and Zone 9 includes the western coastal areas of Britain and Ireland.

Each plant in the directories has been allocated a zone range (for example, Z7-9) within which it is most likely to thrive. However, these zones can give only a very approximate indication of appropriate climates for the plants listed. Within any one zone several micro-climates can occur, and other factors, such as site, aspect and soil, may also affect a plant's growth.

Zone	
1	Below -45°C/-50°F
2	-45° to -39°C/-50° to -40°F
3	-39° to -35°C/-40° to -30°F
4	-35° to -29°C/-30° to -20°F
5	-29° to -23°C/-20° to -10°F
6	-23° to -18°C/-10° to 0°F
7	-18° to -12°C/0° to 10°F
8	-12° to -6°C/10° to 20°F
9	-6° to -1°C/20° to 30°F
10	-1° to 4°C/30° to 40°F
11	Above 4°C/40°F

PICTURE CREDITS